The WILD VEGETARIAN Cookbook

The WILD VEGETARIAN Cookbook

A Forager's Culinary Guide (in the Field or in the Supermarket) to Preparing and Savoring Wild (and Not So Wild) Natural Foods, with More than 500 Recipes

"*Wildman*" STEVE BRILL

Foreword by
ARTHUR SCHWARTZ

THE HARVARD COMMON PRESS
Boston, Massachusetts

THE HARVARD COMMON PRESS
535 Albany Street
Boston, Massachusetts 02118
www.harvardcommonpress.com

Printed in the United States of America

Printed on acid-free paper

Library of Congress Cataloging-in-Publication Data

Brill, Steve
  The wild vegetarian : A forager's culinary guide (in the field or in the supermarket) to preparing
and savoring wild (and not so wild) natural foods, with more than 500 recipes / by "Wildman"
Steve Brill ; foreword by Arthur Schwartz.
    p. cm.
  Includes index.
  ISBN 1-55832-214-0 (cl : alk. paper)
    1. Vegetarian cookery. 2. Cookery (Wild foods) I. Title.

TX837.B824 2002
641.5'636–dc21   2001051929

Special bulk-order discounts are available on this and other Harvard Common Press books.
Companies and organizations may purchase books for premiums or resale, or may arrange
a custom edition, by contacting the Marketing Director at the address above.

10 9 8 7 6 5 4 3 2 1

Book design by Susan McClellan
Illustrations by Linda Hillel

Jacket design by Deborah Kerner/Dancing Bears Design
Jacket photographs by Alexandra Grablewski, except fiddlehead photograph by PhotoDisc

This book is dedicated to all the nonviolent environmental activists worldwide who have risked physical injury, financial loss, and their liberty to keep our planet green, vibrant, and alive.

CONTENTS

The plants in this book appear in the chronological order in which they are
ready to be foraged during the year and during each season.

FOREWORD

CALL ME FORAGER. THAT'S MY NAME IN THE New York City Parks Department book of department nicknames, courtesy of former Parks Commissioner Henry Stern, but inspired by "Wildman" Steve Brill.

It wasn't until I read the introduction to this book that I realized it has been nearly 20 years since I took my first foraging walk with the Wildman. I don't remember where exactly we went that first time out, but, courtesy of Steve Brill, I now know places around my great and vast city where I can find all sorts of delicious wild foods. On the beach in Breezy Point, in the Rock-aways, a section of Gateway National Park where Fort Tilden used to be, there are rose hips to make a vitamin-C-rich tea, beach plums for jelly, and lemony sorrel for salads and seasoning. Amazingly, within earshot of traffic on the Long Island Expressway, in the center of Queens, peppery watercress surrounds an underground mineral spring that wells up in a sandy, wild section of Alley Pond Park. You can even drink the water!

Because the Wildman taught me, either first hand or through his first book, *Identifying and Harvesting Edible and Medicinal Plants in Wild (and Not So Wild) Places*, I can now tell the difference between young dandelions and new green shoots of chicory. I have gathered gingko nuts in tranquil Greenwood ceme-tery, in the heart of Brooklyn. I have trespassed in a private, but neglected, row-house garden to harvest chickweed (delicious and worth the risk of arrest!). I know the difference between the very similar leaves of wild onions and wild garlic. I invariably notice that there are succulent leaves of purslane growing in the cracks of the sidewalk everywhere. And before they fall and stain the street, I gather the mulberries from a tree on my corner in Brooklyn. Yes, more than one tree grows here.

No one thinks of New York as having much green space. "Out-of-towners," which is how New Yorkers refer even to foreigners, don't realize that not only do we have many huge parks besides Manhattan's Central Park, but also that there are numerous "vest-pocket" or small neighborhood parks, and even several bird and animal wilderness refuges. It doesn't matter where you live on this planet. Nature is so persistent and var-ied that any of us can forage for our dinner.

This was an amazing fact to me back in 1983, when I first met the Wildman. It was a new idea, too, to then–Parks Commissioner Henry Stern, who hap-pened to be an old friend. How fortunate for Wildman that Henry didn't get it. Henry thought Wildman was destroying the parks by taking groups of New Yorkers through them and pointing out the edibles, picking the weeds and gathering the nuts, berries, seeds, and occasional wild mushroom. Henry had the Wildman arrested by a park ranger while the Wildman was dig-ging up a dandelion. The media loved the story. The arrest made Wildman famous. It made Henry look like a dope and a bully. How could picking dandelion greens be hurting the environment, as Stern said?

To help them both, I called Henry. "You don't get it," I said. "This guy lives on the edge. He isn't mak-ing a fortune on the parks. He barely pays his rent. He eats only what he finds. And toward the public good, he is teaching people an appreciation of the parks that they would never otherwise have."

Henry is actually smart, and a good politician.

Instead of continuing to prosecute the Wildman, he made him an official park guide, an employee of the city. Everyone benefited. Indeed, Wildman Steve Brill got to go home with a paycheck.

At the time, I was the executive food editor of the New York *Daily News*. Back then, the New York Public Library organized a fundraiser called "The Night of 100 Dinners," in which 100 of the city's more famous hosts and hostesses welcomed paying guests into their homes for an evening of good food and conversation. My publisher, James Hoge, generously offered to organize one in his grand apartment on Gramercy Park and he asked me to plan it and cook it.

As the food editor of the nation's greatest tabloid newspaper (well, at least the most famous), I came up with a theme that echoed the street-corner newsboys of old and parodied my newspaper's famous in-your-face and often alliterative headlines (Remember the one about our former president? "Ford To New York: Drop Dead.") The dinner was called "Extra, Extra, Eat All About It: Fine Food from the Five Boroughs."

The idea was that everything we ate would be grown or produced in New York City. We planned on serving a Brooklyn bouillabaisse, using fish and shellfish brought in by the charter boats of Sheepshead Bay. The smoked salmon for an appetizer was processed in Brooklyn. Pastries and cakes were easy. New York has more than its share of great bakeries. For dessert, we set out a Viennese table, a buffet with dozens of sweets from every borough.

The dinner was in early November, so vegetables were a problem. We were able to buy some cool weather crops, broccoli and winter squash, from the last working farm left in the city, a small plot on Staten Island. But where would we find salad?

Wildman Steve Brill to the rescue! We went for a foraging trip through several parks and a number of verdant side streets (that's when I had to trespass to gather chickweed) and found garlic mustard, field garlic (it looks like scallions), and winter cress, to name of few of our greens. The Wildman knew where to find each and every one, and at the end of a long day of food gathering, we returned to his apartment for a snack.

The two most amazing things about the Wildman's apartment, which was amazing in many ways, was that the main furniture in his foyer was a second refrigerator-freezer where he stored, like a squirrel, all the nuts, seeds, and other edibles he needed for the winter, when the rewards of foraging are meager at best, and that every surface of his bedroom was covered with models of mushrooms that he had painstakingly sculpted and painted with the accuracy and delicacy of John James Audubon.

During the 20 years that Wildman Steve Brill has been leading foraging tours, now not just in New York but all over the Mid-Atlantic and New England, he has also been cooking the foods he finds in the wild. This book probably does not represent the culmination of his explorations in the kitchen. He is a man in constant search of knowledge and increased deliciousness. I could not ask for more, however. *The Wild Vegetarian* is absolutely *the* definitive book on the subject of cooking foods from the wild.

ARTHUR SCHWARTZ
JANUARY 2002

PREFACE

THE PHRASE "THE ENVIRONMENT" MEANS MANY things to many people. To some, it conjures up an image of distant rainforests in need of protection. To others, it might also encompass the nearby parks and local woodlands where people go for recreation, or it might even include neighborhood lawns, backyards, street trees and shrubs, and empty lots.

Few people realize that the local environment also has sources of foods that are delicious, healthful, and organic, including herbs, greens, fruit, berries, nuts, seeds, and even mushrooms. My previous book, *Identifying and Harvesting Edible and Medicinal Plants in Wild (and Not So Wild) Places* (William Morrow & Company, 1994) shows you how to have fun foraging for edible wild plants safely and profitably throughout North America. The present volume explains in detail the way you can use these wild foods to create delicious and healthful meals.

ACKNOWLEDGMENTS

I WOULD LIKE TO THANK ALL THE WILD PLANTS and fungi that grow in such abundance throughout North America, even up to my doorstep (a hen-of-the-woods mushroom comes up every year on an ornamental crabapple tree on the lawn of my old apartment building, and wine-cap stropharia mushrooms fruit in great quantity on the grounds of the co-op where I'm about to move), for presenting themselves in such abundance, and for tasting so good. This book could not have been written without them. I hope everyone who enjoys them can return the favor by working to preserve their habitats and the planet that's home to us all.

My thanks to Leslie-Anne Skolnik, soon to be my wife, for contributing Turkish recipe ideas, part of her heritage, to this book, and for being so supportive of my work from the moment I met her blooming in Central Park on a field walk I was leading in 1998.

Leslie put me in touch with literary agent Sheree Bykofsky, who did a great job helping me fine-tune the book proposal and winning the book contract with this publishing house.

I want to thank Arthur Schwartz for writing the wonderful foreword to this book, for foraging with me in the winter, for writing about me in the *New York Daily News* back in 1985 when I was unknown, for giving me national publicity when I was arrested by undercover park rangers for eating a dandelion in Central Park in 1986, and for having me on his WOR radio show in New York so many times.

My thanks to everyone at Harvard Common Press: Pam Hoenig, my editor, and Bruce Shaw, the president, who chose to publish the book and gave it full support. Thanks to managing editor Valerie J. Cimino, production editor Jodi Marchowsky, and copyeditor Maggie Carr for improving all aspects of the book. Also, thanks to artist Linda Hillel for the beautiful illustrations.

Finally, my thanks to all the participants of my public Wild Food and Ecology Tours for supporting my educational efforts, and for working against stiff resistance to make my tours available to school classes and other organizations. Without their help, I'd probably be working at a "real" job instead of teaching foraging and ecology, and writing books such as this one.

The WILD

VEGETARIAN

Cookbook

INTRODUCTION

FORAGING AND ME

I T BEGAN IN MY TWENTIES WITH A DAY OF household chores—vacuuming, laundry, and shopping. A girlfriend had promised me a sumptuous gourmet dinner in exchange for the work, but she changed her mind right after I had carried out the last load of garbage. Not unexpectedly, this relationship didn't last long, but my appetite for gourmet food did.

Taking a break from my unsuccessful effort at becoming a world-class chess player, I made my first culinary attempt in the mid-1970s, when I followed a cookie recipe from the side of an oatmeal box. The surprising success of this project led me to send away for free recipe booklets, and then to experiment with library cookbooks. Chess fell by the wayside and I was soon preparing delicious meals for more appreciative lady friends (although I have yet to entice anybody to help with household chores).

Enter Carleton Fredricks, the granddaddy of radio health-show gurus, and I began applying the principles of alternative nutrition to my recipes. Interesting explorations of exotic ingredients from New York City's health food stores and ethnic food stores soon followed.

I took a crucial step toward becoming hooked on wild foods when, while riding my bicycle in a local park in Hollis, Queens, I saw some Greek women in traditional black garb who were busily foraging for plants. I stopped to ask them what they were doing, but their answers were all Greek to me. Nevertheless, the ladies showed me how to recognize and collect delicious, fresh, organic wild grape leaves, which I stuffed when I got home. And they were great!

Using contemporary field guides to identify edible

wild plants and avoid poisoning myself, I discovered some obstacles. The authors were botanists who wouldn't recognize a kitchen if one fell on their heads. And wild food cookbooks offered recipes for death: Boil the nutrition out of your greens or cook them in enough bacon fat to induce cardiac arrest. Add refined sugar or white flour to everything else. So I sprang into the empty ecological niche and began creating healthful wild food recipes.

In 1982 the name "Wildman" came to me during a session of transcendental meditation, influenced by my lifelong love of jazz and my familiarity with "The Wild Man Blues" by Jelly Roll Morton and Louis Armstrong. I let go of my current activities—unsuccessful struggles to cater healthy meals, teach cooking, or cook professionally—and started leading foraging tours in and around New York City.

My big break came at four P.M. on March 29, 1986, when two undercover park rangers who had infiltrated a Central Park tour arrested and handcuffed me for eating a dandelion. The police fingerprinted me and charged me with criminal mischief for removing vegetation from the park. But because I had eaten all the evidence, they released me with a desk appearance ticket, pending trial. I informed the press and immediately appeared on page 1 of the *Chicago Sun-Times* courtesy of the Associated Press, page 2 of the *New York Daily News*, in the *New York Times*, on CBS-TV *Evening News with Dan Rather*, Kathie Lee and Regis's TV talk show, and much more. The press ate up Wildman's Five-Boro Salad (page 159), which I served to reporters and passersby on the steps of the Manhattan Criminal Court House on the day of my arraignment. Because of all the publicity, Parks Commissioner Henry Stern turned over a new leaf. He dropped all charges and hired me to lead the same tours I was leading when he had had me arrested.

Appearances on *Eyewitness News, LateNight with David Letterman*, MTV, *The Joan Rivers Show*, and *The Today Show* followed, as did my first book contract.

I left the New York City Parks Department in 1990 when the administration changed, and these days I lead freelance tours throughout Greater New York every Saturday, Sunday, and holiday, spring through fall. Private tours and lectures for schools, museums, environmental groups, libraries, garden clubs, Ys, and other organizations fill my weekdays. I've hosted local environmental cable TV and radio series and dream of having my own national TV show. I'm still experimenting with wild plant recipes, and I've organized a collection of my best recipes with the ideas behind them. Here they are.

FORAGING AND YOU

OBVIOUSLY YOU CAN'T WALK OUT THE DOOR and taste every wild plant you see. Many wild plants and mushrooms (which are fungi, not plants) are delicious and healthful, but others may taste awful, make you sick, or kill you. *Use only those wild foods that you've identified with 100 percent certainty.* This is your responsibility, even when you attend an expert's field walk. Furthermore, since anyone may suffer an adverse reaction to any new food, wild or cultivated, eat small portions of any new food at first. *It's the reader's responsibility to identify and use the information in this book sensibly.*

Unlike my previous book, this volume doesn't provide the complete information about plant identification that is necessary to forage safely. Use my previous book or other field guides, and identify any wild plant you're going to eat with complete certainty before you consume it. Always collect at least 50 feet from heavy traffic, wash all plants under running water before you use them, and make sure the plants aren't contaminated with pesticides, herbicides, or other things.

I lead wild food and ecology field walks throughout Greater New York (see wildmanstevebrill.com for the schedule), and other instructors lead tours throughout the country. If there is no foraging teacher in your area, it will take time and patience to locate and positively identify your region's wild edibles. Meanwhile, you may purchase identical or similar ingredients in supermarkets, gourmet shops, or ethnic stores. You may also substitute alternative ingredients, which I list in the recipes and in the Equivalents table (page 474). The results will differ somewhat, but they'll still be delicious.

What Makes Wild Foods Special

BACK BEFORE THE INVENTION OF AGRICULTURE, and even before the day the first Big Mac slithered and slopped down the assembly line, people depended on wild foods for survival. Because wild plants have to cope with herbivores, competing plants, weather, and changing climate to survive, they've evolved extraordinary fitness. That's why they contain concentrations of high-quality carbohydrates, fats, and proteins, as well as vitamins, minerals, and fiber, thus serving themselves and us. By the way, many of the flavors we enjoy, such as sourness, pungency, saltiness, bitterness, and the taste of onions, garlic, wintergreen, licorice, and mint, are qualities plants have adapted in order to discourage herbivores.

Because we co-evolved with these plants, our present nutritional needs reflect what we found in the environment, not what we find in the candy store. For example, somewhere in our history we lost the common mammalian ability to synthesize vitamin C because a chance mutation destroyed this trait in an ancestor. But because this nutrient is so common in wild foods, natural selection didn't kill off our ancestors who had this gene, and because the gene happened to be dominant (when paired with a recessive gene, only the dominant gene expresses its trait) the trait spread throughout the population. Foraging populations normally don't get scurvy (acute vitamin C deficiency), because wild foods contain vitamin C, but agricultural societies were often plagued by this illness until comparatively modern times when scientists recognized that certain foods (long known to foraging societies) cure and prevent this condition.

Plants use fiber for structural support and to discourage some herbivores. Although we can't digest fiber, our digestive system depends on the large quantities of it that are present in natural, unprocessed foods to push food through the intestines. Remove the fiber by refining food, and your stools become hardened and you slow the time it takes for material to travel through your bowels. As a result you risk actual physical damage as well as increasing exposure to accumulating bacterial toxins (given a chance, bacteria multiply geometrically). The lack of sufficient fiber contributes to today's epidemics of constipation, hemorrhoids, diverticulosis, diverticulitis, and bowel cancer. These illnesses don't exist in foraging societies.

So why did we abandon foraging for healthier foods and domesticate plants? Because agriculture supports larger populations. The historical mechanism was probably that when societies competed and waged war, those with the larger populations usually won. It is ironic that people in foraging societies had much more leisure time than did their agricultural and industrial counterparts, and suffered less malnutrition than did agricultural people in preindustrial times, and indeed less than do many people in modern society. (It's difficult to be healthy on a high-fat, refined/processed food diet.)

Because we buy and sell food according to its weight, size, and appearance instead of based on flavor or nutrient content, producers breed bigger plants with less flavor and nutrition. Agribusiness uses herbicides and pesticides that kill beneficial insects, earthworms, and other vital soil organisms, making it necessary to use artificial fertilizer in order to force damaged soil to produce poor-quality crops. Misuse of the science of biotechnology aggravates the situation. Just taste a commercially produced vegetable and compare it to the same food grown by an organic gardener. Or compare wild watercress, strawberries, or blueberries with their supermarket counterparts. Participants in my field walks rave about the flavor of wild foods and deplore the blandness of supermarket fare. Finding, identifying, collecting, and using wild foods is an exciting way to provide delicious meals, enhance your health, get some exercise, and put you in touch with your environment.

HOW TO PREPARE HEALTHY, TASTY FOOD

HOW DO YOU MAKE FOOD THAT'S GOOD FOR you and tastes good too? Begin with the finest ingredients whenever possible: fresh wild foods, homegrown organic garden produce, or fresh ingredients from a certified organic farm. When you prepare food, focus on bringing out the ingredients' outstanding qualities—flavor, texture, and appearance. Cook food until it's just done. Use ingredients that complement each other.

The world's great cuisines were all developed by home cooks using local ingredients and seasonings. They provide cooking techniques and ideas for combining foods. Choose proportions, cooking methods, and seasonings that are appropriate to your ingredients and respectful (but not slavishly imitative) of the cuisines you're emulating. This prospect intimidated me when I was a beginner, but after a while, it becomes second nature. Like removing the training wheels of a bicycle as you gain confidence, as you work with the recipes that follow you will build confidence in putting together high-quality, healthy wild (and not-so-wild) ingredients with sound culinary and nutritional principles.

Wholeness is a mainstay of all natural foods cooking. A diet of whole foods best approximates the quantities and proportions of carbohydrates, fats, proteins, vitamins, minerals, trace minerals, enzymes, and fiber we ate as we evolved and adapted to the foods our natural environment offered. Although different individuals of different sexes, ages, states of health, and genetic inheritance have different nutritional needs, a whole foods diet provides an excellent starting point for achieving better health.

Ingredients should be as close as possible to their living state. You can use them raw, chop or grind them, and heat them without overcooking them, but avoid using refined ingredients. After industrial processing, the original ingredients are often unrecognizable, and their flavors and nutrients are sacrificed in the interest of furthering shelf life and profit.

Grain ground into flour, for example, retains most of its original properties, although the increased surface area of flour unduly speeds digestion and absorption as compared to that of cooked whole grain. But refining grain into white flour removes all the fiber your digestive system needs to operate properly. The valuable germ layer is removed (and fed to hogs!), along with all the B vitamins, vitamin E, and trace minerals, leaving only starch and protein. "Enriching" white flour only restores a legally mandated minimum of these nutrients. Should you feel enriched if you find a few of your precious valuables in a pile of rubble after a tornado has flattened your home? Degrading sugarcane into white sugar yields similar results.

Why are carbohydrates refined and the healthful oils and germ removed? Because eventually products that retain their wholeness become rancid, whereas refined flour has a longer shelf life and therefore is more profitable. Refined foods are usually white, nutritionally meaningless but culturally and commercially desirable because there is a psychological association between sunlight and the day, whereas dark foods connote darkness and night.

Refined carbohydrates rush into the bloodstream and raise the blood sugar (whole foods, on the other hand, take time to digest), forcing the pancreas to produce unusually great amounts of insulin quickly. To burn these empty calories, you need vitamins and minerals, which must come from your body (remember, they've been removed from the food). You usually can't burn all the calories at once, so the body stores them as fat, which is very difficult to break down. (That's why it's so hard to lose weight.) Your blood sugar levels go down because all that insulin more than does its job, and you're soon hungry again.

The overprocessing of other foods is just as bad. Take vegetable oil, for instance. Subjecting vegetables to solvents or high temperatures to extract oil, then filtering them, saves industry money in the production of oil and leads to a clear, beautiful-looking but unhealthful, insipid product that easily goes rancid. The preservatives added to prevent spoilage are often carcinogenic. A healthier alternative is the unrefined

product, which is darker and tastier, and can be found at health food stores. It needs to be refrigerated.

Artificial flavors and colors are commercially convenient because they're cheaper to use than are their natural counterparts. Ubiquitous in candy, chips, and soda, artificial colors are made by heating coal in the absence of oxygen to produce coal tar, which is then further treated. These carcinogenic chemicals are suitable for dying clothing, but not for eating. One artificial color, yellow dye number 14, becomes toxic when exposed to sunlight, so farmers put it on manure heaps to kill flies. Do you want this chemical in your body?

Evolution has endowed us with molecules to transport the broken-down products of natural foods into our cells, to be reassembled and used as needed according to our genetic codes. We haven't developed the mechanisms to handle coal tar and other laboratory chemicals, which we haven't been eating for millions of years. These substances enrich the food business at the expense of our health.

Margarine (along with the hydrogenated oils used in supermarket cookies, crackers, cakes, and baked goods) is another example of a lab-created food. It is derived from vegetable oil, which chemists solidify by bubbling hydrogen through it. The molecules of natural vegetable oils (with the exceptions of monounsaturated olive and canola oils) are polyunsaturated: All the places that could be filled with hydrogen are empty. That's why they're unsaturated. Saturated fats such as animal fat, coconut oil, and avocado oil hold as much hydrogen as possible. The body has evolved mechanisms to handle these natural fats, within limits. Consuming too much saturated animal fat is a well-established risk factor for heart disease, obesity, and a variety of associated ills.

But margarine's partially saturated fat is new. No natural fat molecule has some potential hydrogen bonds occupied with hydrogen while others remain empty. Our bodies have had millions of years to adapt to saturated and polyunsaturated fats but only decades to handle margarine. Furthermore, margarine and its ilk are configured into the mirror image of normal fats. Biochemically, it's like forcing a left-handed glove onto a right hand; we have no effective way of handling these alien molecules. As a result, they give rise to free radicals, which are highly active electrically charged molecules that steal electrons from other molecules, destroying their normal functions and turning them into free radicals themselves. The resulting DNA damage leads to mistakes when cells divide. Enough of these inheritable errors accumulating over generations of damaged cells can lead to the creation of cancer cells. And free radicals killing cells in artery walls leads to the spread of lesions that fill with cholesterol, contributing to cardiovascular disease. (This condition is exacerbated if one consumes a high-fat diet or if the presence of the wrong genes raises one's low-density cholesterol level.)

On the other hand, nuts such as black walnuts, butternuts, acorns, and hickory nuts provide the high-quality essential fatty acids the body can't synthesize. These nutrients regulate cholesterol, prevent arterial plaque, and keep the immune system and the brain healthy. Other natural foods make you healthy in other ways, and major new discoveries involving health benefits of components of natural foods burst into the media almost every year. For example, just before this book went to press, scientists discovered a powerful antioxidant called lycopene, which is present in tomatoes, and that helps prevent cancer and heart disease. The autumn olive (page 415) has 17 times the lycopene of tomatoes.

The recipes in this book omit animal products. I gradually became a vegetarian as I discovered that the high fat content of animal products was dangerous. Modern livestock has been bred to contain far more fat than the wild game our Paleolithic ancestors occasionally caught. The hormone residues in animal products and the low fiber content are also very dangerous. Not to mention the artificial growth hormones and the antibiotics—and *E. coli*, mad cow disease, salmonella, and other very nasty things. And the relationship between a diet high in animal fat and cardiovascular disease and cancer is unequivocal.

Meat-eating also often degrades the environment. It's wasteful because raising animals converts vegetable products such as grain, which we could eat directly, into meat very inefficiently. Livestock raised in large factory farms wastes water resources and produces excrement that pollutes the environment. Live-stock grazing on public lands damages the environment directly when ranchers act irresponsibly. (But not all ranchers and farmers are irresponsible. I'd rather see cows grazing in a meadow than a housing development.) As the Farm Service Agency would say, our safe food supply is best ensured by small family farms. Factory farmers inhumanely crowd animals together and mistreat them. To keep these abused animals alive, they pump them full of antibiotics, creating a milieu where pathogens can evolve antibiotic resistance, and when we eat these animals or their by-products we risk breeding super-pathogens that are immune to the drugs that could otherwise save our lives.

Even if you do eat animal products, you'll probably enjoy an occasional vegetarian meal. That was how I first approached vegetarianism. Today I consume no animal products whatsoever. Animal products aren't necessary to make great-tasting, healthful meals. It was a long time coming, but now even the conservative medical establishment admits the benefits of reducing one's consumption of animal products and increasing the consumption of fruits, vegetables, whole grains, and legumes.

Non-vegetarians worry about protein deficiency in vegetarian diets. All of us require the 23 essential amino acids the body can't synthesize. By combining whole grains and legumes (or legumes plus seeds) in the diet, we can get all 23. Root vegetables, nuts, and cattail flower (and seed-) heads also supply protein in the absence of animal products. Vitamin B12 is absent in non-animal foods (foods previously touted as sources of B12 contain inactive B12 analogs), but this vitamin can be in supplement form. Eating a variety of vegetarian foods provides other important vitamins, minerals, and trace minerals, as well as fiber in much better balance than is present in diets based on meat and refined foods.

If you gradually improve your diet, add some exercise and stretching to your routine, get some meaningful contact with nature, and do some meditation (or whatever gives you inner fulfillment), you'll notice an improvement in your health, and you will attain a greater feeling of well-being.

In America, many of us tend to take food for granted. Many people never cook. I myself had a real aversion to cooking until my late twenties, even though I didn't know anything about cooking. People in other cultures take a far greater interest in food. In China, for example, family life—centered on the table—led to the creation of one of the great world cuisines, on the one hand, and, it is ironic that this tradition evolved into the Chinese take-out joints in America! Still, a lot of U.S. families—old and young—have farming roots—a tradition of raising and preparing foods that was central to family life. The same goes for the immigrant backgrounds that enrich our cuisine.

We have many ways of understanding food, food preparation, and nutrition. Although cooking is an art form, the science of nutrition can also analyze food and food preparation methods and their effects on the body. Science is supposed to be an objective search for the truth based on evolving theoretical frameworks that we can verify or refute experimentally. But establishment nutritional science has long been mired in dogma because of its ties to the profit-oriented food industry and medical-pharmaceutical institutions. Alternative nutrition takes account of research that is not profitable to the food and medical industries, and for that reason it sometimes takes decades for these findings to be accepted. When I first started studying health in the mid-1970s, the medical establishment opposed many of the same "alternative" ideas it promotes today. Anyone who recommended a lowfat diet with lots of fruits and vegetables was considered a quack. Acupuncture was superstition, chiropractic was fraud, and exercise was undervalued. Artificial flavors and colors, pesticides, herbicides, and preservatives were supposed to be harmless. Although research results are sometimes contradictory, I think a "natural" diet and lifestyle is our best bet for staying healthy.

Alternative nutrition, on the other hand, also includes rigid schools of thought that are not always amenable to new scientific research. Although dogmatic, they also contain elements of truth: Macrobiotics, for example, embodies an ancient Japanese philosophical system, based on even more ancient antecedents, sensibly urging "closeness to nature." According to its prescriptions, one should eat locally grown food in season, minimize refined foods and animal products, and avoid synthetic chemicals. This advice is consistent with the best of scientific nutrition and conservation, as well as with the seasonal realities of foraging.

But macrobiotics also categorically denies the scientifically proven value of all vitamin and mineral supplements. And it shoehorns all aspects of reality, including food, into the concepts of yin and yang—a system of thinking that is too simplistic and reductionist for me to digest. Food that originates from a different latitude from your home is supposed to be harmful, so northerners should avoid (tropical) oranges and potatoes (originally Peruvian), even though harm from these foods has not been demonstrated experimentally. Furthermore, in tune with ancient Japan, macrobiotic cuisine tends to be high in salt and low in healthful raw salads. (Before modern sanitation, raw food was often contaminated with pathogens, which cooking, pickling, and fermentation killed or reduced. Alcohol was much safer to drink than was water.)

At the other extreme from macrobiotics are a variety of live food and natural hygiene philosophies that emphasize consuming raw food because it's more "natural" than "dead" cooked food. Some variants eliminate all cooked food. Cooking does reduce vitamin content, and raw food does contain healthful enzymes that are sensitive to heat and that cooking destroys. So I include raw vegetable salads and fresh fruit in my diet every day. Some people I know claim to thrive on vegetarian diets that consist of purely raw food with no vitamin B12 or other supplements.

But you can't digest grains and beans, which are important vegetarian sources of protein, vitamins, minerals, and fiber, without cooking them (although you can sprout many grains and some beans, making them more digestible to consume raw). Some healthful root vegetables, such as burdock and potatoes, are very difficult to digest or are simply inedible or somewhat poisonous eaten raw. Lightly cooked stinging nettles, which are very high in nutrients, are delicious. Raw, they'll sting you. Mushrooms, which are tasty

and healthful, should always be cooked. All species, including commercial mushrooms and those wild species that won't make you sick immediately if you eat them uncooked, contain carcinogenic hydrazines —substances NASA uses in rocket fuel—which are destroyed by cooking. (Some otherwise edible wild species make people sick if they are eaten raw; others may or may not be edible raw.)

We originally learned which wild plants to eat, grow, and use for medicine from discoveries indigenous cultures made over the centuries as they struggled to survive. There's even paleontological evidence that *Homo erectus*, one of *Homo sapiens*'s nearest predecessors, used fire. All these societies cooked food— no trivial matter when they had to gather and chop firewood. None of these societies ate mushrooms raw. This is where I disagree with proponents of all-raw-foods diets. It isn't natural for humans to eat only raw foods. We shouldn't sweep all this experience away in the name of unsubstantiated dogma.

Both conventional and alternative systems of health and nutrition are less than perfect. Your best bet is to study these fields widely, seeking what makes the most sense and works best for you, and remain flexible as you learn.

Although the art of cooking seems mysterious at first, its elements are easy to define. You can prepare foods using different methods, with a variety of equipment, ingredients, and seasonings. The great world cuisines came into being when people in diverse ecosystems and climates experimented with limited regional food resources and technologies over long periods of time, and shared their knowledge through trading.

The Chinese method of stir-frying, for example, was developed where large populations made firewood scarce. Brief cooking over a hot flame, stirring constantly to avoid burning, maximized fuel efficiency.

The Greeks create wonderful dishes with olive oil, mint, marjoram, flour, and other locally available ingredients. Likewise, Meso-Americans create fantastic dishes with indigenous corn and chiles. French cuisine, which we associate with expensive restaurants, originated in the kitchens of family farmers, as did Italian, English, and many other cuisines. Diverse regions and ethnic groups, including those of the Caribbean, India, Italy, the Middle East, Japan, North America, and Southeast Asia, among others, have contributed ideas we can draw from. And we must thank the Native Americans for showing us how to use our own native wild edible plants.

Regional cuisines realized a quantum leap forward when New World ingredients reached the Old World and vice versa, and when Asia exchanged food ingredients with the rest of the world. The tomatoes of Italian cuisine, potatoes of Irish dishes, and hot peppers of Indian food all come from the Americas. Turkey, a crossroads between the East and West, developed an original cuisine long ago based on elements of the Middle East, Greece, Asia, and the West before incorporating New World ingredients such as eggplants, bell peppers, and tomatoes. Such revolutionary developments transformed medieval cuisine into the Old World and New World ethnic cuisines we recognize today.

When populations, along with their cuisines, were dislocated or immigrated and different ethnic groups were thrown together in regions with different food resources, new creativity with food burst forth. In the Americas, for example, French and African influences transformed Haitian and other Caribbean cuisines into what they are today, while a melding of Spanish and Native American cooking styles and ingredients led to modern Mexican and Tex-Mex (another hybrid in the making) food.

Substituting healthful vegetarian and wild ingredients for animal products and refined food and using healthful cooking methods and proportions in modern kitchens offer us the opportunity to create new recipes in the spirit (if not the letter) of preexisting cuisines.

FOOD PREPARATION METHODS

RAW FOOD

Many foods are wonderful raw. Nothing can beat eating wild berries off the bushes. You can combine raw ingredients to make salads, grind raw nuts into nut butter, or dry and grind sprouted grains into what are called *essine* breads.

FERMENTATION

In fermentation, "friendly" microorganisms act on food, as when yeast creates the bubbles of carbon dioxide that make bread rise. Commercial yeast has been bred for this purpose, but you can also invite wild yeast from the air to leaven your sourdough breads and pancakes. Other yeasts have been bred for making wine and other alcoholic beverages. Yogurt is a healthful fermented food. Asian fermented foods (available in health food and ethnic stores) include miso, a soybean paste that tastes like soy sauce, and tempeh, a yeasty tasting cake of fermented soybean grits. Fermented foods provide microorganisms that have proven to be beneficial because they displace pathogens and may even synthesize some nutrients. These microorganisms, together with minerals and enzymes, substantiate the traditional claims of the health benefits of fermented foods.

Pickling, which sometimes involves fermentation, originated as a means of preserving food before the advent of refrigeration. The highly acidic or saline brine stops the microorganisms that cause spoilage from proliferating.

WATER-BASED COOKING

Water-based cooking is one of the healthiest ways to cook. It retains nutrients and flavor, if done correctly.

Steaming

You can steam many foods by setting them above a boiling liquid on a steamer rack—this method is good for cooking thick foods such as root vegetables and stems, and also for making Boston brown bread. Most people don't know that washed leafy green vegetables retain enough water that you can steam them for from 3 to 10 minutes in a heavy, covered pot without the need for a steamer or any added water. The flavor or nutrition concentrates in the greens, rather than dissipating into the water. This "waterless steaming" method is one of the simplest and best ways of preparing lamb's-quarters, chickweed, and spinach, although I usually add some seasonings when the vegetables are done. Steaming is not a good way to cook very bitter wild greens like dandelions or winter cress, because the bitterness concentrates.

Boiling

Boiling vegetables for too long and in too much water is usually a beginner's mistake that ruins their flavor and nutrition (steaming often retains more flavor and nutrition). However, you must boil some wild vegetables if they're too bitter or toxic to prepare otherwise (for instance, milkweed and pokeweed). In such situations, make sure the water is boiling rapidly before you add the vegetables, and keep it boiling rapidly, especially if the procedure calls for changing the water. In such cases, seasonings are added after cooking and the vegetables will taste great.

Simmering

Soups and sauces are made by gently simmering ingredients in a water-based liquid (you may also precook some of the ingredients first), taking care not to overcook them. Nutrients and flavors that leave the solid ingredients go into the liquid. You may thicken some sauces and concentrate the flavors by boiling them down: this is called *reducing*. But doing so also "reduces" the nutrient content of your wild foods. (Flour, arrowroot, kudzu, potato starch, powdered dried sassafras leaves [called filé powder], or puréed ingredients also make good thickeners.)

Whole grains or beans are cooked by gently simmering them in a measured amount of water or water-based liquid, which is absorbed and softens them.

OIL-BASED COOKING

Oil-based cooking involves a higher temperature (approximately 375 degrees) than does water-based cooking, since boiling water can't surpass 212 degrees at sea level. The oil imparts flavor and crispness to the food. Unfortunately, high temperatures degrade oil, making this cooking method less healthful than water-based cooking. Sautéing is the most desirable way of cooking with oil, especially if you use olive oil or peanut oil, which best resist degradation by heat. Used in moderation along with other cooking methods, sautéing poses no real dangers. It's better to eat oil-cooked foods in moderation.

Deep-Frying

You can make delicious food by heating a pot of vegetable oil (don't use olive oil, which burns) to 375 degrees (use a liquid thermometer to help you regulate the temperature) and cooking vegetables coated with batter until they are lightly browned and crisp, 3 to 5 minutes. Drain the food on paper towels and serve it immediately.

Use this method only for special occasions, such as when the daylily, wisteria, or black locust flowers bloom. Deep-frying is expensive and messy; you're consuming lots of unhealthful cooked oil, and you are taking in too many fat calories, so the flavor had better be worth it.

Sautéing

Sautéing is the most common way to cook with oil. You heat a frying pan for a few minutes over medium heat, add the oil, wait until it's hot (don't let the oil get hot enough to smoke), and stir in the other ingredients. Continue to cook the food over medium heat, stirring occasionally, for from 5 to 20 minutes, until it is done. You want to keep the food sizzling slightly while sautéing to maintain crispness, without burning it. Too much food in too small a pan lowers the temperature of the oil and causes sogginess.

You can't properly sauté food that's dripping with water. (Pat food dry with a paper towel or spin it in a salad spinner first.) The residual water will reach 212 degrees (sautéing occurs at higher temperatures) and start to boil. Turning up the flame just makes the water boil faster, and the food will become soggy with oil.

Braising

This technique combines moist heat and oil cooking. You sauté food briefly, add a liquid such as a sauce, cover the pot, and simmer the food over low heat until it is done.

Stir-Frying

If you like Asian cuisine, knowing how to stir-fry is essential. Chop or slice ingredients and set them aside in separate bowls beforehand. Heat a wok (it is better than a frying pan because more surface area is exposed to the heat) over high heat and add more than enough peanut oil to coat the surface. When the oil is very hot, add one batch of solid ingredients (don't overload the wok) and cook the food, stirring constantly, over high heat until it is just tender, 1 to 3 minutes. Remove the food from the wok and then add the next ingredient until you've gone through the entire assembly line. Then you might reassemble all the ingredients in the pan with a sauce and heat the mixture through.

TOASTING

This method heats food over an open fire, in a pan on the stovetop, or in the oven, without any liquid. You can toast nuts or seeds in a hot frying pan on the stovetop, stirring often (if you add some oil or other liquid, you're roasting the food), or do the same in a roasting pan or cookie sheet in the oven.

BAKING

Baking refers to anything cooked in the oven, whether or not liquid is involved. This makes sense, because when you bake breads, cakes, or casseroles you may be using both solid and liquid ingredients.

BROILING AND GRILLING

You can broil food by exposing it to direct high heat in your oven's broiler (grilling food outdoors over hot coals is similar). You may or may not marinate the food in advance for added flavor.

COOKING IN MICROWAVE OVENS

It has become very popular to save time by bombarding food with very high-energy microwaves. This cooking method breaks down chemical bonds in food that normal cooking doesn't, creating multitudes of novel, unknown, and untested chemicals that don't occur in nature. Because I don't want such potentially hazardous chemicals in my body, I never cook with a microwave oven (also, some things taste awful microwaved). Time will tell if long-range consumption of microwaved food leads to illness, but I don't want to be one of the industry's guinea pigs.

COOKING EQUIPMENT

WHAT KIND OF COOKING EQUIPMENT SHOULD you use? Whether you keep your purchases to a minimum or try to equip your kitchen as completely as possible, it pays to buy high-quality equipment rather than cheap junk that burns, damages, or contaminates your food, or that quickly wears out and breaks.

Since I cook regularly and like gadgets, I've accumulated lots of cooking paraphernalia. Some of the basics include high-quality, sharp chopping and paring knives (Japanese knives often offer the best quality for your money), heavy pots and pans (lightweight cookware usually distributes heat poorly and burns the food), mixing bowls, casserole dishes, cookie sheets, roasting pans, measuring cups and spoons, wooden spoons, various spatulas, thick oven gloves, colanders, strainers, and food storage containers.

Caution: Avoid cookware with an aluminum surface that comes into contact with the food, unless you want this unhealthful metal in your body. Teflon is another unnecessary substance that may also contaminate food.

Depending on your tastes and budget, you may want to invest in the following: some funnels, a can opener, blender, salad spinner (to rid your washed vegetables of extra water), nutcracker, garlic press, flour sifter, pie tins, bread pans, ladles, grater, scale, spice (or coffee) grinder, rice cooker, muffin tins, cookie sheets, casserole dishes, heavy saucepans, cast-iron skillets, tortilla press, heat diffuser, cheesecloth, parchment paper, ravioli press, kitchen timer, racks, apple corer, tongs, scissors, citrus squeezer, pastry sheets, rolling pin, wok, food processor, grain mill, dehydrator, pasta machine, ice cream machine, mixer, juicer, and dishwasher. (Have I left anything out?)

UNCOMMON INGREDIENTS

SINCE I BEGAN COOKING, PROFESSIONALS AND amateurs have begun incorporating relatively new natural, healthful ingredients, often from other cultures, into their recipes. Some of these ingredients you can buy only in widely scattered ethnic specialty stores, but many now occupy the shelves of health food stores, grocery stores, and supermarkets. New ingredients are always fun to try, even when you have to buy them instead of gathering them.

Most people today are familiar with tofu. This mild-tasting, easily digestible soybean curd cake takes on the flavors of the other ingredients and seasonings that are used with it. So don't spare the seasonings when you use tofu. Its texture varies from extra-firm (good sliced, marinated, and grilled—you can turn it with a spatula without breaking it) to firm, soft, and silken (great in ice creams, sauces, salad dressings, or whipped into puddings with fruit, sweetener, and flavorings). You can apply virtually any cooking method to tofu. And the way you prepare it influences its texture as well as its final flavor.

As a soybean product, this excellent source of calcium provides high-quality complete protein if your diet also includes whole grains. Soybean products (in addition to members of the cruciferous or mustard family) contain phytoestrogens, inactive plant estrogens that block normal estrogen and super-estrogens (DDT, Agent Orange, and other environmental contaminants) from entering your cells and forcing them to proliferate. Cells making copies of copies of themselves accumulate mistakes that may lead to cancer, and foods such as soybean products and whole grains reduce your risk.

ALTERNATIVES TO TABLE SALT

It's unhealthy to take in too much sodium as it leads to high blood pressure in susceptible people. It overworks the kidneys, which must excrete the excess sodium. And you lose one precious potassium atom along with every sodium atom you excrete, leading to electrolyte imbalance. Many alternatives to table salt also contain sodium, but they provide so much flavor that you can use them sparingly, thereby reducing your sodium intake to reasonable levels.

Anyone who's eaten Chinese food is familiar with *soy sauce*. Because this cheap commercial imitation of traditional shoyu is loaded with sodium, sugar, and preservatives, health-conscious people prefer natural tamari soy sauce, sold in health food stores, which also tastes better. (Tamari is so unfamiliar to people who don't shop in health food stores that the editor of my previous book wanted to delete the word, imagining that I was endorsing a brand-name product!)

Miso, a by-product of traditional tamari manufacture, is a thick, salty paste that comes in many forms. The darker-colored, saltier kinds taste more like strong soy sauce, while the light-colored, mellow ones taste sweeter and contain less sodium. The brands that come in tubs and must be refrigerated are much better than those in plastic bags that you may store unrefrigerated.

To use miso, you can blend it into the recipe with a food processor or blender, or mix it with some of the liquid with a whisk or fork. To retain maximum flavor and nutrients in miso, you usually mix it into the liquid of a soup or stew after the cooking is done. One trick is to dip a strainer into the pot and incorporate the miso by stirring the miso against the strainer's sides with a whisk or wooden spoon.

Bragg's Liquid Aminos (Paul Bragg, barely remembered today, was an important early-twentieth-century alternative health pioneer), is a unique brand-name product. This watery, dark liquid—available in health food stores—provides a meat-like flavor that's excellent in vegetarian meat-analog recipes. Vege-Sal is my favorite seasoned salt substitute, although health food stores also sell other great formulations.

SEASONINGS FOR ALL SEASONS

Food seasoning is a very personal matter. I like strong seasonings, but others find anything more than the slightest flavoring too strong, especially when it comes to garlic or hot peppers. Decades of research confirm how greatly people's sense of taste varies. In a recent study, some people were unable to detect a flavor constituent extracted from broccoli and related vegetables, while others found it terribly bitter. This difference was demonstrated to be inherited.

Although initial sensitivity to various flavors is genetic, your taste perception will change as you continue to experiment with new foods and recipes. If you're used to a high sugar and salt diet, it may take a while to readjust to the flavor of natural foods, from a matter of weeks to a couple of months.

Seasonings can make the difference between a pedestrian dish and a wonderful one. Often, you'll want to use these flavorings to complement the main ingredients and bring out their flavors, adding just enough so you barely detect them. You don't want to drown out the flavors of the main ingredients. On the other hand, there are times when the seasonings predominate. You should clearly taste the spices in curries and the chile in chilis. The flavorings should step forward in lemon rice, saffron rice, pesto (intensely garlicky), and vanilla ice cream.

What are herbs and spices? Definitions vary: to a botanist, an herb is any nonwoody plant. In herbal medicine, it's a biologically active plant. To cooks, an herb may be any plant seasoning, although some people define herbs as leafy plant seasonings, distinct from spices, which include seeds, pods, roots, and barks. Others distinguish spices from herbs by their greater pungency. Choose your own definition.

The first step in learning how to use herbs is to have them on hand. Keep fresh garlic in a paper bag, like onions, or in a special garlic container away from the light. Store fresh parsley, dill, ginger, and cilantro in the refrigerator, along with any other fresh wild (or commercial) culinary herbs that are in season and that you can identify with certainty, plus any culinary herbs from a garden.

If you want to keep them for future use, you can dry most fresh leafy herbs in a food dehydrator or by leaving them in a paper bag in a warm, dry, well-ventilated room for a couple of weeks. *Note:* Basil loses much of its flavor when you dry it, so I freeze the leaves on a cookie sheet to keep them from freezing into a solid lump. I then pack the frozen leaves in a food storage container, and remove some at the last minute as needed.

Purchase as many of the other culinary herbs as possible. Store them in tightly closed airtight jars with easily visible labels. I write the herb names on masking tape with magic markers. These labels are easy to remove when the jar is empty.

You can't have too many herbs and spices. They last for years, and the worst that can happen as they age is that they become weaker; you can mitigate this problem by simply using larger quantities.

Refer to the Herb and Spice User's Guide (page 448) for the traditional uses of herbs, as well as my own suggestions. Prepare your own herb and spice mixes, such as curry and chili powders, and experiment with original combinations. Keep the herbs handy. I arrange mine alphabetically inside kitchen cabinets (light eventually degrades dried herbs), with leafy herbs (that is, marjoram, rosemary, and thyme) on one set of shelves; barks, seeds, and pods (that is, cardamom, cinnamon, nutmeg, star anise) on another, and combinations in a third cabinet. If your herb cabinet is deep, keep rows of smaller jars in front of the larger ones.

In India, cooks place open jars of the herbs they tend to use together in covered tins. Use any scheme that increases accessibility. Being able to see the selection and smell your herbs makes it easier to choose the right ones.

When you purchase dried herbs, beware of rip-offs. Avoid supermarket herbs unless you have an appetite for irradiated food. Most commercial herbs are irradiated to "preserve" them—a great way for the nuclear industry to profit from nuclear wastes! Because the government has ties to the food industry, food companies are not required to provide warnings on labels of irradiated food. These herbs aren't radioactive, but the treatment alters their chemical composition, creating potentially dangerous, new, unknown chemical by-products.

Herb stores or health food stores that supply certified organic herbs in bulk (instead of prepackaged herbs) offer the best buys. Ethnic markets often sell fresh and dried herbs at great prices. Make sure the dried herbs' colors correspond to those of the fresh herbs. If you dry green leaves, they usually remain green. Brown dried leaves were decaying and browning before they were dried (garbage in, garbage out). If you're buying dried leaves, make sure that half of what you're buying isn't dried twigs or other plant debris.

I like to buy spices whole and grind them in a spice grinder or coffee grinder right before using them. Whole spices and herbs retain more flavor than do powdered ones, especially if you store them for months. When you grind dried leafy herbs and most dried seeds and spices, the volume stays the same. Exceptions include black and white peppercorns and mustard seeds, which expand to twice their volume ground; celery seeds, which expand by 50 percent, and flaxseeds (which are actually used for purposes other than flavor), which increase two and a half times in volume. In my recipes, in these cases, you will find in the ingredient list the final ground volume listed first, followed by the measured amount of seeds needed to yield this volume of ground spice.

You may also purchase a great variety of wonderful natural extracts, which are flavors dissolved in a natural medium, vanilla extract being the most familiar. Extracts are fun and easy to use. Choose natural extracts over extracts made with unhealthful artificial flavors. One company I've found that offers a great selection of unadulterated extracts is Bickford Flavors, (800) 283-8322.

Chiles

Many vegetarian cookbooks over-recommend using cayenne pepper for pungency. Cayenne is used in herbal home remedies to increase circulation, and it can replace black pepper, which may cause stomach irritation in sensitive people if it is used excessively. But cayenne pepper can taste too harsh, and it's often inferior to various other hot seasonings.

To my palate, the fresh chiles available in any grocery store or supermarket taste better than cayenne pepper. The smallest peppers are usually the hottest. Cut the peppers open and discard the irritatingly hot seeds and ribs. Wear rubber gloves when handling chiles or wash your hands three times afterward. If you handle hot peppers and accidentally touch your eyes, you'll regret it.

Asian specialty stores also sell excellent-tasting chili pastes. My favorite is called chili paste with soybean. *Caution:* Many canned products in ethnic stores often contain undesirable additives such as preservatives, artificial colors, and sugar. If you're health-conscious, read the labels before buying.

CRACKING THE EGG MYTH

Some people believe cooking without eggs greatly limits the variety of dishes you can create. And all the health food store egg substitutes I've tried lay eggs— they don't work! Supermarket egg replacers contain unhealthful artificial and refined ingredients. Instead, to substitute for 1 egg white, grind 1½ tablespoons flaxseeds or chia seeds (also available in health food stores) in a spice or coffee grinder and add 1½ tablespoons water. To substitute for 1 egg yolk, mix together 2 tablespoons lecithin granules (a food supplement extracted from soybeans) and 1 tablespoon corn oil, flaxseed oil, or olive oil. In baking, add a pinch more extra leavening, such as baking soda, as well.

The lecithin in egg yolks creates their flavor and color, provides the nutrients choline and inositol, and helps normalize cholesterol levels. (I began using lecithin as an egg yolk substitute after adding it to oatmeal as a nutritional food supplement, noticing the egg yolk flavor, and recalling the egg yolk connection.) Flaxseeds and chia seeds provide bulk that prevents constipation. Many of the recipes in this book rely on these ingredients to advantage.

VEGETARIAN MEAT

It's easy to create more-than-reasonable meat substitutes. Take a thick-textured ingredient, season it with the flavorings associated with a particular type of meat (see the Herb and Spice User's Guide, page 448), add some vegetable oil if appropriate, and use the substitute in a recipe that usually includes meat. You'll be astonished with the results.

Vegetarian cooks have been doing this with texturized vegetable protein (TVP) and tofu for years. TVP, made from soybeans, has a meaty flavor and texture to begin with. Adding meat flavors makes it even better. You buy it dry, so you need to soak it in hot stock, almost any savory sauce, or hot water for 10 minutes. After you drain it, you can sauté it for 10 to 15 minutes, or include it in soups, stews, sauces, casseroles, or other dishes.

To make *tofu* work, use the extra-firm variety, drain it for a long time, cut it into meat-sized chunks, and don't spare the seasonings. Marinating the tofu before cooking it works well, as does cooking the tofu until it's slightly browned. Even better, if you have the time, drain it, freeze it, and let it defrost first beforehand. This process will give your tofu an even more meaty texture.

Sauté tofu, simmer it in liquid dishes, stir-fry it, or bake it. You can also deep-fry tofu, although you will be taking in more vegetable oil and calories than with other cooking methods.

Tempeh is another ingredient some people use as a meat subtitute. Made from fermented soy grits, tempeh is good sautéed or baked with plenty of seasoning (you may also marinate it first). Personally, I don't care for tempeh's bitter-fermented flavor, which I can taste no matter how I try to cover it up, so I prefer other meat substitutes.

Wheat gluten, a.k.a. seitan, is another meat substitute, made by repeatedly kneading and washing whole wheat flour under cold water to remove everything but the protein. Seitan is also sold in health food stores, often frozen. Again, you can sauté, simmer, bake, or deep-fry this chewy textured wheat protein with appropriate flavorings or sauces to create a meat substitute, or add it to stews.

Many people, myself included, are allergic to wheat (which is why I personally don't use wheat in recipes).

When I started switching from the typical American diet to a whole-foods approach and began substituting whole wheat flour for white flour, I began getting headaches as I developed an allergy from repeated exposure. As a result, I don't recommend the frequent use of wheat gluten as a meat substitute, and I don't include seitan or whole wheat recipes in this book.

Some *wild mushrooms*, again with the appropriate seasonings, make ideal meat substitutes. The chicken mushroom, fried chicken mushroom, beefsteak mushroom, oyster mushroom, and lobster mushroom didn't get their names for nothing. (See Under the Mushroom Cloud, page 28, for more information about using marinated mushrooms as meat substitutes.)

IN THE SOY COW'S PASTURE—THE VEGAN DAIRY

Many cuisines traditionally rely on dairy products. After years of limiting myself to nondairy recipes, it struck me that I might be able to re-create the essential flavors and textures of dairy products with the wide range of nondairy vegan ingredients available in health food stores. (Vegans consume no animal products whatsoever—that means no eggs, cheese, butter, or honey.)

Essential to this new vegan cuisine is tofu. I've been criticized for using it too often, but most people take for granted the inordinately high use of dairy products in conventional cooking. Properly prepared, tofu provides an excellent alternative to a variety of dairy products.

Don't Laugh at Mock Cheese

Cheese, for example, includes dairy solids. Extra-firm tofu can substitute for hard cheeses, soft and silken tofu for softer varieties. And you can use the various tofus sliced, grated, puréed, raw, sautéed, or baked to create different textures.

Health food stores already sell tofu cheeses, but cheese analog manufacturers use the cheapest ingredients to stay competitive, and the results are terrible. Many brands even contain casein, defeating their own purpose (unless their intent is to snow consumers who don't know that casein comes from milk).

How do you make flavorless tofu resemble cheese more closely? You replace each of the cheese's flavor and texture components individually to achieve a whole that is greater than the sum of its parts:

Cheese is acidic. Using an obvious acidic ingredient like lemon juice makes tofu taste lemony, not cheesy. Cider vinegar, the standard health-food cuisine standby, has a distinct, overpowering flavor I don't care for; it's too strong and obvious. (In the nineteenth century, people used it to clean walls. Believing the human body to be filthy, puritanical and prudish people used cider vinegar to clean their insides and restore health. It's because of this long-forgotten simple-minded idea that cider vinegar still reigns supreme in health food stores and health food cookbooks.) But combining two milder, more subtle vinegars such as brown rice vinegar, wine vinegar, or umeboshi plum vinegar solves the problem of creating unobtrusive acidity.

Cheese is fermented. So is brewer's yeast. When I first started cooking, this was a vile-tasting nutritional supplement you swallowed for its B-complex vitamins. Today manufacturers produce brewer's yeast without the bitterness, and I use it in many tofu cheese recipes for its cheesy flavor. Sweet-tasting light-colored mellow miso, also fermented, works in some tofu cheese recipes, where it also mimics the saltiness of real cheese. Cheese is salty, so when I don't use miso, I use coarse kosher salt, which is chemical-free (commercial salt includes toxic aluminum as an anti-caking agent), and also used in dairy cheese, to achieve cheese's saltiness. (Umeboshi plum vinegar, which provides acidity, is also salty.) Sea salt, also good, is more expensive than is kosher salt, and "land" salt is really just sea salt that is mined from areas where ancient oceans have dried up. They're both simply sodium chloride.

Cheese is usually sharp. Like cider vinegar, cayenne pepper (popular because it has real medicinal properties), the health food stand-by, is too harsh and obvious. A combination of Tabasco sauce and paprika—especially "hot" paprika—does the job. (Some dairy cheeses also include paprika.) For additional sharpness, I sometimes also add undetectably small amounts of white pepper. Other spices also sometimes help. Turmeric colors yellow tofu cheeses, and its flavor also makes a positive contribution. Very small amounts of fenugreek and mace can also be helpful. In Tofu Herb Cheese (page 131), you use the same herbs you use in dairy herb cheese, that is, garlic, parsley, dill, rosemary, or tarragon.

Dairy cheese contains butterfat. Corn oil and flaxseed oil, the most buttery tasting vegetable oils, fill this niche, although olive oil also works sometimes. Some tofu cheeses also benefit from the addition of lecithin granules, which impart a rich, egg-yolk-like flavor.

You'll enjoy the tofu cheese recipes based on the above principles by themselves, but they're even better in traditional dishes that call for cheese (see the Quick Guide to Making Dairy-Free Cheese, page 467, for a compilation of all the mock cheese recipes in this book).

Milking the Soy Cow

There's an increasing proliferation of soy milk, nut milk, and the like available that you can substitute for cow's milk, and all of it is available in health food stores, and even in some supermarkets. Try different brands to determine which ones you like. My favorite is a soy and rice blend.

Avoid using soy milk with lemon juice, lime juice, vinegar, or other acidic substances, especially when the soy milk is hot. The curds will separate from the whey. (If you drain and press these curds, you'll get tofu.)

You can also make delicious nut milk yourself by soaking nuts in hot water for an hour or overnight, puréeing the mixture in a blender, and straining out the solids through cheesecloth or nylon cloth.

Dairy-Free Ice Cream

When I became a vegan, I thought I would be giving up forever the homemade ice cream I used to make with fresh cream and wild berries. After years of abstinence, I found ways to re-create incredibly good ice cream without dairy products. As with nondairy cheese making, you have to replace each of the dairy components with something similar.

A combination of soy milk and silken tofu substitutes partially for the milk and cream. Milk and cream also contain fat, but most vegetable oils impart the wrong flavors for ice cream. Canola oil, a monounsaturated oil that reduces the risk of heart disease, is much more healthful than is butterfat, and its lack of flavor makes it the perfect source for ice cream's necessary fat content.

Rich-tasting French ice cream includes raw egg yolks, an excellent source of cholesterol and salmonella bacteria. Lecithin granules (made from soybeans and providing an egg yolk flavor) provide a sound alternative. Lecithin is also an emulsifier: Like soap, its molecules can bind to both water and fats, allowing these substances, which normally repel each other, to mix.

Ice cream is sweet, and white sugar is unhealthful, so I use liquid stevia or vegetable glycerin instead. Puréed dates (which also add thickness), honey, maple syrup, rice syrup, or barley malt also work as sweeteners. Salt enhances sweetness, so a small amount of kosher salt or sea salt is appropriate.

Additional flavors often fit in well. Vanilla extract or fresh vanilla beans enhance most ice creams. Sweet herbs or spices (such as cinnamon, sassafras, nutmeg, wild ginger or regular ginger, various types of mints) and other seasonings such as freshly grated orange or lemon rind and ground Kentucky coffee tree seeds can also be good. So can a variety of natural flavor extracts. Blueberry, blackberry, and cherry extracts, for example, intensify the flavors of ice creams that contain those fruits.

Berries and sliced fruits, of course, are great in ice cream. And so are edible wildflowers such as black locust, redbud, wisteria, and elderberry. I usually purée half the fruit or flowers with the other ingredients in a blender, and then add the rest later. Sometimes carob powder, nuts, or nut butter go into the blender, sometimes chopped nuts go in after puréeing.

A modern ice cream machine works very effectively for making nondairy ice cream. The bowl's walls contain a gel you can chill below freezing in a freezer beforehand, and an electric-powered rotor keeps stirring, preventing ice crystals from forming. The much larger old-fashioned, labor-intensive machines used cumbersome salted ice water for refrigeration, and you'd turn a crank. I currently own a Krups machine, which is excellent, although replacement parts are all but impossible to get (I have heard Cuisinart is very good too). Previously, I had a gelato machine that had too little gel to freeze the ice cream completely, and a weak motor that cut off way too early.

GETTING SAUCY

A SAUCE IS A LIQUID (ALTHOUGH SCIENTIFICALLY it's a mixture or suspension), usually flavored and often thickened, that usually accompanies or becomes part of other foods. Although you can make an unlimited number of great-tasting sauces with natural ingredients, many people still make traditional sauces with unhealthful traditional ingredients.

Some traditional sauces, such as tomato sauce, are perfectly natural and healthful. So is Wild Applesauce (page 341), so long as you substitute more healthful sweeteners for white sugar. But others, such as hollandaise sauce and cream sauces, for example, are loaded with white flour and high-fat butter, egg yolks, and cream. How necessary are these ingredients?

To make traditional cream sauce, you cook refined white flour in butter to make a roux, then stir in milk or cream, plus various other ingredients or seasonings. But you can substitute a light whole-grain flour—for the white flour—such as brown rice flour, oat flour, or barley flour, or substitute kudzu or arrowroot (also excellent thickeners used in other kinds of sauces), which you don't have to cook in butter. Corn oil or flaxseed oil, which taste buttery, replace butter without adding saturated fat. You may also substitute olive oil, with its own wonderful flavor.

Soy milk, with a little added oil and perhaps a tiny amount of liquid stevia or other sweetener, substitutes for the dairy products and their saturated fat and milk sugar. Puréeing silken tofu in water provides an equally healthful alternative to the soy milk in sauces.

The silken tofu base works especially well in Indian yogurt sauces, which often consist of yogurt, water, clarified butter, and chickpea flour. Lemon juice, lime juice, or Sumac Concentrate (page 281) provide the acidity of yogurt, chickpea flour still acts as a thickener, and peanut oil or sesame oil (both used in traditional Indian cooking), as well as corn oil or flaxseed oil, substitute for the clarified butter (ghee).

Many traditional sauces are oversalted, but you can reduce the salt to taste and use herbs and spices to add flavor.

Hollandaise sauce, with its egg yolks and melted butter, is another delicious nutritional nightmare we can rescue. Healthy Hollandaise Sauce (page 130) uses lecithin granules (the soy-derived nutritional supplement that gives egg yolks their color and flavor) in place of egg yolks. Lecithin is also an emulsifier, a substance that helps fats mix with water. Water plus corn oil, flaxseed oil, or olive oil supplants the melted butter, while the secondary ingredients and seasonings remain essentially unchanged. This sauce can be simply mixed in a blender—a much easier prospect than slowly incorporating the melted butter into the egg yolks at just the right temperature.

This book contains many examples of natural sauces for main courses, for desserts, and more. Enjoy them as is, transpose ingredients, or start out with my ideas and then develop your own originals.

WILDMAN'S BAKERY

SOON AFTER LEARNING HOW UNNATURAL AND unhealthy refined carbohydrates were, I switched to whole wheat flour. From a culinary and personal standpoint, an equal exchange of one flour for another didn't quite work. My breads and pastries were often too heavy. I could see why conventional chefs stick to refined white flour.

After giving up wheat entirely I began experimenting with other flours. In baked goods that don't have to rise much, such as pie crusts, cookies, pancakes, pastries, tarts, and biscuits, non-wheat flours yield lighter results.

Wheat is a relatively new food for humans. It dates back only about 10,000 years, to the beginning of agriculture, when our ancestors discovered that they could cultivate a rare hybrid of wild wheat grasses that bore seeds that were too heavy to disperse successfully without our intervention. The seeds of the parent grasses were too small to be harvested effectively (foraging for wild seeds is much more labor-intensive than is gathering shoots, greens, root, fruits, berries, nuts, or mushrooms), and the hybrid's offspring soon died out in nature owing to poor dispersal. Humans and the large-kernel hybrid wheat helped each other. We haven't yet had time to adapt biochemically to this new food. Its highly allergenic protein, gluten, makes many people sick. (The same is true of dairy products. For example, East Asian people and Native Americans, who have not used milk as adults until modern times, tolerate dairy products especially poorly.)

Because the recipes in this book reflect cooking experiments I've undertaken to feed myself, they're largely wheat-free—this should be good news for other wheat-intolerant people. Also, reducing exposure to gluten will help prevent future sensitivity in susceptible people who are not yet allergic. Cooking with flours other than wheat also opens up largely unexplored culinary territory, and it's fun to try new possibilities. If you wish, you may still substitute whole wheat flour for the other flours in the recipes. The way to substitute one flour for another is by weight, not by volume, so an inexpensive cooking scale is a good investment (see the Flour Substitutions Chart, page 481, for details).

NONSTICK BAKING (MORE OR LECITHIN)

One of the most useful baking aids I've found is liquid lecithin, which is available in health food stores. Mix a small amount in a jar with a slightly larger volume of any light vegetable oil, and rub a little on your baking surfaces with a paper towel. It will create a nonstick surface without the risks of Teflon or the unnatural ingredients that are present in commercial nonstick sprays.

Another method to circumvent stickiness, if your recipe doesn't have lots of liquid, is to put parchment paper on the baking surface, such as on a cookie sheet or in a cake pan.

GETTING A RISE OUT OF BREAD MAKING

The best thing about wheat is that it contains the proteins glutenin and gliadin, which, when combined with liquid and agitated, produce gluten: elastic strands that trap carbon dioxide bubbles and allow breads to rise. Flours made from rye, sweet brown rice, buckwheat, oats, corn, or barley, all of which contain little or none of these two proteins, all have their own flavors and textures. In baking, they work best with the addition of a starchy ingredient such as arrowroot, kudzu, or potato starch, which makes them more workable. This is especially true with rye flour.

You usually have to knead yeast-leavened wheat bread to develop the gluten so it can trap carbon dioxide bubbles, because kneading makes the gluten elastic. With non-wheat yeast-leavened bread or with baking-soda-leavened bread, it's enough just to mix the ingredients. Overmixing baking-soda-leavened bread is bad because it makes the baking soda release its carbon dioxide bubbles while you mix, instead of while the bread is baking.

Quick breads rely on the chemical action of baking soda instead of the metabolism of yeast to produce the carbon dioxide bubbles that make bread rise. To provide the correct acidity for this process, many of my quick bread and muffin recipes require cream of tartar (a by-product of winemaking) or lemon or lime juice. These substitutions are generally better than commercial baking powder, which contains unhealthful aluminum and refined cornstarch. However, some health food stores sell acceptable baking powder formulations. To substitute one for the other, see the Equivalents table (page 472).

Commercial baking yeast has been bred to leaven bread. (*Note:* unless you rarely bake, it's more economical to buy it in a jar rather than in individual paper packets.) You dissolve it in a lukewarm liquid that includes a sweetener. I use a natural sweetener such as fruit juice because it's more healthful than the standard white sugar. Then you mix the yeast with the wet ingredients and enough of the flour and other dry ingredients to make a dough. After letting the dough

rise, covered, in a warm place (about 80 degrees) for about 45 minutes, until it doubles in volume, you add the remaining dry ingredients plus fruit, nuts, or any additional ingredients you want. You then place the dough in the baking container, let it rise for another 45 minutes, glaze it with oil or other glazes if appropriate, and bake it. I often place a pan of hot water in the bottom of the oven to keep the bread from getting too crusty. After baking the bread, let it cool on racks to prevent water condensation from giving it a soggy bottom.

Wild yeast is also wonderful to use for making sourdough breads, pancakes, and muffins. Following cookbook methods for creating wild yeast sourdough starter didn't work for me, and commercial sourdough preparations tasted too weak. Then I discovered an easy way to befriend wild yeast (see page 42), and made my first Sourdough Rye Bread recipe (page 318). On the first day I made sourdough bread, long before I became the "Wildman," I embarked on a Queens–Long Island (I live in Queens) day tour with a bicycle club. Unfortunately, no one except the leader and I showed up. Perhaps on account of this, she seemed rather uncommunicative and unfriendly. She proceeded to get us lost 30 miles out on Long Island in the middle of nowhere, hadn't brought a map, and probably wouldn't have known how to read one if she had one. To make matters worse, my bike broke down, and it was impossible to repair outside of a bike shop. She biked home to Queens to get her car and drive me back, but she decided to have a lengthy dinner with her parents before returning. I waited four hours, and it began to pour even though a zero percent chance of rain had been forecast. The only thing that saved me was the hearty, delicious sourdough rye bread I had brought along. Since then, I've improved the recipe with the addition of wild ingredients.

Many conventional breads contain milk, but soy milk or nut milks work equally well. Ground flaxseeds or chia seeds plus lecithin granules replace egg whites and yolks, and corn oil or flaxseed oil, which taste buttery, replace butter. These changes work equally well in recipes for cakes, cookies, and pastries. The addition of wild or cultivated nuts, seeds, fruits, seaweed, mushrooms, or seasonings provides plenty of room for innovation.

THE CRUST OF THE MATTER

Pie or pastry crusts may be pressed or rolled. A single crust of the press-in type, which you don't necessarily cook, consists of a mixture of pulpy ingredients that are thick enough to form a thin sheet that isn't too sticky when you pinch it between your thumb and forefinger. The crust often contains puréed thick fruit such as figs, prunes, dates, bananas, pawpaws, raisins, commercial currants, or wild raisins; ground nuts or seeds, or nut butter; often sweet bread crumbs; optional seasonings; and an additional sweetener if desired. You press this mixture into an oiled pie tin or baking dish with your fingers, add a filling that needs no cooking (you may precook the filling), chill, slice, and serve the pie.

You may also roll out a crust. I begin with a light whole-grain flour such as buckwheat, sweet brown rice, cornmeal, or oat flour. I often also add arrowroot or kudzu to the flour, to improve crust texture and workability. I sometimes include ground almonds or other nuts, as well as seasonings, if their flavors fit into my plan. Then I mix in enough corn oil or flaxseed oil (the closest-tasting substitutes for the traditional butter) to create a granular texture similar to that of cornmeal.

Traditional cooks add water. I find that adding other liquids is sometimes better. Because I don't use strong, concentrated sweeteners in the filling, I compensate by making sweet pastries sweeter by adding fruit juice (for vegetable pastry crusts, water, vegetable stock, or soy milk is fine). Add enough liquid so the dough forms a thin sheet (³⁄₁₆ inch is often best) when you pinch it between your thumb and forefinger, but not so much that it becomes sticky. Dough you've chilled beforehand (or begin with chilled ingredients) is more easily workable, but you can usually get away without this step. Or you can freeze the dough for future use.

Roll out the crust on a pastry sheet or on a clean, thick, canvas-like cloth. Enclose your rolling pin in a cloth sleeve. Both the pastry sheet and the rolling pin sleeve are available in cookware and hardware stores. Sprinkle arrowroot, kudzu, potato starch, or flour on the pastry sheet and sleeve to prevent sticking. Shape the pastry into a ball with your hands, flatten it into a thick disk in the center of the pastry sheet, sprinkle it with arrowroot or the alternatives, and roll out the dough from the center of the disk to the periphery with the rolling pin. After each stroke, change the direction in which you roll the pastry so that it spreads out evenly in a circle. Of course, if you're making a crust for a rectangular pastry dish, favor strokes that tend to create a rectangular shape. Sprinkle the dough with more arrowroot or the alternatives after every few strokes, to prevent sticking. When the dough is ³⁄₁₆ inch thick (use a ruler), trim it with a pizza cutter or butter knife if necessary, and save the trimmings for rolling out in your next crust.

To transfer the crust, roll it around the rolling pin without removing it from the pastry sheet, suspend it above the oiled pie pan or baking dish, and unroll it so that the pastry falls onto the pie pan sandwiched between the pie tin and the pastry sheet. Peel off the pastry sheet, lift and push any elevated parts of the pastry inward toward the border between the bottom and sides of the pan without stretching the dough, and trim away any excess pastry (which you can reuse) using a pizza cutter or butter knife.

If you're making a double crust, preheat the oven, roll out the top crust, and punch some small holes in the bottom with a fork to prevent the crust from buckling during baking. Sprinkle the bottom crust with arrowroot or its alternative to absorb liquid and prevent sogginess, pour in the filling, moisten the top edges of the bottom crust with water (so the top crust will stick to it), position the top crust over the filling, transferring it as already described, press the edges of the two crusts together with a fork or with your fingers, trim off the excess dough, cut a few slits in the top crust to let steam escape, and bake the pie immediately.

To create the right crispness and lightness, bake this type of pastry in a hot oven (425 degrees) until the crust is very lightly browned, 6 to 8 minutes. Use an oven thermometer to make sure the temperature inside the oven is correct. Turn the baking dish once or twice, and check the pie often to avoid burning the crust. If you're making a single-crust pie and you've precooked the filling, remove the crust from the oven immediately, allow it to cool, and then pour in the filling. If you need to continue cooking the filling, or the filling and the top crust, open the oven door for a minute or two to lower the oven temperature to 350 degrees to prevent burning, and cook the pie until it is done, when the filling is bubbly, turning the pie occasionally to prevent any parts of the crust from burning.

BE MY DUMPLING!

I'VE ALWAYS LOVED STUFFED DUMPLINGS (CALLED won tons in Chinese cuisine, and kreplach in Jewish circles), which are filled dough that you boil or steam (you can also bake them with excellent results,

but then they're no longer dumplings—they're pastries), but when I switched to wheat-free baking, problems arose. Whole wheat flour and white flour contain enough gluten-forming proteins to make dough elastic. When I put my gluten-free doughs in a Chinese dumpling press or Italian dumpling-making device and tried to seal them, the dough would tear. When I boiled these dumplings, they'd void their fillings into the water. Steaming them improved things, but the resulting dumplings were far from perfect.

The solution lies in using the most inexpensive, unassuming device, an Italian ravioli punch. This is simply a serrated cookie cutter that cuts a sheet of pastry dough into squares about 2½ inches across. You spread a tablespoon of filling on one square, moisten the edges with water, place another dough square on top of it, and press the edges together with the punch or using your fingers. There's no stretching, so the dough doesn't tear. Repeat the process until you've used all the dough and filling. And you may substitute a cookie cutter, a small bowl, or a large glass for the ravioli punch.

By varying the dough type and filling, you can make a fantastic variety of dumplings, which you may then steam or boil for 15 to 20 minutes, until the dough no longer tastes raw.

PUDDING IT ALL TOGETHER

A PUDDING IS USUALLY AN UNHEALTHFULLY sweet, thickened dessert, often loaded with sugar, white flour, milk or cream, butter, and eggs—all of which are unnecessary. Light whole-grain flours, such as sweet brown rice flour, oat flour, barley flour, cornmeal, or buckwheat flour, make excellent thickeners, as do kudzu, arrowroot, puréed silken tofu, and agar. Soy milk, nut milk, or puréed silken tofu mixed with some corn, sesame, or flaxseed oil plus a natural sweetener usurp the milk, cream, and sugar, while lecithin granules do a remarkable job replacing the flavor of egg yolks.

Fruits, berries, nuts, seeds, bread crumbs, coconut, carob powder, corn, the soy cheese recipes in this book, or even noodles may be added to puddings. Some puddings may be raw, you may simmer others, or bake them, usually uncovered, in a moderate oven, for 20 to 50 minutes, until they are thickened. Eating such desserts is like pudding yourself in heaven.

STOP WINING AND START WINEMAKING!

WINE IS SURPRISINGLY GOOD AND EASY TO make with wild ingredients. Simply pour a gallon of boiling or room-temperature water over 2 to 6 cups of wild flowers, berries, or leaves, along with 3 pounds of white sugar (otherwise I never use this unhealthful refined carbohydrate, but in this case it acts as a health food for the yeast, which converts the sugar to alcohol), the appropriate seasonings, and lemon juice or chopped-up whole lemons, limes, or oranges. When this mixture approaches room temperature, stir in ½ teaspoon wine yeast, cover the container loosely, and stir the mixture twice a day for a week. Don't use metal containers, which create disagreeable flavors. Glass, ceramic, or plastic is fine.

Next, strain out the solids through a cheesecloth-lined colander, pour the liquid into a jug, and seal the jug with an airlock stopper (a U-shaped stopper that you can buy in a winemaking store). When the yeast converts the sugar into alcohol, this stopper allows the carbon dioxide by-product to escape (otherwise, the jug would explode) while keeping oxygen out. This oxygen-free process is fermentation. If oxygen gets in, the wrong microorganisms could engage in oxygen-dependent respiration and ruin the wine. Winemaking stores throughout the country sell inexpensive airlocks and wine yeast. I patronize a local establishment, Milan Lab, 57 Spring Street, New York, NY 10012, (212) 226-4780. They do a mail-order business, and they may be able to direct you to a winemaking store in your area.

Two to four weeks later, after the sugar is converted to alcohol and the bubbling stops, close the jug tightly with a regular stopper and age the wine for from six weeks to two years. Storing wine in a cool cellar is supposed to be best, but I live in an apartment without such amenities, and my wines come out perfectly well. After aging the wine, you may siphon off (or pour off) the wine and discard the sediment that settles to the bottom of the jug, and you're done.

See A Quick Guide to Wild Wine on page 469 for specific ingredients and fermentation times for each wild wine. Winemaking can seem tricky for some people, but keep all your equipment clean and you'll have no problems.

Wine, of course, contains alcohol, which has all the harmful effects of white sugar and also kills brain cells, damages the liver, and overworks the kidneys. Of course, the less you consume, the less damage you'll incur. I don't drink any alcoholic beverages, but I use the wine I make to flavor soups, sauces, and other recipes. Alcohol has a lower boiling point than water does, so much of the alcohol cooks off when you cook with wine.

The alcohol industry touts wine's cardiac benefits and healthful antioxidants. But the beneficial substance, resveratrol, comes from the skin of the grapes, which you can simply eat, and it's also present in

Japanese knotweed (see page 98), a delicious rhubarb-like edible wild plant. Nevertheless, a dash of wild wine in a recipe does amazing things. And if you switch from commercial to wild wine, you avoid all the dangerous pesticide residues and unhealthful chemical additives that our domestic winemaking industry inflicts on its customers.

COOKING WITH WILD FOODS

WHEN YOU APPLY THE IDEAS I'VE DESCRIBED in the preceding sections to wild foods that you've identified and harvested correctly, even more scrumptious possibilities pop into existence, and understanding the special culinary characteristics of wild herbs, greens, shoots, flowers, fruits, berries, nuts, seeds, roots, seaweed, and mushrooms will empower you to take full advantage of their potential.

Wild ingredients generally provide more intense flavors than do their commercial counterparts, the result of their need to chemically adapt to their environment in order to survive. Agricultural producers, on the other hand, have spent generations selecting wild foods to grow larger, and as a result many food crops now contain more water and less flavor. Compare the flavor of a small wild strawberry to that of a larger commercial one and you'll certainly agree. Because wild foods taste so much stronger, it's easier to feature the flavor of a wild food in a recipe when that's your intention. On the other hand, if you're creating a balance of many flavors, or the wild ingredient isn't your main focus, you many want to use less of it, or cook it in such a way that it doesn't overpower the other ingredients. Always consider the special qualities of each wild ingredient and treat it accordingly.

WILD FOOD SEASONS

Wild leaf and stem vegetables come into season as winter ends and peak in mid-spring, although there are plenty of wild vegetables in the summer and fall, and a few grow during the winter when it's above freezing. Edible flowers bloom mostly in springtime. Most root vegetables are in season from fall through early spring, although the leaves that tell you where to dig usually disappear in winter, and the ground is frozen. A few roots continue in season from spring to fall.

Fruits and berries come into season by the start of summer and continue until the beginning of winter. A few even persist into the winter. Most nuts and seeds ripen at the end of summer and autumn. Gourmet mushrooms peak in the fall, but some come up in spring and summer, and a couple of species even appear in very rainy weather in the winter. Seaweed is best in the spring, before epiphytes (plants that grow on other plants) infest it and animals chew holes in it, although you can still harvest some in summer, fall, and sometimes even in the winter.

AW, SHOOT!

Wild shoots (the new growth of an edible stem, sometimes with edible young leaves) and leafy greens come in a profusion of flavors and strengths. A good number of these—such as fiddleheads, purslane, Hercules'-club, chickweed, sweet cicely leaves, Solomon's-seal and false Solomon's-seal, violets, and others—are mild to moderately flavored. Seasoning them delicately and cooking them briefly, 5 to 10 minutes, often brings out their best, although they may sometimes stand out to advantage even among strong seasonings. They also fit well into many recipes as a secondary ingredient.

Curly dock, wood sorrel, sheep sorrel, greenbrier, and Japanese knotweed contribute wonderful sour flavors. You may prepare them by themselves and glory in their sourness, as in a dish of lightly seasoned steamed greens or a very simple soup. You may also offset them with mild ingredients, as in tossed salads, or contrast them with sweeter foods, as when you cook them in flavored rice with currants or raisins.

Bitter greens provide the greatest culinary challenge of the wild vegetable group. Incorrectly prepared dandelion greens, garlic mustard leaves, chicory, sow thistle, or winter cress can ruin many a dish. Collected in season (many of these greens are good only when they are harvested very young) and prepared correctly, they'll add just the right brash bite to your repast.

People used to attack the bitterness of these vegetables by boiling them to death, ruining them in the process. Instead, add some bitter greens sparingly to tossed salads, along with many differently flavored ingredients, and chop these vegetables well, or cook them for no less than 15 minutes, using appropriate seasonings. Onions, garlic, hot peppers, curry powder, Cajun-style or Caribbean seasonings, and other flavor combinations all work with these vegetables. If you sauté them with such seasonings for 10 minutes and simmer them in a sauce for another 10 minutes, all traces of bitterness vanish, and your dinner guests will be astonished that you have produced an outstanding dish from hated "weeds."

Many wild shoots and greens are pungent. All members of the onion family, the related daylily, and the many wild mustards (some of which are also bitter) fit into this category. You may use them in small or large quantities, depending on how much you enjoy spiciness, in salads or cooked vegetable dishes. You may cook them briefly, until they are just wilted, or prepare them according to the procedures for bitter greens, again according to your tastes.

Some wild vegetables require special preparation.

Cow parsnip stems, for example, are so strongly flavored that you should cook them the same way you cook bitter greens, even though they're not bitter. Stinging nettles need to be cooked briefly to disarm the stinging hairs. Glasswort, a flowering plant covered by seawater during high tide, adapts by maintaining high sodium levels. Use it as a flavorful salt substitute in recipes where you don't add other sources of sodium. And don't forget to remove the thorns of prickly pears and Hercules'-club before removing your gloves, or you'll live to regret it.

Pokeweed shoots contain a poison that you must disperse by repeated boiling in fresh baths of rapidly boiling water (see page 165), and you must dissipate milkweed's less dangerous but bitter sap the same way (page 170). Afterward, you squeeze out the excess water and either add seasonings or use the precooked vegetable in other recipes.

NOW YOU SEA WEEDS, NOW YOU DON'T

Wild seaweeds (which are algae, not flowering plants), which you can collect along America's coasts, are sometimes the same species you purchase in health food stores or Asian specialty stores, or eat in Chinese, Japanese, or Korean restaurants. Some American wild species are relatives of commercial species; others are neglected commercially.

If they're dried, usually you must soak seaweeds in room temperature water for 10 to 15 minutes (unnecessary for dulse, an exception). Drain and discard the soaking water, rinse the seaweed to get rid of excess sodium, and cook it in moist heat, that is, with grains, in soups, sauces, or stews. Seaweeds lend themselves especially well to East Asian cuisine.

Some seaweeds expand more after soaking than do others, and some are saltier, tougher, or more tender than others. Prepare them according to their individual properties and your own taste.

THE ROOT OF WILD FOOD CUISINE

Wild roots are sometimes tougher and are always more flavorful than are commercial root vegetables. Collect roots in season (many species are inedibly woody at certain times of the year) and eliminate any injured, knobby areas, which tend to be fibrous. Slice the roots diagonally, Asian style, and razor thin, or use the finest slicing disk of a food processor, to make the roots easier to tenderize by cooking. Thin slicing also stretches the ingredient (digging up roots is labor-intensive), and a super-thin slice of a wild root usually provides more flavor to the dish than would a thick slice of a comparable commercial root.

Add those species of roots that are edible raw to salads sparingly, after chopping the roots very fine. The firm grain of wild roots is especially advantageous in soups or stews. Wild roots never become mushy the way commercial roots do. Thinly sliced and simmered for close to 20 minutes, they provide much-needed texture, along with plenty of flavor, to these liquidy dishes. Every root vegetable has its own peculiarities, so be sure to check out the description of a root's culinary properties before adding it to a dish.

GETTING FRUITY

Wild fruits and berries are usually more flavorful, less sweet, and smaller than the commercial fruits you're used to. They're so tasty, they're the perfect focus of a dessert, and you can use them more sparingly to stretch them (collecting some wild berries and fruits takes time), because the flavor is so much more penetrating.

Sour seasonings, such as lemon and lime juice, enhance sweet ingredients. This is apropos for mul-berries, wild persimmons, and many commercial fruits that don't provide their own acidity, but inappropriate for other wild fruits that are already sour.

Some fruits and berries contain inedible seeds that are impractical to remove by hand. An inexpensive food mill (a rotating plate attached to a crank, set in a bowl, that pushes the pulp through a strainer) will remove seeds. You often cook the resulting pulp with a thickener to make sauces, fillings, and jams.

Keeping such considerations in mind, you will have vastly superior results using wild fruits and berries in recipes calling for commercial ingredients.

THE POWER OF A FLOWER

Chefs who serve dishes with currently popular edible flowers in gourmet restaurants are missing the boat by using only a few commercially available species. The wild species they omit are great. A good number of common, renewable wildflowers make exceptionally good, exotic-tasting food ingredients. In season every spring, they range in taste quality from sweet to pungent to mild, and you should use them accordingly.

The common blue violet, for example, has such a mild flavor that I use it mainly for its color. That's because American wild violets are odorless, unlike their European relatives. The daylily's flower, which is large enough to stuff, is sweet and hot. Milkweed's flower buds and flowers taste more like vegetables. Wisteria blossoms taste sweet and perfumed, while the redbud flower, which makes great pickles, is sweet and sour. Black locust blossoms are like sweetened green peas, and elderberry blossoms, which shouldn't be eaten raw, taste like vanilla.

Most species of flowers make superb additions to salads, pancake batter, muffins, fritters, and oatmeal. They make top-rate wildflower wines as well as exotic ice creams and shakes. You may add them to soup at the end of the cooking time, and nothing beats them as garnishes. Most freeze well. Freeze them on cookie sheets before packing them into freezer containers. Then they won't stick together, and you can add them to recipes as needed.

GOING NUTS IN THE WOODS

Although each species of wild nut has its own unique flavor, you can usually use most wild nuts the same way you'd use their commercial siblings. The wild pecan, hazelnut, and Asian chestnut, although tastier than their commercial counterparts, are very similar to the ones you buy in the store. The acorn, an exception, requires special preparation (page 292), and the black walnut is so flavorful, you should use it more sparingly than you would commercial walnuts (or mix 1 part black walnuts with 3 parts commercial walnuts in a recipe that calls for only regular walnuts) if you don't want the black walnuts to overshadow the other ingredients.

UNDER THE MUSHROOM CLOUD

Many Americans are as scared of wild mushrooms as they would be if they saw a mushroom cloud looming in the sky—an attitude people in mushroom-loving countries cannot understand. The fungus kingdom is as vast as the plant kingdom, featuring a huge variety of flavors and textures. If you've identified your wild species with certainty, collected them with an expert, grown "wild" species from a kit, or depleted your life savings buying wild mushrooms in a gourmet store, you're in for an unbelievable treat.

Although I describe the mushrooms that appear in the recipes in this book, it's beyond my scope here to teach you everything you need to know to collect wild mushrooms safely (some species, of course, contain deadly toxins). Two books I recommend for this purpose are *Mushrooms Demystified* by David Aurora (Ten Speed Press, 1986), comprehensive but too large to carry into the field; and *The National Audubon Society Field Guide to North American Mushrooms* (Alfred A. Knopf, 1997), much smaller but more portable. There's also a mushroom section on my Web site, wildmanstevebrill.com, outlining the basics of mycology (the study of mushrooms) and providing mushroom links and many other resources. If you can locate a mycological society (mushroom club) in your area, join it.

Because wild mushrooms are so variable, you must prepare them according to their individual properties. You cannot sauté all species in olive oil with onions and garlic as you would commercial mushrooms and expect exceptional results. Although some species are great sautéed, others require moist cooking and shine only in soups, stews, sauces, and grain pilafs. Even species with caps you can sauté to advantage may have tougher stems that also require moist heat to tenderize them.

The seasonings and cooking methods that work with some mushrooms flop with others. The French prize some mushroom species that the Chinese disdain, and vice versa. The former stand out sautéed in olive oil with onions and garlic, while the latter taste best stir-fried or simmered in soups and seasoned with soy sauce, ginger, dark sesame oil, or other Chinese flavorings. The converse won't kill you, but it could taste so bad you'd wish you were dead. So learn which cuisines use and which disdain the species you're going to prepare, and apply procedures akin to the ones that have been developed over the centuries.

Marination followed by baking, broiling, or grilling is another way to tenderize and flavor wild mushrooms. Many nonpoisonous species are too woody and bitter to eat no matter how you prepare them. But other "unworthy" species such as very young Berkeley's polypore (or choice species such as chicken mushrooms that are past their prime but not yet maggot-ridden or rotten) become transformed into choice delicacies after such preparation. Better yet, their meaty texture, along with marinade flavorings associated with meat as listed in the Herb and Spice User's Guide (page 448), create meat substitutes that are better than any you can buy. Refer to each species' culinary characteristics to bring out its best qualities.

IMPROVISATION

AFTER YOU'VE TRIED FOLLOWING SOME OF THE recipes in this book, you may begin to improvise. If you're a beginner, start with small changes, varying the amounts of seasonings or substituting equivalent ingredients. Later on, you can make greater changes. In bread making, for example, you may substitute one flour for another by weight, substitute a different oil or liquid ingredients by volume, use different seasonings, and switch the additional ingredients, such as nuts or berries. The result may be a completely different recipe that's just as good if not better than the original.

Discipline yourself to write down what you're doing in case you want to duplicate the result. More often than not, your original inspiration will lead to a result you will not be able to duplicate without notes.

Had I followed my own advice consistently since I began cooking, this would probably be my second cookbook.

By switching around nearly all the ingredients and some of the seasonings, I've created successful new recipes loosely based on traditional ones that include animal products and refined ingredients. The Equivalents table (page 472) provides information to help you choose your own alternates.

TO SUM UP

WHEN YOU BEGIN USING WILD PLANTS AND mushrooms, follow the natural cooking principles I have described and try out the recipes that follow. You'll have a great time, and you'll be eating exciting, tasty dishes that will increase your chances of living a longer, healthier life.

Remember to collect wild foods with an expert or to use my previous book, *Identifying and Harvesting Edible and Medicinal Plants in Wild (and Not So Wild) Places* (William Morrow & Co., 1994) or other field guides—but use them carefully, and *don't eat anything unless you've identified it with 100 percent certainty*.

If you're not confident of your identification, if you haven't located a certain wild plant called for in a recipe, or if you live in a region where the plant doesn't grow, most of the recipes list commercially available ingredients you may substitute.

Unwild Food Recipes

BEFORE BRINGING IN THE RECIPES THAT INCLUDE wild ingredients, I present some "unwild" recipes for unbelievably good tofu mock cheeses, and others for food products you can use as ingredients in later recipes. The tofu-based cheeses don't melt, but they taste so much like dairy cheeses that you can enjoy them as such, or use them to replace cheese in most dishes.

TOFU CREAM CHEESE

This is the first mock cheese I ever created. I originally used it as a spread and then discovered it works as a cheese sauce (thickened with kudzu or arrowroot if desired) in cooked dishes. You can also use it in place of cream cheese, as a spread, and as an ingredient in other recipes.

> One 19-ounce package silken tofu, well drained
> 2 tablespoons olive oil
> ¾ teaspoon hot paprika
> 1 ½ teaspoons brewer's yeast
> ½ teaspoon salt
> ½ teaspoon turmeric
> 1 tablespoon umeboshi plum vinegar or red wine vinegar
> 1 tablespoon brown rice vinegar
> 1 tablespoon lecithin granules
> ½ teaspoon Tabasco sauce

In a food processor, combine all the ingredients and process until smooth, or mash the ingredients in a medium-size bowl with a whisk or fork. Tofu Cream Cheese will keep, tightly covered, in the refrigerator for up to a week.

MAKES 2 CUPS

TOFU COTTAGE CHEESE

This simple recipe makes an excellent lowfat, animal-free substitute for cottage cheese. Enjoy it as is, mix it with wild berries or jam, or use it in wild (and unwild) food recipes. It's especially good mixed with cooked wild mushrooms and heated through.

> One 16-ounce package soft tofu, drained and grated (2 ¼ cups)
> 2 tablespoons lecithin granules
> 1 tablespoon brewer's yeast
> ½ teaspoon salt
> ½ teaspoon hot paprika
> 1 tablespoon umeboshi plum vinegar or red wine vinegar
> 1 tablespoon brown rice vinegar
> 1 tablespoon corn oil
> ¼ teaspoon Tabasco sauce
> ⅛ teaspoon liquid stevia

1. Preheat the oven to 350 degrees.
2. Mix together all the ingredients in a medium-size bowl until they are well combined.
3. Transfer the mixture to a 14 x 9 x 2-inch oiled baking dish and bake, stirring occasionally, until enough liquid has cooked off that the mixture has the texture of commercial cottage cheese, about 20 minutes.
4. Let the mixture cool completely before serving. Tofu Cottage Cheese will keep, tightly covered, in the refrigerator for up to a week.

MAKES 2 CUPS

TOFU SHARP CHEESE

Here's a simple mock grated cheese that's great on pasta, or used to replace Parmesan or Romano cheese, but with a cheesy flavor all its own.

One 16-ounce package extra-firm tofu, drained
 and grated (3 cups)

2 tablespoons brewer's yeast

2 tablespoons corn oil

1 tablespoon umeboshi plum vinegar or red wine
 vinegar

1 tablespoon brown rice vinegar

1 teaspoon salt

½ teaspoon hot paprika

¼ teaspoon freshly ground fenugreek seeds

½ teaspoon freshly ground white pepper
 (¼ teaspoon peppercorns)

½ teaspoon ground mace

½ teaspoon Tabasco sauce

1. Preheat the oven to 350 degrees.

2. Mix all the ingredients together in a medium-size
bowl until well combined.

3. Transfer the mixture to a 14 x 9 x 2-inch oiled baking dish and bake it, uncovered, until it is dry and
somewhat firm, about 30 minutes, stirring occasionally.

4. Let the cheese cool completely before serving. Tofu
Sharp Cheese will keep, tightly covered, in the refrigerator for up to a week.

MAKES 2⅔ CUPS

TOFU RICOTTA CHEESE

This dairy-free version of ricotta cheese is great in
Italian pasta dishes as well as in desserts, with wild or
unwild ingredients.

Two 19-ounce packages soft tofu, well drained

¼ cup lecithin granules

2 tablespoons corn oil

2 tablespoons red wine vinegar

½ teaspoon salt

1 teaspoon sweet paprika

¼ teaspoon liquid stevia

1. Preheat the oven to 300 degrees.

2. In a food processor, combine half the tofu along
with the remaining ingredients and process until
smooth.

3. Grate the remaining tofu and add it to the puréed
tofu mixture.

4. Transfer the mixture to a 14 x 9 x 2-inch oiled baking dish and bake it until some of the liquid has
cooked off and the texture resembles that of commercial ricotta, about 30 minutes, stirring occasionally.

5. Let the mixture cool completely before using it.
Tofu Ricotta Cheese will keep, tightly covered, in the
refrigerator for up to a week and in the freezer for up
to 6 months.

MAKES 2⅔ CUPS

TOFU SLICED CHEESE

Marination is the key to imparting a cheese flavor to
tofu, and baking supplies the proper texture. Use this
cheese in sandwiches or baked dishes.

1 cup corn oil

¼ cup red wine vinegar

¼ cup brown rice vinegar

1 tablespoon Tabasco sauce

4 teaspoons paprika

1¼ teaspoons turmeric

1 tablespoon freshly ground yellow mustard seeds
 (1½ teaspoons seeds)

½ teaspoon ground mace

¼ teaspoon freshly ground fenugreek seeds

One 16-ounce package extra-firm tofu, drained
 and cut into slices about ¼ inch thick

1. In a 14 x 9 x 2-inch glass baking dish, mix together all the ingredients, except the tofu.

2. Submerge the tofu in the marinade, cover the dish, and chill the tofu for at least 6 hours and up to overnight. Stir once or twice if possible.

3. Preheat the oven to 375 degrees. Drain the tofu and save the marinade for another use.

4. Transfer the tofu slices to a wire rack set over an oiled cookie sheet and bake them until they are somewhat firm, about 20 minutes. Eat Tofu Sliced Cheese hot or cold. Tofu Sliced Cheese will keep, tightly covered, in the refrigerator for up to a week, or in the freezer for 6 months.

MAKES 7 SLICES

TOFU GRATED CHEESE

Here's a delicious, slightly sharp, grated mock cheese you can use anytime a recipe calls for cheese.

2 tablespoons olive oil or corn oil

One 16-ounce package extra-firm tofu, drained and grated (3 cups)

2 teaspoons brewer's yeast

½ teaspoon turmeric

½ teaspoon Tabasco sauce

½ teaspoon salt

¼ teaspoon hot paprika

1 tablespoon umeboshi plum vinegar or red wine vinegar

1 tablespoon brown rice vinegar

1. Heat the oil in a large skillet over medium heat and cook the tofu, brewer's yeast, turmeric, Tabasco, salt, and hot paprika for 10 minutes, stirring often.

2. Add the vinegars and cook the mixture for another 5 minutes, stirring often. Store Tofu Grated Cheese, tightly covered, in the refrigerator for up to 2 weeks and in the freezer for up to 6 months.

MAKES 3 CUPS

PANIR TOFU CHEESE

This tofu cheese resembles panir so closely that you can use it in Indian dairy recipes and nobody will be the wiser.

2 tablespoons corn oil

One 16-ounce package creamy-style firm tofu, drained and diced

1 tablespoon brewer's yeast

½ teaspoon freshly ground fenugreek seeds

½ teaspoon ground mace

½ teaspoon salt

¼ teaspoon vanilla extract

¼ teaspoon liquid stevia

1 tablespoon fresh lime or lemon juice

1 tablespoon red wine vinegar

1 tablespoon brown rice vinegar

Heat the oil in a medium-size skillet over medium heat, add the tofu, brewer's yeast, fenugreek, mace, salt, vanilla, and liquid stevia, and cook, stirring, for 3 minutes. Add the lime juice and vinegars and cook, stirring, for another 3 minutes. Panir Tofu Cheese will keep, tightly covered, in the refrigerator for up to a week and in the freezer for up to 6 months.

MAKES 2 CUPS

TOFU WHIPPED CREAM

This mock whipped cream is good served with fruit, or used as a topping for desserts. Sumac concentrate lends a sourness that is different from the more obvious lemon juice.

> One 19-ounce package silken tofu, well drained
> ½ cup pitted dates
> 2 tablespoons lecithin granules
> 2 tablespoons canola oil or safflower oil
> 1 tablespoon Sumac Concentrate (page 281)
>   or fresh lemon juice
> 2 teaspoons vanilla extract
> ½ teaspoon liquid stevia or 2 tablespoons honey,
>   barley malt, or rice syrup
> ¼ teaspoon butterscotch extract or lemon extract
>   (optional)
> ¼ teaspoon salt

In a food processor, combine all the ingredients and process until smooth. Tofu Whipped Cream will keep, covered, in the refrigerator for 5 days.

MAKES 2½ CUPS

TOFU SOUR CREAM

I'm very proud of coming up with this simple mixture to serve as an excellent nondairy alternative to sour cream.

> 3½ cups silken tofu, well drained
> ¼ cup Sumac Concentrate (see page 281) or fresh
>   lime juice
> 2 tablespoons brown rice vinegar or wine vinegar
> ¼ cup lecithin granules
> 2 tablespoons mellow (light-colored) miso
> 2 tablespoons chopped fresh dill, or 2 teaspoons
>   dillweed, ground
> 2 tablespoons corn oil

In a food processor or using a whisk, potato masher, or fork, purée all ingredients. Tofu Sour Cream will keep, tightly covered, in the refrigerator for 5 to 7 days; it doesn't freeze well.

MAKES 4 CUPS

TOFU FETA SPREAD

Here's a cheese spread that is reminiscent of feta cheese.

> One 19-ounce package soft tofu, well drained
> 2 tablespoons brewer's yeast
> 2 tablespoons corn oil
> 1 tablespoon red wine vinegar
> 1 tablespoon brown rice vinegar
> ½ teaspoon salt
> 1 teaspoon freshly ground white poppy seeds
>   (optional)
> ½ teaspoon freshly ground white pepper
>   (¼ teaspoon peppercorns)
> ⅛ teaspoon ground mace
> ⅛ teaspoon freshly ground fenugreek seeds

In a food processor, combine all the ingredients and process until smooth. Tofu Feta Spread will keep, tightly covered, in the refrigerator for up to a week.

MAKES 2¾ CUPS

TOFU EGG FILLING

Use this tofu-based egg substitute in any recipe that calls for hard-boiled eggs, especially stuffings and fillings. Although its flavor closely approaches that of eggs, Tofu Egg Filling won't act as a thickener the way raw eggs do.

You can also sauté the ingredients in the corn oil and eat Tofu Egg Filling in place of eggs.

1 tablespoon corn oil

One 16-ounce package soft tofu, drained and
    grated

½ cup fresh Bread Crumbs (page 40)

2 tablespoons lecithin granules

2 ½ tablespoons freshly ground flaxseeds
    (1 tablespoon seeds)

½ teaspoon Vege-Sal or ¼ teaspoon salt, or to taste

½ teaspoon dried sage, finely crumbled

1 teaspoon freshly ground black pepper
    (½ teaspoon peppercorns), or to taste

½ teaspoon turmeric

½ teaspoon freshly grated nutmeg

¼ teaspoon freshly ground fenugreek seeds

In a medium-size bowl, mix together all the ingredients until they are well combined. Tofu Egg Filling will keep, tightly covered, in the refrigerator for 6 days, or in the freezer for 6 months.

MAKES 2¼ CUPS

EGGPLANT PURÉE

This mild Turkish dip is perfect served as an accompaniment to wild mushrooms or wild vegetables.

    3 medium-size eggplants

    2 tablespoons corn oil

    1 tablespoon any whole-grain flour

    ¾ cup Tofu Cream Cheese (page 30)

    1 teaspoon Vege-Sal or ½ teaspoon salt, or to taste

1. Prick the eggplants with a fork and toast them directly over a stovetop burner over high heat, or place the eggplants on a baking sheet and cook them under a preheated broiler until they are blackened, turning them with large tongs or a fork every few minutes.

2. Submerge the blackened eggplants in a large bowl of cold water and remove the skins with your fingers. Squeeze any excess water out of the eggplants, and then slice them thin.

3. Meanwhile, in a medium-size skillet over low heat, heat the oil, add the flour, and cook it for 4 minutes, stirring occasionally. Stir in the Tofu Cream Cheese, Vege-Sal, and sliced eggplant and bring the mixture to a boil, stirring often. Reduce the heat to low and simmer the mixture, covered, for 10 minutes, stirring often.

4. Chill the purée and serve it as an appetizer. The purée may be arranged in a ring, with cooked wild mushrooms in the center. Eggplant Purée will keep, tightly covered, in the refrigerator for 5 days.

MAKES 4¼ CUPS

BUCKWHEAT NOODLES

If you own a pasta machine you can use this recipe, which contains no wild ingredients, to make whole-grain noodles that you can then use in wild or unwild recipes. Use finely ground flour and be sure to sift the flour so it can pass through the pasta machine's extruder.

    ¾ pound buckwheat flour plus ¾ pound sweet
        brown rice flour, or 1 ½ pounds any whole-grain
        flour

    6 tablespoons arrowroot or kudzu

    ¾ cup plus 3 tablespoons freshly ground flaxseeds
        (6 tablespoons seeds)

    1 ½ teaspoons dried oregano, finely crumbled

    1 ½ teaspoons dried rosemary or savory, finely
        crumbled

    3 tablespoons olive oil, plus 1 tablespoon for
        serving

    1 cup boiling water

1. Sift together the flour, arrowroot, ground flaxseeds, and herbs in a large bowl. Stir in the 3 tablespoons olive oil. Mix in the boiling water until the mixture is well combined.

2. Use your pasta machine according to the manufacturer's instructions to form noodles or other pasta, or roll out the dough with a rolling pin and cut it into noodles (you may need more water to make a workable dough for hand-rolling).

3. Place the pasta in a saucepan of rapidly boiling salted water with a dash of olive oil to prevent the pasta from sticking, and boil the pasta until it is al dente, about 5 minutes.

4. Drain the noodles in a colander, toss them with 1 tablespoon olive oil or other oil, and serve, or add the noodles to another recipe immediately. If you let this pasta sit, the noodles may stick together.

MAKES 1¾ POUNDS; SERVES 6

Note: If you're going to cook the noodles in another recipe, boil them a few minutes less.

GARLIC BUTTER SAUCE

Here's a great-tasting dairy-free substitute for garlic butter. Use it on popcorn, for sautéing vegetables, or to add flavor to any dish. The flaxseed oil or corn oil and the lecithin granules provide the buttery flavor. The seasonings increase the flavor's complexity, and the miso (which also adds saltiness) and poppy seeds add body.

1 cup canola oil

1 cup flaxseed oil or corn oil

2 tablespoons roasted garlic

¼ cup chopped fresh parsley leaves

3 tablespoons mellow (light-colored) miso

1 tablespoon freshly ground white or black poppy
  seeds (optional)

1 teaspoon freshly ground white pepper
  (½ teaspoon peppercorns)

½ teaspoon freshly grated nutmeg

½ teaspoon turmeric

In a blender, combine all the ingredients and blend until smooth. Garlic Butter Sauce will keep, tightly covered, in the refrigerator for 2 to 4 weeks.

MAKES 2½ CUPS

MOCK YOGURT SAUCE

Many cultures cook with yogurt. Here's a vegan substitute you can either cook with or enjoy as is.

¼ cup fresh dill leaves, chopped

1 clove garlic, peeled

2 tablespoons lecithin granules

2 tablespoons fresh lemon juice

2 tablespoons corn oil or flaxseed oil

One 19-ounce package silken tofu, drained

1 teaspoon Vege-Sal or ½ teaspoon salt

In a food processor, combine all the ingredients and process until smooth. Mock Yogurt Sauce will keep, tightly covered, in the refrigerator for 5 days.

MAKES 2 CUPS

MOCK EGG SAUCE

This combination of seasonings, which are traditional for lamb, works perfectly with the egg-like flavor of the lecithin granules and corn oil. Any cook who goes back to egg sauce with high-cholesterol eggs after trying this simpler, more healthful recipe will have egg on his or her face. Serve Mock Egg Sauce over vegetables or mushrooms.

One 16-ounce package silken tofu, drained
1 cup Vegetable Stock (page 40) or water
¼ cup Sumac Concentrate (page 281) or fresh
   lemon juice
¼ cup lecithin granules
2 tablespoons corn oil
2 tablespoons kudzu or arrowroot
2 tablespoons dark-colored miso or 1 tablespoon
   tamari soy sauce, or to taste
1 teaspoon dried rosemary, finely crumbled
1 teaspoon dried tarragon, finely crumbled
½ teaspoon dried sage, finely crumbled
½ teaspoon freshly ground juniper berries
½ teaspoon turmeric
¼ teaspoon freshly ground white pepper
   (⅛ teaspoon peppercorns)
Pinch of cayenne pepper, or to taste

1. In a food processor, combine all the ingredients and process until smooth.
2. Transfer the mixture to a medium-size saucepan and bring the pot to a boil over medium-high heat, stirring constantly. Reduce the heat to low, cover, and simmer for 10 minutes. Mock Egg Sauce will keep, tightly covered, in the refrigerator for 5 days.

MAKES 3⅓ CUPS

CHILI POWDER

No wild ingredients here, but this hot seasoning is suitable for Mexican and Tex-Mex recipes that may or may not include wild plants.

¾ cup plus 2 tablespoons ground chiles of your
   choice, or to taste
½ cup cumin seeds
½ cup dried oregano
3 tablespoons coriander seeds
1 teaspoon cloves
1 teaspoon allspice berries

Combine all the ingredients in spice grinder and grind them into a powder. Chili Powder will keep indefinitely in a tightly closed jar, although the spices will get weaker after 6 months.

MAKES 2 CUPS

GARAM MASALA

This classic blend of spices is essential in Indian cuisine.

½ cup cumin seeds (optional)
½ cup coriander seeds
¼ cup black peppercorns
¼ cup cloves
4 cinnamon sticks
1 tablespoon freshly ground cardamom seeds

1. In a hot skillet over medium heat, toast all the ingredients except the cardamom seeds for 2 to 3 minutes, stirring or shaking the pan constantly.
2. Turn off the heat, stir in the cardamom seeds, and continue to stir the mixture for 1 minute.
3. Remove the pan from the heat and grind all the spices together in a spice grinder. Garam Masala will keep indefinitely in a tightly closed jar, although the spices will get weaker after 6 months.

MAKES 1¾ CUPS

CURRY PASTE

Here's a handy condiment to have around if you're a curry lover. You can add it to any wild or unwild savory dish that benefits from a little spicing up.

4 teaspoons coriander seeds
2 tablespoons yellow mustard seeds
1 ¼ teaspoons turmeric
12 cloves garlic, crushed into a paste
¼ cup chili paste

1. In a small skillet over medium heat, toast the coriander seeds and yellow mustard seeds until the mustard seeds pop, 2 to 3 minutes. Transfer the seeds from the pan to a small bowl.
2. Place the turmeric in the hot pan and stir until it becomes fragrant, 1 to 2 minutes. Transfer the turmeric to the bowl, add the garlic and chili paste, and mix the ingredients until they are well combined. Curry Paste will keep, tightly covered, in the refrigerator for up to 2 months.

MAKES ⅔ CUP

HOMEMADE KETCHUP

Making your own ketchup is fun and easy.

Four 6-ounce cans tomato paste
1 cup apple juice
¼ cup red wine vinegar, or to taste
2 teaspoons dried oregano, finely crumbled
¼ teaspoon freshly ground cumin seeds
½ teaspoon freshly grated nutmeg
½ teaspoon freshly ground white pepper
    (¼ teaspoon peppercorns), or to taste
2 teaspoons freshly ground mustard seeds
    (1 teaspoon seeds)

½ teaspoon finely chopped wild garlic bulb (page 160) or 1 clove regular garlic, crushed
½ teaspoon Vege-Sal or ¼ teaspoon salt, or to taste
¼ teaspoon Tabasco sauce or dash of cayenne pepper, or to taste
¼ teaspoon liquid stevia or 1 tablespoon vegetable glycerin, honey, barley malt, or rice syrup

In a medium-size saucepan over medium heat, bring all the ingredients to a boil, stirring often. Reduce the heat to low and simmer the mixture, covered, for 10 minutes, stirring often. Adjust the vinegar, Vege-Sal, and Tabasco sauce to taste. Homemade Ketchup will keep, tightly covered, in the refrigerator for 2 weeks.

MAKES 3 CUPS

CASHEW BUTTER

Besides using cashew butter on bread or crackers, you can also use this creamy spread, which has no wild ingredients, to thicken soups, sauces, and icing recipes. To make cashew milk, add equal parts water and cashew butter.

8 cups raw cashews
5 tablespoons canola oil or safflower oil
½ teaspoon salt

In a food processor, combine all the ingredients until the mixture is smooth, 5 to 10 minutes. Cashew Butter will keep, tightly covered, in the refrigerator for up to 2 months.

MAKES 6 CUPS

CRUNCHY ALMOND BUTTER

Why buy this popular spread in the health food store or supermarket when it is cheaper to make it fresh in minutes in a food processor?

7 cups raw whole almonds
¼ cup almond oil
1 teaspoon salt

1. In a food processor using the chopping blade, process 6 cups of the almonds with the almond oil and salt until the mixture is smooth.
2. Add the remaining 1 cup almonds and process until they are finely chopped. (If you want smooth almond butter, add all the almonds at the beginning.) Crunchy Almond Butter will keep, tightly covered, in the refrigerator for up to 2 months.

MAKES 4 CUPS

CRUNCHY PEANUT BUTTER

If you own a food processor, you can make a superior peanut butter in minutes. I'm sure you won't lack uses for it.

4 cups unsalted dry-roasted peanuts
¼ cup peanut oil
½ teaspoon salt
¼ teaspoon freshly ground black pepper
(⅛ teaspoon peppercorns; optional)
⅛ teaspoon freshly ground cloves (optional)

1. In a food processor using the chopping blade, process 3 cups of the peanuts along with the peanut oil and salt, until the mixture is smooth. Include the black pepper and cloves if you want a slightly spicy flavor.
2. Add the remaining 1 cup peanuts and process until

they are finely chopped. (If you prefer smooth peanut butter to crunchy peanut butter, add all the peanuts at the beginning.) Crunchy Peanut Butter will keep, tightly covered, in the refrigerator for up to 2 months.

MAKES 3 CUPS

TAHINI

Tahini, or sesame paste, is a basic ingredient in Middle Eastern dishes. It's wonderful in sauces and is a popular spread. You can buy tahini in health food stores, ethnic stores, and supermarkets, but it's quick, easy, and fun to make yourself.

1 cup unhulled (whole) raw sesame seeds
¼ cup sesame oil
½ teaspoon salt, or to taste

1. Toast the sesame seeds in a medium-size skillet over medium heat, stirring constantly, until the seeds pop and become fragrant, 3 to 5 minutes.
2. Transfer the seeds to a food processor immediately to prevent their burning. Add the sesame oil and salt, and process the mixture until it is fairly smooth, or grind it by hand with a mortal and pestle. Tahini will keep, tightly covered, in the refrigerator for up to a month.

MAKES ¾ CUP

PITA BREAD

This basic Middle Eastern bread, cooked in the traditional manner, uses whole-grain flour instead of white flour. It doesn't contain any wild food, but you can split it open and stuff it with hummus, sprouts, and wild greens.

1 ½ tablespoons dry active yeast

3 ½ cups lukewarm water

3 tablespoons olive oil

2 teaspoons salt

3-pound mixture of any whole-grain flour (that is,
    1 pound each buckwheat, sweet brown rice, and
    oat flour)

1 cup arrowroot or kudzu

¼ cup corn oil, or as needed

1. In a large bowl, dissolve the yeast in the lukewarm water and let the mixture sit until it is bubbly, about 5 minutes. Add the olive oil and salt, and then mix in the flour and arrowroot. Knead the dough for 5 minutes.

2. Cover the dough and let it stand in a warm place to rise until it is doubled in volume, 40 minutes to 1 hour.

3. Punch down the dough and divide it into 9 equal portions. Roll each portion into a ball and using the heel of your hand flatten each ball into a ¼-inch-thick disk.

4. Place the disks on an oiled cookie sheet, cover them with a damp towel, and let the dough rise in a warm place for 40 minutes to 1 hour.

5. Preheat the oven to 525 degrees. Brush the disks lightly with the corn oil and bake them until the bottoms are browned, about 5 minutes. Check carefully to prevent burning. Turn the loaves over with a metal spatula, brush them with corn oil again if desired, and bake them for another 5 minutes. Let the loaves cool on a wire rack.

6. Cut a slit into the edge of the pita with a knife and create a pouch between the two faces of the bread. Stuff the pita with wild greens, alfalfa sprouts, hummus (page 132), or falafel (page 283), if desired.

M A K E S   9   L O A V E S

CORN TORTILLAS

Traditional Mexican flatbread is very easy to make and fun to use with sauces and fillings. A special corn flour for tortillas, called *masa harina*, is available in Mexican specialty stores, in gourmet food stores, through some mail-order catalogs, and in some supermarkets. If you use ordinary corn flour, the more finely ground varieties are best.

2 ½ cups (1 ¼ pounds) masa harina or ordinary
    corn flour, or a combination of cornmeal and
    any whole-grain flour

¼ teaspoon salt

¾ cup plus 2 tablespoons water, or as needed

1. In a medium-size bowl, mix the *masa harina* and salt with enough water to make a dough that isn't wet enough to be sticky and not dry enough to be crumbly. Divide the dough evenly into 10 pieces and roll each piece into a ball.

2. Put each ball between 2 sheets of wax paper and press the dough into a disk 6 inches across using a tortilla press, rolling pin, or heavy book. Peel off 1 sheet of the wax paper from the dough disk.

3. Put the disk face-down on a hot griddle or frying pan and peel off the remaining sheet of wax paper. Cook the tortillas, one at a time, over medium-high heat until dry and lightly browned on each side, 1½ to 2 minutes per side. You can keep tortillas warm in a preheated 200-degree oven in a covered baking dish; refrigerate them, wrapped in plastic, for up to a week; or freeze them, wrapped in plastic, for up to 6 months and then reheat them briefly on a hot griddle before using them.

M A K E S   1 0   T O R T I L L A S

CHEESE BREAD FOR MAKING BREAD CRUMBS

There are no wild ingredients or cheese in this basic bread recipe, but it's very quick, easy, and good. When I make it, I eat some of the bread right away and grind the rest into bread crumbs in a food processor, to use later in other recipes. The bread crumbs freeze well.

DRY INGREDIENTS

3 1/3 cups (1 pound) sweet brown rice flour, 4 cups (1 pound) oat flour, and 1 3/4 cups plus 2 tablespoons (1/2 pound) barley flour, or 2 1/2 pounds any whole-grain flour

1/2 cup arrowroot or kudzu

1 1/2 teaspoons baking soda

1 teaspoon salt

WET INGREDIENTS

2 cups Tofu Cream Cheese (page 30)

1/4 cup corn oil

1 1/2 tablespoons fresh lemon juice

1. Preheat the oven to 350 degrees.
2. Sift together the dry ingredients in a large bowl.
3. Mix together the wet ingredients in a medium-size bowl.
4. Pour the wet ingredients into the dry ingredients and mix them together. Don't overmix.
5. Transfer the batter to 2 oiled 6½ x 4⅜ x 2½-inch loaf pans and bake the loaves until a toothpick inserted into the center emerges clean, about 30 minutes. Let the bread cool on racks.

MAKES 2 LOAVES

VEGETABLE STOCK

This broth is a mineral-rich base for soups and sauces. You simply overcook whatever vegetables you have on hand (avoid very strong-tasting ones such as cabbage, cauliflower, and broccoli) along with savory seasonings, then strain the vegetables out. Drink it as broth in cold weather, give it to someone who's ill, or use it as a base for soups, stews, or sauces.

Any combination of aromatic wild or cultivated vegetables or scraps (i.e., tough stems), coarsely chopped, in any amount; these may include carrots and carrot tops, onions (including the skin), garlic (including the skin), potatoes, common plantain, bell peppers, celery, seaweeds, tough mushroom stems such as oyster mushroom stems (page 404)

Savory herbs of your choice, such as 1 teaspoon to 1 tablespoon each dried or fresh parsley, basil, goutweed (page 130), savory, rosemary, black peppercorns, marjoram, thyme, common spicebush berries (page 314), bayberry leaves (page 185) or bay leaves

Salt to taste

1. Simmer the vegetables and herbs together in a soup pot with water to cover for 1 to 2 hours.
2. Strain the mixture through a cheesecloth-lined colander and discard the vegetables.
3. Salt to taste, if desired. Vegetable Stock will keep, tightly covered, in the refrigerator for up to 10 days, or in the freezer for up to a year.

WINTER
WILD FOODS

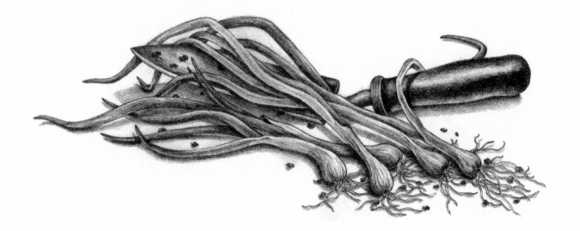

WINTER, OF COURSE, IS THE WORST TIME for foraging. Nevertheless, there are many cold-resistant plants (some of which are covered in the Autumn section) that you can find during warm spells in the winter, especially if you live in an area with warm winters. All the root vegetables are available in the winter, although you'll need to be able to identify the above-ground parts to find the roots, and you won't be able to dig up roots if the ground is frozen or covered with lots of snow. With the unfortunate global warming we humans are inducing, wild foods are easier to find during the increasingly mild winters.

SOURDOUGH STARTER FOR DUMMIES

In the early 1980s I was introduced to a naturally fermented health drink called rejuvelac in a course taught by Steve Meyerowitz, the Sproutman. Simple to make, this fermented health drink also provides a foolproof starting point for inaugurating a sourdough starter that yields wonderfully tangy sourdough breads, pancakes, and muffins.

After you experience genuine wild sourdough baked goods, you'll never even think of using commercial starter again. You'll want to maintain your starter forever, and you may even give some away as a gift to grateful culinary friends. Here's everything you need to know about creating, using, and maintaining a wild yeast starter. The steps are many, but each one is very simple.

Never use up all of your starter. Use some for your recipes, and add more rye or some other whole-grain flour and water to the remainder to replenish it. If you use the starter daily, store it at room temperature, beat it twice a day (I know this sounds cruel), and replenish it as necessary. If you use your starter less frequently, store it in the refrigerator, beat it every few days to keep the flour and water from separating, and feed it with additional flour and water once a week to keep it from starving to death (now that would really be cruel). Six to 12 hours before you plan on using your starter again, feed it, add enough water to restore it to a thick batter, beat it, and let it stand at room temperature. You can use it again as soon as it bubbles actively.

To turn a normal yeast bread recipe into a sourdough recipe, replace the dry yeast required for 2 medium-size loaves with 1 cup starter and omit ½ cup of the flour and ½ cup of the water from the recipe.

¼ cup wheat berries (available in health food stores)
½ cup water, plus more as needed
1 cup rye flour (or half as much rye flour as the amount of starter you want to make)

1. In a small bowl, soak the wheat berries in the ½ cup water overnight.
2. Drain the wheat berries and then tie them in a mesh bag, cheesecloth, nylon stocking (a clean one!), or any other porous cloth container and hang the sprout sack where it can drain at room temperature. Rinse the bag with water twice a day for about 3 days, until the sprouts on the wheat berries are as long as the wheat berry itself.
3. In a blender, combine the sprouts with twice their volume of water and blend on the lowest speed for a few seconds, just to break up the sprouts. Don't overblend.
4. Put the sprout-water combination in a non-metal (glass, plastic, or ceramic—metal kills wild yeast) jar or food container and cover the container with cheesecloth or a towel (it should not be airtight). Let the mixture sit at room temperature for about 3 days, stirring it twice a day with a non-metal implement, until the liquid bubbles and tastes sour.
5. Strain out and discard the sprouts. The liquid is now called rejuvelac.
6. Using a non-metal implement, stir in the rye flour and enough additional water to make a thick batter. Something close to an equal volume of liquid to flour usually does the trick. Cover the starter loosely, let it sit at room temperature, and stir it twice a day. When it bubbles actively, it's ready to use.

Note: Don't fill your starter container to the top when storing it. The starter may expand, pop the lid, and make a mess.

WILD CABBAGE
Brassica oleracea

WILD CABBAGE IS A EUROPEAN PLANT THAT grows in sandy fields, such as those near the seashore, similar to the fields in which the plant evolved. If garden cabbage is planted in the vicinity of the seashore, it may escape cultivation and revert to its primordial form, growing a stalk rather than a head. You can find wild cabbage everywhere throughout the United States.

Cabbage likes cold weather and grows in late fall, early spring, and during warm spells in the winter. You can collect it during any of these seasons.

Wild cabbage grows to about 2½ feet tall, with alternating, long-oval, toothed leaves that grow to about 8 inches long on a stalk. Beginning with a low basal rosette of leaves emerging from a slender taproot, the plant develops a flower stalk in early spring, when it races to its full height. The radially symmetrical, four-petaled yellow flowers, ¼ inch across, emerge alternately from the flower stalk. The slender, cylindrical seed pods are about ¾ inch long.

Don't confuse wild cabbage with skunk cabbage, a poisonous plant that has much larger leaves, a totally different flower structure, and the strong smell of skunk. The only similarity between the two is in their names.

Use wild cabbage leaves the same way you would use cultivated cabbage—in salads, soups, slaws, or stuffed. The flavor is similar to that of cultivated cabbage, only sharper.

STUFFED WILD CABBAGE

In this version of a traditional dish, vegan ingredients are used instead of cheese, and wild cabbage, if you can find it, instead of the cultivated variety.

28 medium-size wild or cultivated cabbage leaves
STUFFING
 ½ cup Tofu Cottage Cheese (page 30)
 ½ cup any cooked grain
 6 tablespoons almonds, toasted (page 158)
  and chopped
 1 teaspoon Bragg's Liquid Aminos or Vege-Sal
  or ½ teaspoon salt, or to taste
 ½ teaspoon chili paste or ⅛ teaspoon cayenne
  pepper, or to taste

 Puffball Marinara (page 397) or any other tomato
  sauce
TOPPING
 2 cups fresh Bread Crumbs (page 40)
 ¼ cup olive oil
 ½ teaspoon Vege-Sal or ¼ teaspoon salt, or to taste

1. Preheat the oven to 350 degrees.

2. *To prepare the cabbage leaves:* Wash the cabbage leaves and shake or spin off the excess water. In a large heavy saucepan without a steamer rack cook the cabbage leaves, covered, over low heat until they are just wilted, 5 to 10 minutes. You want the leaves to be soft enough to roll, but not so soft that they tear easily.

3. *To make the stuffing:* Mix the stuffing ingredients together and place about 1 tablespoon of stuffing in the center of each leaf. Fold each leaf's sides over the stuffing and roll up the leaf from base to tip. Repeat the process until you have used up all the leaves and stuffing.

4. Place the rolled leaves in a 14 x 9 x 2-inch oiled

baking dish and pour the tomato sauce over them.

5. *To make the topping:* Mix together the topping ingredients and sprinkle the topping over the tomato sauce. Bake the stuffed cabbage until the sauce is bubbling, about 25 minutes.

SERVES 6

WILD CABBAGE CRUNCH

Although I'd been hunting for wild plants since the late 1970s, I finally discovered wild cabbage for the first time in 1998. It had invaded a local urban seashore park, recently having escaped cultivation, but it wasn't able to escape ending up in this slaw!

4 cups chopped or shredded wild or cultivated
    cabbage leaves
1 cup Wild Mustard Seed Mayonnaise (page 206)
    or Green Mayonnaise (page 93)
½ cup raisins
½ cup walnuts, chopped
1 medium-size red bell pepper, seeded and chopped
2 tablespoons finely chopped onion
1 tablespoon chopped fresh dill
1 teaspoon caraway seeds
½ teaspoon Vege-Sal or ¼ teaspoon salt, or to taste
½ teaspoon freshly ground black pepper
    (¼ teaspoon peppercorns)

Toss together all the ingredients in a large bowl until well combined. Chill the salad before serving to allow the flavors to blend.

SERVES 6

SASSAFRAS
Sassafras albidum

THIS IS ONE OF THE EASIEST TREES TO RECOGNIZE, with three kinds of leaves: oval, mitten-shaped, and two-lobed (subdivisions), all 3 to 5 inches long, with smooth (untoothed) edges. The deeply grooved bark has long, flattened ridges occasionally broken by horizontal cracks. Scrape the bark with a knife and you'll find a reddish brown color underneath and detect a sweet fragrance, which is also apparent when you scratch and sniff a twig.

In the winter, look for the green saplings among the parent trees. The branches of young and old trees alike arch upward like a candelabra. Look for this medium-sized tree along the edges of forests or trails, and in thickets throughout eastern North America. The tree may also be cultivated, anywhere in North America, and it's in season all year.

Pull up the smaller saplings, 3 to 6 feet tall. If you have other people to help pull and the soil is loose or rain-softened, you can harvest the larger saplings.

Sassafras is famous as a tea and a tonic, but it is underappreciated as a seasoning. Wash the soil off the sapling's root and peel off the outer layer (the cambium). If an adult tree has been felled recently by a storm, you can cut through the outer bark and harvest the cambium (inner "bark") that surrounds the wood that forms the core of the tree. The cambium tastes like a combination of cinnamon and root beer. You can use the cambium fresh, finely chopped, or dried and ground into a powder. It adds a wonderful exotic touch to any recipe that calls for cinnamon.

You can also make a delicious detoxifying and

tonic herb tea by simmering the whole root of a sapling or recently felled tree or the cambium in water for 20 minutes, covered, over low heat. If you chill this tea and add some sparkling water plus honey to taste, you'll make an excellent mock root beer. You can also use the young leaves as a thickener in gumbo by drying them and grinding them into a powder (called filé powder) in a spice grinder or blender.

SASSAFRAS PEANUT SAUCE

You can cook nearly anything in this Caribbean sauce. It imparts a peanut-coconut flavor, with sassafras adding an even more exotic touch. You can cook vegetables or tofu in this sauce, or pour it over already cooked food, such as noodles, rice, or vegetables.

> 2 tablespoons peanut oil
> 2 medium-size red onions, chopped
> 3 large cloves garlic, chopped
> 1 cup unsalted dry-roasted peanuts, finely chopped
> 1 cup unsweetened coconut milk
> ½ cup water
> 3 tablespoons fresh lime juice
> ½ teaspoon ground dried cambium of sassafras
> ½ teaspoon salt
> ¼ teaspoon liquid stevia

1. Heat the peanut oil in a large skillet over medium heat. Cook the onions and garlic, stirring, for 10 minutes. Add the remaining ingredients, bring the pot to a boil, reduce the heat to low, and simmer for 10 minutes.
2. Carefully transfer the mixture to a blender or food processor and process it until it is smooth, if you prefer. Serve Sassafras Peanut Sauce hot or at room temperature. Sauce will keep, tightly covered, for 7 days

in the refrigerator.

MAKES 2⅓ CUPS

SASSAFRAS ICE CREAM

Because sassafras imparts its sweet, spicy flavor to this ice cream, no other special ingredients need be added to this basic vegan ice cream formulation.

> 2 cups drained silken tofu
> 1½ cups soy milk or nut milk
> ½ cup canola oil or safflower oil
> ¾ cup raw cashews
> ¼ cup vegetable glycerin, barley malt, or honey, or to taste
> 2 tablespoons lecithin granules
> 2 teaspoons ground dried cambium of sassafras
> 2 teaspoons vanilla extract
> ½ teaspoon salt
> 1 teaspoon liquid stevia (optional)
> ¼ teaspoon butterscotch extract (optional)

1. In a blender, combine all the ingredients and process until smooth.
2. Chill the mixture (or begin with chilled ingredients) if required by your ice cream machine.
3. Pour the mixture into an ice cream machine and freeze it according to the manufacturer's instructions.

MAKES 5½ CUPS; SERVES 5 TO 6

OH! MY DARLING ICE CREAM

Here's an unusual orange ice cream based on seedless clementine tangerines and seasoned with sassafras, a match made in heaven.

2 ½ cups soy milk or nut milk

1 cup drained silken tofu

½ cup canola oil

¼ cup vegetable glycerin, honey, barley malt, or
    rice syrup

¼ cup lecithin granules

2 teaspoons ground dried cambium of sassafras

2 teaspoons vanilla extract

1 teaspoon liquid stevia (optional)

¼ teaspoon salt

Freshly grated rind of 1 clementine
    (1 ½ teaspoons)

7 clementines, peeled, or 1 ⅓ cups good, sweet-
    tasting orange segments, seeds removed

1. In a blender, combine all the ingredients, except for 2 of the clementines or ½ cup of the orange segments, and process until smooth.

2. Chill the mixture (or begin with chilled ingredients) if required by your machine.

3. Pour the mixture into an ice cream machine and freeze it according to the manufacturer's instructions.

4. Chop the remaining clementines or orange sections coarsely, stir them into the ice cream, and return the ice cream to the freezer to freeze completely.

MAKES 6 CUPS; SERVES 6

MOUNTAIN
WATERCRESS

Cardamine rotundifolia

H ERE'S AN OVERLOOKED DELICACY THAT I first discovered thriving in a moist meadow in a neighborhood park in New York in December 1998.

This small plant forms dense mats in such habitats. It begins in late fall and very early spring as a low basal rosette (the leaves emerge from one point on the ground in a circle) with long-stalked, roundish leaves about 1¼ inches across, bearing tiny, paired projections on some of the leafstalks. The plant persists through mild winters.

Before spring progresses very far, the herb reaches its full height of 6 to 24 inches. The rounded leaves alternate along the stalk, which also bears alternating four-petaled white flowers that are less than ¼ inch across. Some other mustards resemble this plant, but they're edible as well. By mid-spring, mountain watercress has dispersed its seeds from its tiny elongated pods, and disappears.

The leaves and stems of this delicate, barely pungent vegetable, which grows in the Northeast, lend themselves well to salads, soups, and almost any vegetable dish. Unlike other, more robust members of its tribe, it must not be overpowered by other ingredients in a recipe. Cook this herb for no longer than 10 minutes.

LAST CHANCE/
FIRST CHANCE GREEN SALAD

Here's a wonderful salad I first made with mostly wild leafy greens collected at the beginning of winter, just before the first hard frost wiped out the last hardy plants. The same wild greens also come into season in early spring.

2 cups bite-size pieces arugula

1 cup chopped sow thistle leaves (page 47)

1 cup chopped chickweed leaves (page 53)

1 cup packed mountain watercress or watercress
    leaves (page 387), chopped

½ cup packed winter cress leaves (page 49),
chopped

¼ to ½ cup Gingko Cheese Dressing (page 436)
or any salad dressing

Toss all the ingredients, except the dressing, together in a large salad bowl. Serve the mixed greens tossed with the dressing.

SERVES 6

SOW THISTLE

Sonchus species

HERE'S ANOTHER "WEED," DESPISED BY FARMERS and gardeners alike, that makes for wonderful eating. Sow thistle is a coarse, prickly, bitter green only fit for pigs—when it's mature. Young plants, which abound in late fall until they're killed by heavy frosts, persist during mild winters and reappear in early spring. The leaves taste so good after you sauté them with seasonings and complete the cooking in a sauce, you'll have an irresistible urge to pig out.

Sow thistle's flowers resemble those of the related dandelion, but the sow thistle plant is much taller when mature, growing from 1 foot to 8 feet tall, depending on the species. The leaves are sharply toothed, even prickly in one species (snip off its spines with scissors), but less deeply toothed than the dandelion's. Unlike the similar wild lettuce, another edible relative, there's no thin line of bristles on the midrib of the leaf's underside.

The leaves growing on sow thistle's flower stalk lack stems, and instead attach themselves by clasping (partially encircling) the stalk. The leaves have a milky white sap, like dandelions and the wild lettuces.

This European invader grows throughout North America and many other parts of the world. I've even seen it growing literally on the equator in Ecuador.

SOW IN WINE

My basic method of preparing bitter wild greens, sautéing and simmering, works beautifully with sow thistle. This unappreciated "weed" tastes especially good simmered in a French-style wine sauce.

6 tablespoons olive oil

16 cups packed sow thistle leaves (cut off the prickles of the prickly species with scissors), chopped

3 tablespoons peeled and chopped fresh ginger

8 cloves garlic, or to taste, chopped

2 to 4 small chiles, seeds and ribs removed and chopped, or ¼ to ½ teaspoon cayenne pepper, to your taste

SAUCE

2 cups water

½ cup Mulberry Wine (page 222) or red wine

¼ cup drained silken tofu

3 tablespoons mellow (light-colored) miso

2 tablespoons corn oil or flaxseed oil

2 tablespoons lecithin granules

5 teaspoons kudzu or arrowroot

1 teaspoon dried rosemary, finely crumbled

1 teaspoon dried tarragon, finely crumbled

½ teaspoon anise seeds

½ teaspoon caraway seeds

1. Heat the olive oil in a large skillet over medium heat and cook the sow thistle, stirring, for 5 minutes. Add the ginger, garlic, and chiles and cook, stirring, for another 5 minutes.

2. *To make the sauce:* In a blender, combine the sauce ingredients and process the mixture until it is smooth. Pour the sauce over the sow thistle mixture and bring the pot to a boil over medium heat, stirring constantly. Reduce the heat to low, cover, and simmer for 10 minutes.

3. Serve Sow in Wine hot, with homemade bread or grains.

SERVES 6

SHEPHERD'S PURSE

Capsella bursa-pastoris

HERE'S ANOTHER COLD-WEATHER PLANT THAT shelters itself by hugging the ground and spreading its leaves around in a circle—the very common basal rosette formation. The leaves are toothed, like the edible dandelion's, but not as sharp, and they point outward, not toward the leaf's base. The leaves have no milky white sap.

This despised garden weed produces surprisingly mild-flavored leaves in late fall and very early spring (also during very mild winters). Later on, when the flower stalk appears, the leaves get unpalatably tough and coarse.

The flower stalk, which appears in early spring, grows to about 2 feet tall. The alternating flowers are ¼ inch across, with four white petals arranged in the shape of a cross, a typical feature of the mustard family. The distinctive, tiny, flattened, triangular seedpods were supposed to resemble shepherd's purses, back in "the day." This European plant grows in lawns and disturbed habitats throughout North America.

The young leaves are great in salads, especially when they are used to offset the very strong flavors of other early spring greens. They're also fine sautéed, steamed, or simmered in a sauce, and they usually cook in 10 to 15 minutes.

SHEPHERD'S PURSE SAUTÉ

Many cultures have discovered how tasty greens can be when they're cooked with cheese. The same also follows for wild greens cooked with tofu cheese. Add the appropriate seasonings, and you have an easy dish everyone will enjoy.

> ¼ cup olive oil
> 4 cups shepherd's purse leaves, chopped
> 1 teaspoon peeled and finely chopped fresh ginger
> 1 small chile, seeds and ribs removed and finely chopped, or ¼ teaspoon cayenne pepper, or to taste
> 4 cloves garlic, or to taste, chopped
> ½ teaspoon dried rosemary, finely crumbled
> ½ teaspoon dried thyme, finely crumbled
> 3 cups Tofu Cottage Cheese (page 30)
> 1 cup Homemade Ketchup (page 37)
> 1 cup unsalted dry-roasted peanuts, chopped

1. Heat the olive oil in a large skillet over medium heat. Add the shepherd's purse, ginger, and chile and cook, stirring, for 5 minutes. Add the garlic, rosemary, and thyme and cook, stirring, for another 5 minutes.

2. Add the remaining ingredients and bring the mixture to a boil. Reduce the heat to low, cover, simmer for 10 minutes, and serve.

SERVES 6 TO 8

WINTER CRESS

Barbarea vulgaris

WINTER CRESS IS A BITTER, COLD-WEATHER wild vegetable with a strong, cabbage-like flavor that reminds me of the Three Stooges—I love it, but my past girlfriends always hated it. You have to pick the leaves in the winter, early spring, or very late fall, when other wild greens are few and far between, and then you have to cook them thoroughly, with lots of spices or in a sauce. Then it's marvelous.

Its cold-weather form is a basal rosette of leaves emerging from one point on the ground. The leaves are glossy, dark green, hairless, and 4 to 12 inches long. Each leaf bears a large, rounded lobe or subdivision at its tip, with pairs of increasingly smaller lobes continuing toward the leaf's base.

By mid-spring, winter cress grows a flower stalk that is 2 to 3 feet tall with clusters of alternating four-petaled yellow flowers shaped like crosses, a typical feature of the mustard family. By that time the leaves are way too bitter for most people to eat. Its slender, cylindrical seedpods are nearly 1½ inches long.

Look for winter cress in wet, sunny places. It's very common throughout the eastern half of the country.

WINTER CRESS POTATO SOUP

Potatoes and seasonings tame the bitterness of winter cress to create an elegant, easy-to-make vegetable soup. Because winter cress tastes a little like cabbage, I use traditional cabbage seasonings, and they work perfectly.

3 tablespoons olive oil

2 teaspoons caraway seeds

4 cups packed winter cress leaves, chopped

4 cloves garlic, finely chopped

8 cups Vegetable Stock (page 40)

4 cups sliced potatoes

2 teaspoons paprika

1 teaspoon dried sage, finely crumbled

¼ cup kudzu or arrowroot

1 cup drained silken tofu

¼ cup dark-colored miso

1 teaspoon freshly ground black pepper
   (½ teaspoon peppercorns)

1. Heat the olive oil in a large skillet, over medium heat. Cook the caraway seeds in the hot oil for 1 minute, stirring. Add the winter cress and cook, stirring, for 8 minutes. Add the garlic and cook, stirring, for another 2 minutes.

2. Meanwhile, in a medium-size saucepan, bring 5 cups of the stock to a boil, add the potatoes, paprika, and sage, reduce the heat to medium, and simmer for 10 minutes.

3. In a blender, process the remaining 3 cups stock with the kudzu, tofu, miso, and black pepper until the mixture is smooth. Add this mixture to the stock and potatoes in the saucepan along with the sautéed seasoned winter cress. Heat the soup through and serve it hot.

SERVES 8 TO 12

WINTER CRESS KIMCHI

Here's a spicy Korean pickling method that works wonderfully for pungent winter cress. I think if they gave this dish a chance, my ex-girlfriends who hate winter cress might change their minds.

6 quarts packed winter cress leaves, coarsely
   chopped
3 cloves garlic, chopped
1 large red onion, coarsely chopped
3 tablespoons dill seeds or caraway seeds
3 tablespoons kosher (coarse) salt or sea salt
2 tablespoons chili paste or ½ teaspoon cayenne
   pepper, or to taste

1. Mix all the ingredients together in a large bowl.

2. Place a plate with a diameter smaller than that of
the top of the bowl on top of the winter cress mixture.
Put a weight (for example, an unopened bottle of fruit
juice) on top of the plate to compress the mixture.
The salt will draw out the liquid and create the pickle juice.

3. After 1 hour remove the winter cress mixture and
pack it tightly into a jar. Make sure the liquid covers
the leaves. Store the kimchi in the refrigerator until
you are ready to use it.

4. When you're ready to eat this condiment, place it
in a colander and hold it under cold running water to
rinse off the salt. Winter Cress Kimchi will keep for
many weeks in the refrigerator.

MAKES 4 CUPS

CREAMED WINTER CRESS

Winter cress's bitterness vanishes when you cook it in
a seasoned cream sauce, transforming this despised but
nutritious "weed" into a delicate gourmet vegetable.

SAUCE
   2 cups water
   4 teaspoons kudzu or arrowroot
   ½ cup drained silken tofu
   ¼ cup miso

SAUTÉ
   2 tablespoons peanut oil or olive oil
   2 tablespoons flaxseed oil or corn oil
   2 teaspoons cumin seeds
   2 small chiles, seeds and ribs removed and
      chopped, or ¼ teaspoon cayenne pepper, or to
      taste
   2 large cloves garlic, chopped
   ¼ cup fresh basil leaves, chopped, or 4 teaspoons
      dried, finely crumbled
   6 tablespoons brewer's yeast
   ½ teaspoon freshly ground coriander seeds
   ¼ teaspoon freshly ground cloves
   12 cups packed winter cress leaves, chopped

1. *To make the sauce:* Place the sauce ingredients in a
blender and process until smooth.

2. *To make the sauté:* Heat the peanut oil and flaxseed
oil in a large skillet over medium heat and cook the
cumin seeds for 2 minutes, stirring often. Add the
chiles, garlic, and basil and cook, stirring, another
minute. Add the brewer's yeast, ground coriander, and
ground cloves and cook, stirring, another minute. Add
the winter cress and cook, stirring, for 5 minutes.

3. Stir in the sauce and bring the pot to a boil, stirring
constantly. Reduce the heat to low, covered, and simmer for 15 minutes. Serve Creamed Winter Cress hot
with brown rice or homemade bread.

SERVES 6

BANDHGOBI

Indian cooking methods bring out the best properties
of winter cress. (**Note:** If really spicy food is not for
you, cut the seasonings in half.) Serve Bandhgobi as a
side dish.

2 tablespoons peanut oil

2 tablespoons peeled and chopped fresh ginger

2 teaspoons black mustard seeds

1 teaspoon turmeric

1 teaspoon chili paste or ⅛ teaspoon cayenne
   pepper, or to taste

2 jalapeños or other small chiles, seeds and ribs
   removed and finely chopped

1 teaspoon Vege-Sal or ½ teaspoon salt, or to taste

8 cups (1 pound) packed winter cress leaves

Heat the peanut oil in a large skillet over medium heat and cook the ginger, black mustard seeds, turmeric, chili paste, jalapeños, and Vege-Sal for 2 to 3 minutes, stirring. Stir in the winter cress and cook, covered, over low heat for 10 minutes.

SERVES 4 TO 6

CURRIED WINTER CRESS

Winter cress benefits greatly from spices, and what cuisine has given us greater command of spices than Indian cuisine? This recipe transforms a vegetable that many find difficult to enjoy into a gourmet delight. Serve Curried Winter Cress hot as a side dish.

1 cup drained silken tofu

½ cup water

Juice of 1 lime

1 teaspoon Vege-Sal or ½ teaspoon salt, or to taste

2 tablespoons peanut oil

1 tablespoon peeled and chopped fresh ginger

2 cloves garlic, chopped

2 small chiles, seeds and ribs removed and chopped

1 teaspoon chili paste or ¼ teaspoon cayenne
   pepper, or to taste

2 teaspoons turmeric

1 ½ teaspoons coriander seeds

1 teaspoon yellow mustard seeds

1 teaspoon cumin seeds

1 teaspoon cardamom seeds or ground cardamom

1 teaspoon ground cinnamon

6 curry leaves (optional; available in Indian
   specialty stores)

4 cups packed winter cress leaves

1. In a blender, process the tofu with the water, lime juice, and Vege-Sal until smooth.

2. Heat the peanut oil in a large saucepan over medium-low heat and cook the ginger, garlic, chiles, chili paste, turmeric, coriander seeds, yellow mustard seeds, cumin seeds, cardamom seeds, cinnamon, and curry leaves, if you are using them, for 3 minutes, stirring constantly. Add the tofu mixture and winter cress and bring the pot to a boil over medium heat. Reduce the heat to low and simmer, covered, for 15 minutes.

SERVES 4 TO 6

WINTER CRESS INDIAN STYLE

Indian cooking methods and pungent seasonings again make perfect culinary sense for this strong-tasting wild vegetable, because the seasonings offset the vegetable's intensity.

2 tablespoons peanut oil

1 tablespoon coriander seeds

2 teaspoons cumin seeds

4 cloves garlic, crushed

1 small chile, seeds and ribs removed and chopped

6 cups packed winter cress leaves

3 tablespoons fresh lemon juice

3 tablespoons drained silken tofu

2 tablespoons water

½ teaspoon Vege-Sal or ¼ teaspoon salt, or to taste

1. Heat the peanut oil in a large skillet over medium heat. Cook the coriander seeds, cumin seeds, garlic, and chile for 1 minute, stirring. Stir in the winter cress and cook, covered, over low heat for 5 minutes.

2. Meanwhile, in a blender or food processor, process the lemon juice, tofu, water, and Vege-Sal together or mix them with a whisk or fork until smooth. Stir the sauce into the winter cress mixture and heat it through. Serve Winter Cress Indian Style hot with whole grains or Indian bread.

SERVES 6

KENTUCKY COFFEE TREE

Gymnocladus dioica

THIS 40- TO 100-FOOT-TALL NATIVE TREE, A member of the legume family, has impressive double-compound leaves. Each huge leaf is around 3 feet long and is completely divided into segments along an axis, and the leaflets are divided again.

The dark brown seedpods are 4 to 10 inches long, 2 to 3 inches wide, and 1 to 2 inches thick, curved on one edge and straight on the other. Inside the seedpods is *poisonous* sticky green pulp and 6 to 10 flattened seeds about ¾ inch across and ¼ inch thick. The pods ripen in the fall and drop to the ground in the early spring, but you can find many bare seeds, which never seem to perish, on the ground all year, even under the snow. *There are other poisonous legumes with pods, so be absolutely sure of your identification.*

Although this attractive tree is native to the Southeast west of the Appalachians, landscapers have planted it in parks and cultivated areas throughout the country.

The seeds of this plant make the world's best caffeine-free coffee substitute. Crack the pod with a hammer, discard the poisonous green pulp, and rinse the seeds. Toast the seeds, which are poisonous eaten raw, covered in the oven (or they may pop all over your oven, like popcorn), for 3 hours at 300 degrees. Grind the seeds at low speed in a blender, ½ cup at a time, and then use the grounds like coffee.

Gourmet cooks often use coffee to season chocolate recipes, and the seeds of the Kentucky coffee tree work the same way. I use them with carob in icings, cakes, and ice cream. One toasted seed, ground in a spice grinder (don't do more than 1 seed at a time or you'll wreck your grinder), flavors a recipe that serves 6.

CAROB ICE CREAM

The seed of the Kentucky coffee tree makes this carob-flavored ice cream taste more like chocolate than ever.

2 cups soy milk or nut milk

1 cup well-drained silken tofu

½ cup carob powder

½ cup raisins

½ cup Cashew Butter (page 37) or ½ cup plus
*   2 tablespoons raw cashews*

½ cup canola oil

¼ cup vegetable glycerin, honey, barley malt, or
*   rice syrup*

2 tablespoons lecithin granules

2 teaspoons vanilla extract

8 common spicebush berries (page 314) or
　　½ teaspoon freshly ground allspice berries
1 Kentucky coffee tree seed (not the pod), toasted
　　(page 51) and ground
½ teaspoon salt
¼ teaspoon freshly ground cloves
1 teaspoon liquid stevia

1. In a blender, combine all the ingredients and process until smooth.

2. Chill the mixture (or begin with chilled ingredients) if required by your ice cream machine.

3. Pour the mixture into the ice cream machine and freeze it according to the manufacturer's instructions.

MAKES 5½ CUPS; SERVES 5 TO 6

CHICKWEED

Stellaria species

CHICKWEED IS ONE OF THE MOST COMMON AND widespread of the wild vegetables. Loaded with nutrients, it gets awful press from lawn chemical companies, but it's one of the best free foods anywhere. Children, even those who hate vegetables, invariably love chickweed, especially after I show them how it gets its name: I hop around and cackle into their faces like a chicken, then grab a piece with my mouth and gobble it up. Kids, chickens, other birds, and I all think this plant is super.

This small plant usually stays close to the ground, befitting a species that can grow during warm spells in the winter, although you can find it any month of the year. Pairs of tiny, oval to spade-shaped, smooth-edged leaves arise from a weak, sprawling, faintly hair-ridged, wirelike stem.

This European annual, which grows worldwide, flowers in early spring and fall. The tiny white, radially symmetrical flowers have five petals that are split so deeply that they look like ten. Five tiny green, leaflike sepals surround the flower.

One species has nearly stalkless leaves, another is long stalked, and yet another is so hairy you have to cook it (you can enjoy the other species cooked or raw).

Raw, chickweed tastes like a combination of corn on the cob and sprouts; cooked, its flavor resembles that of spinach. It's so tender, you can eat the stems and the leaves. The mild flavor stands out in both lightly and heavily seasoned dishes. Add it to salads, soups, creamed soups, or any vegetable dish.

CHICKWEED BEAN SPREAD

Here's a hearty bean spread you can make for cold days from late fall through early spring. Serve it on whole-grain bread or use it as a dip, and you'll never think that vegetarian food doesn't stick to your ribs again.

BEANS

1 cup dried adzuki beans or other dried beans,
　　picked over and rinsed
4 cups water, or as needed
1 tablespoon brown rice vinegar or red wine vinegar
1 tablespoon olive oil
1 teaspoon bayberry leaves (page 185) or bay
　　leaves
1 teaspoon dried tarragon, finely crumbled
1 teaspoon dried savory, finely crumbled
1 teaspoon dried epazote leaves, stems, or flowers
　　(page 177; optional)

TO FINISH

2 tablespoons chopped fresh dill

2 to 4 cloves garlic, or to taste

1 to 2 small chiles, seeds and ribs removed and chopped, or ¼ to ½ teaspoon cayenne pepper, to your taste

1 cup chickweed leaves and stems, chopped (chop by hand, not in a food processor)

4 scallions, chopped (chop by hand, not in a food processor)

¼ cup dark-colored miso

2 tablespoons fresh lemon juice

2 tablespoons olive oil

1. Place the beans in a medium-size saucepan with 1½ cups of the water, bring the pot to a boil over high heat, remove it from the heat, cover it, and let the beans soak for 1 hour.

2. Drain the beans in a colander, discard the soaking water, and return the beans to the saucepan with the remaining 2½ cups water. Add the remaining bean cooking ingredients, bring the pot to a boil over high heat, reduce the heat to low, cover, and simmer the beans until they are tender, about 1 hour.

3. Drain the beans, discarding the bayberry leaves and reserving ¼ cup of the cooking liquid. In a food processor, combine the beans along with the reserved liquid and the remaining ingredients, and process until smooth (or mash with a potato masher or fork in a medium-size bowl). The flavor will be enhanced if you let the spread sit so the ingredients can mix and marry. Chickweed Bean Spread will keep, tightly covered, in the refrigerator for 5 days.

MAKES 3⅓ CUPS

CHICKWEED AND DAYLILY EARLY SPRING SPREAD

As soon as the very first edible plants of springtime appear, you can use them to make a fantastic spread or dip. If you omit the olives, you'll have an all-raw food recipe.

2 cups chickweed stems and leaves

1 cup daylily shoots (page 64)

1 medium-size red onion, coarsely chopped

1 large clove garlic, chopped

2 ripe avocados, peeled, pitted, and coarsely chopped

One 6-ounce jar low-sodium pitted olives (optional), drained and coarsely chopped

Juice of 1 lemon

1 teaspoon Vege-Sal or ½ teaspoon salt, or to taste

½ teaspoon freshly ground black pepper (¼ teaspoon peppercorns)

¼ teaspoon freshly ground fenugreek seeds

1. Coarsely chop the chickweed and daylily shoots by hand (they won't chop well in a food processor).

2. Mix the chickweed and daylily shoots with the remaining ingredients until well combined. Chickweed and Daylily Early Spring Spread will keep, tightly covered, in the refrigerator for 5 days.

SERVES 4

GRANDMA WILDMAN'S CONVALESCENT SOUP

Chickweed, a powerhouse of vitamins and minerals, unites with other natural remedies in this soothing, fortifying soup. It is great to feed someone who is trying to recover from a cold or the flu.

8 cups Vegetable Stock (page 40)

¼ cup kudzu or arrowroot

2 tablespoons olive oil

2 to 4 cloves garlic, to taste, chopped

1 cup very thinly sliced burdock root (page 139)

2 tablespoons tamari soy sauce, or to taste

1 teaspoon dried rosemary, finely crumbled

1 teaspoon dried tarragon, finely crumbled

¾ teaspoon freshly ground celery seeds
  (½ teaspoon seeds)

½ teaspoon freshly ground white pepper
  (¼ teaspoon peppercorns) or pinch of cayenne
  pepper (optional)

2 cups Buckwheat Noodles (page 34) or store-
  bought flat noodles

4 cups chickweed stems and leaves, chopped by
  hand (not in a food processor)

1. In a blender or with a whisk in a small bowl, blend 2 cups of the stock with the kudzu .

2. Heat the olive oil in a large saucepan over medium heat, add the garlic, and cook it for 30 seconds, stirring constantly. Add the kudzu mixture, the remaining 6 cups stock, and the remaining ingredients, except the noodles and chickweed. Bring the pot to a boil over medium heat, stirring constantly. Reduce the heat to low and simmer, covered, for 13 minutes.

3. Add the homemade noodles (if you're using store-bought noodles, add them earlier, following the directions on the box, so they will finish cooking when the soup is done), return the pot to a boil, reduce the heat to low, and simmer, covered, for another 4 minutes.

4. Add the chickweed and simmer, covered, for another 3 minutes. Serve hot.

SERVES 6

CHICKWEED DELIGHT

Some people insist on enjoying chickweed only raw. "Why meddle with perfection?" they ask. Never one to leave well enough alone, I wondered what would happen if one were to cook mild-tasting chickweed (which I do regularly use raw in salads) with comparatively strong seasonings. Surprisingly, chickweed's flavor doesn't get drowned out. Instead the spices take on a fresh, mellow quality.

3 tablespoons peanut oil

3 tablespoons flaxseed oil or corn oil

½ teaspoon cumin seeds

4 small chiles, seeds and ribs removed and
  chopped, or ½ teaspoon cayenne pepper, or to
  taste

6 large cloves garlic, or to taste, chopped

¼ cup fresh basil leaves, chopped, or 4 teaspoons
  dried, finely crumbled

6 tablespoons brewer's yeast

½ teaspoon freshly ground coriander seeds

¼ teaspoon freshly ground cloves

½ teaspoon Vege-Sal or ¼ teaspoon salt, or to taste

16 cups chickweed stems and leaves, well chopped
  by hand (not in a food processor)

1. Heat the peanut oil and flaxseed oil together in a skillet over medium heat for 2 minutes, stirring often. Add the cumin seeds, chiles, garlic, and basil and cook, stirring, for 1 minute. Add the brewer's yeast, ground coriander and cloves, and Vege-Sal and cook, stirring, for another minute.

2. Add the chickweed, and cook, stirring, for 2 minutes more. Reduce the heat to low and cook, covered, until the chickweed is tender, 5 to 10 minutes.

SERVES 6

ROCKWEED,
BLADDERWRACK

Fucus vesiculosis

M Y TOUR PARTICIPANTS ARE ALWAYS SURPRISED that this coarse-looking seaweed, which coats rocks along the seashore, is edible. Rockweed looks like branching brown ribbons, each with a vein running down the middle. Near the tips you'll see distinctive elliptical yellow-brown flotation bladders, accounting for one of this plant's names. You can harvest this seaweed along most rocky shores all year, but if you collect it in the winter, wait for a warm day, so your hands don't freeze.

Rockweed is strong-tasting and salty, with a pronounced, somewhat fishy flavor. That makes it wonderful for flavoring mock seafood dishes. Wash it thoroughly under running water to get rid of excess salt. Add it sparingly to soups, and simmer it until it is tender, about an hour. To preserve it for future use, you can also dehydrate it in a food dehydrator (or hang it on a rack in a well-ventilated place until it feels dry), season it, and bake it with a tiny amount of oil until it is crisp.

VEGETARIAN WORCESTERSHIRE SAUCE

The English traditionally make this well-known seasoning with walnut ketchup and essence of anchovy. You can approach the first flavor with tomato ketchup plus walnut extract. Rockweed imparts the flavor of fish. The result is a high-grade vegetarian Worcestershire sauce.

2 cups brown rice vinegar

2 shallots, chopped

3 tablespoons Homemade Ketchup (page 37)

2 tablespoons tamari soy sauce

2 tablespoons ground dried rockweed

½ teaspoon walnut extract

¼ teaspoon cayenne pepper

1. Mix all the ingredients together in a tightly closed jar and refrigerate.

2. Shake the jar twice a day if possible for 2 weeks.

3. Strain the sauce through a fine mesh sieve. Vegetarian Worcestershire Sauce will keep, tightly covered, in the refrigerator for up to 2 months.

MAKES 2 ½ CUPS

VEGETARIAN CHINESE FISH SAUCE

Rockweed's fishy flavor makes it ideal for creating a vegan version of the classic Chinese fish sauce. After you briefly stir-fry the ingredients in Chinese recipes, you may finish cooking them by simmering them in this sauce, or serve the sauce over potatoes or other cooked vegetables.

6 cups Vegetable Stock (page 40)

½ cup kudzu or arrowroot

2 cups Autumn Olive Wine (page 423) or rice wine

2 tablespoons ground dried rockweed

¼ cup dark-colored miso

1 tablespoon tamari soy sauce

1 ½ teaspoons toasted sesame oil

3 tablespoons peanut oil

2 cups packed wild garlic leaves (page 160), chopped, or chopped scallions

8 cloves garlic, chopped

2 small chiles, seeds and ribs removed and chopped

1. Bring the stock to a boil in a large saucepan.

2. In a blender, blend the kudzu, wine, rockweed, miso, tamari, and sesame oil. Stir the mixture into the boiling stock and bring the pot back to a boil over high heat, stirring constantly. Reduce the heat to low and simmer, covered, while you continue with the next step.

3. Heat the peanut oil over high heat in a wok or medium-size skillet. Stir-fry the wild garlic leaves, garlic, and chiles for 2 minutes. Add these vegetables to the stock mixture and simmer, covered, over low heat, for 10 minutes. Use the sauce hot or cold. Vegetarian Chinese Fish Sauce will keep, tightly covered, in the refrigerator for up to a week.

MAKES 7 CUPS

FIELD GARLIC, ONION GRASS, WILD ONION, WILD SCALLION

Allium vineale

THIS COMMON LAWN WEED, WHICH IS WIDE-spread across the country, is very easy to recognize. It looks like bunches of chives and smells of onion or garlic. The plant has rounded, hollow leaves, as opposed to the flat leaves of ordinary grass. The underground bulb looks like a miniature head of garlic. In the summer, when the plant attains its full height of 2 to 3 feet, rounded seedheads of tear-shaped seeds underlie tiny pink, six-petaled flowers. It grows

in the fall and spring, sticking around somewhat battered through the winter as well.

Other smelly members of the onion/garlic family are also good to eat, but similar-looking plants that have no odor are poisonous.

Use field garlic's leaves as you would scallions or chives, harvesting them in early spring, autumn, and during mild winters, at which time the bulbs are most similar to onions. Peel the outer layer of the bulbs to get rid of the dirt. In warm weather, the leaves get too tough to eat, and the bulbs become hot, like garlic. At this time, you can harvest the spicy seeds and use them as you would garlic.

I tell kids this plant will give them a super power, but it will turn them into supervillains, not superheroes. After they eat it, they attain "death breath." If blowing into your friends' faces doesn't kill them, it will make them wish they were dead!

GARLIC-ALMOND PASTE

You can make this condiment with field garlic, wild garlic, ramp bulbs (page 116), or cultivated garlic. Use it as a side dish or a spread.

2 tablespoons field garlic bulbs, peeled

2 cloves garlic, peeled

1 cup raw almonds

2 slices bread, torn into small pieces, or ½ cup fresh Bread Crumbs (page 40)

2 tablespoons corn oil

½ teaspoon Angostura bitters or Vegetarian Worcestershire Sauce (page 56)

¼ teaspoon almond extract

¼ teaspoon salt, or to taste

¼ teaspoon chili paste or pinch of cayenne pepper (optional)

In a food processor, chop the field garlic and garlic. Add the remaining ingredients and process until smooth. Garlic-Almond Paste will keep, tightly covered, in the refrigerator for 2 weeks.

MAKES 1 CUP

INDIAN HERB CHEESE SPREAD

In India, people make this cheese spread with high-fat yogurt cheese and eat it with homemade millet bread. Here's a vegan version that substitutes flavored silken tofu for the cheese, and field garlic for the chives.

2 cloves garlic, peeled
4 chiles, seeds and ribs removed
¼ cup chopped fresh dill
¼ cup fresh cilantro leaves
1 small red onion, peeled
2 tablespoons finely chopped field garlic leaves
2 cups well-drained silken tofu
2 tablespoons fresh lemon juice
2 tablespoons corn oil
1 tablespoon lecithin granules
2 teaspoons mellow (light-colored) miso or Vege-Sal or 1 teaspoon salt, or to taste
2 teaspoons brewer's yeast
¼ teaspoon turmeric

1. In a food processor, chop the garlic and chiles. Add the dill and cilantro and chop again. Add the red onion and chop again.
2. Add the remaining ingredients and process until well blended. Indian Herb Cheese Spread will keep, tightly covered, in the refrigerator for 5 to 7 days.

MAKES 2 CUPS

HERB BUTTER

When I first started cooking, I used to grind herbs and mix them into butter in the French tradition. Here's a similar, more healthful vegetarian spread that is enhanced with wild garlic. It's great as a spread and in baked dishes that call for seasoned butter. But if you want to sauté something, use Spiceberry Butter Sauce (page 316), corn oil or flaxseed oil (the most buttery flavored oils), or olive oil instead, because this mock herb butter is not oil based. Nonetheless, you can use this herb butter to enhance flavor in such dishes at the end of the cooking process.

1 teaspoon field garlic bulbs, peeled
¼ cup chopped fresh parsley leaves or goutweed leaves (page 130)
1 small red onion, peeled
1 cup well-drained silken tofu
1 tablespoon flaxseed oil or corn oil
1 tablespoon mellow (light-colored) miso
1½ teaspoons lecithin granules
½ teaspoon dried tarragon, finely crumbled
½ teaspoon dried oregano, finely crumbled
½ teaspoon dried marjoram, finely crumbled
½ teaspoon paprika
¼ teaspoon turmeric
¼ teaspoon chili paste or ⅛ teaspoon cayenne pepper, or to taste

1. In a food processor, chop the field garlic bulbs, add the parsley, and chop again. Add the onion and chop once more.
2. Add the remaining ingredients and process until smooth. Herb Butter will keep, tightly covered, in the refrigerator for 1 week.

MAKES 1 CUP

MISO SAUCE

This spicy Asian sauce is great served with vegetables, loaves, and burgers.

8 cups Vegetable Stock (page 40)
½ cup Wild Crabapple Blossom Wine (page 425)
* or white wine*
½ cup kudzu or arrowroot
1 tablespoon peeled and chopped fresh ginger
2 tablespoons field garlic seeds or 4 cloves garlic,
* peeled*
¾ cup brown rice miso
¼ cup garlic mustard seeds (page 252) or other
* edible wild mustard seedpods (page 206), or*
* 2 tablespoons freshly ground black mustard*
* seeds (1 tablespoon seeds)*
1 tablespoon chili paste or 1 teaspoon cayenne
* pepper, or to taste*

1. Mix 6 cups of the stock with the wine in a large saucepan and bring the mixture to a boil over medium heat.

2. Meanwhile, in a blender process the remaining 2 cups stock with the kudzu, ginger, and field garlic until smooth. Stir this mixture into the boiling stock in the saucepan, return the pot to a boil, and simmer, uncovered, over low heat for 5 minutes, stirring often.

3. Pour 2 cups of this mixture back into the blender and process it with the remaining ingredients until smooth. Stir this mixture back into the saucepan, remove the pot from the heat, and serve. Miso Sauce will keep, tightly covered, in the refrigerator for 10 days.

MAKES 9 CUPS

WILD SPEARMINT
Mentha spicata

LIKE OTHER EDIBLE MINTS, THIS FRAGRANT species has a square stem, opposite (paired) leaves, and bilaterally symmetrical flowers. Wild spearmint grows 10 to 20 inches tall, with toothed, stalkless leaves, and blooms in the summer. It grows in wet areas and ditches throughout the country.

Identical to garden spearmint, this garden escapee has been a favorite for millennia. The leaves are great in all kinds of desserts, and they make excellent sauces. Companion flavorings such as marjoram and lemon or lime juice bring out the herb's best qualities.

MONSIEUR WILDMAN'S FRENCH DRESSING

Here's a recipe using cultivated mint that I made for my cooking class in 1981, before I became the "Wildman." With slight modifications and the option of substituting wild spearmint, this dressing is just as good today. Add 1 to 2 tablespoons of the dressing to a serving of any tossed salad.

1 cup olive oil
1 cup canola oil, walnut oil, sunflower seed oil,
* or any vegetable oil*
6 tablespoons fresh lemon juice
1 small white onion, peeled
¼ cup mellow (light-colored) miso
2 cloves garlic, peeled
2 tablespoons chopped fresh wild spearmint
* leaves or 2 teaspoons dried, finely crumbled*

2 tablespoons chopped fresh basil leaves or
*   2 teaspoons dried, finely crumbled*
4 teaspoons hot paprika
4 teaspoons freshly ground yellow mustard seeds
*   (2 teaspoons seeds)*
⅛ teaspoon liquid stevia or 2 teaspoons honey,
*   barley malt, or rice syrup*

In a blender, combine all the ingredients and process until smooth. Monsieur Wildman's French Dressing will keep, tightly covered, in the refrigerator, for up to 1 month.

MAKES 2¾ CUPS

MINT-LIME SAUCE

Here's a recipe that's structurally similar to my Healthy Hollandaise Sauce (page 130), but it uses lime juice instead of lemon juice, and it adds spearmint to complement the lime flavor. Serve this sauce hot or cold over vegetables, grains, or beans. Don't bring this sauce to a boil or the liquid may separate out.

¼ cup fresh wild spearmint leaves
One 19-ounce package silken tofu, drained
½ cup fresh lime juice
½ cup flaxseed oil or corn oil
¼ cup water
3 tablespoons lecithin granules
1 teaspoon freshly ground yellow mustard seeds
*   (½ teaspoon seeds)*
1 teaspoon freshly ground white pepper
*   (½ teaspoon peppercorns)*
1 teaspoon freshly grated nutmeg
½ teaspoon dried marjoram, finely crumbled
½ teaspoon salt

In a food processor, chop the mint leaves. Add the remaining ingredients and process until smooth. Mint-Lime Sauce will keep, tightly covered, in the refrigerator for 5 to 7 days.

MAKES 5 CUPS

WILD SPEARMINT–MANGO SHERBET

Wild spearmint melds with fresh mangoes to create this refreshing, healthful summer treat.

2 cups water
½ cup raw cashews
½ cup canola oil
¼ cup vegetable glycerin, honey, barley malt, or
*   rice syrup*
¼ cup lecithin granules
1 teaspoon liquid stevia (optional)
1 tablespoon chopped fresh wild spearmint leaves
*   or 1 teaspoon dried, finely crumbled*
1 teaspoon ground cinnamon
½ teaspoon mango extract (optional)
¼ teaspoon freshly ground cloves
½ teaspoon salt
2 medium-size ripe mangoes, peeled, seeded, and
*   chopped*

1. In a blender, combine all the ingredients, except one of the mangoes, and process until smooth.
2. Chill the mixture (or begin with chilled ingredients) if required by your ice cream machine.
3. Pour the mixture into the ice cream machine along with the remaining chopped mango, and freeze according to the manufacturer's instructions.

MAKES 6 CUPS; SERVES 6

WILD SPEARMINT–PINEAPPLE SORBET

Pour wild spearmint, pineapple, and a few other ingredients from a blender into an ice cream machine, and you can have a delicious, healthful cold dessert with next to no effort.

3 cups pineapple chunks

1½ cups water

½ cup raw cashews

½ cup canola oil

¼ cup vegetable glycerin, honey, barley malt,
*   or rice syrup*

¼ cup lecithin granules

3 tablespoons chopped fresh wild spearmint leaves
*   or 1 tablespoon dried, finely crumbled*

1 teaspoon liquid stevia (optional)

½ teaspoon salt

1. In a blender, combine all the ingredients and process until smooth.

2. Chill the mixture (or begin with chilled ingredients) if required by your ice cream machine.

3. Pour the mixture into the ice cream machine and freeze according to the manufacturer's instructions.

MAKES 5½ CUPS; SERVES 5 TO 6

GARLIC MUSTARD
Alliaria esculente

THIS WIDESPREAD EUROPEAN PLANT GROWS IN various partially shaded habitats throughout eastern North America. In the cold weather of late fall, winter, and early spring, the stalked, heart-shaped, dark green, heavily veined, scallop-edged leaves radiate into a circle along the ground from one point. In mid-spring, more triangular leaves alternate from a 3-foot-tall flower stalk. If you crush a leaf, you'll notice the garlicky odor.

You can also eat the alternating tiny white four-petaled flowers that bloom in the spring, or the tiny black seeds (see page 206) that fall out of the thin brown cylindrical seedpods on the dead stalk in the summer. Be careful not to let the seeds fall to the ground when you try to gather them.

Perfect for salads, the pungent, bitter leaves are tricky to cook because they quickly shrink and concentrate their bitterness. Although they're edible in the late fall, winter, and early spring, mid-spring is their best season. Then, tender new leaves on the flower stalk combine sweet and pungent flavors with a mild bitterness.

The white taproot, which is in season during late fall, winter, and early spring, tastes like horseradish. Use it in soups and sauces in any recipe that needs spiciness.

GARLIC MUSTARD CREAM SAUCE

This low-calorie, mild, horseradish-flavored sauce takes minutes to prepare. Serve it over tofu, tempeh, or vegetables.

¾ cup well-drained silken tofu

¼ cup garlic mustard roots

1 slice bread, torn into pieces

1 pitted date (optional)

2 teaspoons corn oil or flaxseed oil

½ teaspoon freshly ground yellow mustard seeds
*   (¼ teaspoon seeds)*

¼ teaspoon Vege-Sal or ⅛ teaspoon salt, or to taste

In a blender, combine all the ingredients and process until the garlic mustard is finely chopped. Garlic Mustard Cream Sauce will keep, tightly covered, in the refrigerator for 5 to 7 days.

MAKES 1 ½ CUPS

REMOULADE SAUCE

This uncooked French sauce will add zest to any dish. Use it hot or cold on vegetables or tempeh, fill an avocado with it, or use it as a dip for artichokes or raw vegetables.

1 tablespoon garlic mustard roots

1 clove garlic, crushed into a paste

2 small chiles, seeds and ribs removed, or
*   ¼ teaspoon cayenne pepper, or to taste*

¾ cup drained silken tofu, diced

1 tablespoon olive oil

2 tablespoons fresh lemon juice

1 tablespoon corn oil

1 tablespoon balsamic vinegar

2 teaspoons freshly ground mustard seeds
*   (1 teaspoon seeds)*

1 ½ teaspoons lecithin granules

½ teaspoon Vege-Sal or ¼ teaspoon salt, or to taste

¼ teaspoon turmeric

In a food processor, chop the garlic mustard root, garlic, and chiles. Add the remaining ingredients and process until the ingredients are well mixed. Remoulade Sauce will keep, tightly covered, in the refrigerator for 5 to 7 days.

MAKES 1 CUP

GARLIC MUSTARD SAUTÉ

Garlic mustard leaves provide the pungent flavors of both garlic and mustard. This recipe further reduces the leaves' bitterness by adding other flavors. Serve this dish hot over brown rice.

SAUTÉ

¼ cup olive oil

6 cups garlic mustard leaves

8 cloves garlic, chopped

SAUCE

1 ½ cups Vegetable Stock (page 40)

1 cup drained silken tofu

2 tablespoons chopped fresh parsley leaves

2 tablespoons mellow (light-colored) miso

1 tablespoon garlic mustard taproots

1 tablespoon sesame seeds, toasted (page 73)

1 tablespoon brown rice vinegar

1 teaspoon brewer's yeast

1 teaspoon wasabi (Japanese horseradish) powder,
*   or to taste*

1 teaspoon chili paste or ¼ teaspoon cayenne
*   pepper, or to taste*

1. *To make the sauté:* Heat the olive oil in a medium-size skillet over medium heat. Cook the garlic mustard leaves for 4 minutes, stirring. Add the garlic and cook, stirring, another minute.

2. *To make the sauce:* In a blender, combine all the sauce ingredients and process until smooth. Pour the sauce over the sautéed leaves and bring the pot to a boil. Reduce the heat to low and simmer, covered, for 5 minutes.

SERVES 6

EARLY SPRING WILD FOODS

E ARLY SPRING IS THE BEST TIME FOR GATHERING cold-resistant wild vegetables. Many of these species protect themselves from increasing populations of herbivores by becoming very bitter by the time the weather becomes warm. That's why many wild food cooks tell you to boil these plants to death. Instead, learn to recognize the plants when they first appear, and you'll be sure to enjoy them before they grow so bitter. I'm arbitrarily leaving out many of the root vegetables that are also in season in early spring, and I am covering them instead in their other season, autumn.

DAYLILY SHOOT

Hemerocallis fulva

THE DAYLILY IS VERY COMMON AND WELL known, as both a cultivated plant and a wild plant. Imported from Asia as a food, it soon became a favorite show flower. But the shoots, which are in season in early spring, as well as the flower buds and flowers (see page 212 for details), which are in season around the summer solstice, still provide one of the finest foods on the planet. (Although the tubers are edible, they're too small, and cleaning them is too labor-intensive to be worth the trouble.)

The daylily is easiest to identify in early summer, when it flowers. The large, spectacular funnel-shaped, short-stemmed, reflexed (bent backwards) orange flowers, 6 to 15 per plant, stand erect on a leafless 3-foot-tall flower stalk. What look like six petals are really three petals and three nearly identical sepals (the modified leaves that constitute the outside of the flower bud) that are 4 inches long. The petals surround 6 long (male) stamens, covered with pollen, and a single (female) pistil. The narrow, sword-like leaves all emerge from the ground. Several feet long, they bend backward under their own weight.

Underground are almond-sized potato-like tubers that are attached to the plant's base by cord-like rhizomes (underground stems). In early spring, when the shoot is edible, the rhizomes and tubers help distinguish the daylily from other poisonous plants, which lack tubers. The daylily shoot consists of unbranched narrow, pointed, sword-like emerald green leaves that emerge from the ground in dense stands. Collect them when they are up to 8 inches tall. If they grow any

longer they begin to become coarse and acrid. *Caution: Eat small amounts of this plant the first time. It gives 1 out of 50 people indigestion.*

EARLY SPRING STIR-FRY

This Asian treatment enhances some of the best wild and cultivated vegetables that you can get in the early part of the growing season.

SAUCE

> 1 teaspoon freshly ground cumin seeds
>
> 1 teaspoon freshly ground fennel seeds
>
> 1½ teaspoons freshly ground celery seeds (1 teaspoon seeds)
>
> 1 teaspoon finely chopped common spicebush berries (page 314) or freshly ground allspice berries
>
> ¼ cup tamari soy sauce

STIR-FRY

> ¾ cup peanut oil mixed with ¼ cup toasted sesame oil
>
> 4 cups daylily shoots, chopped
>
> 4 cups snow peas, trimmed of strings
>
> 1 cup chicory (page 70) or dandelion leaves (page 71), chopped
>
> 1 cup garlic mustard leaves (page 61) or other mustard greens
>
> 3 cups Jerusalem artichokes (page 361), sliced
>
> 2½ cups chopped field garlic leaves (page 57), wild garlic leaves (page 160), or scallions
>
> 1 daikon (Japanese radish), chopped
>
> 2 small yellow squash, ends trimmed and sliced
>
> 1 medium-size carrot, sliced
>
> ½ cup garlic mustard roots (page 61), chopped
>
> Two 16-ounce packages firm tofu, drained and cubed

1. *To make the sauce:* Mix the sauce ingredients together and set aside.

2. *To make the stir-fry:* Assemble the stir-fry ingredients, heat a wok over high heat, and add 2 to 3 tablespoons of the mixed oils to the wok. Stir-fry the ingredients consecutively in the hot oil, as specified below, removing each ingredient when it is done and adding a little more oil before cooking each new ingredient.

3. Stir-fry the daylily shoots, then the snow peas, 3 minutes each.

4. Stir-fry the chicory leaves for 2 minutes.

5. Stir-fry the garlic mustard leaves for 1 minute.

6. Stir-fry each of the remaining ingredients for 3 minutes.

7. When all the ingredients are cooked, return them all to the wok, mix them together well with the sauce, heat them through if necessary, and serve the stir-fry over brown rice.

SERVES 10 TO 12

DAYLILY CHOLENT

This warming traditional Jewish dish will heat the blood during the last bitterly cold spells of March, when the daylily is one of the few wild edibles to brave the elements. Slow cooking gives the ingredients a chance to blend and meld.

2½ cups (1 pound) dried lima beans, picked over
   and rinsed

3 tablespoons olive oil

3 medium-size onions, chopped

4 cloves garlic, crushed

4 cups daylily shoots, chopped

1½ teaspoons Vege-Sal or ¾ teaspoon salt

2 teaspoons paprika

1 teaspoon freshly ground cumin seeds

1 teaspoon dried marjoram, finely crumbled

1 teaspoon dried thyme, finely crumbled

1 teaspoon freshly ground black pepper
   (½ teaspoon peppercorns), or to taste

½ teaspoon crushed red pepper or cayenne pepper, or
   to taste

2 bayberry leaves (page 185) or 1 bay leaf

4 medium-size potatoes (1¼ pounds), coarsely chopped

4 cups boiling water, or as needed

1. Cover the beans with water in a large saucepan and bring the pot to a boil for 2 minutes. Remove the pot from the heat and let the beans stand, covered, for 1 hour.

2. Preheat the oven to 250 degrees.

3. Meanwhile, heat the olive oil in a large skillet over medium heat. Add the onions, garlic, and daylilies and cook them, stirring, for 5 minutes.

4. Drain the lima beans and mix them with the sautéed vegetables, the seasonings and herbs, and the potatoes in a 3-quart Dutch oven or casserole dish. Cover the vegetables completely with the boiling water, stir well, and bake the casserole, covered, for 6 to 8 hours or overnight (or cook the vegetables in a slow cooker set on medium heat overnight). Add more water if necessary. Serve Daylily Cholent hot with whole-grain bread.

SERVES 8 TO 10

CURRIED DAYLILY SOUP

Westerners often make curries with curry powder, but in India, cooks use individual whole spices to create curries. Except for the substitution of silken tofu and lime juice for the yogurt, this is how Indian cooks would make curried daylily shoots if daylilies grew in India.

3 cups water

1 cup drained silken tofu

1 ½ tablespoons dried chickpeas, ground into
   a flour in a spice grinder, or 2 tablespoons
   chickpea flour

1 tablespoon fresh lime juice

1 tablespoon tamari soy sauce, 2 teaspoons
   Vege-Sal, or 1 teaspoon salt, or to taste

2 tablespoons peanut oil

One 1-inch cinnamon stick

3 cloves

1 teaspoon fenugreek seeds

½ teaspoon yellow mustard seeds

½ teaspoon turmeric

1 teaspoon chili paste or ½ teaspoon cayenne
   pepper, or to taste

2 ¼ cups daylily shoots, chopped

1. In a blender, combine the water, tofu, chickpea flour, lime juice, and tamari and process until smooth. 2. Heat the peanut oil, cinnamon, cloves, fenugreek seeds, yellow mustard seeds, turmeric, and chili paste together in a large saucepan over medium heat, stirring constantly, until the mustard seeds splatter. Add the tofu mixture and bring the pot to a boil over medium heat, stirring often. Reduce the heat to low and simmer, covered, for 10 minutes. Stir in the daylily shoots and simmer for another 10 minutes. Serve the curried daylily shoots hot as a soup, or with whole grains or Indian bread.

SERVES 4 TO 6

DAYLILY RICE

Adding sautéed daylily shoots to brown rice transforms that vegetarian staple into a truly extraordinary dish.

2 tablespoons olive oil

4 cups daylily shoots, chopped

1 tablespoon chopped garlic

2 chiles (optional), or to taste, seeds and ribs
   removed and chopped

2 teaspoons dried oregano, finely crumbled

1 teaspoon dried sage, finely crumbled

1 teaspoon dried lemon thyme or thyme, finely
   crumbled

1 ¾ cups basmati brown rice

¼ cup wild rice (page 353)

3 ½ cups water

1 tablespoon tamari soy sauce

Heat the olive oil in a large pot over medium heat. Add the daylily shoots, garlic, and chiles and cook, stirring, for 5 minutes. Add the remaining ingredients and bring the pot to a boil. Reduce the heat to low and simmer, covered, until all the water is absorbed, about 40 minutes.

SERVES 6 TO 8

SWEET CREAMED DAYLILY SHOOTS

A sauce of chestnuts puréed in coconut milk transforms the new daylily growth of early spring into a luxuriant dish.

¾ cup reconstituted dried or cooked wild American
   chestnuts (page 348) or cultivated Asian chestnuts

½ cup unsweetened coconut milk

¼ cup water

1 tablespoon Blackberry Spice Wine (page 278) or
   red wine

¼ teaspoon freshly ground cloves

½ teaspoon freshly grated nutmeg

½ teaspoon ground dried wild ginger (page 111) or
* regular ground ginger*

1 tablespoon tamari soy sauce

2 tablespoons sesame oil

6 cups daylily shoots

4 cloves garlic, finely chopped

4 small chiles, seeds and ribs removed and chopped,
* or ¼ teaspoon cayenne pepper, or to taste*

1. Place the chestnuts, coconut milk, water, wine, cloves, nutmeg, ginger, and tamari in a medium-size saucepan, cover, bring the pot to a simmer, and let the chestnuts simmer until they are tender, 10 to 20 minutes.

2. Meanwhile, heat the sesame oil in a large skillet over medium heat and cook the daylilies, garlic, and chiles, stirring, for 5 minutes. Add the chestnut mixture, reduce the heat to low, and simmer, covered, for 10 minutes. Serve Sweet Creamed Daylily Shoots hot on a bed of brown rice or other grain.

S E R V E S   4   T O   6

DAYLILY KIMCHI

This simple East Asian pickling method works perfectly with this Asian wild vegetable. The salt pulls water out of the weighted-down vegetables and also preserves them.

8 cups daylily shoots, partially pulled apart

1 medium-size red onion, chopped

2 small carrots, grated

3 tablespoons chili paste or 1 ½ teaspoons cayenne
* pepper*

6 cloves garlic, crushed

2 ½ tablespoons salt

1 tablespoon peeled and grated fresh ginger

1. Mix everything together in a large bowl.

2. Put a plate with a diameter a little smaller than the top of the bowl on top of the mixture. Put a weight (such as an unopened container of juice) on top of the plate. Leave it there for 1 hour.

3. Remove the plate and use the kimchi at once or store it, tightly packed, in the refrigerator. It will keep for months.

4. Just before serving, rinse the kimchi in a colander to remove excess salt. Serve as an appetizer or side dish.

M A K E S   4   C U P S

DAYLILY, NOODLE, AND CHEESE CASSEROLE

Try this recipe with tofu dairy alternatives and homemade noodles. Whether you're a vegan or an open-minded dairy product consumer, you're in for a treat.

4 cups tightly packed daylily shoots, chopped

¾ pound Buckwheat Noodles (page 34) or store-
* bought noodles*

1 cup Tofu Cottage Cheese (page 30)

1 cup Tofu Cream Cheese (page 30)

1 ¼ cups Tofu Sour Cream (page 33)

1 teaspoon Vege-Sal or ½ teaspoon salt, or to taste

½ teaspoon freshly ground black pepper
* (¼ teaspoon peppercorns)*

⅓ cup field garlic leaves (page 57), chopped, or
* chopped fresh chives or scallions*

1 tablespoon corn oil

1. Preheat the oven to 350 degrees.

2. Rinse the daylily shoots and shake or spin off any excess water. Place the daylily shoots in a medium-size saucepan over low heat and cook, covered, until they are just wilted, 5 to 10 minutes.

3. Cook the noodles in rapidly boiling salted water for 2 minutes less than directed in the recipe or on the package. Drain the noodles in a colander, and stop the cooking by plunging the colander into a bowl of cold water. Drain the noodles again.

4. Meanwhile, in a large bowl stir together the cottage cheese and cream cheese, with 1 cup of the sour cream. Stir in the cooked noodles and pour the mixture into a 3-quart oiled casserole dish. Sprinkle the noodle mixture with the Vege-Sal, pepper, and field garlic leaves, pour the remaining ¼ cup sour cream on top, and dot the casserole with the corn oil. Bake, uncovered, until bubbly, about 30 minutes.

SERVES 6

MASHED POTATOES WITH DAYLILY SHOOTS

Sautéed daylily shoots make plain old mashed potatoes seem luxurious.

2 tablespoons olive oil

4 cups daylily shoots

1 medium-size red onion, chopped

5 cloves garlic, or to taste, chopped

3 cups boiled potato chunks

1 cup Tofu Sour Cream (page 33)

*1 teaspoon chili paste or ¼ teaspoon cayenne
   pepper, or to taste*

½ teaspoon Vege-Sal or ¼ teaspoon salt, or to taste

*½ teaspoon freshly ground white pepper
   (¼ teaspoon peppercorns)*

1. Heat the olive oil in a medium-size skillet over medium heat. Cook the daylily shoots and onion, stirring, for 5 minutes. Add the garlic and cook, stirring, for another 5 minutes. Don't let the garlic brown or it will become bitter.

2. In a food processor, purée the cooked potatoes (or mash the potatoes in a large bowl with a potato masher or fork) with the sour cream, chili paste, Vege-Sal, and white pepper until the potatoes are smooth. Stir in the sautéed vegetables and heat the mixture through.

SERVES 4 TO 6

CHINESE DAYLILY SHOOTS

Here's a simple stir-fried side dish featuring this overlooked superfood.

SAUCE

2 cups Vegetable Stock (page 40)

2 tablespoons kudzu or arrowroot

*2 tablespoons any miso or 1 tablespoon tamari soy
   sauce, or to taste*

*1 teaspoon chili paste or ¼ teaspoon cayenne
   pepper, or to taste*

½ teaspoon freshly ground star anise

½ teaspoon freshly ground cloves

STIR-FRY

3 tablespoons peanut oil

7 cups daylily shoots, sliced

1 tablespoon toasted sesame oil, or as needed

*One 28.5-ounce can sliced bamboo shoots
   (4 cups), drained*

1 teaspoon peeled and finely chopped fresh ginger

5 cloves garlic, finely chopped

1. *To make the sauce:* In a blender process all the sauce ingredients together until smooth. Transfer the sauce to a medium-size saucepan and bring it to a boil over medium heat, stirring often. Reduce the heat to low and simmer, covered, for 5 minutes.

2. *To make the stir-fry:* Heat 2 tablespoons of the peanut oil in a wok or large skillet over high heat. Stir-fry the daylily shoots for 3 minutes. Remove the daylily shoots from the pan and set them aside.

3. Add the remaining 1 tablespoon peanut oil and the sesame oil to the wok and let the wok heat up. Add the bamboo shoots and ginger and stir-fry them for 2 minutes. Add the garlic and stir-fry for 1 minute more.

4. Add the daylilies and sauce and bring the mixture to a boil. Reduce the heat to low and simmer, covered, for 5 minutes. Serve hot over brown rice.

SERVES 6 TO 8

CURRIED DAYLILIES

The daylily is a jack-of-all-ingredients, and master of all recipes, too! You'll delight at how well it fits into a traditional-style Indian dish.

SAUTÉ

- *¼ cup sesame oil*
- *8 cups daylilies, sliced*
- *2 medium-size carrots, sliced*
- *4 celery stalks, sliced*
- *1 cup texturized vegetable protein (TVP), soaked for 10 minutes in ¾ cup hot water and drained, with its soaking water reserved*
- *½ cup raw cashews or peanuts*

SAUCE

- *¾ cup drained silken tofu*
- *¼ cup dark-colored miso*
- *2 tablespoons Curry Paste (page 37)*
- *Juice of 1 lime*
- *1 tablespoon kudzu or arrowroot*

1. *To make the sauté:* Heat the sesame oil in a large skillet over medium heat. Add the remaining sauté ingredients and cook, stirring, for 10 minutes.

2. *To make the sauce:* In a blender, combine all the sauce ingredients and process until smooth.

3. Pour the sauce into the skillet and bring the mixture to a boil over medium heat, stirring often. Reduce the heat to low, cover the pan, and simmer the mixture for another 10 minutes. Serve over brown rice or with Indian bread.

SERVES 6

DAYLILY WINE

Here's a hearty cooking wine you can make with one of the most common wild and cultivated plants. Use it to season vegetables and grain dishes.

- *6 cups sugar*
- *1 gallon boiling water*
- *8 cups daylily shoots*
- *Juice of 2 lemons*
- *1 tablespoon dried tarragon*
- *1 tablespoon dill seeds*
- *1 tablespoon poppy seeds*
- *½ teaspoon champagne yeast or other wine yeast*

1. Dissolve the sugar in the water in a non-metal (plastic, glass, or ceramic) food container and add the daylily shoots, lemon juice, and herbs.

2. When the mixture has cooled to lukewarm, stir in the yeast and cover the container with a non-airtight cover, cheesecloth, or a towel. Allow the mixture to ferment for a week at room temperature, stirring it twice a day.

3. Strain the mixture through cheesecloth, transfer the liquid to a jug, and seal the jug with an airlock stopper (which lets carbon dioxide bubbles escape but keeps oxygen out).

4. When the bubbling stops and fermentation ends about 2 or 3 weeks later, seal the jug with a cork and let the wine age for 6 months to 2 years before using it. Siphon the wine to get rid of the sediment, if desired.

MAKES 1 GALLON

CHICORY

Cichorium intybus L.

THIS PLANT PRODUCES THE BEAUTIFUL, SKY blue flowers with fringed petals that you see along roadsides, in fields, and in disturbed areas in the summer. At that time, the plant is inedible. Collect the leaves when they first appear in early spring, growing along the ground in the form of a basal rosette. Later the plant becomes intensely bitter. You can also use the new growth in late fall. The basal leaves, 3 to 6 inches long, are deeply toothed. The teeth point outward, not toward the leaf base, like dandelion leaves. Unlike wild lettuce, which has a fibrous root, chicory has a deep taproot, which some people toast until it is black, grind, and use as a coffee substitute.

Chicory's bitterness, which you can attenuate with other ingredients and seasonings, adds a savory quality to any dish. You can sauté chicory and then braise it in a sauce. Cook it for at least 15 to 20 minutes.

REFRIED BEANS WITH CHICORY

The flavor of wild chicory is a perfect match for this hearty Mexican classic. You can season the beans as strongly as you wish—people's preferences for spiciness vary greatly.

6 tablespoons olive oil

4 cups very young wild chicory, dandelion (page 71), or sow thistle leaves (page 47)

2 medium-size red onions, chopped

2 small chiles, or to taste, seeds and ribs removed and finely chopped

8 cloves garlic, or to taste, chopped

4 cups cooked kidney beans or other beans, drained

¼ cup Mulberry Wine (page 222) or red wine

¼ cup tomato paste

1 tablespoon freshly ground cumin seeds

2 teaspoons dried oregano, finely crumbled

1 teaspoon freshly ground black pepper (½ teaspoon peppercorns)

½ teaspoon Vege-Sal or ¼ teaspoon salt, or to taste

1. Heat 2 tablespoons of the olive oil in a large skillet over medium heat. Add the chicory, onions, and chiles and cook, stirring, for 10 minutes. Add the garlic and cook, stirring, for another 2 minutes.

2. Add the remaining ingredients, partially mashing the beans with a potato masher, wooden spatula, or wooden spoon as you stir them in. Reduce the heat to low and cook, covered, for 10 minutes. Serve with rice or rolled up in tortillas.

SERVES 6

CHICORY AND BROCCOLI HOLLANDAISE

Wild chicory sautéed with broccoli and smothered in my version of hollandaise sauce makes another fabulous vegetable side dish created with "weeds."

6 tablespoons olive oil, or as needed

1 large head broccoli, stems and florets sliced

8 cups very young wild chicory, dandelion (page
    71), or sow thistle leaves (page 47)
1 small chile, seeds and ribs removed and finely
    chopped, or ¼ teaspoon cayenne pepper, or to
    taste
6 cloves garlic, or to taste, chopped
2 tablespoons tamari soy sauce
2 tablespoons White Oak Wine (page 176) or
    sherry
2 cups Healthy Hollandaise Sauce (page 130)

1. Heat the olive oil in a large skillet over medium heat. Cook the broccoli, chicory, and chile for 5 minutes. Add the garlic and cook, stirring, for another 5 minutes. Add the tamari and wine, reduce the heat to low, and simmer, covered, for 10 minutes.

2. Stir in the hollandaise sauce and heat the mixture to serving temperature over medium heat, stirring often. Serve hot with whole grains or whole-grain bread. Chicory and Broccoli Hollandaise will keep, tightly covered, in the refrigerator for 5 to 7 days.

SERVES 8 TO 10

COMMON
DANDELION

Taraxacum officinale

EVERYONE KNOWS THIS PLANT WHEN ITS YELLOW composite flowers (which you can eat, if you discard the very bitter leaflike green sepals beneath the flower) appear in early spring. But to use the plant you need to be able to recognize the young leaves, which you can collect before the plant blooms or when new growth occurs in late fall.

Dandelion means "lion's tooth," and the hairless leaves (chicory, page 72, has some hair on the leaves), usually 3 to 12 inches long, sport sharp, recurved teeth pointing toward the leaf's base. The leaves form a basal rosette, radiating in a circle along the ground from a beige taproot. The whole plant exudes a white sap when cut.

Using this rather bitter green with several other ingredients and the correct seasonings and cooking it for a relatively long time make it so good that I'd eat it even if it meant getting arrested again.

CURRIED DANDELIONS

Dandelion leaves are moderately bitter even when they're at their best, but you would never know it when you apply Indian methods to this common, super-nutritious, easy-to-recognize wild vegetable.

3 tablespoons corn oil, peanut oil, sesame oil, or
    olive oil
9 cups young common dandelion leaves
4½ teaspoons chopped garlic
1½ cups water
¾ cup drained silken tofu
2 tablespoons mellow (light-colored) miso
1½ tablespoons fresh lime juice
1½ tablespoons Curry Powder (page 112), or to taste

1. Heat the oil in a large skillet over medium heat. Cook the dandelion leaves and garlic, stirring, for 10 minutes, being careful not to let the garlic burn.

2. Meanwhile, in a blender, combine the remaining ingredients and process until smooth. Add the purée to the dandelions and bring the mixture to a boil. Reduce the heat to low and simmer, covered, for 10 minutes.

SERVES 6

DANDELIONS AND VEGETABLES SMOTHERED IN HOLLANDAISE SAUCE

Plain ole dandelions rise to new heights of excellence in the company of other vegetables and my mock hollandaise sauce.

>   3 tablespoons olive oil, or as needed
>   3 cups dandelion leaves, chopped
>   One 16-ounce package firm tofu, drained and diced
>   1 medium-size red onion, chopped
>   2 medium-size zucchini, ends trimmed and sliced
>   1 medium-size yellow or red bell pepper, seeded and cut into strips
>   4 cloves garlic, chopped
>   1 tablespoon arrowroot or kudzu
>   2 cups Healthy Hollandaise Sauce (page 130)

1. Heat the olive oil in a large skillet over medium heat. Add the dandelion leaves, tofu, and onion and cook, stirring, for 10 minutes. Add the zucchinis, bell pepper, and garlic and cook, stirring, for another 5 minutes.

2. In a small bowl, mix the arrowroot with the hollandaise sauce and stir the mixture into the vegetables. Reduce the heat to low and simmer, covered, for 10 minutes.

SERVES 6

DANDELION FRIED RICE

Pieces of shrimp or pork usually enhance the flavor of fried rice. Pieces of dandelion greens and bits of texturized vegetable protein seasoned with Chinese flavors perform the same function remarkably well, producing a dish that can serve as a meal in itself.

>   5 tablespoons peanut oil
>   2 cups dandelion leaves, coarsely chopped
>   2 small chiles, seeds and ribs removed and chopped, or ¼ teaspoon cayenne pepper, or to taste
>   4 large cloves garlic, chopped
>   1 tablespoon peeled and chopped fresh ginger
>   5 scallions, chopped
>   ½ cup texturized vegetable protein (TVP)
>   1 tablespoon toasted sesame oil
>   2 cups brown basmati rice or other brown rice
>   2¾ cups water
>   2 tablespoons tamari soy sauce, or to taste
>   1 teaspoon brown rice vinegar

1. Heat 2 tablespoons of the peanut oil over high heat in a wok or large skillet. Stir-fry the dandelion leaves for 90 seconds. Add the chiles, garlic, and ginger and stir-fry for another 30 seconds. Remove the cooked vegetables from the wok and set them aside.

2. Heat another 2 tablespoons of the peanut oil over high heat in the wok. Stir-fry the scallions and TVP for 2 minutes. Remove them from the wok and set them aside.

3. Heat the remaining 1 tablespoon peanut oil with the sesame oil in the wok over high heat and stir-fry the rice for 2 minutes.

4. Transfer the cooked vegetables and the remaining ingredients to a large saucepan and bring the pot to a boil over medium heat. Reduce the heat to low and cook, covered, until all the water is absorbed and the rice is tender, about 40 minutes.

SERVES 6 TO 8

DANDELION COLUMBO

Like the curries of India, *columbo* is a traditional blend of herbs. Originating in Sri Lanka and Senegal, it migrated to the French Antilles islands of Martinique and Guadeloupe. After a Haitian friend described it to me, I applied *columbo* to wild dandelions, and now I'm offering it to you. Simple!

2 tablespoons peanut oil

6 cups dandelion leaves, wild chicory leaves
    (page 72), or other bitter greens, chopped

1 medium-size head cauliflower, stems and florets
    sliced

6 cloves garlic, chopped

2 small chiles, seeds and ribs removed, or ¼
    teaspoon cayenne pepper, or to taste

1 teaspoon freshly ground coriander seeds

1 teaspoon turmeric

2 teaspoons freshly ground yellow mustard seeds
    (1 teaspoon seeds)

1 cup unsweetened coconut milk

½ cup drained silken tofu

¼ cup water

1 ½ tablespoons mellow (light-colored) miso

½ teaspoon rum extract or 2 tablespoons rum or
    any wild wine or sherry (optional)

1. Heat the peanut oil in a large skillet over medium heat. Add the dandelion leaves, cauliflower, garlic, and chiles and cook, stirring, for 10 minutes.

2. Meanwhile, place the remaining ingredients in a blender and process until smooth. Pour the purée into the skillet and bring the mixture to a boil. Reduce the heat to low and cook the mixture, covered, until the cauliflower is tender, another 10 minutes.

SERVES 6

DANDELION GREENS WITH SESAME SEEDS

Very young dandelion leaves impart a bitter flavor that may be wonderful or terrible, depending on how you prepare and season them. The four other ingredients in this recipe optimize the dandelion's flavor. This simple side dish is equally good if you use very young wild chicory or very young wild lettuce leaves.

¾ cup sesame seeds

1 ½ tablespoons olive oil

7 ½ cups packed dandelion or wild chicory leaves
    (page 72)

6 cloves garlic, chopped

2 ½ teaspoons Bragg's Liquid Aminos or tamari
    soy sauce

1. In a medium-size dry skillet, toast the sesame seeds over medium heat, stirring or shaking them constantly, until they are lightly browned and fragrant, 2 to 3 minutes. Immediately remove the sesame seeds from the pan and set them aside.

2. Heat the olive oil in a large skillet over medium heat and cook the dandelion leaves and garlic for 15 minutes, stirring the vegetables often and being careful not to let the garlic burn. Stir in the Bragg's Liquid Aminos and toasted sesame seeds and serve hot.

SERVES 6

WILD CARROT
Daucus carota

Here's a wild food most people don't know that they know. They're familiar with

Queen Anne's lace, with its flat-topped white cluster of tiny flowers, often with a dark purple floret in the middle. The plant grows 2 to 3 feet tall in fields, disturbed areas, and along roadsides. You can see it throughout the country every summer.

What most people recognize is the second-year form of this biennial (two-year plant). Although the flower is edible (but not especially good) and you can use the seeds, which cluster on top of the stalk like an abandoned bird's nest, the beige taproot is the best part to harvest in the fall and early spring (and in the winter, if you can find it).

Look for a basal rosette of much-divided lacy leaves that look just like the carrot leaves you see in the store. The leafstalks of wild carrot are slightly hairy, and the root smells like carrots. Once the flower stalk starts to grow, by mid-spring, the root gets too tough to eat.

Poison hemlock and other deadly relatives have similar flowers, leaves, and roots, but they lack the carrot odor and the hairy leafstalks. Nonetheless, this is not a plant for beginners.

Crunchier than cultivated carrots, the strong-flavored wild carrot root is better in cooked dishes than the familiar orange strain.

WILD CARROT AND CRESS SALAD

Here's a quick, simple seasonal salad, made all the more crunchy by the inclusion of wild carrots.

¾ cup grated wild carrot taproots

¾ cup Tofu Grated Cheese (page 32)

3 tablespoons raisins

2 cloves garlic, crushed

3 tablespoons Sumac Concentrate (page 281) or fresh lemon or lime juice

1 cup wild watercress (page 387) or cultivated watercress leaves, chopped

Vege-Sal or salt and freshly ground black pepper to taste

1. Toss the carrots, Tofu Grated Cheese, raisins, garlic, and sumac concentrate together in a medium-size bowl until they are well combined.

2. Serve the salad on a bed of watercress leaves, sprinkled with Vege-Sal and pepper.

SERVES 6

TURKISH LENTIL SOUP

This traditional lentil soup, flavored with wild carrots and hen-of-the-woods mushrooms, is as delightful as it is simple. The vinegar makes the lentils cook more quickly. Adding the Vege-Sal when the soup is done prevents the salt from making the lentils tough.

9 cups Vegetable Stock (page 40)

2 cups dried lentils, picked over and rinsed

1 tablespoon red wine vinegar

4 bayberry leaves (page 185) or 2 bay leaves, enclosed in a tea ball or tea bag if desired

2 tablespoons corn oil

¾ cup (¼ pound) hen-of-the-woods mushrooms (page 363) or other mushrooms, sliced

1 medium-size onion, chopped

4 cloves garlic, chopped

2 wild carrot taproots, finely chopped

3 medium-size ripe tomatoes, chopped

2 tablespoons chopped fresh cilantro or parsley leaves

1 teaspoon dried marjoram, finely crumbled

½ teaspoon freshly ground black pepper (¼ teaspoon peppercorns)

1 teaspoon Vege-Sal or ½ teaspoon salt, or to taste

1. In a stockpot, bring the stock to a boil.

2. Add the lentils, vinegar, and bayberry leaves to the boiling stock, reduce the heat to low, and simmer the lentils, covered, for 10 minutes.

3. Meanwhile, heat the corn oil in a medium-size skillet over medium heat. Add the mushrooms, onion, and garlic and cook, stirring, for 5 minutes. Add these vegetables to the lentils along with the remaining ingredients, except the Vege-Sal. Return the pot to a boil, reduce the heat to low, and simmer, covered, until the lentils are tender, about 10 minutes more.

4. Stir in the Vege-Sal and remove the bayberry leaves.

SERVES 6 TO 8

WILD CARROT SOUP

The great flavor and texture of wild carrots shine in this truly superior soup.

6 cups Vegetable Stock (page 40)

¼ cup olive oil

4 cups wild carrot taproots, sliced

1 ½ teaspoons freshly ground celery seeds
*   (1 teaspoon seeds)*

1 tablespoon chopped fresh dill or 1 teaspoon
*   dillweed, finely crumbled*

1 cup Tofu Cream Cheese (page 30)

1 teaspoon miso

1. In a stockpot, bring the stock to a boil.

2. Heat the olive oil in a large skillet over medium heat. Cook the carrots, stirring, for 10 minutes.

3. Add the carrots to the boiling vegetable stock along with the ground celery seeds and dill and simmer 10 more minutes.

4. Carefully transfer the mixture to a blender and process it in batches with the Tofu Cream Cheese and miso until smooth. Hold down the blender cover with a towel and begin on low speed to prevent eruptions.

SERVES 6 TO 8

THAI PUMPKIN SOUP

This delicate, creamy pumpkin soup benefits greatly from the inclusion of wild carrots.

¼ cup olive oil

2 stalks celery, sliced

¾ cup wild carrot taproots, chopped

1 medium-size onion, chopped

1 habañero or other chile, seeds and ribs removed
*   and chopped*

2 cloves garlic, chopped

1 teaspoon peeled and chopped fresh ginger

5 common spicebush berries (page 314), finely
*   chopped, or ½ teaspoon freshly ground allspice*
*   berries*

½ teaspoon freshly ground cloves

4 cups Vegetable Stock (page 40)

4 cups water

4 cups cooked pumpkin

One 14-ounce can unsweetened coconut milk

½ cup mellow (light-colored) miso

1. Heat the olive oil in a large pot over medium heat. Add the celery, wild carrots, onion, habañero, garlic, ginger, and spicebush berries and cook, stirring, for 10 minutes. Add the remaining ingredients except the miso and bring the pot to a boil over medium heat, stirring often. Reduce the heat to low and simmer, covered, for 10 minutes.

2. Add the miso and then carefully transfer the mixture to a blender, processing it in batches. Begin at low

speed and hold down the cover with a towel to prevent eruptions.

SERVES 6 TO 8

CARROT-BARLEY PILAF

Wild carrots cooked with barley and seasonings make a hearty, satisfying dish.

½ cup dried kelp or other seaweed
3¾ cups Vegetable Stock (page 40) or water
2 cups barley
½ cup wild carrot taproots, grated
2 tablespoons chopped fresh parsley leaves
2 teaspoons dried oregano, finely crumbled
1 tablespoon freshly ground celery seeds
  (2 teaspoons seeds)
2 teaspoons freshly grated nutmeg
2 small chiles, seeds and ribs removed and chopped,
  or ½ teaspoon cayenne pepper, or to taste
2 tablespoons olive oil
2 tablespoons Bragg's Liquid Aminos or tamari soy
  sauce, or to taste
4 cloves garlic, chopped

1. Soak the kelp in water to cover for 5 minutes to rehydrate it.
2. Drain and rinse the kelp, chop it, and combine it with all the other ingredients in a large saucepan. Bring the pot to a boil over medium heat, reduce the heat to low, and simmer, covered, until all the liquid is absorbed, about 1 hour.

MAKES 8 CUPS; SERVES 6 TO 8

WILD CARROT TZIMMES

Tzimmes, which means "uproar" or "fuss" in Yiddish, is a slow-cooked dish that may include meat, vegetables, or fruit. This recipe lends itself especially well to wild carrots. Tougher than commercial carrots, these taproots shine in long-cooking recipes.

4 cups wild carrot taproots, grated or finely
  chopped
¾ cup cored and grated green apples
2 tablespoons olive oil
¾ cup Vegetable Stock (page 40)
¼ cup raisins
1 tablespoon barley
4 cloves garlic, chopped
1 teaspoon ground cinnamon
½ teaspoon fennel seeds
1 ½ teaspoons freshly grated nutmeg
1 teaspoon Vege-Sal or ½ teaspoon salt, or to taste

Place all the ingredients in a large, heavy saucepan and bring the pot to a simmer. Cook the mixture over very low heat until all the liquid is absorbed, about 1 hour, stirring occasionally. (You may want to put a heat diffuser under the saucepan to prevent scorching on the bottom of the pot.)

SERVES 6

WILD CARROT CROQUETTES

These meat-free burgers showcase the flavor and crunchiness of the wild ancestor of all cultivated carrots.

3 tablespoons sesame oil
1 pound wild carrot taproots, grated
1 medium-size onion, minced

2 cloves garlic, minced

4 large potatoes, sliced, boiled until soft in water to
cover (about 10 minutes), drained, and mashed

2 tablespoons soy flour or any whole-grain flour

2 tablespoons chopped fresh parsley leaves

5 tablespoons freshly ground flaxseeds
(2 tablespoons seeds)

1 tablespoon arrowroot or kudzu

1 teaspoon tamari soy sauce

1 teaspoon dried rosemary, finely crumbled

1 teaspoon freshly ground black pepper
(½ teaspoon peppercorns)

1 teaspoon hot paprika

1. Preheat the oven to 350 degrees.

2. Heat the sesame oil in a large skillet over medium
heat. Add the carrots, onion, and garlic and cook, stirring often, until the onions and garlic begin to brown,
10 to 15 minutes.

3. In a large bowl, combine the cooked vegetables well
with the remaining ingredients, except the paprika.

4. Form the mixture into patties 1⅛ inches thick.
Place the patties on an oiled cookie sheet and sprinkle
them with the paprika. Bake the patties until they are
lightly browned underneath, about 45 minutes.

SERVES 6

WILD CARROT CAKE

Wild carrots are especially good in carrot cake because
they provide more flavor than commercial carrots do,
and they're still crunchy after cooking. Unlike in
more usual cakes, in this recipe you add the icing
before you bake the cake.

ICING

Two 19-ounce packages silken tofu, drained

¾ cup dates, chopped

¼ cup fresh lemon or lime juice

2 tablespoons arrowroot or kudzu

2 tablespoons fresh Bread Crumbs (page 40)

1 tablespoon almond oil

2 teaspoons vanilla extract

2 teaspoons ground cinnamon

1 teaspoon liquid stevia or 2 tablespoons honey,
barley malt, or rice syrup

½ teaspoon orange extract

½ teaspoon salt

CAKE

4 cups (19 ounces) sweet brown rice flour and
4 cups (1 pound) oat flour, or 35 ounces any
whole-grain flour

1 cup arrowroot or kudzu

¾ cup plus 3 tablespoons freshly ground flaxseeds
(6 tablespoons seeds)

2 teaspoons freshly ground star anise

1 teaspoon freshly ground coriander seeds

1 ½ teaspoons freshly grated nutmeg

2 teaspoons salt

1 teaspoon baking soda

2 ¼ cups plus 2 tablespoons apple juice

1 cup corn oil or other vegetable oil

¼ cup fresh lime or lemon juice

½ cup lecithin granules

2 teaspoon liquid stevia

1 ½ cups raisins

1 ½ cups wild carrot taproots, grated

1. Preheat the oven to 350 degrees.

2. To make the icing: In a food processor, combine the
icing ingredients and process until smooth.

3. To make the cake: Mix together the flour, arrowroot,
ground flaxseed, spices, salt, and baking soda in a large
bowl.

4. In a blender, combine the apple juice, corn oil, lime juice, lecithin granules, and liquid stevia and process until smooth. Mix the wet ingredients into the dry ingredients, being careful not to overmix. Stir in the raisins and grated wild carrots.

5. Divide the batter evenly between 2 oiled 12-inch round cake pans. Pour the icing over the cake batter in each pan. Bake the cakes until the bottom of each one is lightly browned, about 40 minutes. Let the cakes cool on wire racks before serving.

MAKES 2 CAKES

WILD CARROT SANDWICH SPREAD

This simple spread takes seconds to make, it's healthy, and kids love it. You can also use it to fill sandwiches.

> 1 cup Tofu Cream Cheese (page 30)
> ½ cup wild carrot taproots, grated
> ½ cup raisins

Mix all the ingredients together until they are well combined. Wild Carrot Sandwich Spread will keep, covered, in the refrigerator for 5 to 7 days.

MAKES 2 CUPS

HEDGE MUSTARD

Sisymbrium officinale

THIS IS ANOTHER GREAT MUSTARD PLANT THAT almost no one knows about. It begins as a basal rosette with hairy, lobed (partially subdivided) leaves that are 3 to 5 inches long. It then develops a stiff flower stalk with a few branches and small, four-petaled yellow flowers that bloom in late spring. The flowers are followed by long, slender seedpods. The spicy, decorative flowers and immature seedpods don't offer much food, but the leaves, which taste like pungent Chinese mustard, do. Gather the leaves in the spring and early summer.

INDIAN EGGPLANT

Traditionally made with spinach, this dish tastes even better made with wild greens and mushrooms.

SAUCE

> ⅔ cup water
> ⅓ cup drained silken tofu
> 2 tablespoons chopped fresh cilantro leaves
> 1 tablespoon fresh lime juice
> 2 teaspoons corn oil
> 1 teaspoon Vege-Sal or ½ teaspoon salt, or to taste
> ½ teaspoon turmeric

SAUTÉ

> 2 tablespoons mustard oil or peanut oil
> 2 teaspoons cumin seeds
> 1 teaspoon cloves
> 1 teaspoon black mustard seeds
> 1 tablespoon peeled and chopped fresh ginger
> 4 cups oyster mushrooms (page 404) or other mushrooms, sliced
> 1 small red onion, chopped
> 4 cloves garlic, chopped
> 4 small chiles, seeds and ribs removed and chopped
> 1 medium-size eggplant, diced
> 6 cups hedge mustard leaves or lamb's-quarters leaves (page 287), chopped

1. *To make the sauce:* In a blender, combine the sauce ingredients and process until smooth.

2. *To make the sauté:* Heat the mustard oil in a large skillet over medium heat, add the cumin seeds, cloves, black mustard seeds, and ginger, and cook, stirring constantly, until the mustard seeds pop, 2 to 3 minutes. Add the mushrooms, onion, garlic, and chiles and cook, stirring, for 5 minutes. Add the sauce and the remaining ingredients, bring the pan to a boil, reduce the heat to low, cover, and simmer the vegetables for 15 minutes.

3. Serve with brown rice or Indian bread.

SERVES 6

HEDGE MUSTARD MASALA

Hedge mustard greens are common, easy to collect, and delicious teamed up with wild meadow mushrooms in this Indian-style dish. If you're sensitive to hot dishes, use fewer chiles and less black pepper.

SAUTÉ

> ¼ cup peanut oil
>
> 2 tablespoons yellow or black mustard seeds
>
> 1 tablespoon cumin seeds
>
> 2 teaspoons cloves
>
> 1 teaspoon coriander seeds
>
> 1 teaspoon caraway seeds
>
> 1 teaspoon black peppercorns, or to taste
>
> 5 small chiles, or to taste, seeds and ribs removed and chopped
>
> 12 cups meadow mushrooms (page 382) or other mushrooms, sliced
>
> 10 cups hedge mustard leaves or other garlic mustard greens (page 61), chopped

SAUCE

> 2½ cups water

> ¼ cup Crunchy Peanut Butter (page 38)
>
> ¼ cup drained silken tofu
>
> ¼ cup mellow (light-colored) miso
>
> 3 tablespoons corn oil or flaxseed oil
>
> 2 tablespoons freshly ground white or black poppy seeds
>
> 1 teaspoon turmeric

1. *To make the sauté:* Heat the peanut oil in a large skillet over medium heat and cook the mustard seeds, cumin seeds, cloves, coriander seeds, caraway seeds, and peppercorns, stirring constantly, until the mustard seeds pop, about 2 minutes. Add the chiles, mushrooms, and hedge mustard and cook, uncovered, over medium heat, stirring often, until all the liquid is absorbed or evaporated, about 15 minutes.

2. *To make the sauce:* In a blender, combine all the sauce ingredients and process until smooth. Stir the sauce into the vegetables, bring the mixture to a boil, and cook the vegetables in the sauce for another 5 minutes, uncovered, over medium heat, stirring often. Serve hot with Indian bread or brown rice.

SERVES 6

SAUTÉED HEDGE MUSTARD WITH TOFU

Here's a quick wild green side dish you'll love.

> 4½ tablespoons Spiceberry Butter Sauce (page 316)
>
> 9 cups hedge mustard leaves
>
> One and a half 16-ounce packages firm tofu, drained and diced
>
> ½ teaspoon Vege-Sal or ¼ teaspoon salt, or to taste
>
> ½ teaspoon freshly ground black pepper (¼ teaspoon peppercorns)

Heat the Spiceberry Butter Sauce in a large skillet over medium heat. Add the hedge mustard, tofu, Vege-Sal, and pepper and cook, stirring, for 10 minutes. Serve hot.

SERVES 6

CREAM OF HEDGE MUSTARD

Oats bind wild hedge mustard and cauliflower in a whole that's greater than the sum of the parts in this simple cream soup.

12 cups Vegetable Stock (page 40) or water

¼ cup sesame oil

1 head cauliflower, chopped

8 cloves garlic, chopped

8 cups hedge mustard leaves or other wild mustard greens (page 61)

1 ½ cups rolled oats (not the quick-cooking kind)

1 teaspoon dried thyme, finely crumbled

2 teaspoons Vege-Sal or 1 teaspoon salt, or to taste

1 teaspoon freshly ground black pepper (½ teaspoon peppercorns)

1. In a stockpot, bring the stock to a boil.
2. Heat the sesame oil in a large skillet over medium heat. Cook the cauliflower, stirring, for 10 minutes.
3. Add the remaining ingredients to the vegetable stock and simmer the mixture for 10 minutes.
4. Carefully transfer the mixture to a blender and process, working in batches, until smooth. Begin on low speed and hold down the blender cover with a towel to prevent eruption. Serve hot.

SERVES 8 TO 10

HORSERADISH
Armoracia lapathifolia

HORSERADISH IS A LARGE MUSTARD PLANT, growing up to 4 feet tall, with slightly toothed leaves that are 2 feet long and more than 4 inches wide. The alternating white four-petaled flowers, with petals arranged like a cross, bloom from spring to summer. The flowers are replaced by tiny egg-shaped pods. Underground the plant features a large taproot. The root and the leaves have the familiar fiery taste we associate with horseradish.

This European garden herb sometimes spreads into the wild, where you can harvest it without trespassing. Use the young leaves or large taproot anytime you want intense pungency. Both are great in salads and sauces. Avoid cooking horseradish, since the oils responsible for the flavor are volatile and will dissipate quickly.

HORSERADISH DRESSING

When I finally found wild horseradish in an unpolluted spot after years of searching, this salad dressing was the first recipe I made.

1 cup olive oil

1 cup canola oil

½ cup red wine vinegar

¼ cup mellow (light-colored) miso

¼ cup Homemade Ketchup (page 37)

¼ cup horseradish root

In a blender, combine all the ingredients and process

until smooth. Horseradish Dressing will keep, covered, in the refrigerator for up to 2 weeks.

MAKES 3¼ CUPS

SOLOMON'S-SEAL

Polygonatum species

and

FALSE SOLOMON'S-SEAL

Smilacina racemosa

THE SHOOTS OF SOLOMON'S-SEAL LOOK LIKE long green pencils poking out of the soil. The plant can be found in partially sunny areas of the woods of eastern North America in early spring. That's the time to gather the shoots of this plant and its similar-looking relative, false Solomon's-seal.

Later in the spring, alternating, long-oval, alternating, pointed, smooth-edged leaves about 4 inches long, with parallel veins, unfurl from the now arching stem, which grows to between 2 and 4 feet long. Alternating white six-petaled flowers dangle beneath Solomon's-seal's stem, while a showy cluster of white flowers grace the tip of false Solomon-seal's stem. You can also tell the plants apart by their roots. Solomon's-seal has a knobby white horizontal rhizome (an underground stem). Although it is edible, you shouldn't dig up the rhizome because you'll be killing a threatened plant (you shouldn't even eat the renewable stem in places where the plant isn't very common). *False Solomon's-seal's rhizome is yellow and poisonous.*

The shoots of both plants impart an asparagus-like quality to any dish. Use them before the leaves unfurl.

Discard the rolled-up leaves that grow at the shoot's tip, because they can be very bitter and acrid.

Everyone on my field walks loves these plants. You can use them raw or cook them using just about any method. They cook in about 10 minutes.

SOLOMON'S BIRYANI

Solomon's-seal shoots fit perfectly in this traditional Indian layered rice dish.

SOLOMON'S-SEAL LAYER

    4 cups young Solomon's-seal shoots or false
        Solomon's-seal shoots

    1 cup raw cashews, chopped

    4 cloves garlic, crushed

    ½ teaspoon Vege-Sal or ¼ teaspoon salt, or to taste

    ½ teaspoon freshly ground black pepper
        (¼ teaspoon peppercorns)

TOFU LAYER

    1¾ cups drained silken tofu

    2 tablespoons corn oil

    2 tablespoons brown rice vinegar or wine vinegar

    2 tablespoons lecithin granules

    ½ teaspoon Tabasco sauce or pinch of cayenne
        pepper

RICE LAYER

    2 cups cooked brown basmati rice or other brown
        rice

    3 tablespoons fresh lemon juice

    1 tablespoon sesame oil

    ½ teaspoon saffron threads, finely crumbled

    ½ teaspoon freshly ground cardamom seeds

    1 teaspoon freshly ground yellow mustard seeds
        (½ teaspoon seeds)

    1 teaspoon freshly ground black pepper
        (½ teaspoon peppercorns)

1. *To make the Solomon's-seal layer:* Rinse the Solomon's-seal's stems, shake off the excess water, and place them in medium-size, heavy saucepan. Cover the pot and steam the stems over medium heat with just the water still clinging to them until they are just tender, 10 to 20 minutes. Chop the shoots and mix them with the cashews, garlic, Vege-Sal, and black pepper.

2. *To make the tofu layer:* In a food processor, combine all the tofu layer ingredients and process until smooth, or mix the ingredients in a medium-size bowl with a whisk or fork until smooth. Set this mixture aside.

3. *To make the rice layer:* In a small bowl, mix 1 cup of the brown rice with the remaining rice layer ingredients. Set this mixture aside.

4. Preheat the oven to 350 degrees

5. Layer a 3-quart oiled casserole dish with the seasoned rice, Solomon's-seal mixture, the remaining 1 cup plain brown rice, and the tofu mixture. Bake the casserole, uncovered, for 35 minutes.

SERVES 6

CHINESE CLAY POT

Stews with ingredients that are first lightly stir-fried and then simmered in a sauce are served in Chinese restaurants as "clay pots." Here's a wild food variation on the theme.

6 to 8 tablespoons peanut oil, or as needed

2 cups Solomon's-seal or false Solomon's-seal shoots, chopped

6 cloves garlic, finely chopped

2 small chiles, or to taste, seeds and ribs removed and finely chopped

2¾ cups drained firm tofu

3 cups ramp leaves (page 116) or chopped onions

3 cups seeded and diced red or green bell peppers (2 peppers)

1 cup oyster mushrooms (page 404) or other edible wild or cultivated mushrooms, sliced

1 large zucchini, ends trimmed and diced (3 cups)

1¼ cups cooked lotus seeds (available in Asian food stores; cook by simmering for 30 minutes in boiling salted vegetable stock or water to cover) or cooked navy beans, drained

6 cups boiling Vegetarian Chinese Fish Sauce (page 56) or other Chinese sauce

1. Heat 1½ tablespoons of the peanut oil in a wok or large skillet over high heat. Stir-fry the Solomon's-seal shoots for 30 seconds. Add the garlic and chiles and stir-fry for another 30 seconds. Remove the vegetables from the wok and set them aside.

2. Add more peanut oil if needed and let the wok heat up. Stir-fry the tofu for 2 minutes, remove it from the wok, and set it aside.

3. Add more peanut oil if needed and let the wok heat up. Stir-fry the ramps for 1 minute, remove them from the wok, and set them aside.

4. Add more peanut oil if needed and let the wok heat up. Stir-fry the bell peppers and oyster mushrooms for 1 minute, remove them from the wok, and set them aside.

5. Add more peanut oil if needed and let the wok heat up. Stir-fry the zucchini for 1 minute. Return all the stir-fried ingredients to the wok, add the lotus seeds and fish sauce, and simmer the vegetables and tofu over medium heat for 10 minutes. Serve hot on brown rice.

SERVES 8

SOLOMON'S-SEAL CAMELINE

A medieval bread-crumb-thickened sauce is a fit accompaniment for this New World vegetable.

1 tablespoon peeled and chopped fresh ginger

2 cloves garlic, chopped

1 cup fresh Bread Crumbs (page 40)

½ cup red wine vinegar

2 teaspoons ground cinnamon

*2 teaspoons freshly ground black pepper
(1 teaspoon peppercorns)*

½ teaspoon freshly ground cloves

½ teaspoon Vege-Sal or ¼ teaspoon salt, or to taste

*3 cups Solomon's-seal or false Solomon's-seal
shoots, chopped*

1. Preheat the oven to 350 degrees.

2. In a large bowl, combine everything except the Solomon's-seal shoots. Stir in the Solomon's-seal shoots.

3. Transfer the ingredients to a 14 x 9 x 2-inch oiled baking dish, cover, and bake for 20 minutes.

SERVES 4 TO 6

ORPINE

Sedum purpureum

THIS THICK-STEMMED ORNAMENTAL GONE WILD is distinct, beautiful, and delicious. Growing 1 to 1½ feet high, it has succulent, oval, coarsely toothed leaves 1 inch to a little over 2 inches long, usually grouped in whorls of three, but sometimes alternate. A dense flower head of small lavender pink five-petaled flowers blooming from summer to early fall tops the plant. Look for the plant in cultivated areas, fields, disturbed areas, and mountains in the Northeast. Roseroot (*Sedum rosea*), a smaller version, is also edible. You can collect the leaves from spring to fall.

The leaves have a mild flavor, and they're chewy.

Almost any cooking method will do, so long as you don't drown out the mild flavor with too many strong-tasting ingredients.

BLACK BEANS 'N' RICE

Mild-flavored and juicy, orpine makes this traditional Hispanic dish taste even better.

*3 cups cooked black beans or other cooked beans,
drained*

3 cups orpine leaves, chopped

*¾ cup Red Hot Chile Sauce (page 162) or Steve's
Salsa (page 374)*

2 cups Tofu Grated Cheese (page 32)

1. Preheat the oven to 350 degrees.

2. Layer a 3-quart oiled casserole dish with the ingredients in the order listed. Bake the casserole, covered, for 40 minutes.

SERVES 6 TO 8

STINGING NETTLE

Urtica dioica

THIS COARSE-LOOKING PLANT GROWS 2 TO 4 feet tall, with stalked, oval to heart-shaped, coarsely toothed and pointed opposite leaves that are 2 to 4 inches long. In late spring and early summer, strands of tiny green flowers hang from the leaf axils (where the leaves join the stem) of the female plants. The plant is covered with tiny stinging hairs. Look for nettles in rich, disturbed soil, along riverbanks, in thickets, and along partially sunny trails in the woods.

Slender nettle (*U. gracilis*) is smaller, with fewer stinging hairs. Wood nettle (*Laportea canadensis*) has much larger oval, alternate (unpaired) leaves. Use the leaves of these plants in the same way you would use stinging nettle leaves. But if a plant looks like a nettle and has no stinging hairs, it's no nettle. *Urtica* comes from the Latin *urare*, "to burn."

Use the leaves from early spring until just before the plant flowers in late spring, and then again in late fall if you can find new growth. Stinging nettles are surprisingly wonderful if you collect them carefully and prepare them properly. Nevertheless, people often collect them out of season, let themselves get stung, boil the leaves (the worst way to prepare them), and then complain that nettles taste awful.

Stinging nettle's tiny hypodermic needles inject you with formic acid, histamine, acetylcholine, serotonin, 5-hydroxytryptamine, and other unknown compounds—but only if you touch the plant. If you collect the young plants wearing rubber gloves, wash the leaves carefully, and cook the nettles gently, they're delicious, full of nutrients, including iron and beta-carotene, and perfectly safe. Steaming the leaves until they are just wilted, gently sautéing them, or simmering them in soups is fine. Nettles cook in 5 to 10 minutes.

You can also dry nettles for long-term storage. Use a food dehydrator or place the leaves in a paper bag for a couple of weeks. Store dried nettles in a tightly covered jar. They can be reconstituted for use in soups and stews, or used to make a nutritious tea.

STINGLESS NETTLE PÂTÉ

This mild, creamy spread, inspired by a traditional recipe from the former Soviet Georgia, gets its color and flavor from stinging nettles. Use this pâté on crackers, muffins, or bread.

10 cups stinging nettle leaves
3 cloves garlic, peeled
1 small chile, seeds and ribs removed, or
   1 teaspoon chili paste
1 small onion, peeled
1 ripe avocado, peeled and pitted
½ cup walnuts
¼ cup black walnuts (page 375) or wild hazelnuts
   (page 299)
1 tablespoon red wine vinegar
2 tablespoons mellow (light-colored) miso
½ teaspoon freshly ground coriander seeds
½ teaspoon hot paprika

1. Shake or spin the excess water off the washed nettles and place the leaves in a large, heavy pot with no additional water. Cover the pot and cook the nettles over low heat until they are just wilted, about 10 minutes.

2. Chop the garlic and chile in a food processor. Add the cooked nettles and the remaining ingredients and process until smooth. Stingless Nettle Pâté will keep, tightly covered, in the refrigerator for 5 to 7 days.

MAKES 3½ CUPS

NETTLE, WHERE IS THY STING?

This simple recipe takes the sting out of stinging nettles. Substituting healthful silken tofu, olive oil, and cashews for high-fat cream and using an Indian condiment called *chonce* for seasoning yields one of the best Indian-style soups you've ever tasted.

3 cups stinging nettle leaves
3 cups water
1 cup raw cashews

½ cup drained silken tofu

2 tablespoons olive oil or corn oil

¼ cup mellow (light-colored) miso

¼ cup Chonce (page 162)

1. Shake any excess water off the washed leaves. Place the leaves in a medium-size, heavy saucepan and cook them, covered, over low heat until the leaves are just wilted, about 10 minutes.

2. Transfer the nettles to a blender, add the remaining ingredients, and process until smooth.

3. Return the mixture to the saucepan and bring the pot to a boil over medium heat, stirring often. Reduce the heat to low and simmer for 2 minutes.

MAKES 5 CUPS; SERVES 6

SESAME RICE WITH STINGING NETTLES

Mild-flavored stinging nettles combine with sesame seeds to make a simple but unique vegetable-rice dish.

2 ¾ cups water

1 ½ cups brown basmati rice

¼ cup wild rice (page 353)

¼ cup amaranth (page 338)

½ cup dried stinging nettle leaves

¼ cup sesame seeds, toasted (page 73)

⅓ cup preserved radish in chili, chopped (optional; a spicy pickle available in Chinese grocery stores)

2 tablespoons tamari soy sauce

5 teaspoons olive oil

1 teaspoon toasted sesame oil

2 cloves garlic, chopped

Place all the ingredients in a large saucepan, cover, and bring to a boil. Reduce the heat to low and gently simmer the mixture until all the water is absorbed and the rice is tender, about 40 minutes.

MAKES 6½ CUPS; SERVES 6

NO-SUFFERIN' SUCCOTASH

Traditionally, cooks who know what they're doing combine nettles with dairy products, but this principle also works with tofu cheeses. Here this overlooked "weed" adds a gourmet touch to my version of a Native American classic.

1 ½ cups cooked lima beans or other beans

1 cup corn kernels, cut fresh off the cob

½ cup Tofu Cream Cheese (page 30)

1 ½ cups stinging nettle leaves

⅓ cup Vegetable Stock (page 40) or water

2 tablespoons corn oil or olive oil

5 tablespoons freshly ground flaxseeds (2 tablespoons seeds)

2 tablespoons Homemade Ketchup (page 37)

1 tablespoon lecithin granules

4 field garlic bulbs (page 57) or 2 cloves garlic, peeled

½ teaspoon chili powder (page 36)

½ teaspoon freshly ground black pepper (¼ teaspoon peppercorns) or cayenne pepper, or to taste

1. Preheat the oven to 375 degrees.

2. Place the lima beans and corn in an oiled 1-quart baking dish.

3. In a food processor, process the remaining ingredients until just chopped. Pour the mixture over the limas and corn and mix well. Bake the succotash, uncovered, until it is just set, about 45 minutes.

SERVES 6

GREEN NETTLE BAKE

The super-nutritious nettle adds its distinctive flavor to a woodsy green sauce in this baked noodle and mock cheese casserole.

5 ounces Buckwheat Noodles (page 34) or store-bought flat noodles

SAUCE

2 cups lightly steamed (not boiled!) stinging nettle leaves

1 cup soy milk or nut milk

5 tablespoons freshly ground flaxseeds (2 tablespoons seeds)

1 tablespoon lecithin granules

1 tablespoon miso

1 tablespoon olive oil

2 cloves garlic, peeled

1 teaspoon dried rosemary, finely crumbled

1 teaspoon dried sage, finely crumbled

½ teaspoon freshly grated nutmeg

1 teaspoon freshly ground yellow mustard seeds (½ teaspoon seeds)

½ teaspoon chili paste or ¼ teaspoon cayenne pepper, or to taste

1 cup Tofu Grated Cheese (page 32)

1. Preheat the oven to 375 degrees.

2. Cook the noodles in rapidly boiling salted water to which you've added a dash of oil. Remove the pot from the heat after about 2 minutes (before the noodles are al dente). After draining the noodles in a colander, lower the colander into a bowl of cold water to halt the cooking. Drain the noodles again, and place them in a 3-quart oiled casserole dish.

3. *To make the sauce:* In a blender, combine the sauce ingredients and process until smooth. Pour the sauce over the noodles. Cover the top of the casserole evenly with the Tofu Grated Cheese. Bake the casserole for 35 minutes. Serve hot.

SERVES 4 TO 6

CREAMED NETTLES

A cream sauce based on silken tofu brings out the best in this flavorful wild vegetable.

2 ½ tablespoons olive oil

1 clove garlic, crushed

1 ½ tablespoons any whole-grain flour

1 cup drained silken tofu

½ cup Vegetable Stock (page 40) or water

1 ½ tablespoons fresh lime or lemon juice

2 teaspoons tamari soy sauce

½ teaspoon freshly grated nutmeg

½ teaspoon freshly ground black pepper (¼ teaspoon peppercorns)

4 cups stinging nettle leaves, chopped

1. Heat the olive oil in a large skillet over medium-low heat. Add the garlic and flour and cook, stirring, for 5 minutes.

2. Meanwhile, in a blender, combine the tofu, stock, lime juice, tamari, nutmeg, and pepper and process until smooth. Stir this mixture into the skillet ingredients and bring the mixture to a simmer over low heat, stirring often. Stir in the nettles and bring the skillet to a boil. Reduce the heat to low, and simmer, covered, until the nettles are just wilted, about 5 minutes. Serve Creamed Nettles hot over noodles or whole grains.

SERVES 4

STINGING NETTLES INDIAN STYLE

Stinging nettles shouldn't sting you after you cook them, but you might just be stung if you add enough chile peppers to this savory Indian recipe.

SAUCE

½ cup dried chickpeas, ground into a flour in a
    spice grinder, or ¼ cup chickpea flour

2 tablespoons Garam Masala (page 36)

2 teaspoons Vege-Sal or 1 teaspoon salt, or to taste

½ teaspoon turmeric

1 cup drained silken tofu

Juice of 1 lime (2 tablespoons)

3 cups water

¼ cup corn oil

4 cloves garlic, chopped

2 small chiles, seeds and ribs removed and chopped

8 cups stinging nettle leaves, chopped

1. *To make the sauce:* In a small skillet, toast the chickpea flour over medium heat, stirring constantly, until it is lightly browned and fragrant, 3 to 4 minutes. Immediately remove the flour from the pan and, using a blender, mix the flour with the garam masala, Vege-Sal, turmeric, tofu, lime juice, and water until smooth.
2. Heat the corn oil in a large skillet over medium heat and cook the garlic and chiles, stirring, for 1 to 2 minutes. Stir in the nettles and then add the puréed sauce. Bring the pot to a boil over medium heat, stirring constantly. Reduce the heat to low, cover, and simmer for 5 minutes. Serve over rice.

SERVES 6

SCOTTISH NETTLE PUDDING

You must give the Scots credit for bravery. They live in a land full of stinging nettles, yet they walk around wearing kilts. Maybe eating the cooked nettles in this pudding fortifies them.

¼ cup olive oil or corn oil

3 cups stinging nettle leaves, chopped

3 cups ramp bulbs (page 116), chopped, or 2 cups
    chopped leeks

2 large red onions, sliced

6 cloves garlic, chopped

1 large carrot, sliced

3½ cups Vegetable Stock (page 40) or water

2 cups rolled oats (not the quick-cooking kind)

1 tablespoon Vegetarian Worcestershire Sauce
    (page 56; optional)

1 tablespoon Bragg's Liquid Aminos, 2 teaspoons
    Vege-Sal, or 1 teaspoon salt, or to taste

1 teaspoon dried rosemary, finely crumbled

1 teaspoon dried tarragon, finely crumbled

1 teaspoon freshly ground dill seeds

1 teaspoon freshly ground black pepper
    (½ teaspoon peppercorns)

1. Heat the olive oil in a large skillet over medium heat. Add the nettles, ramps, onions, garlic, and carrots and cook, stirring, for 5 minutes. Add the remaining ingredients and bring the pot to a boil over medium heat, stirring constantly. Reduce the heat to low and simmer the mixture, covered, for 5 minutes.
2. Turn off the heat and let the pudding rest, covered, for 15 minutes. Serve Scottish Nettle Pudding with Mint-Lime Sauce (page 60), Healthy Hollandaise Sauce (page 130), or any other sauce in this book.

SERVES 6

THE IMAM FAINTED

This Turkish appetizer gets its name because it's so good that a legendary imam (an Islamic religious official) who tasted it swooned. If the imam had known he was eating stinging nettles, he might have fainted even more quickly. Nevertheless, cooked, the nettles add to the charm and flavor of the recipe.

½ cup olive oil, or as needed

2 medium-size onions, sliced

4 cups stinging nettle leaves, chopped

2 medium-size ripe tomatoes

8 cloves garlic, chopped

2 tablespoons chopped fresh parsley leaves

2 tablespoons fresh lemon juice

1 teaspoon Vege-Sal or ½ teaspoon salt

5 drops liquid stevia or 1 teaspoon honey

3 medium-size eggplants

½ teaspoon freshly ground black pepper

   (¼ teaspoon peppercorns), or to taste

1. Heat 2 tablespoons of the olive oil in a large skillet over medium heat. Add the onions, nettles, tomatoes, and garlic, and cook, stirring, for a few minutes. Stir in the parsley, lemon juice, Vege-Sal, and stevia and set aside.

2. Cut off the tip of the eggplants to remove the brown coverings connected to the stems. Cut each eggplant in half lengthwise and create a pouch for the filling along the cut face by cutting a slit from ½ inch from the tip to ½ inch from the end of each eggplant half. Don't cut all the way through to the skin.

3. Heat the remaining 6 tablespoons olive oil, or as much as is needed, in the same skillet over medium heat and lightly brown the eggplants for 5 minutes on each side. Remove the eggplants from the skillet.

4. When the eggplants have cooled, fill the slits with the stuffing, spreading any remaining stuffing on top of the cut side of the eggplants.

5. Pressure-cook the stuffed eggplants piled on a wire rack over water for 10 minutes, or steam the stuffed eggplants until they are tender, about 40 minutes, adding more water if needed.

6. Serve this dish chilled, sprinkled with the black pepper. The Imam Fainted will keep, tightly covered, in the refrigerator for 5 days.

SERVES 6

NETTLE-STUFFED POTATOES

The strong flavor of steamed nettles, along with Tofu Sharp Cheese, contrasts perfectly with the mildness of baked potatoes. This is an elegant side dish.

4 baking potatoes, baked until tender

3 cups lightly steamed stinging nettle leaves, chopped

1 cup Tofu Sharp Cheese (page 30)

1 teaspoon olive oil or corn oil

1 teaspoon tamari soy sauce

1. Preheat the oven to 350 degrees.

2. Cut the potatoes in half lengthwise and scoop out most of the pulp. Don't scoop all the way to the skin or break the skin.

3. Chop the potato pulp and mix it with the remaining ingredients. Stuff the potato skins with the mixture.

4. Bake the stuffed potatoes, uncovered, skin side down, in a 14 x 9 x 2-inch oiled baking dish until they are heated through, about 20 minutes.

SERVES 8

WILD RAVIOLI

This whole-grain ravioli filled with stinging nettles and chicken mushrooms is marvelous served with tomato sauce, or used in any number of Italian baked dishes. This recipe will convince you that a ravioli press, which is simply an inexpensive, open serrated square with a handle, is a worthwhile investment.

DOUGH

1 ½ cups plus 3 tablespoons (½ pound) sweet brown rice flour, 2 cups (½ pound) oat flour, and 1 ¾ cups plus 2 tablespoons (½ pound) barley flour, or 1 ½ pounds any whole-grain flour

1 cup arrowroot or kudzu

2 teaspoons dried rosemary, finely crumbled

1 teaspoon freshly ground dill seeds

2 teaspoons freshly ground white pepper (1 teaspoon peppercorns)

1 teaspoon Vege-Sal or ½ teaspoon salt

¼ teaspoon turmeric

2 cups water, as needed

3 tablespoons olive oil

FILLING

1 ⅓ cups chicken mushrooms (page 321) or other edible wild or cultivated mushrooms, cooked and finely chopped

1 cup Tofu Cream Cheese (page 30)

⅔ cup lightly steamed stinging nettle leaves, finely chopped

⅔ cup finely chopped cooked beets

4 cloves garlic, finely chopped

1 tablespoon finely chopped fresh dill or parsley leaves

2 teaspoons chili paste or ¼ teaspoon cayenne pepper, or to taste

1 ½ teaspoons tamari soy sauce, or to taste

1 teaspoon freshly grated nutmeg

1 teaspoon dried savory, finely crumbled

1. *To make the dough:* In a large bowl, mix together the dry ingredients for the dough. Add the water and olive oil, using just enough water to make a dough that is wet enough so it doesn't crack when you pinch a piece, but not so wet as to make it sticky. Knead the dough briefly.

2. *To make the filling:* In a medium-size bowl, mix together the filling ingredients.

3. On a floured pastry sheet, using a rolling pin covered with a floured sleeve, roll out half the dough into a rectangle ³⁄₁₆ inch thick. Cut the dough into squares 2¾ inches across with a pizza cutter or butter knife.

4. Put ½ tablespoon of the filling in the center of a square, moisten the edges, place another square on top, and press the top and bottom together with a ravioli press (or use a glass that is 2½ inches in diameter). Repeat the process until you've used up all the dough and filling.

5. Cook the ravioli in rapidly boiling salted water for 7 minutes. Remove them carefully with a slotted spoon.

6. Serve the ravioli hot with tomato sauce or another sauce of your choosing, or use the ravioli in other pasta recipes.

MAKES 2 DOZEN RAVIOLI

BAKED WILD RAVIOLI

This simple recipe uses three other recipes from this book to create a traditional Italian dish you can make with wildly untraditional ingredients.

6 cups Puffball Marinara (page 397)

15 Wild Ravioli (above), cooked and drained

1 ½ cups Tofu Grated Cheese (page 32)

1. Preheat the oven to 350 degrees.

2. Spread half the tomato sauce over the bottom of a 14 x 9 x 2-inch oiled baking dish.

3. Arrange the ravioli on top of the tomato sauce. Pour the remaining tomato sauce over the ravioli.

4. Sprinkle on the Tofu Grated Cheese. Bake the ravioli for 35 minutes. Serve hot.

SERVES 5

WOOD NETTLE
Laportea canadensis

SIMILAR TO STINGING NETTLE (PAGE 83), BUT with its own delicate flavor, this plant sports fewer stinging hairs than does its notorious cousin, but it's just as good. Use the leaves of both plants steamed, simmered in soups, or sautéed.

ALL-WILD SPRING CURRY

Here's a dish worthy of an accomplished forager, since all the main ingredients are wild. The curry spices, in a combination called *sambar*, make this Indian dish especially good. The spicy-flavored hedge mustard adds its pungency to that of the chiles.

¼ cup dried chickpeas

1½ teaspoons black peppercorns

1 teaspoon fenugreek seeds

1 tablespoon turmeric

2 teaspoons Vege-Sal or 1 teaspoon salt

¼ cup drained silken tofu

1½ cups water

2 tablespoons fresh lemon juice

2 tablespoons corn oil

¼ cup peanut oil

2 teaspoons coriander seeds

2 teaspoons black mustard seeds

1½ teaspoons cumin seeds

3 small chiles, or to taste, seeds and ribs removed and chopped

4 cloves garlic, chopped

½ cup burdock root (page 139), very thinly sliced

5 cups cattail shoots (page 189), sliced

2 cups wood nettle, stinging nettle (page 83), or slender nettle leaves (page 84), chopped

1⅔ cups hedge mustard (page 78) or other mustard greens, chopped

½ cup ramp bulbs (page 116) or shallots, sliced

2 tablespoons chopped fresh goutweed (page 130) or parsley leaves

1. Toast the chickpeas in a small skillet over medium heat, stirring constantly, until they are slightly browned and fragrant, 3 to 4 minutes. Remove the chickpeas from the skillet immediately. When they are cool, grind the chickpeas with the peppercorns and fenugreek seeds in a spice grinder or coffee grinder. Then place this mixture in a blender with the turmeric, Vege-Sal, tofu, water, lemon juice, and corn oil and process until smooth. Set aside.

2. Heat the peanut oil in a large skillet over medium heat, add the coriander seeds, black mustard seeds, and cumin seeds and cook, stirring constantly, until the mustard seeds pop, 2 to 3 minutes. Add the chiles, garlic, and burdock and cook, stirring, for another 5 minutes. Stir in the cattail shoots, wood nettles, field pennycress, hedge mustard, ramps, and goutweed and cook, stirring, for another 5 minutes.

3. Add the tofu mixture and bring the pot to a boil. Reduce the heat to low and simmer the vegetables,

covered, for 10 minutes. Serve hot on brown rice or with Indian bread.

SERVES 4 TO 6

WOOD NETTLE POTATO CASSEROLE

Although nettles have a wonderfully strong, earthy flavor, toning it down a little with other ingredients makes this vegetable even better.

¼ cup olive oil

4 medium-size potatoes, sliced

4 cups wood nettle, stinging nettle (page 83), or slender nettle leaves (page 84), chopped

1 medium-size onion, chopped

4 cloves garlic, chopped

3 tablespoons preserved radish in chili (available in Chinese grocery stores), chopped, or chopped radish

SHAGGY MANE SAUCE

2 cups Vegetable Stock (page 40)

5 tablespoons raw cashews

3 tablespoons dark-colored miso

1 ½ tablespoons arrowroot or kudzu

½ teaspoon dried marjoram, finely crumbled

½ teaspoon caraway seeds

½ teaspoon freshly grated nutmeg

½ teaspoon freshly ground black pepper (¼ teaspoon peppercorns), or to taste

¾ cup shaggy mane mushrooms (page 399) or other edible wild or cultivated mushrooms, sliced

1. Preheat the oven to 350 degrees.

2. Heat the olive oil in a large skillet over medium heat. Add the potatoes, wood nettles, onion, garlic, and radish and cook, stirring, for 10 minutes.

3. *To make the sauce:* In a blender, combine all the sauce ingredients, except the mushrooms, and process until smooth. Pour the sauce into a medium-size saucepan, add the mushrooms, and bring the pot to a boil over medium heat, stirring constantly. Reduce the heat to low, and simmer the sauce, covered, for 5 minutes, stirring often.

4. Cover the bottom of a 3-quart oiled casserole dish with about one quarter of the sauce and arrange half the sautéed vegetables over that. Cover that layer of vegetables with half the remaining sauce, layer the remaining vegetables over that, and cover them with the remaining sauce. Bake the casserole, covered, until it is bubbly, about 35 minutes.

SERVES 6

STUFFED YAMS HARISSA

Harissa is a well-known Tunisian hot sauce. The same elements that make it so good add just the right touch to yams stuffed with wood nettles and dulse. (Handling uncooked wood nettles without gloves is the kind of touch you don't want to experience.)

3 yams

¼ cup olive oil

2 tablespoons freshly ground coriander seeds

1 ½ teaspoons freshly ground cumin seeds

1 teaspoon dried mint, finely crumbled

1 teaspoon freshly ground caraway seeds

2 cups tightly packed wood nettle, stinging nettle (page 83), or slender nettle leaves (page 84), chopped

⅓ cup tightly packed dried dulse (page 174)

4 cloves garlic, chopped

2 small chiles, seeds and ribs removed and chopped

½ cup Tahini (page 38)

1. Preheat the oven to 350 degrees. Brush the yams with 1 tablespoon of the olive oil and bake them on a rack over an oiled cookie sheet until tender, about 1 hour. Remove the yams but leave the oven on.

2. Meanwhile heat the remaining 3 tablespoons olive oil in a large skillet over medium heat, add the coriander, cumin, mint, and caraway seeds and cook for 1 minute, stirring constantly. Add the nettles, dulse, garlic, and chiles and cook, stirring, for 5 minutes.

3. When the yams are cool enough to handle, cut them in half lengthwise and scoop out most of the pulp with a spoon. Don't scoop all the way to the skin or break the skin.

4. Mix the yam with the sautéed ingredients and tahini, mound the mixture back into the yam skins, and bake the stuffed yams, covered, in a 14 x 9 x 2-inch oiled casserole dish until they are heated through, 20 minutes. Serve hot.

SERVES 6

SWEET CICELY, ANISE ROOT

Osmorhiza species

THIS IS A GROUP OF CLOSELY RELATED PLANTS that smell and taste like anise or licorice. (This *isn't* anise, even though it has the same fragrance and flavor.) The delicate-looking basal leaves (at the base of the plant), which can grow up to a foot long, divide repeatedly, like parsley.

In mid-spring, the plant bolts up to 1 to 3 feet in height and displays a flat-topped cluster of sparse white five-petaled flowers. These are followed by the appearance of tapered, thin, prickly, seeds that penetrate your clothes in the summer and fall. *Be sure you're not collecting a poisonous plant with umbrella-like flowers by mistake.*

You can eat the leaves (and even the flowers), which are especially good in salads, but I think the best parts are the fleshy roots, which arise from a woody, gnarled rhizome (underground stem) and are in season in the fall and early spring (and during mild winters). Discard the underground stem and use the taproots as you would other root vegetables. I find the taproots a little stringy raw, so I usually cook them.

ALOO CHAT

If you're a potato lover, you'll go crazy over this simple Indian potato salad. For variety, you may substitute other cooked root vegetables, such as beets, burdock (page 139), wild parsnips (page 426), or common evening primrose (page 430), for the potatoes. Serve Aloo Chat as an appetizer, side dish, or snack.

> 4 medium-size potatoes, diced, cooked in water to cover until tender, and drained
> ¼ cup sweet cicely leaves (fennel leaves are an excellent alternative), finely chopped
> 2 teaspoons fresh lemon juice
> 2 small chiles, seeds and ribs removed and minced
> ½ teaspoon turmeric
> ½ teaspoon Vege-Sal or ¼ teaspoon salt, or to taste
> 1 teaspoon freshly ground black pepper
>   (½ teaspoon peppercorns)

Combine all the ingredients in a medium-size bowl. Serve Aloo Chat at room temperature, with Wild Currant Chutney (page 236), if desired.

SERVES 4 TO 6

SWEET CICELY RAITA

Indian raitas are flavorful condiments that stimulate the appetite and aid digestion. The licorice-like flavor of sweet cicely fits into this simple recipe beautifully.

½ cup sweet cicely leaves

½ cup raw almonds

⅔ cup well-drained silken tofu

1 cup soy milk or nut milk

1 tablespoon fresh lemon juice

1 tablespoon mellow (light-colored) miso

2 teaspoons corn oil

½ teaspoon sweet paprika

½ teaspoon Tabasco sauce or ⅛ teaspoon cayenne pepper, or to taste

1. In a food processor, chop the sweet cicely leaves and almonds.

2. Add the remaining ingredients and process until smooth. Sweet Cicely Raita will keep, tightly covered, in the refrigerator for 5 days.

MAKES 2 CUPS

ANISE-PEANUT SAUCE

Peanut lovers will delight in this sauce, which gets additional flavor from sweet cicely. Use Anise-Peanut Sauce on vegetables or tofu and in Chinese dishes.

¼ cup olive oil, or as needed

2 medium-size onions, chopped

4 cloves garlic, chopped

1 tablespoon peeled and chopped fresh ginger

½ cup sweet cicely taproots (avoid the gnarled, stringy underground stems), chopped

1 cup barley flour or 4.5 ounces any other whole-grain flour

8 cups Vegetable Stock (page 40)

1 teaspoon dill seeds or 1 tablespoon chopped fresh dill

1 teaspoon freshly ground coriander seeds

1 teaspoon freshly ground white pepper (½ teaspoon peppercorns)

½ teaspoon ground mace

½ cup unsalted dry-roasted peanuts, chopped

¼ cup mellow (light-colored) miso

¼ cup smooth peanut butter

1. Heat the olive oil in a large skillet over medium heat, add the onions, garlic, ginger, sweet cicely, and flour, and cook, stirring constantly, for 5 minutes.

2. Meanwhile, combine 6 cups of the stock, the dill seeds, coriander, pepper, and mace in a large saucepan and bring the pot to a boil. Slowly stir the cooked vegetable mixture into the boiling liquid, stirring constantly. Reduce the heat to low, add the peanuts, and simmer for 10 minutes, stirring often.

3. Meanwhile, in a blender, process the miso and peanut butter with the remaining 2 cups stock until smooth. Stir this mixture into the simmering ingredients, remove the sauce from the heat, and serve it hot. Anise-Peanut Sauce will keep, tightly covered, in the refrigerator for 1 week.

MAKES 12 CUPS; SERVES 12

GREEN MAYONNAISE

Sweet cicely leaves enhance this tofu mayonnaise by contributing their pale green color and delicate anise flavor.

2 cloves garlic, peeled

½ cup sweet cicely leaves

¼ cup fresh parsley leaves

¼ cup fresh dill leaves

One 19-ounce package silken tofu, well drained

¼ cup olive oil

Juice of 1 lime

2 tablespoons red wine vinegar

2 tablespoons lecithin granules

*1½ teaspoons chili paste or ¼ teaspoon cayenne
    pepper, or to taste*

1 tablespoon freshly ground yellow mustard seeds

1 teaspoon dried tarragon, finely crumbled

*2 teaspoons freshly ground white pepper
    (1 teaspoon peppercorns)*

1. Chop the garlic in a food processor or by hand. Add the sweet cicely leaves, parsley, and dill and chop again.

2. Add the remaining ingredients and process until smooth (or mash everything together with a whisk or fork). Green Mayonnaise will keep in the refrigerator, covered, for up to a week.

MAKES 3 CUPS

JENNY'S WILD SPAGHETTI SAUCE

Finding a dense stand of sweet cicely on one of my tours inspired a participant to create this tomato sauce, which she describes as tasty and mildly seasoned with just a hint of anise.

Two 15-ounce cans tomato sauce

*Four 3-inch-long sweet cicely taproots (avoid the
    gnarled, stringy underground stems), chopped*

*8 field garlic bulbs (page 57) or 1 small onion, or
    to taste, chopped*

12 bayberry (page 185) or 8 bay leaves, crushed

2 cloves garlic, or to taste, crushed

1 teaspoon dried oregano, finely crumbled

4 teaspoons Vege-Sal or 2 teaspoons salt, or to taste

Place all the ingredients in a large saucepan and bring the pot to a boil. Reduce the heat to medium-low, cover, and simmer the sauce for 30 minutes. Jenny's Wild Spaghetti Sauce will keep, tightly covered, in the refrigerator for 10 days.

MAKES 4 CUPS

WILD TOMATO SAUCE

Here's a more complicated wild version of traditional Italian tomato sauce, made even better with the addition of wild bayberry leaves and sweet cicely. Use this sauce on pasta, veggie loaves, burgers, or with vegetables.

¼ cup olive oil

4 celery stalks, sliced

*2 medium-size red bell peppers, seeded and sliced
    into strips*

*1 cup sweet cicely taproots (avoid the gnarled,
    stringy underground stems)*

12 shallots, chopped

8 cloves garlic, crushed

Four 25.5-ounce jars tomato sauce

¾ cup White Oak Wine (page 176) or sherry

¼ cup fresh basil leaves, chopped

¼ cup fresh parsley leaves, chopped

*3 tablespoons powdered dried boletes (page 267)
    or other mushroom*

1 tablespoon bayberry (page 185) or bay leaves

1½ teaspoons dried tarragon, finely crumbled

1 teaspoon dried sage, finely crumbled

1 teaspoon dried marjoram, finely crumbled

1 teaspoon Vege-Sal or ½ teaspoon salt, or to taste

1 teaspoon freshly ground white pepper

    (½ teaspoon peppercorns)

1. Heat the olive oil in a large skillet over medium heat. Add the celery, red peppers, sweet cicely, shallots, and garlic and cook, stirring, for 10 minutes.

2. Meanwhile, bring the remaining ingredients to a simmer in a large saucepan over low heat, stirring occasionally. If you have a heat diffuser, put it under the saucepan to help prevent the bottom from getting scorched.

3. Add the sautéed ingredients to the saucepan and simmer the sauce, covered, for 1 hour over low heat, stirring occasionally. Wild Tomato Sauce will keep, tightly covered, in the refrigerator for 10 days or in the freezer for months.

MAKES 6 QUARTS

SWEET CICELY POTATOES

The addition of a sweet cicely sauce and Indian spices makes this ordinary potato dish anything but plain.

POTATOES

    3 tablespoons peanut oil

    ½ teaspoon black mustard seeds

    ½ teaspoon cumin seeds

    1 teaspoon turmeric

    6 small red potatoes, cooked in water to cover
        until tender, drained, and sliced

    4 cloves garlic, chopped

    2 small chiles, seeds and ribs removed and chopped

SAUCE

    1¾ cups water, or as needed

    1 cup sweet cicely leaves (with the flowers, if
        they're in season)

    3 scallions or chives or ½ small onion, chopped

    ¼ cup unsweetened shredded coconut

    ⅓ cup drained silken tofu

    1 tablespoon fresh lemon or lime juice

    1 tablespoon corn oil

    2 teaspoons Vege-Sal or 1 teaspoon salt, or to taste

    ¼ teaspoon cayenne pepper, or to taste

1. In a skillet, heat the peanut oil over medium heat and cook the mustard seeds, cumin seeds, and turmeric, stirring constantly, until the mustard seeds pop, 2 to 3 minutes. Add the potatoes, garlic, and chiles and cook, stirring, for 10 minutes.

2. Meanwhile, in a blender, combine the sauce ingredients and process until smooth, using enough water to make the blender work.

3. Stir the sauce into the potato mixture and bring the pot to a boil over high heat, stirring constantly. Reduce the heat to medium and cook, stirring frequently, until the sauce is reduced and thick, about 10 minutes.

SERVES 6

SWEET CICELY BREAD

Sweet cicely imparts its wonderful licorice flavor to this simple yeast bread.

    2 teaspoons (1 package) active dry yeast

    1 cup lukewarm apple juice

    ⅓ cup corn oil

    2 tablespoons fresh lemon juice

    ½ teaspoon anise extract (optional)

    ½ teaspoon liquid stevia or 2 tablespoons honey

    3¼ cups plus 2 tablespoons (1 pound) sweet brown
        rice flour and 1¾ cups plus 2 tablespoons
        (½ pound) barley flour, or 1½ pounds any
        whole-grain flour

    ½ cup arrowroot or kudzu

2 ½ tablespoons freshly ground flaxseeds
   (1 tablespoon seeds)
1 tablespoon poppy seeds
1 teaspoon freshly ground coriander seeds
½ teaspoon salt
½ cup sweet cicely taproots (avoid the gnarled,
   stringy underground stems), chopped
1 ½ teaspoons lecithin granules
1 teaspoon freshly grated lemon rind

1. In a large bowl, mix the yeast in the apple juice until the yeast is dissolved. Let the mixture stand for 5 minutes. Stir in the corn oil, lemon juice, anise extract, if you are using it, liquid stevia, and 1½ cups of the sweet brown rice flour.

2. Mix in the remaining flour and then the remaining ingredients. Knead the dough briefly, and then let it sit, covered, in a warm place (80 to 85 degrees) until it is doubled in volume, about 1½ hours.

3. Punch down the dough, place it an oiled 6½ x 4⅜ x 2½-inch loaf pan, cover it, and let it rise again in a warm place for 45 minutes.

4. Meanwhile, preheat the oven to 375 degees. Set a pan of hot water on the bottom of the oven to keep the bread from becoming too crusty.

5. Bake the bread until a cake tester or toothpick inserted in the center comes out dry, about 40 minutes.

6. Remove the loaf from the pan and let it cool on a wire rack before slicing it.

MAKES 1 LOAF

Note: If you prefer an extra-soft crust, brush the top of the bread with corn oil when you remove the loaf from the oven.

SWEET CICELY AND SOURDOUGH CORNBREAD

Sweet cicely's anise flavor makes it an ideal addition to sourdough cornbread. **Note:** Completely avoid metal containers and implements, which kill sourdough microorganisms.

2 ½ cups (1 pound) yellow cornmeal
4 cups oat flour or 1 pound any other whole-grain
   flour
1 cup kudzu or arrowroot
5 tablespoons freshly ground flaxseeds
   (2 tablespoons seeds)
1 tablespoon lecithin granules
2 teaspoons salt
1 teaspoon freshly grated nutmeg
½ teaspoon turmeric
2 ½ cups water
1 cup Sourdough Starter (page 42)
3 tablespoons corn oil
2 cups sweet cicely taproots (avoid the gnarled,
   stringy underground stems), finely chopped
   or grated
½ cup raisins

1. In a large bowl, mix together the cornmeal, flour, kudzu, ground flaxseeds, lecithin, salt, and spices.

2. In another large bowl, mix together the water, sourdough starter, and 2 tablespoons of the corn oil. Mix two-thirds of the dry mixture into the wet mixture. Allow the dough to rise, covered, at room temperature, for 6 hours or up to overnight.

3. Add the remaining third of the dry mixture, the sweet cicely, and raisins to the dough. Divide the mixture evenly between 2 oiled non-metal 6½ x 4⅜ x 2½-inch loaf pans and shape the dough into loaves. Brush the top of each loaf with the remaining 1 tablespoon

corn oil. Cover the loaves and allow them to rise at room temperature for 4 hours or up to overnight.

4. Preheat the oven to 350 degrees. Set a tray of hot water on the bottom of the oven to keep the crust soft.

5. Bake the loaves until each one has pulled away from the sides of the pan slightly, about 50 minutes.

6. Remove the loaves from the pans and let them cool on wire racks before slicing them.

MAKES 2 LOAVES

INDIAN ICE CREAM

This most unusual ethnic ice cream uses black pepper as the main seasoning, although sweet cicely also makes an essential contribution.

> 1 cup unsweetened coconut milk
> 1 ½ cups soy milk or nut milk
> 1 ripe papaya, peeled and seeded
> ½ cup canola oil
> ¼ cup sweet cicely taproot (avoid the gnarled, stringy underground stems)
> ¼ cup vegetable glycerin, barley malt, or honey
> ¼ cup lecithin granules
> 1 teaspoon liquid stevia (optional)
> 2 teaspoons vanilla extract
> 4 teaspoons freshly ground black pepper (2 teaspoons peppercorns), or to taste

1. In a blender, combine all the ingredients and process until smooth.

2. Chill the mixture (or begin with chilled ingredients) if required by your ice cream machine.

3. Pour the mixture into the ice cream machine and freeze it according to the manufacturer's instructions.

MAKES 5 ½ CUPS; SERVES 5 TO 6

SWEET CICELY–PISTACHIO ICE CREAM

The subtle anise flavor of sweet cicely leaves adds to the flavor of the pistachio nuts while coloring this dairy-free ice cream pale green.

> 2 cups soy milk or nut milk
> ½ cup well-drained silken tofu
> ½ cup raw cashews
> ½ cup canola oil
> ½ cup sweet cicely leaves
> ¼ cup vegetable glycerin, barley malt, or rice syrup
> ¼ cup lecithin granules
> 2 teaspoons vanilla extract
> 1 teaspoon liquid stevia
> ½ teaspoon lime or lemon extract
> ¼ teaspoon anise extract (optional)
> ½ teaspoon salt
> ¼ teaspoon freshly ground cardamom seeds
> 2 cups shelled unsalted pistachio nuts, toasted (page 158) and chopped

1. In a blender, combine all the ingredients, except for 1 cup of the pistachios, and process until smooth.

2. Chill the mixture (or begin with chilled ingredients) if required by your ice cream machine.

3. Stir in the remaining 1 cup pistachio nuts.

4. Pour the mixture into the ice cream maker and freeze it according to the manufacturer's instructions.

MAKES 6 CUPS; SERVES 6

JAPANESE KNOTWEED

Polygonum cuspidatum

HERE'S ONE OF THE PREMIER WILD FOODS OF early spring. It is so abundant and invasive that gardeners and landscapers detest it. It starts out resembling a fat, reddish asparagus stalk, its hollow, jointed stems popping up in dense stands in early spring. This is the time to harvest it, and there's more than enough for any kind of recipe you can imagine. Having escaped from cultivation, Japanese knotweed invades gardens, disturbed habitats, roadsides, cultivated parks, riverbanks, and fields throughout the United States.

You can eat the shoot when it is up to 1 to 2 feet tall, but you should remove the leaves. The eight-inch shoots are optimal, because as the shoots get bigger they soon get tough, especially the skin, which you then must peel. By mid-spring, the plant is too tough to eat. By summertime, it reaches 10 feet, and before autumn, it is covered with showy strands of delicate tiny white flowers, which are soon replaced with the translucent three-sided seeds of autumn. In the winter, the dead stalks look like a bamboo jungle—hollow, woody, and with jointed stems. But the rhizomes (underground stems) live on underground.

Japanese knotweed is very sour, like its relative, rhubarb, so use it sparingly (especially the first time you use it, because, like rhubarb, it may act as a laxative in some people). Combine Japanese knotweed with mild or sweet ingredients to create contrast. It also works well in soups and stews, adding a piquant flavor, okra-like thickening, and a surprisingly soft

texture. It cooks in 5 to 10 minutes.

If you catch the larger hollow stalks just before they get too tough to use (at less than 1½ feet long), you can peel off the tough skin and stuff the stalks.

KNOT SOUP

Is this soup or is it knot soup? Maybe it's both. Either way, the tangy flavor of Japanese knotweed mellowed by vegetable broth and Tofu Cream Cheese yields a winner you'll knot regret having made.

> 4 cups Vegetable Stock (page 40)
> 3½ cups young Japanese knotweed shoots no longer than 8 inches, sliced
> 1 cup Tofu Cream Cheese (page 30)

1. Place the stock and knotweed in a large saucepan and bring the pot to a boil. Reduce the heat to medium and simmer the knotweed until it is tender, about 5 minutes.
2. Stir in the Tofu Cream Cheese and serve the soup hot.

SERVES 4 TO 6

STEAMED KNOTWEED SESAME

Japanese knotweed, with its soft texture and lemony flavor, is great in vegetable dishes. The seasonings in this steamed side dish complement this vegetable perfectly.

> 8 cups young Japanese knotweed shoots no longer than 8 inches
> 3 tablespoons tamari soy sauce
> 1 tablespoon chili paste or ¼ teaspoon cayenne pepper, or to taste

6 cloves garlic, crushed into a paste

6 tablespoons sesame seeds, toasted (page 73)

Mix together all the ingredients except the sesame seeds in a large, heavy saucepan. Cook the knotweed, covered, over low heat until it is tender, 10 to 20 minutes. Serve the cooked knotweed hot, sprinkled with the sesame seeds.

SERVES 6

BAKED KNOTWEED

Japanese knotweed becomes soft, sour, and incredibly flavorful when you simply bake it with olive oil and seasonings.

6 cups Japanese knotweed shoots, peeled if larger
than 8 inches long

2 tablespoons olive oil

1 tablespoon tamari soy sauce

2 teaspoons dried rosemary, finely crumbled

2 teaspoons freshly ground dill seeds

2 teaspoons freshly ground yellow mustard seeds
(1 teaspoon seeds)

1 teaspoon freshly ground black pepper
(½ teaspoon peppercorns)

1. Preheat the oven to 375 degrees.

2. Place the Japanese knotweed shoots in a 3-quart oiled casserole dish.

3. Combine the remaining ingredients in a small bowl and stir them into the knotweed shoots. Bake the knotweed, covered, until it is tender, about 30 minutes. Serve hot.

SERVES 4 TO 6

KNOT ZITI

This really only looks like ziti (it's "knot" ziti). It's a baked Italianesque dish featuring stuffed Japanese knotweed shoots layered over noodles and covered with tomato sauce and tofu cheese.

1 pound dried flat noodles

1 tablespoon olive oil

1¾ cups Tofu Cottage Cheese (page 30)

¾ cup pine nuts or chopped raw cashews

12 cups large, plump Japanese knotweed stalks
about 1 inch in diameter, peeled if longer than
8 inches

1½ cups Wild Tomato Sauce (page 94)

1¼ cups Tofu Cream Cheese (page 30)

1. Preheat the oven to 350 degrees.

2. Cook the noodles in plenty of boiling salted water. Two minutes before they would be al dente, drain the noodles in a colander and then plunge the colander into a bowl of cold water to halt the cooking. Drain the noodles again, and toss them with 1 teaspoon of the olive oil.

3. In a medium-size bowl, mix together the Tofu Cottage Cheese and pine nuts.

4. Cut the knotweed shoots into lengths that will fit into your baking dish. Hollow out the knotweed shoots using the handle of a wooden spoon or a chopstick. Stuff the shoots with the Tofu Cottage Cheese mixture.

5. Layer a 14 x 9 x 2-inch oiled baking dish with the noodles, stuffed knotweed, tomato sauce, and Tofu Cream Cheese. Sprinkle the top with the remaining 2 teaspoons olive oil. Bake the ziti, uncovered, until bubbly, about 45 minutes.

SERVES 6 TO 8

KNOTWEED RYE BAGELS

This is one of the most fun recipes to bake, and the results are unbelievable. I'm from New York, the bagel capital of the world, and Japanese knotweed is a bagel flavoring you'll never find in any of the city's best (or even its worst) bagel bakeries. **Note:** Never allow sourdough to come in contact with metal implements or containers, which are deadly to wild yeast.

8½ cups plus 2 tablespoons (2 pounds) rye flour

5 tablespoons freshly ground flaxseeds (2 tablespoons seeds)

2 tablespoons poppy seeds

1 cup arrowroot or kudzu

2 teaspoons dried marjoram, finely crumbled

4 teaspoons freshly ground yellow mustard seeds (2 teaspoons seeds)

1 tablespoon Vege-Sal or 1 ½ teaspoons salt, or to taste

2 cups water

1 cup Sourdough Starter (page 42)

1 tablespoon corn oil

1 small red onion, finely chopped

1 cup finely chopped Japanese knotweed shoots 8 inches or shorter (only larger shoots going out of season need be peeled)

1 tablespoon lecithin granules

2 cloves garlic, crushed into a paste or finely chopped

1. Mix together the flour, ground flaxseeds, poppy seeds, arrowroot, marjoram, ground yellow mustard seeds, and Vege-Sal in a medium-size bowl.

2. In a large bowl, mix together the water, sourdough starter, and corn oil. Stir two-thirds of the dry mixture into the wet mixture. Cover the dough and allow it to rise at room temperature for 4 hours or overnight. The longer it rises or the higher the room temperature, the more sour it will taste.

3. Add the remaining dry mixture, the onion, knotweed, lecithin, and garlic to the dough.

4. Divide the dough into 12 parts, shaping each piece into a ball and flattening it partially. Punch a hole in each piece of dough with a floured finger, and shape the dough into a bagel. Cover the bagels with a damp towel and let them rise at room temperature for 4 hours or overnight.

5. Preheat the oven to 375 degrees. Bring a large pot of salted water to a boil. Drop in the bagels, bring the water back to a boil, and let the bagels boil for 7 minutes.

6. Drain the bagels, place them on an oiled cookie sheet, and bake them until they are brown and crusty, about 35 minutes.

MAKES 1 DOZEN BAGELS

BANANA-KNOTWEED MUFFINS

Japanese knotweed's sour flavor is the perfect foil for the sweet bananas in these fluffy muffins.

1 ½ cups (6 ounces) oat flour and 1 ¼ cups (6 ounces) sweet brown rice flour, or ¾ pound any whole-grain flour

¼ teaspoon arrowroot or kudzu

2 ½ tablespoons freshly ground flaxseeds (1 tablespoon seeds)

1 ½ teaspoons lecithin granules

¾ teaspoon baking soda

½ teaspoon salt

1 teaspoon freshly grated nutmeg

¼ teaspoon freshly ground cardamom seeds

¼ cup apple juice or other unsweetened fruit juice

3 tablespoons soy milk or nut milk

3 tablespoons corn oil

1 tablespoon fresh lemon juice

2 teaspoons vanilla extract

½ teaspoon banana extract (optional)

½ teaspoon liquid stevia or 2 tablespoons honey, barley malt, or rice syrup

3 medium-size ripe bananas, peeled and sliced

3 common spicebush berries (page 314), finely chopped, or ¼ teaspoon freshly ground allspice berries

⅔ cup Japanese knotweed shoots, peeled if longer than 8 inches and chopped

1. Preheat the oven to 350 degrees.

2. Mix together the flour, arrowroot, ground flaxseeds, lecithin, baking soda, salt, and spices in a large bowl.

3. In a blender, combine the apple juice, soy milk, corn oil, lemon juice, vanilla, banana extract, if you are using it, liquid stevia, bananas, and spicebush berries and process until smooth.

4. Mix the wet ingredients and the Japanese knotweed into the dry ingredients. Don't overmix. Pour the batter into an oiled muffin tin. Set a pan of water on the bottom of the oven to keep the muffins soft. Bake the muffins until a toothpick inserted in the center emerges clean, 15 to 20 minutes.

5. Loosen the muffins from the tin by running a butter knife around the edge of each muffin. Remove the muffins and let them cool on wire racks.

MAKES 1 DOZEN MUFFINS

JAPANESE KNOTWEED CHUTNEY

Japanese knotweed's sour flavor makes it ideal for the complex of elements that make up a chutney. Serve this chutney as a condiment with Indian dishes.

1 teaspoon coriander seeds

6 cups Japanese knotweed shoots, peeled if longer than 8 inches and chopped

1 cup ramp bulbs (page 116) or shallots, chopped

2 green apples, cored and chopped

1 cup cultivated currants

½ cup fresh basil leaves, finely chopped

¼ cup natural cherry juice concentrate

1 ½ teaspoons ground dried wild ginger (page 111) or peeled and finely chopped cultivated fresh ginger

4 cloves garlic, crushed into a paste

4 common spicebush berries (page 314), finely chopped, or ½ teaspoon freshly ground allspice berries

1 teaspoon ground cinnamon

1 teaspoon freshly ground cloves

½ teaspoon Vege-Sal or ¼ teaspoon salt

1. Toast the coriander seeds over medium heat in a small skillet, stirring or shaking the skillet constantly, until the seeds are fragrant, about 2 minutes. Grind the toasted seeds in a spice grinder or coffee grinder (or with a mortar and pestle).

2. Place the ground coriander and the remaining ingredients in a large saucepan and bring the pot to a boil. Reduce the heat to medium and simmer the mixture for 10 minutes. Serve chilled. Japanese Knotweed Chutney will keep, covered, in the refrigerator for up to 10 days.

MAKES 4 CUPS

JAPANESE KNOTWEED SALAD DRESSING

Salad dressings usually benefit from sour ingredients, and therefore people traditionally use lemon juice, lime juice, or vinegar. Japanese knotweed, as creamy as it is sour, more than fills the bill. And the monounsaturated olive and canola oils that form the dressing's base are the most healthful vegetable oils you can use.

> 2 ½ cups young Japanese knotweed shoots no
>   longer than 8 inches
> 1 cup olive oil
> 1 cup canola oil
> ½ cup brown rice vinegar or red wine vinegar
> ¼ cup mellow (light-colored) miso
> 4 cloves garlic, or to taste
> 1 tablespoon chili paste or ½ teaspoon cayenne
>   pepper, or to taste

1. Cook the knotweed, covered, without water in a medium-size, heavy saucepan over low heat until it is tender, about 10 minutes.

2. Transfer the knotweed to a blender, add the remaining ingredients, and process until smooth. Japanese Knotweed Salad Dressing will keep, covered, in the refrigerator for up to 10 days.

MAKES 3¾ CUPS

JAPANESE KNOTWEED MARMALADE

Japanese knotweed's lemony flavor and creamy texture lends itself to spreads, jams, and fillings. This invasive, often hated, wild plant is at its best in this sweet-sour spread.

> 2 cups Japanese knotweed shoots, peeled if longer
>   than 8 inches and thickly sliced
> 1 ½ cups apple juice or freshly squeezed orange
>   juice
> 1 ½ tablespoons agar flakes
> 1 tablespoon freshly grated orange rind or
>   ½ teaspoon orange extract

> 1 tablespoon vegetable glycerin, barley malt, or
>   honey
> 1 teaspoon ground cinnamon
> 1 teaspoon vanilla extract
> ½ teaspoon lemon extract
> ¼ teaspoon liquid stevia (optional)

1. Stir together all the ingredients in a medium-size saucepan and bring the pot to a boil over medium heat. Reduce the heat to low and simmer, covered, for 10 minutes.

2. Transfer the mixture to a blender and process for 1 second on low speed if you prefer a smoother marmalade (if you like a chunky marmalade, don't process the mixture). Japanese Knotweed Marmalade will keep, covered, in the refrigerator, for up to 2 weeks.

MAKES 2¼ CUPS

PEAR BROWN BETTY

If you don't find pears growing in the wild, you'll still love this dish made with ripe cultivated pears. The sour-tasting Japanese knotweed shoots contrast quite well with the sweet-tasting fruit.

CRUMB LAYER
> 2 ½ cups fine cake crumbs
> 1 cup walnuts
> ½ cup oat bran or wheat bran
> ⅛ teaspoon salt
> ¼ cup corn oil
> ½ teaspoon amaretto extract or vanilla extract

FRUIT LAYER
> 8 cups cored and sliced ripe pears
> 1 cup Japanese knotweed shoots, peeled if longer
>   than 8 inches and chopped
> ½ cup unsweetened pear or apple juice

¼ cup Blackberry Spice Wine (page 278) or red
   wine

1 tablespoon fresh lemon juice

½ teaspoon liquid stevia (optional)

3 tablespoons arrowroot or kudzu

2 teaspoons ground cinnamon

1 teaspoon freshly ground fennel seeds

1 teaspoon freshly grated nutmeg

1. Preheat the oven to 375 degrees.

2. *To make the crumb layer:* In a medium-size bowl, mix together the crumb layer ingredients.

3. *To make the fruit layer:* In a large bowl, mix together the fruit layer ingredients.

4. Spread half the crumb layer mixture over the bottom of a 14 x 9 x 2-inch oiled baking dish. Pour the fruit layer over the crumb layer, and top with the remaining crumb layer mixture. Bake the Brown Betty, uncovered, until bubbly, about 45 minutes. Serve hot or cold.

SERVES 8

JAPANESE KNOTWEED–KIWI PIE

Sour Japanese knotweed shoots and sweet kiwi fruit make perfect partners in this pie thickened with agar.

CRUST

1 ⅔ cups buckwheat flour or ½ pound any other
   whole-grain flour

⅔ cup ground almonds or other nuts

¼ cup arrowroot or kudzu

½ teaspoon freshly ground coriander seeds

½ teaspoon ground cinnamon

⅓ cup flaxseed oil or corn oil

½ cup apple juice

FILLING

8 kiwis, peeled and sliced

2 ½ cups young Japanese knotweed shoots no
   longer than 8 inches

2 cups apple juice

6 tablespoons agar flakes

2 tablespoons vegetable glycerin, barley malt, or
   honey

2 teaspoons ground cinnamon

2 teaspoons vanilla extract

1 teaspoon lemon extract

½ teaspoon liquid stevia (optional)

2 cups walnuts, chopped

1. *To make the crust:* In a large bowl, mix the flour, almonds, arrowroot, ground coriander, and cinnamon together.

2. In a small bowl, mix the flaxseed oil and apple juice together. Stir the wet ingredients into the dry ingredients until well combined.

3. Chill, if desired. Preheat the oven to 425 degrees. Divide the dough in half and roll half into a pie crust ³⁄₁₆ inch thick on a floured pastry sheet, using a rolling pin covered with a floured sleeve. Roll the dough and pastry sheet around the rolling pin and transfer the crust to an oiled 9-inch pie pan. Unroll the crust over the pie pan, peel off the pastry sheet, and push the crust into place. Repeat this process with the remaining dough and a second pie pan.

4. Bake the crusts until they are lightly browned, about 8 minutes, turning the pie pans occasionally. Watch carefully that the crusts don't burn. Remove the crusts from the oven.

5. *To make the filling:* In a large saucepan over medium heat, combine all the filling ingredients except the walnuts and simmer, covered, for 10 minutes. Remove the pot from the heat.

6. When the filling is lukewarm, pour it into the pre-baked pie crusts, top each pie evenly with the walnuts, and chill until set.

MAKES 2 PIES

STRAWBERRY-KNOTWEED COBBLER

Traditional Western cuisine combines rhubarb with strawberries. Japanese knotweed, a better-tasting, more nutritious relative of rhubarb, makes this union even better. Layered between Tofu Cottage Cheese, bread crumbs, and walnuts, it can't be beat.

2 cups fresh Bread Crumbs (page 40)

¼ cup corn oil

2 cups Tofu Cottage Cheese (page 30)

3 cups Japanese knotweed shoots, peeled if longer than 8 inches and sliced

2 ½ cups Super Strawberry Jam (page 208) or store-bought

1 cup walnuts, chopped

1. Preheat the oven to 350 degrees.
2. Mix the bread crumbs with the corn oil in a small bowl until well combined.
3. Layer a 3-quart oiled casserole dish with the Tofu Cottage Cheese, Japanese knotweed, strawberry jam, oiled bread crumbs, and walnuts, pressing everything down with the palm of your hand. Bake the cobbler, uncovered, until bubbly, about 30 minutes. Serve chilled. Do not freeze.

SERVES 6

JAPANESE KNOTWEED ICE CREAM

Like its milder-flavored relative rhubarb, sour-tasting Japanese knotweed is equally at home in vegetable dishes and desserts. This pale green-yellow ice cream has a wonderfully mild, lemony flavor.

2 cups Japanese knotweed shoots, peeled if longer than 8 inches

1 cup apple juice

1 cup drained silken tofu

½ cup raw cashews

1 ½ cups soy milk or nut milk

¼ cup canola oil

¼ cup vegetable glycerin, barley malt, or honey

1 teaspoon liquid stevia

2 teaspoons vanilla extract

1 teaspoon lemon extract

½ teaspoon salt

2 tablespoons lecithin granules

1. In a medium-size saucepan, simmer the Japanese knotweed in the apple juice over medium heat until tender, about 10 minutes.
2. Transfer the knotweed and apple juice to a blender, add the remaining ingredients, and process until smooth.
3. Chill the mixture until it is cold (1 hour in the freezer or 4 hours in the refrigerator).
4. Pour the mixture into an ice cream machine and freeze it according to the manufacturer's instructions.

MAKES 5½ CUPS; SERVES 5 TO 6

JAPANESE KNOTWEED SHERBET

Japanese knotweed lends its lemony flavor and thickening qualities to this sweet-tasting sherbet.

3 cups Japanese knotweed shoots, peeled if longer
than 8 inches and coarsely sliced
1⅓ cups orange juice (freshly squeezed is best)
1½ cups apple juice or other unsweetened fruit
juice
½ cup fresh lemon juice
¼ cup canola oil
¼ cup vegetable glycerin, honey, barley malt, or
rice syrup
1 tablespoon freshly grated orange rind
2 teaspoons vanilla extract
1 teaspoon lemon extract
1 teaspoon liquid stevia (optional)
½ teaspoon salt

1. In a medium-size saucepan, simmer the Japanese knotweed shoots in the orange juice, apple juice, and lemon juice over medium heat, covered, until they are tender, about 10 minutes.

2. Transfer the knotweed and the juices to a blender, add the remaining ingredients, and process until smooth.

3. Chill the mixture until it is cold (1 hour in the freezer or 4 hours in the refrigerator).

4. Pour the mixture into an ice cream machine and freeze it according to the manufacturer's instructions.

MAKES 5 CUPS; SERVES 5

WATERLEAF

Hydrophyllum species

HERE'S AN APTLY NAMED GROUP OF PLANTS. They grow near the water, and the leaves bear what look like water stains. The waterleaf grows 1 to 2 feet tall, with densely clustered white, blue, or purple bell-shaped flowers that have five parts, with stamens and pistils (male and female flower parts) protruding.

The leaves may have many lobes (subdivisions), or they may be shaped like maple leaves, depending on the species. Use the hairless varieties raw or cooked like parsley (you may enjoy all the species cooked) in early spring, before the flowers appear; the flavor is similar to parsley, but waterleaf carries exotic overtones. Sauté the leaves and add them to soups, sauces, stews, entrées, and, of course, include them in salads. I dry large quantities of the leaves every spring and use them like dried parsley until the following year.

TRUE GRITS

Here's a natural way to make the best-tasting grits you'll ever eat. The Fakin' Bacon (a vegetarian bacon substitute that is available in health food stores) does its job wonderfully when you mix it with other ingredients. The silken tofu, lecithin granules, and flaxseeds more than substitute for the more usual eggs. The waterleaf adds an exotic touch.

2 cups water

¾ cup yellow corn grits

1 ⅓ cups drained silken tofu, finely chopped

¼ cup lecithin granules

¼ cup Fakin' Bacon Bits

¼ cup waterleaf leaves, chopped

2 tablespoons flaxseeds or chia seeds

2 tablespoons corn oil or olive oil

2 cloves garlic, chopped

½ teaspoon Vege-Sal or ¼ teaspoon salt

½ teaspoon hot paprika

¼ cup turmeric

½ teaspoon freshly ground white pepper
   (¼ teaspoon peppercorns)

Combine all the ingredients in a large saucepan and bring the pot to a boil over medium heat, stirring constantly. Reduce the heat to low, cover, and simmer until the grits are soft, 15 to 20 minutes. Serve hot.

SERVES 4 TO 6

COMMON BLUE VIOLET

Viola papilionacea

THIS EASY-TO-RECOGNIZE, FAMILIAR ORNAMENTAL is also very common in the wild, and quite good to eat. The odorless, heart-shaped leaves on long stalks form a basal rosette radiating from a gnarled underground emetic rhizome (horizontal stem) the width of a pencil. The violet five-petaled bilaterally symmetrical flower, which begins to appear early in the spring, reaches nearly an inch across. Inside, bushy stamens form a "beard."

Other species of violets (not the African violet, which is a houseplant that's not a violet) are also edible. One has a white flower. But another, with yellow flowers, may make you throw up. And larkspur (*Delphinium tricorne*), with different leaves and an erect spur sticking out from the back of the otherwise violet-like flower, is poisonous.

Look for violets in cultivated areas, lawns, parks, open areas in the woods, and meadows.

Violets have exceptionally delicious leaves and flowers, which you can collect from early spring to late spring. Sometimes you can also find new growth in the fall. The flowers have a very mild flavor, but they add wonderful color. The leaves taste mild at first, then become somewhat hot as you chew them. They may be eaten raw in salads. And they're slightly mucilaginous, so they thicken soups a little bit like okra does. The leaves cook in 5 to 10 minutes, and you can add them to soups, stews, and virtually any kind of vegetable dish. Use any method you wish to cook them. Dried, they reconstitute exceptionally well.

CHICKEN MUSHROOM SOUP WITH BROWN RICE

As a kid, I usually insisted on eating junk food, but I'd always eat canned chicken soup with rice. Here's a homemade version, greatly improved by the substitution of chicken mushrooms and the addition of violet leaves.

12 cups chicken mushrooms (page 321) or other
   mushrooms, sliced

8 cups Vegetable Stock (page 40) or water

4 cups common blue violet leaves or other greens

2 cups short-grain brown rice

One 22.5-ounce jar tomato sauce

One 33.8-ounce package soy milk or nut milk

2 medium-size onions, chopped

½ cup Redbud Wine (page 159) or red wine

5 cloves garlic, crushed

¼ cup field garlic leaves (page 57) or scallion
    greens, chopped

1 tablespoon tamari soy sauce

2 teaspoons freshly ground fennel seeds

1 teaspoon dried thyme, finely crumbled

2 teaspoons freshly ground black pepper
    (1 teaspoon peppercorns)

Combine all the ingredients in a large saucepan and bring the pot to a boil over medium heat, stirring occasionally. Reduce the heat to low and simmer, covered, for 35 minutes. This soup freezes well and will keep in the freezer for 6 months.

SERVES 8

VIOLET SAAG

A *saag* is an Indian dish of cooked leafy greens, often including panir cheese. If you like Indian food, I guarantee that if you prepare this mildly seasoned violet dish, your enthusiasm for violets will never saag.

SAUCE

4 cups common blue violet leaves

1½ cups water

5 tablespoons raw cashews

¼ cup drained silken tofu

2 tablespoons fresh lemon juice

2 tablespoons corn oil

2 teaspoons salt

SPICES

2 tablespoons toasted sesame oil

2 cloves garlic, chopped

1 small chile, seeds and ribs removed and chopped,
    or ¼ teaspoon cayenne pepper, or to taste

1½ teaspoons ground cinnamon

1½ teaspoons freshly ground cumin seeds

2 teaspoons freshly ground black mustard seeds
    (1 teaspoon seeds)

1 teaspoon freshly ground bayberry (page 185) or
    bay leaves

1 teaspoon freshly ground coriander seeds

1 teaspoon freshly ground cloves

1 teaspoon freshly ground black pepper
    (½ teaspoon peppercorns)

½ teaspoon freshly ground cardamom seeds

½ teaspoon ground mace

2 cups Panir Tofu Cheese (page 32)

1. *To make the sauce:* Rinse the violet leaves and spin or shake off any excess water. Place the violet leaves in a medium-size, heavy saucepan and cook them, covered, over low heat until they are just wilted, about 10 minutes. Remove the pot from the heat and let the cooked leaves sit, covered, for another 5 minutes.

2. Meanwhile, in a blender, combine all the sauce ingredients and process until smooth. Add the violet leaves to the blender and process again until smooth.

3. *To prepare the spices:* Heat the sesame oil in a large skillet over medium heat, add all the spices, and cook for 1 minute, stirring constantly. Add the sauce and Tofu Panir Cheese, and bring the mixture to a boil over medium heat, stirring constantly. Reduce the heat to low and simmer, covered, for 5 minutes. Serve Violet Saag hot over rice or with Indian bread.

SERVES 4 TO 6

VIOLET POLENTA CASSEROLE

This great dish is beautiful garnished with violet flowers.

> 2 cups yellow cornmeal
>
> 4 cups cold Vegetable Stock (page 40) or water
>
> 2 teaspoons Vege-Sal or 1 teaspoon salt, or to taste
>
> 1 teaspoon freshly ground black pepper
>   (½ teaspoon peppercorns)
>
> 1½ tablespoons corn oil or flaxseed oil
>
> 3 cups common blue violet leaves, 2 cups chopped
>   and 1 cup left whole
>
> 1¼ cups (½ pound) Tofu Cream Cheese (page 30)
>
> 1½ cups (1 pound) Tofu Grated Cheese (page 32)

1. Mix the cornmeal with the cold stock, Vege-Sal, and pepper in a large, heavy saucepan and bring the pot to a boil over high heat, stirring constantly with a whisk. (If you don't have a heavy saucepan, put a heat diffuser under the saucepan you are using, to prevent scorching.) When the pot reaches a boil and the mixture thickens, reduce the heat to medium and simmer, covered, for 15 minutes, stirring often with a wooden spoon. Add the corn oil and simmer for another 10 minutes.

2. Preheat the oven to 350 degrees.

3. Layer a 3-quart oiled casserole dish with half the polenta (cornmeal mush), half the chopped violet leaves, half the Tofu Cream Cheese, half the Tofu Grated Cheese, followed by the remaining polenta, chopped violet leaves, Tofu Cream Cheese, and Tofu Grated Cheese. Bake the polenta, covered, until bubbly, about 40 minutes.

4. Serve hot, garnished with the whole violet leaves.

SERVES 6

VIOLET PANSOTTI

When I first made these traditional Italian dumplings many years ago, I stuffed them with cheese, hard-boiled eggs, and spinach. Using Tofu Grated Cheese, violet leaves, and lotus seeds instead makes the dumplings even tastier and more healthful.

FILLING

> ½ cup pine nuts
>
> 1 cup common blue violet leaves along with some
>   flowers
>
> 1 cup cooked lotus seeds (available in Asian food
>   stores; cook by simmering for 30 minutes in
>   boiling salted vegetable stock or water to cover)
>   or lima beans, drained
>
> ¼ cup lecithin granules
>
> 4 cloves garlic, chopped
>
> ½ teaspoon Vege-Sal or ¼ teaspoon salt, or to taste

> 1 recipe Wild Ravioli dough (page 89)
>
> Black Walnut Sauce (page 377)

1. *To make the filling:* In a medium-size bowl, mix together the filling ingredients.

2. On a floured pastry sheet using a rolling pin enclosed in a floured sleeve, roll out half the ravioli dough, making a rectangle ³⁄₁₆ inch thick. Cut as many 3-inch squares as possible in the dough, using a pizza cutter or butter knife.

3. Put about 1 tablespoon of filling on one square of dough. Moisten the edges of the dough with water, place another square on top, and press the top and bottom together with a ravioli press, cookie cutter, or a glass that is 2½ inches in diameter. Repeat the process until all the squares are used, and then roll out the scraps of dough and repeat the process again until all the filling and dough are used up.

4. To cook the ravioli, bring a large pot of salted water to a boil, add the ravioli, and let them boil for 10 minutes. Drain the ravioli and serve them hot with the warmed sauce.

MAKES 20 DUMPLINGS

CURLY DOCK, YELLOW DOCK

Rumex crispus

HERE'S ANOTHER REALLY IMPORTANT EDIBLE plant. It's tasty, healthful, and easy to recognize, and because it is common and widespread, it is a cinch to collect in quantity.

In early spring, you'll first notice a basal rosette of long, hairless leaves with very wavy edges, growing up to 2 feet long and 3½ inches wide, emerging from a large yellow taproot. In mid-spring, a central flower stalk with alternate leaves starts its growth, which may reach 5 feet.

In the summer, dense, erect clusters of tiny green flowers emerge from the leaf axils (where they meet the stems), followed by tiny rust brown seeds in late summer and fall.

Curly dock grows throughout North America in disturbed habitats, fields, thickets, and along roadsides.

Don't confuse curly dock, with its delicious, sour leaves, with Moe dock or Larry dock. (Nyuck! Nyuck! Nyuck!) The sour-tasting leaves are great eaten raw in salads, steamed, or cooked in soups. The leaves cook in 3 to 5 minutes. Crisp-textured when raw, the leaves become very soft after brief cooking, and even more sour. Use the leaves from early to mid-spring, after

which time they become too bitter. Collect the new growth in late fall. You can easily dry the leaves, which reconstitute quickly in soups, stews, and grain dishes. Curly dock also makes a great vegetable flour.

CURLY DOCK–BURDOCK RICE

Wild food students often confuse curly dock with burdock, even though the former is in the buckwheat family, and the latter is related to artichokes. (The word *dock* means to "get rid of or remove," as when someone's pay is docked, and it also applies to gardeners who try to eliminate burdock from their gardens.) Here's a simple rice dish enhanced with the sour flavor of curly dock leaves and the hearty taste of burdock root.

6 cups water
3 cups curly dock leaves
2 cups sweet brown rice
1 ⅓ cups burdock root (page 139), thinly sliced
½ cup wild rice
½ cup brown basmati rice
1 large onion, chopped
4 large cloves garlic, minced
2 tablespoons olive oil
1 tablespoon tamari soy sauce
1 teaspoon dried rosemary, finely crumbled
1 teaspoon dried thyme, finely crumbled
1 teaspoon dried sage, finely crumbled
½ teaspoon cayenne pepper or to taste

Combine all the ingredients in a large saucepan and bring the pot to a boil. Reduce the heat to low, and simmer, covered, until all the liquid is absorbed and the rice is tender, about 40 minutes.

SERVES 8

QUINOA WITH CURLY DOCK

Quinoa is a South American relative of lamb's-quarters, spinach, and beets. You may prepare its mild-tasting, nutritious seeds as you would grains. Curly dock, with its biting, lemony flavor, adds just the right amount of zing to this dish. I came up with this recipe one day when I used curly dock leaves in a salad and had the stems left over.

> 4 cups Vegetable Stock (page 40) or water
>
> 1¾ cups quinoa
>
> 2 cups curly dock stems or leaves, chopped
>
> 2 tablespoons sesame oil
>
> ¼ cup amaranth (page 338)
>
> 4 cloves garlic, crushed into a paste
>
> 1 teaspoon dried marjoram, finely crumbled
>
> 1 teaspoon dried sage, finely crumbled
>
> 1 teaspoon dried savory, finely crumbled

Combine all the ingredients in a large saucepan and bring the pot to a boil. Reduce the heat to low, and simmer, covered, until all the liquid is absorbed and the grains are tender, about 30 minutes.

SERVES 4 TO 6

GREEN WILD NOODLES

This recipe makes it worth it to buy a pasta machine. It uses healthful whole-grain flour along with dried curly dock or other greens.

> 3⅓ cups (1 pound) buckwheat flour and 3 cups
>
> plus 3 tablespoons (15 ounces) sweet brown
>
> rice flour, or 31 ounces any whole-grain flour
>
> 3 cups (1 ounce) dried curly dock, ground into
>
> a powder in a blender or spice grinder
>
> ½ cup plus 1 tablespoon arrowroot or kudzu

> 1¼ cups plus 2½ tablespoons freshly ground
>
> flaxseeds (9 tablespoons seeds)
>
> 2 teaspoons dried oregano, finely crumbled
>
> 2 teaspoons dried rosemary, finely crumbled
>
> 2 teaspoons dried savory, finely crumbled
>
> 2 teaspoons Vege-Sal or 1 teaspoon salt
>
> ¼ cup olive oil
>
> 1 cup plus 2 tablespoons water

1. Sift together the flour, curly dock powder, arrowroot, ground flaxseeds, herbs, and Vege-Sal. Mix in 3 tablespoons of the olive oil. Add the water. You will have a very dry dough.

2. Use a pasta machine, following the manufacturer's instructions, to form noodles, or roll out the dough with a rolling pin and cut the dough into noodles. (If you plan to roll out the dough by hand, you may need to add more water to the dough.)

3. To cook the noodles, bring a large pot of salted water to a boil. Add the noodles and let them boil until they are al dente, about 7 minutes. (If you're going to cook the noodles in another recipe, boil them for only 5 minutes.) Drain the noodles in a colander, toss them with the remaining 1 tablespoon olive oil, and serve them or use them in another recipe immediately.

MAKES 11 CUPS; SERVES 8

DOCKED POTATOES

Sour curly dock leaves and Tofu Cottage Cheese add a gourmet touch to plain baked potatoes.

> 6 medium-size potatoes, baked until tender (see
>
> note on page 111)
>
> 3 cups curly dock leaves
>
> 1¾ cups Tofu Cottage Cheese (page 30)
>
> ¼ cup corn oil

6 cloves garlic, crushed into a paste

1 tablespoon Vegetarian Worcestershire Sauce
(page 56)

1 teaspoon dried tarragon, finely crumbled

1 teaspoon chili paste or ¼ teaspoon cayenne
pepper, or to taste

1 teaspoon Vege-Sal or ½ teaspoon salt, or to taste

1 teaspoon freshly ground white pepper
(½ teaspoon peppercorns), or to taste

1. Preheat the oven to 350 degrees.

2. When they are cool enough to handle, cut the potatoes in half lengthwise and scoop out most of the pulp, being careful not to break the skin.

3. Mix the potato pulp with the remaining ingredients and mound the mixture back into the potato skins. Bake the stuffed potatoes, covered, in a 14 x 9 x 2-inch oiled casserole dish or baking dish for 30 minutes.

SERVES 6

Note: To bake potatoes, scrub them, rub them with Spiceberry Butter Sauce (page 316), Herb Oil (page 112), or olive oil, and bake them in a preheated 450-degree oven on a rack set over a cookie sheet, until they are tender, about 1 hour.

IMAM

Here's a wild version of a classic Turkish vegetable casserole. Curly dock does a more than adequate job replacing the traditional lemon juice as the source of tartness.

⅓ cup olive oil, or as needed

5 medium-size zucchini, ends trimmed and sliced
lengthwise

1 medium-size eggplant, sliced into medium-thick
rounds

4 medium-size carrots, sliced

1 large onion, chopped

6 cloves garlic, chopped

4 medium-size ripe tomatoes, chopped

4 cups curly dock leaves, chopped

¼ cup fresh parsley leaves, chopped

2 teaspoons Vege-Sal or 1 teaspoon salt, or to taste

2½ cups walnuts, chopped

1. Preheat the oven to 350 degrees.

2. Heat the olive oil in a large skillet over medium heat. Add the zucchini, eggplant, carrots, onion, and garlic and cook, stirring, for 10 minutes.

3. Transfer the vegetables to a food processor, add the remaining ingredients, except the walnuts, and process until smooth, or chop fine with a knife. Mix in the walnuts.

4. Transfer the vegetable and walnut mixture to a 14 x 9 x 2-inch oiled baking dish and bake it until bubbly, about 30 minutes. Serve hot as a dip. Imam will keep, tightly covered, in the refrigerator for 5 days.

MAKES 2 CUPS

WILD GINGER

Asarum species

ONE OF MY FAVORITE WILD SEASONINGS, WILD ginger is a small plant with a pair of heart-shaped leaves that emerges on a long stalk from the ground. Hanging from the crotch between the two leaves you'll find a single deep purple brown flower, consisting of three parts.

The stem, a brittle underground horizontal rhizome the thickness of a pipe cleaner, exudes a strong ginger fragrance. You'll find the plant in partially sunny wooded areas throughout eastern North America, as well as in cultivated areas anywhere (landscapers have planted it in Central Park, for example).

Once you locate this widespread, common plant you can begin using the rhizome in all recipes that call for ginger. I add it to desserts, curries, and various other ethnic dishes. Wild ginger is not related to commercial (Asian) ginger, but the various native and European wild ginger species provide a similar but more subtle flavor. Unlike commercial ginger, you don't peel wild ginger.

To store the rhizome long-term, dehydrate it (after scrubbing off the soil) in a food dehydrator, or pat the rhizome dry with paper towels and dry it in a paper bag for a couple of weeks. Keep dehydrated rhizomes stored in a tightly covered jar. Grind the dried rhizome into a powder in a spice grinder before using.

CURRY POWDER

For years I was frustrated because I had lost this original formula for curry powder and never could re-create it. Finally, when I had my refrigerator replaced I found the index card with the recipe underneath the old refrigerator. I've been using this recipe in wild and non-wild curry dishes ever since.

 6 *tablespoons coriander seeds*
 6 *tablespoons turmeric*
 3 *tablespoons cumin seeds*
 3 *tablespoons cardamom seeds*
 2 *tablespoons ground cinnamon*
 4 *dried chiles or 1 tablespoon cayenne pepper*
 2 *tablespoons ground dried wild ginger or regular*
   ginger

Simply grind the whole spices and chiles in a spice grinder and mix them with the ground ginger. Store Curry Powder in a tightly closed jar at room temperature. After a few months, it'll lose some strength, so you'll have to use more Curry Powder to achieve the same effect.

MAKES 1½ CUPS

FIVE-SPICE POWDER

This is a traditional Chinese seasoning combination using American wild ginger.

 2 *tablespoons cinnamon stick pieces*
 2 *tablespoons ground dried wild ginger or regular*
   ginger
 2 *tablespoons star anise*
 2 *tablespoons fennel seeds*
 2 *tablespoons cloves*
 ¼ *teaspoon black peppercorns*

Grind all the ingredients into a powder using a spice grinder. Store Five-Spice Powder in a tightly covered jar.

MAKES ⅔ CUP

HERB OIL

Use this spread for bread, popcorn, potatoes, avocados, or whatever you'd normally use butter for. Be ready for a spicy kick.

 2½ *cups olive oil*
 ½ *cup mellow (light-colored) miso*
 4 *large cloves garlic, peeled*
 2 *tablespoons finely chopped fresh wild ginger or*
   2 *teaspoons ground dried wild ginger*

2 tablespoons chili paste or 1 teaspoon cayenne
pepper, or to taste

2 tablespoons chopped fresh parsley leaves

1 teaspoon common spicebush berries (page 314),
finely chopped, or freshly ground allspice berries

Place all the ingredients in a blender and process until smooth. Herb Oil will keep, tightly covered, in the refrigerator for 6 to 8 weeks.

MAKES 3⅓ CUPS

SESAME-MISO SAUCE

I used cultivated fresh commercial ginger when I first developed this Asian-style sauce for my pre-Wildman cooking classes in 1980, but the sauce is even better with wild ginger. You can use this sauce on stir-fried dishes or as a marinade.

½ cup sesame seeds

1½ cups Vegetable Stock (page 40)

½ cup dark-colored miso

2 tablespoons apple juice

2 tablespoons freshly grated orange rind or lemon
rind

1½ tablespoons finely chopped fresh wild ginger

1 tablespoon chopped fresh wild spearmint (page
59) or other mint leaves or 1 teaspoon dried

1. Toast the sesame seeds in a dry small, heavy skillet over medium heat, stirring constantly, until the seeds become fragrant and begin to pop. Do not overcook or stop stirring the sesame seeds or they'll burn. Transfer the toasted seeds to a small bowl.

2. When the sesame seeds have cooled, process them in a blender with the remaining ingredients until smooth. Sesame-Miso Sauce will keep, tightly cov-

ered, in the refrigerator for up to 1 week.

MAKES 3 CUPS

INDIAN FRIED RICE

If you cook rice by boiling it, how do you make fried rice? You fry rice with seasonings or additional ingredients either before (as below) or after you boil the rice. With wild ginger and Indian seasonings to add such elegance to brown basmati rice, wild rice, and amaranth, how can you go wrong with this recipe?

¼ cup mustard oil (available in Indian grocery
stores), corn oil, or peanut oil

2 teaspoons yellow mustard seeds

1 teaspoon cloves, left whole or freshly ground

1 teaspoon Vege-Sal or ½ teaspoon salt, or to taste

1 teaspoon turmeric

½ teaspoon ground dried wild ginger

½ teaspoon coriander seeds, left whole or freshly
ground

4 cloves garlic, chopped

1 tablespoon chili paste or ½ teaspoon cayenne
pepper, or to taste

1½ cups brown basmati rice or other brown rice

¼ cup wild rice (page 353)

¼ cup amaranth (page 338)

1¾ cups boiling water

1. Heat the oil in a medium-size skillet over medium heat, add the yellow mustard seeds, cloves, Vege-Sal, turmeric, wild ginger, and coriander, and cook, stirring often, until the mustard seeds pop, about 2 minutes.

2. Add the remaining ingredients, except the boiling water, and cook the mixture over medium heat, stirring often, for another 5 minutes.

3. Transfer the mixture to the saucepan containing the

boiling water and bring the pot back to a boil over medium heat. Reduce the heat to low, cover, and simmer the grains until all the water is absorbed, about 40 minutes.

SERVES 4 TO 6

PORK MARINADE

Season firm-textured, bland mushrooms, well-drained firm tofu, or some other bland, firm-textured food with ingredients people often use to season pork, and you'll get an excellent meat substitute.

> ¼ cup olive oil
> 2 tablespoons white wine
> 3 tablespoons tamari soy sauce
> 2 tablespoons prepared mustard
> 1 teaspoon minced fresh wild ginger
> ½ teaspoon Vegetarian Worcestershire Sauce
>   (page 56)
> ¼ teaspoon liquid stevia or 2 tablespoons honey,
>   barley malt, or rice syrup

Mix together all the ingredients in a small bowl. Pork Marinade will keep, tightly covered, in the refrigerator for up to 4 weeks.

MAKES ¾ CUP (ENOUGH TO MARINATE
ONE 19-OUNCE PACKAGE OF TOFU)

MOCK DUCK

After tasting mock duck in vegetarian Chinese restaurants, I decided to try making it myself. You can purchase soy skins, which are skimmed from the surface of boiling soy milk, in Asian grocery stores. My version of mock duck tastes more like Western duck than Chinese duck does because of the Western seasonings, which include wild ginger.

> 2 cups soy skins
> ¾ cup Vegetable Stock (page 40)
> 1 tablespoon flaxseed oil or corn oil
> 1 teaspoon hot paprika
> 1 teaspoon dried savory, finely crumbled
> 1 teaspoon dried thyme, finely crumbled
> 1 teaspoon Tabasco sauce
> ¼ teaspoon ground dried wild ginger

1. Preheat the oven to 350 degrees.
2. Mix all ingredients together in a 1½-quart oiled casserole dish and bake for 30 minutes. Serve Mock Duck hot or cold as an appetizer.

SERVES 6

WILD GINGERBREAD

This traditional whole-foods gingerbread is great made with wild ginger, and it's quite straightforward and easy to make.

DRY INGREDIENTS

> 2 cups (9.5 ounces) sweet brown rice flour and
>   1⅔ cups (½ pound) buckwheat flour, or
>   17.5 ounces any whole-grain flour
> 1¼ cups freshly ground flaxseeds (½ cup seeds)
> 2 tablespoons lecithin granules
> 1½ teaspoons ground dried wild ginger
> 1 teaspoon baking soda
> ½ teaspoon cream of tartar
> ½ teaspoon ground cinnamon
> ½ teaspoon freshly ground cloves
> ½ teaspoon salt

WET INGREDIENTS

> 2 cups freshly squeezed orange juice, or other fruit
>   juice
> ½ cup corn oil, flaxseed oil, or other vegetable oil

1. Preheat the oven to 300 degrees.

2. In a large bowl, mix the dry ingredients together.

3. In a medium-size bowl, mix the wet ingredients together.

4. Mix the wet ingredients into the dry ingredients. Don't overmix.

5. Press the batter evenly into an oiled 9 x 5 x 3-inch loaf pan and bake the gingerbread until a toothpick inserted into the center emerges clean, about 1 hour. Let the gingerbread cool completely before slicing it.

MAKES 1 LOAF

VANILLA PUDDING

Here's a simple soy pudding flavored with wild ginger that everyone will love.

½ vanilla bean

3 cups drained silken tofu

¼ teaspoon ground dried wild ginger

½ teaspoon salt

2 tablespoons tapioca pearls

2 tablespoons lecithin granules

2 tablespoons almond oil

1 teaspoon liquid stevia

1. Preheat the oven to 350 degrees.

2. Split the vanilla bean lengthwise with a sharp paring knife and scrape out the pulp.

3. In a blender or with a hand mixer or whisk, purée the pulp with the remaining ingredients (you can use the rest of the bean in herb tea).

4. Transfer the mixture to a 10 x 6½ x 2-inch oiled baking dish and bake the pudding, uncovered, until it is set, about 50 minutes. Serve hot or chilled.

SERVES 6

INSTANT MARZIPAN

My dad always brought this German almond paste confection home for my sister and me when he returned from a business trip. Decades later I was delighted when I managed to create a healthful version of this childhood treat.

1 ¾ cups almonds

½ cup well-drained silken tofu

½ teaspoon vanilla extract

1 tablespoon almond oil

1 teaspoon almond extract

2 drops bitter almond essential oil (optional)

1 teaspoon liquid stevia or 2 tablespoons honey

¼ teaspoon ground dried wild ginger

⅛ teaspoon salt

3 tablespoons carob powder, or as needed

1. In a food processor, grind the almonds finely. Add the remaining ingredients, except the carob powder, and process into a paste.

2. Roll the mixture into 2 dozen small balls and roll each ball in the carob powder. Refrigerate Instant Marzipan in a tightly covered container for up to 1 week.

MAKES 2 DOZEN BALLS

HERCULES'-CLUB, DEVIL'S-WALKING STICK
Aralia spinosa

THE CELEBRATED CLUB THAT HERCULES WIELDED was studded with spiky thorns, and so is the small tree that bears its name. The tree grows anywhere from 6 to 30 feet tall, and the twice-compound (segmented) leaves, also thorny, may reach 6 feet in length! In late summer, tiny white flowers cluster in halos, accounting for another common name for the plant, angelica tree (not the herb angelica). In the fall, *poisonous* black berries replace the flowers. Look for the plant in thickets, at the edge of trails, and in openings in the woods in eastern North America, and throughout the country in cultivated parks, where landscapers plant it.

Harvest the shoots (young growth) in the spring. Hercules'-club is not something you want to touch unless you're wearing gloves. Peel the thorns off the shoots and cook the shoots (10 to 15 minutes of any kind of cooking usually does it). Hercules'-club shoots add a special touch to any dish. They taste a little like asparagus, but more exotic.

CURRIED RICE WITH HERCULES'-CLUB

In this deluxe rice dish some of the finest Indian seasonings are counterbalanced with springtime wild ingredients.

½ cup peanut oil

3 cups ramp leaves (page 116) or 2 cups chopped shallots or onions

2 cups Hercules'-club shoots, thorns removed and sliced

½ cup raw cashews

4 cloves garlic, chopped

1 tablespoon peeled and chopped fresh ginger

2 teaspoons cumin seeds

One 1-inch cinnamon stick

1 teaspoon coriander seeds

1 teaspoon turmeric

2 teaspoons chili paste or ½ teaspoon cayenne pepper, or to taste

1 teaspoon Vege-Sal or ½ teaspoon salt, or to taste

½ teaspoon freshly ground black pepper (¼ teaspoon peppercorns)

½ teaspoon saffron threads soaked in ½ cup hot water

2 cups brown basmati rice or other long-grain brown rice

3½ cups boiling water

⅔ cup raisins

1. Heat the peanut oil in a large skillet over medium-low heat. Add the ramp leaves, Hercules'-club, cashews, garlic, ginger, cumin seeds, cinnamon stick, coriander seeds, turmeric, chili paste, Vege-Sal, and black pepper and cook for 5 minutes.

2. Meanwhile, in a blender purée the saffron and its soaking water.

3. Add the rice to the sautéing ingredients and cook, stirring, until the oil is absorbed, another 5 minutes. Add the saffron mixture, boiling water, and raisins and simmer, covered, over low heat, until all the liquid is absorbed and the rice is tender, about 40 minutes.

SERVES 4 TO 6

RAMP, WILD LEEK
Allium tricoccum

YOU MAY RECOGNIZE THIS PREMIER MEMBER OF the onion/garlic family by its stalked, elongated, oval, smooth-edged leaves, 4 to 12 inches long and 1 to 2½ inches wide, which emerge in dense stands from the floor of moist, open woodlands throughout eastern

North America every spring. Crush any part of the plant, and its familial affinity will hit you right in the nose. Lily-of-the-valley, beautiful but deadly, has similar leaves but no odor.

The leaves of this plant die back when the trees' leaves keep the sun from reaching them, but a smooth, slender, erect flower stalk 6 inches to 1½ feet tall supports a small umbrella-like cluster of six-petaled flowers in the summer, followed by tiny, shiny black seeds that remind me of BBs.

Underground, you'll find white bulbs, usually clustered, which are edible in the spring (when you collect the leaves), summer, and fall (as well as during mild winters, if you can find them). When there are no leaves, look for the flower or seed stalk or a straw-like skeleton.

There are no two ways about it: Whether you use the leaves or the bulbs, this is simply the best-tasting member of the entire onion family, wild or cultivated. You can use the leaves or bulbs raw or cooked. Ramps cook in 5 to 15 minutes, and any cooking method works. Ramps are terrific, and so is the resulting ramp breath.

If you can't find ramps in the wild, you may purchase them in gourmet stores. Otherwise substitute shallots.

RAMP GUACAMOLE

Ramps and garlic mustard add even more zing to this traditionally pungent spread. I use it on Sourdough Rye Bread (page 318) and as a dip for vegetables. You can also serve it on a bed of wild watercress or other greens.

1 ripe avocado, peeled and pitted
1 cup ramp leaves

Juice of ½ lemon
2 tablespoons minced garlic mustard roots (page 61) or horseradish root (page 80)
1 teaspoon Vege-Sal or ½ teaspoon salt, or to taste

In a food processor, combine all the ingredients and process with the chopping blade until well mixed (or mince the ramps with a knife and mash them together with the other ingredients using a potato masher or fork). Ramp Guacamole will keep, tightly covered, in the refrigerator for 1 week.

SERVES 4

RAMP DIP

This simple dip combines the flavor of "cheese" with that of wild leeks.

3 cloves garlic, peeled
1 small chile, seeds and ribs removed, or ¼ teaspoon cayenne pepper, or to taste
⅓ cup ramp leaves
1½ tablespoons chopped fresh basil leaves
1½ cups Tofu Cream Cheese (page 30)
1 teaspoon freshly ground coriander seeds
¼ teaspoon freshly ground cumin seeds
¼ teaspoon freshly ground caraway seeds
½ teaspoon freshly ground black pepper (¼ teaspoon peppercorns)

1. Chop the garlic, chile, ramp leaves, and basil in a food processor or by hand.
2. Add the remaining ingredients and process (or mash well with a potato masher or fork) until well mixed. Ramp Dip will keep, tightly covered, for 5 to 7 days.

MAKES 1⅔ CUPS

DEATH BREATH DIP

It's easy for me to get kids to eat vegetables. When we find ramps, I tell them that this vegetable will give them a super power. After they eat the ramps, I reveal that they've been transformed into supervillains with the power of death breath, and I suggest they test their power by blowing in their friends' faces. This ramp dip tastes great, and it's as good at producing death breath as anything I've ever created. Serve it with chips, bread sticks, or vegetables.

2 large cloves garlic, peeled

Two 19-ounce packages silken tofu, well drained

½ cup loosely packed dried ramp leaves, ground into 2 tablespoons of powder, or 1 ½ cups chopped fresh ramp leaves

¼ olive oil

1 ½ teaspoons hot paprika

1 tablespoon brewer's yeast

2 teaspoons Vege-Sal or 1 teaspoon salt, or to taste

1 teaspoon turmeric

2 tablespoons umeboshi plum vinegar or red wine vinegar

1 tablespoon brown rice vinegar

2 tablespoons lecithin granules

½ teaspoon Tabasco sauce, or to taste

One 6-ounce jar low-sodium pitted olives, drained

1. In a food processor, chop the garlic well.

2. Add the remaining ingredients, except the olives, and process until smooth.

3. Add the olives and process until they are finely chopped. Death Breath Dip will keep, tightly covered, in the refrigerator for 5 to 7 days.

MAKES 4½ CUPS

RAMP SPREAD

This spicy spread is ideal in sandwiches or as a dip.

2 cloves garlic, peeled

12 ramp bulbs (remove the hard cores, which form after the plant flowers in the summer)

One 6-ounce jar mild low-sodium pitted olives, drained

1 ripe avocado, peeled and pitted

2 tablespoons mellow (light-colored) miso

Juice of 1 lemon

1 tablespoon preserved radish in chili (available in Asian specialty stores) or 1 fresh radish, chopped

1 teaspoon turmeric

1 teaspoon Vege-Sal or ½ teaspoon salt, or to taste

1. In a food processor fitted with the chopping blade, chop the garlic, ramp bulbs, and olives fine (or chop them by hand).

2. Add the remaining ingredients and process or hand-chop until the avocado is puréed. Ramp Spread will keep, tightly covered, in the refrigerator for up to a week.

MAKES 1¾ CUPS

LOOING SAUCE—CHINESE MASTER SAUCE

The Chinese use this sauce for both marinating and cooking. Afterward, they recover and recycle it, using it over and over again, so long as they're marinating vegetables and not meat or poultry.

4 cups Vegetable Stock (page 40)

½ cup ramp leaves, chopped

½ cup tamari soy sauce

½ cup dark-colored miso

½ cup Ramp Wine (page 129) or white wine

¼ cup sweet cicely taproots (avoid the gnarled, stringy underground stems; page 92), chopped, or 2 teaspoons freshly ground star anise

1 ½ tablespoons peeled and chopped fresh ginger

Place all the ingredients in a medium-size saucepan and bring the pot to a boil over medium heat. Reduce the heat to medium-low and simmer for 10 minutes. Looing Sauce will keep, tightly covered, in the refrigerator for 1 week, or in the freezer for 6 months.

MAKES 6¼ CUPS

SESAME RAMP SAUCE

In this sauce with an East Asian motif, the tahini (sesame butter) tones down the wild leek's strong flavor while providing thickness. Heat Sesame Ramp Sauce and pour it over steamed vegetables, tofu, tempeh, burgers, veggie loaves, or Chinese-style stir-fry dishes.

¼ cup sesame oil

3 cups ramp bulbs or leaves, chopped

3 tablespoons peeled and chopped fresh ginger

8 cloves garlic, chopped

2 cups Vegetable Stock (page 40) or water

¾ cup Ramp Wine (page 129) or white wine

1 cup plus 2 tablespoons Tahini (page 38)

3 tablespoons dark-colored miso, 2 teaspoons Vege-Sal, or 1 teaspoon salt, or to taste

1. Heat the sesame oil in a medium-size skillet over medium heat and cook the ramps, ginger, and garlic, stirring, for 5 minutes. Add the stock and wine and bring the pot to a boil over medium heat. Reduce the heat to low and simmer, uncovered, for 5 minutes.

2. Transfer the mixture to a food processor or blender, add the tahini and miso, and process until smooth. Sesame Ramp Sauce will keep, tightly covered, in the refrigerator for 1 week.

MAKES 4½ CUPS

AIOLI WITH RAMPS

Traditional aioli, or garlic mayonnaise, is an unhealthful mixture of butter and egg yolks. Here's a wonderful version, flavored with wild leeks, that's good for you.

6 cloves garlic, peeled

½ cup ramp leaves

¾ cup olive oil

⅔ cup drained silken tofu

3 tablespoons lecithin granules

3 tablespoons fresh lime juice

¼ teaspoon turmeric

½ teaspoon freshly ground white pepper (¼ teaspoon peppercorns)

¼ teaspoon Tabasco sauce or pinch of cayenne pepper

¼ teaspoon Vege-Sal or ⅛ teaspoon salt, or to taste

1. Chop the garlic in a food processor.

2. Add the remaining ingredients and process until the ramp leaves are chopped and everything is well mixed. (If you don't have a food processor, chop the garlic and ramps by hand and whip them together with the other ingredients using a whisk or fork.) Aioli with Ramps will keep, tightly covered, in the refrigerator for up to a week.

MAKES 1⅓ CUPS

GREEK TOMATO SAUCE

The difference between Greek tomato sauce and its more familiar Italian cousin is in the choice of seasonings and thickener.

  2 cups Ramp Wine (page 129), any other wild
    wine, or sherry
  ¼ cup olive oil
  ¼ cup arrowroot or kudzu
  4 cloves garlic, crushed
  1 ½ teaspoons dried oregano, finely crumbled
  2 tablespoons Bragg's Liquid Aminos or tamari
    soy sauce, 4 teaspoons Vege-Sal, or 2 teaspoons
    salt, or to taste
  ½ teaspoon ground cinnamon
  2 common spicebush berries (page 314), finely
    chopped, or ¼ teaspoon freshly ground allspice
    berries
  12 medium-size ripe tomatoes, cut into pieces
  ¾ cup ramp leaves
  ¼ cup fresh parsley leaves

1. In a blender, combine the wine, olive oil, arrowroot, garlic, oregano, Bragg's Liquid Aminos, cinnamon, and spicebush berries and process until smooth.
2. Add the tomatoes, ramps, and parsley in batches and process until the vegetables are coarsely chopped (use low speed for a few seconds).
3. Transfer the mixture to a large, heavy stockpot and bring the pot to a boil over medium heat, stirring often. Reduce the heat to low and simmer, stirring often, for 30 minutes. Greek Tomato Sauce will keep, tightly covered, in the refrigerator for 10 days, or in the freezer for 6 months.

MAKES 6 CUPS

BÉARNAISE SAUCE À LA BRILL

This mock French béarnaise sauce uses American wild leeks instead of shallots, as well as tofu and lecithin granules instead of egg yolks. Ramps beat out shallots hands down for flavor, the tofu provides texture, while the lecithin adds the flavor of raw egg yolk without the cholesterol or danger of salmonella.

  2 tablespoons chopped fresh parsley leaves
  4 cloves garlic, peeled
  1 ½ cups olive oil
  ⅔ cup well-drained silken tofu
  ¼ cup fresh lemon juice
  ¼ cup red wine vinegar
  1 tablespoon ramp bulbs
  1 tablespoon lecithin granules
  1 teaspoon mellow (light-colored) miso
  ½ teaspoon turmeric
  1 teaspoon freshly ground yellow mustard seeds
    (½ teaspoon seeds)
  ½ teaspoon dried thyme, finely crumbled
  ½ teaspoon dried marjoram, finely crumbled

1. In a food processor (or by hand), chop the parsley and garlic.
2. Add the remaining ingredients and process until smooth (or chop the vegetables by hand and mix in the ingredients with a whisk or fork).
3. Transfer the mixture to a medium-size saucepan and heat the sauce through over medium-low heat, stirring often. Don't allow the sauce to come to a boil or it will lose its texture. (If the sauce comes to a boil, beat in more tofu.) Béarnaise Sauce à la Brill will keep, tightly covered, in the refrigerator for 5 days.

MAKES 4 CUPS

RAMP BARBECUE SAUCE

For any dish that benefits from a strong onion/garlic flavor, the ramp, or wild leek, reigns supreme. Use this sauce on vegetables, veggie loaves, burgers, patties, mushrooms. Or on any vegetables you might barbecue, use this sauce as both a marinade and a sauce.

2 tablespoons olive oil

4 teaspoons freshly ground black mustard seeds (2 teaspoons seeds)

¾ cup ramp leaves or bulbs, chopped

2 cloves garlic, chopped

1⅔ cups canned tomato purée or tomato sauce

¼ cup apple juice

¼ cup Blackberry Spice Wine (page 278) or red wine

1 teaspoon chili paste or ¼ teaspoon cayenne pepper, or to taste

1 teaspoon tamari soy sauce, or to taste

1. Heat the olive oil in a large skillet over medium heat. Add the black mustard and cook, stirring, until they pop, 2 to 3 minutes. Add the ramps and garlic and cook, stirring, for 5 minutes.

2. Add the remaining ingredients and bring the pot to a boil. Reduce the heat to medium-low and simmer, uncovered, for 15 minutes. Ramp Barbecue Sauce will keep, tightly covered, in the refrigerator for a week, or in the freezer for 6 months.

MAKES 2⅔ CUPS

RAMP CHUTNEY

If you love onions and garlic, wild or otherwise, this chutney is for you.

4 chiles, seeds and ribs removed

2 teaspoons chili paste or ½ teaspoon cayenne pepper, or to taste

2 tablespoons ramp bulbs

1 cup unsweetened shredded coconut

2 tablespoons mellow (light-colored) miso, or to taste

2 teaspoons sunflower oil, walnut oil, or corn oil

In a food processor, combine all the ingredients and process them until they are finely chopped. Ramp Chutney will keep, tightly covered, in the refrigerator for up to 1 month.

MAKES 1¼ CUPS

RAMP PESTO

Pesto gets its name because Italians used to grind the ingredients together with a mortar and pestle. Using a food processor makes preparation simple, and adding ramps, the world's best-tasting onion species, makes this famous sauce taste even better. Of course, if you don't have a food processor, you can still grind your pesto by hand. Serve Ramp Pesto on pasta, popcorn, vegetables, and bread or add it to soups or stews for extra flavor.

8 large cloves garlic, or to taste, peeled

½ cup ramp bulbs

½ cup fresh parsley leaves

½ cup fresh basil leaves

1 teaspoon Vege-Sal or ½ teaspoon salt, or to taste

3 cups pine nuts or walnuts

1 cup olive oil, or as needed

1. In a food processor, chop the garlic and ramps together

2. Add the parsley, basil, and Vege-Sal and process again until finely chopped.

3. Add the pine nuts and process until they are finely chopped.

4. Pour in enough olive oil through the feed tube while processing to make a thick or thin paste, according to your preference. Store Ramp Pesto in a covered container in the refrigerator with some olive oil on top, and it will last for months.

MAKES 2¾ CUPS

HOT AND WILD SAUCE

This fiery condiment goes well with Indian and Mexican dishes.

4 cloves garlic, peeled
6 common spicebush berries (page 314) or
*   1½ teaspoons allspice berries*
6 chiles, seeds and ribs removed
2 cups ramp bulbs
1 cup red wine vinegar
1 tablespoon Homemade Ketchup (page 37) or
*   tomato paste*
2 teaspoons mellow (light-colored) miso, 1 teaspoon
*   Vege-Sal, or ½ teaspoon salt, or to taste*
1 teaspoon freshly ground cumin seeds

1. In a food processor, combine the garlic, spicebush berries, and chiles and process them into a paste. Add the remaining ingredients and process until the ramp bulbs are finely chopped.

2. Chill this sauce and serve it as a condiment. Hot and Wild Sauce will keep, tightly covered, in the refrigerator for 1 week.

MAKES 1¾ CUPS

RAMP DRESSING

This is my favorite dressing for air-popped popcorn, and it's also great as a spread on bread. It tastes a little like Italian pesto, although it includes ramps and no basil or cheese.

2 cups olive oil
½ cup finely crumbled dried ramp leaves
10 cloves garlic, peeled
¼ teaspoon wasabi (Japanese horseradish) powder,
*   or to taste*
⅔ cup dark-colored miso
¼ cup chili paste or 1 teaspoon cayenne pepper,
*   or to taste*
2 tablespoons brewer's yeast

In a blender, combine all the ingredients and process until smooth. Ramp Dressing will keep, tightly covered, in the refrigerator for up to 1 month.

MAKES 2⅔ CUPS

SPICEBERRY-RAMP SALAD DRESSING

Ramps and spiceberries enhance the flavor of this creamy-textured salad dressing, one of my favorites.

1 cup olive oil
1 cup canola oil
5 tablespoons red wine vinegar
3 tablespoons fresh lime juice
4 ramp bulbs
2 tablespoons lecithin granules
1 tablespoon mellow (light-colored) miso
4 common spicebush berries (page 314)
2 cloves garlic, peeled

1 teaspoon chili paste or ¼ teaspoon cayenne
   pepper, or to taste
2 teaspoons freshly ground mustard seeds
   (1 teaspoon seeds)
½ teaspoon turmeric
½ cup well-drained silken tofu

1. In a blender, combine all the ingredients, except the tofu, and process until smooth.
2. Add the tofu and process again until smooth. Spiceberry Ramp Salad Dressing will keep, tightly covered, in the refrigerator for up to 2 weeks.

MAKES 3½ CUPS

SPICY SALAD DRESSING

Wild foods are at an ebb in the winter, so here's a dressing in which you can use dried wild greens to add flavor to any salad even in the dead of winter.

½ cup olive oil
½ cup canola oil
½ cup balsamic vinegar
¼ ripe avocado, peeled and pitted
2 tablespoons Curry Powder (page 112), or to
   taste
1 tablespoon mellow (light-colored) miso
1 tablespoon ground or finely crumbled dried ramp
   leaves or bulbs or 3 tablespoons fresh ramp
   leaves
2 cloves garlic, peeled

In a blender, combine all the ingredients and process until smooth. Spicy Salad Dressing will keep, tightly covered, in the refrigerator for up to 10 days.

MAKES 2 CUPS

CREAMY RAMP DRESSING

This is one of my favorite salad dressings. It has a creamy texture and piquant flavor, and it takes only a few minutes to make.

½ cup olive oil
½ cup canola oil
½ cup balsamic vinegar
¼ cup ramp bulbs
4 cloves garlic, peeled
¼ cup mellow (light-colored) miso
1 tablespoon chili powder (page 36) or ½ teaspoon
   cayenne pepper

In a blender, combine all the ingredients and process until smooth. Creamy Ramp Dressing will keep, tightly covered, in the refrigerator for up to 1 month.

MAKES 2 CUPS

RAMP LEAF SALAD DRESSING

Ramps in any form will add zing to any recipe. This dressing will spice up even the plainest salad.

1 cup olive oil
Juice of 1 lemon
1 cup ramp leaves
¼ cup mellow (light-colored) miso
¼ cup lecithin granules
1 teaspoon chili paste or ½ teaspoon Tabasco sauce
2 cloves garlic, peeled

In a blender, combine all the ingredients and process until smooth. Ramp Leaf Salad Dressing will keep, tightly covered, in the refrigerator for up to 2 weeks.

MAKES 2 CUPS

RAMP BULB AND CHEESE SALAD

The hotness of ramp bulbs, the creamy texture of Tofu Cottage Cheese, and the crunchiness of sunflower seeds produce a delightful salad.

1 head romaine lettuce, torn into bite-size bits
1 ½ cups Tofu Cottage Cheese (page 30)
1 cup shelled raw sunflower seeds, toasted (page 158)
½ cup ramp bulbs, chopped
1 medium-size red bell pepper, seeded, and sliced into strips
1 medium-size carrot, grated
4 cloves garlic, chopped

Toss together all the ingredients in a large serving bowl. Serve with Gingko Cheese Dressing (page 436) or any other salad dressing.

SERVES 6

EGG-FREE SALAD

Ramp bulbs add piquancy to this genuine-seeming eggless egg salad.

2 cups ramp bulbs, chopped
3 cups Tofu Egg Filling (page 33)
4 teaspoons chopped fresh parsley leaves
1 cup Green Mayonnaise (page 93) or other vegan mayonnaise
8 cups any salad greens

In a large bowl, mix together the ramp bulbs, Tofu Egg Filling, parsley, and Green Mayonnaise. Serve the mixture on a bed of salad greens. Egg-Free Salad will keep, tightly covered, in the refrigerator for up to 5 days.

SERVES 6

RAMP VICHYSSOISE

This French potato and leek soup is greatly improved by the addition of native American wild leeks—which are no more closely related to cultivated leeks than to any other member of the onion family, but are much tastier.

6 medium-size potatoes, sliced
2 quarts Vegetable Stock (page 40)
4 cups ramp leaves, sliced
3 cups drained silken tofu
4 teaspoons caraway seeds
1 tablespoon corn oil
1 ½ teaspoons fresh lime juice
2 teaspoons Vege-Sal or 1 teaspoon salt, or to taste
1 teaspoon hot paprika
½ teaspoon freshly ground white pepper (¼ teaspoon peppercorns)
¼ cup chopped scallions or fresh chives

1. In a large saucepan, bring stock to a boil. Reduce heat and simmer the potatoes in the stock for 10 minutes.
2. Add the remaining ingredients, except the scallions, and simmer, covered, until the potatoes are tender, about another 10 minutes.
3. Transfer the mixture in batches to a blender and process until smooth. Start on low speed and hold down the blender cover with a towel to prevent eruptions.
4. Garnish the soup with the scallions and serve hot or cold.

SERVES 6 TO 8

WILD RICE WITH WILD LEEKS

Mixing brown rice with wild rice makes the brown rice taste even better, and adding amaranth, wild leeks, and herbs improves it even more.

1 cup medium-grain brown rice

2 cups ramp bulbs, chopped

3⅞ cups water

½ cup wild rice (page 353)

½ cup amaranth (page 338)

2 cloves garlic, chopped

2 teaspoons dried sage, finely crumbled

2 teaspoons dried thyme, finely crumbled

2 teaspoons dried rosemary, finely crumbled

2 tablespoons olive oil

1 tablespoon tamari soy sauce

Dash of Tabasco sauce

In a large saucepan, combine all the ingredients and bring the pot to a boil. Reduce the heat to low, and simmer, covered, until all the water is absorbed and the rice is tender, about 40 minutes.

MAKES 6 CUPS; SERVES 6

RAMP RISOTTO

Ramps and black walnuts make this the best baked rice and cheese casserole you've ever tasted.

2 tablespoons olive oil

4 cups ramp leaves, chopped

2 large cloves garlic, chopped

3⅔ cups water

2 cups Tofu Cottage Cheese (page 30)

1 cup long-grain brown rice

1 cup brown basmati rice

¾ cup black walnuts (page 375), pine nuts,
   or regular walnuts

2 tablespoons tamari soy sauce

1 tablespoon freshly grated lemon rind

1 tablespoon chili paste or ½ teaspoon cayenne
   pepper, or to taste

1. Preheat the oven to 375 degrees.

2. Heat the olive oil in a large skillet over medium heat, add the ramps and garlic, and cook, stirring, for 5 minutes.

3. Mix the ramps and garlic with the remaining ingredients in a 3-quart oiled casserole dish and bake, covered, until all the water is absorbed, 1¼ to 1½ hours.

SERVES 6 TO 8

RAMPAROLE

Here's another quick, easy way to showcase the best qualities of ramps.

18 cups ramp leaves

2 cups Tofu Cottage Cheese (page 30)

⅔ cup cooked corn kernels

1 cup Mock Egg Sauce (page 35)

2 tablespoon olive oil

1¾ cups fresh Bread Crumbs (page 40)

1. Preheat the oven to 375 degrees.

2. Wash off the ramp leaves, shake off any excess water, and place the ramps in a large, heavy saucepan, Cover the pot and cook the ramps over low heat until they are just wilted, 10 to 15 minutes.

3. Mix the ramp leaves with the Tofu Cottage Cheese, cooked corn, and egg sauce in a 3-quart oiled casserole dish.

4. Mix the olive oil with the bread crumbs and spread this mixture over the top of the vegetable mixture. Bake the casserole, uncovered, for 30 minutes.

SERVES 6

MEDIEVAL-STYLE WILD LEEKS

Medieval people may have cooked the plants we know as cultivated leeks with seasonings similar to those in this recipe, using poppy seeds as a thickener. American wild leeks replace cultivated leeks here, and corn oil and silken tofu serve as healthful alternatives to butter and cream.

¼ cup corn oil

10 cups ramp leaves, chopped

6 cloves garlic, chopped

6 tablespoons freshly ground white or black poppy seeds

2 teaspoons ground cinnamon

2 teaspoons ground ginger

2 teaspoons Vege-Sal or 1 teaspoon salt, or to taste

1 teaspoon saffron threads, finely crumbled

2 teaspoons freshly grated nutmeg

2 teaspoons freshly ground black pepper (1 teaspoon peppercorns)

½ teaspoon freshly ground cloves

2 cups water

2 tablespoons red wine vinegar

⅔ cup drained silken tofu

1. In a large skillet over medium heat, heat the corn oil. Add the ramps and garlic and cook, stirring, for 5 minutes.

2. Meanwhile, in a blender, combine the remaining ingredients and process until smooth. Pour the purée over the ramp mixture and bring the pot to a boil over medium heat, stirring constantly. Reduce the heat to low, cover, and simmer for 5 minutes.

SERVES 6

BAKED RAMPS

This variation of a classic onion lover's recipe works even better with the finest member of the onion family. The recipe uses an odd measurement of ramps (1⅓ cups) because that's what I happened to have in the refrigerator when I invented this recipe.

1 ⅓ cups ramp bulbs

1 tablespoon olive oil

1 teaspoon chili paste or Curry Paste (page 37; available in Indian specialty stores) or ½ teaspoon Tabasco sauce

1 teaspoon dried rosemary, finely crumbled

1 teaspoon tamari soy sauce

1. Preheat the oven to 350 degrees.

2. Place the ramps in a 1½-quart oiled casserole dish.

3. In a small bowl, mix together the remaining ingredients. Pour half the sauce over the ramps and bake them, covered, for 1 hour, basting them every 20 minutes with the remainder of the sauce.

SERVES 4

BROCCOLI INDIAN STYLE

Wild leeks add extra life to the Indian seasonings and sauce that flavor this familiar vegetable.

3 tablespoons peanut oil

1 tablespoon coriander seeds

2 ½ teaspoons cumin seeds

½ cinnamon stick

2 teaspoons black peppercorns

1 teaspoon cardamom seeds

3 cloves

4 cloves garlic, chopped

3 small chiles, or to taste, seeds and ribs removed
  and chopped

1 large head broccoli, stems and florets sliced

8 ramp bulbs, sliced

SAUCE

  1 ½ cups water

  ½ cup drained silken tofu

  ½ cup raw cashews

  2 tablespoons corn oil

  2 tablespoons fresh lemon juice

  2 teaspoons Vege-Sal or 1 teaspoon salt

  ½ teaspoon freshly grated nutmeg

1. Heat the peanut oil in a large saucepan over medium heat, add the coriander seeds, cumin seeds, cinnamon stick, peppercorns, cardamom seeds, and cloves, and cook for 2 minutes, stirring often. Add the garlic, chiles, broccoli, and ramp bulbs and cook, stirring, for 5 minutes.

2. *To make the sauce:* In a blender, combine all the sauce ingredients and process until smooth. Pour the sauce over the broccoli mixture. Bring the pot to a boil, reduce the heat to low, cover, and simmer until the broccoli is tender, 5 to 10 minutes.

SERVES 4 TO 6

VEGAN SCRAMBLED EGGS WITH RAMPS

This vegan recipe tastes so much like scrambled eggs, I was going to announce that you couldn't possibly lay an egg when you prepare it. But maybe I should say that you'll lay an egg every time!

  One 19-ounce package soft tofu, drained

  2 tablespoons olive oil

  2 tablespoons flaxseed oil or corn oil

24 ramp bulbs or 3 medium-size red onions, chopped

1 teaspoon turmeric

4 cloves garlic, chopped

One 19-ounce package silken tofu, drained

2 tablespoons Black Locust Blossom Wine (page
  182) or white wine

5 tablespoons freshly ground flaxseeds
  (2 tablespoons seeds)

1 tablespoon chopped fresh cilantro leaves

1 teaspoon Vege-Sal or ½ teaspoon salt, or to taste

2 teaspoons freshly ground black pepper
  (1 teaspoon peppercorns)

½ teaspoon dried sage, finely crumbled

½ teaspoon freshly grated nutmeg

¼ teaspoon freshly ground fenugreek seeds

¼ cup lecithin granules

1. In a food processor or with a grater, grate the soft tofu.

2. Heat the olive oil and flaxseed oil together in a large skillet over medium heat and add the grated tofu, ramps, and ½teaspoon of the turmeric. Cook the mixture, stirring often, for 5 minutes. Add the garlic and cook, stirring, for another 2 minutes.

3. Meanwhile, in a food processor, combine the silken tofu, wine, ground flaxseeds, cilantro, Vege-Sal, pepper, sage, nutmeg, the remaining turmeric, the fenugreek seeds, and lecithin granules and process until smooth. Stir this sauce into the skillet with the ramp mixture, reduce the heat to low, cover, and cook for 15 minutes. Serve over toast.

SERVES 4 TO 6

RAMP BULBS GREEK STYLE

Mediterranean seasonings complement the foremost representative of the onion family, creating a quick, simple cold appetizer that will delight all onion lovers. Serve Greek-style ramps on a bed of lettuce with olives.

   2 cups ramp bulbs
   ¼ cup chopped celery
   2 cloves garlic, crushed into a paste
   2 tablespoons olive oil
   2 tablespoons fresh lemon juice
   2 tablespoons water
   1 tablespoon Ramp Wine (page 129) or white wine
   1 tablespoon red wine vinegar
   1 teaspoon freshly ground black pepper
      (½ teaspoon peppercorns)
   ½ teaspoon freshly ground coriander seeds
   ½ teaspoon freshly ground fennel seeds
   ½ teaspoon dried thyme, finely crumbled
   ½ teaspoon Vege-Sal or ¼ teaspoon salt, or to taste
   1 bayberry leaf (page 185)

Place all the ingredients in a small saucepan over medium heat and bring the pot to a boil. Reduce the heat to medium-low, and simmer, covered, for 15 minutes. Remove the bayberry leaf and chill the dish before serving.

MAKES 2 CUPS

WILD LEEK CHILI
This spicy vegetarian chili will knock your socks off.

   ¼ cup olive oil, or as needed
   6 celery stalks, sliced
   8 wild carrots (page 73) or 4 cultivated carrots, sliced
   1 green bell pepper, seeded and sliced into strips
   25 ramp bulbs or 2 large onions, chopped
   1 cup hen-of-the-woods mushroom (page 363) or other mushrooms, sliced
   5 cloves garlic, or to taste, chopped
   Two and a half 22.5-ounce jars tomato sauce
   1 cup Blackberry Spice Wine (page 278) or red wine
   3 ounces low-sodium pitted olives, drained
   ¼ cup Chili Powder (page 36), or to taste
   1 tablespoon Vege-Sal or 1 ½ teaspoons salt, or to taste

1. Heat the olive oil in a large skillet over medium heat. Add the celery, wild carrots, green pepper, and ramps, and mushrooms and cook, stirring often, for 10 minutes. Add the garlic and cook, stirring, for another 5 minutes.
2. Meanwhile, bring the rest of the ingredients to a boil in a large pot over medium heat, stirring often. Add the cooked vegetables to the tomato sauce mixture, reduce the heat to low, and simmer, covered, for 1 hour. Serve this chili hot over rice.

MAKES 2 QUARTS

Note: Chili improves as the flavors blend. Store in the refrigerator overnight or for a few days before serving.

RAMP BULB PICKLES
Ramp bulbs are naturally spicy, so their flavor shines through the vinegar and the spices of this recipe, resulting in superb pickles. And they'll last for months refrigerated (if you don't finish them off a lot sooner).

   4½ cups ramp bulbs
   1½ cups brown rice vinegar or other mild-flavored vinegar
   1½ cups water
   1 tablespoon ground bayberry (page 185) or bay leaves

1 tablespoon Vege-Sal or ½ teaspoon salt

2 teaspoons coriander seeds

1 teaspoon dried rosemary

1 teaspoon liquid stevia or 2 tablespoons honey or
barley malt

1. Place the ramp bulbs, vinegar, and water in a large saucepan and bring the pot to a simmer over medium heat. Reduce the heat to medium-low and let the mixture simmer, covered, for 15 minutes. Drain the ramps, reserving the vinegar-water mixture.

2. Put the ramps in a jar, along with a fork to prevent the glass from cracking.

3. Pour enough of the vinegar-water mixture over the ramp bulbs to cover them.

4. Stir in the remaining ingredients and remove the fork.

5. Cover the jar with a tight-fitting lid, and refrigerate the pickled ramps overnight before eating them.

MAKES 4 ½ CUPS

RAMP WINE

Wild leeks make a pungent white cooking wine that is great for savory recipes that can benefit from more than a hint of onions and garlic. As with all ramp recipes, be prepared for the vegetable's distinct aroma while the wine is fermenting.

6 cups sugar

1 gallon boiling water

2 cups ramp leaves or bulbs

6 cloves garlic, peeled

1 tablespoon celery seeds

½ teaspoon champagne yeast or other wine yeast

1. In a non-metal (plastic or ceramic) food container, dissolve the sugar in the boiling water, and add the ramps, garlic, and celery seeds.

2. When the mixture has cooled to lukewarm, stir in the yeast and cover the container with a non-airtight cover, cheesecloth, or towel. Allow the mixture to ferment for a week at room temperature, stirring it twice a day.

3. Strain the liquid through cheesecloth, transfer the liquid to a jug, and seal the container with an airlock stopper (which lets carbon dioxide bubbles escape but keeps oxygen out).

4. When the bubbling stops and fermentation ends about 3 weeks later, seal the jug with a cork and age the wine for 6 months to a year before using it. Siphon the wine to get rid of the sediment, if desired.

MAKES 1 GALLON

WILD MINT

Mentha arvensis

EDIBLE MINT SPECIES SMELL LIKE MINT, HAVE square stems, opposite (paired) leaves, and clusters of small, bilaterally symmetrical flowers. Wild mint's leaves and unbranched stems are downy, and its bell-shaped pale violet to white flowers cluster in the leaf axils (where the leaves join the stem). Look for this plant in damp soil and along shorelines from spring to fall on the East Coast and California. The whole plant is so strongly flavored of mint, it reminds me of candy whenever I bite into it. This is one of the best mint species for making desserts and sweet sauces. You mainly use the leaves, although flowers and other tender parts are useable. Even the tough parts make great herb tea.

CLEMENTINE'S DELIGHT PUDDING

You'll be as delighted as Clementine once you try this pudding based on the sweet, small, seedless tangerine named after the darling of the nineteenth-century ballad. And wild mint enhances the pudding's flavor.

2 ¼ cups soy milk or nut milk

¾ cup raw cashews

½ cup canola oil

¼ cup vegetable glycerin, honey, barley malt, or rice syrup, or to taste

¼ cup lecithin granules

¼ cup kudzu or arrowroot

2 teaspoons vanilla extract

Freshly grated rind of 1 clementine orange or tangerine

1 teaspoon dried wild mint (page 129) or other mint, finely crumbled, or 1 tablespoon finely chopped fresh leaves

1 teaspoon liquid stevia (optional)

¼ teaspoon orange extract (optional)

¼ teaspoon salt

¼ teaspoon ground cinnamon

7 clementine oranges or tangerines, peeled and seeds (if any) removed

1 cup fresh Bread Crumbs (page 40)

1. Place all the ingredients, except for 2 of the clementines and the bread crumbs, in a blender and process until smooth.

2. Divide the remaining clementines into sections and stir them into the purée along with the bread crumbs. Transfer the mixture to an oiled baking dish and bake, uncovered, until set, about 40 minutes. Serve hot or cold.

SERVES 6

GOUTWEED

Aegopodium podagraria L.

THIS PLANT HAS COMPOUND PALMATE LEAVES (the leaf divisions all connect to one point, like the fingers connecting to the palm of your hand), and the serrated lobes are sometimes divided into two, sometimes three lobes. Leaves and stems emerge from the ground in early spring, and by late spring there's a flower stalk over a foot tall with a cluster of umbrella-like white flowers. Tiny cylindrical seeds replace the flowers in late summer. The whole plant smells like celery or parsley when crushed.

A garden escapee, it grows in partially shaded wooded areas and cultivated parks and is most common in the Northeast.

Caution: Don't confuse goutweed with other plants that have umbrella-shaped flower clusters but different leaves, which may be poisonous.

This common wild green tastes like an exotic combination of parsley and celery leaves. Using it in place of parsley will transform an ordinary dish into something special.

HEALTHY HOLLANDAISE SAUCE

Traditional hollandaise sauce is loaded with egg yolks. This version omits the cholesterol by substituting lecithin granules to create the egg yolk flavor, and using silken tofu to provide a creamy texture. The goutweed replaces the parsley, providing a more exotic flavor. Serve this sauce on cooked asparagus, artichokes, cauliflower, avocado, or any cooked cultivated or wild vegetable.

Hollandaise sauce was one of my favorite gourmet recipes when I used to eat eggs, so I was very happy to find a way to make a simple vegan version. Cooking traditional hollandaise sauce over high heat destroys it. High heat destroys the texture of Healthy Hollandaise Sauce, but you can prevent that by adding 2 tablespoons arrowroot to the sauce before cooking it further.

One 19-ounce package silken tofu, well drained
½ cup water
½ cup fresh lemon juice (2 large lemons)
½ cup corn oil, flaxseed oil, or olive oil
¼ cup goutweed leaves
3 tablespoons lecithin granules
1 teaspoon freshly ground yellow mustard seeds
* (½ teaspoon seeds)*
1 teaspoon freshly ground white pepper
* (½ teaspoon peppercorns)*
½ teaspoon freshly grated nutmeg
¼ teaspoon turmeric
1 teaspoon Vege-Sal or ½ teaspoon salt, or to taste

1. In a food processor or blender, combine all the ingredients and process until smooth.

2. Transfer the mixture to a saucepan and heat it all the way through over low heat. Do not bring the sauce to a boil or it will lose its texture and become watery. Healthy Hollandaise Sauce will keep, tightly covered, in the refrigerator for up to 1 week.

MAKES 5½ CUPS

TOFU HERB CHEESE

Here's another dairy-free cheese with tofu as the base and the other components of cheese, such as the fermentation flavor, sourness, fattiness, color, and sharpness provided by appropriate nondairy ingredients. As in dairy-based herb cheeses, the addition of the herbs further increases the flavor. Enjoy this cheese as is, or use it as a spread, or wherever cheese is called for.

4 cloves garlic, peeled
2 tablespoons chopped goutweed leaves
One 19-ounce package soft tofu, well drained
2 tablespoons lecithin granules
1 tablespoon brewer's yeast
1 teaspoon dried rosemary, finely crumbled
½ teaspoon dried sage, finely crumbled
½ teaspoon hot paprika
1 teaspoon Vege-Sal or ½ teaspoon salt
1 teaspoon freshly ground white pepper
* (½ teaspoon peppercorns)*
¼ teaspoon turmeric
2 tablespoons olive oil
1 tablespoon red wine vinegar
1 tablespoon brown rice vinegar
½ teaspoon Tabasco sauce

1. Finely chop the garlic and goutweed in a food processor or by hand.

2. Add the remaining ingredients and process (or mash with a potato masher or fork) until they are well blended. Tofu Herb Cheese will keep, tightly covered, in the refrigerator for up to a week. It also freezes well.

MAKES 2 CUPS

ALL-PURPOSE HERB STUFFING

This traditional-style stuffing is great for stuffing vegetables, mushrooms, and veggie loaves. Goutweed and carrot seeds add greatly to the flavor of this stuffing.

Use it in any recipe that calls for stuffing.

> ¼ cup corn oil or olive oil
>
> 1 small onion, chopped
>
> 2 cloves garlic, crushed
>
> 4 cups fresh bread cubes
>
> 1 celery stalk, sliced
>
> ¼ cup goutweed leaves, chopped
>
> 1 teaspoon tamari soy sauce, or to taste
>
> 1 teaspoon dried sage, finely crumbled
>
> 1 teaspoon dried rosemary, finely crumbled
>
> 1 teaspoon dried marjoram, finely crumbled
>
> 1 teaspoon hot paprika
>
> ½ teaspoon dried thyme, finely crumbled
>
> ½ teaspoon freshly ground black pepper
>   (¼ teaspoon peppercorns)
>
> ¼ teaspoon freshly ground wild carrot seeds (page
>   73; optional)

1. Heat the oil in a small skillet over medium heat and add the onions and garlic. Cook them, stirring, until they are slightly browned, about 10 minutes.

2. Mix the onions and garlic with the remaining ingredients in a large bowl.

MAKES 4 CUPS

WILD HUMMUS

Goutweed brightens the flavor of this traditional Middle Eastern spread.

> 2 teaspoons any wild garlic bulbs (page 160), or
>   2 cloves regular garlic, peeled
>
> 1 tablespoon chopped fresh basil leaves or
>   1 teaspoon dried, finely crumbled
>
> 2 tablespoons chopped goutweed leaves
>
> ½ medium-size red onion

> 2 ½ cups cooked chickpeas, drained
>
> ½ cup Tahini (page 38)
>
> ¼ cup mellow (light-colored) miso
>
> 3 tablespoons fresh lemon juice
>
> 2 tablespoons olive oil
>
> 1 teaspoon dried oregano, finely crumbled
>
> 1 teaspoon chili paste or ½ teaspoon cayenne
>   pepper, or to taste
>
> ½ teaspoon freshly ground cumin seeds

1. In a food processor, chop the garlic, fresh basil, and goutweed. Add the onion and process again.

2. Add the remaining ingredients and process until smooth. Wild Hummus will keep, tightly covered, in the refrigerator for up to a week.

MAKES 3 ½ CUPS

GARLIC BUTTER

Use this buttery vegan spread on wild and unwild bread, for sautéing, or on popcorn.

> 1 cup flaxseed oil or corn oil
>
> ½ cup olive oil
>
> ¼ cup goutweed leaves
>
> ¼ cup mellow (light-colored) miso
>
> 1 teaspoon dried tarragon, finely crumbled
>
> 1 teaspoon freshly ground white pepper
>   (½ teaspoon peppercorns)
>
> 6 cloves garlic, roasted and peeled

In a blender, combine all the ingredients and process until smooth. Garlic Butter will keep, tightly covered, in the refrigerator for up to 2 weeks.

MAKES 2 CUPS

OSTRICH FERN FIDDLEHEAD

Matteuccia pensylvanica

HERE'S OUR BEST EDIBLE FERN AND ONE OF THE most sought after wild foods; it is even available seasonally in green markets. The mature feathery vegetative fronds resemble ostrich feathers and are 2 to 6 feet tall, with toothed leaflets arising from the stem in a curved arch. The fronds arise from the ground configured like a vase. Stiff, leathery reproductive fronds, with their rounded podlike spore containers, grow within the vegetative fronds and barely reach 2 feet in height.

The fiddlehead, the only edible part (mature fronds are poisonous), has a firm, stout, hairless stalk covered with brown papery scales. (Many other species, though not poisonous, are fuzzy and awful tasting.) The fiddlehead tapers toward a curled top that looks like the top of a violin. The plant grows in swamps, and it can be collected for less than 2 weeks every spring before the season ends.

Caution: Never take more than half of each bunch of fiddleheads or you may deplete the perennial underground rhizome's energy reserves and injure the plant.

Gourmet chefs have been using ostrich fern's fiddleheads for years. Because of their delicate flavor, you should season fiddleheads very gently and avoid drowning out their flavor with too many other ingredients. You may sauté them; simmer them in soups, stews, or sauces; or use them raw (with caution—some people reportedly don't tolerate raw fiddleheads) in salads. Fiddleheads cook in about 10 to 20 minutes.

SPRINGTIME MEDLEY SOUP

This soup largely consists of common wild foods you can find in the wild in the springtime. There's no better way to celebrate the season than to partake of nature's wild harvest.

> 6 cups Vegetable Stock (page 40)
> 1 cup barley
> ¼ cup burdock root (page 139), very thinly sliced on the diagonal
> 1 ½ teaspoons chopped fresh wild spearmint (page 59) or other mint leaves
> ½ teaspoon dried rosemary, finely crumbled
> ¼ teaspoon dried sage, finely crumbled
> ¼ teaspoon dried oregano, finely crumbled
> ½ tablespoon tamari soy sauce, or to taste
> ¾ cup sliced carrots
> 2 cups ramp leaves (page 116), thinly sliced, or shallots, sliced
> 1 cup daylily shoots (page 64) or scallions, sliced
> ½ cup ostrich fern fiddleheads, chopped
> ¼ cup sliced Japanese knotweed shoots (page 98) or rhubarb stalks

1. Bring the stock and barley to a boil in a large saucepan over medium heat. Reduce the heat to medium-low and simmer, covered, for 50 minutes.
2. Add the burdock, spearmint, rosemary, sage, oregano, and tamari and simmer for 10 minutes. Add the carrots and simmer for 5 minutes. Add the remaining ingredients and simmer for 5 minutes more.

SERVES 8

POLENTA WITH OYSTERS AND FIDDLEHEADS

This Italian setting for oyster mushrooms and fiddleheads brings out the best in all the ingredients. For even more flavor, you may first parch the cornmeal for 30 minutes in a roasting pan in a preheated 350-degree oven, stirring occasionally.

POLENTA

4 cups yellow cornmeal

5 cups boiling water

Vege-Sal or salt, as needed

VEGETABLES

2½ cups tempeh (fermented soybean grits)
cut into strips 1½ x ½ inch

2 tablespoons any whole-grain flour

¼ cup corn oil or olive oil

6 cups oyster mushrooms (page 404), sliced

4 cups ostrich fern fiddleheads, chopped

4 cloves garlic, crushed

1 teaspoon dried rosemary, finely crumbled

½ teaspoon freshly ground black pepper
(¼ teaspoon peppercorns), or to taste

½ cup White Oak Wine (page 176) or sherry

1 tablespoon tamari soy sauce

1. *To make the polenta:* In a large saucepan, gradually stir the cornmeal into the boiling water over low heat, using a whisk at first and switching to a wooden spoon when the mush begins to thicken. Continue to cook the cornmeal over low heat, stirring often, until it is very thick, about 40 minutes.

2. Empty the polenta onto a cutting board and allow it to cool. Salt it to taste and use it as is, or sauté it in corn oil.

3. *To prepare the oysters and fiddleheads:* Roll the tempeh in the flour. Heat the olive oil in a large skillet over medium heat, add the tempeh and mushrooms and cook, stirring occasionally, for 10 minutes. Add the fiddleheads, garlic, rosemary, and pepper and cook, stirring, for another 5 minutes.

4. Add the wine and tamari, reduce the heat to low, cover, and simmer the vegetables for 10 minutes, stirring occasionally.

5. Serve the vegetables over the polenta.

SERVES 6 TO 8

SCALLOPED FIDDLEHEADS

Fiddleheads have such a mild, delicate flavor that I used to have a hard time using them. The solution is to strive for simplicity, as in, for example, this casserole of fiddleheads, sauce, and oiled bread crumbs.

4 cups ostrich fern fiddleheads, coarsely chopped

1½ cups Tofu Cream Cheese (page 30)

1½ cups fresh Bread Crumbs (page 40)

2 tablespoons corn oil

1. Preheat the oven to 350 degrees.

2. Place the fiddleheads in a 3-quart oiled casserole dish.

3. Spread the Tofu Cream Cheese over the fiddleheads.

4. Combine the bread crumbs with the corn oil and spread this mixture over the layer of Tofu Cream Cheese. Bake the casserole, uncovered, until it is lightly brown on top, 30 to 40 minutes.

SERVES 6

FIDDLEHEADS WITH SESAME NOODLES

You'll love the delicate flavor of fiddleheads when they're served on noodles after simmering in sesame sauce.

1 cup Tahini (page 38)

¼ cup mellow (light-colored) miso

¼ cup fresh cilantro or parsley leaves

¼ cup fresh lemon juice

8 cloves garlic, peeled

2 teaspoons freshly ground cumin seeds

2 teaspoons chili paste or ¼ teaspoon cayenne
pepper, or to taste

1 ¼ cups water

8 cups ostrich fern fiddleheads, chopped

4 cups Buckwheat Noodles (page 34) or store-
bought noodles

2 teaspoons olive oil

1. In a blender, combine the tahini, miso, cilantro, lemon juice, garlic, cumin, chili paste, and water and process until smooth.

2. Transfer the sauce to a large saucepan and bring the pot to a gentle boil over medium heat. Reduce the heat to low, add the fiddleheads, and simmer them until they are tender, 5 to 10 minutes.

3. Meanwhile, cook the noodles as directed in boiling salted water, drain them, and toss them with the olive oil.

4. Serve the fiddleheads and sauce over the noodles.

SERVES 6

OSTRICH-STUFFED EGGPLANT

Ostrich fern fiddleheads with seasoning and Tofu Cream Cheese make a wonderful stuffing for this Middle Eastern appetizer.

2 large eggplants

4 cups ostrich fern fiddleheads, coarsely chopped

1 cup Tofu Cream Cheese (page 30)

6 cloves garlic, crushed

2 tablespoons chopped fresh basil leaves

2 teaspoons dried oregano, finely crumbled

2 teaspoons Vege-Sal or 1 teaspoon salt

1 teaspoon freshly ground fennel seeds

2 tablespoons sesame seeds

1. Preheat the oven to 350 degrees. Prick the eggplants with a fork to prevent them from exploding. Place the eggplants on a rack set over a cookie sheet, and bake until they are tender, about 50 minutes.

2. When the eggplants are cool enough to handle, cut them in half lengthwise and use a spoon to remove most of the pulp, being careful not to break the skin. In a large bowl, mix the eggplant pulp with the remaining ingredients, except the sesame seeds.

3. Mound the stuffing back into the eggplant halves and sprinkle the sesame seeds on top.

4. Arrange the stuffed eggplants on an oiled cookie sheet, and bake them for 30 minutes. Serve hot or cold.

SERVES 8

WILD RICE WITH FIDDLEHEADS

The hearty flavor of wild rice and the mild taste of ostrich fern fiddleheads make for a winning combination.

2 ⅔ cups water

1 cup brown basmati rice

1 cup wild rice (page 353)

2 cups ostrich fern fiddleheads, chopped

1 tablespoon corn oil or flaxseed oil

1 teaspoon dried marjoram, finely crumbled

1 teaspoon dried tarragon, finely crumbled

¾ teaspoon freshly ground celery seeds
(½ teaspoon seeds)

2 teaspoons Vege-Sal or 1 teaspoon salt, or to taste

1 teaspoon Tabasco sauce, or to taste

Bring all the ingredients to a boil in a large saucepan set over medium heat. Reduce the heat to low, cover, and simmer until all the water is absorbed and the rice is tender, about 40 minutes.

SERVES 6

FIDDLEHEAD CASSEROLE

Baking fiddleheads over noodles with a mildly seasoned sauce brings out the best these infant ferns have to offer.

> 4 cups Buckwheat Noodles (page 34)
> Olive oil
>
> SAUCE
>
> 2 cups water
> 3 tablespoons arrowroot or kudzu
> 4 cloves garlic, peeled
> ¼ cup corn oil or olive oil
> ¼ cup mellow (light-colored) miso
> ½ cup drained silken tofu
> 2 tablespoons chopped fresh parsley leaves
> ¼ teaspoon ground dried wild ginger (page 111)
>   or regular ground ginger
> ½ teaspoon freshly ground black pepper
>   (¼ teaspoon peppercorns)
>
> 4 cups ostrich fern fiddleheads, coarsely chopped

1. Preheat the oven to 350 degrees.
2. Cook the noodles in rapidly boiling salted water with a dash of olive oil for 2 minutes. Drain the noodles in a colander and then lower the colander in a bowl of cold water to halt the cooking.
3. Meanwhile, in a blender, combine all the sauce ingredients and process until smooth.
4. Layer a 3-quart oiled casserole dish with half the noodles, one third of the sauce, half the fiddleheads,

half the remaining sauce, the remaining noodles, the remaining fiddleheads, and the remaining sauce. Bake the casserole until it is bubbly, about 30 minutes.

SERVES 6

FIDDLEHEADS ALMONDINE

This combination of yellow peppers, almonds, and a mild cream sauce showcasing fiddleheads is a great way to enjoy the arrival of spring.

> SAUTÉ
>
> ¼ cup almond oil or olive oil
> 8 cups ostrich fern fiddleheads, coarsely chopped
> One 16-ounce package extra-firm tofu, drained
>   and diced
> 2 yellow bell peppers, seeded and sliced into strips
> 2 teaspoons peeled and finely chopped fresh ginger
>
> SAUCE
>
> 2½ cups water
> 1 cup drained silken tofu
> ¼ cup mellow (light-colored) miso
> 2 tablespoons lecithin granules
> 2 tablespoons corn oil
> 2 tablespoons chopped fresh dill
> 2 tablespoons chopped fresh wild mint (page 129)
>   or other mint leaves
> Juice of ½ lemon (2 tablespoons)
> 1 teaspoon freshly grated nutmeg
> 1 teaspoon almond extract
> 1 teaspoon freshly ground white pepper
>   (½ teaspoon peppercorns)
>
> 1 cup slivered almonds
> 1 tablespoon poppy seeds

1. *To make the sauté:* Heat the oil in a large skillet over medium heat. Add the remaining sauté ingredients and cook, stirring, for 10 minutes.

2. *To make the sauce:* In a blender, combine the sauce ingredients and process until smooth.

3. Stir the sauce and the remaining ingredients into the sautéed ingredients and bring the pot to a boil over medium heat, stirring often. Reduce the heat to low, cover, and simmer for 10 minutes. Serve Fiddleheads Almondine over brown rice or with homemade bread.

SERVES 6

WILD VEGETABLE PIE

This savory pie includes some of the best wild vegetables of springtime.

CRUST

1 ⅔ cups (½ pound) buckwheat flour and 3 ⅓ cups (1 pound) sweet brown rice flour, or 1 ½ pounds any other whole-grain flour

½ cup arrowroot or kudzu

1 teaspoon dried marjoram, finely crumbled

1 teaspoon dried savory, finely crumbled

1 teaspoon dried rosemary, finely crumbled

½ teaspoon Vege-Sal or ¼ teaspoon salt, or to taste

¼ cup olive oil

¾ cup plus 2 tablespoons water

GRAVY

2 tablespoons olive oil

6 tablespoons sweet brown rice flour or any other whole-grain flour

¾ teaspoon freshly ground celery seeds (½ teaspoon seeds)

½ teaspoon dried sage, finely crumbled

½ teaspoon dried thyme, finely crumbled

2 cups boiling Vegetable Stock (page 40)

2 tablespoons Bragg's Liquid Aminos or tamari soy sauce, 1 teaspoon Vege-Sal, or ½ teaspoon salt, or to taste

2 teaspoons chili paste or ½ teaspoon cayenne pepper, or to taste

FILLING

2 cups sliced potatoes, cooked until tender in water to cover and drained

2 cups sliced cow parsnip stalks (page 146) or celery

1 cup ramp leaves (page 116) or chopped onions

1 cup curly dock (page 109) or spinach leaves, chopped

1 cup ostrich fern fiddleheads, coarsely chopped

3 cloves garlic, crushed

1. *To make the crust:* In a large bowl, mix together the flours, arrowroot, marjoram, savory, rosemary, and Vege-Sal. Stir in the olive oil. Mix in the water and knead the dough briefly. Chill the dough while you prepare the gravy and filling.

2. *To prepare the gravy:* Heat the olive oil over medium heat in a large saucepan. Add the sweet brown rice flour, ground celery seeds, sage, and thyme, and cook for 3 to 4 minutes, stirring constantly. Slowly add the boiling vegetable stock, Bragg's Liquid Aminos, and chili paste, stirring constantly. (If lumps form, carefully purée the gravy in a blender, holding down the lid with a towel and beginning on low speed to prevent eruption.) Reduce the heat to low and simmer, covered, for 5 to 10 minutes, stirring occasionally.

3. *To make the filling:* Add all the filling ingredients to the gravy.

4. Preheat the oven to 425 degrees.

5. Divide the dough into 4 parts. On a floured pastry sheet, using a rolling pin enclosed in a floured sleeve, roll out one part of dough ⅜ inch thick, or big enough to fill a 9-inch pie pan. Roll the dough and pastry sheet around the rolling pin, transfer the dough to an oiled 9-inch pie tin, peel off the pastry sheet, and push the dough into place.

6. Pour in half the filling mixture.

7. Roll out another portion of the dough to serve as the top crust. Moisten the edge of the lower crust with water. Transfer the top crust to the pie. Press the edges together to seal them, and trim off the excess dough.

8. Repeat steps 5 through 7 with the remaining filling and dough for the second pie and cut slits into the top crust to let the steam escape. Bake the pies for 5 minutes at 425 degrees, and then reduce the oven temperature to 350 degrees and bake the pies until the filling is bubbly, another 45 minutes.

MAKES TWO 9-INCH PIES; SERVES 8

BAKED TOFU PIE

This casserole consists of layers of tofu and delicately flavored wild vegetables in a creamy peanut sauce.

4 cups ostrich fern fiddleheads

Three 16-ounce packages extra-firm tofu, well
drained and sliced ½ inch thick along the
largest surface

4 cups daylily shoots (page 64)

4 cups cooked chicken mushrooms (page 321)

¼ cup tamari soy sauce

4 cups Anise-Peanut Sauce (page 93)

1. Preheat the oven to 350 degrees.

2. Layer a 3-quart oiled casserole dish with fiddleheads, tofu slices, daylily shoots, and cooked chicken mushrooms.

3. In a medium-size bowl, mix together the tamari and

Anise Peanut Sauce and pour it over the other ingredients. Bake the casserole, covered, for 45 minutes.

SERVES 6

SHEEP SORREL
Rumex acetosella L.

HERE'S A PLANT WITH A STALKED LEAF THAT can grow up to 4 inches long and ¾ inch wide and resembles a sheep's face. The base has two lateral lobes, like ears, and the tip is pointed, like a nose. Basal rosettes of these leaves emerge from the ground in early spring and late fall. Later in the spring the same leaves, as well as clusters of tiny reddish flowers (followed by inconspicuous papery fruits) grow on a slender, upright flower stalk that can reach 20 inches in height.

Wood sorrel (*Oxalis* species) doesn't look like sheep sorrel at all (see page 183). It has three leaves shaped like hearts. Although more delicate, it has the same lemony flavor as sheep sorrel, and you can usually interchange these two widespread plants in recipes.

Look for sheep sorrel in meadows and fields with acidic soil throughout the United States. Collect the leaves in spring, summer, and fall. This sour-flavored plant is stronger tasting and better than cultivated sorrel (also called schav). Use sheep sorrel in recipes with mild-tasting ingredients, where a tang is welcome. It's great raw in salads, and you can apply any cooking method to it. It cooks in 5 to 10 minutes.

SHEEP SORREL SPREAD

Sheep sorrel's piquant, lemony flavor adds distinction to this avocado-based spread. It's great on bread, crackers, and muffins.

2 medium-size red onions, peeled

2 medium-size ripe avocados, peeled and pitted

2 cups sheep sorrel, wood sorrel (page 183), or garden sorrel leaves

¼ cup wild onion (page 57) or wild garlic leaves (page 160), chives, or scallion greens, chopped

One 6-ounce jar low-sodium pitted olives, drained

Juice of 1 lemon

2 tablespoons mellow (light-colored) miso

1 teaspoon chili paste or ¼ teaspoon cayenne pepper, or to taste

Chop the onions by hand. In a food processor, combine the onions and the remaining ingredients and chop them fine. Sheep Sorrel Spread will keep, tightly covered, in the refrigerator for up to 10 days.

MAKES 3 ¾ CUPS

CREAM OF SORREL SOUP

This thick soup uses potatoes for thickness and sheep sorrel and other vegetables for flavor.

8 cups Vegetable Stock (page 40)

6 medium-size potatoes, chopped

2 tablespoons olive oil

6 celery stalks, sliced

2 frying peppers or 1 green bell pepper, seeded and sliced into strips

6 cloves garlic, crushed

4 small chiles, seeds and ribs removed and finely chopped

8 cups sheep sorrel or wood sorrel (page 183) leaves

2 teaspoons dried tarragon, finely crumbled

2 teaspoons dried sage, finely crumbled

1 tablespoon dried oregano, finely crumbled

2 teaspoons freshly grated nutmeg

1 teaspoon freshly ground fenugreek seeds

½ cup mellow (light-colored) miso

1. Bring the stock and potatoes to a boil in a large saucepan over medium heat. Reduce the heat to medium-low and simmer the potatoes for 20 minutes.
2. Meanwhile, heat the olive oil in a medium-size skillet over medium heat, add the celery and frying peppers, and cook, stirring, for 10 minutes. Add the garlic and chiles and cook, stirring, for another 2 minutes.
3. Add the sautéed ingredients and all the remaining ingredients, except the miso, to the potatoes and stock and simmer the mixture for 10 minutes more.
4. Carefully transfer the soup to in a blender in batches, adding the miso, and process until smooth. Start on low speed and hold down the lid with a towel at first, to prevent eruptions.

SERVES 12

BURDOCK ROOT
Arctium species

THIS MAJOR WILD FOOD HAS LONG-STALKED, wedge-shaped leaves reminiscent of an elephant's ears, 2 feet long and 1 foot across. Unlike similar-looking leaves, they're white and fuzzy underneath. The basal rosette of leaves stays close to the ground the first year and the beginning of the second. Then, in mid-spring of year two, a central flower stalk 2 to 9 feet tall appears. The flowers resemble purple shaving brushes, and the fruits that follow are globular brown burrs that stick to clothing and anything else that brushes up against them. After dispersing its seeds, this biennial dies. Look for burdock in disturbed habitats, along roadsides, and in vacant lots and fields. It grows throughout North America, except in the Deep South.

You can harvest the deep, large, beige taproot when the plant is in the basal rosette form (as soon as the flower stalk appears, the root becomes tough and woody) from early spring to late fall. Its hearty flavor is a little like that of potatoes, although the plant is related to artichokes.

Scrub the root with a coarse copper scouring pad, but don't peel it. Slice it razor-thin on a diagonal, Asian style, or process it using the finest slicing disk of a food processor. Simmer the root until it is tender, about 20 minutes. You may also sauté the root for the first 10 minutes, but then add liquid and cook it in moist heat for another 10 minutes, or it may not get tender. You can dry thinly sliced burdock root in a food dehydrator, or by leaving the slices in a paper bag for a few weeks.

The immature flower stalk (see page 198) can also be gathered in late spring, before the flowers appear, while the flower stalk is still tender and very flexible. Peeled and parboiled for 1 minute to get rid of the bitterness, it tastes like artichoke heart, and it will enhance any traditional recipe that calls for artichoke hearts. Cook burdock for another 5 to 10 minutes after parboiling it for 1 minute.

PICKLED BURDOCK ROOT

People used to pickle food to preserve it before they had refrigeration, because vinegar stops bacteria from growing. Pickling makes food tasty and healthful, unless the pickled food is overly salted or chemically contaminated. The process works especially well with burdock root.

4 cups burdock root, cut into finger-size pieces
1 cup brown rice vinegar
1 cup water
18 common spicebush berries (page 314) or 2 tablespoons allspice berries
2 tablespoons bayberry leaves (page 185) or bay leaves
1 tablespoon star anise
2 tablespoons peeled and sliced fresh ginger
2 teaspoons black mustard seeds
1 teaspoon cloves
1 teaspoon Vege-Sal or ½ teaspoon salt

1. Steam the burdock on a steamer rack until it is tender enough to pierce with a fork, 30 to 40 minutes. Drain the burdock and transfer it to a jar, placing a fork in the jar to keep it from shattering.
2. Meanwhile, mix together the vinegar and water in a small saucepan and bring the pot to a boil. Pour the mixture over the burdock and stir in the remaining ingredients.
3. Remove the fork, cover the jar, and refrigerate the pickles at least 12 hours before serving. Pickled Burdock Root lasts for weeks, refrigerated.

MAKES 4 CUPS

BURDOCK ROOT SOUP

This simple soup, made with stock, a root vegetable, thickener, and seasonings, shows how good the basics can be if the ingredients are wild. The ingredients are available very early and very late in the growing season.

    2 tablespoons dark-colored miso
    6 tablespoons arrowroot or kudzu
    9 cups Vegetable Stock (page 40)
    2 cups burdock root, very thinly sliced
    One 19-ounce package soft tofu, drained and diced
    2 cloves garlic, chopped
    2 teaspoons freshly ground black pepper
        (1 teaspoon peppercorns)
    1 teaspoon paprika
    1 teaspoon dried marjoram, finely crumbled
    1 teaspoon dillweed, finely crumbled
    2 ½ cups chickweed (page 53), chopped

1. Place the miso, arrowroot, and some of the stock in a blender and process until smooth.

2. Transfer the mixture to a large saucepan, add the remaining stock and the rest of the ingredients, except the chickweed, and bring the pot to a boil. Reduce the heat to low and simmer the soup for 20 minutes. Add the chickweed and simmer the soup for another 2 minutes.

SERVES 8 TO 10

CURRIED BURDOCK SOUP

Burdock root has a potato-artichoke flavor, a firm texture, and lots of vitamins and minerals. It's expensive to buy but abundant in urban and suburban environments throughout most of the United States. Simple and spicy, this soup will warm you up and stimulate your taste buds.

    2 tablespoons peanut oil
    2 teaspoons cumin seeds
    1 teaspoon yellow or black mustard seeds
    1 teaspoon turmeric
    1 teaspoon fenugreek seeds
    3 cloves
    1 teaspoon Vege-Sal or ½ teaspoon salt, or to taste
    ¼ teaspoon freshly ground cardamom seeds
    ¾ teaspoon chili paste or ½ teaspoon cayenne
        pepper, or to taste
    2 cups burdock root, very thinly sliced
    ¾ cup drained silken tofu
    4 cups boiling water
    2 teaspoons fresh lime juice

1. Heat the peanut oil in a large saucepan over low heat. Add the cumin seeds, mustard seeds, turmeric, fenugreek seeds, cloves, Vege-Sal, ground cardamom, and chili paste and cook, stirring, for 1 to 2 minutes. Add the burdock and cook the mixture for another 2 to 3 minutes, stirring a few times.

2. Meanwhile, in a blender, combine the tofu and 2 cups of the boiling water and process until smooth, holding down the lid with a towel to prevent eruption. Pour the tofu mixture into the burdock mixture, add the lime juice and remaining water, and bring the pot to a boil. Reduce the heat to low, cover, and simmer until the burdock is tender, about 20 minutes.

SERVES 4 TO 6

BURDOCK AND DAYLILY STEW

Burdock and daylilies are both Asian immigrants that grow side by side throughout much of America. At the beginning of the foraging season, they can also reside side by side in this stew.

9 cups Vegetable Stock (page 40)

6 cups texturized vegetable protein (TVP)

2 cups burdock root, very thinly sliced

¼ cup arrowroot or kudzu

¼ cup fresh cilantro or parsley leaves, chopped

6 large cloves garlic, crushed

2 teaspoons chili paste or 1 teaspoon cayenne
pepper, or to taste

2 teaspoons Vege-Sal or 1 teaspoon salt, or to taste

1 ½ teaspoons dried rosemary, finely crumbled

1 ½ teaspoons dried tarragon, finely crumbled

1 teaspoon sweet paprika

2 teaspoons freshly ground black mustard seeds
(1 teaspoon seeds)

2 teaspoons freshly ground black pepper
(1 teaspoon peppercorns), or to taste

½ teaspoon turmeric

½ teaspoon freshly grated nutmeg

2 cups daylily shoots (page 64), chopped

1. In a large stockpot, bring the stock to a boil. Soak the TVP in the boiling stock for 10 minutes.

2. Add the remaining ingredients, except the daylily shoots, and return the pot to a boil over medium heat. Reduce the heat to low and simmer, covered, for 10 minutes, stirring occasionally.

3. Add the daylily shoots and continue to simmer, stirring occasionally, until the burdock root is tender, about another 10 minutes. Serve Burdock and Daylily Stew with rice.

SERVES 8 TO 10

BURDOCK RICE

Here's a totally different burdock dish with rice that demonstrates how versatile these two foods can be.

3 ¾ cups water

1 ½ cups brown basmati rice

¾ cup dried burdock root

¼ cup amaranth (page 338)

¼ cup wild rice (page 353)

2 tablespoons tamari soy sauce

5 teaspoons olive oil

1 teaspoon toasted sesame oil

1 teaspoon Tabasco sauce

1 teaspoon fennel seeds

1 teaspoon dried rosemary, finely crumbled

½ teaspoon dried sage, finely crumbled

Place all the ingredients in a large saucepan and bring the pot to a boil. Reduce the heat to low, and simmer the mixture, covered, until the burdock and grains are tender, about 50 minutes.

MAKES 6 CUPS; SERVES 6

SESAME RICE WITH BURDOCK

Brown rice never need be dull when you're a forager. Sesame seeds and burdock root supply outstanding flavor to this version. Serve this dish whenever you need a filling and nutritious grain dish.

3 ¾ cups water

2 cups burdock root, very thinly sliced

1 cup brown basmati rice

1 cup long-grain brown rice

¼ cup sesame seeds, toasted (page 73)

2 tablespoons tamari soy sauce

1 teaspoon sesame oil

1 teaspoon toasted sesame oil

1 teaspoon dried rosemary, finely crumbled

¼ teaspoon ground dried wild ginger (page 111) or
regular ginger

1 teaspoon chili paste or ¼ teaspoon cayenne
   pepper, or to taste

Bring all the ingredients to a boil in a large saucepan over medium heat. Reduce the heat to low, cover, and simmer until the burdock and rice are tender, about 40 minutes.

SERVES 6

KINPIRA GOBO

Beginners usually get into trouble when they sauté burdock root (*gobo* in Japanese) instead of simmering or steaming it, because sautéing is a more difficult way to make the root tender. The trick is to slice the root razor-thin and braise it after sautéing it, as in this spicy traditional Japanese side dish.

2 tablespoons toasted sesame oil

2 cups burdock root, very thinly sliced

2 cups thinly sliced carrots

2 tablespoons peeled and thinly sliced fresh ginger

1 clove garlic, peeled

¼ cup sesame seeds

½ cup Redbud Wine (page 159), mirin (Japanese
   rice wine), or white wine

2 tablespoons tamari soy sauce

1 tablespoon chili paste or 1 ½ teaspoons cayenne
   pepper, or to taste

1. Heat the sesame oil in a large skillet over medium heat. Add the burdock, carrots, ginger, and garlic and cook for 10 minutes, stirring often. Remove and discard the garlic as soon as it turns slightly brown.
2. Meanwhile, toast the sesame seeds in a small skillet over medium heat, stirring constantly, until the sesame seeds pop and become slightly brown and fragrant.

Remove the toasted seeds from the skillet immediately and set them aside.
3. Add the wine and tamari to the sautéed vegetables and bring the pot to a boil. Reduce the heat to low, cover, and simmer until the burdock is tender, about another15 minutes.
4. Stir in the sesame seeds. Serve Kinpira Gobo hot as an appetizer, a condiment, or a side dish.

MAKES 2½ CUPS

BURDOCK CHEESE BREAD

Burdock root and soy cheese shine through the piquant flavor of sourdough in this multi-grain bread. Moist, rich, and flavorful, this bread is one of my favorites.

4⅓ cups (1 pound) sweet brown rice flour, 4 cups
   (1 pound) oat flour, and 1 ¾ cups plus 2
   tablespoons (½ pound) barley flour, or 2 ½
   pounds any whole-grain flour

½ cup arrowroot or kudzu

1 ¾ cups water

1 cup Sourdough Starter (page 42)

3 tablespoons corn oil

2 cups steamed sliced burdock root

1 ½ cups Tofu Grated Cheese (page 32)

1 tablespoon Vege-Sal or 1 ½ teaspoons salt, or to
   taste

2 teaspoons freshly ground black pepper
   (1 teaspoon peppercorns)

1 teaspoon paprika

1. Mix together all the flours in a large nonmetal bowl. In another large bowl, combine half the flour mixture with the arrowroot and then add the water, sourdough starter, and 2 tablespoons of the corn oil.

Cover the dough and allow it to rise for 4 hours or up to overnight at room temperature.

2. Mix in the burdock root, Tofu Grated Cheese, Vege-Sal, and pepper and brush with the remaining 1 tablespoon corn oil.

3. Divide the dough between 2 oiled 6½ x 4⅜ x 2½-inch loaf pans and shape the dough into loaves. Sprinkle the tops with the paprika, cover the loaves, and allow them to rise at room temperature for 4 hours or up to overnight.

4. Preheat the oven to 350 degrees and place a pan of hot water on the bottom of the oven, to keep the bread from becoming too crusty. Bake the bread until it pulls away from the sides of the pan slightly and sounds somewhat hollow when you tap it on the bottom, about 50 minutes. Remove the loaves from the pans and let them cool on a wire rack before slicing.

MAKES 2 LOAVES

Note: Never allow sourdough to come in contact with metal implements or containers or you'll kill the wild yeast.

MID- *to* LATE SPRING WILD FOODS

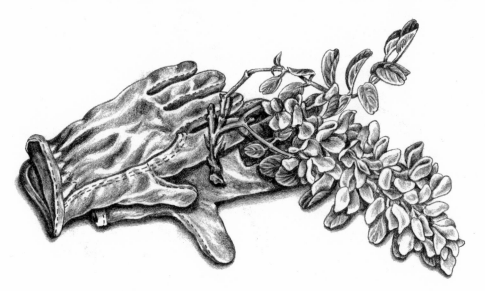

NATURE PROVIDES A GREATER ABUNDANCE OF wild vegetables and edible flowers in mid- to late spring than at any other time of the year. You can be busy collecting and cooking every day without exhausting all the possibilities. In addition to the species I cover in this section, a number of the early spring plants remain in season in mid-spring, and a small number of gourmet mushrooms also begin to appear.

COW PARSNIP
Heracleum maximum

THIS HUGE, COARSE-LOOKING PLANT HAS woolly, toothed leaves up to 3 feet long, divided into three sections, like maple leaves. The leaves begin along the ground as a basal rosette, then alternate along a flower stalk in mid-spring, when their swollen, stalkless bases (deadly water hemlock lacks stalkless bases) clasp (partially surround) the stem. An umbrella-like flower stalk up to 8 inches across supports many tiny white flowers later in the spring. The plant grows in wet areas, in partially sunny areas in the woods, along the edges of woods, and in old meadows from coast to coast in the northern states, Canada, and Alaska.

Don't handle cow parsnip with sweaty hands if you're going to be exposed to the sun; you may get a rash.

Although it's related to the common parsnip and the spicy-smelling taproots are edible cooked, the best parts of the cow parsnip are the immature leaf stalks and flower stalks, gathered in season in mid-spring. They're crunchy and have an intense celery flavor that you may want to tone down with creamy sauces, or by preparing them in combination with many other ingredients. They're too strong to eat raw.

SACRED COW PARSNIP

The herders who settled in India in ancient times worshipped the cattle that provided their sustenance. Their descendants still consider cows sacred. When you discover how good this Indian-style cow parsnip dish tastes, your taste buds will want to worship this sacred wild vegetable.

¼ cup dried chickpeas, ground into ¼ cup chick-pea flour in a spice grinder, coffee grinder, or blender
1 tablespoon turmeric
3 tablespoons peanut oil
1 tablespoon ground cinnamon
1 tablespoon coriander seeds
2 teaspoons cumin seeds
2 teaspoons black mustard seeds
½ teaspoon cardamom seeds or ground cardamom
1 tablespoon peeled and chopped fresh ginger
3 small chiles, or to taste, seeds and ribs removed and chopped
6 cloves garlic, chopped
4 cups sliced young cow parsnip stalks
1 head cauliflower, stems and florets sliced
⅔ cup drained silken tofu
Juice of 1 lemon
2 teaspoons Vege-Sal or 1 teaspoon salt, or to taste
2 cups water
½ cup unsalted dry-roasted peanuts, chopped

1. Toast the chickpea flour in a large skillet over medium heat until it is lightly browned, about 1 minute, stirring constantly. Remove the toasted flour from the skillet at once and set it aside.
2. Add the turmeric to the skillet and stir it, away from the heat, until it is fragrant, about 1 minute. Add it to the chickpea flour.
3. Wipe the skillet out well. Heat the peanut oil over medium heat and cook the cinnamon, coriander seeds, cumin seeds, black mustard seeds, and cardamom until the mustard seeds pop, 2 to 3 minutes.
4. Add the ginger, chiles, garlic, cow parsnip, and

cauliflower and cook, stirring, for 10 minutes.

5. Meanwhile, in a blender, combine the tofu, lemon juice, Vege-Sal, water, and chickpea flour mixture and process until smooth. Add this mixture to the sautéed vegetables, reduce the heat to low, cover, and simmer for 20 minutes.

6. Serve Sacred Cow Parsnip hot on brown rice or with Indian bread, garnished with the peanuts.

SERVES 6

COW PARSNIP PILAF

The powerful celery-like flavor of cow parsnip leaf-stalks comes shining through in this wonderful whole-grain pilaf.

1 ½ cups brown basmati rice or other long-grain
   brown rice
¼ cup wild rice (page 353)
¼ cup amaranth (page 338)
2 cups sliced cow parsnip stalks
1 cup ramp leaves (page 116) or scallions, chopped
3 large cloves garlic, chopped
1 tablespoon olive oil
1 tablespoon Bragg's Liquid Aminos or tamari soy
   sauce, or to taste
¾ teaspoon freshly ground celery seeds
   (½ teaspoon seeds)
1 teaspoon freshly ground black pepper
   (½ teaspoon peppercorns)

1. Preheat the oven to 375 degrees.

2. Combine all the ingredients in a 3-quart oiled casserole dish and bake, covered, until all the liquid is absorbed and the grains are tender, about 1½ hours.

SERVES 6

COW PARSNIP CHEESE BUNS

Cow parsnips have a celery-like texture, but much more flavor than celery. They stand out in this baked recipe.

2 ½ cups (¾ pound) sweet brown rice flour and
   3 cups (¾ pound) oat flour, or 1 ½ pounds any
   whole-grain flour
2 cups sliced young cow parsnip stalks
½ cup arrowroot or kudzu
1 tablespoon caraway seeds
½ tablespoon baking soda
1 teaspoon salt
2 cups Tofu Cream Cheese (page 30)
4 to 5 ½ tablespoons corn oil
1 ½ tablespoons fresh lemon juice

1. In a medium-size bowl, mix ¼ cup of the flour with the cow parsnip stalks.

2. In a large bowl, combine the remaining flour, the arrowroot, caraway seeds, baking soda, and salt.

3. In a medium-size bowl, mix together the Tofu Cream Cheese, ¼ cup of the corn oil, and the lemon juice. Stir this mixture into the dry ingredients, being careful not to overmix. Stir in the cow parsnip stalks, being careful not to overmix.

4. Preheat the oven to 350 degrees and set a pan of hot water in the bottom of the oven to keep the crust of the buns soft.

5. Roll the dough into about 20 balls, arranging them on 2 oiled cookie sheets. Brush them with the remaining 1½ tablespoons corn oil, if desired. Bake the buns until they are lightly browned underneath, about 30 minutes. Let them cool on wire racks.

MAKES ABOUT 20 BUNS

MOREL

Morchella species

MORELS ARE AMONG THE MOST PRIZED OF WILD mushrooms. The cap, honeycombed with pits and ridges, is contiguous with the stalk, so if you cut one of these mushrooms lengthwise, it's hollow from top to bottom, with no division between the cap and stem.

False morels (Gyromitra species), which are sometimes poisonous, and thimble-caps (Verpa species), have a separation between the stem and cap. They aren't hollow all the way through when you split them lengthwise.

Morels grow in the spring in a wide variety of habitats throughout North America. Old apple orchards, areas near dead elm trees, and regions with limestone in the soil are especially good places to look. People also find morels in woods, and along the edges of trails. Morels sometimes come up in the same place year after year.

Living in New York City, I find large quantities of a variety of mushrooms in our many parks, but morels are rare here, or I don't have the eye for them. We find them only rarely on my tours, and people who know where they grow don't give away the locations.

Nevertheless, a roofer friend was at work in an affluent neighborhood in Queens, New York, when he saw a troop of morels on his client's manicured lawn. He was so shocked, he almost fell off the roof. But he did bring the mushrooms home and enjoyed them thoroughly.

In the Midwest, morels are so prolific there are morel-hunting contests. Morels are also common in the Pacific Northwest.

And these mushrooms come up after forest fires. In the nineteenth century, the Russian government had to pass a law making it illegal to burn down the forests in order to harvest morels the following year.

German folklore attributes the origin of morels to the devil. Offended by a very wrinkled old woman, he transformed her into this mushroom. Ever since, calling a woman a *morel* in Germany has been a major insult.

It can be difficult to distinguish one morel species from another, but all species provide a rich, earthy flavor that makes them all especially good. You can sauté them, bake them, steam them, or include them in soups, casseroles, stews, or sauces. Never eat morels raw or undercooked (cook them for at least 15 minutes) or you may get quite ill.

BAKED MOREL CASSEROLE

Morels are considered the best-tasting mushrooms of springtime. These potato and vegetable patties more than showcase these prized mushrooms.

Mushroom Spore Print

THE SPORE PRINT is one more means of identifying a mushroom. To make a spore print, place the cap, gills down, on heavy white paper and cover with a bowl or cup to keep air currents from blowing the spores away. The next day, you'll see fine powder, the spore print, on the paper.

4 cups morels or other wild or commercial
   mushrooms
1 bell pepper, seeded and finely chopped
1 onion, finely chopped
2 cloves garlic, finely chopped
2 tablespoons olive oil
1 ¼ tablespoons silken tofu, drained
1 tablespoon fresh lime juice
½ teaspoon Vege-Sal or ¼ teaspoon salt, or to taste
1 tablespoon finely chopped fresh parsley leaves
¼ teaspoon freshly ground white pepper
   (⅛ teaspoon peppercorns)
1 tablespoon corn oil
½ tablespoon lecithin granules
3 ½ cups mashed boiled potatoes
2 tablespoons any wild onion leaves (page 57),
   chives, or scallions, chopped

1. Preheat the oven to 350 degrees.
2. In a saucepan over medium heat, sauté the morels, bell pepper, onions, and garlic in olive oil for 5 minutes.
3. Stir in silken tofu, lime juice, Vege-Sal, parsley, and white pepper, reduce the heat to low, and simmer, covered, for 5 minutes.
4. Meanwhile, in a large bowl, mix the corn oil and lecithin granules with the potatoes and transfer half of the mixture into an oiled baking dish.
5. Layer the mushrooms and vegetables on top and cover with the remaining mixture. Garnish with the wild onion leaves.
6. Bake the casserole, covered, for 20 minutes.

SERVES 6

FAIRY RING MUSHROOM
Marasmius oreades

THERE ARE ONLY A FEW GREAT SPRINGTIME mushrooms, and this is one of them. Its cap is ⅜ inch to 1⅝ inches across, bell-shaped to convex, beige, with a knob on top. Underneath the cap are broad whitish gills, usually free from the stem, sometimes attached. Unlike similar-looking mushrooms or fairy rings, there's always quite a bit of space between the gills, and the spore print is white. The straight, dry, rubbery stalk is ⅜ inch to 3 inches long. The fairy ring mushroom grows on lawns, where the fungus decomposes organic matter. You can find it throughout North America in the spring and summer.

Although no poisonous mushrooms have the exact same features as the fairy ring mushroom, it's not hard for unsupervised beginners to confuse the fairy ring mushroom with toxic mushrooms growing in the same habitat.

Fairy ring mushrooms are small but very tasty. Try the caps sautéed in olive oil with garlic (the stems are too tough for anything but stock). And you can stretch your supply by letting the mushroom suffuse its excellence into other ingredients in a soup, stew, or stuffing. Unlike most other species of mushrooms, if you dehydrate this mushroom (or find it dehydrated) and soak it in water, it revives completely within minutes.

❧ BEETS STUFFED WITH FAIRY RINGS

Here's an example of how a little fairy ring mushroom can go a long way toward transforming a recipe.

3 medium-size beets

1 ½ tablespoons olive oil

1 cup fairy ring mushroom caps or other mushrooms, chopped

2 cloves garlic, chopped

½ cup fresh Bread Crumbs (page 40)

¼ cup Mint-Lime Sauce (page 60), Healthy Hollandaise Sauce (page 130), or any other creamy sauce in this book

½ teaspoon freshly ground black pepper (¼ teaspoon peppercorns)

1. Preheat the oven to 350 degrees. Rub the beets with ½ tablespoon of the olive oil and bake them in a 14 x 9 x 2-inch oiled baking dish, covered, until tender, about 1 hour.

2. Meanwhile, heat the remaining 1 tablespoon olive oil in a medium-size skillet, add the mushrooms and garlic, and cook, stirring, for 5 minutes.

3. When the beets are cool enough to handle, cut them in half and scoop out most of the pulp with a grapefruit knife or spoon, leaving a ¼-inch-thick wall of pulp adjacent to the skin.

4. Chop the scooped-out beet pulp and mix it with the mushroom mixture, bread crumbs, the Mint-Lime Sauce, and pepper.

5. Return the beet shells to the baking dish and pile the stuffing into them. Bake the stuffed beets, covered, for 20 minutes.

SERVES 6

WINE-CAP STROPHARIA MUSHROOM
Stropharia rugoso-annulata

THIS SPECTACULAR CHOICE MUSHROOM, WHICH you can find in quantity throughout the United States in the spring and fall (sometimes even in the summer), has a cap that is red-brown to tan and can sometimes grow to the size of a dinner plate, but is usually 2 to 5 inches across, bell-shaped when young, flat when old. The crowded broad lilac-colored gills attach to the stem. The spore print is a very dark purple-brown. The white stem is 4 to 6 inches long, ⅜ to ¾ inch wide, emanating from an enlarged base. Penetrating the wood chips, where the mushroom grows, you'll see threads of white fungus coming from the mushroom's base. A distinctive membranous ring with radial lines on the mushroom's upper surface grows on the upper stalk.

This large decomposer mushroom doesn't take to traditional Western onion-garlic seasonings. Cooked with a minimum of oil and ample quantities of lemon juice, wine (it is a wine-cap, after all), nutmeg, and fennel, its flavor is outstanding. Braise it, bake it, or add it to soups. It cooks in 15 to 20 minutes. Unless you're using this mushroom with other ingredients, it gives off too much liquid to sauté properly, but it dehydrates well, and after cooking it, you can also freeze it for up to 2 years in a very cold freezer.

❧ WINE CAPS IN WINE

Here's a basic way to make this mushroom shine. After you've cooked wine caps with these seasonings, you can add them to another recipe just before it is done, or enjoy the mushroom as a side dish. You won't believe how good it tastes.

1 ½ teaspoons olive oil

12 cups sliced wine-cap stropharia mushrooms

6 tablespoons fresh lemon or lime juice

6 tablespoons White Oak Wine (page 176) or white wine

1 tablespoon freshly grated nutmeg

1 ½ teaspoons freshly ground fennel seeds

1 tablespoon Vege-Sal or 1 ½ teaspoons salt

1. Heat the olive oil in a large skillet over medium heat. Cook the mushrooms, stirring often, until they begin to release liquid, 3 to 5 minutes.

2. Stir in the remaining ingredients and bring the pot to a boil. Reduce the heat to low and simmer, covered, for 15 minutes.

3. Uncover and cook the mushrooms over high heat, stirring constantly, until all the liquid is evaporated or absorbed, another 5 to 10 minutes.

SERVES 6

WINE CAPS AND CAULIFLOWER INDIAN STYLE

Here's a side dish where the mild flavor of cauliflower offsets the stronger influences of the wild mushrooms and Indian seasonings. Wine-cap stropharia mushrooms have enough of a penetrating flavor to withstand the pungent spices.

2 tablespoons peanut oil

2 teaspoons Garam Masala (page 36) or Curry Powder (page 112)

1 teaspoon black mustard seeds

1 teaspoon cumin seeds

½ teaspoon freshly ground black pepper (¼ teaspoon peppercorns)

1 clove garlic, chopped

1 ½ pounds cauliflower, broken into florets

2 ½ cups sliced wine-cap stropharia mushrooms

1. Heat the peanut oil in a large skillet over medium heat. Add the garam masala, black mustard seeds, cumin seeds, and black pepper and cook, stirring constantly, until the mustard seeds pop, 2 to 3 minutes.

2. Add the remaining ingredients and cook the vegetables, stirring, for another 15 minutes, until the water from the mushrooms has evaporated.

SERVES 6

WISTERIA
Wisteria species

THIS LONG-LIVED, THICK, SMOOTH-BARKED, woody, twining vine, with alternate feather-compound leaves (leaves segmented along an axis) that grow to 2 feet long, produces dense, drooping clusters of fragrant and edible bilaterally symmetrical lilac blossoms every spring. In the summer, you'll find fuzzy, knobby green pods 4 to 6 inches long with poisonous seeds inside.

Look for this cultivated ornamental in landscaped parks and gardens. It also escapes cultivation and grows wild along the edges of trails, in partially sunny woods and thickets, along streams, and along the edges of woodlands. You can find it anywhere in the United States.

The blossom's lush, perfumed flavor is so strong, you should use wisteria sparingly, or subdue it by combining it with other ingredients. I especially like using the blossoms to make ice cream. They also add an exotic touch to various desserts, hot cereal, pancake batter, and fritters. You may also use wisteria in most recipes that call for black locust blossoms (page 179) or redbud blossoms (page 156).

WISTERIA SOURDOUGH PANCAKES

The sweetness of wisteria blossoms offsets the sourness of the sourdough in this flavorful, hearty pancake. The longer you let the first batter ferment, the sourer it becomes.

> ½ cup Sourdough Starter (page 42)
>
> 1 cup water
>
> ¼ cup sesame oil or other vegetable oil
>
> 1 cup raisins
>
> 1½ cups apple juice
>
> 2 cups buckwheat flour or 9.6 ounces any other whole-grain flour
>
> 1½ teaspoons freshly ground coriander seeds
>
> 2 tablespoons poppy seeds
>
> 1 teaspoon freshly ground star anise
>
> 1 teaspoon freshly grated nutmeg
>
> ½ teaspoon salt
>
> 1 cup pecans, chopped
>
> 2 cups wisteria blossoms

1. In a large non-metal bowl, mix together the sourdough starter, water, and oil and set the mixture aside at room temperature for 4 to 6 hours or overnight. Do not use a metal container or utensils, because they will kill the sourdough microorganisms.

2. Meanwhile, in a small bowl, soak the raisins in the apple juice.

3. In a large bowl, mix together the flour, spices, and salt.

4. Mix the apple juice, raisins, and pecans, into the sourdough mixture, and then mix in the flour mixture. Finally, gently mix in the wisteria blossoms. (At this point you can freeze the batter for future use.)

5. Heat an oiled griddle or skillet over medium-low heat and pour on a few tablespoons of the batter. Spread out the batter with a spatula.

6. When the underside of the pancakes is lightly browned, turn with a spatula and let the other side brown. Remove the pancakes to a plate and keep warm in a low oven until all the batter has been used up. Serve the pancakes hot with jam or syrup.

MAKES 2 DOZEN PANCAKES; SERVES 12

WISTERIA RASGOOLA

Perfumed wisteria blossoms enhance the flavor of these sweet, delicate Indian cheese balls, while the simple apricot sauce provides a perfect setting for them.

CHEESE BALLS

> 1 cup sweet brown rice flour
>
> One 19-ounce package soft tofu, drained and grated
>
> ½ cup unsweetened apricot juice
>
> ¼ cup kudzu or arrowroot
>
> 1 cup fresh Bread Crumbs (page 40)
>
> 1 teaspoon liquid stevia
>
> ½ teaspoon salt
>
> ¼ teaspoon ground dried wild ginger (page 111) or regular ground ginger
>
> ¼ teaspoon freshly ground cardamom seeds
>
> 2 cups Panir Tofu Cheese (page 32)
>
> ½ cup wisteria blossoms

SAUCE

2 cups unsweetened apricot juice

1 cup water

½ cup fresh Bread Crumbs (page 40)

1 ½ tablespoons kudzu or arrowroot

1 tablespoon fresh lemon juice

1 teaspoon liquid stevia

1. *To make the cheese balls:* Preheat the oven to 350 degrees. Toast the rice flour in a roasting pan for 30 minutes, stirring occasionally. Remove the flour from the oven but leave the oven on.

2. Mix the rice flour in a large bowl with the remaining cheese ball ingredients, except the Panir Tofu Cheese and wisteria. Stir in the Panir Tofu Cheese and wisteria.

3. Roll the mixture into about 3 dozen balls that are 1¼ inches in diameter, and arrange the balls on an oiled cookie sheet. Bake the cheese balls until they are lightly browned underneath, about 25 minutes.

4. *To make the sauce:* In a blender, combine all the sauce ingredients and process until smooth. Transfer the mixture to a medium-size saucepan and bring it to a boil over medium heat, stirring constantly. Reduce the heat to low, cover, and simmer for 10 minutes.

5. Serve the cheese balls hot or cold, covered with the sauce, which may be hot or cold.

MAKES ABOUT 3 DOZEN BALLS

WISTERIA AND SWEET CICELY ICE CREAM

Sweet cicely, wisteria blossoms, and lemon verbena are perfect partners in this soy-based ice cream.

1 cup apple juice

¾ cup sweet cicely taproots (avoid the gnarled,

stringy underground stems; page 92)

1 ½ cups soy milk or nut milk

1 cup well-drained silken tofu

½ cup raw cashews

¼ cup canola oil

¼ cup vegetable glycerin, honey, barley malt, or rice syrup

1 tablespoon chopped fresh lemon verbena or mint leaves or 1 teaspoon dried, finely crumbled

2 tablespoons lecithin granules

2 teaspoons vanilla extract

2 teaspoons freshly grated orange rind or ½ teaspoon orange extract

½ teaspoon salt

1 teaspoon liquid stevia

2 cups wisteria blossoms

1. Place the apple juice and sweet cicely in a small saucepan and bring the pot to a boil. Reduce the heat to medium-low, and simmer, covered, for 5 minutes.

2. Carefully transfer the sweet cicely mixture to a blender, add the remaining ingredients, except for 1 cup of the wisteria blossoms, and process until smooth.

3. Chill the mixture until cold (1 hour in the freezer, 4 hours in the refrigerator). Stir in the remaining 1 cup wisteria.

4. Pour the mixture into an ice cream maker and freeze it according to the manufacturer's instructions.

MAKES 5 CUPS; SERVES 5

WISTERIA-LIME ICE CREAM

The sweet, perfumed flavor of wisteria flowers complements the sour flavor of lime juice in this piquant ice cream.

2 ½ cups soy milk or nut milk

1 cup drained silken tofu

½ cup raw cashews

½ cup canola oil or safflower oil

¼ cup vegetable glycerin, honey, barley malt, or
  rice syrup

¼ cup lecithin granules

2 teaspoons vanilla extract

1 teaspoon liquid stevia

½ teaspoon salt

Juice of 1 lime

½ cup wisteria blossoms

1. In a blender, combine all the ingredients except the wisteria and process until smooth.

2. Chill the mixture (or begin with chilled ingredients) if required by your ice cream machine

3. Pour the mixture into the ice cream machine, along with the wisteria blossoms, and freeze it according to the manufacturer's instructions.

MAKES 5 ½ CUPS; SERVES 5 TO 6

WISTERIA LOVERS' ICE CREAM

Here's the ultimate ice cream for anyone who loves wisteria.

2 cups soy milk or nut milk

2 cups well-drained silken tofu

¼ cup canola oil or safflower oil

¼ cup vegetable glycerin, honey, barley malt, or
  rice syrup

1 tablespoon freshly grated orange rind, 1 teaspoon
  ground dried orange rind, or ½ teaspoon orange
  extract

2 tablespoons lecithin granules

2 teaspoons vanilla extract

½ teaspoon blueberry extract (optional)

1 teaspoon liquid stevia

2 cups wisteria blossoms

1. In a blender, combine all the ingredients, except for 1 cup of the wisteria blossoms, and process until smooth.

2. Chill the mixture (or begin with chilled ingredients) if required by your ice cream machine. Stir in the remaining 1 cup wisteria blossoms.

3. Pour the mixture into the ice cream machine and freeze it according to the manufacturer's instructions.

MAKES 5 ½ CUPS; SERVES 5 TO 6

WISTERIA WINE

This blossom makes a strong-flavored sweet wine that is great for desserts. Use it sparingly.

6 cups sugar

1 gallon boiling water

2 quarts wisteria blossoms

1 lemon, including the rind, chopped and crushed

1 orange, including the rind, chopped and crushed

2 tablespoons common spicebush berries (page
  314) or 1 teaspoon allspice berries

8 bayberry leaves (page 185) or 4 bay leaves

2 tablespoons dried tarragon, finely crumbled

½ teaspoon champagne yeast or other wine yeast

1. Dissolve the sugar in the boiling water in a nonmetal (plastic or ceramic) food container and add the wisteria, fruit, spices, and herbs.

2. When the wisteria mixture is lukewarm, stir in the yeast and cover the container with a non-airtight cover, cheesecloth, or towel.

3. Allow the wisteria mixture to ferment for a week at

room temperature, stirring twice a day.

4. Strain the wisteria mixture through cheesecloth, transfer the liquid to a jug, and seal the jug with an airlock stopper (which lets carbon dioxide bubbles escape but keeps oxygen out).

5. When the bubbling and fermentation ends about 2 weeks later, seal the jug with a cork and age the wine for 2 to 6 months before using it.

6. Siphon the wine to get rid of the sediment, if desired.

MAKES 1 GALLON

SEA LETTUCE

Ulva lactuca

SEA LETTUCE LOOKS SO MUCH LIKE GREEN plastic wrap (it can grow up to 3 feet across) washed up on the seashore that the only thing you could confuse this tasty seaweed with would be green plastic wrap washed up on the seashore.

Place sea lettuce in a colander set into a bowl and rinse it thoroughly under running water, as it is often engrained with sand. Refrigerate the sea lettuce and use it within 2 days, or dehydrate it at once (and later soak it in water to reconstitute it). It's highly perishable.

Sea lettuce is a little too tough to eat raw, but if you sauté it in olive oil with some garlic, you'll have a colorful, high-mineral vegetable dish. You can also simmer it for 20 minutes in soups or stews.

MISO SOUP WITH SEA LETTUCE

Japanese miso soup relies on a delicate balance of mild-flavored ingredients and seasonings, and sea lettuce is just right for this traditional dish.

> 1 tablespoon sesame oil
>
> 2 cups dried sea lettuce
>
> 1 ½ tablespoons peeled and finely chopped fresh ginger
>
> 3 cloves garlic, finely chopped
>
> 7 ½ cups Vegetable Stock (page 40)
>
> 2 ¾ cups enoki mushrooms (page 429) or other mushrooms, chopped
>
> 2 cups drained soft tofu, diced
>
> 1 ½ teaspoons red miso or other miso

1. Heat the sesame oil in a medium-size skillet over medium heat, add the sea lettuce, ginger, and garlic, and cook, stirring, for 5 minutes.

2. Meanwhile, combine the stock, mushrooms, and tofu in a large saucepan, bring to a boil, reduce the heat to medium-low, and simmer, covered, for 5 minutes.

3. Add the sautéed vegetables to the stock mixture and simmer, covered, for another 5 minutes.

4. Remove the pot from the heat, lower a strainer partway into the stock, and stir in the miso against the strainer's sides using a wooden spoon.

SERVES 6

REDBUD

Cercis canadensis

THIS SMALL TREE, WHICH REACHES ONLY UP TO 50 feet but is usually smaller, has distinct alternate heart-shaped leaves that grow from 2 to 6 inches across and are smooth edged with a pointy tip. In the spring, thousands of fragrant, small, bilaterally symmetrical clusters of purple-red blossoms decorate the twigs and branches before the leaves have grown. Later in the spring, flattened pinkish green pods replace the flowers. Look for this native tree in landscaped areas throughout the country and in thickets throughout eastern North America. If you live on the West Coast, you can use the very similar *Cercis occidentalis* the same way.

The sweet-tangy flowers, with a hint of the flavor of green peas, are among the best of wild foods. You can use the flowers in almost any dish, from main courses to breads to desserts. When we find this tree in flower on a school tour, the kids are in heaven. You can also add the sour-flavored pods raw to salads, or stir-fry or sauté them (or add them to soups) the way you would snow peas. Unfortunately, the pods are labor intensive to collect and are in season for such a short time before becoming tough and leathery that I rarely get a chance to use them.

REDBUD PICKLES

Redbud blossoms are tasty, but they're only in season for a few weeks every year. These pickles last for months in the refrigerator, and pickling adds a new flavor to this wild food delicacy. Serve Redbud Pickles as an appetizer or use them to garnish savory entrées.

> 1 ½ cups water
> 4 cups redbud flowers
> 1 teaspoon coriander seeds
> 1 teaspoon fennel seeds
> ½ teaspoon black peppercorns
> 4 bayberry (page 185) or bay leaves
> ¾ cup red wine vinegar
> 1 teaspoon Vege-Sal or ½ teaspoon salt

1. Bring the water to a boil in a saucepan and steam the redbud flowers on a steamer rack for 15 minutes.
2. Enclose the coriander seeds, fennel seeds, peppercorns, and bayberry leaves in a tea bag or tea ball, or tie them up in a piece of cheesecloth.
3. Transfer the redbud flowers and the water, along with the vinegar, the bag of spices, and Vege-Sal to a jar. Refrigerate the pickles overnight before serving. Redbud Pickles will keep, tightly covered, in the refrigerator for up to 3 months.

MAKES 2 CUPS

BRAISED VEGETABLES WITH PANIR CHEESE

Here's one of the best Indian stews you've ever tasted. Even though it's vegan, it's quite filling. And the flowers of the redbud tree make it even more exciting.

SAUCE
> 1 cup plus 3 tablespoons water
> ¼ cup tomato paste
> 2 tablespoons lecithin granules
> 2 tablespoons drained silken tofu
> 3 tablespoons almonds

1 tablespoon corn oil

½ tablespoon fresh lemon juice

¼ teaspoon Vege-Sal or ⅛ teaspoon salt

SAUTÉ

6 tablespoons peanut oil

1 medium-size onion, finely chopped

2 tablespoons freshly ground coriander seeds

2 tablespoons freshly ground cumin seeds

½ teaspoon turmeric

1 teaspoon freshly ground black pepper
   (½ teaspoon peppercorns)

3 tablespoons peeled and finely chopped or
   grated fresh ginger

2 cloves garlic, finely chopped

1 chile, or to taste, seeds and ribs removed and
   finely chopped

1 medium-size potato, coarsely chopped

1 small eggplant, diced

3 medium-size zucchini, ends trimmed and
   coarsely sliced

1 Panir Tofu Cheese (page 32)

1 cup redbud flowers

1 cup water

1 tablespoon Vege-Sal or 1 ½ teaspoons salt, or to
   taste

1 teaspoon Garam Masala (page 36)

1. *To make the sauce:* In a blender, combine all the sauce ingredients and process until smooth.

2. *To make the sauté:* Heat the peanut oil in a large skillet over medium heat and cook the onion until it is lightly browned, about 15 minutes, stirring. Stir in the coriander seeds, cumin seeds, turmeric, black pepper, ginger, garlic, and chile and cook another 2 minutes, stirring constantly. Slowly pour in the sauce. Add the potato and bring the pot to a boil. Reduce the heat to low, cover, and cook the potatoes for 10 minutes.

3. Transfer the potato mixture to a large saucepan, stir in the remaining ingredients, and simmer until the vegetables are soft, 30 to 40 minutes.

SERVES 6 TO 8

REDBUD CORNBREAD

This bread combines the tangy taste of redbuds with the down-home flavor of cornbread.

4 cups (2 ½ pounds) yellow cornmeal

3 cups (14.25 ounces) sweet brown rice flour and
   1 cup (4.3 ounces) barley flour, or 18.55
   ounces any whole-grain flour

½ cup plus 2 tablespoons freshly ground flaxseeds
   (¼ cup seeds)

2 tablespoons cream of tartar

1 tablespoon baking soda

2 teaspoons freshly grated nutmeg

1 ½ teaspoons turmeric

2 ½ cups apple juice

1 ½ cups soy milk or nut milk

1 cup corn oil

3 cups redbud flowers

¼ cup lecithin granules

1 teaspoon finely chopped common spicebush
   berries (page 314) or 1 teaspoon freshly ground
   allspice berries

½ teaspoon sweet paprika

1. Preheat the oven to 350 degrees.

2. Mix together the cornmeal, flour, ground flaxseeds, cream of tartar, baking soda, nutmeg, and turmeric in a large bowl.

3. In a medium-size bowl, mix together the apple juice, soy milk, and corn oil. Stir the wet ingredients into the dry ingredients, being careful not to overmix.

Stir the redbud flowers, lecithin, and spicebush berries into the batter.

4. Pour the batter into 3 oiled 8½ x 4½ x 2½-inch loaf pans. Sprinkle the top of each loaf with the paprika. Place a pan of hot water in the bottom of the oven to keep the crust soft. Bake the cornbread until a toothpick inserted in the center emerges clean, about 55 minutes.

5. Remove the loaves from pans and let them cool on a wire rack.

MAKES 3 LOAVES

REDBUD ICE CREAM

Redbud flowers' sweet flavor and crunchy texture are ready-made for ice cream.

2 ½ cups soy milk or nut milk

1 cup drained silken tofu

½ cup raw cashews

½ cup canola oil

¼ cup vegetable glycerin, barley malt, or honey

1 teaspoon liquid stevia

2 teaspoons vanilla extract

1 teaspoon freshly grated lemon rind or ¼ teaspoon lemon extract

1 teaspoon freshly grated nutmeg

½ teaspoon salt

¼ cup lecithin granules

3 cups redbud blossoms

1. In a blender, combine all the ingredients, except for 1 cup of the redbuds, and process until smooth.

2. Chill the mixture (or start with chilled ingredients) if required by your ice cream machine. Stir in the remaining 1 cup redbud blossoms.

3. Pour the mixture into the ice cream machine and

freeze it according to the manufacturer's instructions.

MAKES 5½ CUPS; SERVES 5 TO 6

CASHEW ICE CREAM

This ice cream will knock the socks off anyone who loves cashews. The redbud flowers add a nice touch of elegance.

2 ½ cups soy milk or nut milk

1 cup drained silken tofu

1 cup raw cashews

½ cup canola oil or safflower oil

¼ cup vegetable glycerin, honey, barley malt, or rice syrup

¼ cup lecithin granules

2 tablespoons fresh lemon juice

1 teaspoon liquid stevia

½ teaspoon salt

1 cup raw cashews, toasted (see note) and chopped

1 cup redbud flowers

1. In a blender, combine all the ingredients except the toasted cashews and redbuds and process until smooth.

2. Chill the mixture (or begin with chilled ingredients) if required by your ice cream machine. Stir in the toasted cashews and redbud flowers.

3. Pour the mixture into the ice cream machine and freeze it according to the manufacturer's instructions.

MAKES 6½ CUPS; SERVES 6

Note: To toast nuts, put them in a roasting pan in a preheated 375-degree oven, stirring frequently, until they are lightly browned and crisp (about 1 to 1½ hours for raw cashews; times will vary greatly for other types of nuts).

REDBUD WINE

Here's an excellent red table wine and cooking wine that is strongly flavored but not overpowering. You'll love it. Use cold water rather than boiling water in order to retain the flowers' delicate flavor. If you have trouble getting the sugar to dissolve, heat the water just until the sugar dissolves, then cool the liquid to lukewarm before adding the blossoms.

> *6 cups sugar*
>
> *1 gallon water*
>
> *1 quart redbud blossoms*
>
> *1 lemon, including the rind, chopped and crushed*
>
> *1 orange, including the rind, chopped and crushed*
>
> *2 tablespoons cloves*
>
> *8 bayberry leaves (page 185) or 4 bay leaves*
>
> *2 tablespoons coriander seeds*
>
> *½ teaspoon champagne yeast or other wine yeast*

1. Dissolve the sugar in the water in a non-metal (plastic or ceramic) food container. Add the redbud blossoms, fruits, cloves, bayberry leaves, and coriander seeds.

2. Stir in the yeast and cover the container with a non-airtight cover, cheesecloth, or towel.

3. Allow the mixture to ferment for a week at room temperature, stirring twice a day.

4. Strain the mixture through cheesecloth, transfer the liquid to a jug, and seal the jug with an airlock stopper (which lets carbon dioxide bubbles escape but keeps oxygen out).

5. When the bubbling stops and fermentation ends about 2 weeks later, seal the jug with a cork and let the wine age for 8 to 12 weeks before using it.

6. Siphon the wine to get rid of the sediment, if desired.

MAKES 1 GALLON

GREENBRIER
Smilax species

HERE'S A HIGH-CLIMBING, THORNY, GREEN woody vine with alternate heart-shaped to rounded, smooth-edged, pointed leaves. Greenbrier grabs on to other plants with its wiry tendrils. In the spring, clusters of small, inconspicuous six-petaled flowers appear, followed by rubbery blue berries in the summer and fall.

This divine vine provides fantastic-tasting leaves, tendrils, and shoots (tender, growing vine tips) in mid-spring, all very delicate, with sour overtones. By late spring and into the summer, only the newest leaves, shoots, and tendrils are still soft enough to eat. One of our best salad greens, greenbrier is also scrumptious lightly cooked. Unlike most wild greens, this one is perishable. Use it within a few days of collecting it.

WILDMAN'S FIVE-BORO SALAD

Here's the all-wild salad I served to the press and passersby on the steps of the Manhattan Criminal Courthouse in 1986 when I was arraigned, after being arrested by undercover park rangers for eating a dandelion in Central Park. Although the salad is just as good now as it was then, it makes me wish I could have all that publicity again!

> *2 cups cattail shoots (page 189), sliced*
>
> *1½ cups tender young greenbrier leaves, shoots, and tendrils*
>
> *1 cup common blue violet leaves (page 106), chopped*

1 cup curly dock leaves (page 109), chopped

1 cup ramp leaves (page 116), chopped

½ cup sheep sorrel leaves (page 138), chopped

¼ cup dandelion flowers (page 71), all green parts removed

¼ cup common blue violet flowers (page 106)

¼ cup black locust blossoms (page 179)

Toss together all the ingredients in a large serving bowl. Serve this salad with any of the salad dressings in this book.

SERVES 6

BABA GHANOUSH

When you add tart-flavored greenbrier shoots and leaves to this traditional Middle Eastern recipe, you'll enjoy it even more.

3 small eggplants

4 cloves garlic, peeled

2 tablespoons chopped fresh parsley leaves

¼ cup Tahini (page 38)

2 tablespoons fresh lemon juice

1 tablespoon mellow (light-colored) miso,
    1 teaspoon Vege-Sal, or ½ teaspoon salt,
    or to taste

½ teaspoon freshly ground cumin seeds

2 teaspoons chili paste or ¼ teaspoon cayenne pepper, or to taste

¼ cup sesame seeds, toasted (page 73)

1 cup tender young greenbrier leaves, shoots (stem tips), and tendrils

1. Preheat the oven to 375 degrees. Prick the eggplants with a fork so they won't explode in the oven, and bake them on a wire racks set over an oiled cook-

ie sheet until they are soft and shriveled, about 1 hour. Plunge the eggplants into cold water to cool, and then peel them, discarding the skin.

2. In a food processor, combine the garlic and parsley and process into a paste. Add the remaining ingredients except the sesame seeds and greenbrier and process until smooth. Stir in the sesame seeds and chill.

3. Serve Baba Ghanoush with Pita Bread (page 38) and garnish it with the greenbrier. Baba Ghanoush will keep, tightly covered, in the refrigerator for 5 days.

SERVES 6

WILD GARLIC

Allium canadense

THIS PLANT IS VERY SIMILAR TO FIELD GARLIC (see page 57), except that its leaves are flat, not round, the plant reaches only 14 inches in height, the flowers are sparser, and the leaves don't reappear in the fall. Wild Garlic grows in eastern North America, and its flavor is even better than that of its relatives. Again, use the leaves and bulbs in place of chives and garlic, respectively. Before using the bulbs, clean them off and peel off any skin that contains dirt.

SAVORY TOFU SPREAD

This spicy dip also makes a great spread for sandwiches, and it makes simple baked potatoes, baked beets, or steamed vegetables irresistible.

1 ½ teaspoons wild garlic bulbs, cleaned and any skin with dirt removed

1 small red onion, cut into several pieces

One 19-ounce package silken tofu, well drained

2 tablespoons Fakin' Bacon Bits (optional)

1 tablespoon umeboshi plum vinegar

1 tablespoon red wine vinegar

1 tablespoon corn oil or olive oil

1 ½ teaspoons caraway seeds

1 ½ teaspoons lecithin granules

2 teaspoons sweet white miso or other miso

2 teaspoons brewer's yeast

1 teaspoon Tabasco sauce or ¼ teaspoon cayenne
    pepper, or to taste

1 teaspoon toasted sesame oil

½ teaspoon hot paprika

¼ teaspoon freshly ground fenugreek seeds

1 cup low-sodium pitted olives, drained

1. In a food processor, chop the garlic. Add the onion and chop. Add the remaining ingredients, except the olives, and process until smooth.

2. Add the olives and process until they are well chopped. Savory Tofu Spread will keep, tightly covered, in the refrigerator for up to a week.

MAKES 3 ½ CUPS

NO CHEESE SPREAD

Here's a cheesy spread flavored with the combination of ingredients I've found to be so effective in creating mock cheese, but with wild garlic leaves and caraway seeds for extra zip, and puréed avocado as a thickener. Use No Cheese Spread as a spread on breads or as a dip for vegetables.

One 19-ounce package silken tofu, well drained

1 medium-size ripe avocado, peeled and pitted

½ cup wild garlic leaves, chopped

¼ cup mellow (light-colored) miso

2 tablespoons lecithin granules

1 tablespoon corn oil, flaxseed oil, or olive oil

1 tablespoon red wine vinegar

2 tablespoons brown rice vinegar

4 teaspoons brewer's yeast

1 teaspoon caraway seeds

1 teaspoon hot paprika

½ teaspoon turmeric

½ teaspoon Tabasco sauce

In a food processor, combine all the ingredients and process until smooth, or potato masher with a whisk or fork until smooth. No Cheese Spread will keep, tightly covered, in the refrigerator for up to a week.

MAKES 3 CUPS

AVOCADO DIP

This simple mixture featuring wild garlic is wonderful as a sandwich spread or as a dip.

1 medium-size ripe avocado, peeled, pitted, and
    mashed

1 cup Red Hot Chile Sauce (page 162)

1 cup Tofu Grated Cheese (page 32)

2 teaspoons wild garlic bulbs, cleaned, any dirty
    skin peeled away, and chopped

Mix together all the ingredients, using a food processor or mixing by hand, and serve. Avocado Dip will keep, tightly covered, in the refrigerator for 5 to 7 days.

MAKES 3 CUPS

RED HOT CHILE SAUCE

This simple hot sauce is great served with tortillas or other Mexican dishes. Smother beans with it or pour it over the fillings for enchiladas or tacos.

1½ cups dried chiles (you may choose a
*   combination, hot or mild, according to your*
*   taste; larger chiles are usually mild, while*
*   the small ones are fiery)*
3 cups boiling water
¼ cup tomato paste
1 tablespoon wild garlic bulbs, cleaned, any skin
*   with dirt removed, and finely chopped, or*
*   4 cloves regular garlic, finely chopped*
1 teaspoon Vege-Sal or ½ teaspoon salt, or to taste
1 teaspoon dried oregano, finely crumbled
¼ teaspoon freshly ground cumin

1. Dry-toast the chiles in a large skillet over medium heat until the chiles are slightly browned and fragrant, 2 to 3 minutes, stirring very often. Don't let the chiles blacken and burn or they'll become bitter.
2. Remove the toasted chiles from the skillet and allow them to cool. Break open the chiles and remove the stems, seeds, and ribs. (You're best off working with gloves on when you do this, to avoid getting the burning capsaicin on your fingers; or wash your hands three times after you're done—and don't touch your eyes!) Rinse the chiles with cold water, drain them, and then put them in a saucepan with the boiling water. Remove the pot from the heat, cover, and allow the chiles to soak for 1 hour.
3. Add the remaining ingredients and bring the pot to a boil. Reduce the heat to low, and simmer, covered, for 10 minutes.
4. Transfer the mixture to a blender and process until smooth. Red Hot Chile Sauce will keep, tightly cov-

ered, in the refrigerator for up to 10 days. You can also store it in the freezer for months.

MAKES 5½ CUPS

WILD AIOLI

This wild garlic mayonnaise uses potatoes and lecithin granules instead of egg yolks. If you love garlic or hate crowds, this one is for you. It's perishable, so use it within 6 days.

1 tablespoon wild garlic bulbs, cleaned and any
*   skin with dirt peeled away*
¾ cup olive oil
½ cup diced cooked potato
2 tablespoons lecithin granules
2 tablespoons mellow (light-colored) miso
1 teaspoon fresh lemon juice
½ teaspoon freshly ground black pepper
*   (¼ teaspoon peppercorns)*

1. Chop the wild garlic in a food processor or by hand.
2. Add the remaining ingredients and process until smooth, or mash them together with a potato masher or fork until smooth. Wild Aioli will keep, tightly covered, in the refrigerator for 6 days.

MAKES 1⅔ CUPS

CHONCE

This unusual hot seasoning includes ingredients associated with Indian, Mediterranean, and health-conscious cuisines. Even plain macrobiotic food won't taste bland when you season it with chonce. Add this seasoning to soups, grains, spreads, or sauces. Try it and take a chonce! I like the flavor so much, I raid the refrigerator to snap up a spoonful by itself every now and then (don't tell anyone!).

3 tablespoons peanut oil

3 tablespoons corn oil or flaxseed oil

2 teaspoons cumin seeds

¼ teaspoon crushed red pepper

¼ cup fresh basil leaves or 4 teaspoons dried

1 tablespoon wild garlic bulbs, cleaned and any skin
  with dirt removed, or regular garlic, chopped

½ teaspoon freshly ground coriander seeds

6 tablespoons brewer's yeast

¼ teaspoon ground cloves

1 teaspoon tamari soy sauce

1. In a small skillet over low heat, heat the oils together. Add the cumin seeds and crushed red pepper and cook them for 2 to 3 minutes, stirring constantly. Add the basil and wild garlic and cook for another minute, stirring.

2. Add the remaining ingredients, remove the pot from the heat, and allow the mixture to sit in the hot pan for another 2 minutes, stirring often. Chonce will keep, tightly covered, in the refrigerator, for up to 2 weeks.

MAKES ½ CUP

WILD GARLIC OIL

Here is a simple way to flavor olive oil with wild garlic. Using the oil imparts the health benefits of garlic while guaranteeing you a seat on the New York City subway. Use the oil sparingly (it's strong tasting) uncooked, or for cooking, to impart an onion/garlic flavor to foods. It's especially good for dipping bread.

½ cup wild garlic bulbs, cleaned and any skin with
  dirt peeled away, avoiding cutting into the bulbs

½ cup olive oil, or as needed

1. Put the bulbs in a jar and cover them with olive oil. Tightly cover the jar and store it in the refrigerator for up to 2 weeks, shaking the jar every morning and evening. (You can use the oil after a few hours, but it won't be full strength.)

2. Strain out the garlic and use it in other recipes. Store the flavored oil in a jar in the refrigerator. (Recent reports warn that the traditional practice of storing oil containing vegetable particles at room temperature risks botulism.) Wild Garlic Oil will keep, tightly covered, in the refrigerator for 6 weeks.

MAKES ½ CUP

WILD GARLIC SALAD

Sweet-tasting grapes, spicy wild garlic, crunchy carrots, crunchy walnuts, and mild greens contrast with each other to create a perfect balance in this salad.

4 cups mesclun salad green mix

2 cups wild garlic leaves and bulbs, bulbs cleaned,
  any skin with dirt peeled away, and chopped

2 cups seedless grapes, sliced

2 cups walnuts, chopped

1 medium-size carrot, grated

Black Walnut Salad Dressing (page 376)

Toss together all the salad ingredients in a large serving bowl. Serve with the dressing on the side.

SERVES 6

SPAGHETTI WITH WILD GARLIC

This is one of the simplest and best ways to serve spaghetti.

> 12 ounces Buckwheat Noodles (page 34) or store-bought spaghetti
> ¼ cup olive oil
> 1 tablespoon wild garlic bulbs, cleaned, any dirty skin peeled away, and crushed
> 3 tablespoons chopped fresh parsley leaves
> Salt and freshly ground black pepper to taste

1. Cook the spaghetti in rapidly boiling salted water with a dash of oil until al dente, about 7 minutes, and drain.

2. Meanwhile, heat the remaining olive oil in a medium-size skillet over medium heat, add the wild garlic and parsley and cook, stirring, until the garlic is slightly brown (but don't let the garlic burn).

3. Add the drained spaghetti to the skillet, toss to coat it with the oil, and serve at once.

SERVES 4

TOFU GROUND BEEF

Use this hot Mexican filling in enchiladas, stuffed peppers, and avocados, or in any recipe that calls for ground beef. Mixing in some Tofu Cream Cheese (page 30) works especially well and also smooths out the spiciness.

> 2 tablespoons olive oil
> 1 medium-size onion, chopped
> 1 tablespoon wild garlic bulbs, cleaned, peeled of any dirty skin, and finely chopped
> One 16-ounce package extra-firm tofu, drained and grated in a food processor or finely chopped

> 1 ½ teaspoons freshly ground celery seeds (1 teaspoon seeds)
> 1 teaspoon hot paprika
> 1 teaspoon dried thyme, finely crumbled
> 1 teaspoon Bragg's Liquid Aminos or Vege-Sal or ½ teaspoon salt, or to taste
> ½ cup Red Hot Chile Sauce (page 162)

1. Heat the olive in a large skillet over medium heat. Add the onion, wild garlic, tofu, celery seeds, paprika, and thyme and cook, stirring, for 10 minutes.

2. Stir in the Bragg's Liquid Aminos and the Red Hot Chile Sauce, reduce the heat to low, cover, and simmer for 10 minutes.

MAKES 3 CUPS

POKEWEED

Phytolacca americana

THIS REDDISH-STAINED, NON-WOODY PLANT grows from 4 to 8 feet tall and branches like a tree, and then dies to the ground, all in one season. Its stalked, alternate, oval emerald green smooth-edged leaves grow to 8 to 10 inches long. Short-stalked, small, five-petaled radially symmetrical flowers with green centers bloom in the summer and fall, dangling from long racemes (common stems). The flowers are replaced by purple–black berries ⅓ inch in diameter in the fall, each with an indentation, as though someone has poked it. Underground is a huge, fleshy perennial taproot that is *toxic*.

Pokeweed is one of the best-tasting vegetables on the planet. The flavor defies comparison with any other vegetable. Gourmet stores in Europe (where the plant is grown as a crop) and supermarkets in the South (where it's been popular since the days of the pioneers) sell it canned. *Make sure you collect only the young stems and leaves only in the spring, never the roots, flowers, berries, or summer or fall plants, which are poisonous. Avoid plants that are more than 8 inches tall. Never eat pokeweed raw or out of season. Prepare pokeweed as directed below, or you may get very sick. Always discard the cooking water from preparing boiled pokeweed. Beginners should use this potentially dangerous gourmet vegetable only under expert supervision.*

BASIC POKEWEED PREPARATION

This recipe is a must for anyone using pokeweed. It makes the plant safe and delicious.

> 8 cups young pokeweed leaves and stems from plants that are up to 8 inches tall, collected only in springtime (and without any pieces of the toxic taproot), coarsely chopped
> 4 cloves garlic (optional), chopped
> 2 tablespoons olive oil (optional)
> 2 teaspoons tamari soy sauce (optional)
> ¼ cup red wine vinegar (optional)

1. Bring 1 large pot of water and 1 medium-size pot of water to a rapid boil over high heat. Place the pokeweed in the medium-size pot and let it boil for 1 minute. Drain the pokeweed in a colander, discarding the cooking water.

2. Transfer some of the boiling water from the large pot to the medium-size pot, add the pokeweed to it immediately before it can cool, bring the medium-size pot back to a boil over high heat, and let the poke-

weed boil for another minute. Drain it again, discarding the cooking water.

3. Refill the medium-size pot again with boiling water, add the pokeweed immediately, bring to a boil again, and let the pokeweed boil for 15 minutes. Drain the pokeweed again, pressing the pokeweed against the colander with a slotted spoon to press out as much water as possible. Discard the cooking water.

4. Meanwhile, if desired, gently heat the garlic in the olive oil, stirring, until it is lightly browned, 2 to 3 minutes. Stir the oil, garlic, tamari, and vinegar into the drained, cooked pokeweed greens and serve hot.

MAKES 2⅔ CUPS

Note: Omit step 4 only if you're planning to use the pokeweed in another recipe with different seasonings.

POKEWEED RELISH

This is a wonderful condiment to serve with savory dishes as long as you harvest and prepare pokeweed correctly (see Basic Pokeweed Preparation, above).

> 1 medium-size ripe avocado, peeled, pitted, and chopped
> 1½ tablespoons Sumac Concentrate (page 281) or fresh lime juice
> 1 cup cooked and drained unseasoned pokeweed
> ½ cup unsalted dry-roasted peanuts, chopped
> ½ cup Homemade Ketchup (page 37)
> One 6-ounce jar low-sodium pitted olives, drained and chopped
> 2 tablespoons minced red onion
> 1 tablespoon preserved radish with chili (available in Asian ethnic stores) or minced radish, or
> ½ teaspoon cayenne pepper

In a medium-size bowl, combine all the ingredients and chill until ready to serve.

MAKES 3 ½ CUPS

POKEWEED CRÊPES

A thin batter of whole-grain flour, a liquid, an oil, and seasonings can produce wonderful crêpes. You can stuff these main-course crêpes with any kind of savory stuffing moistened with a sauce. Here's a simple example with a pokeweed filling. Be sure to harvest and prepare the pokeweed properly (see page 165) or you could poison yourself.

CRÊPES

¾ cup plus 1 ½ tablespoons (¼ pound) brown rice
  flour and 1 cup (¼ pound) buckwheat flour, or
  ½ pound any whole-grain flour
½ cup arrowroot or kudzu
2 ¼ cups soy milk or nut milk, or as needed
1 tablespoon freshly grated lemon rind or
  1 teaspoon dried
1 tablespoon chopped fresh parsley leaves
1 teaspoon dried tarragon, finely crumbled
1 teaspoon Vege-Sal or ½ teaspoon salt
½ teaspoon freshly ground white pepper
  (¼ teaspoon peppercorns)
Oil for cooking the crêpes

FILLING

1 ¾ cups cooked brown rice
1 cup cooked and drained unseasoned pokeweed
  (page 165)
½ cup walnuts, chopped
½ cup Béarnaise Sauce à la Brill (page 120) or
  other sauce
1 tablespoon tamari soy sauce, or to taste
5 cloves garlic, or to taste, chopped

½ teaspoon chili paste or ⅛ teaspoon cayenne
  pepper, or to taste

¾ cup Tofu Sour Cream (optional; page 33)

1. *To make the crêpes:* In a blender, combine all the batter ingredients and process until smooth, using just enough soy milk to make a thin batter.

2. Pour a circle of batter onto a hot, oiled griddle and spread the batter with a metal spatula to make a thin pancake. When the underside is lightly browned, flip the crêpe over with the spatula and brown the other side. (If the crêpes brown unevenly, place a heat diffuser under the griddle.) Repeat the process with the remaining batter. Remove the finished crêpes to a plate, piling them on top of each other.

3. Preheat the oven to 350 degrees.

4. *To make the filling:* Combine all the filling ingredients.

5. Put a couple of tablespoons of filling along one edge of each crêpe and roll it up. Place the filled crêpes in a 14 x 9 x 2-inch oiled baking dish and bake them until they are heated through, about 15 minutes.

6. Serve Pokeweed Crêpes, topped with the Tofu Sour Cream, if desired.

MAKES 12 CRÊPES; SERVES 4 TO 6

POKE-QUETTES

If pokeweed doesn't kill you (follow instructions on page 165 to make sure it doesn't), it can be one of the best foods you've ever tasted. And its distinctive flavor pervades these hearty croquettes.

4 cups cooked millet or other grain
2 cups cooked and drained unseasoned pokeweed
  (page 165)

1 cup Tofu Cream Cheese (page 30)

1 cup walnuts, chopped

1 cup fresh Bread Crumbs (page 40)

2 tablespoons chopped fresh parsley or dill leaves

2 tablespoons chopped fresh basil leaves

6 cloves garlic, chopped

1 tablespoon chili paste or ½ teaspoon cayenne
   pepper, or to taste

2 teaspoons dried marjoram, finely crumbled

2 teaspoons Vege-Sal or 1 teaspoon salt, or to taste

2 teaspoons paprika

2 teaspoons freshly ground black mustard seeds
   (1 teaspoon seeds)

2 teaspoons freshly ground white pepper
   (1 teaspoon peppercorns)

1. Preheat the oven to 350 degrees.

2. Mix together all the ingredients. Using a circular cookie cutter or working by hand, shape the mixture into 18 croquettes that are about 3 inches in diameter and ¾ inch thick.

3. Arrange the croquettes in a single layer on 2 oiled cookie sheets and bake them until they are lightly browned underneath, 40 to 50 minutes, turning them halfway through the baking time. Serve with Sesame Ramp Sauce (page 119) or any of the other sauces in this book.

MAKES 18 CROQUETTES; SERVES 6 TO 8

POKE LOAF

Pokeweed has such a wonderful flavor that it improves any dish, as you'll see when you make this vegetable loaf.

2 cups cooked and drained unseasoned pokeweed
   (page 165)

2 cups cooked brown rice or other grains

2 cups fresh Bread Crumbs (page 40)

1 cup walnuts, chopped

¼ cup lecithin granules

¼ cup dark-colored miso, 4 teaspoons Vege-Sal, or
   2 teaspoons salt, or to taste

5 tablespoons freshly ground flaxseeds
   (2 tablespoons seeds)

1 tablespoon hot paprika

4 cloves garlic, crushed

2 teaspoons dried oregano, finely crumbled

2 teaspoons freshly ground black mustard seeds
   (1 teaspoon seeds)

2 teaspoons freshly ground black pepper
   (1 teaspoon peppercorns)

1 ½ teaspoons freshly ground celery seeds
   (1 teaspoon seeds)

½ teaspoon freshly ground allspice berries or 6
   common spicebush berries (page 314), finely
   chopped

½ teaspoon ground mace

1 cup Ramp Barbecue Sauce (page 121) or
   Puffball Marinara (page 397)

1. Preheat the oven to 350 degrees.

2. Mix together all the ingredients, except half the barbecue or marinara sauce.

3. Press the mixture into an oiled 9¼ x 5½ x 2¼-inch loaf pan (or an equivalent casserole dish). Spread the remaining sauce on top. Bake the vegetable loaf, uncovered, until it is lightly browned and firm, about 1 hour. Serve hot from the oven.

SERVES 6 TO 8

POKEWEED BAKED EGGS

The flavor of eggs adds to the richness of this poke-weed casserole, even though the dish is animal-free. The secret lies in the flavor of the seasonings and the flavor and texture of the other ingredients. As a vegan who has loved eggs since childhood, I make this recipe whenever pokeweed is in season, and with defrosted cooked pokeweed during the rest of the year.

EGG LAYER

One 19-ounce package silken tofu, drained

½ cup flaxseed oil or corn oil

¼ cup dry Bread Crumbs (page 40)

¼ cup lecithin granules

2 ½ tablespoons freshly ground flaxseeds
    (1 tablespoon flaxseeds)

½ teaspoon dried tarragon, finely crumbled

¼ teaspoon turmeric

¼ teaspoon paprika

½ teaspoon freshly ground yellow mustard seeds
    (¼ teaspoon seeds)

⅛ teaspoon ground mace

⅛ teaspoon freshly ground fenugreek seeds

½ teaspoon Vege-Sal or ¼ teaspoon salt, or
    to taste

1 teaspoon freshly ground black pepper
    (½ teaspoon peppercorns)

2 cups cooked and drained seasoned pokeweed
    (page 165)

1 tablespoon olive oil

¼ cup dry Bread Crumbs (page 40)

1. Preheat the oven to 375 degrees.
2. *To make the egg layer:* In a 1½-quart oiled casserole dish, mix together all the egg layer ingredients with a whisk, mixer, or fork.

3. Spread the pokeweed evenly over the egg layer.
4. Mix the olive oil with the bread crumbs and press the mixture evenly over the pokeweed layer. Bake the casserole, uncovered, for 30 minutes.

SERVES 6

FRIED CHICKEN MUSHROOM

Lyophyllum decastes

THE FRIED CHICKEN MUSHROOM IS COMPLETELY different from the chicken mushroom (see page 321), and it doesn't even taste like fried chicken (at least, not to me). Its cap, which measures 1 to 5 inches across, is convex to almost flat, beige to yellow brown to grayish, with a margin that is in-curved at first, then upturned as the mushroom ages. The broad, whitish gills attach or sometimes slightly descend the stalk. The spore print is white. The whitish stalk is 2 to 4 inches long, ¼ to ¾ inch wide.

You can find shopping bags full of this mushroom anywhere in America, spring and fall (sometimes in the summer), growing on the ground in grassy areas or overgrown places and on disturbed soil, where the fungus decomposes organic material.

The fried chicken mushroom is considered second-rate, and it is when you sauté it with onions and garlic. But Asian cooks consider it first-rate because that's how it tastes when they use it correctly—in soups, stew, and sauces. Its sweet flavor, chewy texture, and slight okra-like thickening effect make it perfect for such dishes. This mushroom cooks in 15 to 20 minutes. Because you can find it in such large quantities, it's often worthwhile to use the caps and stems separately, adding the caps to your best recipes, and keeping the stems for dishes you're going to purée.

SWEET-AND-SOUR POWER

I first made this mouthwatering Southeast Asian–style dish with cultivated peaches and mushrooms in the 1970s. When I switched to using wild peaches and the fried chicken mushroom, the dish got even better.

¾ cup apple juice

¾ cup red wine vinegar

2 teaspoons arrowroot or kudzu

¼ cup peanut oil, or as needed

3 cups fried chicken mushrooms, chopped

1 small onion, sliced

3 frying peppers, seeded and sliced into strips

2 cups drained and diced firm tofu

2 tablespoons peeled and finely chopped fresh
ginger

5 medium-size ripe peaches, pitted and diced

1 cup almonds, chopped

½ cup alfalfa sprouts

2 tablespoons chopped fresh wild spearmint (page
59) or other mint leaves, or 2 teaspoons dried,
finely crumbled

2 teaspoons freshly ground cloves

2 teaspoons Angostura bitters (optional)

2 teaspoons Vege-Sal or 1 teaspoon salt, or to taste

⅛ teaspoon cayenne pepper

1. Assemble all the ingredients.

2. In a blender, blend the apple juice, vinegar, and arrowroot.

3. Heat the peanut oil in a wok or large skillet over high heat, add the mushrooms, and stir-fry them for 5 minutes. Set them aside.

4. Add more oil to the wok, if necessary, and stir-fry the onions and peppers for 3 minutes. Set them aside.

5. Stir-fry the tofu and ginger for 3 minutes.

6. Add all cooked ingredients and the remaining ingredients to the wok and bring the contents to a boil over medium heat. Reduce the heat to low and simmer, covered, for 10 minutes, stirring often. Serve over noodles.

SERVES 6 TO 8

COMMON MILKWEED

Asclepias syriaca

THIS THICK-STEMMED, UNBRANCHED NON-woody plant, which exudes a milky fluid when cut, grows from 3 to 5 feet tall. Its velvety, thick, elliptical, opposite leaves grow 4 to 9 inches long and 2 to 4½ inches wide. The flower buds, which form in the spring, look like loose clusters of miniature broccoli heads. These buds give way to globular clusters of showy, radially symmetrical, five-petaled pink flowers. The flowers are replaced, in turn, in the summer by warty, cucumber-shaped seedpods filled with silky seeds.

Poisonous dogbane (*Apocynum* species) looks just like milkweed when the plants are immature. The only difference is that milkweed's stalk has minute hairs, while dogbane's stalk is bald, but you may need a hand lens to see the distinction. When the plants are mature, dogbane has different flowers and pods than milkweed has, and dogbane branches whereas milkweed does not.

Butterfly weed or pleurisy root (*Asclepias tuberosa*) is a poisonous milkweed with orange flowers and a *clear* sap. There are other poisonous milkweed species on the West Coast. *Beginners should collect common milkweed only under supervision.* Look for common milkweed in disturbed habitats, fields, poor or sandy soil, and along roadsides throughout the eastern United States.

Common milkweed provides three excellent cooked vegetables—the young shoots in mid-spring, the flower buds with immature leaves from the tops of the plants in late spring, and the flowers in early summer. The very young, firm seedpods of mid-summer are also edible cooked, but they're labor intensive to collect. You must boil milkweed in three changes of water (except the mature flowers, which you need only parboil for just 1 minute) to eliminate the slightly toxic but very bitter sap. After you squeeze out the excess water and season milkweed, it's great.

Eat small amounts of common milkweed the first time. This plant doesn't agree with everyone.

COMMON MILKWEED BASIC PREPARATION

Use the young shoots when they are up to 6 inches tall, the smaller leaves and tender sections of stem near the top of older plants, along with any unopened flower buds; or the firm, small, young pods. The basic preparation yields a great side dish, but you may also use the cooked milkweed in other recipes.

12 cups young common milkweed

4 cloves garlic, chopped

1 tablespoon olive oil

1 tablespoon tamari soy sauce

1 tablespoon brown rice vinegar or red wine vinegar

1. Bring a large pot and a medium-size pot of water to a rapid boil over high heat. Place the milkweed in the medium-size pot and let it boil for 1 minute. Drain the milkweed in a colander, discarding the cooking water.

2. Transfer some of the boiling water from the large pot to the medium-size pot, add the milkweed to the medium-size pot, and bring the pot back to a boil. Boil the milkweed for a minute. Drain it again, discarding the cooking water.

3. Refill the medium-size pot again with boiling water, add the milkweed, and bring the pot back to a boil. Boil the milkweed for 15 minutes. Drain it again, pressing the milkweed against the colander with a slotted spoon to press out as much water as possible. Discard the cooking water and transfer the milkweed to a large bowl.

4. Meanwhile, gently heat the garlic in the olive oil in a skillet over medium heat until it is very lightly browned, 2 to 3 minutes. Add the garlic, along with the tamari and brown rice vinegar, to the drained milkweed. (Omit this step if you're using the milkweed in another recipe with different seasonings.) Serve hot.

MAKES 2 CUPS

GINGKO MILKWEED SOUP

Gingkos come into season in the fall, milkweed in mid-spring, but you can freeze (or buy) gingko nuts, or freeze milkweed, and make this cross-seasonal dish anytime.

6½ cups Vegetable Stock (page 40)

¾ cup barley

¼ cup dried wakame or other dried seaweed

2 cloves garlic, crushed

1½ teaspoons chopped fresh dill

½ teaspoon dried tarragon, finely crumbled

⅜ teaspoon freshly ground celery seeds
   (¼ teaspoon seeds)

¾ cup cooked and drained unseasoned common
   milkweed (page 170)

1 medium-size onion, chopped

6 tablespoons toasted and shelled gingko nuts
   (page 435)

1 tablespoon dark-colored miso

1. In a large saucepan, bring the stock to a boil and then reduce the heat to low. Add the barley and simmer, covered, for 30 minutes.

2. Meanwhile, cover the wakame with water and let it soak for 10 minutes. Drain it and rinse it.

3. Add the wakame to the barley and stock along with garlic, dill, tarragon, and celery seeds and simmer the mixture for another 15 minutes. Add the milkweed and gingkos and simmer the mixture for another 5 minutes. Remove the pot from the heat.

4. Lower a strainer into the soup, add the miso, and stir it with a wooden spoon against the side of the strainer until the miso is dissolved. Serve hot.

SERVES 6

CREAM OF MILKWEED SOUP

Here's a quick, simple, and tasty cream soup.

2 cups Vegetable Stock (page 40)

1 tablespoon olive oil

1 small red onion, chopped

2 cloves garlic, chopped

1 celery stalk, sliced

1½ cups cooked and drained unseasoned common
   milkweed (page 170)

1½ cups drained silken tofu

2 tablespoons chopped fresh dill

2 teaspoons tamari soy sauce, or to taste

1 teaspoon chili paste or ¼ teaspoon cayenne
   pepper, or to taste

½ teaspoon freshly ground black pepper
   (¼ teaspoon peppercorns), or to taste

1. In a small saucepan, bring the stock to a boil.

2. In a large saucepan over medium heat, heat the olive oil. Add the onion, garlic, and celery and cook, stirring, for 10 minutes.

3. Transfer the vegetables to a blender along with the stock and remaining ingredients and process until smooth, beginning on low speed and holding down the cover with a towel to prevent eruptions.

4. Transfer the mixture back to the saucepan and gently heat it through over low heat. Serve hot.

SERVES 4 TO 6

SCALLOPED MILKWEED

Milkweed buds melding with other vegetables, nuts, and tofu cheese result in a wonderful casserole.

1 tablespoon olive oil

2 cloves garlic, chopped

2 cups fresh Bread Crumbs (page 40)

2 tablespoons flaxseed oil or corn oil

4 cups cooked and drained seasoned common
   milkweed (page 170)

Kernels cut from 2 ears of corn

2 medium-size ripe tomatoes, chopped

1 cup walnuts, chopped

1 tablespoon tamari soy sauce

2 cups Tofu Cream Cheese (page 30)

1½ cups Tofu Sharp Cheese (page 30)

1. Preheat the oven to 375 degrees.

2. Heat the olive oil over medium heat in a small skillet. Add the garlic and cook it, stirring, until it is lightly browned, 2 to 3 minutes. Do not burn it.

3. Mix the bread crumbs with the flaxseed oil in a small bowl.

4. Mix the cooked milkweed, corn, tomatoes, walnuts, tamari, and Tofu Cream Cheese together in a 3-quart oiled casserole dish. Top the casserole with the oiled bread crumbs. Sprinkle the Tofu Sharp Cheese on top and press it down with your hand. Bake the casserole, uncovered, until bubbly, about 35 minutes.

SERVES 6

MILKWEED BIRYANI

Common milkweed shoots, other wild vegetables, and a mock tofu yogurt make this East Indian layered rice casserole even more exotic. You may also substitute other vegetables for the milkweed, mushrooms, and potatoes, including wild onions (page 57) or ramps (page 116), pokeweed shoots (page 164), daylily shoots (page 64), eggplant, celery, zucchini, green peas, string beans, or green or red bell peppers.

> 2 ½ cups drained silken tofu
> Juice of 3 lemons
> 5 tablespoons peanut oil
> 2 teaspoons Vege-Sal or 1 teaspoon salt
> ½ teaspoon saffron threads
> 6 cups cooked brown basmati rice
> 2 teaspoons black or yellow mustard seeds
> 2 teaspoons cumin seeds
> 1 teaspoon cayenne pepper
> 2 cups cooked and drained unseasoned common
>   milkweed (page 170), chopped
> 2 cups oyster mushrooms (page 404) or other
>   mushrooms

> 2 cups chopped potatoes
> ½ cup chopped dried figs
> ½ cup shelled raw pistachio nuts or cashew pieces

1. Preheat the oven to 350 degrees.

2. In a blender, combine the tofu, 1 tablespoon of the lemon juice, 1 tablespoon of the peanut oil, and 1 teaspoon Vege-Sal and process until smooth.

3. Grind the saffron in a spice grinder and mix it in a small bowl with the remaining lemon juice. Let the mixture stand for 5 minutes or more. Mix the lemon juice–saffron mixture with half the rice.

4. Heat the remaining 4 tablespoons peanut oil in a small skillet over medium heat, add the mustard seeds, cumin seeds, and cayenne, and cook, stirring, constantly, until the mustard seeds pop. Immediately mix the spice blend into the cooked milkweed, oyster mushrooms, and potatoes along with the remaining 1 teaspoon Vege-Sal in a large bowl.

5. Layer a 3-quart oiled casserole dish with the plain rice, vegetables, saffron rice, figs and nuts, and tofu mixture. Bake the casserole, covered, until bubbly, about 50 minutes. Serve hot.

SERVES 6

MILKWEED RICE INDIAN STYLE

This Indian treatment of a plant that is native to America confirms the value of international cooperation.

> ¼ cup peanut oil
> 3 tablespoons coriander seeds
> 2 tablespoons cumin seeds
> 2 teaspoons black mustard seeds
> ¼ teaspoon fennel seeds
> 1 teaspoon poppy seeds

¼ teaspoon freshly ground star anise

One 1-inch cinnamon stick

1 tablespoon Vege-Sal or 1½ teaspoons salt, or to taste

4 cloves garlic, chopped

2 small chiles, seeds and ribs removed and chopped, or ½ teaspoon cayenne pepper, or to taste

2 cups brown basmati rice

1 teaspoon freshly ground cardamom seeds

½ teaspoon saffron threads, finely crumbled

1 teaspoon freshly grated nutmeg

4 bayberry leaves (page 185) or 2 bay leaves, ground

2 cups cooked and drained unseasoned common milkweed (page 170)

3¾ cups boiling water

1. Heat the peanut oil in a large skillet over medium heat and cook the coriander seeds, cumin seeds, black mustard seeds, fennel seeds, poppy seeds, ground star anise, cinnamon stick, and Vege-Sal until fragrant, about 2 minutes, stirring constantly. Add the garlic and chiles and cook, stirring, for another 2 minutes.

2. Add the rice, cardamom, saffron, nutmeg, and bayberry leaves and cook, stirring, for 3 to 4 minutes.

3. Combine the rice-and-spice mixture with the cooked milkweed and boiling water in a large saucepan and bring the pot to a boil over medium heat. Reduce the heat to low, and simmer, covered, until all the water is absorbed and the rice is tender, about 40 minutes.

SERVES 4 TO 6

MILKWEED ITALIANO

Milkweed is a wonderful vegetable. This Italian treatment is only one of the many delicious ways to use it.

8 cups Buckwheat Noodles (page 34) or store-bought flat noodles

2 cups Puffball Marinara (page 397)

2 cups cooked and drained, seasoned common milkweed (page 170)

1 head cauliflower, broken into florets and steamed for 10 minutes

1 tablespoon Vegetarian Worcestershire Sauce (page 56)

2 teaspoons poppy seeds

½ teaspoon Tabasco sauce or dash of cayenne pepper, or to taste

¼ teaspoon Vege-Sal or ⅛ teaspoon salt, or to taste

1 cup Tofu Cream Cheese (page 30)

2 cups fresh Bread Crumbs (page 40)

2 tablespoons corn oil

½ teaspoon freshly ground black pepper (¼ teaspoon peppercorns)

1½ cups Tofu Grated Cheese (page 32)

1. Preheat the oven to 350 degrees.

2. Cook the noodles in rapidly boiling salted water with a dash of oil for 3 minutes less than directed. Drain the noodles in a colander and then lower the colander into a bowl of cold water to halt the cooking. Drain the noodles again. Place the noodles in a 14 x 9 x 2-inch oiled baking dish, and cover them with the marinara sauce.

3. Arrange the cooked milkweed on top of the noodles and tomato sauce.

4. Mix the cauliflower with the Vegetarian Worcestershire Sauce, poppy seeds, Tabasco, and Vege-Sal, and spread the mixture evenly on top of the milkweed.

5. Spread the Tofu Cream Cheese on top of the cauliflower mixture with a large rubber spatula.

6. Mix the bread crumbs with the corn oil and spread

them on top of the Tofu Cream Cheese.

7. Sprinkle the black pepper on top of the bread crumbs and press everything down with the palm of your hand. Top with the Tofu Grated Cheese. Bake, uncovered, until bubbly, about 40 minutes.

SERVES 8

MILKWEED WITH PASTA

After one of my tours, Leslie Skolnik discovered that cooked milkweed with simple seasonings goes perfectly with pasta.

> *2 tablespoons olive oil*
> *4 cloves garlic, finely chopped*
> *4 cups cooked and drained unseasoned common*
>   *milkweed (page 170)*
> *Vege-Sal or salt and freshly ground black pepper*
>   *to taste*
> *4 cups freshly cooked Buckwheat Noodles*
>   *(page 34)*

1. Heat the olive oil in a large skillet, add the garlic, and cook, stirring, until it is very lightly browned, 2 to 3 minutes.

2. Add the cooked milkweed, season with Vege-Sal salt and pepper to taste, and toss with the pasta.

SERVES 4 TO 6

DULSE
Palmaria palmata

THIS PURPLE-BROWN SEAWEED, WHICH ATTACHES itself to rocks below the low tide line, grows up to 1 foot across and is so deeply lobed that it resembles broad fingers tapering to a small stalk. At its best in the spring, dulse grows in New England and the Pacific Northwest—places that are inaccessible to me. Fortunately, you can also find this seaweed in great abundance in health food stores.

Enjoy dulse raw, in salads, or as a snack, or cooked. You can sauté it, bake it, or add it to any dish, from Asian recipes to savory breads to soup. Its sharp, nutty flavor lends itself well to nearly any vegetable dish.

To store dulse long-term, dry it in a food dehydrator or in a very low oven with the door open until the seaweed feels soft and dry. Then store the seaweed in an airtight container.

TARAMA SPREAD

Is there something fishy about this Greek recipe? Traditionally, this spread or dip is made with fish roe. Here, dulse seaweed provides the fishy flavor, and umeboshi plums (available in health food stores and Asian groceries) add the zing. Serve Tarama Spread on crackers, bread, chips, or cooked or raw vegetables.

> *2 tablespoons olive oil*
> *1 cup fresh Bread Crumbs (page 40)*
> *½ cup dulse flakes*
> *Juice of 1 lemon*
> *¼ cup pitted umeboshi plums*
> *2 tablespoons lecithin granules*

In a food processor, combine all the ingredients and process until smooth. Tarama Spread will keep, tightly covered, in the refrigerator for 1 week.

MAKES 3½ CUPS

ALMOND SEAWEED SAUCE

Seaweed with almonds sounds like a strange combination, but it works surprisingly well.

1 cup Vegetable Stock (page 40) or water
1 cup almonds
¼ teaspoon dulse powder
¼ teaspoon kelp powder (found at health food stores)
⅜ teaspoon freshly ground celery seeds
   (¼ teaspoon seeds)
2 tablespoons almond oil or vegetable oil
¼ teaspoon paprika
4 teaspoons dark-colored miso

1. In a food processor or blender, blend the vegetable stock, almonds, dulse, kelp, celery seeds, almond oil, and paprika together until very smooth. Turn the blender on and off if necessary to blend the mixture from top to bottom.

2. Add the miso and blend again. Heat the sauce until warm and serve it over vegetables or noodles.

MAKES 2 ½ CUPS

DULSE CORNBREAD

Dulse adds just the right amount of tanginess and saltiness to this cornbread.

2 ¾ cups (11 ounces) oat flour and 2 ⅓ cups
   (11 ounces) sweet brown rice flour, or 22
   ounces any whole-grain flour
3 cups yellow cornmeal
3 ½ teaspoons baking soda
6 tablespoons freshly ground flaxseeds (¼ cup seeds)
1 tablespoon cream of tartar
1 teaspoon ground mace
½ teaspoon turmeric

3 ¼ cups soy milk or nut milk
¾ cup corn oil
½ cup lecithin granules
¼ cup fresh lemon juice
1 teaspoon liquid stevia or 2 tablespoons rice
   syrup, barley malt, or honey
½ cup dulse flakes
1 tablespoon anise seeds

1. Preheat the oven to 350 degrees.

2. In a large bowl, mix together the flour, cornmeal, baking soda, ground flaxseeds, cream of tartar, mace, and turmeric.

3. In a medium-size bowl, mix together the soy milk, corn oil, lecithin granules, lemon juice, and liquid stevia. Stir the wet ingredients into the dry ingredients. Don't overmix. Stir in the dulse flakes and anise seeds. Don't overmix.

4. Transfer the batter to 2 oiled 6½ x 4⅜ x 2½-inch loaf pans and shape it into loaves. Set a pan of water on the bottom of the oven to keep the crust soft. Bake the loaves until a toothpick inserted in the center emerges clean, about 45 minutes. Eat the bread warm or let it cool on a wire rack.

MAKES 2 LOAVES

OAK LEAF
Quercus species

OAK LEAVES ARE DELICIOUS, BUT ONLY IF YOU'RE a caterpillar. But immature white oak leaves make an outstanding table and cooking wine, that is great in soups and sauces. (See page 292 for details about oak trees.)

WHITE OAK WINE

Here's one of the weirdest wild food experiments I've ever conducted: making wine from oak leaves. I was completely astonished that I could make a superb wine that can be used as a table wine, in place of white wine, or a cooking wine that can be used in virtually any savory recipe that calls for wine. The flavor is robust, but not overpowering. The secret is using very young white oak leaves that have not yet developed a high tannin content.

7 cups sugar

1 gallon boiling water

1 gallon immature white oak leaves or leaves of other members of the white oak group, gathered in early spring, just before the leaves have reached full size

¼ cup juniper berries

¼ cup fennel seeds

¼ cup celery seeds

½ teaspoon champagne yeast or other wine yeast

1. Dissolve the sugar in the boiling water in a non-metal (plastic or ceramic) food container and add the oak leaves, juniper berries, fennel seeds, and celery seeds.

2. When the liquid has cooled to lukewarm, stir in the yeast and cover the container with a non-airtight cover, cheesecloth, or towel.

3. Allow the mixture to ferment for a week at room temperature, stirring it twice a day.

4. Strain the mixture through cheesecloth, transfer the liquid to a jug, and seal the jug with an airlock stopper (which lets carbon dioxide bubbles escape but keeps oxygen out).

5. When the bubbling stops and fermentation ends a few weeks later, seal the jug with a cork and let it age for 2 months to 2 years (taste it to determine if it's ready) before using it.

6. Siphon the wine to get rid of the sediment, if desired.

MAKES 1 GALLON

CHINESE SAUCE

Wild white oak wine adds a distinctive touch to this sauce, which can enhance any Chinese dish.

¼ cup arrowroot or kudzu

1 teaspoon Five-Spice Powder (page 112)

2 tablespoons White Oak Wine (opposite)

4 cups Vegetable Stock (page 40)

2 tablespoons dark-colored miso

1. Mix the arrowroot, Five-Spice Powder, and wine with 3½ cups of the stock in a medium-size saucepan. Bring the pot to a boil, reduce the heat to medium-low, and simmer the mixture for 5 minutes, stirring constantly.

2. Blend the remaining ½ cup stock with the miso in a blender, stir the miso mixture into the simmering stock, and remove the pot from the heat. Serve hot.

MAKES 4 CUPS

WILD GRAPE

Vitis species

GRAPES ARE HIGH-CLIMBING, WOODY VINES with stalked, alternate, serrated leaves that vary from 2 to 8 inches across and are partially divided into three lobes, like maple leaves. Some poisonous plants have similar fruit, but different leaves. Porcelain berry

(*Ampelopsis brevipendunculata*) has similar leaves, but the vine isn't woody. Unlike poisonous Canada moonseed (*Menispermum canadense*), the grapevine supports itself with forked (they have split ends consisting of two branches), wirelike tendrils. The grapevine's familiar dark purple fruit has many seeds, whereas Canada moonseed has but one crescent-shaped seed.

Wild grapes, which are in season in autumn, grow in partially sunny areas in the woods, along the edges of woods, roads, and trails, in thickets, and in wetlands throughout the country. Only a small fraction of wild grapevines bear fruit in any one year, and abundant fruit is more likely if the weather has been dry.

Some wild grapes taste great raw, while others are very sour. Use the fruit in jams, jellies, pie and cake fillings, or drinks. Cook wild grapes with a sweetener and, if appropriate, a thickener. Then strain out the seeds with a food mill. Grapes cook in 10 minutes.

In the spring, you can also steam the medium-sized leaves until they're soft enough to eat, but not so soft that they tear easily, 10 to 20 minutes. Then roll the leaves around virtually any stuffing imaginable.

APRICOT-STUFFED GRAPE LEAVES

When we found in-season wild grape vines on a recent tour, I suggested off the top of my head that we prepare a simple stuffing of apricots, walnuts, and bread crumbs. It sounded so good that I tried it myself a few days later, and I certainly wasn't disappointed.

½ cup dried apricots
½ cup unsweetened apricot or other fruit juice, or
   as needed
16 medium-size wild grape leaves, stems removed
½ cup fresh Bread Crumbs (page 40)

½ cup walnuts, toasted (page 158) and chopped
1 tablespoon flaxseed oil, corn oil, or almond oil
½ teaspoon ground cinnamon
½ teaspoon dried wild spearmint (page 59) or
   other mint leaves, finely crumbled
½ teaspoon freshly grated nutmeg

1. Cover the dried apricots with the apricot juice and either soak the fruit overnight, or place the fruit and juice in a saucepan, bring the pot to a boil, remove the pot from the heat, and let the apricots soak, covered, for 1 hour.

2. Meanwhile, steam the grape leaves on a steamer rack over boiling water until they are tender, but not so long that they tear easily, 10 to 20 minutes.

3. In a saucepan, simmer the apricots in their soaking juice, over medium-low heat, covered, for 10 minutes adding more juice or water if necessary.

4. Chop the apricots and mix them with the bread crumbs, walnuts, flaxseed oil, cinnamon, spearmint, and nutmeg. Place about 1 tablespoon of the stuffing at the base of each leaf, fold the leaf's sides toward the leaf's midline, and roll the leaf up from the base to the tip. Serve as an appetizer.

MAKES 16 LEAVES

EPAZOTE, MEXICAN TEA
Teloxys ambrosoides

THIS FRAGRANT PLANT USUALLY GROWS TO 3 feet tall and features elliptical, coarse-toothed, leaves that are 2 to 4 inches long and pointed on both ends. In the summer and fall, spikes of tiny green flowers arch upward from the leaf axil (where the leaf and stem join). The whole plant smells like a cross between pine and turpentine. It grows throughout North America in disturbed soil.

As a seasoning, epazote leaves are a must for Mexican dishes—great in bean dishes, tortillas, stews, and soups. Use them fresh or dried the same way you'd use parsley. But don't eat epazote in large quantities as a vegetable, or the resins may cause nausea. Caution: Avoid this plant if you're a parasite—it may kill you!

GARLIC BEANS

This is a garlic-lover's delight. Cooking garlic without cutting into it turns it into a kinder, gentler herb. Soaking the beans in hot water for 1 hour instead of soaking them overnight, and adding oil, cumin, and epazote reduces gas. Adding the salt after cooking keeps the beans from becoming tough.

1 pound dried black or white beans, rinsed and picked over

16 wild garlic bulbs (page 160), cleaned and any skin with dirt removed, or 1 clove regular garlic, peeled

1 tablespoon chopped fresh epazote leaves or 1 teaspoon dried, finely crumbled

1 teaspoon freshly ground cumin seeds

½ cup olive oil

1 clove garlic, minced

2 teaspoons Vege-Sal or 1 teaspoon salt, or to taste

1. In a large saucepan, cover the beans in water and bring them to a boil. Cook the beans for 2 minutes, remove the pot from the heat, cover, and let the beans stand for 1 hour.

2. Tie the garlic bulbs and epazote up in cheesecloth.

3. Drain the beans, discard the water, and return them to the pot along with the garlic bulbs, epazote, cumin seeds, and 1 teaspoon of the olive oil. Add enough water to cover the beans by 1½ inches. Bring the pot to a boil over medium heat, reduce the heat to low, cover, and simmer until the beans are almost tender, about 1 hour, adding more water if necessary.

4. Meanwhile, heat the remaining olive oil in a small skillet over medium heat, add the minced garlic, and cook it, stirring, until it is very lightly browned. Remove the garlic and discard it before it burns, reserving the oil. Add the garlic-flavored oil to the beans and cook the beans, uncovered, until they are tender, another 25 minutes. Stir in the Vege-Sal. Serve hot.

SERVES 4 TO 6

BLACK BEANS WITH EPAZOTE

Here's another simple recipe that demonstrates that epazote is one of the best seasonings for beans. And, for good measure, it also includes bayberry leaves, which are ideal for beans.

2 cups dried black beans or other beans, rinsed and picked over

11 cups water, or as needed

2 tablespoons chopped fresh epazote leaves or 2 teaspoons dried, finely crumbled

3 bayberry leaves (page 185) or 2 bay leaves

1 head garlic (use elephant garlic, if available), minced

2 chiles (use a more or less pungent variety, according to your taste), seeds and ribs removed and chopped

1 tablespoon olive oil

1 teaspoon Vege-Sal or ½ teaspoon salt, or to taste

1. In a large saucepan, cover the beans with 8 cups of the water and bring the pot to a boil over high heat. Let the beans cook for 2 minutes before removing the pot from the heat. Let the beans stand, covered, for 1 hour.
2. Meanwhile, put the epazote and bayberry leaves in a tea ball or tea bag, or tie them up in a piece of cheesecloth.
3. Drain the beans. Return the beans to the saucepan, along with the epazote, bayberry leaves, garlic, chiles, olive oil, and the remaining 3 cups water. Bring the pot to a boil over high heat, reduce the heat to low, and simmer the beans, uncovered, until they are very soft, 2 to 2½ hours. Add more water toward the end if necessary. Add the Vege-Sal.
4. Mash some of the beans with a wooden spoon to thicken the remaining liquid, if desired.

SERVES 6

BLACK LOCUST
Robinia pseudoacacia L.

B LACK LOCUST IS ONE OF MY FAVORITE TREES. Growing up to 80 feet tall, it has deeply furrowed, dark brown bark. The alternate leaves are 6 to 12 inches long and feather-compound (divided along an axis), with 7 to 21 elliptical, smooth-edged leaflets.

Clusters of fragrant, showy white, bilaterally symmetrical flowers droop from the branches every spring. Short, flat, dark brown pods replace the flowers in the fall. This tree grows in dry forests, thickets, and overgrown fields throughout eastern North America, and it has been planted in parks and landscaped areas in other regions.

The blossoms of this tree have a sweet, pea-like flavor, without the perfume-like quality of wisteria or the tartness of redbud flowers, two of the plant's edible relatives. You can sprinkle the blossoms on salads, and they're also great added to almost any dessert. Vanilla is the flavoring of choice to complement these delectable flowers.

LOCUST CORN DUMPLINGS
These hearty, whole-grain corn dumplings owe their flavor to traditional seasonings plus black locust flowers.

1 cup (6.4 ounces) yellow cornmeal and 1 ½ cups (9.6 ounces) sweet brown rice flour, or 1 pound any whole-grain flour
2 ½ tablespoons freshly ground flaxseeds (1 tablespoon seeds)
1 teaspoon dried wild spearmint (page 59) or other mint, finely crumbled
1 teaspoon cream of tartar
½ teaspoon baking soda
¼ teaspoon salt, or to taste
¼ teaspoon ground mace
¼ teaspoon freshly ground dill seeds or 1 tablespoon finely chopped fresh dill
½ teaspoon freshly ground yellow mustard seeds (¼ teaspoon seeds)
2 tablespoons corn oil
¾ cup soy milk, almond milk, or water
1 cup black locust blossoms
⅔ cup fresh corn kernels (cut from 1 ear of corn)
1 small red onion, minced
1 ½ teaspoons lecithin granules
Vegetable Stock (page 40), as needed

1. Mix together the cornmeal, flour, ground flaxseeds, spearmint, cream of tartar, baking soda, salt, mace, and ground dill and yellow mustard seeds in a large bowl. Add the corn oil. Mix in the soy milk. Add the locust blossoms, corn, onion, and lecithin granules, and combine. Do not overmix.

2. In a large saucepan, bring the stock to a boil.

3. Meanwhile, form the mixture into 20 dumplings.

4. Place the dumplings on a steamer rack over boiling vegetable stock and steam for 25 minutes. Serve hot.

MAKES 20 DUMPLINGS; SERVES 6

EGGLESS NOG

Who needs to use eggs in an eggnog when you can use black locust blossoms and a bunch of wonderful-tasting natural ingredients instead?

¼ cup raw cashews

¼ cup lecithin granules

2 ½ tablespoons freshly ground flaxseeds (1 tablespoon seeds)

1 teaspoon ground cinnamon

1 teaspoon freshly grated nutmeg

½ teaspoon salt

3 ½ cups soy milk or nut milk

¼ cup canola oil

2 tablespoons vegetable glycerin, barley malt, honey, or rice syrup

2 teaspoons vanilla extract

½ teaspoon amaretto extract or almond extract

1 cup black locust blossoms

In a blender, combine all the ingredients and process until smooth. Chill before serving.

SERVES 4

LOCUST FRUIT BAKE

This dessert casserole combines the black locust's sweet flavor with a variety of fruits. Because the black locust flower's season is so short, I normally double this recipe and freeze some for future reminiscences of springtime. This recipe can also be made with wisteria or redbud blossoms.

4 cups black locust blossoms

2 ½ cups dry Bread Crumbs (page 40)

One 16-ounce package soft tofu, drained and mashed

2 pints fresh strawberries, hulled and chopped

1 medium-size ripe mango, peeled, pitted, and chopped

4 medium-size apricots, pitted and sliced

2 medium-size ripe peaches, pitted and sliced

1 green apple, cored and sliced

1 ripe banana, peeled and sliced

1 teaspoon vanilla extract

1 ½ teaspoons ground cinnamon

1 ½ teaspoons liquid stevia or ¼ cup pure maple syrup or honey

½ teaspoon almond extract

½ teaspoon maple extract (optional)

½ cup homemade or store-bought jam of any flavor (optional)

1 ½ cups walnuts, toasted (page 158) and chopped

1. Preheat the oven to 350 degrees.

2. Mix the ingredients together, except the jam and nuts, in a 14 x 9 x 2-inch oiled baking dish. Bake the casserole, uncovered, for 1 hour.

3. Top the casserole with the jam and nuts and serve it hot or cold.

SERVES 10

BLACK LOCUST CRUMBLE

The black locust tree's sweet white flowers make a perfect topping for a layered baked dish of pastry, Tofu Grated Cheese, and apples.

FRUIT LAYER

5 Granny Smith apples, cored and sliced, or 7 cups cored and sliced wild apples (page 340)

½ cup raisins

½ cup apple juice

2 tablespoons fresh lemon juice

2 tablespoons kudzu or arrowroot

2 teaspoons ground cinnamon

2 teaspoons freshly grated nutmeg

¼ teaspoon freshly ground cardamom seeds

CRUMBLE LAYER

1 cup plus 1 tablespoon (4.5 ounces) yellow cornmeal

3 tablespoons corn oil

1 ¼ cups Tofu Grated Cheese (page 32)

½ cup hazelnuts or other nuts, chopped

⅓ cup apple juice

1 ½ teaspoons finely chopped fresh mint leaves or ½ teaspoon dried, finely crumbled

2 cups black locust blossoms

1. Preheat the oven to 375 degrees.

2. *To make the fruit layer:* Mix together the fruit layer ingredients and place them in a 14 x 9 x 2-inch oiled baking dish.

3. *To make the crumble layer:* Mix together the crumble layer ingredients and spread them evenly over the fruit layer. Bake the fruit crumble until the fruit layer is bubbly and the crumble layer is lightly browned, 35 to 40 minutes.

4. Remove the pan from oven, let the fruit crumble cool for 5 to 10 minutes, and garnish it with the black locust blossoms. Serve hot or cold.

SERVES 6

BLACK LOCUST VANILLA PUDDING

Black locust blossoms' sweet flavor, enhanced with the flavor of vanilla plus the richness of tapioca, makes a fabulous pudding. All you have to do is put the ingredients into a blender, then bake them in the oven.

3 cups soy milk or nut milk

1 cup raw cashews

1 cup dates

¼ cup walnut oil, sesame oil, or canola oil

¼ cup vegetable glycerin, honey, barley malt, or rice syrup

¼ cup lecithin granules

Pulp scraped from 1 vanilla bean

2 teaspoons vanilla extract

1 teaspoon liquid stevia (optional)

¼ teaspoon salt

2 cups black locust blossoms

½ cup tapioca pearls

1. Preheat the oven to 375 degrees.

2. In a blender, combine all the ingredients, except for 1 cup of the black locust blossoms and the tapioca, and process at high speed until smooth.

3. Stir in the remaining ingredients and pour the mixture into a 3-quart oiled casserole dish. Bake the pudding, uncovered, until set, about 50 minutes. Eat it hot or cold.

SERVES 6

LOCUST BLOSSOM ROLLS

Black locust blossoms meld with figs and pecans to fill a scrumptious pastry roll.

> 2 cups dried figs
>
> 1 cup apple juice
>
> 1 ½ cups pecans
>
> 2 teaspoons vanilla extract
>
> 2 cups black locust blossoms
>
> 1 ¾ cups pastry dough from Wild Apricot Cobbler
> recipe (page 228)

1. In a medium-size saucepan, bring the figs and apple juice to a boil, and then remove the pot from the heat. Cover the pot and let the figs soak for 30 minutes. Drain the figs, saving the juice for another recipe.

2. Chop the figs along with the pecans in a food processor or by hand. Mix in the vanilla and black locust blossoms.

3. Preheat the oven to 400 degrees.

4. Divide the pastry dough into 3 balls. Roll one dough ball into a flat rectangle ³⁄₁₆ inch thick.

5. Spread one-third of the fig filling over the dough, leaving a small margin along the edges and a few inches near one of the shorter ends free of filling. Moisten the edges of the dough with water and roll up the pastry toward the empty edge. Pinch down the open ends.

6. Repeat steps 4 and 5 with the remaining 2 balls of dough and filling.

7. Transfer the rolls to an oiled cookie sheet and bake them until they are lightly browned, 15 to 20 minutes.

8. Let the rolls cool on a wire rack before serving.

MAKES 3 ROLLS

VANILLA–LOCUST ICE CREAM

Black locust blossoms enhance the flavor of a fresh vanilla bean to create the most vanilla-like ice cream you've ever tasted.

> 2 ½ cups soy milk or nut milk
>
> ¾ cup drained silken tofu
>
> ½ cup raw cashews
>
> ½ cup canola oil
>
> ¼ cup vegetable glycerin, honey, barley malt, or
> rice syrup
>
> ¼ cup lecithin granules
>
> 2 teaspoons vanilla extract
>
> 1 teaspoon liquid stevia
>
> ½ teaspoon salt
>
> Pulp scraped from ½ vanilla bean
>
> 2 cups black locust blossoms

1. In a blender, combine all the ingredients, except for 1 cup of the black locust blossoms, and process until smooth.

2. Chill the mixture (or begin with chilled ingredients) if required by your ice cream machine.

3. Pour the mixture into the ice cream machine along with the remaining 1 cup black locust blossoms, and freeze according to the manufacturer's instructions.

MAKES 6 CUPS; SERVES 6

BLACK LOCUST BLOSSOM WINE

These wonderful flowers make a superb table wine and cooking wine, similar to white wine. The flowers' flavor adds a delicate bouquet to any dish, and this is one of the best wines to serve with light vegetarian meals. Unlike most wine recipes, in this one you start with cold water, in order to retain the flowers' flavor. If you have trouble getting the sugar to dissolve in cold water, heat the water just until the sugar dissolves and then cool the mixture to lukewarm before adding the blossoms.

6 cups sugar

1 gallon water, at room temperature

2 quarts black locust blossoms

1 lemon, including the rind, chopped and crushed

1 orange, including the rind, chopped and crushed

2 tablespoons peeled and coarsely chopped fresh
ginger

2 tablespoons star anise

2 tablespoons coriander seeds

½ teaspoon champagne yeast or other wine yeast

1. Dissolve the sugar in the water in a non-metal (plastic or ceramic) food container and add the locust blossoms, fruits, ginger, and spices.

2. Stir in the yeast and cover the container with a non-airtight cover, cheesecloth, or towel.

3. Allow the mixture to ferment for a week at room temperature, stirring it twice a day.

4. Strain the mixture through cheesecloth, transfer the liquid to a jug, and seal the jug with an airlock stopper (which lets carbon dioxide bubbles escape but keeps oxygen out).

5. When the bubbling stops and fermentation ends about 2 weeks later, seal the jug with a cork and age the wine for 2 to 6 months before using it.

6. Siphon the wine to get rid of the sediment, if desired.

MAKES 1 GALLON

WOOD SORREL
Oxalis species

THIS DELICATE GREEN IS VERY COMMON, EASY to recognize, and a favorite with kids. It reminds me of my girlfriend, because its three leaves are all shaped like hearts. Don't confuse wood sorrel with clover, which has oval leaves.

This small group of plants usually grows no larger than 12 inches high. The five-petaled flower is radially symmetrical. Different species have different-colored flowers. The plant grows throughout America in partially shaded woodlands, on lawns, in disturbed areas, and in fields. It is in season from spring to fall.

The leaves of this plant have a strong lemony flavor, like the leaves of the unrelated sheep sorrel (page 138). Eat the leaves, flowers, and small capsule-shaped fruits raw or cooked.

WOOD SORREL DUMPLINGS
Wood sorrel provides a fitting focal point for these scrumptious corn dumplings.

DRY INGREDIENTS

1⅓ cups (5.5 ounces) oat flour and ¾ cup plus
½ tablespoon (5 ounces) yellow cornmeal, or
10.5 ounces any whole-grain flour

½ teaspoon baking soda

½ teaspoon dried sage, finely crumbled

½ teaspoon dried thyme, finely crumbled

2½ tablespoons freshly ground flaxseeds
(1 tablespoon seeds)

1 teaspoon cream of tartar

WET INGREDIENTS

   ¾ cup soy milk or nut milk

   1 tablespoon corn oil

   1 teaspoon tamari soy sauce

   1 cup cooked sweet brown rice

   3 tablespoons minced wood sorrel leaves

   1 ½ teaspoons lecithin granules

   1 teaspoon chili paste or ¼ teaspoon cayenne
     pepper, or to taste

   4 cups simmering Vegetable Stock (page 40) or
     water, if necessary

1. Mix together the dry ingredients in a large bowl.

2. Mix together the wet ingredients in a small bowl. Mix the wet ingredients into the dry ingredients, being careful not to overmix. Mix in the remaining ingredients, except for the stock. Shape the dough into round dumplings that are 1 inch in diameter.

3. Simmer the dumplings in the stock for 15 minutes, or add the dumplings to soups or stews 15 minutes before the end of the cooking time.

SERVES 6

GLASSWORT

Salicornia species

THIS LEAFLESS, CYLINDRICAL, COLONIAL succulent plant, with opposite branches and miniscule, nearly invisible flowers, grows to about 6 inches in height. Adapted to the seashore, it has virtually no leaves. It lives on tidal flats and near the ocean on all U.S. seacoasts, where the plant is sometimes covered by water. The stem is best eaten in the spring, when it is green. It turns a translucent pinkish color in autumn.

Glasswort tolerates saltwater by concentrating sodium within itself; hence it tastes like a salty pickle. The stems and branches are used as salty additions to soups and, not surprisingly, make great pickles. You can also dehydrate glasswort, grind it into a powder, and use it like seasoned salt. This green is not as good raw, because it can make your throat burn.

GLASSWORT PICKLES

Glasswort gets its name because it used to be used for glass manufacture, but you may prefer to use it to make these pickles, which taste much better than glass.

   1 cup glasswort stems

   1 cup water

   ¼ cup red wine vinegar

   1 tablespoon olive oil

   2 small chiles, or to taste, seeds and ribs removed
     and chopped

   1 tablespoon peeled and sliced fresh ginger

   2 teaspoons white peppercorns, or to taste

   2 teaspoons yellow mustard seeds

   1 teaspoon cloves

   4 common spicebush berries (page 314) or
     ¼ teaspoon allspice berries

1. In a small saucepan, bring the glasswort and water to a simmer and let the glasswort simmer for 5 minutes.

2. Pour the glasswort, water, and the remaining ingredients into a jar with a tight-fitting lid, along with a fork to prevent the glass from cracking. You may enclose the flavorings in a tea bag or tea ball, or tie them up in a piece of cheesecloth if you wish. Then you'll be able to remove the flavorings more easily later on. Cover the jar and store the mixture, refrigerated, overnight.

3. Remove the herbs, if you wish. Glasswort Pickles will keep, tightly covered, in the refrigerator for up to 1 month.

MAKES 1 CUP

GLASSWORT SOFRITO

Glasswort and epazote make this spicy Puerto Rican side dish all the more piquant.

- 2 tablespoons olive oil
- 2 medium-size green bell peppers, seeded and sliced into strips
- 2 medium-size ripe tomatoes, sliced
- 2 cups low-sodium pitted olives, drained and sliced
- ⅔ cup chopped glasswort stems
- ½ cup ramp bulbs (page 116) or shallots, chopped
- 3 small chiles, or to taste, seeds and ribs removed and chopped
- 4 cloves garlic, chopped
- 2 teaspoons dried oregano, finely crumbled
- 1 teaspoon freshly ground cumin seeds
- 1 teaspoon dried epazote (page 177) or sage, finely crumbled
- ⅔ cup Fakin' Bacon Bits (a vegetarian bacon substitute available in health food stores)

Heat the olive oil in large skillet over medium heat. Add the remaining ingredients and cook, stirring, for 10 minutes. Serve Glasswort Sofrito hot as a side dish.

SERVES 6

BAYBERRY
Myrica species

BAYBERRY BUSHES HAVE GRAY BARK AND alternate, oblong, slightly toothed leaves that are 1 to 4 inches long. Female bushes get covered with hard, round gray berries about ¼ inch across in the summer and fall. Various species grow from 3 to 26 feet tall, but every part of the plant smells like bay leaves when crushed. Bayberries grow in the sand near the ocean throughout America's coastal areas, and you may often find them in overgrown fields, too.

Bayberry leaves are America's answer to Asian bay leaves. When you use bayberry leaves in place of cultivated bay leaves to flavor soups, stews, and tomato sauce, you'll soon realize that our herb is superior. Use bayberry leaves fresh or dried (drying preserves them). Bayberry leaves are smaller than bay leaves, so use 3 to 4 bayberry leaves in place of 1 bay leaf. Like bay leaves, bayberry leaves should be removed after cooking.

SAVORY SEASONING

Here's a seasoning that you can use in a variety of main courses. And it lives up to its name.

- ¼ cup celery seeds
- ¼ cup ground kelp
- ¼ cup black peppercorns
- ¼ cup yellow mustard seeds
- ¼ cup ground chiles
- 4 teaspoons ground mace
- 4 teaspoons cardamom seeds
- 4 teaspoons cloves

4 teaspoons ground dried wild ginger (page 111)
  or regular ground ginger
24 dried bayberry leaves

Grind all the ingredients together in a spice grinder. Store the seasoning in a tightly sealed jar for up to 1 year.

MAKES 2 CUPS

RUSSIAN TOMATO SAUCE

Unlike familiar Italian tomato sauce, the traditional Russian version contains lots of dill, parsley, and cilantro instead of basil and oregano. It's just as good as what you're used to, only different. And wild bayberry leaves make it even better. You can freeze this sauce for up to 6 months.

¼ cup olive oil
12 shallots, chopped
2 celery stalks, sliced
8 cloves garlic, chopped
Four 22.5-ounce jars tomato sauce
¾ cup Wineberry Wine (page 246) or red wine
¼ cup tomato paste
¼ cup fresh parsley leaves, chopped
¼ cup fresh dill leaves, chopped
¼ cup fresh cilantro leaves, chopped
1 teaspoon Vege-Sal or ½ teaspoon salt, or to taste
1 teaspoon black peppercorns
4 bayberry leaves, enclosed in a tea ball or tea bag
  if desired

1. Heat the olive oil in a large skillet over medium heat, add the shallots and celery, and cook, stirring, for 5 minutes. Add the garlic and cook, stirring, for another 5 minutes. Transfer to a stockpot, add the remaining ingredients, and bring the pot to a boil over medium heat, stirring often.

2. Reduce the heat to low and simmer the sauce, covered, for 1 hour.

3. Remove and discard the bayberry leaves. Russian Tomato Sauce will keep, tightly covered, in the refrigerator for 10 days.

MAKES 16 CUPS

ZUCCHINI TOMATO SAUCE

Use this deluxe tomato sauce in a wide range of recipes, or freeze or can it for future use.

¼ cup olive oil
3 medium-size red onions, sliced
3 medium-size zucchini, ends trimmed and sliced
6 frying peppers or 3 large green bell peppers,
  seeded and sliced into strips
9 cloves garlic, crushed into a paste
2 bayberry leaves
½ cup Ramp Wine (page 129) or sherry
2 tablespoons chopped fresh basil leaves
2 teaspoons dried tarragon, finely crumbled
2 teaspoons dried oregano, finely crumbled
2 teaspoons dried sage, finely crumbled
1 tablespoon chili paste or 1 teaspoon cayenne
  pepper, or to taste
Three 26-ounce jars tomato sauce
1 tablespoon Vege-Sal or 1 ½ teaspoons salt,
  or to taste

1. Heat the olive oil in a large skillet over medium heat. Add the onions, zucchinis, and frying peppers and cook, stirring, for 10 minutes. Add the garlic and cook, stirring, for another 10 minutes.

2. Put the bayberry leaves in a tea ball or tea bag, or

tie them up in a piece of cheesecloth. Place the bayberry leaves in a large saucepan with the sautéed vegetables and the remaining ingredients, except the Vege-Sal. Bring the pot to a boil over medium heat, stirring often. Reduce the heat to low, cover, and simmer for 30 minutes, stirring often.

3. Remove the bayberry leaves, and season the sauce with the Vege-Sal. Zucchini Tomato Sauce will keep, tightly covered, in the refrigerator for 10 days.

MAKES 12 CUPS

COCONUT RICE

Coconut milk is a common ingredient in lands where coconuts grow, so it's no wonder that this rice recipe tastes like something originating in Southeast Asia, despite its wild American seasonings.

6 bayberry leaves

2 cups brown basmati rice

One 14-ounce can unsweetened coconut milk
(1⅔ cups)

⅓ cup Wineberry Wine (page 246) or red wine

2 cups water

2 small chiles, seeds and ribs removed and chopped,
or ½ teaspoon cayenne pepper, or to taste

1 tablespoon tamari soy sauce

4 cloves garlic, minced

1 teaspoon vanilla extract

1 teaspoon dried lemon verbena or mint, finely
crumbled

½ teaspoon ground dried wild ginger (page 111) or
regular ground ginger

1 teaspoon Vege-Sal or ½ teaspoon salt

Put the bayberry leaves in tea bag or tea ball or tie them up in a piece of cheesecloth. Place the bayberry

leaves in a large saucepan with the remaining ingredients. Bring the pot to a boil over medium heat, reduce the heat to low, and simmer, covered, until all the liquid is absorbed and the rice is tender, about 40 minutes. Remove and discard the bayberry leaves before serving.

SERVES 6

EXOTIC RICE

Here's a sweet rice pilaf filled with fruits, nuts, and onions, and flavored with wild bayberry leaves.

3¾ cups plus 2 tablespoons water

1⅔ cups sweet brown rice

⅓ cup wild rice (page 353)

½ cup cultivated currants

½ cup unsweetened shredded coconut

½ cup raw cashews

1 small red onion, chopped

2 tablespoons canola oil

1 tablespoon Garam Masala (page 36)

4 bayberry leaves

1 teaspoon Vege-Sal or ½ teaspoon salt

In a large saucepan bring all the ingredients to a boil over medium heat. Reduce the heat to low, cover, and simmer until all the water is absorbed and the rice is tender, about 40 minutes. Remove and discard the bayberry leaves before serving.

SERVES 6

WINTER CASSEROLE

Here's a quick, simple, hearty, and nutritious casserole you can put together in minutes any time of the year, even in the winter, when few wild plants are in season.

6 medium-size potatoes, sliced

1 head cauliflower, broken into florets

One 16-ounce package firm tofu, drained and
diced

3 cups Russian Tomato Sauce (page 186)

1. Preheat the oven to 350 degrees.

2. Mix together all the ingredients in an oiled 3-quart
casserole dish and bake the casserole, covered, for 1
hour, until potatoes are tender.

SERVES 6

PERILLA,
BEEFSTEAK LEAF,
SHISO

Perilla frutescens

PERILLA IS A DISTINCTIVELY COLORED MINT THAT
escapes people's gardens and can wind up growing
in disturbed soil and wet areas anywhere in the country. As with all mints, it has a square stem and opposite leaves, as well as long clusters of small, bilateral
flowers that bloom in the summer. The stalked, oval,
deeply toothed leaves are 3 to 4½ inches long, and the
plant reaches a height of 6 to 8 inches. Perilla is easy
to recognize because the whole plant is red.

People who shop in health food stores or eat in
Japanese restaurants often see perilla leaves, also
called beefsteak or shiso leaves, surrounding pickled
umeboshi plums. Perilla is more savory tasting and less
minty than are other mint species—and it is great in
Asian dishes. Use the delicate leaves from spring to
fall, fresh or dried.

WILD OMELET

Who says you can't make an omelet without breaking
an egg? Here's a way you can duplicate the flavor and
texture of an omelet with animal-free, cholesterol-free
ingredients. Fill the omelets with the filling suggested
below, or with any cooked vegetables, and serve them
with or without a sauce.

FILLING

2 tablespoons olive oil

½ medium-size green bell pepper, seeded and sliced
into strips

½ cup fresh perilla leaves, chopped

½ cup dried dulse (page 174), broken apart

4 ramp bulbs (page 116) or ½ small onion,
chopped

2 cloves garlic, chopped

1 teaspoon chili paste or ¼ teaspoon cayenne
pepper, or to taste

¼ teaspoon Vege-Sal or ⅛ teaspoon salt, or to taste

OMELETS

1⅔ cups drained silken tofu

2 tablespoons fresh Bread Crumbs (page 40)

2 tablespoons lecithin granules

1 tablespoon kudzu or arrowroot

1 tablespoon corn oil

1 teaspoon freshly ground black pepper
(½ teaspoon peppercorns)

½ teaspoon freshly grated nutmeg

¼ teaspoon freshly ground fenugreek seeds

¼ teaspoon Vege-Sal or ⅛ teaspoon salt, or to taste

2 tablespoons olive oil

1. *To make the filling:* Heat the olive oil in a medium-
size skillet over medium heat, add the filling ingredients, and cook them, stirring, for 10 minutes.

2. *To make the omelets:* In a food processor, combine all the omelet ingredients, except the olive oil, and process until smooth, or beat the ingredients together in a medium-size bowl with a whisk or fork.

3. Heat 1 tablespoon of the olive oil in a medium-size skillet over medium heat. Pour in half the omelet batter. Cook the omelet over medium-low heat until it is lightly browned, about 4 minutes. Flip it over with a metal spatula, and cook the other side until it is lightly browned.

4. Keep the omelet warm and repeat step 3, cooking the remaining batter using 1 tablespoon olive oil.

5. Place half the filling on half of an omelet, and fold the other half of the omelet over it. Repeat with the remaining omelet and filling. Transfer the omelets to plates and serve.

MAKES 2 OMELETS

SHISO SANDWICH

These red-leaved mint plants, which escape cultivation and grow wild, also provide a green that is a welcome change from the lettuce that usually inhabits sandwiches.

6 tablespoons fresh shiso leaves, chopped

2 tablespoons chopped Glasswort Pickles (page 184) or dill pickles

½ cup vegan mayonnaise, homemade (page 31) or store-bought

6 thick slices bread, toasted, if desired

3 pieces Tofu Sliced Cheese (page 31), cut to the same size as the bread slices

1. In a small bowl, mix together the shiso leaves, glasswort pickles, and mayonnaise.

2. Divide half the mixture among 3 slices of the bread. Place a slice of Tofu Sliced Cheese on top of the vegan

mayonnaise mixture, cover that with the remaining shiso mixture, and top that with a piece of bread.

MAKES 3 SANDWICHES

CATTAIL

Typha species

THESE FAMILIAR GRASS-LIKE PLANTS OF THE wetlands are among the very best of edible wild plants. Cattails have pointed, sword-like leaves emerging from the ground (reeds or *Phragmites* species have leaves emerging from a central stalk) in the spring. The plants can reach 9 feet in height. By late spring a tight, cylindrical green flower head, at first enclosed by the leaves, embraces a central flower stalk. The flower head is soon covered with yellow pollen. Later it becomes the familiar sausage-shaped brown ornamental (providing important positive identification) in the summer, and a fluffy white seed head in the fall and winter. Horizontal beige rhizomes (underground stems) create a network growing through the mud. Cattails grow throughout the United States and worldwide in freshwater marshes, and they tolerate some salinity.

In the spring you can peel away the shoot's outer leaves in the spring and pull out the tender white core. Then peel any layers you can't pinch through, and use the core raw or cooked like cucumbers (that's what the shoots taste like) or zucchini. You can harvest cattail shoots until the green flower head begins to form; at that point, the core becomes too hard to eat. Cattail shoots cook in 5 to 10 minutes, and you can apply virtually any cooking method to them.

Steam or bake the immature green flower head for

15 minutes, like corn on the cob, and serve it with a sauce (otherwise, it's a little dry) such as Spiceberry Butter Sauce (page 316). Cattail shoots taste a little like chewy corn grits. If the wind doesn't blow it away first, shake the pollen from many mature golden flower heads into a paper bag and use it as flour. It's quite tasty and colors baked goods golden, too.

CATTAIL RELISH

This tasty condiment goes well with any dish, and it makes a great dip for vegetables. It is especially good with artichokes.

> 4 cloves garlic, peeled
> 2 cups peeled cattail shoots
> ½ cup fresh Bread Crumbs (page 40)
> 2 tablespoons fresh lime juice
> 2 teaspoons tamari soy sauce, or to taste
> 1 teaspoon freshly ground black pepper
>   (½ teaspoon peppercorns)
> ⅛ teaspoon cayenne pepper, or to taste
> 2 tablespoons olive oil, or as needed

1. Chop the garlic in a food processor or by hand. Add the cattail shoots and chop them too.
2. Mix in the remaining ingredients, including just enough olive oil to form a paste. Cattail Relish will keep, tightly covered, in the refrigerator for up ro 10 days.

MAKES 2 CUPS

CATTAIL TZATZIKI

This spicy Greek appetizer is a great showcase for springtime cattail shoots. In other times of the year, when cattails are out of season, you may substitute purslane (page 269). Adjust the amount of garlic to suit your taste.

> 1 to 2 large cloves garlic, to your taste, peeled
> 4 common spicebush berries (page 314) or
>   ½ teaspoon allspice berries
> 2 tablespoons chopped fresh dill
> 4 cups drained silken tofu
> ¼ cup fresh lime juice
> 2 tablespoons olive oil
> ½ teaspoon Vege-Sal or ¼ teaspoon salt, or to taste
> ½ teaspoon freshly ground black pepper
>   (¼ teaspoon peppercorns)
> 2 cups peeled and sliced cattail shoots
> ½ cup chopped ramp leaves (page 116) or scallions

1. Chop the garlic and spicebush berries in a food processor or by hand. Add the dill and chop again. Add the tofu, lime juice, olive oil, Vege-Sal, and pepper and process until smooth or whisk until smooth.
2. Mix in the cattail shoots and serve the tzatziki cold, garnished with the ramps. Cattail Tzatziki will keep, tightly covered, in the refrigerator for up ro 5 days.

SERVES 6

CATTAIL RAITA

Use this Indian dish as an accompaniment to very spicy food to give your palate a chance to recover between hot mouthfuls. Or just enjoy it in its own right. Cattail shoots replace the traditional cucumbers, and silken tofu, lime juice, and sesame oil stand in for the traditional yogurt.

> ¾ cup peeled and sliced cattail shoots
> ¾ cup drained silken tofu
> 2 tablespoons sesame oil
> 1 tablespoon fresh lime juice or red wine vinegar
> 1 clove garlic, or to taste, crushed into a paste
> 1 teaspoon Vege-Sal or ½ teaspoon salt, or to taste

½ teaspoon cumin seeds or fennel seeds

2 tablespoons chopped fresh cilantro leaves

¼ teaspoon cayenne pepper, or to taste

1. In a food processor, combine all the ingredients, except the cilantro and cayenne, and process until smooth, or place the ingredients in à medium-size bowl and mash them until smooth.

2. Garnish the raita with the cilantro and cayenne. Chill the mixture before serving. Cattail Raita will keep, tightly covered, in the refrigerator for 7 days.

MAKES 1¾ CUPS

GREEN CATSAUCE

Raw cattail shoots provide thickness and flavor in a sauce that will season any vegetable dish or entrée.

1 cup water

½ cup drained silken tofu

2 tablespoons mellow (light-colored) miso

2 tablespoons chopped fresh dill or parsley leaves

1½ tablespoons lecithin granules

1 tablespoon fresh lemon or lime juice

1 tablespoon brown rice vinegar or red wine vinegar

1 tablespoon corn oil or olive oil

½ teaspoon freshly ground white pepper
(¼ teaspoon peppercorns)

¼ teaspoon freshly ground celery seeds
(⅛ teaspoon seeds)

¼ teaspoon freshly ground yellow mustard seeds
(⅛ teaspoon seeds)

1 cup peeled and diced cattail shoots

1. In a blender, combine all the ingredients, except the cattails, and process until smooth. Add the cattails and blend until they are very finely chopped.

2. Transfer the mixture to a medium-size saucepan and heat the sauce through over medium-low heat. Serve hot. Green Catsauce will keep, tightly covered, in the refrigerator for 5 days.

MAKES 2⅓ CUPS

CATATO SALAD

This mid-spring wild potato salad is undoubtedly the cattail's meow.

4 cups sliced cooked potatoes

2 cups peeled cattail shoots, sliced

¼ cup hedge mustard leaves (page 78) or chopped arugula

¼ cup fresh wild spearmint (page 59) or other mint leaves

1¼ cups Wild Mustard Seed Mayonnaise (page 206)

Toss together all the ingredients with the mayonnaise in a large bowl until they are well coated with the mayonnaise. Catato Salad will keep, tightly covered, in the refrigerator for 5 days.

SERVES 6

GREEK CATTAIL SALAD

This simple springtime salad is a sort of Greek cucumber salad with cattail shoots replacing the cucumbers.

3 cups peeled cattail shoots, chopped

6 radishes, ends trimmed and thinly sliced

1 cup wild onion leaves (page 57), sliced, or thinly sliced onions

1 teaspoon chopped fresh dill

1 cup Tofu Cream Cheese (page 30)

Mix together all the ingredients. Chill the salad before serving.

SERVES 4 TO 6

THE CAT'S MEOW

Cattail shoots, with their cucumber flavor and slightly crunchy texture, are great in salads such as this one. Caution: Never let an animal rights activist catch you pulling cattail!

⅔ cup Tofu Cream Cheese (page 30)
¼ cup olive oil
Juice of 1 lemon
1 teaspoon prepared mustard
Vege-Sal or salt and freshly ground black pepper or cayenne pepper to taste
1 cup peeled and diced cattail shoots
1 cup sheep sorrel (page 138), curly dock (page 109), or garden sorrel leaves, or other greens, chopped

1. Combine the Tofu Cream Cheese, olive oil, lemon juice, mustard, and salt and pepper in a small bowl.
2. Pour the Tofu Cream Cheese mixture over the cattail shoots and sheep sorrel, toss to combine, and chill before serving.

SERVES 4 TO 6

TURQUOISE

This cold soup is named after the color that gave the land of Turkey its name. Adapted from a traditional dish containing yogurt and cucumber, Turquoise is superb with cattail shoots and vegetarian mock yogurt. I especially appreciate it during very hot weather.

1 ½ cups water
¼ cup drained silken tofu
3 tablespoons olive oil
1 tablespoon corn oil
1 tablespoon fresh lemon or lime juice
2 tablespoons chopped fresh dill
1 clove garlic, peeled
2 cups peeled cattail shoots, grated or finely chopped
6 ice cubes (optional)
1 tablespoon chopped fresh mint or cilantro leaves

1. In a food processor or blender, combine the water, tofu, olive oil, corn oil, lemon juice, dill, and garlic and process until smooth.
2. Transfer the mixture to a large bowl and mix in the cattail shoots. Serve the soup chilled, with the ice cubes, if desired. Garnish it with the mint leaves.

SERVES 6

RAW CATTAIL SOUP

When I was invited to a raw food potluck dinner, creating an extraordinary recipe posed a psychological challenge for me because I disagree with the theory that it's more healthful to eat only raw food. I was quite pleased to come up with a successful wild variant of a traditional raw dish, an iced Greek yogurt and cucumber soup. The party guests consumed my soup completely soon after it was served.

2 ½ cups almonds
10 cups water, or as needed
2 cups peeled and thinly sliced cattail shoots
¼ cup fresh wild spearmint (page 59) or other mint leaves, finely chopped
Juice of ½ lemon

1. Cover the almonds with the water in a large bowl and soak the almonds, refrigerated, for from 6 hours to overnight.

2. In a blender, place the soaked almonds, about 2 cups at a time, with about 3 cups of the soaking water at a time and process until all the almonds have been puréed.

3. Pour the purée into a colander lined with cheesecloth or thin nylon fabric set over a bowl. Twist the top of the cheesecloth and squeeze out any remaining water.

4. Discard the pulp and mix the remaining ingredients with the almond milk. Serve this soup chilled.

SERVES 6

CATTAIL FRIED RICE

This savory version of a well-known Chinese dish combines leftover rice with wild plants.

1 tablespoon toasted sesame oil
½ cup peeled and chopped cattail shoots
1 cup ramp bulbs (page 116) or shallots, chopped
2 cloves garlic, chopped
3 cups cooked brown rice
2 tablespoons tamari soy sauce
1 tablespoon chili paste or ½ teaspoon cayenne
    pepper, or to taste

Heat the sesame oil in a large skillet over medium heat. Add the cattails, ramps, and garlic and cook, stirring, for 5 minutes. Add the remaining ingredients and cook until the rice is hot. Serve hot.

SERVES 4

WILD SUEY

Chop suey isn't genuine Chinese food. It was invented for Americans. So it's only appropriate to include America's wild plants in this version.

¼ cup peanut oil, or as needed
2 tablespoons toasted sesame oil, or as needed
1½ cups peeled and sliced cattail shoots
1 medium-size onion, chopped
2 celery stalks, sliced
2 cups daylily shoots (page 64), sliced
2 frying peppers, seeded and chopped
1 medium-size zucchini, ends trimmed and sliced
½ cup mung sprouts or any bean sprouts
2 cups oyster mushrooms (page 404), sliced
2 cups field garlic leaves (page 57), other Allium
    species leaves, or chopped scallions
2 cloves garlic, chopped
1 cup alfalfa sprouts
2 tablespoons tamari soy sauce, or to taste
2 teaspoons chili paste or ½ teaspoon cayenne
    pepper, to taste

1. Mix the peanut oil with the sesame oil. Prepare and assemble all the ingredients in advance.

2. Heat 1½ tablespoons of the oil mixture in a wok or large skillet over high heat. Add the cattails and stir-fry them for 2 minutes. Remove them and keep them warm.

3. Add more of the oil mixture if necessary and stir-fry the onion and celery for 4 minutes. Remove the vegetables and keep them warm.

4. Add more of the oil mixture if necessary and stir-fry the daylilies and frying peppers for 3 minutes. Remove the vegetables and keep them warm.

5. Add more of the oil mixture if necessary and stir-fry the zucchini and mung sprouts for 2 minutes. Remove

the vegetables and keep them warm.

6. Add more of the oil mixture if necessary and stir-fry the oyster mushrooms for 4 minutes. Remove the mushrooms and keep them warm.

7. Add more of the oil mixture if necessary and stir-fry both types of garlic and the alfalfa sprouts for 1 minute.

8. Mix all the cooked vegetables together in the wok, season them with the tamari and chili paste, and heat them through if necessary. Serve Wild Suey over hot over brown rice or noodles, with Vegetarian Chinese Fish Sauce (page 56), if desired.

SERVES 6 TO 8

PASTA WITH CAT'S TAIL

Cattail shoots, easy to identify and collect in quantity, fit into virtually any recipe, as demonstrated in this simple pasta dish.

> *24 ounces any homemade pasta (such as*
> *Buckwheat Noodles, page 34) or store-bought*
> *macaroni*
> *½ cup olive oil*
> *6 cups peeled and sliced cattail shoots*
> *4 cloves garlic, finely chopped*
> *½ cup fresh parsley, goutweed (page 130), or*
> *waterleaf leaves (page 105), finely chopped*
> *Vege-Sal or salt and freshly ground black pepper to*
> *taste*

1. Cook the pasta in rapidly boiling salted water with 1 tablespoon of the olive oil until the pasta is al dente. Drain the pasta.

2. Meanwhile, heat the remaining 7 tablespoons olive oil in a large skillet over medium heat, add the cattail shoots, and cook, stirring, for 10 minutes. Add the gar-

lic and cook, stirring, for another 2 minutes. Add the drained pasta, parsley, and salt and pepper to taste. Toss to combine the pasta and vegetables, and serve at once.

SERVES 6 TO 8

CATATOUILLE

Catatouille is a superior version of ratatouille. Wouldn't you rather eat a stew based on tail-of-cat rather than tail-of-rat?

> *¼ cup olive oil*
> *4 cups peeled and sliced cattail shoots*
> *1 small eggplant, diced*
> *1 medium-size green bell pepper, seeded and*
> *sliced into strips*
> *1 medium-size onion, sliced*
> *6 cloves garlic, finely chopped*
> *2 medium-size ripe tomatoes, chopped*
> *1 tablespoon chopped fresh basil leaves*
> *2 teaspoons dried thyme, finely crumbled*
> *1 tablespoon tamari soy sauce, 2 teaspoons*
> *Vege-Sal, or 1 teaspoon salt, or to taste*
> *1 teaspoon dried marjoram, finely crumbled*
> *1 teaspoon dried oregano, finely crumbled*
> *1 teaspoon freshly ground black pepper*
> *(½ teaspoon peppercorns)*
> *⅛ teaspoon cayenne pepper*

Heat the olive oil in a large skillet over medium heat. Add the cattail shoots, eggplant, green pepper, onion, and garlic, and cook, stirring, for 10 minutes. Add the remaining ingredients and simmer, covered, over low heat until the vegetables are tender, 10 to 15 minutes. Serve Catatouille over pasta or grains.

SERVES 4 TO 6

CATTAIL POLLEN CORNBREAD

This is one of the best cornbreads I've ever made. The flaxseeds and lecithin provide egg texture and flavor, the fresh corn increases the corn flavor, and the cattail pollen adds a wild touch.

DRY INGREDIENTS

4 cups (1 pound, 9.6 ounces) yellow cornmeal, 3 cups (14.25 ounces) sweet brown rice flour, and 1 cup (4.3 ounces) barley flour, or 2 ¾ pounds any whole-grain flour

½ cup plus 2 tablespoons freshly ground flaxseeds (¼ cup seeds)

2 tablespoons cattail pollen (from about a dozen cattail flower heads)

1 tablespoon chopped fresh lemon verbena or mint leaves

2 tablespoons cream of tartar

1 tablespoon baking soda

2 teaspoons freshly ground coriander seeds

1 teaspoon freshly ground fennel seeds

1 teaspoon turmeric

4 teaspoons Vege-Sal or 2 teaspoons salt

WET INGREDIENTS

2 ¼ cups apple juice or other unsweetened fruit juice

¾ cup corn oil

½ teaspoon lemon extract or freshly grated rind of 1 lemon

2 ⅓ cups corn kernels (cut from 4 ears of corn)

¼ cup lecithin granules

½ teaspoon sweet paprika

1. Preheat the oven to 350 degrees.
2. Sift the dry ingredients together in a large bowl.
3. Mix the wet ingredients together in a medium-size bowl. Mix the wet ingredients into the dry ingredients, being careful not to overmix. Stir in the corn and lecithin granules, being careful not to overmix.
4. Divide the batter among 3 oiled 8½ x 4½ x 2½-inch loaf pans. Sprinkle each loaf with paprika. Set a pan of hot water on the bottom of the oven to keep the crust soft. Bake the loaves until a toothpick inserted into the center emerges clean, about 50 minutes.
5. Remove the loaves from the pans and let them cool on a wire rack before slicing.

MAKES 3 LOAVES

AMERICAN ELDERBERRY FLOWER
Sambucus canadensis

THIS THORNLESS SHRUB, WHICH GROWS UP TO 13 feet tall, has smooth, gray bark and opposite, feather-compound (divided along an axis) leaves. Five to eleven long-stalked opposite, coarsely toothed, pointed leaflets 3 to 4 inches long make up each leaf. Flat-topped to rounded clusters of tiny white, branched flowers 6 inches across appear in late spring and early summer. Purple black round berries ⅛ inch across replace the flowers in late summer and fall.

Look for elderberry bushes in wet areas, such as marshes and riverbanks, in moist woods, in thickets, and along roadsides in eastern North America. An edible dark blue elder (*Sambucus cerulea*) grows in western North America. *Avoid species with red fruit, which may make you sick. Use only the flowers and ripe berries. The rest of the shrub is poisonous. Be sure to pick out any stray stems or leaves.*

The fresh flowers provide a sweet, vanilla-like

flavor. They are great cooked (avoid using them raw) in all desserts and hot cereals. They're also superb in fritters. Avoid rank-tasting older, yellowing flowers. The berries are flavorful, but not sweet. They're much better tasting cooked; some people get nauseous from the raw fruit. Use the fruit like raisins, but include a sweetener (see page 18 for recipes).

ELDERBLOW BREAKFAST CEREAL

Elderblow refers to the elderberry bush's white flower clusters. Here's a cereal I make every year when the elderberry flowers are in season.

> One 33.8-ounce container soy milk or nut milk
> 1 ¾ cups rolled oats (not the quick-cooking kind)
> 1 cup amaranth (page 338)
> ½ cup raisins
> ½ cup almonds, toasted (page 158) or raw
> 2 tablespoons vegetable glycerin, honey, barley
>   malt, rice syrup, or maple syrup
> 2 teaspoons vanilla extract
> ½ teaspoon salt
> ½ teaspoon liquid stevia (optional)
> ¼ teaspoon orange extract
> 1 ¼ cups elderberry flowers
> ¼ cup oat bran or wheat bran

1. Place all the ingredients except the elderberry flowers and oat bran in a large saucepan and bring the pot to a boil over medium heat, stirring constantly. Reduce the heat to low and simmer, covered, for 10 minutes.
2. Stir in the remaining ingredients, remove the pot from the heat, and let the cereal steep, covered, for 10 to 15 minutes. Serve hot.

SERVES 4 TO 6

FOUR-GRAIN CEREAL

Elderberry blossoms enhance any hot cereal, and this combination of oats, millet, amaranth, and buckwheat is no exception.

> One 33.8-ounce container soy milk or nut milk
> 1 ½ cups rolled oats (not the quick-cooking kind)
> 1 cup amaranth (page 338)
> ½ cup millet
> ½ cup buckwheat or kasha
> ½ cup raisins
> ½ cup raw cashews, toasted (page 158), if desired
> 2 tablespoons vegetable glycerin, honey, barley
>   malt, rice syrup, or maple syrup
> 2 teaspoons vanilla extract
> ½ teaspoon salt
> ½ teaspoon liquid stevia (optional)
> ¼ teaspoon lemon extract
> 1 ¼ cups elderberry flowers
> ¼ cup oat bran or wheat bran

1. Bring all the ingredients except the elderberry flowers and oat bran to a boil in a large saucepan over medium heat, stirring constantly. Reduce the heat to low and simmer, covered, for 10 minutes, stirring occasionally.
2. Stir in the remaining ingredients, remove the pot from the heat, and let the cereal rest, covered, for 10 to 15 minutes. Serve hot.

SERVES 4 TO 6

ELDERBLOW PANCAKES

These pancakes owe their delicate, sweet flavor to elderberry flowers, also called elderblow. You won't believe how good they taste.

1 teaspoon active dry yeast

1 cup lukewarm apple juice

2 ½ cups soy milk or nut milk

¼ cup corn oil

2 teaspoons vanilla extract

¼ teaspoon lime extract or lemon extract (optional)

½ teaspoon liquid stevia or 2 tablespoons barley
    malt, rice syrup, honey, or maple syrup

1 ¼ cups (6 ounces) sweet brown rice flour and 1 ¼
    cups (6 ounces) buckwheat flour, or ¾ pound
    any whole-grain flour

½ cup arrowroot or kudzu

2 tablespoons lecithin granules

1 tablespoon white poppy seeds or black poppy seeds

½ teaspoon salt

½ teaspoon freshly grated nutmeg

2 cups elderberry flowers

1. Dissolve the yeast in the lukewarm apple juice for 5 minutes.

2. Combine the yeast mixture well with the remaining ingredients except the elderberry flowers. Let the dough rise, covered, for 1 hour in a warm place, or overnight in the refrigerator.

3. Stir in the elderberry flowers. Heat an oiled griddle and drop the batter by the small ladleful onto the griddle. Cook each pancake until the underside is browned. Turn the pancake over with a metal spatula, press down, and cook it until it is lightly browned on the other side. Repeat this process until you've used up all the batter. You may keep finished pancakes warm in a slow oven. Serve Elderblow Pancakes topped with any of the jams in this book.

MAKES 15 FRITTERS; SERVES 6 TO 8

SUPER VANILLA ELDER FLOWER ICE CREAM

Elderberry flowers have a sweet, vanilla-like flavor, which makes them a great match for vanilla ice cream. Warning: You'll never like commercial vanilla ice cream again after you try this one.

2 cups soy milk or nut milk

1 cup fresh young elderberry flowers

One 1 ½-inch piece vanilla bean

1 ¼ cups well-drained silken tofu

½ cup canola oil

¼ cup vegetable glycerin, rice syrup, barley malt,
    or honey

¼ cup lecithin granules

2 teaspoons vanilla extract

½ teaspoon liquid stevia (optional)

½ teaspoon salt

1. Bring the soy milk and elderberry flowers to a boil in a medium-size saucepan over medium heat, stirring constantly. Pay attention because soy milk boils over very easily. Remove the pot from the heat, cover, and let the elderberry flowers steep for 5 minutes.

2. Split the vanilla bean in half lengthwise and scrape out the pulp. In a blender, combine the pulp along with the soy milk, elderberry flowers, and the remaining ingredients and process until smooth.

3. Chill the mixture until it is cold (1 hour in the freezer or 4 hours in the refrigerator).

4. Pour the mixture into an ice cream machine and freeze it according to the manufacturer's instructions.

MAKES 5 CUPS; SERVES 5

BURDOCK FLOWER STALK

Arctium species

BURDOCK FLOWER STALKS, WHICH ITALIANS CALL *cardunes*, provide a wonderful alternative to the related artichoke heart. (See page 139 for detailed information about this plant.) Cut the flower stalks off before the flowers bloom, when the stalks are still very flexible. Peel the flower stalks and then parboil them for 1 minute to get rid of the bitterness.

CARDUNES SCALOPPINI

Burdock flower stalks (*cardunes*) are especially tasty in this Italian casserole of zucchini, tofu cheese, and bread crumbs.

> 3 cups peeled and sliced immature (soft, flexible) burdock flower stalks (cardunes)
>
> 3 tablespoons olive oil
>
> 1 large zucchini, ends trimmed and thinly sliced
>
> 2 tablespoons chopped fresh parsley leaves
>
> 4 cloves garlic, chopped
>
> 1 teaspoon chili paste or ¼ teaspoon cayenne pepper, or to taste
>
> 2 teaspoons dried oregano, finely crumbled
>
> ½ teaspoon freshly ground fennel seeds
>
> 1 teaspoon dried rosemary, finely crumbled
>
> 1 teaspoon Vege-Sal or ½ teaspoon salt, or to taste
>
> 1 teaspoon freshly ground black pepper (½ teaspoon peppercorns)
>
> 2 tablespoons Wild Crabapple Blossom Wine (page 425) or white wine

> 4 cups Buckwheat Noodles (page 34) or any store-bought noodles
>
> 2 cups fresh Bread Crumbs (page 40)
>
> 2 tablespoons corn oil
>
> 3 cups Tofu Cream Cheese (page 30)

1. Boil the peeled burdock flower stalks for 1 minute in rapidly boiling salted water to remove the bitterness. Drain the *cardunes*.

2. Preheat the oven to 350 degrees.

3. Heat the olive oil in a large skillet over medium heat and add the burdock, zucchini, parsley, garlic, chili paste, oregano, fennel seeds, rosemary, Vege-Sal, and black pepper and cook, stirring, for 5 minutes. Stir in the wine, reduce the heat to low, and simmer, covered, for 5 minutes.

4. Meanwhile, cook the noodles in rapidly boiling salted water for 2 minutes less than directed. Drain the noodles in a colander and lower the colander into a bowl of cold water to halt the cooking.

5. Mix the bread crumbs with the corn oil in a medium-size bowl.

6. Layer a 14 x 9 x 2-inch oiled baking dish with the noodles, cooked vegetables, Tofu Cream Cheese, and oiled bread crumbs. Bake the casserole, uncovered, until bubbly, about 40 minutes.

SERVES 6

CARDUNES IN WINE

This wonderful, simple side dish is similar to one for artichoke hearts that the Romans enjoyed two thousand years ago. Hail, Caesar!

> 2 tablespoons olive oil
>
> 4 cloves garlic, crushed
>
> 2 cups peeled and sliced immature (soft, flexible)

burdock flower stalks (cardunes), parboiled in
water for 1 minute and drained

2 teaspoons dried oregano, finely crumbled

¼ teaspoon Vege-Sal or ⅛ teaspoon salt, or to taste

½ teaspoon freshly ground black pepper
(¼ teaspoon peppercorns), or to taste

¾ cup Vegetable Stock (page 40)

1 tablespoon Wineberry Wine (page 246) or red
wine

Heat the olive oil in a large skillet over medium heat. Add the garlic and parboiled burdock and cook, stirring, for 5 minutes. Add the remaining ingredients and cook, uncovered, stirring often, until all the liquid is absorbed or evaporated, 5 to 10 minutes.

SERVES 4 TO 6

BERKELEY'S POLYPORE

Bondarzewia berkeleyi

THIS HUGE, BEIGE TO LIGHT BROWN MUSHROOM can weigh over 50 pounds when mature. It begins as a misshapen lump emerging from the base of oaks or other deciduous trees, which it parasitizes. Later, this fungus develops many overlapping, short-stalked, flat shelves that are 3 to 10 inches wide, which eventually become pitted or rough. White spores emerge from pores, the openings of tubes, on the caps' and stalks' undersides. The tubes are .11 to .19 inches long, the pores .02 to .07 inches across. The whole mushroom attaches to the tree's trunk or roots with a thick, yellow-brown stalk that is 2 to 4 inches long and 1¼ to 2 inches thick.

The mushroom, which persists until the fall, is only good to eat when it's very young, in very late spring or early summer, when you can still pinch through the flesh. Later the mushroom becomes leathery and bitter. Berkeley's polypore is considered a trash mushroom because it has hardly any flavor, and it's inedible when mature. But, like tofu, it can absorb other flavors. Marinate the very young mushroom with traditional meat seasonings and you can create unsurpassed vegetarian mock meats. You can use any part of the mushroom that is tender enough to pinch through.

STUFFED PEPPERS CHINESE STYLE

Among the Asian ingredients in these stuffed peppers is the Berkeley's polypore mushroom. Generally considered as tasteless as some of my jokes, it's especially good marinated with Chinese herbs—then it develops a meatlike texture.

MARINADE

1 clove garlic, chopped

¾ teaspoon peeled and chopped fresh ginger

¾ teaspoon freshly ground star anise

¾ teaspoon fennel seeds

One ½-inch piece cinnamon stick

½ teaspoon cloves

¼ cup Autumn Olive Wine (page 423), white
wine, or mirin

¼ cup sesame oil

2 tablespoons toasted sesame oil

2 tablespoons tamari soy sauce

2 tablespoons brown rice vinegar or other vinegar

1 cup sliced very young Berkeley's polypore mushrooms

6 bell peppers

1 ¾ cups cooked brown rice

½ cup cooked beans (any type), drained

½ cup gingko nuts, shelled and cooked (page 435),
or cooked peas, drained

¼ cup Looing Sauce (page 118; optional)

1. *To make the marinade:* Put the marinade herbs and spices in a tea bag or tea ball, or tie them up in a piece of cheesecloth. Whisk together the other marinade ingredients in a medium-size bowl. Stir in the mushrooms and spices and refrigerate the mixture, covered, for 6 hours or overnight, stirring once or twice if possible.

2. Preheat the oven to 325 degrees. Drain the mushrooms, reserving the marinade, and then bake the mushrooms on a wire rack over an oiled cookie sheet for 25 minutes. Then increase the oven temperature to 350 degrees and cook the mushrooms for another 10 minutes. Thoroughly pat dry with paper towels to remove excess marinade.

3. Put the reserved marinade into a clear measuring cup and pour off the oil, which will rise to the top. Use that oil in another recipe.

4. Cut off the tops of the peppers, remove the seeds and ribs, rub the inside and outside with some of the marinade remaining in the measuring cup, and pour ½ cup of the remaining marinade into an oiled 2-quart casserole dish.

5. *To make the stuffing:* Chop the mushrooms and then mix them with the stuffing ingredients. (You may substitute ¼ cup of the remaining marinade for the Looing Sauce.) Stuff the peppers with the stuffing, stand them upright in the casserole dish, and bake them for 1 hour. Serve hot.

SERVES 6

PORKY'S POLYPORE

Here's a marinade with pork seasonings that makes this meaty-textured mushroom taste absolutely piggy. Serve Porky's Polypore hot as a side dish, or use it in recipes that call for meat. If you can't find young Berkeley's polypore, you can also use other edible polypore species or chicken mushrooms (page 321).

1 tablespoon peeled and sliced fresh ginger

2 teaspoons cloves

1 teaspoon black peppercorns

1 ¼ cups corn oil or flaxseed oil

½ cup Blackberry Spice Wine (page 278) or red
wine

½ cup Vegetarian Worcestershire Sauce (page 56)

¼ cup red wine vinegar

¼ cup Bragg's Liquid Aminos or tamari soy sauce

¼ teaspoon liquid stevia or 1 tablespoon barley
malt, rice syrup, or honey

4 cups sliced very young Berkeley's polypore
mushrooms

1. Put the ginger, cloves, and black peppercorns in a tea ball or tea bag, or tie them up in a piece of cheesecloth. Whisk together the remaining marinade ingredients in a large bowl and then stir in the mushrooms and spices. Cover and let the mushrooms marinate in the refrigerator for 6 hours to overnight, stirring once or twice if possible.

2. Preheat the oven to 375 degrees. Drain the mushrooms in a colander and bake them for 25 minutes on a wire rack set over an oiled cookie sheet. When the mushrooms are done, squeeze them in a few layers of paper towels to get rid of the excess liquid.

MAKES 1 CUP

CHINESE BEEF AND VEGETABLES

When I first used marinated Berkeley's polypore, it came out tasting like pork. So I was surprised when I added it to this Chinese stir-fry entrée it came out tasting just as good, but like beef.

6 tablespoons peanut oil, or as needed

4 scallions, sliced

2 tablespoons peeled and chopped fresh ginger

4 large mildly hot chiles, seeds and ribs removed and chopped

4 cloves garlic, chopped

One 19-ounce package soft tofu, drained and coarsely diced

2 celery stalks, sliced

2 medium-size red bell peppers, seeded and chopped

2 cups snow peas

2 medium-size ripe tomatoes, sliced

½ cup black walnuts (page 375)

2 ½ cups Porky's Polypore (page 200), diced

¼ cup Vegetarian Chinese Fish Sauce (page 56)

2 tablespoons tamari soy sauce

1. Heat 1 tablespoon of the peanut oil in a wok or large skillet over high heat. Stir-fry the scallions, ginger, chiles, and garlic for 2 minutes and set aside.

2. Add another 1 to 2 tablespoons of the peanut oil to the wok and stir-fry the tofu for 3 minutes; set aside.

3. Adding more oil if necessary, stir-fry the celery for 3 minutes and set aside.

4. Adding more oil if necessary, stir-fry the bell peppers for 3 minutes and set aside.

5. Adding more oil if necessary, stir-fry the snow peas for 3 minutes and set aside.

6. Adding more oil if necessary, stir-fry the tomatoes

and black walnuts for 2 minutes.

7. Return all the cooked ingredients to the wok along with the mushrooms, Vegetarian Chinese Fish Sauce, and tamari, heat through, and serve immediately.

SERVES 6 TO 8

MUSHROOM-STUFFED ZUCCHINI

Using wild mushrooms instead of ground meat in this classic Turkish dish creates a light, tasty vegetable dish. Serve Mushroom-Stuffed Zucchini cold as an appetizer.

5 medium-size zucchini

1 cup Porky's Polypore (page 200), made with finely chopped mushrooms

¼ cup cooked brown rice

⅓ cup Wild Tomato Sauce (page 94)

¼ cup fresh dill leaves, chopped

¼ cup fresh mint leaves, chopped

2 cloves garlic, chopped

1 teaspoon Vege-Sal or ½ teaspoon salt, or to taste

1 teaspoon freshly ground black pepper (½ teaspoon peppercorns), or to taste

1 tablespoon olive oil

3 cups water, or as needed

1. Cut the zucchini in half lengthwise and scoop out the insides, leaving a ¼-inch-thick shell to stuff. An apple corer is the best implement for this, but a serrated grapefruit spoon or regular spoon will also work. Reserve the zucchini pulp for another use.

2. In a medium-size bowl, mix together the remaining ingredients except the olive oil and water and stuff the zucchinis. Dot the top of the stuffed zucchini with the olive oil.

3. Place the zucchini boats on a steamer rack and steam until the zucchini are tender, about 20 minutes.

SERVES 5

CURRIED POLYPORE

Marinated with Madras curry and baked, Berkeley's Polypore is great as a side dish, or use it as a meat substitute in Indian recipes.

4 dried chiles

2 tablespoons coriander seeds

1 tablespoon cumin seeds

1 tablespoon black peppercorns

2 teaspoons black or yellow mustard seeds

2 teaspoons turmeric

10 cloves garlic, peeled

2 tablespoons peeled and chopped fresh ginger

3 cups corn oil

½ cup red wine vinegar

½ cup brown rice vinegar

¼ cup Bragg's Liquid Aminos or tamari soy sauce

8 cups sliced young Berkeley's polypore mushrooms

1. Toast the dried chiles in a small skillet over medium heat until darkened and fragrant, turning them often, 3 to 4 minutes. Don't let them blacken and burn. Remove them from the pan.

2. Toast the coriander seeds, cumin seeds, peppercorns, and mustard seeds in the skillet over medium heat, stirring constantly, until the mustard seeds pop, 2 to 3 minutes. Immediately remove the spices from the pan.

3. Remove the seeds and ribs from the chiles and grind the chiles in a spice grinder or coffee grinder (or with a mortar and pestle) along with the toasted spices.

4. In a blender, combine all the ingredients, except the mushrooms, and process until smooth. Marinate the mushrooms in the purée for 6 hours to overnight in the refrigerator, stirring once or twice if possible. Drain the mushrooms in a colander and save the marinade for reuse.

5. Preheat the oven to 350 degrees. Bake the mushrooms on a wire rack set over an oiled cookie sheet for 30 minutes. Press the mushrooms in several layers of paper towels to remove excess oil. Serve hot as a side dish or use in other recipes.

MAKES 3 ½ CUPS

FRIED NO-RICE WITH MUSHROOMS

Here's a riceless fried rice dish that features millet and amaranth instead of rice. And the marinated, seasoned mushrooms make this dish even richer.

2 tablespoons olive oil

1 tablespoon toasted sesame oil

1 ¾ cups millet

¼ cup amaranth (page 338)

3 ¾ cups water

3 cups Porky's Polypore (page 200)

2 tablespoons tamari soy sauce

1 teaspoon Tabasco sauce

1 teaspoon dried rosemary, finely crumbled

1 teaspoon dried tarragon, finely crumbled

1 teaspoon dried savory, finely crumbled

1. Heat the olive oil and sesame oil together in a large skillet over medium heat. Add the millet and amaranth and cook, stirring, until coated and fragrant, about 5 minutes.

2. Add the remaining ingredients and bring the pot to a boil over medium heat. Reduce the heat to low and simmer, covered, until all the liquid is absorbed and the grains are tender, about 40 minutes.

SERVES 6 TO 8

PENNYROYAL
Hedeoma pulegioides

THIS IS ONE OF THE MOST FRAGRANT AND flavorful members of the mint family. When another botanist first showed it to me at the beginning of winter, it was already dead and withered, but its strong, exotic fragrance persevered. Like the other mints, it has opposite leaves, a square stem, and bilaterally symmetrical flowers. Only 6 to 18 inches tall, the erect, hairy stem bears small lance-shaped leaves ½ to 1½ inches long. The bluish violet to pinkish flowers cluster in the leaf axils (where the leaves emerge from the stem). You can find pennyroyal from spring to fall in dry woods, on mountains, along paths, and in fields throughout the eastern United States.

Use the stems, leaves, and flowers in desserts or beverages where you want pennyroyal to be a main flavor, and you'll always succeed.

PENNYROYAL ICE CREAM

Pennyroyal is one of my favorite wild herbs. It has such a heavenly flavor. You'll love the ice cream based on it.

3 cups soy milk or nut milk
½ cup canola oil
½ cup raw cashews
½ cup drained silken tofu
¼ cup lecithin granules
¼ cup pitted dates
Juice of ½ lemon
4 teaspoons chopped fresh pennyroyal or
*   1 ¼ teaspoons dried, finely crumbled*
2 teaspoons liquid stevia or 2 tablespoons honey,
*   barley malt, or rice syrup*
2 teaspoons vanilla extract
¼ teaspoon praline extract (optional)
½ teaspoon salt
½ cup pecans, chopped

1. In a blender, combine all the ingredients, except the pecans, and process until smooth.
2. Chill the mixture (or start with chilled ingredients) if your ice cream machine requires it.
3. Pour the mixture into the ice cream machine along with the pecans and freeze the ice cream according to the manufacturer's instructions.

MAKES 6 CUPS; SERVES 6

SUMMER
WILD FOODS

THIS IS THE TIME WHEN FRUITS
and berries, as well as the summer
mushrooms, make their first appearances. Some spring greens also
continue in season, so there's plenty to drive
the wild cook wild.

WILD MUSTARD SEED

Brassicacae

S OME WILD MUSTARDS HAVE SEEDS YOU CAN
gather in abundance and use as you'd use commercial mustard seeds. They're as sharp as commercial
mustard seeds, but each variety has its own flavor.

This is a large family. Some of the edible species in
this book are garlic mustard (page 61), hedge mustard
(page 78), watercress (page 387), wild cabbage (page
43), shepherd's purse (page 48), and wild radish (page
443). If the seeds are too small or elusive, you can use
the seedpods, as long as they're still tender enough to
eat.

WILD MUSTARD SEED
MAYONNAISE

Wild mustard seeds provide an unparalleled contribution
to this wild mayonnaise, and you'll never miss the egg
yolks—they're really unnecessary. Use it on vegetables
and in sauces, sandwiches, and salad dressings.

> 1 to 2 cloves garlic, to your taste, peeled
> ¼ cup fresh parsley leaves
> One 19-ounce package silken tofu, drained
> ¼ cup olive oil
> ¼ cup mellow (light-colored) miso
> 2 tablespoons lecithin granules
> 1 teaspoon freshly ground wild mustard seeds
>   (garlic mustard seeds are my favorite here)
> 2 teaspoons freshly ground white pepper
>   (1 teaspoon peppercorns)

> 1 teaspoon dried tarragon, finely crumbled
> ½ teaspoon turmeric
> Juice of 1 lime (2 tablespoons) or 2 tablespoons
>   fresh lemon juice
> 2 tablespoons red wine vinegar
> ¼ teaspoon red pepper flakes or pinch of cayenne
>   pepper
> ¼ teaspoon liquid stevia (optional)

In a food processor fitted with the chopping blade,
finely chop the garlic and parsley together. Add the
remaining ingredients and process until smooth. Wild
Mustard Seed Mayonnaise will keep, tightly covered,
in the refrigerator for up to a week.

MAKES 2 CUPS

COMMON
STRAWBERRY

Fragaria virginiana

A DULTS AND KIDS ADORE THIS WILD PLANT,
one of the most familiar and tastiest on the
planet. Growing 2 to 6 inches tall, this small plant has
a long-stalked, palmate-compound leaf (the leaflets all
originate at one point) arranged in sets of three. Close
to an inch long, the pointed leaflets are deeply and
evenly toothed. Half to one inch across, the white,
five-petaled, radially symmetrical flower arises on a
separate stalk in mid-spring. The familiar red fruit,
much smaller than the cultivated version, ripens in
late spring or early summer, and goes out of season less
than two weeks later.

Nothing poisonous looks like the common strawberry, but there's a similar wood strawberry (*Fragaria*

vesca), which is in season much longer, is edible and colorful, but has absolutely no flavor (about as tasteless as some of my jokes). Look for the common strawberry in fields and meadows, at the edges of trails, and along borders of woods throughout the country.

Its small size makes collecting so labor-intensive that I often reward my patience by eating the strawberries I want to cook with as I gather them. Still, their superior flavor makes the effort worthwhile. Any recipes you prepare with wild strawberries will be outstanding. If you can't find wild strawberries or they're out of season, use cultivated strawberries souped up with some natural strawberry extract to recoup some of their lost flavor.

FRUITBERRY SHAKE

Adults and kids will love this quick, simple, summertime blender drink, especially if you include wild berries.

> 2 cups apple juice or other unsweetened fruit juice
> 1 cup wild strawberries
> ½ cup fresh blueberries, picked over for stems
> ½ cup drained silken tofu
> 1 ripe banana, peeled
> 3 apricots, pitted
> 2 tablespoons fresh lemon juice
> 1 teaspoon vanilla extract
> 1 teaspoon ground cinnamon
> 1 teaspoon dried wild spearmint (page 59) or other mint, finely crumbled
> 1 teaspoon strawberry extract (optional)
> 1 teaspoon blueberry extract (optional)
> ¼ teaspoon liquid stevia or 2 tablespoons honey

In a blender, combine all the ingredients and process until smooth.

SERVES 5

Note: If you like your drinks chunky, withhold the fruit until the other ingredients are thoroughly blended. Then add the fruit and blend very briefly on low speed.

SESAME MILK SMOOTHIE

Blending sesame milk with wild fruit and herbs creates an incredibly delicious drink.

> 1 cup sesame seeds
> 3 cups water
> 2 ripe wild peaches (page 232), peeled, pitted, and cut up
> 1 cup wild strawberries
> 2 tablespoons frozen apple juice concentrate, honey, barley malt, or rice syrup
> 1 teaspoon ground cinnamon
> 1 teaspoon freshly grated nutmeg
> ¼ teaspoon ground dried wild ginger (page 111) or regular ground ginger

1. Toast the sesame seeds in a medium-size skillet over medium heat, stirring or shaking the skillet constantly, until the sesame seeds pop and smell fragrant. Transfer them immediately to a blender and process them with the water until well blended. Strain the mixture through a colander lined with cheesecloth and discard the sesame seeds.

2. Return the sesame water to the blender, add the remaining ingredients, and process until smooth.

SERVES 6

WILD STRAWBERRY SAUCE

Here's a quick, simple, healthful sauce you can make with wild strawberries. I first threw this together as a topping while I was making pancakes, but you can use it on ice cream or other desserts.

2 ½ cups wild strawberries
2 tablespoons kudzu or arrowroot
½ teaspoon freshly grated lemon rind
½ teaspoon tangerine or orange extract or
    2 teaspoons freshly grated orange rind
2 tablespoons vegetable glycerin, honey, barley
    malt, or rice syrup
½ teaspoon liquid stevia (optional)

1. Mix all the ingredients together in a medium-size saucepan and bring the pot to a boil over medium heat, stirring often and mashing the strawberries somewhat as they cook.
2. Reduce the heat to low and simmer, covered, for 5 minutes. Serve hot or cold over desserts. Wild Strawberry Sauce will keep, tightly covered, in the refrigerator for up to a week.

MAKES 2 CUPS

SUPER STRAWBERRY JAM

This strawberry jam recipe doesn't taste like familiar strawberry jam. It tastes like strawberries! If you have the patience to pick enough tiny wild strawberries (without eating them all before you get back to the kitchen), you're in for an extraordinary treat.

1 tablespoon agar flakes
6 tablespoons apple juice or other unsweetened
    fruit juice
4 cups wild strawberries

1 tablespoon freshly grated lemon rind
⅓ cup vegetable glycerin, barley malt, honey,
    or rice syrup, or to taste
1 teaspoon liquid stevia (optional)
⅛ teaspoon ground dried wild ginger (page 111)
    or regular ground ginger
¼ teaspoon freshly ground coriander seeds

1. Bring the agar and apple juice to a boil over medium heat, stirring often. Reduce the heat to low and simmer until the agar is dissolved, about 5 minutes. Add the remaining ingredients and bring the pot to a boil over medium heat, stirring often. Reduce the heat to low and simmer, covered, for another 5 minutes, stirring often.
2. Test the mixture for firmness (agar's thickening effect varies according to its fineness) by putting a large metal spoon with a small amount of jam in the freezer for a couple of minutes, until the jam is chilled. If the jam is the right thickness, your recipe is done. If it's too watery, stir in more agar, simmer the jam for another 5 to 10 minutes, and test it again. If it's too thick, stir in some fruit juice or water and test the jam again immediately.
3. Store Super Strawberry Jam the refrigerator in a tightly covered container for up to 10 days.

MAKES 4 CUPS

STRAWBERRY CRUMBLE

Here's a simple layered dessert that can't be beat.

FRUIT LAYER
    4 cups red mulberries (page 214) or other fruit
    2 cups wild strawberries
    ½ cup apple juice
    2 tablespoons arrowroot or kudzu

1 teaspoon ground cinnamon

1 teaspoon dried wild spearmint (page 59) or other
   mint, finely crumbled

½ teaspoon ground dried wild ginger (page 111) or
   regular ground ginger

½ teaspoon liquid stevia or 2 tablespoons honey,
   barley malt, or rice syrup

½ teaspoon lemon extract

CRUMBLE TOPPING

   3 cups fresh Bread Crumbs (page 40)

   1 cup walnuts, chopped

   2 tablespoons corn oil

   ¼ teaspoon salt

1. Preheat the oven to 350 degrees.

2. *To make the fruit layer:* Mix together the fruit layer ingredients and pour the fruit mixture into a 3-quart casserole dish.

3. *To make the crumble topping:* Mix together the topping ingredients and press the crumble mixture on top of the fruit layer. Bake the dessert until bubbly, about 40 minutes. Serve hot or cold.

SERVES 6

WILD STRAWBERRY ICE CREAM

After I gave up dairy products, I told myself that it was impossible to make natural, dairy-free ice cream, so I did without this delicious food for eight years. I was completely mistaken. Every element in dairy-based ice cream has a healthy vegan counterpart. And vegan ice cream doesn't taste like insipid commercial "dietetic" ice cream! See for yourself:

   1 ½ cups soy milk or nut milk

   1 ½ cups drained silken tofu

½ cup canola oil

¼ cup vegetable glycerin, barley malt, or honey

¼ cup lecithin granules

2 tablespoons chopped fresh lemon balm or
   other wild mint leaves (page 129) or
   2 teaspoons dried, finely crumbled

2 teaspoons vanilla extract

1 teaspoon strawberry extract (optional)

½ teaspoon orange extract or 2 teaspoons freshly
   grated orange rind

½ teaspoon salt

1 teaspoon liquid stevia (optional)

2 cups wild strawberries

1. In a blender, combine all the ingredients except for 1 cup of the strawberries, and process until smooth.

2. Add the remaining strawberries and blend a few seconds on low speed until they are just chopped.

3. Chill the mixture (or use chilled ingredients) if required by your ice cream machine.

4. Pour the mixture into the ice cream machine and freeze it according to the manufacturer's instructions.

MAKES 5½ CUPS; SERVES 5 TO 6

PEANUT BUTTER AND WILD STRAWBERRY JELLY ICE CREAM

Homemade strawberry jam and fresh peanut butter go together as well in this ice cream as they do in sandwiches. Here's an unusual and healthy dessert for kids of all ages.

   2 ½ cups soy milk or nut milk

   ½ cup canola oil or safflower oil

   ¾ cup well-drained silken tofu

   ¼ cup vegetable glycerin, honey, barley malt, or
      rice syrup

¼ cup lecithin granules

2 teaspoons vanilla extract

½ teaspoon salt

¾ cup Crunchy Peanut Butter (page 38)

2 cups Super Strawberry Jam (page 208)

1. In a blender, combine all the ingredients, except the peanut butter and jam, and process until smooth.
2. Add the peanut butter and blend on low speed until the peanut butter is just blended in.
3. Chill the mixture (or begin with chilled ingredients) if required by your ice cream machine
4. Stir in the jam.
5. Pour the mixture into the ice cream machine and freeze it according to the manufacturer's instructions.

MAKES 6 CUPS; SERVES 6

WILD STRAWBERRY SHERBET

It takes a lot more time to gather the wild strawberries than it does to make the sherbet, but the effort is worth it.

3 cups wild strawberries

2 cups cold water

½ cup raw cashews

½ cup canola oil

¼ cup lecithin granules

¼ cup vegetable glycerin, honey, barley malt, or rice syrup

1 teaspoon liquid stevia (optional)

½ teaspoon salt

¼ teaspoon amaretto extract (optional)

1. In a blender, combine all the ingredients and process until smooth.
2. Chill the mixture (or begin with chilled ingredients) if required by your ice cream machine.

3. Pour the mixture into the ice cream machine and freeze it according to the manufacturer's instructions.

MAKES 5½ CUPS; SERVES 5 TO 6

SWEET CHERRY
Prunus avium

THIS IS A EUROPEAN CHERRY TREE, ESCAPED from cultivation, probably spread by birds. Reaching a height of 70 feet, it has long-oval, toothed, alternate leaves close to 3 inches long. The bark is smooth, shiny, and dark reddish brown, with horizontal whitish streaks. The long stalks of several of the red fruits (each with one stone) attach to the same point on the twig. There isn't a long common fruit stalk, as there is on the native species (see black cherry, page 253).

Sweet cherries ripen close to the summer solstice. The trees are most common in eastern North America, but they can escape cultivation anywhere. Look for them in forests or at the edges of woods and fields. It's best to pick from smaller, younger trees because you can reach the fruit more easily. Wild cherries aren't as sweet or juicy as the ones you buy, but they are smaller, with a more intense flavor, so they are better for cooking. If it's a good year for them, collect the fruit in quantity, and use it the same way you'd use cultivated cherries: in fruit salads, jams and jellies, ice cream, cakes, pies, smoothies, or pastries.

WILD FRUIT SOUP

Drink this Scandinavian-style cold soup on a hot day just before the summer solstice, when wild sweet cherries and wild strawberries ripen. You'll have something cold to take your mind off the heat.

> 3 large green apples, cored and sliced
> 3 ripe bananas, peeled and sliced
> 2 cups wild strawberries (page 206)
> 3 cups water
> 1 cup drained and diced soft tofu
> 1 cup sweet cherries, pitted
> 1 ripe wild peach (page 232), peeled, pitted, and sliced
> ½ cup shelled raw sunflower seeds, toasted (page 73)
> Juice of 1 orange
> 1 tablespoon freshly grated orange rind
> 1 tablespoon chopped fresh mint leaves
> 1 teaspoon ground cinnamon
> ¼ teaspoon freshly ground cloves

1. In a blender, combine 2 of the apples, 2 of the bananas, and 1 cup of the strawberries and process until smooth, using just enough of the water to allow the blender to work.

2. In a large saucepan, combine the purée with the remaining ingredients and bring to a boil over medium heat, stirring occasionally. Reduce the heat to low and simmer, covered, until the fruit is tender, 5 to 10 minutes, stirring occasionally. Serve chilled.

SERVES 6 TO 8

WILD CHERRY ICE CREAM
Wild sweet (European) cherry trees don't produce fruit every year, but when they do, this is a great way to use them. Otherwise, you'll also love this recipe if you make it with cultivated cherries.

> 2 cups soy milk or nut milk
> ½ cup canola oil
> ½ cup drained silken tofu
> ½ cup raw cashews
> ¼ cup vegetable glycerin, honey, barley malt, or rice syrup
> ¼ cup lecithin granules
> 1 tablespoon fresh lemon juice
> 1 teaspoon liquid stevia (optional)
> 1 teaspoon cherry extract (optional)
> ½ teaspoon salt
> 2 cups pitted sweet cherries, chopped

1. In a blender, combine all the ingredients, except for 1 cup of the cherries, and process until smooth.

2. Chill the mixture (or begin with chilled ingredients) if required by your ice cream machine.

3. Pour the mixture into the ice cream machine along with the remaining 1 cup cherries, and freeze the ice cream according to the manufacturer's instructions.

MAKES 6 CUPS; SERVES 6

SWEET CHERRY JAM
Because wild sweet cherries are actually less sweet and more flavorful, they make a wonderfully tasty jam.

> 6 cups sweet cherries
> ½ cup natural cherry juice concentrate
> 2 tablespoons red wine
> 4 teaspoons agar
> 1 teaspoon ground dried wild ginger (page 111) or regular ground ginger
> 1 teaspoon freshly ground coriander seeds
> 1 teaspoon dried wild spearmint (page 59) or other mint, finely crumbled

1. Bring all the ingredients to a boil in a large saucepan over medium heat, stirring often. Reduce the heat to low and simmer, covered, for 10 minutes, stirring often.

2. Strain out the cherry pits using a food mill or colander.

3. Test the jam for firmness (agar's thickening effect varies according to its fineness) by putting a large metal spoon with a small amount of jam in the freezer for a couple of minutes until the jam is chilled. If the jam is the right thickness, your recipe is done. If it's too watery, stir in more agar, simmer the jam for another 5 to 10 minutes, and test it again. If the jam is too thick, stir in some fruit juice or water and test the jam again immediately.

4. Store Sweet Cherry Jam, tightly covered, in the refrigerator for up to a week, or you can keep it in the freezer for up to 6 months.

MAKES 4 CUPS

DAYLILY FLOWER
Hemerocallis fulva

THE SAME PLANT THAT PROVIDED SHOOTS VERY early in the spring provides edible flowers in the summer (see page 64 for details). Their sweet and spicy flavor makes them a favorite among Chinese cooks, who call them "golden needles."

You may prepare daylily flowers the same way you would prepare squash flowers—deep-fried in batter, simmered for 5 minutes in soups, or stuffed and baked. They're even good raw, in salads. They're perishable, so use them the day you collect them, or freeze or dehydrate them. Of course, you may substitute squash flowers or tiger lily flowers for daylilies if daylilies are out of season or you can't find them.

HOT-AND-SOUR SOUP
Daylily flowers live just one day. Be there that day (actually, different flowers open and die every day over a period of a few weeks toward the beginning of summer), and you'll be able to make a piquant Chinese soup featuring these delectable flowers.

> 8 cups Vegetable Stock (page 40)
> ½ cup arrowroot or kudzu
> 2 common spicebush berries (page 314), finely chopped, or ½ teaspoon freshly ground allspice berries
> ¼ cup balsamic vinegar
> ¼ cup Wisteria Wine (page 154) or red wine
> 2 tablespoons water
> 1 teaspoon liquid stevia or 2 tablespoons barley malt or honey
> 1 teaspoon dried tarragon, finely crumbled
> 1 teaspoon chili paste or ½ teaspoon cayenne pepper, or to taste
> 1 teaspoon tamari soy sauce
> ¼ teaspoon orange extract
> ½ teaspoon turmeric
> 1 packed cup daylily flowers

1. In a blender, combine 3 cups of the stock, the arrow-root, and spicebush berries and process until smooth.

2. Transfer the purée to a large saucepan, add the remaining ingredients, except the daylily flowers, and bring the pot to a boil over medium heat, stirring constantly. Reduce the heat to low and simmer, covered, for 10 minutes, stirring often.

3. Stir in the daylily flowers and simmer for another 5 minutes. Serve hot.

SERVES 6 TO 8

STUFFED DAYLILY BLOSSOMS

You can fill daylily flowers, which grow everywhere, with any number of stuffings and then bake them. Here's one of my favorite versions.

2 tablespoons olive oil

2 cups lamb's-quarters leaves (page 287), spinach, or other wild or cultivated greens, chopped

2 cloves garlic, chopped

1 cup cooked brown rice or other grain

2 tablespoons Blackberry Spice Wine (page 278) or red wine

½ cup Tofu Grated Cheese (page 32)

½ teaspoon dried thyme, finely crumbled

1 teaspoon freshly ground yellow mustard seeds (½ teaspoon seeds)

1½ teaspoons lecithin granules

½ teaspoon tamari soy sauce, or to taste

⅜ teaspoon freshly ground celery seeds (¼ teaspoon seeds)

½ teaspoon freshly ground black pepper (¼ teaspoon peppercorns), or to taste

24 daylily flowers

1. Preheat the oven to 350 degrees.

2. Heat the olive oil in a medium-size skillet over medium heat, add the lamb's-quarters and garlic, and cook, stirring, until the lamb's-quarters is just wilted, 3 to 5 minutes.

3. In a large bowl, mix the lamb's-quarters mixture with the remaining ingredients except the daylily flowers.

4. Gently fill the flowers with the stuffing. Fold the tips of the petals around the stuffing. Place the stuffed daylily flowers with the stems pointed upward (to keep the stuffing inside) on an oiled cookie sheet or 14 x 9 x 2-inch baking dish and bake for 20 minutes. Serve hot.

MAKES 24; SERVES 6

DAYLILY SUPREME

Daylily flowers stuffed with Tofu Egg Filling create a unique focus for this Italianesque casserole. Have all your ingredients ready before you collect the daylily flowers so you can make the dish the same day. Daylily flowers wilt at the end of the day.

7 cups (1 pound) Buckwheat Noodles (page 34) or store-bought flat noodles

Dash of olive oil

2½ cups Wild Tomato Sauce (page 94)

28 daylily flowers

2¼ cups Tofu Egg Filling (page 33)

3 cups Tofu Cream Cheese (page 30)

3 tablespoons corn oil

3 cups fresh Bread Crumbs (page 40)

1. Cook the homemade noodles for 5 minutes (or cook store-bought noodles for 2 minutes less than directed) in plenty of rapidly boiling salted water with the dash of olive oil. Drain the noodles in a colander and then lower the colander into a bowl of cold water to halt the cooking.

2. Preheat the oven to 350 degrees.

3. Mix the noodles with the tomato sauce in a 14 x 9 x 2-inch oiled baking dish.

4. Stuff the daylily flowers with the Tofu Egg Filling, fold the petals over the open end of each flower, and press each flower, open side down, into the noodle and tomato sauce mixture.

5. Spread the Tofu Cream Cheese over the stuffed daylily flowers.

6. Mix the corn oil with the bread crumbs and spread this mixture on top of the other ingredients, pressing down with the palm of your hand. Bake the casserole until bubbly, about 30 minutes.

SERVES 6

DAYLILY BREAD ROLLS

Each daylily flower blooms but once a year, and you can celebrate this beginning-of-summer day by making these rolls, which incorporate the spicy sweet daylily.

1 ¾ cups lukewarm apple juice

4 teaspoons (2 packages) active dry yeast

4 ⅓ cups (21 ounces) buckwheat flour, 4 cups
*   (1 pound) oat flour, and 1 ½ cups plus 3*
*   tablespoons (½ pound) sweet brown rice flour,*
*   or 45 ounces any whole-grain flour*

½ cup arrowroot or kudzu

2 ½ tablespoons freshly ground flaxseeds
*   (1 tablespoon seeds)*

1 tablespoon poppy seeds

1 ½ teaspoons lecithin granules

½ teaspoon salt

1 teaspoon freshly grated nutmeg

¾ cup corn oil, or as needed

½ cup soy milk, nut milk, or water

¼ teaspoon liquid stevia or 1 tablespoon honey

1 ½ cups packed daylily flowers, chopped

2 teaspoons freshly grated lemon rind or
*   ⅔ teaspoon dried*

1. In a blender, process the lukewarm apple juice and yeast and let the yeast stand for 5 minutes to dissolve.

2. Mix the flours, arrowroot, ground flaxseeds, poppy seeds, lecithin, salt, and nutmeg together in a large bowl.

3. In another large bowl, mix together the yeast mixture, ½ cup of the corn oil, the soy milk, and liquid stevia.

4. Stir 3 cups of the dry ingredients into the wet ingredients. Incorporate the remaining dry ingredients and knead the dough for 5 minutes. Cover the dough and let it rise in a warm place for 40 to 60 minutes.

5. Punch down the dough and knead in the daylily flowers and lemon rind. Divide the dough into 21 equal pieces and roll each piece into a ball ½ inch in diameter. Brush the dough balls with the remaining ¼ cup corn oil and arrange 3 balls in each cup of an oiled 8-section muffin tin. Allow the dough to rise, covered with a damp towel, for another 40 to 60 minutes in a warm place.

6. Preheat the oven to 400 degrees. Set a pan of water in the oven to keep the crust soft. Bake the rolls until they pull away from the sides of the tin slightly and sound hollow when tapped, about 15 minutes. Place the rolls on wire racks to cool. Brush the rolls with additional corn oil for even richer, softer rolls (optional).

MAKES 7 CLOVERLEAF ROLLS

MULBERRY
Morus species

RED, WHITE, AND PINK MULBERRIES RAIN ONTO the ground and streets at the end of spring and the beginning of summer every year. The medium-size trees grow in cultivated areas, fields, open areas in woods, trailsides, backyards, roadsides, fencerows, empty lots, and at the edges of woods throughout the country. The roughly oval, toothed leaves are 2 to 6 inches long and sometimes deeply lobed.

The berries look like elongated raspberries hanging individually from slender stalks (black raspberries, which are stalkless, grow on thorny bushes, not trees—see page 226). Whichever color they are, they're soft, sticky, and juicy when ripe. Although you can pick the berries one at a time, I collect great quantities in moments by shaking the branches over a drop cloth. Pick out the larger debris and rinse the berries in a colander set inside a bowl. Then spread out the berries on a tray to complete the sorting process.

Mulberries perish within a couple of days, so eat them, cook them (they cook in 5 minutes), dehydrate them, or freeze them right away. Each color berry has its own flavor, and there's great variation from tree to tree, so it's worthwhile to note your favorite neighborhood trees. Mulberries taste a little like their relative the fig, but they are juicier. Since mulberries often lack the tart component of other berries, complementing their sweetness with the addition of sour ingredients such as lemon juice enhances their flavor.

SATTOO

You can make this porridge, which originates in India, with various combinations of flour and wild or cultivated fruit and nuts in season. The ingredient combination below represents the ingredients I had on hand at the time I created the recipe.

> ½ cup (3.2 ounces) yellow cornmeal, ½ cup (2.95 ounces) barley flour, and ½ cup (3 ounces) millet flour or 9.15 ounces any combination of whole-grain flours
> ½ cup corn oil
> 4 cups water

> ¼ teaspoon liquid stevia or 2 tablespoons honey, maple syrup, barley malt, or rice syrup
> ¼ cup raisins or cultivated currants
> ¼ cup black walnuts (page 375) or other nuts, chopped
> ½ cup mulberries of your choice
> ½ cup blackberries or other berries
> ½ cup pitted and sliced apricots or other fruit
> ½ cup cored and sliced apples or other fruit

1. In a saucepan, cook the flour with the corn oil for 10 minutes over medium-low heat, stirring often.
2. Slowly incorporate the water and liquid stevia, stirring constantly. Bring the pot to a boil over medium heat, reduce the heat to low, and simmer, covered, for 20 minutes, stirring often. Pour the mixture into an oiled 9-inch pie tin and chill.
3. Top the grain layer with the fruit and nuts, cut the porridge into 6 wedges, and serve.

SERVES 6

MULBERRY FRUIT SALAD

Mulberries are good in virtually any fruit recipe, and this fruit and vegetable salad is no exception.

DRESSING
> 1 cup well-drained silken tofu
> 2 tablespoons corn oil
> 1 ½ teaspoons lecithin granules
> 1 teaspoon freshly ground yellow mustard seeds (½ teaspoon seeds)
> ½ teaspoon freshly ground white pepper (¼ teaspoon peppercorns)
> 1 teaspoon dried mint, finely crumbled
> 1 tablespoon fresh lime juice
> 1 tablespoon red wine vinegar

SALAD

    1 cup mulberries of your choice
    1 cup cored and diced apples
    1 cup sliced celery
    1 cup raisins
    1 cup grated carrots
    1 cup Tofu Grated Cheese (page 32)
    ½ cup black walnuts (page 375) or hazelnuts, chopped
    ½ cup regular walnuts, chopped

1. *To make the dressing:* In a food processor, combine the dressing ingredients and process until smooth.
2. *To make the salad:* In a large bowl, stir the dressing together with the salad ingredients. Serve chilled.

SERVES 6

MULBERRY-PAPAYA SALAD

The sweetness of mulberries is a perfect match for the creamy texture of papayas, with crunchy hazelnuts adding the finishing touch to this great fruit salad.

    2 medium-size ripe papayas, peeled, seeded, and diced
    1 cup mulberries of your choice
    2 tablespoons natural cherry juice or other fruit juice concentrate
    1 cup hazelnuts, chopped
    2 teaspoons ground cinnamon
    2 teaspoons dried mint, finely crumbled
    ½ teaspoon liquid stevia or 2 tablespoons honey, barley malt, or rice syrup (optional)

Mix together all the ingredients in a medium-size serving bowl. Chill and serve.

SERVES 6

COLD MULBERRY SOUP

Here's a cold summer refresher that won't keep you in the hot kitchen for more than a few minutes.

    4 cups water
    2 tablespoons Sumac Concentrate (page 281) or fresh lemon or lime juice
    2 tablespoons kudzu or arrowroot
    2 tablespoons vegetable glycerin, honey, barley malt, or rice syrup
    ½ teaspoon liquid stevia (optional)
    ⅛ teaspoon salt
    1 cup red mulberries
    1 cup drained silken tofu, coarsely diced

1. In a blender or large bowl, combine all the ingredients, except the mulberries and tofu, and process or beat with a whisk until smooth.
2. Transfer the mixture to a large saucepan, add the mulberries and tofu, and bring the pot to a boil over medium heat, stirring occasionally. Reduce the heat to low, and simmer, covered, for 5 minutes.
3. Chill the soup completely before serving.

SERVES 6

BARBECUE SAUCE WITH WILD WINE

Mulberry wine lends a special flavor to any marinated and barbecued food it touches. Marinate vegetables, tofu, tempeh, mushrooms, or other food in this sauce overnight, of if you are barbecuing outdoors or on a stovetop grill, baste your food with this sauce.

    ½ cup tomato juice
    ¼ cup Mulberry Wine (page 222) or red wine
    2 tablespoons tamari soy sauce

1 teaspoon dried tarragon, finely crumbled

2 cloves garlic (optional), crushed into a paste

1 teaspoon freshly ground black pepper
   (½ teaspoon peppercorns)

2 teaspoons chili paste or ½ teaspoon cayenne
   pepper

In a small bowl, mix all the ingredients together. Barbecue Sauce with Wild Wine will keep, tightly covered, in the refrigerator for 1 week.

MAKES ⅞ CUP

MULBERRY-KIWI JAM

After you shake several quarts of mulberries down from the tree onto a drop cloth, this freezable recipe will help you dispose of any of these wonderful but perishable berries you can't eat at once. The kiwis' tartness complements the mulberries' sweetness.

2 cups apple juice

½ cup mulberry juice (which drains from the
   berries after you store them in a container) or
   other unsweetened fruit juice

2 ½ tablespoons agar powder

8 cups mulberries of your choice

8 kiwis, peeled and chopped (1 ½ cups)

Juice of 1 lemon (2 tablespoons)

1 teaspoon dried mint, finely crumbled

1 teaspoon vanilla extract

½ teaspoon common spicebush berries (page 314),
   finely chopped, or freshly ground allspice berries

1 teaspoon freshly grated nutmeg

1. In a stockpot, bring the apple juice, mulberry juice, and agar to a boil over medium heat, stirring often. Reduce the heat to low and simmer, covered, for 5

minutes, stirring often. Add the remaining ingredients, return the pot to a boil over medium heat, reduce the heat to low, and simmer, covered, for another 5 minutes, stirring often.

2. Test the jam for firmness (agar's thickening effect varies according to its fineness) by putting a large metal spoon with a small amount of jam in the freezer for a couple of minutes, until the jam is chilled. If the jam is the right thickness, your recipe is done. If it's too watery, stir in more agar, simmer the jam for another 5 to 10 minutes, and test it again. If the jam is too thick, stir in some fruit juice or water and test it again immediately.

MAKES 10 CUPS

Note: To prepare kiwis, stand each of them on end and horizontally slice off a piece of the top, like a boiled egg. Scoop out the flesh with a serrated grapefruit spoon or a teaspoon, as people do with medium-boiled eggs. (There are special kiwi knives, but they're hard to find outside of New Zealand.)

MULBERRY SAUCE

This is one of my favorite toppings for pancakes, ice cream, and fruit salads.

3 cups mulberries of your choice

1 cup apple juice

2 tablespoons fresh lemon juice

1 tablespoon vegetable glycerin, honey, barley
   malt, maple syrup, or rice syrup

1 ½ tablespoons kudzu or arrowroot

1 teaspoon dried wild spearmint (page 59)
   or other mint, finely crumbled

½ teaspoon ground cinnamon

¼ teaspoon maple extract (optional)

Bring all the ingredients to a boil in a medium-size saucepan over medium heat, stirring constantly. Reduce the heat to low and simmer, covered, for 5 minutes. Serve hot or cold. Mulberry Sauce will keep, tightly covered, in the refrigerator for up to a week.

MAKES 3 CUPS

MULBERRY MUFFINS

You can make these great light muffins very quickly, before your mulberries perish, or substitute other berries if mulberries aren't in season.

DRY INGREDIENTS

6¾ cups sweet brown rice flour or 2 pounds any other whole-grain flour

½ cup plus 2 tablespoons freshly ground flaxseeds (¼ cup seeds)

1 teaspoon cream of tartar

½ teaspoon baking soda

½ teaspoon salt

1 teaspoon ground dried wild ginger (page 111) or regular ground ginger

2 teaspoons freshly grated nutmeg

1 teaspoon dried mint, finely crumbled

WET INGREDIENTS

3 cups soy milk or nut milk

2 tablespoons sesame oil or corn oil

½ cup apple juice

1 teaspoon liquid stevia or 2 tablespoons honey

2 cup mulberries of your choice

½ cup lecithin granules

1. Preheat the oven to 425 degrees.
2. Mix the dry ingredients together in a large bowl.
3. Mix the wet ingredients together in another bowl.

4. Toss the mulberries with 2 tablespoons of the dry ingredients so they don't make the muffins soggy.
5. Stir the wet ingredients into the remaining dry ingredients, being careful not to overmix. Stir the berries and lecithin into the batter just until it is well combined. Pour the batter into 2 oiled 12-section muffin tins, filling each compartment three-quarters full. Set a pan of water on the bottom of the oven to keep the crust soft. Bake the muffins until a toothpick inserted into the center emerges clean, about 35 minutes.
6. Remove the muffins from the pans and let them cool on wire racks.

MAKES 24 MUFFINS

RED MULBERRY COBBLER

Too many mulberries to devour falling from your neighborhood trees? "Dispose" of them deliciously with this recipe. You'll be surprised how good mulberries taste in this dessert, and how much like cottage cheese the Tofu Cottage Cheese tastes here.

1 tablespoon kudzu or arrowroot

8 cups red mulberries

4 cups Tofu Cottage Cheese (page 30)

¼ cup natural cherry juice or other fruit juice concentrate

1 teaspoon liquid stevia or 2 tablespoons honey, barley malt, or rice syrup

2 tablespoons apricot kernel oil, almond oil, canola oil, or peanut oil

2 cups fresh Bread Crumbs (page 40)

½ teaspoon ground cinnamon

1. Preheat the oven to 375 degrees.
2. Mix the kudzu with the mulberries in a 14 x 9 x 2-inch oiled baking dish.

3. Stir in the Tofu Cottage Cheese, cherry juice concentrate, and liquid stevia.

4. Mix the apricot kernel oil with the bread crumbs and press the bread crumb mixture into the fruit mixture. Sprinkle the cinnamon on top. Bake the cobbler, uncovered, until bubbly, about 40 minutes. Serve hot or cold. Don't freeze it.

SERVES 6

MULBERRY CRUMBLE

This is one of the best desserts you'll ever make, and it's a very easy one also.

FRUIT LAYER

    6 cups mulberries of your choice

    ½ cup fresh orange juice

    2 tablespoons kudzu or arrowroot

    1 ½ tablespoons chopped fresh wild spearmint (page 59) or other mint leaves

    2 teaspoons vanilla extract

    ½ teaspoon almond extract

    ½ teaspoon liquid stevia or 2 tablespoons honey, barley malt, or rice syrup

CRUMBLE TOPPING

    2 ½ cups fresh Bread Crumbs (page 40)

    ¼ cup corn oil or flaxseed oil

    1 cup shelled raw pistachio nuts or other nuts, chopped

    ½ teaspoon salt

    1 teaspoon ground cinnamon

1. Preheat the oven to 350 degrees.

2. *To make the fruit layer:* Combine the fruit layer ingredients in a bowl and then pour the mixture into a 3-quart casserole dish.

3. *To make the crumble topping:* Combine the crumble topping ingredients except the cinnamon. Press the crumble mixture on top of the fruit layer. Sprinkle the cinnamon on top. Bake for 40 minutes. Serve hot or cold.

SERVES 6

MULBERRY RICE PUDDING

Mulberries, be they red, white, or pink, brighten a variety of desserts, and this rice pudding is no exception.

    2 cups sweet brown rice

    4 cups soy milk or nut milk

    1 teaspoon turmeric

    1 teaspoon ground dried wild ginger (page 111) or regular ground ginger

    One 3-inch-long sassafras root (page 44) or 1 cinnamon stick

    ½ cup chickpea flour, yellow cornmeal, or any whole-grain flour

    4 ¼ cups apple juice or other unsweetened fruit juice

    3 cups mulberries of your choice

    1 cup raisins

    1 cup pine nuts or other nuts

    2 tablespoons sesame oil

    1 tablespoon vanilla extract

    1 teaspoon lime extract or lemon extract

    2 teaspoons freshly grated nutmeg

1. In a large saucepan, combine the rice, soy milk, turmeric, ginger, and sassafras and bring the pot to a simmer over medium heat. Reduce the heat to low, and cook, covered, for 40 minutes.

2. Preheat the oven to 350 degrees.

3. Remove the sassafras and mix in the chickpea flour.

Stir in the remaining ingredients and transfer the mixture to a 14 x 9 x 2-inch oiled baking dish. Bake the pudding, covered, until it is moderately firm, about 1 hour. Serve hot or cold.

SERVES 10 TO 12

MULBERRY CUSTARD

I was especially happy when I discovered a way to make genuine-tasting custards without eggs, milk, or sugar. Making such a custard with wild mulberries makes me even happier and I'm sure it will have the same effect on you.

Two 19-ounce packages silken tofu, drained
¼ cup lecithin granules
2 tablespoons natural cherry juice concentrate, honey, barley malt, or rice syrup
3 tablespoons fresh lemon juice
2 tablespoons flaxseed oil or corn oil
2 tablespoons kudzu or arrowroot
1 teaspoon vanilla extract
1 teaspoon liquid stevia (optional)
½ teaspoon amaretto extract (optional)
½ teaspoon salt
4 cups mulberries of your choice

1. Preheat the oven to 375 degrees.
2. Place all the ingredients except the mulberries in a large bowl or food processor and process or mix until smooth.
3. Stir in the mulberries. Pour the mixture into 6 oiled custard dishes (or pour it into a 3-quart oiled casserole dish) and bake until a butter knife inserted into the center emerges clean, about 30 minutes. Serve hot or cold.

SERVES 6

RED MULBERRY TAPIOCA PUDDING

Here's a fast, simple pudding you'll love that you can make with the abundance of mulberries you can collect every year.

2 ½ cups soy milk or nut milk
½ cup drained silken tofu
¼ cup almond oil
½ cup pitted dates
¼ cup lecithin granules
¼ cup tapioca pearls
1 teaspoon liquid stevia or 2 tablespoons honey, barley malt, or rice syrup
2 teaspoons vanilla extract
1 teaspoon ground cinnamon
½ teaspoon salt
3 cups red mulberries

1. In a blender, combine all the ingredients, except the mulberries, and process until smooth.
2. Transfer the mixture to a large saucepan, stir in the mulberries, and bring the pot to a boil over medium heat, stirring constantly. Reduce the heat to low and simmer, covered, for 10 minutes. Serve hot or cold.

SERVES 6

SWEET NOODLES WITH MULBERRIES

Traditionally made with sugar and butter, this Jewish dessert benefits nutritionally and flavor-wise by the addition of vegan ingredients and mulberries.

NOODLE CASSEROLE
8 cups Buckwheat Noodles (page 34) or store-bought flat noodles

¼ cup corn oil

2 teaspoons ground cinnamon

Freshly grated rind of 1 lemon

1 cup mulberries of your choice

1 cup raisins

1 cup almonds, toasted (page 158) and chopped

SYRUP

1 cup water

½ cup natural cherry juice concentrate

¼ cup fresh lemon juice

4 teaspoons arrowroot or kudzu

¼ teaspoon caramel extract or vanilla extract

⅛ teaspoon salt

1 recipe Tofu Whipped Cream (page 32)

1. Preheat the oven to 300 degrees.

2. *To make the noodle casserole:* Cook the noodles in rapidly boiling salted water for 2 minutes. Drain the noodles and mix in 2 tablespoons of the corn oil, the cinnamon, and lemon rind.

3. Layer a 14 x 9 x 2-inch oiled baking dish with one-third of the noodles, one-third of the mulberries, one-third of the raisins, and one-third of the almonds. Repeat the layers until you've used up everything. Bake the noodle casserole for 15 minutes, uncovered.

4. *To make the syrup:* Combine the syrup ingredients in a medium-size saucepan and bring the pot to a boil over medium heat, stirring often. Reduce the heat to low and simmer, covered, for 5 minutes.

5. When the noodle casserole comes out of the oven, pour the syrup on top and bake the casserole again, covered, for another 10 minutes.

6. Serve hot or cold with the Tofu Whipped Cream.

SERVES 6

MULBERRY CREAM PIE

Mulberries set in a sweet cream filling are more than suitable for any pie crust from this book or elsewhere.

16 cups mulberries of your choice

4 cups well-drained silken tofu

2 cups pecans, chopped

1½ cups raisins

½ cup apple juice

¼ cup kudzu or arrowroot

2 tablespoons sesame oil

2 tablespoons lecithin granules

1 tablespoon vanilla extract

½ teaspoon orange extract

1 tablespoon finely chopped fresh lemon balm or other mint leaves

1 teaspoon ground dried wild ginger (page 111) or regular ground ginger

Two 9-inch pie shells

1. Preheat the oven to 350 degrees.

2. Mix all the ingredients except the pie shells together.

3. Pour the filling into the pie shells and bake until the filling is set, about 40 minutes. Let the pies cool before slicing.

MAKES TWO 9-INCH PIES;

SERVES 8 TO 12

MULBERRY COOKIES

Mulberry trees, easy to recognize, widespread, and abundant, drop an astounding quantity of wonderful fruit but only for a short time in late spring and early summer. Make multiple quantities of these cookies, freeze what you can't eat fresh, and extend the summer solstice through the rest of the year.

1 cup plus 2 ½ teaspoons (5 ounces) sweet brown
    rice flour and 1 ½ cups (6 ounces) oat flour, or
    11 ounces any whole-grain flour
1 cup (6.4 ounces) yellow cornmeal
¼ cup arrowroot or kudzu
7 ½ tablespoons freshly ground flaxseeds
    (3 tablespoons seeds)
1 ½ tablespoons lecithin granules
1 teaspoon ground dried wild ginger (page 111) or
    regular ground ginger
½ teaspoon salt
1 cup pomegranate juice, grape juice, or other
    liquid sweetener
¼ cup corn oil
½ teaspoon liquid stevia or 2 tablespoons honey,
    barley malt, or rice syrup
2 cups mulberries of your choice
4 common spicebush berries (page 314), finely
    chopped, or ¼ teaspoon freshly ground allspice
    berries
1 cup walnuts, chopped
1 ½ teaspoons freshly grated lemon rind or ½
    teaspoon dried

1. Preheat the oven to 350 degrees.
2. In a large bowl, mix together the flours, cornmeal,
arrowroot, ground flaxseeds, lecithin, ginger, and salt.
3. In a medium-size bowl, mix together the pomegranate juice, corn oil, and liquid stevia. Mix the wet
ingredients into the dry ingredients. Then stir in the
remaining ingredients.
4. Drop the batter by the spoonful onto an oiled cookie sheet. Bake the cookies until they are lightly
browned underneath and a toothpick inserted into
the center emerges clean, 15 to 20 minutes.

MAKES 3 DOZEN COOKIES

MULBERRY-KIWI ICE CREAM

Sweet, whole mulberries add an extra sparkle to this
lemony ice cream.

2 ½ cups soy milk or nut milk
1 ¼ cups well-drained silken tofu
½ cup canola oil
¼ cup vegetable glycerin, honey, barley malt,
    or rice syrup
2 kiwis
¼ cup lecithin granules
2 tablespoons fresh lemon juice
2 teaspoons vanilla extract
1 teaspoon liquid stevia or 2 tablespoons honey,
    barley malt, or rice syrup
½ teaspoon lemon extract (optional)
1 cup mulberries of your choice

1. In a blender, combine all the ingredients, except
the mulberries, and process until smooth.
2. Chill the mixture (or begin with chilled ingredients) if required by your ice cream machine.
3. Pour the mixture into the ice cream machine and
freeze according to the manufacturer's instructions.
4. Stir in the mulberries.

MAKES 6 ½ CUPS; SERVES 6

MULBERRY WINE

Here's an unusual delicate-flavored wine that is
equally good in main courses, side dishes, and
desserts.

6 cups sugar
1 gallon boiling water
4 cups mulberries of your choice
Juice of 2 lemons

3 tablespoons chopped fresh wild spearmint (page 59) or other mint leaves or 1 tablespoon dried

2 cinnamon sticks

½ teaspoon champagne yeast or other wine yeast

1. Dissolve the sugar in the water in a non-metal (plastic or ceramic) food container, add the mulberries, mashing them slightly with a hand blender or potato masher, and add the lemon juice, mint, and cinnamon sticks.

2. When the mixture is lukewarm, stir in the yeast and cover the container with a non-airtight cover, cheesecloth, or towel.

3. Let the mixture ferment for 7 to 10 days at room temperature, stirring twice a day.

4. Strain the mixture through cheesecloth, transfer the liquid to a jug, and seal the jug with an airlock stopper (which lets carbon dioxide bubbles escape but keeps oxygen out).

5. When the bubbling stops and fermentation ends a couple of weeks later, seal the jug with a cork and let the wine age for 10 weeks to 6 months before using it.

6. Siphon the wine to get rid of the sediment if desired.

MAKES 1 GALLON 2 CUPS

JUNEBERRY

Amelanchier species

AMELANCHIER IS A GENUS OF SHRUBS OR SMALL trees with smooth gray bark distinguished by vertical darker gray stripes. The opposite, stalked, long-oval, finely toothed, pointed leaves, which are light green underneath, grow to about 2 inches long.

Long-stalked, white, five-petaled, radially symmetrical flowers ¾ inch across, arising alternately from a long common stalk called a raceme, bloom in early spring. The flowers are replaced by round, blue black berries ¼ to ⅓ inch across, usually in early summer. (One exotic species has red berries that ripen in autumn.) The flower has five parts. A flaring calyx, or crown, on the side away from the stalk distinguishes this fruit from similar poisonous ones.

Look for the various species anywhere there's enough sunlight for shrubs. The plants grow in thickets, at the edges of woods, in wetlands and dry soil, and they're very common planted in cultivated areas.

The juneberry is one of the tastiest, most underappreciated of the wild berries. The fruit tastes like a combination of apples and blueberries, while the soft seeds taste like almonds. You can collect these berries in large quantity every year and use them raw or cooked for 5 to 10 minutes in any recipe that calls for berries. They're an especially good alternative to blueberries.

JUNEBERRY PANCAKES

Juneberries make this already perfect batter even better. Lecithin granules and flaxseeds handily replace the egg yolks and whites.

1 ¼ cups (6 ounces) sweet brown rice flour and 1 ¼ cups (6 ounces) buckwheat flour, or ¾ pound any whole-grain flour

½ cup plus 2 tablespoons freshly ground flaxseeds (¼ cup seeds)

6 tablespoons lecithin granules

2 teaspoons dried lemon balm or other mint, finely crumbled

1 teaspoon ground cinnamon

½ teaspoon freshly grated nutmeg

1 ¼ teaspoons cream of tartar

½ teaspoon baking soda

½ teaspoon salt

3 ½ cups soy milk or nut milk

½ cup corn oil

2 teaspoons vanilla extract

1 cup juneberries

1. Mix together the flours, ground flaxseeds, lecithin, lemon balm, cinnamon, nutmeg, cream of tartar, baking soda, and salt in a large bowl. Stir in the soy milk, corn oil, and vanilla, being careful not to overmix. Stir in the juneberries.

2. Pour a circle of batter onto a hot, lightly oiled griddle and cook each pancake until it is lightly brown underneath. Turn the pancake over with a metal spatula and cook it until it is lightly browned on the other side. Repeat until all the batter is used up. Serve the pancakes hot with any fruit sauce or syrup.

MAKES ABOUT 14 PANCAKES;

SERVES 6 TO 8

JUNEBERRY-ALMOND COOKIES

Juneberries and almonds are distant relatives that deserve to be reunited. One taste of these scrumptious cookies will be all the proof you need. The lecithin granules and flaxseeds more than replace the standard eggs, while the corn and almond oil add to the cookies' richness. The flavor of the juneberries and almonds, combined with the seasonings, will make these some of the best cookies you've ever tasted.

1 ¾ cups (7 ounces) oat flour and 1 ½ cups

(7 ounces) sweet brown rice flour, or

14 ounces any whole-grain flour

2 cups ground almonds (almond meal)

¼ cup arrowroot or kudzu

¼ cup lecithin granules

7 ½ tablespoons freshly ground flaxseeds

(3 tablespoons seeds)

½ teaspoon salt

1 teaspoon cream of tartar

½ teaspoon baking soda

½ teaspoon freshly grated nutmeg

¼ teaspoon freshly ground cardamom seeds

1 cup apple juice

¼ cup corn oil

¼ cup almond oil

2 teaspoons vanilla extract

1 teaspoon almond extract

2 teaspoons liquid stevia or 2 tablespoons honey,

barley malt, or rice syrup

2 cups juneberries

2 teaspoons freshly grated lemon rind

1. Preheat the oven to 375 degrees.

2. In a large bowl, mix together the flours, ground almonds, arrowroot, lecithin, ground flaxseeds, salt, cream of tartar, baking soda, nutmeg, and cardamom.

3. In a medium-size bowl, mix together the apple juice, oils, extracts, and liquid stevia. Mix the wet ingredients into the dry ingredients, being careful not to overmix. Stir in the juneberries and lemon rind, being careful not to overmix.

4. Spoon round dollops of the cookie dough onto 2 oiled cookie sheets and flatten the dough to shape it into cookies. Bake the cookies until they are lightly browned underneath, 15 to 20 minutes. Let them cool on wire racks.

MAKES 2 DOZEN COOKIES

JUNEBERRY ICE CREAM

Juneberries are as fantastic in ice cream as they are in other desserts, and they also provide thickness.

2 ½ cups soy milk or nut milk

½ cup canola oil

¼ cup vegetable glycerin, honey, barley malt, or rice syrup

¾ cup raw cashews

½ cup drained silken tofu

¼ cup lecithin granules

1 teaspoon liquid stevia

1 teaspoon vanilla extract

½ teaspoon salt

2 cups juneberries

1. In a blender, combine all the ingredients, except for 1 cup of the juneberries, and process until smooth.

2. Chill the mixture (or begin with chilled ingredients) if required by your ice cream machine.

3. Pour the mixture into the ice cream machine along with the remaining 1 cup juneberries, and freeze the ice cream according to the manufacturer's instructions.

MAKES 6 CUPS; SERVES 6

COMMON MILKWEED FLOWER

Asclepias syriaca

COMMON MILKWEED FLOWERS ARE AMONG THE most beautiful and sweetly fragrant of wild vegetables (see page 169 for a complete description). You have to parboil them for 1 minute to rid them of their bitter sap. Then squeeze them to remove any excess water and season them properly. Then you can include these flowers in a great variety of vegetable dishes.

MILKWEED FLOWER SAUTÉ

Here's one very simple way to prepare milkweed flowers that brings out their best qualities. Serve as a side dish or use it as an ingredient in other recipes.

6 cups common milkweed flowers, stems mostly removed

6 quarts rapidly boiling water

4 teaspoons olive oil

4 cloves garlic, finely chopped

4 small chiles, or to taste, seeds and ribs removed and finely chopped

¼ cup Black Locust Blossom Wine (page 182) or sherry

1 teaspoon tamari soy sauce, or to taste

1. Add the milkweed flowers to the rapidly boiling water and boil them, covered, for 1 minute after the water returns to a full boil. Drain the milkweed flowers in a colander and press out as much water as possible with a potato masher, slotted spoon, wooden spoon, or fork.

2. Heat the olive oil in a large skillet over medium heat, add the milkweed flowers, garlic, and chiles, and cook, stirring, for 3 minutes. Add the wine and tamari, reduce the heat to low, and cook, covered, for 5 more minutes.

SERVES 6

MILKWEED FLOWER–STUFFED CELERY

Sautéed milkweed flowers and Tofu Egg Filling make a wonderful stuffing for celery.

> 6 celery stalks, leaves and small stems removed
>
> 1 cup Tofu Egg Filling (page 33)
>
> 1 cup Milkweed Flower Sauté (page 225)

1. Cut off the narrower one-third of each celery stalk (save this part for another use) and cut the remaining two thirds of each stalk in half.
2. Mix the Tofu Egg Filling with the milkweed flower sauté and stuff the celery with it.
3. Place the stuffed celery on a steamer rack and steam it until the celery is tender, 15 to 20 minutes.
4. Chill the stuffed celery completely before serving.

SERVES 6

BLACK RASPBERRY

Rubus occidentalis

BLACK RASPBERRIES ARE AMONG THE BEST OF the brambles, and the earliest to appear. Like other brambles (*Rubus* species), they're arching, thorny shrubs with palmate-compound leaves (leaf subdivisions originate from the same point). A waxy, blue-green bloom you can rub off with your finger covers this sparsely thorny shrub. The three sharply double-toothed leaflets are white underneath. The hollow (blackberries aren't hollow) purple-black faceted berries, which are ½ inch across, appear in early summer. Look for these tasty berries in thickets from the East Coast to the Rockies, but not in the Deep South.

Of course, if black raspberries don't grow in your area, you can substitute your local raspberries for black raspberries in the recipes below.

WILD BERRY BAKE

This baked dessert combines the tartness of black raspberries with the sweetness of juneberries.

BOTTOM LAYER

> 2 ½ cups cornbread bread crumbs or fresh Bread Crumbs (page 40)
>
> 3 tablespoons corn oil
>
> 1 teaspoon freshly grated nutmeg
>
> ½ teaspoon freshly ground anise seeds
>
> ½ teaspoon liquid stevia or 1 tablespoon honey, barley malt, or rice syrup

TOP LAYER

> 4 cups juneberries (page 223) or blueberries
>
> 2 cups wild black raspberries
>
> 6 tablespoons kudzu or arrowroot
>
> 2 cups chopped hazelnuts or other nuts
>
> 2 cups apple juice
>
> 2 teaspoons ground cinnamon
>
> 1 teaspoon ground dried wild ginger (page 111) or regular ground ginger
>
> ½ teaspoon liquid stevia or 1 tablespoon honey, barley malt, or rice syrup

> 1 recipe Tofu Whipped Cream (page 32)

1. Preheat the oven to 350 degrees.
2. *To make the bottom layer:* Mix the bottom layer ingredients together and press them into a 14 x 9 x 2-inch oiled baking dish.
3. *To make the top layer:* Mix the top layer ingredients together.

4. Spread the top layer mixture evenly over the bottom layer. Bake the dessert until bubbly, 40 to 60 minutes.

5. Serve Wild Berry Bake hot or cold, topped with Tofu Whipped Cream.

SERVES 10 TO 12

BLACK RASPBERRY PASTRY ROLL

Wild black raspberries are similar to their cultivated counterparts, only better tasting. Use them the same way, but expect even better results. Pastry makes a perfect match for wild berries, stretching the hard-won fruit in the process.

> *2 cups (10 ounces) buckwheat flour and 1 cup*
> *plus 1 tablespoon (4 ounces) sweet brown rice*
> *flour, or 14 ounces any whole-grain flour*
> *1 teaspoon baking soda*
> *2 teaspoons cream of tartar*
> *½ teaspoon salt*
> *½ teaspoon almond extract*
> *3 tablespoons almond oil or corn oil*
> *½ cup plus 2 tablespoons raspberry juice, apple*
> *juice, soy milk, or nut milk, or as needed*
> *2 cups wild black raspberries*
> *¼ teaspoon liquid stevia or 1 tablespoon honey,*
> *barley malt, or rice syrup*
> *½ teaspoon ground cinnamon*
> *1 teaspoon freshly grated nutmeg*

1. Preheat the oven to 375 degrees.

2. In a large bowl, mix together the flours, baking soda, cream of tartar, salt, and almond extract. Cut in the almond oil. Mix in enough fruit juice to make a dough that's neither crumbly nor sticky.

3. On a floured pastry sheet, roll out the dough into 2 rectangles ¼ inch thick, using a rolling pin enclosed in a floured sleeve.

4. Mix the black raspberries and liquid stevia together in a medium-size bowl and distribute the mixture along one long edge of each of the pastry rectangles. Moisten the edges of the pastry rectangles and roll them up, pinching down the ends. Sprinkle cinnamon and nutmeg on top and bake the rolls for 25 minutes. Serve hot or cold.

MAKES 2 PASTRY ROLLS; SERVES 6

WILD APRICOT
Prunus armeniaca

THIS SMALL TREE HAS ALTERNATE, WEDGE-shaped, finely toothed, pointed leaves close to 2 inches long. Showy pink, five-petaled, radially symmetrical blossoms cover the branches in early spring, before the leaves appear. The familiar fruit comes into season at the beginning of summer in areas where early spring frosts haven't destroyed the flowers. Look for this European tree, escaped from cultivation, in sandy fields and thickets anywhere with moderate winters throughout the country.

Wild apricots are much tastier than their Asian commercial forerunners. The climate in my area, New York City, is too cold to make good apricot crops possible more than once in many years. But in one good year, all 30 participants on a tour came home with 11 pounds of this luscious fruit from one tree. You can eat wild apricot raw, or actually improve it by dehydrating and reconstituting it before cooking.

STUFFED APRICOTS

Here's a vegan adaptation of a simple, especially tasty Turkish dessert.

17 fresh wild apricots (about 1 pound)
¾ cup unsweetened apricot juice
2 tablespoons fresh lemon juice
17 whole almonds
2 ½ cups Tofu Whipped Cream (page 32)

1. In a medium-size saucepan, simmer the apricots in the apricot and lemon juices for 10 minutes over low heat, covered. Drain the apricots and allow them to cool. (Set aside the juices for another use.)
2. Make a small hole in the top of each apricot, squeeze out the pit, and replace it with an almond.
3. Serve Stuffed Apricots on a bed of the Tofu Whipped Cream.

SERVES 4 TO 6

WILD APRICOT JAM

Whether you make this jam with cultivated organic or wild apricots, it's still great. Wild Apricot Jam tastes like essence of apricots, not like commercial jam.

2 ½ cups pitted fresh wild apricots
⅓ cup unsweetened peach juice or other fruit juice
1 tablespoon agar powder
¼ teaspoon freshly grated nutmeg
½ teaspoon freshly ground cloves
½ teaspoon liquid stevia or 2 tablespoons honey, barley malt, or rice syrup

1. Simmer all the ingredients together in a medium-size saucepan over low heat for 10 minutes, stirring occasionally.

2. Test the jam for firmness (agar's thickening effect varies according to its fineness) by putting a large metal spoon with a small amount of jam in the freezer for a couple of minutes until the jam is chilled. If the jam is the right thickness, your recipe is done. If the jam is too watery, stir in more agar, simmer the jam for another 5 to 10 minutes, and test it again. If the jam is too thick, stir in some fruit juice or water and test it again immediately.

3. Let the jam cool to room temperature. Store Wild Apricot Jam tightly covered, in the refrigerator for up to a week or keep it in the freezer for up to 6 months.

MAKES 1½ CUPS

WILD APRICOT COBBLER

If you can locate a wild apricot tree, or even if you can't, this dessert will delight anyone partial to apricots who tries it.

FRUIT LAYER

¼ cup unsweetened apricot juice
¼ cup Blackberry Spice Wine (page 278) or red wine
¼ teaspoon liquid stevia or 2 tablespoons honey or barley malt
1 tablespoon fresh lemon juice
2 tablespoons kudzu or arrowroot
½ teaspoon freshly grated lemon rind
1 teaspoon freshly grated nutmeg
1 teaspoon almond extract
4 cups pitted wild apricots, fresh or rehydrated, sliced

TOPPING

2 ½ cups plus 2 tablespoons oat flour or 10.5 ounces any other whole-grain flour
2 tablespoons lecithin granules

1 teaspoon ground cinnamon

½ teaspoon ground dried wild ginger (page 111) or regular ground ginger

¾ teaspoon cream of tartar

⅜ teaspoon baking soda

¼ teaspoon salt

¾ cup apple juice

3 tablespoons corn oil

2 teaspoons fresh lemon juice

1 teaspoon vanilla extract

1. Preheat the oven to 350 degrees.

2. *To make the fruit layer:* Mix together all the fruit ingredients, except the apricots, in a medium-size bowl. Stir in the apricots and place the fruit layer in a 14 x 9 x 2-inch oiled baking dish.

3. *To make the topping:* In another medium-size bowl, mix together the flour, lecithin, cinnamon, ginger, cream of tartar, baking soda, and salt.

4. In a small bowl, mix together the apple juice, corn oil, lemon juice, and vanilla. Mix the wet ingredients into the dry ingredients.

5. Spread the pastry mixture over the apricot mixture. Bake the cobbler until it is bubbly and lightly browned on top, about 40 minutes.

6. Let Wild Apricot Cobbler cool for 10 minutes before cutting it into 6 servings. Serve hot or cold.

SERVES 6

APPLE-APRICOT LAYER CAKE

This cake, which contains layers of fruit alternating with layers of pastry dough, emerges from the oven with flying colors, and tart apricots are outstanding when you eat them in this kind of concoction.

FRUIT LAYER

4 cups dried wild apricots

2 cups apple juice

8 cups cored and sliced Granny Smith apples

½ teaspoon ground dried wild ginger (page 111) or regular ground ginger

1 teaspoon liquid stevia or ¼ cup honey, rice syrup, or barley malt

CAKE

3½ cups plus 2 tablespoons (1 pound) sweet brown rice flour and 3½ cups plus 3½ tablespoons (1 pound) barley flour, or 2 pounds any whole-grain flour

1¼ cups freshly ground flaxseeds (½ cup seeds)

2 teaspoons cream of tartar

1 teaspoon baking soda

½ teaspoon freshly ground cloves

1 teaspoon freshly grated nutmeg

½ teaspoon salt

¼ cup lecithin granules

¾ cup corn oil, sesame oil, or other vegetable oil

1 cup apple juice

¼ cup soy milk or nut milk

1. *To make the fruit layer:* Cover the apricots with the apple juice in a large saucepan and bring the pot to a boil. Remove the pot from the heat, and let the mixture stand for 1 hour. (Or let it soak overnight without heating.)

2. In another large bowl, mix together the apricots and their soaking liquid, the apples, ginger, and liquid stevia.

3. Preheat the oven to 350 degrees.

4. *To make the cake:* In a large bowl, mix together the flour, ground flaxseeds, cream of tartar, baking soda, cloves, nutmeg, salt, and lecithin. Mix in the oil, apple juice, and soy milk. Knead or mix well.

5. Place one-third of the fruit mixture in a 14 x 9 x 2-inch oiled baking dish.

6. Roll out one-third of the dough ¼ inch thick on a floured sheet with a rolling pin in a floured sleeve. Place the rolled out dough over the fruit layer.

7. Repeat steps 5 and 6 until you've used up all the ingredients. Bake the cake until it is lightly browned, about 50 minutes. Serve hot or cold.

SERVES 10

WILD APRICOT ICE CREAM

Apricots provide their own thickener, pectin, so you need only sweeten and add seasonings before running them through an ice cream machine to create one of the best desserts you've ever savored.

2 cups dried wild apricots

3 cups unsweetened apricot juice

2 cups soy milk or nut milk

½ cup canola oil

¼ cup vegetable glycerin or barley malt

2 teaspoons vanilla extract

1 teaspoon mango extract (optional)

½ teaspoon liquid stevia

½ teaspoon salt

1. Bring the apricots and apricot juice to a boil in a large saucepan. Remove the pot from the heat and let the apricots steep, covered, for 30 minutes. (Or soak the apricots in the apricot juice overnight without heating.)

2. Simmer the soaked apricots in the apricot juice for 5 minutes.

3. Remove the apricots from the juice and chop half of them.

4. In a blender, combine all the ingredients, except

the chopped apricots, process until smooth, and chill for 1 hour in the freezer or 4 hours in the refrigerator.

5. Stir in the chopped apricots.

6. Pour the mixture into an ice cream maker and freeze it according to the manufacturer's instructions.

MAKES 6 CUPS; SERVES 6

APRICOT SHERBET

You can make this simple sherbet with the juice squeezed from wild apricots or cultivated apricots, or with apricot juice you purchase. You'll especially appreciate this icy dessert on the hottest days of summer.

1 ½ cups soy milk or nut milk

1 cup unsweetened apricot juice

½ cup raw cashews

½ cup drained silken tofu

½ cup canola oil

¼ cup vegetable glycerin, honey, barley malt, or rice syrup

¼ cup lecithin granules

1 teaspoon liquid stevia (optional)

2 tablespoons fresh lemon juice

½ teaspoon salt

1. In a blender, combine all the ingredients and process until smooth.

2. Chill the mixture (or begin with chilled ingredients) if required by your ice cream machine.

3. Pour the mixture into the ice cream machine, and freeze it according to the manufacturer's instructions.

MAKES 5½ CUPS; SERVES 5 TO 6

RED-CRACKED BOLETE

Boletus chrysenteron

THIS MUSHROOM HAS A VELVETY, DRY, OLIVE-brown cap 1¼ to 3¼ inches wide, with characteristic cracks that are reddish inside. As a bolete, it releases its spores (which are olive-brown) from yellow pores under the cap. The tubes that lead to them are sunken near the stalk, which is 1⅝ to 2⅜ inches long, ¼ to ⅜ inch thick, yellowish above and reddish near the base. The whole mushroom slowly discolors bluish when bruised. Growing under deciduous trees in eastern North America, the mushroom appears from summer to fall.

This delicate-flavored, soft mushroom adds a touch of class to any main course dish, almost like an exotic seasoning. It's great in soups or stews, but don't use strong seasonings or you'll drown out its flavor. Use the cap and the stem, if it is insect-free.

CAULIFLOWER CASSEROLE

This simple casserole owes its excellence to red-cracked boletes.

> *2 tablespoons olive oil*
>
> *1½ cups red-cracked boletes, sliced*
>
> *2 cloves garlic, chopped*
>
> *1 medium-size head cauliflower, broken into florets*
>
> *One 16-ounce package extra-firm tofu, drained and coarsely diced*
>
> *1 cup Tofu Cream Cheese (page 30)*
>
> *2 tablespoons corn oil or olive oil*
>
> *2 cups fresh Bread Crumbs (page 40)*

1. Preheat the oven to 350 degrees.

2. Heat the olive oil in a medium-size skillet over medium heat. Add the mushrooms and garlic and cook, stirring, for 5 minutes.

3. Mix the mushrooms and garlic with the cauliflower, tofu, and Tofu Cream Cheese in a 1½-quart oiled casserole dish.

4. In a small bowl, combine the corn oil with the bread crumbs. Press the mixture on top of the cauliflower mixture. Bake until bubbly, about 40 minutes. Serve hot.

SERVES 6

CHANTERELLE

Cantharellus cibarius

THIS BRIGHT YELLOW TO ORANGE MUSHROOM has a convex to slightly funnel-shaped cap that is ⅜ to 6 inches wide, with a wavy margin. Underneath the cap grow shallow, thick-edged, forked (branched) gills that run down the stem. The gills release pale yellow to buff spores. The stem is 1 to 3 inches long and ¼ to 1 inch thick. The whole mushroom is supposed to smell like apricots, although the specimens I find have a faint, generally sweet aroma. Chanterelles grow on the ground, singly or in troops, in oak forests and near conifers in the summer in the Northeast, the fall in the Northwest, and the late fall and winter in California.

Don't confuse the chanterelle with the poisonous jack-o-lantern (Omphalotus olearius), which is much larger, has sharp, deep gills, and grows in clusters emerging from the bases of trees or from tree roots.

Chanterelles are among the world's most prized mushrooms, with a delicate yet penetrating flavor.

They take exceptionally well to a full range of cooking methods. Nevertheless, some people do get indigestion after eating them, especially if the mushrooms are undercooked. Cook the caps and stems (if insect-free) for 15 to 20 minutes, and start by eating small amounts.

CHANTERELLE CUSTARD

Baking chanterelles with a custard topping shows off their elegance to advantage.

SAUTÉ

> 3 tablespoons olive oil
>
> 6 cups (½ pound) chanterelles, sliced
>
> 6 tablespoons ramp bulbs (page 116) or shallots, chopped
>
> 6 cloves garlic, finely chopped
>
> ¾ teaspoon dried thyme, finely crumbled
>
> ¾ teaspoon dried tarragon, finely crumbled
>
> ¾ teaspoon chili paste or pinch of cayenne pepper, or to taste
>
> ¾ teaspoon Vege-Sal or ¼ teaspoon salt, or to taste
>
> ½ teaspoon freshly ground black pepper (¼ teaspoon peppercorns), or to taste

CUSTARD

> 1½ cups drained silken tofu
>
> ¾ cup soy milk or nut milk
>
> 6 tablespoons corn oil
>
> 3 tablespoons lecithin granules
>
> 1 tablespoon mellow (light-colored) miso
>
> 1½ teaspoons freshly grated nutmeg
>
> ¾ teaspoon paprika

1. Preheat the oven to 350 degrees.

2. *To make the sauté:* Heat the olive oil in a large skillet over medium heat. Add the remaining sauté ingredients and cook, stirring, for 5 minutes. Transfer the

sauté ingredients to a 1½-quart oiled casserole dish.

3. *To make the custard:* In a food processor or a medium-size bowl, combine the custard ingredients and process or beat with a mixer, whisk, or fork until smooth. Pour the custard mixture over the sautéed ingredients. Bake, uncovered, until set, about 30 minutes. Serve hot.

SERVES 6

WILD PEACH

Prunus persica

THE PEACH TREE, CULTIVATED OR ESCAPED from cultivation, is a small tree with slender, curved, lance-shaped, pointed leaves that are 3 to 5 inches long. Pink, five-petaled, radially symmetrical flowers ½ to 2 inches wide appear in early spring. The familiar fruit ripens halfway through summer. Look for peach trees in thickets, fields, roadsides, and disturbed areas throughout the country.

Closely related to apricots and cherries, wild peaches can't be beat. If you can find fruit that has escaped detection from the bugs, you're in for a treat.

STUFFED FRUIT LOAF

This unusual loaf uses wild vegetables in the crust and wild fruits for the filling.

FRUIT FILLING

> 2 cups apple juice or other unsweetened fruit juice
>
> 1 cup dried sliced wild peaches
>
> 1 cup dried sliced beach plums (page 304) or commercial plums or sweet cherries

2 cups drained soft tofu

1 cup tomato sauce

1 teaspoon ground dried wild ginger (page 111) or
　regular ground ginger

1 teaspoon common spicebush berries (page 314),
　finely chopped, or freshly ground allspice
　berries

CRUST

¼ cup olive oil

3 cups oyster mushrooms (page 404) or other
　mushrooms, sliced

¾ cup sliced celery

¾ cup sweet cicely taproots (avoid the gnarled,
　stringy underground stems; page 92) or fennel
　bulb, finely chopped

1 cup daylily shoots (page 64), chopped

1 ¼ cups raw cashew pieces

2 ½ cups cooked adzuki beans or red beans,
　drained and processed into a paste

2 cups cooked brown rice

½ cup Tahini (page 38)

¼ cup alfalfa sprouts

¼ cup chopped fresh parsley leaves

5 tablespoons freshly ground flaxseeds
　(2 tablespoons seeds)

½ teaspoon dried thyme, finely crumbled

1. To start the fruit filling: Cover the dried fruit with the fruit juice in a medium-size saucepan and bring the pot to a boil. Remove the pot from the heat, and let the fruit sit, covered, for 1 hour (or soak the fruit in unheated juice overnight).

2. Preheat the oven to 350 degrees.

3. To make the crust: Meanwhile, heat the olive oil in a large skillet over medium heat. Add the mushrooms, celery, sweet cicely, daylily shoots, and cashews and cook, stirring often, for 10 minutes. Remove the pot

from the heat, add the remaining crust ingredients, and stir to combine.

4. To finish the fruit filling: Return the fruit and juice to a boil, reduce the heat to low, and simmer for 10 minutes. Combine the fruit mixture with the remaining filling ingredients.

5. Press two-thirds of the crust mixture into the bottom and up the sides of 4 oiled 6½ x 4⅜ x 2½-inch loaf pans. Pour in the filling and then cover it with the remaining crust mixture. Bake the fruit loaf until it is lightly browned, about 1 hour. Slice and serve hot.

SERVES 16

PERFECT PEACH JAM

This is one of my oldest recipes, created when I was teaching cooking classes before I became involved with wild edible plants. You can freeze the jam for future use.

6 tablespoons agar flakes

¼ cup apple juice

¼ cup unsweetened grape juice

5 cups (2 ½ pounds) pitted and sliced ripe wild
　peaches

1 tablespoon freshly grated orange rind

¼ teaspoon ground dried wild ginger (page 111) or
　regular ground ginger

1 teaspoon freshly grated nutmeg

1. Bring the agar and fruit juices to a boil in a large pot over medium heat, stirring often. Reduce the heat to low and simmer until the agar dissolves, about 5 minutes, stirring often. Add the remaining ingredients, bring the pot to a boil, reduce the heat to low, and simmer for 5 minutes, stirring often.

2. Test the jam for firmness (agar's thickening effect

varies according to its fineness) by putting a large metal spoon with a small amount of jam in the freezer for a couple of minutes, until the jam is chilled. If the jam is the right thickness, your recipe is done. If it's too watery, stir in more agar, simmer the jam for another 5 to 10 minutes, and test it again. If the jam is too thick, stir in some fruit juice or water and test it again immediately.

3. Store Perfect Peach Jam, tightly covered, in the refrigerator for up to a week.

MAKES 4 CUPS

PECAN–WILD PEACH PIE

Paralleling a well-loved traditional dessert with high-quality, whole-food ingredients in the right proportions, how can you go wrong?

CRUST

> 3⅓ cups (1 pound) sweet brown rice flour and 1⅔ cups (½ pound) buckwheat flour, or 1½ pounds any whole-grain flour
>
> 2 teaspoons freshly ground coriander seeds
>
> 1 teaspoon freshly ground cloves
>
> ½ teaspoon salt
>
> ¼ cup almond oil or corn oil
>
> 1 teaspoon almond extract
>
> 1 cup apple juice

FILLING

> 12 ripe wild peaches, pitted and sliced
>
> 5½ cups pecans, chopped
>
> 1¾ cups apple juice
>
> ½ cup arrowroot or kudzu
>
> 2 tablespoons vanilla extract
>
> 1 tablespoon dried wild mint (page 129) or other mint, finely crumbled
>
> 1 teaspoon butterscotch extract (optional)

> ½ teaspoon liquid stevia or 2 tablespoons honey, rice syrup, or barley
>
> 1 teaspoon ground cinnamon (optional)

1. *To make the crust:* In a large bowl, combine the flours, coriander, cloves, and salt. Stir in the almond oil and almond extract. Stir in the apple juice, or enough to make a dough that's neither crumbly nor sticky. Knead the dough briefly. Chill it briefly.

2. Preheat the oven to 425 degrees.

3. *To make the filling:* Mix together the filling ingredients in another bowl.

4. Divide the dough into 6 balls. Using a rolling pin enclosed in a floured sleeve and working on a floured pastry sheet, roll out 3 of the balls into 10-inch pie crusts that are ⅜ inch thick. Transfer the crusts to 3 oiled 9-inch pie tins, prick the crusts with a fork to let hot air escape, and pour in the filling.

5. Roll out the top crusts with the remaining dough balls. Moisten the edges of the bottom crusts with water, cover the filling with the top crusts, and press the edges down with a fork. Sprinkle cinnamon on top of each pie, if desired.

6. Bake the pies for 10 minutes and then reduce the oven temperature to 350 degrees, opening the oven door for a minute to reduce the temperature quickly, so the browned crust doesn't burn. Rotate the pies so the crusts bake evenly. Bake the pies for another 35 minutes.

7. Chill and serve. These pies freeze well.

MAKES THREE 9-INCH PIES;
SERVES 12 TO 16

WILD PEACH SHERBET

Here is another simple recipe that is simply wonderful made with natural ingredients.

> 4 cups pitted and sliced ripe wild peaches
>
> 2 cups unsweetened peach juice
>
> 2 tablespoons vegetable glycerin, barley malt, or honey
>
> 1 tablespoon fresh lemon juice
>
> 1 tablespoon freshly grated orange rind
>
> 1 teaspoon ground dried wild ginger (page 111) or regular ginger
>
> 1 teaspoon Angostura bitters (optional)
>
> ½ teaspoon freshly ground cloves
>
> ¼ teaspoon salt

1. In a blender, process all the ingredients until smooth in 2 batches.

2. Chill the mixture (or use chilled ingredients) if required by your ice cream machine.

3. Pour the mixture into the ice cream machine and freeze it according to the manufacturer's instructions.

MAKES 6 CUPS; SERVES 6

WILD PEACH ICE CREAM

Peaches are great in my vegan ice cream. You need to use less thickener in this recipe because peaches have a built-in thickening effect.

> 2 cups soy milk or nut milk
>
> ½ cup canola oil
>
> ¼ cup vegetable glycerin, honey, barley malt, or rice syrup
>
> ¼ cup lecithin granules
>
> ¼ cup drained silken tofu
>
> ¼ cup raw cashews

> 1 teaspoon liquid stevia (optional)
>
> 1 teaspoon vanilla extract
>
> 1 teaspoon peach extract (optional)
>
> ½ teaspoon salt
>
> 4 medium-size ripe wild peaches, pitted and chopped

1. In a blender, combine all the ingredients, except for 2 of the peaches, and process until smooth.

2. Chill the mixture (or begin with chilled ingredients) if required by your ice cream machine.

3. Pour the purée and the remaining chopped peaches into the ice cream machine and freeze the ice cream according to the manufacturer's instructions.

MAKES 5½ CUPS; SERVES 5 TO 6

WILD CURRANT
Ribes species

THESE ARCHING BUSHES, WHICH ARE 2 TO 5 feet tall, have alternate leaves that measure a few inches across and look like maple leaves, serrated and with three lobes, or subdivisions. Yellow-white to green to purple, five-petaled flowers with fused bases dangle on long racemes (common linear flower stalks) in the spring. In the summer, the flowers are translucent, replaced by globular berries that are less than ¼ inch across, which may be red, pale yellow, or even black. Gooseberries (*Ribes* species) are similar, but they have thorns you must remove. Look for currants wherever there's moisture, in thickets, woods, on hillsides, prairies, ravines, and canyons throughout the United States.

These berries are so sour raw that I didn't bother to

experiment with them for years—they are nothing like cultivated currants. At last, after finding them in abundance while harvesting other berries, I tried adding them to muffins and discovered that cooking tames their acidity quite handily. And it turns out that wild currants add just the right spark to baked goods, puddings, fruit soups, ice cream, cobblers, and virtually any dessert. I also discovered that the British use currants in baking, and although British cuisine is reputedly the worst in the world, British baking is really quite good. Now I'm disappointed in years when climatic conditions lead to a poor harvest of wild currants.

WILD PEACH AND CURRANT JAM

Fresh fruit and agar, rather than sugar and chemicals, produce a spread that tastes like the fruit it's made from instead of like commercial jam. The sweet peaches and tart wild currants complement each other perfectly. By adding the fruit only toward the end of cooking, you retain more of its flavor and nutrition.

¾ cup unsweetened peach juice

¼ cup fresh lemon juice

3 ⅔ tablespoons agar powder

1 teaspoon liquid stevia or 2 tablespoons honey

1 teaspoon dried lemon verbena or other mint, finely crumbled

1 teaspoon freshly ground star anise

1 teaspoon freshly grated nutmeg

¼ teaspoon freshly ground cloves

14 ripe wild peaches (page 232) or cultivated peaches, pitted and sliced (8 cups)

2 cups wild currants

1. Bring all the ingredients, except the peaches and currants, to a boil in a large saucepan over medium heat, stirring often. Reduce the heat to low and simmer the mixture for 5 minutes, covered. Add the fruit, return the pot to a boil, reduce the heat to low, and simmer for another 5 minutes.

2. Test the jam for firmness (agar's thickening effect varies according to its fineness) by putting a large metal spoon with a small amount of jam in the freezer for a few minutes until the jam is chilled. If the jam is the right thickness, your recipe is done. If the jam is too watery, stir in more agar, simmer the jam for another 5 to 10 minutes, and test it again. If the jam is too thick, stir in some fruit juice or water and test it again immediately.

3. Store Wild Peach and Currant Jam, tightly covered, in the refrigerator for up to a week, or in the freezer for up to 6 months.

MAKES 11 CUPS

WILD CURRANT CHUTNEY

This pungent East Indian relish goes well with any number of main courses, and it will last for weeks in the refrigerator.

5 cups wild currants or gooseberries

2 cups raisins

1 ½ cups apple juice

2 medium-size red onions, chopped

1 cup red wine vinegar

1 cup water

3 tablespoons peeled and chopped fresh ginger

¼ cup freshly ground yellow mustard seeds (2 tablespoons seeds)

2 teaspoons chili paste or ½ teaspoon cayenne pepper

1 tablespoon mellow (light-colored) miso
½ teaspoon turmeric
½ teaspoon freshly ground coriander seeds

Combine all the ingredients in a large saucepan and bring the pot to a boil over medium heat. Reduce the heat to low and simmer, uncovered, until thickened, about 35 minutes, stirring occasionally. Wild Currant Chutney will keep, tightly covered, in the refrigerator for 7 to 10 days.

MAKES 9 CUPS

HOT CROSS BUNS

English cuisine has a bad reputation (some people think the very term an oxymoron), but once you try these traditional buns, updated with healthy ingredients, you'll realize how good traditional-style English baking can be. And you'll be in high-class company: King George II, King George III, and their families bought hot cross buns from the bun house in Chelsea (demolished in 1839), where these delicacies were first created.

½ cup lukewarm apple juice
1½ teaspoons active dry yeast
5 cups (24 ounces) sweet brown rice flour and
    2½ cups (10 ounces) oat flour, or 34 ounces
    any whole-grain flour
½ cup arrowroot or kudzu
½ teaspoon salt, or to taste
1 teaspoon freshly grated nutmeg
½ teaspoon ground mace
¼ teaspoon freshly ground cloves
1½ cups plus 1 tablespoon soy milk or nut milk
¼ cup plus 1½ tablespoons corn oil
2 tablespoons lecithin granules

½ teaspoon liquid stevia
¾ cup wild currants

1. In a blender, dissolve the yeast in the lukewarm apple juice. Blend the mixture, and then let it sit for 5 minutes.
2. In a large bowl, mix together half the flour, the arrowroot, salt, nutmeg, mace, and cloves.
3. Add 1½ cups of the soy milk, ¼ cup of the corn oil, the lecithin, and liquid stevia to the blender and process with the yeast mixture until smooth. Pour the wet mixture into the flour mixture and mix. Cover the bowl and let the dough rise in a warm place for 45 minutes.
4. Roll the currants in 2 tablespoons of the remaining flour.
5. Mix the rest of the flour into the dough and knead it for a few minutes. Fold in the currants. Divide the dough into 18 parts and shape the dough into balls. Place the balls of dough on 2 oiled cookie sheets, leaving plenty of space between the buns. Cover the buns with moist towels, and let the buns rise in a warm place for 45 minutes.
6. Preheat the oven to 425 degrees.
7. Cut an X into the top of each bun with a knife and brush the buns with the remaining 1½ tablespoons corn oil. Set a pan of water in the bottom of the oven to keep the buns soft. Bake them until they are lightly browned, about 15 minutes.
8. Brush the tops of the buns with the remaining 1 tablespoon soy milk and serve them hot, or let them cool on wire racks.

MAKES 18 BUNS

RED CURRANT MUFFINS

Tart wild currants make perfect residents for these exceptional whole-grain muffins.

DRY INGREDIENTS

> 3 ⅓ cups (1 pound) sweet brown rice flour and
> 2 cups (½ pound) oat flour, or 1 ½ pounds any
> whole-grain flour
>
> ½ cup plus 2 tablespoons freshly ground flaxseeds
> (¼ cup seeds)
>
> 1 tablespoon ground cinnamon
>
> 2 teaspoons freshly ground coriander seeds
>
> 1 tablespoon freshly ground fennel seeds
>
> 2 teaspoons cream of tartar
>
> 1 teaspoon baking soda
>
> 1 teaspoon salt

WET INGREDIENTS

> ¾ cup soy milk or nut milk
>
> ¼ cup apple juice or other unsweetened fruit juice
>
> ¼ cup corn oil or flaxseed oil
>
> 2 teaspoons black currant extract (optional)
>
> 2 teaspoons vanilla extract
>
> 1 teaspoon liquid stevia or 2 tablespoons barley malt
>
> 2 cups wild currants
>
> ¼ cup any whole-grain flour
>
> ½ cup lecithin granules

1. Preheat the oven to 350 degrees.

2. In a large bowl, combine the dry ingredients.

3. In a medium-size bowl, mix the wet ingredients together. Stir the wet ingredients into the dry ingredients, being careful not to overmix.

4. Roll the currants in the whole-grain flour so the berries won't create soggy spots in the muffins. Gently fold the currants and lecithin granules into the batter.

5. Spoon the batter into 2 oiled 12-section muffin tins, filling each muffin cup two-thirds full. Bake the muffins until a toothpick inserted in the center emerges clean, about 40 minutes. Let the muffins cool on a wire rack.

MAKES 2 DOZEN MUFFINS

POTATO-CURRANT CAKE

Wild currants resemble small, sour gooseberries, while commercial currants are more like raisins. You can use either (or a combination of both) in this updated English dish from Devonshire. You'll enjoy the results, whichever fruit you use.

> 1 ½ cups oat flour or 6 ounces any other whole-grain flour
>
> ½ cup arrowroot or kudzu
>
> 2 tablespoons lecithin granules
>
> 5 teaspoons caraway seeds
>
> ¼ teaspoon ground cinnamon
>
> ¼ teaspoon common spicebush berries (page 314), finely chopped, or freshly ground allspice berries
>
> ¼ teaspoon ground ginger
>
> ½ teaspoon cream of tartar
>
> ¼ teaspoon baking soda
>
> ¾ cup mashed boiled potatoes
>
> ½ cup apple juice
>
> ¼ cup corn oil
>
> ½ teaspoon liquid stevia or 2 tablespoons barley malt or honey
>
> 1 cup wild currants or gooseberries

1. Preheat the oven to 375 degrees.

2. In a large bowl, mix together the flour, arrowroot, lecithin, caraway seeds, cinnamon, spicebush berries, ginger, cream of tartar, and baking soda.

3. In a medium-size bowl, mix together the mashed potatoes, apple juice, corn oil, and liquid stevia. Mix the potato mixture into the flour mixture. Stir in the currants. Transfer the mixture to a 10 x 6½ x 2-inch oiled baking dish. Set a pan of water in the bottom of the oven to keep the crust soft. Bake the cake for 30 minutes, or until a toothpick inserted in the center emerges clean.

4. Cut the cake into 8 squares and let it cool on a wire rack. Serve with hot herb tea.

MAKES 8 SQUARES

NORTHAMPTONSHIRE CHEESECAKE

Traditional English cuisine commonly employs currants in cakes, and tart wild currants effectively complement the relatively bland tofu in this healthful cheesecake. With this recipe, it will be easy to fool people into thinking you made this cheesecake with cheese.

FILLING

4 cups drained silken tofu

2 tablespoons arrowroot or kudzu

2 tablespoons lecithin granules

2 tablespoons brewer's yeast

1 tablespoon vegetable glycerin, barley malt, or honey

1 tablespoon corn oil

1 tablespoon freshly grated lemon rind

2 teaspoons vanilla extract

1 teaspoon lemon extract

1 teaspoon almond extract

1 teaspoon amaretto extract (optional)

½ teaspoon salt

1 teaspoon liquid stevia or 1 tablespoon honey, barley malt, or rice syrup

¼ teaspoon Tabasco sauce

1 cup wild currants

CRUST

1 cup plus 2 ½ teaspoons (5 ounces) sweet brown rice flour and 1 ¼ cups (6 ounces) buckwheat flour, or 11 ounces any whole-grain flour

⅓ cup ground almonds

2 ⅔ tablespoons arrowroot or kudzu

¼ teaspoon freshly ground cloves

½ teaspoon freshly grated nutmeg

¼ teaspoon salt

2 tablespoons almond oil or corn oil

⅓ cup apple juice

¼ teaspoon orange extract

1. Preheat the oven to 425 degrees.

2. *To make the filling:* In a food processor, combine all the filling ingredients, except the currants, and process until smooth. Mix in the currants.

3. *To make the crust:* Mix together the flours, almonds, arrowroot, cloves, nutmeg, and salt in a large bowl.

4. Mix together the oil, apple juice, and orange extract in a small bowl. Mix the wet ingredients into the dry ingredients.

5. Roll the pastry into a disk 11½ inches in diameter on a floured pastry sheet with a rolling pin enclosed in a floured sleeve. Roll the dough and pastry sheet around the rolling pin and transfer the dough to an oiled 10-inch round cake pan. Trim away any excess dough. Prick the crust with a fork so it doesn't pull away from the bottom of the pan. Bake the crust for 5 minutes. Reduce the oven temperature to 350 degrees and remove the crust from the oven.

6. Fill the partially baked crust with the filling and return the cheesecake to the oven to bake until the filling is set, another 40 minutes, turning the cheesecake occasionally so that the crust will cook evenly. Let the cheesecake cool before serving.

SERVES 6

WINEBERRY

Rubus phoenicolasius

THIS PLANT IS ANOTHER BRAMBLE (*RUBUS* species), a usually thorny, arching plant with palmate-compound leaves. (A palmate-compound leaf, rather than the typical single leaf, consists of a unit of stems branched in palm-like fashion with their own individual leaves, here called "leaflets." This resulted as single leaves evolved into divided ones in order to catch more sunlight and minimize storm damage.) The wineberry has bristly red stems that grow up to 8 feet tall, and three-parted leaves with large, roundish, pointed leaflets that are white underneath. Clusters of small, inconspicuous white flowers appear in the spring, followed by juicy, hollow, large faceted raspberries in the summer. Look for wineberries in moist soil, in thickets, fields, and at the edges of woods or trails throughout the Northeast.

Use this common Asian fruit the same way you'd use commercial raspberries. Wineberries are juicier and more sour, with more flavor than most of their relatives. The seeds are hard, so if you're using the berries puréed, it's better to strain out the seeds.

If this species doesn't grow in your region, substitute your local varieties (various raspberry species grow throughout the United States).

SPICY BARBECUE SAUCE

This hot sauce is great for marinating, basting, and pouring over vegetables or entrées. Use Spicy Barbecue Sauce as a marinade, for outdoor barbecuing or grilling on an indoor broiler, or as a sauce.

½ cup Wineberry Wine (page 246) or red wine

½ cup olive oil

¼ cup Homemade Ketchup (page 37)

1 very small onion, finely chopped

1 tablespoon chili paste or 1 teaspoon cayenne pepper, or to taste

1 tablespoon Bragg's Liquid Aminos or tamari soy sauce, or to taste

In a small bowl, mix together all the ingredients. Spicy Barbecue Sauce will keep, tightly covered, in the refrigerator for up to a week, and frozen for up to 6 months.

MAKES 1½ CUPS

WINEBERRY SALAD DRESSING

This refreshing alternative to vinaigrette (oil and vinegar) salad dressing uses sour-tasting, flavorful wineberries to replace some of the vinegar.

¾ cup peanut oil

¾ cup sesame oil

½ cup wineberries

½ cup red wine vinegar

3 tablespoons any mellow (light-colored) miso

1 teaspoon freshly ground coriander seeds

1 teaspoon freshly ground anise seeds

½ teaspoon freshly ground cardamom seeds

In a blender, combine all the ingredients and process until smooth. Strain out the wineberry seeds through a fine mesh strainer. Wineberry Salad Dressing will keep, tightly covered, in the refrigerator for up to 2 weeks.

MAKES 2¾ CUPS

WINEBERRY JAM

Here's a simple sweet topping for breads and desserts that everyone loves. The thickener, agar, is a seaweed that's more appetizing than gelatin, which is made from cows' hooves and pigs' trotters. And agar solidifies at room temperature, whereas gelatin must be refrigerated.

2 ½ cups wineberry juice (wineberry juice collects
    in the bottom of the container in which you
    store the berries) or orange juice
¼ cup natural black cherry juice concentrate
¼ cup vegetable glycerin, barley malt, rice syrup,
    or honey
2 tablespoons agar powder
1 teaspoon dried pennyroyal (page 203) or other
    mint, finely crumbled
½ teaspoon Grand Marnier extract (optional)
1 ½ cups wineberries

1. Place all the ingredients, except the berries, in a medium-size saucepan and bring the pot to a boil. Reduce the heat to low, and simmer for 10 minutes, stirring often. Add the wineberries and simmer, uncovered, for another 5 minutes.

2. Test the jam for firmness (agar's thickening effect varies according to its fineness) by putting a large metal spoon with a small amount of jam in the freezer for a couple of minutes, until the jam is chilled. If the jam is the right thickness, your recipe is done. If it's too watery, stir in more agar, simmer the jam for another 5 to 10 minutes, and test it again. If the jam is too thick, stir in some fruit juice or water and test the jam again immediately.

3. Store Wineberry Jam, tightly covered, in the refrigerator for up to a week or frozen for up to 6 months.

MAKES 4½ CUPS

WINEBERRY-ALMOND PUDDING

Here's a simple pudding that shows how easy it is to do away with the traditional eggs and sugar, and how good pudding can be with wild berries.

One 19-ounce package silken tofu, drained
1 ⅔ cups Super Strawberry Jam (page 208) or
    other jam
¼ cup Redbud Wine (page 159) or red wine
½ teaspoon strawberry extract (optional)
1 teaspoon freshly grated nutmeg
½ teaspoon freshly ground star anise
4 cups wineberries
1 cup almonds or other nuts, toasted (page 207)
    and chopped

1. Preheat the oven to 350 degrees.

2. Place everything except the wineberries and almonds in a food processor or large bowl and process or beat with an electric mixer or whisk until smooth. Mix in the wineberries.

3. Transfer the mixture to a 1½-quart oiled casserole dish and bake until bubbly, about 30 minutes.

4. Sprinkle the pudding with the almonds. Serve hot or cold.

SERVES 6

WINEBERRY TAPIOCA PUDDING

After decades of popularity, tapioca finally went out of style when I first began cooking. But this natural starchy thickener, made from the tropical manioc root, is as tasty as ever. And tapioca's smoothness and mildness perfectly offset the wineberry's heady tartness in this rich dessert.

One 33.8-ounce container soy milk or nut milk

5 tablespoons tapioca pearls

½ cup natural cherry juice concentrate or other
   fruit juice concentrate

2 tablespoons sesame oil or corn oil

2 teaspoons ground cinnamon

½ teaspoon liquid stevia or 2 tablespoons honey,
   barley malt, or rice syrup

¼ teaspoon almond extract

¼ teaspoon strawberry extract (optional)

¼ teaspoon salt

6 cups wineberries

1 ¾ cups pecans, chopped

1. Place all the ingredients, except the wineberries and pecans, in a large saucepan and bring the pot to a boil over medium heat, stirring often. Reduce the heat to low and simmer, covered, for 10 minutes, stirring occasionally. Add the wineberries and continue to simmer for another 5 minutes.

2. Remove the pot from the heat and add the pecans. Serve hot or cold.

SERVES 6 TO 8

WINEBERRY-FILLED COOKIES

Wineberry jam makes a terrific filling for these cookies, which are also great filled with other jams.

DRY INGREDIENTS

1 ⅔ cups (8 ounces) sweet brown rice flour,
   1 ¾ cups (7 ounces) oat flour, and 1 cup plus
   1 tablespoon (4 ounces) barley flour, or
   19 ounces any whole-grain flour

½ cup arrowroot or kudzu

7 ½ tablespoons freshly ground flaxseeds
   (3 tablespoons seeds)

¾ teaspoon baking soda

1 tablespoon poppy seeds

1 ½ tablespoons lecithin granules

1 teaspoon freshly ground cloves

½ teaspoon freshly ground cardamom seeds

1 teaspoon freshly grated nutmeg

½ teaspoon salt

1 ½ teaspoons freshly grated lemon rind
   or ½ teaspoon dried

WET INGREDIENTS

1 cup plus 2 tablespoons apple juice or other
   unsweetened fruit juice

¼ cup corn oil

1 tablespoon fresh lime or lemon juice

1 teaspoon vanilla extract

½ teaspoon almond extract

¼ teaspoon amaretto extract (optional)

FILLING

1 ½ cups Wineberry Jam (page 241)

1. Preheat the oven to 400 degrees.

2. In a large bowl, combine the dry ingredients.

3. In a small bowl, mix together the wet ingredients. Mix the wet ingredients into the dry ingredients, being careful not to overmix.

4. Roll out half the dough on a floured pastry sheet with a rolling pin enclosed in a floured sleeve, making a circle ³⁄₁₆-inch thick. Using a 3-inch cookie cutter, jar lid, or juice glass, cut out as many cookies as possible. In half the cookies, cut out and remove a circular hole about 1⅛ inches in diameter (a spice jar lid is the right size). Place the shaped dough on an oiled cookie sheet.

5. Continue to reroll and cut the scraps until there is no more dough left.

6. Bake the cookies until they are very lightly browned, 5 to 7 minutes. Don't overcook the cookies or they

will get hard. Let the cookies cool on wire racks.

7. Using a butter knife, spread a tablespoon of the jam on each of the cookies that have no hole, leaving a small area bare near the margin. Press a doughnut-shaped cookie on top of the jam layer of each cookie.

MAKES 2 DOZEN COOKIES

WINEBERRY CREAM PIE

This pie's delectable almond-flavored crust offsets the wineberries' tart, penetrating flavor. Thanks to the seasonings and the pecans, even the otherwise bland tofu contributes to the whole.

CRUST

3 ⅓ cups buckwheat flour or 1 pound any whole-grain flour

2 cups almond meal (you can easily grind raw almonds in a food processor)

½ teaspoon freshly ground anise seeds or star anise

¼ teaspoon salt

¼ teaspoon freshly ground cloves

½ teaspoon freshly grated nutmeg

8 teaspoons almond oil or corn oil

¾ cup apple juice or other unsweetened fruit juice

¼ teaspoon almond extract

Dash of bitter almond extract (optional)

CREAM LAYER

One 19-ounce package silken tofu, drained

1 tablespoon arrowroot or kudzu

1 ½ teaspoons freshly grated orange rind or ¼ teaspoon orange extract

½ teaspoon vanilla extract

¼ teaspoon salt

¼ teaspoon butterscotch extract (optional)

¼ teaspoon liquid stevia or 2 tablespoons honey

¾ cup pecans, chopped

BERRY FILLING

¼ cup wineberry juice (wineberry juice collects in the bottom of the containers in which you store the berries) or other fruit juice

6 tablespoons sweet brown rice flour or 1.75 ounces any other whole-grain flour

¼ cup apple juice

Freshly grated rind of ½ lemon or ¼ teaspoon lemon extract

1 teaspoon dried mint, finely crumbled

¼ teaspoon liquid stevia or 1 tablespoon honey

¼ teaspoon raspberry extract (optional)

¼ teaspoon Grand Marnier extract (optional)

4 ½ cups wineberries

TOPPING

2 teaspoons ground cinnamon

1. *To make the crust:* In a large bowl, mix together the flour, almond meal, anise, salt, cloves, and nutmeg. Mix in the oil and then add the remaining crust ingredients, mixing thoroughly. Chill the dough quickly in the freezer while preparing the other layers.

2. *To make the cream layer:* Place the cream layer ingredients, except the pecans, in a food processor or large bowl and process or beat with an electric mixer or by hand with a whisk until smooth. Stir in the pecans.

3. *To make the berry filling:* In a medium-size bowl, thoroughly mix together the berry filling ingredients, except the wineberries. Gently stir in the wineberries.

4. Preheat the oven to 475 degrees.

5. Divide the pastry dough evenly into 4 pieces. Roll out 2 bottom crusts on a floured pastry sheet with a rolling pin enclosed in a floured sleeve. Transfer the rolled out crusts to 2 oiled 10-inch pie pans. Prick the dough with a fork so it doesn't pull away from the bottom of the pan. Fill each crust with equal portions of the cream filling followed by the berry filling.

6. Roll out the 2 top crusts, moisten the edges of the bottom crusts with water, and cover the fillings with the top crusts. Press the crusts together and trim off the excess dough. Sprinkle the cinnamon on top, if desired.
7. Bake the pies for 10 minutes at 475 degrees, and then reduce the oven temperature to 350 degrees. Bake the pies until the filling is bubbly, another 30 to 40 minutes, rotating the pies so the crusts bake evenly. Serve cold.

MAKES TWO 10-INCH PIES; SERVES 12

Note: You may shape any excess dough into cookies and bake them on a cookie sheet in a preheated 350-degree oven until a toothpick inserted in the center emerges clean, 15 to 20 minutes.

WINEBERRY CRÊPES

These delicate French pancakes, filled with wineberry jam, can't be beat.

CRÊPES

1 cup (¼ pound) oat flour and 1 cup plus
  3 tablespoons (¼ pound) buckwheat flour,
  or ½ pound any whole-grain flour
½ teaspoon salt
½ teaspoon ground cinnamon
½ teaspoon dried wild spearmint (page 59) or
  other mint, finely crumbled
1 ½ cups soy milk or nut milk
2 tablespoons corn oil
1 teaspoon vanilla extract
½ teaspoon almond extract
¼ teaspoon liquid stevia or 1 tablespoon barley
  malt or honey
Oil for cooking the crêpes

FILLING

2 cups Tofu Cottage Cheese (page 30)
1 cup Wineberry Jam (page 241)
½ cup chopped pecans, toasted (page 158)

TOPPING

1 ½ cups Tofu Sour Cream (page 33; optional)

1. Preheat the oven to 350 degrees.
2. *To make the crêpes:* Place the batter ingredients in a blender or large bowl and process or beat with an electric mixer, whisk, or wooden spoon until smooth.
3. *To make the filling:* In a medium-size bowl, mix together the filling ingredients.
4. Pour enough batter onto a hot, oiled griddle to make a thin circle 6 inches in diameter (use a metal spatula to spread out the batter). When the underside of the crêpe is lightly browned, flip the crêpe over with the spatula and cook it until the other side is lightly browned. Remove each crêpe to a plate. Repeat until you've used up all the batter.
5. Put a tablespoon of filling along an edge of each crêpe and roll it up. Repeat with the remaining crêpes and filling.
6. Put the filled crêpes in a 10 x 6½ x 2-inch oiled baking dish and bake them until heated through, about 15 minutes. Serve the crêpes hot topped with Tofu Sour Cream, if desired.

SERVES 6

WINEBERRY LAYER CAKE

Wineberries, the most common wild raspberries of my region, are great in this recipe, but other raspberries or blackberries will also give you excellent results. This layer cake is tastier than conventional cakes, better for you, and more fun to make, especially if you've gathered some of the ingredients yourself.

CAKE

2 cups plus 1½ tablespoons (10 ounces) sweet brown rice flour and 1 cup plus 1 tablespoon (4 ounces) barley flour, or 14 ounces any whole-grain flour

2 tablespoons kudzu or arrowroot

2 teaspoons cream of tartar

½ tablespoon finely chopped fresh wild mint (page 129) or other mint leaves, or ½ teaspoon dried, finely crumbled

1 teaspoon baking soda

1 teaspoon salt

1 teaspoon freshly grated nutmeg

¼ teaspoon freshly ground cardamom seeds

½ cup plus 2 tablespoons apple juice

5 tablespoons almond oil or corn oil

2 tablespoons red wine vinegar

½ teaspoon vanilla extract

1 cup wineberries

½ cup raisins, soaked in hot fruit juice for 30 minutes and drained

½ cup walnuts, chopped

FILLING

2 tablespoons apple juice

2 tablespoons Redbud Wine (page 159) or red wine

½ teaspoon liquid stevia or 2 tablespoons honey, barley malt, or rice syrup

¼ teaspoon ground cinnamon

¼ teaspoon orange extract

7½ teaspoons agar powder

1 cup wineberries

1. Preheat the oven to 325 degrees.

2. *To make the cake:* In a large bowl, mix together the flour, kudzu, cream of tartar, mint, baking soda, salt, nutmeg, and cardamom.

3. In a small bowl, mix together the apple juice, almond oil, vinegar, and vanilla. Mix the wet ingredients into the dry ingredients, being careful not to overmix. Mix in the wineberries, drained raisins, and walnuts.

4. Pour the batter evenly into 2 oiled 9-inch round cake pans. Bake the cakes until a toothpick inserted in the center emerges clean, about 30 minutes. Let the cakes cool on a wire rack.

5. *To make the filling:* In a medium-size saucepan, simmer all the filling ingredients, except the wineberries, together over low heat for 10 minutes, stirring occasionally. Stir in the wineberries, remove the pot from the heat, and let the filling stand for 5 minutes.

6. Test the firmness of the filling by half-filling a metal spoon with the filling and placing it in the freezer for a few minutes, until the filling is chilled. The filling should be as firm as jam. If not, add more agar and simmer the filling for another 10 minutes, or thin the filling by adding more apple juice. Test the filling until the consistency is right.

7. When the cake layers are cool, spread half the filling on one cake, place the other cake on top, and spread the remaining filling on top.

MAKES ONE 2-LAYER CAKE; SERVES 6

WINEBERRY ICE CREAM

The plentiful large, tart fruit of the wineberry, which ripens in midsummer just before the blackberry season, makes a superlative ice cream

1 cup soy milk or nut milk

2 cups well-drained silken tofu

½ cup canola oil or safflower oil

¼ cup vegetable glycerin, honey, rice syrup, or barley malt

¼ cup lecithin granules

2 teaspoons vanilla extract

1 teaspoon raspberry extract (optional)

½ teaspoon salt

3½ cup wineberries

1. In a blender, combine all the ingredients, except for 1½ cups of the wineberries, and process until smooth.
2. Strain the mixture through a fine mesh strainer to remove the seeds.
3. Chill the mixture (or begin with chilled ingredients) if required by your ice cream machine. Stir in the remaining 2 cups wineberries.
4. Pour the mixture into the ice cream machine and freeze it according to the manufacturer's instructions.

MAKES 5½ CUPS; SERVES 5 TO 6

WINEBERRY SHERBET

Here's a wonderfully simple summer refresher you'll love.

2½ cups wineberries

2 cups water

¼ cup canola oil

¼ cup vegetable glycerin, honey, barley malt, or rice syrup

¼ cup raw cashews

1 teaspoon liquid stevia

½ teaspoon salt

½ teaspoon raspberry extract (optional)

1. In a blender, combine all the ingredients and process until smooth.
2. Strain the mixture through a fine mesh strainer and discard the seeds.

3. Chill the mixture (or begin with chilled ingredients) if required by your ice cream machine.
4. Pour the mixture into the ice cream machine, and freeze the sherbet according to the manufacturer's instructions.

MAKES 5½ CUPS; SERVES 5 TO 6

WINEBERRY WINE

These Asian raspberries get their name because they're ideal for wine-making. Serve Wineberry Wine as a table wine, or use it in any recipe that calls for sweet red wine. It's especially good in desserts and sweet sauces.

1 gallon water

6 cups sugar

6 cups wineberries

4 cinnamon sticks, each about 2 inches long

2 tablespoons chopped fresh wild spearmint (page 59) or other mint leaves or 2 teaspoons dried

½ teaspoon champagne yeast or other wine yeast

1. In a large pot, bring the water to a boil and stir in the sugar until it dissolves.
2. Transfer the mixture to a non-metal (plastic or ceramic) food container, add the wineberries, mashing them slightly with a hand blender or potato masher. Add the cinnamon and mint.
3. When the mixture is lukewarm, stir in the yeast and cover the container with a non-airtight cover, cheesecloth, or towel.
4. Allow the mixture to ferment for 7 to 10 days at room temperature, stirring it twice a day.
5. Strain the mixture through cheesecloth, transfer the liquid to a jug, and seal the jug with an airlock

stopper (which lets carbon dioxide bubbles escape but keeps oxygen out).

6. When the bubbling stops and fermentation ends a week or two later, seal the jug with a cork and age the wine for 6 weeks to 6 months before using it.

7. Siphon the wine to get rid of the sediment, if desired.

MAKES 1 GALLON

BEEFSTEAK MUSHROOM

Fistulina hepatica

THE BEEFSTEAK MUSHROOM IS TRULY AMAZING. It's a polypore, so it grows on wood (dead trees), it's shelf shaped rather than umbrella shaped, and tiny pores on its underside emit the spores. This polypore resembles a slab of beefsteak: The rough, spoon-shaped to flat, blood-red cap, which is 3 to 10 inches across, is soft and gelatinous. The flesh is marbled or zoned inside, soft and moist, even bleeding a watery red juice when cut. This fungus appears on dead and living oak trees across the United States in the summer and fall. Alas, it's rare in my region, or I'd have many more recipes for it.

The beefsteak mushroom tastes like beefsteak, and it makes a great meat substitute, seasoned with traditional meat seasonings and cooked almost any way for 15 to 20 minutes.

BEEFED-UP MILLET

Millet is a seed you cook like a grain (or eat raw, if you're a bird). It is higher in protein and less starchy than rice. Pre-toasting it and including some oil with a few other ingredients brings out this grain's best qualities. When you also add the beefsteak mushroom, you get an unusual pilaf everyone will love.

> 1 ¾ cups millet
>
> ¼ cup amaranth (page 338)
>
> 4 cups water
>
> 1 cup chopped beefsteak mushroom or other mushrooms
>
> ½ cup black walnuts (page 375) or regular walnuts
>
> 1 ½ tablespoons sesame oil or corn oil
>
> 1 teaspoon freshly ground fennel seeds
>
> 2 teaspoons freshly ground yellow mustard seeds (1 teaspoon seeds)
>
> 1 teaspoon freshly grated nutmeg
>
> 2 teaspoons Vege-Sal or 1 teaspoon salt, or to taste

1. Preheat the oven to 350 degrees and then toast the millet and amaranth in a roasting pan until fragrant, about 15 minutes, stirring occasionally.

2. Combine the toasted grains with the remaining ingredients in a large saucepan and bring to a boil. Reduce the heat to low and simmer, covered, until all the liquid is absorbed and the grains are tender, 20 to 30 minutes. Serve warm.

SERVES 6

REDDENING LEPIOTA

Lepiota americana

THE LEPIOTAS ARE MUSHROOMS WITH FREE (there's a space between the gills and the stem) white gills, sometimes with a bulbous base on the bottom of the stalk, that decompose dead wood. The spore print is white. **Lepiotas are very similar to Amanitas, which can be poisonous, and there are both edible and poisonous lepiotas, so they're not for unsupervised beginners.** Unlike *Amanitas*, the membranous ring of the lepiotas that encircles the stalk is detachable: You can slide it up and down the stalk like a napkin ring. The reddening lepiota has a scaly reddish brown scaly cap that is 1 to 6 inches wide, convex to nearly flat, with a knob in the center. The spindle-shaped stalk is 3 to 5 inches long and ¼ to ¾ inch across, widening toward the bottom. The whole mushroom bruises red when injured. You can sometimes find reddening lepiotas in large quantities on wood debris in eastern North America in the summer or fall.

This is simply a great-tasting mushroom with an intense flavor and meaty texture. You can use the caps and stems in any kind of recipe and cook them in a variety of ways, always with excellent results.

SAUTÉED MUSHROOMS AND SQUASH

The Japanese sweet kabocha squash, sautéed and smothered in sauce, makes the perfect companion for the reddening lepiota mushroom.

2 tablespoons olive oil

3 cups sliced reddening lepiotas

1 kabocha squash, peeled, seeded, and sliced

1 teaspoon freshly ground cloves

1 teaspoon dried rosemary, finely crumbled

1 teaspoon freshly grated nutmeg

1 cup Mock Yogurt Sauce (page 35)

2 tablespoons tamari soy sauce

2 tablespoons Wineberry Wine (page 246) or red wine

¼ teaspoon liquid stevia

Heat the olive oil in a large skillet over medium heat. Add the mushrooms, squash, cloves, rosemary, and nutmeg and cook, stirring, for 5 minutes. Add the remaining ingredients, reduce the heat to low, cover, and cook for another 8 minutes.

SERVES 4 TO 6

SEA ROCKET

Cakile edentula

THIS SUCCULENT WILD MUSTARD GROWS UP TO about 1 foot tall, with alternate, fleshy, wavy-toothed leaves that are about 3 inches long and 1 inch wide. Small, pink-purple flowers with four petals configured like a cross bloom in the summer and fall, and small, cone-shaped seedpods replace them in autumn. Sea rocket grows closer to the ocean than does any other edible plant. Look for it on sandy beaches on all U.S. coasts, from late spring to early fall.

The leaves and tender, immature seedpods taste a little like wasabe, the hot Japanese horseradish that's used to season sushi. More mature plants are spicier than younger ones. Use sea rocket raw or cooked in any recipe that needs spicing up. It cooks in 5 to 10 minutes.

SEA ROCKET SUSHI

Sea rocket tastes so much like wasabi that it's a natural addition to this popular appetizer. And oyster mushrooms make a magnificent replacement for the traditional raw fish with its attendant traditional parasites.

1 cup basmati brown rice or sweet brown rice

1½ cups plus 1 tablespoon water

¼ cup Wild Crabapple Blossom Wine (page 425) or sake

3 tablespoons brown rice vinegar

1 tablespoon tamari soy sauce

1 teaspoon ground dried wild ginger (page 111) or regular ground ginger

1 teaspoon powdered kelp (optional)

½ teaspoon dillweed, finely crumbled

4 bayberry leaves (page 185) or 2 bay leaves, ground

⅔ cup sliced oyster mushrooms (page 404) or other mushrooms

1 medium-size yellow bell pepper, seeded and slivered

1 medium-size carrot, slivered

2 cloves garlic, crushed into a paste

1 tablespoon wasabi (Japanese horseradish) powder

10 sheets nori or laver seaweed (a sheetlike seaweed that can be found in health food stores and Asian markets)

½ cup fresh sea rocket leaves

1. Place the rice, 1½ cups of the water, the wine, vine-gar, tamari, ginger, and kelp, if you are using it, in a medium-size saucepan and bring the pot to a boil. Reduce the heat to low and simmer, covered, until all the liquid is absorbed and the rice is tender, about 40 minutes. Let the rice cool.

2. Meanwhile, bring a pot of water to a boil, add the dillweed and bayberry leaves, and steam the mushrooms, bell pepper, carrot, and garlic on a steamer rack for 15 minutes. Let the vegetables cool.

3. Mix the wasabi powder with the remaining 1 tablespoon water to make a paste.

4. Hold a sheet of the nori over a burner flame or a kitchen match, using tongs, until the nori turns green. Sprinkle enough water on the nori to moisten it. Spread 3 tablespoons of the cooked rice over a 1-inch-wide strip along one edge of the nori. Spread 1½ tablespoons of the cooked vegetables over the rice, followed by about 2½ teaspoons of the sea rocket leaves and ¼ teaspoon of the wasabi paste.

5. Roll up the sheet of nori. If you're using a sushi mat or a square of wax paper under the sheet of seaweed, start rolling the mat with the seaweed inside and the mat outside, but stop before you tuck the mat under the seaweed. Instead, keep pulling the leading edge of the mat in the same direction you're rolling the sea-weed sheet so that the seaweed continues to get rolled up and the mat moves along parallel to the table. Cut the sushi into serving sizes using large scissors or a very sharp knife. Repeat the filling and rolling process with the remaining ingredients.

SERVES 10

SEA ROCKET TARTAR SAUCE

Spicy sea rocket leaves give this white sauce its punch. Use it on burgers, patties, croquettes, grains, and vegetables.

¾ cup drained silken tofu

½ cup fresh sea rocket leaves or tender immature
  seedpods

¼ cup fresh lemon juice

2 tablespoons chopped shallots or onions

2 tablespoons chopped fresh parsley leaves

1 tablespoon white or red wine vinegar

1 teaspoon freshly ground yellow mustard seeds
  (½ teaspoon seeds)

1 cup low-sodium pitted olives, drained

1. In a blender, combine all the ingredients, except
the olives, and process until smooth. Add the olives
and blend briefly on low speed until the olives are just
chopped.

2. Sea Rocket Tartar Sauce will keep, tightly covered, in the refrigerator for up to a week. It also
freezes well.

MAKES 2¼ CUPS

RICE 'N' ROCKET

This grain pilaf may include wild amaranth, sea rocket, and thyme, or it may be completely tame but still
taste wild.

4 cups water

1¾ cups brown basmati rice

¼ cup amaranth (page 338)

2 cups fresh sea rocket leaves

1½ tablespoons chopped fresh parsley leaves

1½ tablespoons tamari soy sauce, or to taste

1 tablespoon fresh thyme leaves or 1 teaspoon
  dried, finely crumbled

1 tablespoon chili paste or 1 teaspoon cayenne
  pepper, or to taste

2 cloves garlic, chopped

Place all the ingredients in a large saucepan and bring
the pot to a boil. Reduce the heat to low, cover, and
simmer until all the liquid is absorbed and the rice and
grains are tender, about 40 minutes.

SERVES 6

BAKED QUINOA BERBERÉ

Sea rocket adds pungency to the nutty flavor of toasted quinoa and amaranth seeds in this pilaf.

1¾ cups quinoa

¼ cup amaranth (page 338)

3¾ cups water

1 cup raw cashews, chopped

¾ cup sea rocket leaves

½ cup cultivated currants

1 teaspoon peeled and chopped fresh ginger

1 small chile, seeds and ribs removed and chopped,
  or ¼ teaspoon cayenne pepper, or to taste

1½ teaspoons freshly ground coriander seeds

1½ teaspoons freshly ground cardamom seeds

1 teaspoon freshly ground white pepper
  (½ teaspoon peppercorns)

½ teaspoon freshly ground fenugreek seeds

½ teaspoon common spicebush berries (page 314),
  finely chopped, or ½ teaspoon freshly ground
  allspice berries

½ teaspoon freshly grated nutmeg

¼ teaspoon freshly ground cloves

2 tablespoons apricot kernel oil

2 cloves garlic, crushed into a paste

2 teaspoons Vege-Sal or 1 teaspoon salt

1. Preheat the oven to 350 degrees.

2. Meanwhile, toast the quinoa and amaranth in a
medium-size skillet over medium-low heat until the

seeds pop and become fragrant, about 10 minutes, stirring or shaking the skillet constantly.

3. Combine the toasted grain with the remaining ingredients in a 3-quart oiled casserole dish and bake, covered, until all the water has been absorbed and the grains are tender, about 1½ hours.

SERVES 6

WILD THYME
Thymus serpyllum

THIS SPRAWLING MEMBER OF THE MINT FAMILY (square stems, opposite leaves, laterally bisymmetrical flowers) grows in mats trailing over 4 inches to a foot of ground and usually growing 1 to 1½ inches high. Its leaves are only ⅛ inch wide and ½ inch long. Clusters of purple flowers emerge from the top of the plant in summer and fall. The plant smells like commercial thyme, only better. Look for it from spring to fall in disturbed habitats, along roadsides and trailsides, and in fields.

Although wild thyme is technically the same plant you buy in the store, there's a world of difference in the flavor when this exotic garden plant goes feral. Whenever I find it, I have a wild thyme collecting as much as possible without impacting the environment, and drying what I can't use fresh. Great in soups, stews, mock egg dishes, mock fish dishes, stuffing, and on vegetables, it also makes a great herb tea. Its "active" constituent, thymol, even fights the pathogenic bacteria of sore throat.

FOCACCIA WITH TAPENADE

Here's an Italian bread you make like pizza crust, but with its own wonderful flavor and texture. Top it with its compatriot, an olive and wild thyme dip, and you won't be able to stop eating it for a long thyme.

FOCACCIA

> ¾ cup lukewarm apple juice or other unsweetened fruit juice
>
> 1 tablespoon active dry yeast
>
> 1 cup water
>
> 1⅔ cups (½ pound) sweet brown rice flour and 1¾ cups plus 2 tablespoons (½ pound) barley flour, or 1 pound any whole-grain flour
>
> 1 cup arrowroot or kudzu
>
> ½ cup plus 2 tablespoons freshly ground flaxseeds (¼ cup seeds)
>
> 5 tablespoons olive oil
>
> 1 teaspoon Vege-Sal or ½ teaspoon salt

TAPENADE

> 3 cups low-sodium pitted olives, drained
>
> 2½ tablespoons olive oil
>
> 2 tablespoons fresh lemon juice
>
> 2 tablespoons miso
>
> 3 cloves garlic, peeled
>
> ½ teaspoon dried wild thyme, finely crumbled
>
> 1 teaspoon freshly ground black pepper (½ teaspoon peppercorns)
>
> ¼ teaspoon freshly ground cloves
>
> ⅜ teaspoon freshly ground celery seeds (¼ teaspoon seeds)
>
> ¼ teaspoon freshly ground cardamom seeds

1. Preheat the oven to 450 degrees.

2. *To make the focaccia:* Dissolve the yeast in the apple juice for 5 minutes. Mix the yeast mixture with the remaining focaccia ingredients in a large bowl and beat for 5 minutes. Let the dough rise, covered, in a warm place for 1 hour.

3. Punch the dough down and spread it out ⅜ inch thick over an oiled pizza dish or in a cake pan. Bake the loaf until it is lightly brown, about 20 minutes.

4. *To make the tapenade:* In a food processor or by hand, chop the tapenade ingredients together to make a coarse paste.

5. Spread the tapenade over the top of the focaccia and serve hot or cold.

MAKES 2 LOAVES FOCACCIA

AND 3 CUPS TAPENADE

GARLIC MUSTARD SEED

Allaria esculente

LONG AFTER ITS LEAVES BECOME TOO BITTER TO USE, this plant (see page 61 for a description) produces soft, spicy, garlicky seeds. I hadn't discovered them yet when my first wild food book was published, because they're hidden in dry, brown pods on a plant that appears dead (a grade-school child first showed them to me). Now I use the seeds as a seasoning in a variety of dishes. Add them at the end of a recipe for the best results, and never cook them in oil or they'll burn.

Collect the seeds in the summer and fall. To do this, transfer as many dead stalks as possible to a large paper bag. (Don't let the seeds fall to the ground on the way to the bag.) Crumble the pods with your fingers to release all the seeds, spread them over a tray, and use a fan to blow away the light chaff. You can store the seeds in a tightly covered jar for years.

GARLIC MUSTARD SEED RAREBIT

Rarebit is melted cheese, often mixed with sautéed vegetables, and spread on English muffins or toast. Here's my version, seasoned with garlic mustard seeds. Enjoy this quick and healthful sandwich for breakfast, for lunch, or as a snack.

> *1 ½ tablespoons olive oil*
>
> *1 medium-size onion, sliced*
>
> *3 cloves garlic, chopped*
>
> *1 medium-size green bell pepper, seeded and sliced into strips*
>
> *3 ½ cups Tofu Cream Cheese (page 30)*
>
> *¼ cup dry Bread Crumbs (page 40)*
>
> *6 English Oak Muffins (page 294) or 12 slices bread, toasted*
>
> *1 tablespoon garlic mustard seeds*

1. Preheat the oven to 350 degrees.

2. Heat the olive oil in a large skillet over medium heat, add the onion, garlic, and green pepper, and cook, stirring, until the onion is translucent, about 10 minutes.

3. Stir in the Tofu Cream Cheese and bread crumbs, transfer the mixture to a 1½-quart oiled casserole dish, and bake it until bubbly, about 15 minutes.

4. Serve Garlic Mustard Seed Rarebit on English muffins or toast, sprinkled with the garlic mustard seeds, or mix in the garlic mustard seeds and serve it as a dip.

SERVES 6

GARLICKY LEMON RICE

This is a simple, tasty East Indian rice dish that includes American wild rice and European garlic mustard seeds.

  2 tablespoons sesame oil
  2 teaspoons black mustard seeds (1 teaspoon seeds)
  3 ¼ cups plus 2 tablespoons water
  1 ½ cups brown basmati rice
  ½ cup wild rice (page 353)
  ¼ cup fresh lemon juice
  1 teaspoon Vege-Sal or ½ teaspoon salt
  1 teaspoon garlic mustard seeds
  4 teaspoons turmeric

1. In a skillet, heat the sesame oil and black mustard seeds together over medium heat until the seeds pop, stirring or shaking constantly. (Don't include the garlic mustard seeds yet—they'd burn.)

2. Bring all the rest of the ingredients, except the garlic mustard seeds, to boil in a large saucepan. Reduce the heat to low, and simmer, covered, until all the liquid is absorbed and the rice and grains are tender, about 45 minutes.

3. Stir in the garlic mustard seeds and serve.

SERVES 6

GARLIC MUSTARD MILLET

Unlike its relatives, garlic mustard's seeds are soft enough to eat without grinding or cooking. They provide just the right touch to turn plain millet into something special.

  1 ¾ cups millet
  ¼ cup amaranth (page 338)
  3 ⅞ cups water

  1 tablespoon corn oil
  2 teaspoons Vege-Sal or 1 teaspoon salt
  1 tablespoon garlic mustard seeds

In a medium-size saucepan, bring all the ingredients to a boil over medium heat. Reduce the heat to low and simmer, covered, until all the liquid is absorbed and the grains are tender, 20 to 30 minutes.

SERVES 6

BLACK CHERRY
Prunus serotina

THIS NATIVE TREE, WHICH CAN GROW UP TO 70 feet tall, has smooth, silver-gray bark that is streaked with horizontal lines and that cracks and peels. The long, pointed, finely toothed leaves are 2 to 6 inches long and 1 to 1½ inches wide, unlike the European sweet cherry (see page 210). The leaves are glossy dark green on top and lighter underneath. Tiny rust-red hairy glands line the underside's midrib, distinguishing this tree from the chokecherry (*Prunus virginiana*). In the spring, long, showy, drooping clusters of fragrant white radially symmetrical flowers bloom, surrounding a long stalk. Small, round, black fruits, each ⅓ inch across, with 1 hard seed, ripen in the summer. The tree grows throughout eastern North America. Other delicious native and exotic cherry trees grow in other regions, so there's always wild fruit to try in the recipes below.

This native species, not to be confused with the cultivated European black cherry, which also grows in the United States (having escaped from cultivation) provides a bittersweet flavor with a touch of grapefruit—good in a variety of desserts. Collect fruit from the best-tasting trees. Cook the cherries (5 minutes is sufficient), strain out the seeds, add a sweetener (these cherries are tasty, but not sweet), or include sweet ingredients. The contrast between the savory, bitter cherries, and sweet foods such as figs or orange juice brings out the cherries' best qualities. And you may also include a thickener.

BLACK CHERRY JAM

This bittersweet fruit produces an intensely strong tasting spread.

> 4 cups black cherries
> 2 cups natural cherry juice concentrate
> 4 common spicebush berries (page 314), finely chopped, or 1 teaspoon freshly ground allspice berries
> 2 teaspoons freshly ground star anise
> 2 tablespoons chopped fresh wild spearmint (page 59) or other mint leaves
> 2⅔ tablespoons agar powder

1. Place all the ingredients in a large saucepan and bring the pot to a simmer over medium heat. Reduce the heat to low and let the mixture simmer for 10 minutes.
2. Strain out the cherry seeds with a food mill.
3. Test the jam for firmness (agar's thickening effect varies according to its fineness) by putting a large metal spoon with a small amount of jam in the freezer for a couple of minutes, until the jam is chilled. If the jam is the right thickness, your recipe is done. If it's too watery, stir in more agar, simmer the jam for another 5 to 10 minutes, and test it again. If the jam is too thick, stir in some fruit juice or water and test the jam again immediately.

4. Chill. Black Cherry Jam will keep, tightly covered, in the refrigerator for up to 2 weeks, and frozen for months.

MAKES 4 CUPS

BLACK CHERRY CAROB PUDDING

The bittersweet flavor of black cherries is a perfect match for carob's chocolate-like qualities. Where better to combine them than in a pudding?

> 4 cups wild black cherries
> ½ cup natural cherry juice concentrate
> ½ cup water
> 1 cup drained silken tofu
> 1 cup carob powder
> ¼ cup vegetable glycerin, honey, barley malt, or rice syrup
> ¼ cup kudzu, arrowroot, or tapioca pearls
> 2 tablespoons corn oil
> 2 tablespoons lecithin granules
> 2 teaspoons vanilla extract
> ½ teaspoon cherry extract (optional)
> ¼ teaspoon almond extract
> ½ teaspoon freshly grated nutmeg
> 1 cup carob chips

1. In a medium-size saucepan over medium-low heat, simmer the black cherries for 5 minutes in the cherry juice concentrate and water.
2. Strain out the seeds using a food mill or by pressing the pulp through the holes of a colander.
3. In a food processor or large bowl, combine the cherry pulp and the remaining ingredients, except the carob chips, and process or beat together with a whisk until smooth.

4. Transfer the mixture to a medium-size saucepan and bring the pot to a boil over medium heat, adding the carob chips and stirring constantly. Reduce the heat to low and simmer, covered, for 10 minutes, stirring often. Serve hot or cold.

SERVES 6

BLACK CHERRY ICE CREAM

The sweet and creamy ingredients in this ice cream offset the cherries' intense bittersweet flavor perfectly.

2 cups soy milk or nut milk

1 ¼ cups drained silken tofu

½ cup Black Cherry Jam (page 254) or other cherry jam

½ cup canola oil

¼ cup natural cherry juice concentrate

¼ cup vegetable glycerin, honey, barley malt, or rice syrup

2 teaspoons vanilla extract

1 teaspoon cherry extract (optional)

¼ teaspoon almond extract

½ teaspoon salt

1. In a blender, combine all the ingredients and process until smooth.

2. Chill the mixture (or begin with chilled ingredients) if required by your ice cream machine.

3. Pour the mixture into the ice cream maker and freeze it according to the manufacturer's instructions.

MAKES 5½ CUPS; SERVES 5 TO 6

CORNELIAN CHERRY
Cornus mas

THIS SHRUB OR SMALL TREE, WHICH GROWS UP to 30 feet tall, isn't a cherry at all, but an Asian dogwood, with opposite (paired) leaves (cherries have alternate leaves). The short-stalked, glossy, oval leaves grow to about 4 inches long, with pointed tips and prominent curved veins. Unscented tiny yellow four-petaled flowers bloom along the slender green twigs in very early spring. From the middle of the summer to fall, the flowers later develop into oblong, bright red berries that are 1 inch long, with a large, hard pit. This ornamental plant grows in landscaped areas throughout the United States.

Before it is completely ripe, the fruit is very sour and hard. It becomes dark purple-red, very soft, and juicy when ripe, and it continues to ripen after you pick it. The fruit is very tasty (it's the national fruit of Turkey) and quite sour. For the best results, use cornelian cherries with sweet or bland ingredients. After simmering the fruit in sweet fruit juice with a thickener for about 5 minutes, you can remove the pits with a food mill. Cornelian cherry is great in a wide range of desserts.

CORNELIAN CHERRY SODA

When my friend Bruce learned that Russians make beverages with cornelian cherries, he created this delicious soda.

3 cups cornelian cherries

3 cups water

4 cups sparkling water

3 tablespoons honey or other liquid sweetener

½ teaspoon liquid stevia (optional)

1. Place the cornelian cherries and water in a large saucepan and bring the pot to a boil over medium heat. Reduce the heat to low and simmer, covered, for 10 minutes.

2. Put the fruit in a strainer and press the juice out with a potato masher or fork (or use a juicer). Chill the juice.

3. Mix the juice with the remaining ingredients and serve chilled.

SERVES 6 TO 8

CORNELIAN CHERRY KANTEN

Because the cornelian cherry is so sour, the bland tofu and mild cashews in this recipe rebalance the flavor of this non-animal "gelatin" dessert.

3 ¼ cups cornelian cherries

1 cup apple juice

½ cup cornelian cherry juice (the juice collects in the bottom of the container in which you store the cherries) or unsweetened cherry juice

5 teaspoons agar powder

½ teaspoon liquid stevia or 2 tablespoons honey, barley malt, or rice syrup, or to taste

¼ teaspoon almond extract

1 ½ cups drained silken tofu, coarsely diced

1 cup raw cashew pieces

1. In a medium-size saucepan, bring the cornelian cherries, apple juice, cornelian cherry juice, agar, liquid stevia, and almond extract to a boil over medium

heat, stirring often. Reduce the heat to low, cover, and simmer for 10 minutes, stirring often.

2. Pass the mixture through a food mill or push it through a colander to remove the seeds.

3. Return the mixture to the saucepan, add the tofu and cashews, and bring the pot to a boil again over medium heat. Reduce the heat to low and simmer, covered, for 5 minutes, stirring often. Serve hot or cold.

SERVES 6

CORNELIAN PANDOWDY

This dessert will be a favorite for anyone who likes pastries that include sour ingredients.

6 cups cornelian cherries

1 ½ cups (9.6 ounces) yellow cornmeal

6 tablespoons arrowroot or kudzu

1 teaspoon poppy seeds

½ teaspoon freshly ground cardamom seeds

½ teaspoon freshly grated nutmeg

½ teaspoon salt

6 ripe bananas, peeled and sliced

6 tablespoons natural cherry juice concentrate, vegetable glycerin, honey, or barley malt

2 teaspoons liquid stevia

6 tablespoons corn oil

¾ cup plus 2 tablespoons apple juice, or as needed

1. Bring the cornelian cherries to a boil in a large saucepan over medium heat. Reduce the heat to low and simmer, covered, for 5 minutes.

2. Pass the cherries through a food mill or strainer to remove the seeds.

3. Preheat the oven to 350 degrees.

4. Combine the cornmeal, arrowroot, poppy seeds, cardamom, nutmeg, and salt in a medium-size bowl.

5. In a large bowl, mix 6 tablespoons of this mixture with the strained cornelian cherries, bananas, cherry juice concentrate, and 1 teaspoon of the liquid stevia and pour the mixture into a 14 x 9 x 2-inch oiled baking dish.

6. Mix the corn oil and the remaining 1 teaspoon liquid stevia with the remaining dry mixture. Stir in enough of the apple juice to make a dough that's neither crumbly nor sticky. Knead the dough briefly. On a floured pastry sheet with a rolling pin enclosed in a floured sleeve, roll the dough into the shape of the baking dish. Transfer the rolled out dough onto the fruit mixture. Bake the dessert until it is lightly browned, about 35 minutes.

7. Cut the baked dough into 2-inch pieces with a knife and dab it onto the boiling fruit. Cook the dessert for another 15 minutes. Serve hot or cold with vanilla ice cream.

SERVES 6 TO 8

WILD CARROT SEED
Daucus carota

THE SEEDS OF THE WILD CARROT TASTE A LITTLE like caraway seeds or cumin, with a touch of bitterness (see page 73 for a description of this plant). Collect the seeds in summer and fall. They dry quite readily for long-term storage.

Season savory dishes, soups, breads, and casseroles sparingly with wild carrot seeds or they'll overpower the other ingredients. For example, for 1 part caraway seeds, substitute but ¹⁄₁₆ part wild carrot seeds. Wild carrot seeds are also great ground with other herbs to make special seasonings.

SEAFOOD SEASONING
This seasoning combination gives food the hot, spicy Cajun flavor we're used to tasting on Cajun-style seafood. I use it on mushrooms, vegetables, tofu, and popcorn—as well as on mock seafood dishes.

> *3 tablespoons celery seeds*
> *2 tablespoons mustard seeds*
> *2 tablespoons cloves*
> *2 tablespoons bayberry leaves (page 185) or bay leaves*
> *2 teaspoons cardamom seeds*
> *2 teaspoons black or regular caraway seeds*
> *1 teaspoon wild carrot seeds*
> *3 tablespoons sweet paprika*
> *2 teaspoons ground mace*
> *2 teaspoons ground dried wild ginger (page 111) or regular ground ginger*
> *2 teaspoons cayenne pepper*

1. Grind all the whole herbs and spices together in a spice grinder and mix them with the already ground spices.

2. Store Seafood Seasoning in a tightly closed jar. After 3 months, the flavor will begin to weaken, so increase the amount you use in recipes.

MAKES 1 CUP

YEMENITE SEASONING
This is one of the hottest seasonings I've ever made—it's especially for people who like very fiery food. I like to keep a jar of this on hand, but I use it very sparingly, even though I love hot foods.

½ cup black peppercorns (less for a milder seasoning)

2 teaspoons wild carrot seeds

4 teaspoons cumin seeds

2⅔ tablespoons turmeric

4 teaspoons saffron threads

1. Grind the peppercorns, carrot seeds, and cumin seeds together in a spice grinder.

2. Combine the freshly ground spices with the remaining ingredients.

3. Store Yemenite Seasoning in a tightly closed jar. After 3 months, the flavor will begin to weaken, so increase the amount you use in recipes.

MAKES ¾ CUP

CARROT SEED RYE BREAD

This hearty yeast-leavened rye bread demonstrates how well wild carrot seeds act as an alternative to the traditional caraway or poppy seeds.

3 cups Vegetable Stock (page 40) or water

2 tablespoons natural cherry juice concentrate, honey, barley malt, or rice syrup

2¼ teaspoons bread yeast

8 cups (29.5 ounces) rye flour

½ cup brewer's yeast

3 tablespoons plus 2¼ teaspoons freshly ground flaxseeds (1½ tablespoons seeds)

2 large cloves garlic, minced

1 tablespoon lecithin granules

1 teaspoon wild carrot seeds

1 tablespoon Vege-Sal or 1½ teaspoons salt

1 teaspoon freshly ground black pepper (½ teaspoon peppercorns)

Olive oil or water for brushing (optional)

1. In a small saucepan, combine the stock and cherry juice concentrate and heat the mixture to lukewarm over low heat. Remove from heat, add the yeast, stir to dissolve, and let it set for 5 minutes. Transfer the yeast mixture to a large bowl.

2. Stir half the flour into the stock mixture. Let the dough stand in a warm place (80 to 85 degrees) to rise, covered, for 30 minutes.

3. Stir in the remaining flour and all the other ingredients, except the olive oil. Let the dough stand, covered, another 30 minutes in a warm place.

4. Knead the dough for a few minutes.

5. Divide the dough in half and shape it into loaves in 2 oiled 6½ x 4⅜ x 2½-inch loaf pans. Brush the top of each loaf with olive oil or water, if desired. Cover the loaves with a moist towel or place the loaf pans inside a plastic shopping bag without letting the bag touch the dough. Let the loaves stand in a warm place until they stop rising, 30 to 60 minutes.

6. Preheat the oven to 350 degrees. Set a pan of water on the bottom of the oven to keep the crust soft. Bake the loaves until they pull away from the sides of the pan slightly and the loaves sound hollow when you tap them, about 55 minutes.

7. Remove the loaves from the oven and let them cool on wire racks before slicing.

MAKES 2 LOAVES

PUMPERNICKEL CARROT SEED BREAD

Carrot seeds give this whole-food pumpernickel some extra zing.

1½ cups cold apple juice

¾ cup (4.8 ounces) yellow cornmeal

1¾ cups boiling Vegetable Stock (page 40) or water

2 teaspoons caraway seeds

1 teaspoon wild carrot seeds

2 teaspoons Vege-Sal or 1 teaspoon salt

2 tablespoons corn oil, or as needed

4 teaspoons (2 packages) active dry yeast

¼ cup lukewarm water

2 cups mashed boiled potatoes

4 cups (14.8 ounces) rye flour

4 ½ cups brown rice flour or 1 pound, 5.33 ounces
any other whole-grain flour

1. Mix the apple juice with the cornmeal in a large saucepan. Stir in the boiling stock and cook the mixture over medium heat until thick, stirring constantly. Remove from heat, stir in caraway seeds, carrot seeds, Vege-Sal, and corn oil and let the mixture cool to lukewarm.

2. In a small bowl, dissolve the yeast in the lukewarm water for 5 minutes. Add the yeast mixture to the cornmeal mixture, along with the mashed potatoes, and mix well.

3. Mix in the flours and knead the dough for a few minutes. Place the dough in a warm place, covered, until, until the dough stops rising, about 1 hour.

4. Punch the dough down, divide it in half, and shape it into loaves in 2 oiled 6½ x 4⅜ x 2½-inch loaf pans. Cover the loaves with a damp towel or place them in a plastic bag and set them in a warm place until the dough stops rising again, about 45 minutes.

5. Preheat the oven to 375 degrees.

6. Brush the top of each loaf with additional corn oil, if desired. Set a pan of hot water on the bottom of the oven to keep the crust soft. Bake the loaves for 1 hour or until the bread pulls away from the sides of the pan, and the loaves sound hollow when you tap them.

7. Remove the loaves from the loaf pans and let them cool on a wire rack before slicing.

MAKES 2 LOAVES

MAYAPPLE

Podophyllum pelatum

THIS NONWOODY NATIVE PLANT, WHICH GROWS 1 to 1½ feet tall, has two huge, lopsided, umbrella-like, lobed leaves. From where their long stalks fork, a stalked, fragrant, nodding, white six-petaled, waxy flower 2 inches across blooms in the spring. Halfway through the summer, just when the plant dies to the ground, the flower is supplanted by a fragrant, soft, oval, yellow fruit 1½ to 2 inches across. (The rhizomes, underground stems, are perennial.) Look for this plant in partially shaded woodlands in eastern North America, and in landscaped areas and botanical gardens elsewhere.

The leaves and roots are poisonous, and even the unripe green fruit (which continues to ripen after it falls to the ground) can make you quite ill. The ripe yellow fruit, on the other hand, has a lemony flavor with the texture of custard. Remove the seeds, and mayapple is delicious raw or cooked. Add it to puddings, fruit sauces, shakes, pastries, and crisps, along with sweet ingredients to offset its sourness.

MAYAPPLE SALAD DRESSING

Using sour-tasting mayapples in place of lemon juice, and adding wild spearmint, make for a unique salad dressing.

1 ½ cups sesame oil

½ ripe avocado, peeled and pitted

¼ cup ripe yellow mayapples, seeds removed

¼ cup balsamic vinegar

1 small red onion, cut into a few pieces

Juice of 2 limes

2 tablespoons mellow (light-colored) miso

2 tablespoons chopped fresh wild spearmint (page
59) or other mint leaves, or 2 teaspoons dried,
finely crumbled

2 cloves garlic, peeled

½ teaspoon chili paste or ¼ teaspoon cayenne
pepper, or to taste

In a blender, combine all the ingredients and process
until smooth. Mayapple Salad Dressing will keep,
tightly covered, in the refrigerator for up to 10 days.

MAKES 3 CUPS

MAYAPPLE CRISP

Here's a mayapple dessert I created with fruit I gathered in Central Park on a special tour arranged by
German public TV. It's especially good with any of the
ice cream recipes in this book.

FRUIT LAYER

1 ¾ cups ripe yellow mayapple fruit pulp (skins and
seeds removed)

2 medium-size ripe mangoes, peeled, seeded, and
sliced

2 cups common elderberries (page 195) or
cultivated currants

½ cup sweet brown rice flour or 2.33 ounces any
other whole-grain flour

1 tablespoon chopped fresh wild spearmint
(page 59) or other mint leaves

½ teaspoon mango extract (optional)

½ teaspoon liquid stevia or 2 tablespoons barley
malt or honey, or to taste

½ teaspoon freshly ground cardamom seeds

¼ teaspoon ground dried wild ginger (page 111) or
regular ground ginger

CRISP TOPPING

3 cups rolled oats (not the quick-cooking kind)

2 cups walnuts, chopped

3 tablespoons almond oil or corn oil

1 teaspoon ground cinnamon

1 teaspoon vanilla extract

½ teaspoon walnut extract (optional)

½ teaspoon salt

¼ teaspoon liquid stevia or 1 tablespoon barley
malt or honey, or to taste

1. Preheat the oven to 350 degrees.

2. *To make the fruit layer:* Mix together the fruit layer
ingredients in a large bowl. Pour them into a 14 x 9 x
2-inch oiled baking dish.

3. *To make the crisp topping:* Mix together the crisp
topping ingredients and press them on top of the fruit
layer. Bake the dessert until the fruit is bubbly and the
crisp layer is lightly browned, 30 to 40 minutes. Serve
hot or cold.

SERVES 6 TO 8

WILD BLUEBERRY
AND HUCKLEBERRY
Vaccinium species

VARIOUS WILD BLUEBERRY SPECIES CAN BE AS
small as 1½ feet and as large as 14 feet tall. The
alternate leaves of these shrubs are short stalked, elliptical, mostly smooth edged, and 1 to 2 inches long.
The white flowers, which bloom in the spring, look
like bells and can be up to ¾ inch long. The flowers,

with five subdivisions, flare outward toward the tips. The round, blue-black berries have a five-parted "crown," or partial opening, at the end opposite the stalk. *Poisonous berries that look like blueberries lack this "crown."* Blueberry seeds are too small to detect, while huckleberry seeds are crunchy. Both wild blueberries and huckleberries are great wild fruits, smaller but much tastier than commercial varieties. Different species prefer a wide range of habitats across North America, but they all favor acidic soil. Look for them in fields, at the edges of woods, meadows, and bogs, on mountainsides, and in thickets. Use all wild varieties in any berry or fruit recipe, and you won't regret it.

WILD BLUEBERRY–BUCKWHEAT PANCAKES

Bring out the best of wild blueberries first thing in the morning with these pancakes. Baking soda plus cream of tartar replace unhealthful baking powder, while lecithin granules and flaxseeds replace cholesterol-rich eggs.

> 2 ⅓ cups (14 ounces) buckwheat flour
> ½ cup plus 2 tablespoons freshly ground flaxseeds (¼ cup seeds)
> 2 teaspoons cream of tartar
> 1 teaspoon baking soda
> 1 teaspoon salt
> ½ teaspoon freshly grated nutmeg
> 1 ¾ cups soy milk or nut milk
> 2 cups apple juice
> ½ cup peanut oil
> 4 common spicebush berries (page 314), finely chopped, or ½ teaspoon freshly ground allspice berries
> 2 teaspoons vanilla extract

> ½ teaspoon orange extract or ½ tablespoon freshly grated orange rind
> ¼ teaspoon liquid stevia or 2 tablespoons barley malt or honey
> 2 cups wild blueberries or huckleberries, picked over for stems
> ½ cup lecithin granules
> ½ cup pecans, chopped

1. Mix together the flour, ground flaxseeds, cream of tartar, baking soda, salt, and nutmeg in a large bowl.

2. Mix together the soy milk, apple juice, peanut oil, spicebush berries, vanilla, orange extract, and liquid stevia in a medium-size bowl. Mix the wet ingredients into the dry ingredients, being careful not to overmix. Mix in the blueberries, lecithin, and pecans, being careful not to overmix.

3. Spread a few tablespoons of the batter onto a hot, oiled griddle or frying pan over medium-low heat. When the underside of each pancake is browned, turn the pancake over with a metal spatula and cook the other side until it is browned. Repeat until you've used up all the batter. Serve Wild Blueberry–Buckwheat Pancakes hot with Wild Blueberry Jam (below), other jam, or syrup.

MAKES 18 PANCAKES; SERVES 6 TO 8

WILD BLUEBERRY JAM

Despite the many ingredients, this spread is as simple to make as it is delicious to eat.

> 4 cups wild blueberries, picked over for stems
> 3 cups apple juice
> 2 tablespoons vegetable glycerin, barley malt, honey, or rice syrup
> 5 teaspoons agar powder
> ½ teaspoon freshly ground coriander seeds

½ teaspoon dried pennyroyal (page 203) or other
mint, finely crumbled

1 teaspoon freshly grated nutmeg

¼ teaspoon orange extract or ½ teaspoon dried
orange rind

¼ teaspoon liquid stevia (optional)

⅛ teaspoon Grand Marnier extract (optional)

1. Place all the ingredients in a large saucepan, stirring to combine. Bring the pot to a boil over medium heat, stirring often. Reduce the heat to low and simmer, covered, for 10 minutes, stirring often.

2. Test the jam for firmness (agar's thickening effect varies according to its fineness) by putting a large metal spoon with a small amount of jam in the freezer for a couple of minutes, until the jam is chilled. If the jam is the right thickness, your recipe is done. If it's too watery, stir in more agar, simmer the jam for another 5 to 10 minutes, and test it again. If the jam is too thick, stir in some fruit juice or water and test it again immediately.

3. Wild Blueberry Jam will keep, tightly covered, in the refrigerator for up to 1 week, and frozen for up to 6 months.

MAKES 4½ CUPS

BLUEBERRY PUDDING

This recipe is good with cultivated blueberries, and even better with wild blueberries, huckleberries, or the unrelated but similar-tasting juneberries (page 223).

One 19-ounce package silken tofu, drained

2½ cups wild blueberries, picked over for stems

1¼ cups fresh Bread Crumbs (page 40)

½ cup natural cherry juice concentrate

2 tablespoons arrowroot or kudzu

1 tablespoon ground cinnamon

1 tablespoon vanilla extract

1 tablespoon Black Locust Blossom Wine (page
182) or white wine

2 teaspoons freshly grated nutmeg

1 teaspoon liquid stevia or 2 tablespoons honey,
barley malt, or rice syrup

½ teaspoon butter-pecan extract (optional)

1 cup pecans, toasted (page 158) and chopped

1. Bring all the ingredients except the pecans, to a boil in a large saucepan over medium heat, stirring constantly. Reduce the heat to low, and simmer, covered, for 15 minutes, stirring often.

2. Pour into serving bowls and sprinkle on the pecans. Serve hot or cold.

SERVES 4 TO 6

BLUEBERRY CUSTARD

Conventional custards contain unhealthful, high-fat eggs, usually from chickens that have been subjected to unconscionable cruelty. Tasting this superb custard, you'd never know that it's free of both eggs and cruelty.

4 cups well-drained silken tofu

¾ cup plus 1½ teaspoons freshly ground flaxseeds
(5 tablespoons seeds)

⅓ cup kudzu or arrowroot

2 tablespoons flaxseed oil or corn oil

2½ tablespoons lecithin granules

2 teaspoons vanilla extract

1½ teaspoons blueberry extract (optional)

1 teaspoon dried wild spearmint (page 59) or other
mint, finely crumbled

½ teaspoon liquid stevia or 2 tablespoons pure
maple syrup, barley malt, or honey

1 teaspoon freshly grated nutmeg

¼ teaspoon ground dried wild ginger (page 111) or regular ground ginger

¼ teaspoon salt

2 cups wild blueberries or huckleberries, picked over for stems

½ cup chopped pecans (optional)

½ cup unsweetened shredded coconut (optional)

¼ cup sesame seeds (optional)

1. Preheat the oven to 350 degrees.

2. In a food processor, combine all the ingredients, except the blueberries and the optional garnishes of pecans, coconut, and sesame seeds and process until smooth.

3. Pour the mixture into 6 oiled custard cups or a 1½-quart oiled baking dish. Scatter the blueberries on top and bake until the custard is set, about 30 minutes.

4. Serve Blueberry Custard hot or cold, topped with pecans, shredded coconut, and/or sesame seeds, if desired.

SERVES 6

UPSIDE-DOWN BLUEBERRY CAKE

Although this simple cake is simply delicious, you must stand on your head to eat it right side up.

CAKE

7½ tablespoons freshly ground flaxseeds (3 tablespoons seeds)

2¾ cups plus 3 tablespoons buckwheat flour or 14 ounces other whole-grain flour

1 teaspoon ground cinnamon

1½ teaspoons cream of tartar

¾ teaspoon baking soda

½ teaspoon salt

¾ cup apple juice

6 tablespoons corn oil

2 teaspoons vanilla extract

½ teaspoon liquid stevia or 2 tablespoons barley malt or honey

1½ cups pecans, chopped

1½ tablespoons lecithin granules

Freshly grated rind of 1 orange

TOPPING

4 cups wild blueberries, picked over for stems

¼ cup yellow cornmeal

2 tablespoons fresh lemon juice

1 teaspoon blueberry extract (optional)

1 teaspoon freshly grated nutmeg

½ teaspoon ground dried wild ginger (page 111) or regular ground ginger

½ teaspoon liquid stevia or 2 tablespoons barley malt or honey

1. Preheat the oven to 350 degrees.

2. To make the cake: In a large bowl, mix together the ground flaxseeds, flour, cinnamon, cream of tartar, baking soda, and salt.

3. In a medium-size bowl, mix together the apple juice, corn oil, vanilla, and liquid stevia. Stir the wet ingredients into the dry ingredients, being careful not to overmix. Stir in the pecans, lecithin, and orange rind, being careful not to overmix.

4. To make the topping: Mix the topping ingredients together in a large bowl. Pour the mixture into an even layer in an oiled 12-inch round cake pan.

5. Pour the cake batter over the topping. Bake the cake until a toothpick inserted in the center emerges clean, about 55 minutes.

6. Invert the pan onto a wire rack and let it cool before slicing.

SERVES 6 TO 8

WILD BLUEBERRY CHEESECAKE

Tofu provides so many possibilities because it comes in a variety of textures. Having very little flavor of its own, it picks up the flavors of other ingredients. This cake contains many ingredients to simulate the flavor of cheesecake, but it's so simple to mix and bake the cheesecake, it takes longer to assemble the ingredients than to prepare the cake.

Two 19-ounce packages silken tofu, well drained

½ cup fresh Bread Crumbs (page 40)

¼ cup arrowroot or kudzu

¼ cup lecithin granules

¼ cup pitted dates

2 tablespoons corn oil

2 teaspoons liquid stevia

2 teaspoons vanilla extract

1 teaspoon blueberry extract (optional)

1 teaspoon Tabasco sauce

¼ teaspoon almond extract

¼ teaspoon lemon extract

2 teaspoons salt

½ teaspoon hot paprika

¼ teaspoon freshly ground fenugreek seeds

½ teaspoon freshly grated nutmeg

¼ cup fresh lemon juice

2 cups wild blueberries or huckleberries, picked over for stems

1 ½ tablespoons sweet brown rice flour or other whole-grain flour

½ teaspoon ground cinnamon

1 teaspoon brewer's yeast

1 teaspoon cheesecake extract (optional)

1. Preheat the oven to 375 degrees.
2. In a food processor or large bowl, combine all the ingredients, except the blueberries, flour, and cinnamon, and process or beat with an electric mixer or whisk or fork until smooth.
3. Roll the blueberries in the flour and stir them into the mixture.
4. Pour the batter into an oiled medium-size baking pan, sprinkle the cinnamon on top, and bake the cheesecake until it is set, about 45 minutes.
5. Let the cheesecake cool on a wire rack. Chill it until it is completely cool, remove it from the pan, cut it into 6 pieces, and serve.

SERVES 6

WILD BLUEBERRY ICE CREAM

What could be simpler than mixing ingredients in a blender and pouring them into an ice cream machine? Yet doing so with blueberries plus vegetarian thickeners and flavorings makes for an unbelievably scrumptious ice cream.

2 ½ cups soy milk or nut milk

1 cup well-drained silken tofu

½ cup raw cashews

½ cup canola oil or safflower oil

¼ cup vegetable glycerin, barley malt, or honey

¼ cup lecithin granules

2 teaspoons vanilla extract

1 teaspoon blueberry extract (optional)

1 teaspoon liquid stevia (optional)

½ teaspoon salt

2 ½ cups wild blueberries or huckleberries, picked over for stems

1. In a blender, combine all the ingredients, except for 1 cup of the blueberries, and process until smooth.
2. Chill the mixture (or begin with chilled ingredients) if required by your ice cream machine. Stir in

the remaining blueberries.

3. Pour the mixture into the ice cream machine and freeze it according to the manufacturer's instructions.

MAKES 6 CUPS; SERVES 6

ELDERBERRY

Sambucus canadensis

ELDERBERRIES ARE THE SIZE OF CULTIVATED currants but very strongly flavored, crunchy, and not as sweet (see page 195 for a complete description). Raw, they have a slightly rank flavor and give some people indigestion, so always cook them. You may also dehydrate and reconstitute them before you use them.

Here are some recipes that will demonstrate how good elderberries taste if you use them sparingly, with other ingredients, and sweeten the recipe. If you can't find or buy elderberries, substitute cultivated currants and use less sweetener.

ELDERBERRY BREAKFAST CEREAL

Elderberries and black walnuts flavor this healthful, hot multi-grain cereal. Teff is a tasty, nutritious, generally overlooked grain that is available in health food stores. For an even richer flavor, you may parch the teff, cornmeal, and amaranth before making the cereal by toasting the grains for 45 minutes in a roasting pan in a preheated 350-degree oven, stirring the grains occasionally.

One 33.8-ounce package soy milk or nut milk
1 cup whole-grain cornmeal

¾ cup teff
¼ cup amaranth (page 338)
¾ cup black walnuts (page 375) or regular walnuts, chopped
½ cup dried elderberries
½ cup cultivated currants or raisins
1 green apple, cored and sliced
3 tablespoons vegetable glycerin, honey, barley malt, or rice syrup
½ teaspoon liquid stevia (optional)
2 teaspoons vanilla extract
1 teaspoon ground cinnamon
½ teaspoon ground dried wild ginger (page 111) or regular ground ginger
½ teaspoon salt
½ cup lecithin granules (optional)
½ cup oat bran (optional)

1. In a large saucepan, bring all the ingredients, except the lecithin granules and oat bran, to a boil over medium heat stirring often. Reduce the heat to low, cover, and simmer for 15 minutes, stirring often.

2. Remove the pot from the heat and let the mixture stand, covered, for another 15 minutes.

3. Stir in the lecithin and oat bran. Serve hot.

SERVES 6

CZECH ELDERBERRY PANCAKES

An acquaintance once sketched out for me the kind of yeast-leavened pancakes her mother made in the old country. Eliminating the eggs and adding whole-grain flour and wild elderberries results in a filling, satisfying, and healthful breakfast. Czech it out!

1 teaspoon active dry yeast

1 ¼ cups lukewarm apple juice

1 ½ cups soy milk or nut milk

¼ cup corn oil

½ teaspoon liquid stevia or 2 tablespoons barley
  malt, maple syrup, or honey

1 ¼ cups (6 ounces) sweet brown rice flour and
  1 ⅓ cups (6 ounces) barley flour, or ¾ pound
  any whole-grain flour

½ cup arrowroot or kudzu

2 tablespoons lecithin granules

1 tablespoon freshly grated lemon rind

1 tablespoon poppy seeds

1 teaspoon ground cinnamon

1 teaspoon freshly grated nutmeg

¼ teaspoon salt

1 ¼ cups elderberries

¾ cup walnuts, toasted (optional; page 158) and
  chopped

1. Let the yeast dissolve in the apple juice for 5 minutes in a medium-size bowl.

2. Stir in the soy milk, corn oil, and liquid stevia.

3. Mix together the flour, arrowroot, lecithin, lemon rind, poppy seeds, cinnamon, nutmeg, and salt in a large bowl. Stir in the liquid mixture. Cover the bowl and set it in a warm place (80 to 85 degrees) for 1 hour.

4. Stir the elderberries and walnuts into the batter.

5. Pour a circle of batter on a hot, oiled griddle or frying pan and cook each pancake until the underside is lightly browned, 2 to 4 minutes. Turn the pancake over with a metal spatula and brown the other side. Repeat until all the batter is used up (or store the batter for up to 5 days in the refrigerator).

6. Serve Czech Elderberry Pancakes hot with any of the jams in this book or Tofu Sour Cream (page 33).

MAKES 12 PANCAKES

ELDERBERRY CRUNCH BREAD

This bread contains all kinds of things crunchy: sunflower seeds, coconut, granola, and, of course, elderberries.

3 ¾ cups (14 ounces) rye flour and 1 ⅓ cups
  (6 ounces) barley flour, or 1 ¼ pounds any
  whole-grain flour

5 tablespoons freshly ground flaxseeds
  (2 tablespoons seeds)

1 teaspoon baking soda

½ teaspoon salt

3 ¼ cups apple juice or other unsweetened fruit juice

1 teaspoon liquid stevia (optional)

2 tablespoons fresh lemon juice

2 tablespoons corn oil

1 teaspoon coconut extract (optional)

1 teaspoon amaretto extract (optional)

2 cups elderberries

1 cup granola

1 cup shelled raw sunflower seeds

1 cup unsweetened shredded coconut

2 tablespoons lecithin granules

1 teaspoon ground cinnamon

1. Preheat the oven to 350 degrees.

2. Mix the flour, ground flaxseeds, baking soda, and salt in a large bowl.

3. In a medium-size bowl, mix together the apple juice, liquid stevia, if you are using it, lemon juice, corn oil, and extracts. Mix the wet ingredients into the dry ingredients, being careful not to overmix. Stir in the elderberries, granola, sunflower seeds, coconut, and lecithin.

4. Press the dough into 2 oiled 8½ x 4½ x 2½-inch bread pans. Sprinkle the cinnamon on top. Set a pan

of hot water on the bottom of the oven to keep the crust soft. Bake the loaves until a toothpick inserted in the center emerges clean, about 1 hour.

5. Remove the loaves from the oven and let them cool on a wire rack before slicing.

MAKES 2 LOAVES

ELDERBERRY ICE CREAM

Elderberries aren't like sweet berries—they're almost savory. So lemon verbena or other mint leaves provide just the right balance in this vegan dessert.

1 cup elderberries

½ cup apple juice

2 cups well-drained silken tofu

¼ cup canola oil or safflower oil

¼ cup vegetable glycerin, barley malt, or honey

2 tablespoons chopped fresh lemon verbena or other mint leaves, or 2 teaspoons dried, finely crumbled

2 teaspoons vanilla extract

1 teaspoon ground cinnamon

½ teaspoon lemon extract

1 teaspoon liquid stevia

¼ teaspoon salt

1. Place the elderberries and apple juice in a medium-size saucepan over medium heat and bring the pot to a simmer. Reduce the heat to medium-low, and simmer, covered, for 5 minutes.

2. In a blender, combine half the berries, the apple juice, and the remaining ingredients and process until smooth.

3. Chill the mixture completely (1 hour in the freezer, 4 hours in the refrigerator).

4. Pour the mixture into an ice cream machine and freeze it according to the manufacturer's instructions.

5. Stir in the remaining elderberries.

MAKES 5½ CUPS; SERVES 5 TO 6

KING BOLETE

Boletus edulis

THIS WORLD-FAMOUS MUSHROOM, ALSO CALLED the porcino, cèpe, or steinpiltz, has a smooth, moist, reddish brown cap that is 4¼ to 10 inches across, convex to flat, and white inside. It's a bolete, which means it's umbrella shaped (not shelf-like), grows on the ground near trees, and has pores (tiny holes) under the cap. Its pore surface is white, sometimes discoloring brownish. The spores are olive brown. The stalk is 4 to 10 inches long and ¾ to 1⅝ inches across, becoming fatter and also white to brownish toward the bottom. Its upper part is decorated with distinctive whitish webbing pattern. This mushroom and similar choice close relatives grow near deciduous trees and conifers throughout North America in the summer and fall. Avoid the dark-webbed bitter bolete (*Tylopilus felleus*), a nonpoisonous species that is so bitter that one piece will ruin an entire recipe.

One of the tastiest mushrooms in the world, king bolete is good in virtually any mushroom recipe, and you can cook it in a variety of ways. It cooks in 10 to 15 minutes. Often, however, insects have infiltrated the stems, which you'll discard in the field before they make their way into the cap. You may also substitute other choice wild bolete mushrooms or gourmet commercial mushrooms for the king bolete in the following recipes.

BAKED BOLETES IN SOUR CREAM

Finding bolete mushrooms in the summer before the bugs find them is always a great treat (for me maybe, but not for the bugs). Here's a variation on how people prepare boletes in the former Soviet Georgia.

¼ cup olive oil

2 pounds king bolete or other bolete species, sliced

4 cloves garlic, chopped

1 cup Tofu Sour Cream (page 33)

1 cup soy milk or nut milk

¼ cup sweet brown rice flour or any other whole-grain flour

2 tablespoons mellow (light-colored) miso, 2 teaspoons Vege-Sal, or 1 teaspoon salt, or to taste

1 teaspoon freshly ground black pepper (½ teaspoon peppercorns), or to taste

1. Preheat the oven to 400 degrees.
2. Heat the olive oil in a large skillet over medium heat, add the mushrooms and garlic, and cook, stirring, for 5 minutes.
3. Meanwhile, in a blender, combine the Tofu Sour Cream, soy milk, flour, and miso and process until smooth. Stir this mixture into the mushrooms and bring the pot to a boil over medium heat, stirring constantly. Reduce the heat to low and simmer, covered, stirring occasionally, for another 5 minutes.
4. Transfer the mushrooms and sauce to a 10 x 6½ x 2-inch baking dish and bake until the mushrooms are lightly brown on top, about 10 minutes.
5. Serve hot, sprinkled with the black pepper.

SERVES 6

BROILED BOLETES

Boletes are among the best-tasting mushrooms in the world, and broiling them with seasonings places them beyond description. Use any of the choice bolete species in this recipe and you'll find it difficult to conceive that food can taste so good.

½ cup olive oil

1 tablespoon chili paste or ¾ teaspoon cayenne pepper, or to taste

4 cloves garlic, peeled

2 teaspoons mellow (light-colored) miso

1 teaspoon dried rosemary, finely crumbled

½ teaspoon dried thyme, finely crumbled

½ teaspoon turmeric

¼ teaspoon freshly ground juniper berries (optional)

½ teaspoon freshly ground black pepper (¼ teaspoon peppercorns), or to taste

10 cups king bolete or other choice bolete caps

1. Preheat the broiler.
2. In a blender, combine all the ingredients, except the mushroom caps, and process until smooth.
3. In a large bowl, toss this mixture with the mushroom caps to coat well.
4. Broil the mushrooms on a wire rack until they are lightly browned, 4 to 8 minutes. Broilers differ greatly, so check often to make sure the boletes don't begin to burn. Turn the mushrooms with a metal spatula, tongs, or fork and broil them until the other side is lightly browned, another 4 to 8 minutes. Serve Broiled Boletes hot or at room temperature.

SERVES 6

MUSHROOM STEM GRAVY

This rich gravy exploits the stems of bolete mushrooms, which many mushroom hunters discard in favor of the caps because maggots usually infiltrate the stems first. (Not only is maggot-ridden food disgusting; it's probably spoiled.) Use only very fresh bolete stems without insect tunnels, especially if you're a vegetarian. Serve this gravy on vegetables, tofu, tempeh, and vegetable loaves and patties.

  ¼ cup olive oil

  2½ cups king bolete or other choice bolete stems, sliced

  3 cloves garlic, peeled or chopped

  1 tablespoon chopped fresh basil leaves

  1 teaspoon dried oregano, finely crumbled

  ½ teaspoon freshly ground caraway seeds

  *¾ cup barley flour or 3.33 ounces any other
    whole-grain flour*

  3½ cups boiling Vegetable Stock (page 40) or water

  *2 tablespoons Bragg's Liquid Aminos or tamari soy
    sauce, 2 teaspoons Vege-Sal, or 1 teaspoon salt,
    or to taste*

  *2 teaspoons chili paste or ½ teaspoon cayenne
    pepper, or to taste*

1. Heat the olive oil in a large skillet over medium heat. Add the mushroom stems, garlic, basil, oregano, and ground caraway seeds and cook, stirring, for 3 minutes. Stir in the flour and cook for another 3 minutes, stirring often.

2. Gradually stir in the boiling stock, add the Bragg's Liquid Aminos and chili paste, and bring the pot to a boil, stirring constantly. Reduce the heat to low, cover, and simmer for 10 minutes, stirring occasionally. Mushroom Stem Gravy will keep, covered, in the refrigerator for 7 days.

MAKES 3½ CUPS

PURSLANE
Portulaca oleacrea

THIS TRAILING SUCCULENT PRODUCES MATS OF smooth, thick stems with reddish branches that are 4 to 10 inches long. The stalkless fleshy, opposite or alternate, paddle-shaped leaves grow from ½ to 2 inches long. Tiny yellow, five-petaled flowers ⅓ inch wide escape notice in the summer. Late in the summer, fruit capsules ¼ inch long release tiny, round, black seeds that are smaller than mustard seeds. In season in the summer, this exotic plant grows abundantly throughout America in sandy soil. Look for it in gardens, lawns, fields, vacant lots, and disturbed soil.

Use purslane's leaves and stems together. Its distinct sweet-sour flavor makes it a wonderful and nutritious raw addition to salads, and you can include it in a great variety of cooked vegetable dishes, using nearly any cooking method. It cooks in about 10 minutes. You can also cook the seeds the way you would grains, but gathering enough seeds is too labor-intensive to be worthwhile.

PURSLANE-POTATO SALAD
Purslane makes this familiar dish seem ambrosial.

  *6 medium-size red potatoes, sliced, cooked in water
    to cover until tender, and drained*

  2 cups purslane leaves and stems, chopped

  4 scallions, sliced

  1 celery stalk, sliced

  1 cup Wild Mustard Seed Mayonnaise (page 206)

Mix together all the ingredients until well combined. Chill completely before serving.

PURSLANE-ONION SOUP

Purslane has been a food crop in India, was cultivated in gardens in Europe, and became a "weed" in America. This delicious source of omega-3 fatty acids is as protective of your heart as this simple soup is delightful to your taste buds.

4 teaspoons olive oil
2 ½ cups purslane leaves and stems, chopped
¾ cup finely chopped onions
¾ cup any wild or store-bought wine
6 cups soy milk or nut milk
1 ½ teaspoons hot paprika
¾ teaspoon salt, or to taste

1. Heat the olive oil in a large saucepan over medium heat, add the purslane and onions, and cook for 10 minutes, stirring often.
2. Add the wine and bring the pot to a boil. Add the remaining ingredients and cook until hot. Serve hot.

SERVES 6

SEND IT BACK TO INDIA

Grown since antiquity in India, purslane is a delicious wild vegetable, full of iron and essential fatty acids. Yet people try to destroy it when it grows in their tomato patches and lawns. This luscious recipe sends purslane back to India by preparing it with Indian spices and sauce.

1 ½ tablespoons dried chickpeas
1 cup water
Juice of 1 lime
1 teaspoon turmeric
2 tablespoons lecithin granules
⅓ cup drained silken tofu
2 teaspoons Vege-Sal or 1 teaspoon salt
2 tablespoons mustard seed oil (available in Indian grocery stores) or peanut oil
2 teaspoons black mustard seeds
1 ½ teaspoons cumin seeds
1 teaspoon cloves
4 cups purslane leaves and stems, chopped
1 habañero or 2 small chiles, seeds and ribs removed and finely chopped, or ½ teaspoon cayenne pepper, or to taste
2 cloves garlic, chopped
1 tablespoon peeled and finely chopped fresh ginger
One 16-ounce package extra-firm tofu, drained and coarsely diced

1. Toast the chickpeas in a small skillet over medium heat, stirring or shaking the skillet constantly, until the chickpeas are lightly browned and fragrant, 2 to 3 minutes. Remove the chickpeas from the pan and grind them into a powder in a coffee grinder, spice grinder, or blender. In a blender or medium-size bowl, add the water, lime juice, turmeric, lecithin, silken tofu, and Vege-Sal and process or mix until smooth.
2. Heat the mustard oil in a large skillet, add the black mustard seeds, cumin seeds, and cloves, and cook over medium heat, stirring constantly, until the mustard seeds pop, 2 to 3 minutes. Add the purslane, habañero, garlic, and ginger and cook for 5 minutes, stirring occasionally. Add the puréed chickpea mixture and the extra-firm tofu and bring the pot to a boil. Simmer, uncovered, stirring, until the sauce

reduces and thickens, about 10 minutes. Serve hot, over brown rice.

SERVES 4 TO 6

WILD BLACKBERRY

Rubus species

HERE'S ANOTHER BRAMBLE, WITH ARCHING, thorny, woody stems, palmate-compound leaves (subdivisions originate from one point), and a compound fruit, also divided into parts. Various blackberry species can trail along the ground or grow 10 feet tall. The leaf is divided into three to seven oval, sharply toothed, pointed leaflets. The faceted fruit is deep black, and part of the stem, the receptacle, comes off the bush when you pick the berry, so it's not hollow, like the black raspberry. Blackberries grow in fields, thickets, roadsides, fencerows, trailsides, open areas in woods, disturbed habitats, and at the edges of woods throughout North America. You can tell by the number of blackberry recipes in this book how large a quantity of blackberries I manage to collect in New York City most years (I know of some great thickets in empty lots near the seashore). Various species are in season mainly in the summer. Collect only berries that are completely black and come off the bush easily. Unripe berries taste awful.

Ripe blackberries have a complex flavor, with sweet and sour overtones that everyone loves. Use them in any recipe that calls for fruit or berries. They contain no natural thickeners, so add that component where needed. And in puréed recipes, it's much better to strain out the annoyingly hard seeds.

STEVE'S SMOOTHIE

Here's a quick and easy beverage that you'll love.

> 2 cups soy milk or nut milk
> 1 cup wild blackberries
> 1 ripe banana, peeled and cut into a few pieces
> 1 teaspoon ground ginger
> 8 common spicebush berries (page 314), finely chopped, or ¾ teaspoon freshly ground allspice berries
> 2 tablespoons vegetable glycerin, honey, barley malt, or rice syrup
> ½ teaspoon liquid stevia (optional)

In a blender, combine all the ingredients and process until smooth. Pour the mixture through a fine mesh strainer to remove the blackberry seeds.

SERVES 4

WILD BLACKBERRY JAM

This jam is scrumptious as a spread as well as an ingredient in jelly rolls and cake fillings. It also freezes well.

> 6½ cups wild blackberries
> 1 cup apple juice
> 4½ tablespoons agar powder
> ¼ cup natural cherry juice or other fruit concentrate, honey, rice syrup, or barley malt
> Juice of 1 lemon
> 2 teaspoons ground cinnamon
> 1½ teaspoons blackberry extract (optional)
> ½ teaspoon freshly ground cloves
> ½ teaspoon ground dried wild ginger (page 111) or regular ground ginger
> ½ teaspoon liquid stevia (optional)

1. Bring all the ingredients to a boil in a large saucepan over medium-high heat, stirring often. Reduce the heat to medium-low, cover, and simmer for 10 minutes, stirring often.

2. Test the jam for firmness (agar's thickening effect varies according to its fineness) by putting a large metal spoon with a small amount of jam in the freezer for a couple of minutes, until the jam is chilled. If the jam is the right thickness, your recipe is done. If it's too watery, stir in more agar, simmer the jam for another 5 to 10 minutes, and test it again. If the jam is too thick, stir in some fruit juice or water and test it again immediately.

3. Strain the jam through a fine mesh strainer to remove the seeds. Store Wild Blackberry Jam, tightly covered, in the refrigerator for up to 10 days or frozen for up to a year.

MAKES 8 CUPS

BLACKBERRY PANCAKES

These pancakes are unbelievably delicious, and wild blackberries make them even better. As in many of my recipes, flaxseeds and lecithin granules perform superbly in replacing egg whites and yolks, respectively.

1 ¾ cups (7 ounces) oat flour and 1 ½ cups
(7 ounces) buckwheat flour, or 14 ounces
any whole-grain flour
¼ cup lecithin granules
5 tablespoon freshly ground flaxseeds
(2 tablespoons seeds)
1 ½ teaspoons cream of tartar
1 teaspoon baking soda
1 teaspoon ground cinnamon
½ teaspoon salt
½ teaspoon freshly grated nutmeg

3 ½ cups soy milk or nut milk
¼ cup corn oil
2 teaspoons liquid stevia or ¼ cup honey, barley
malt, rice syrup, or maple syrup
½ teaspoon blackberry extract (optional)
2 cups wild blackberries
½ cup walnuts, chopped

1. In a large bowl, mix together the flour, lecithin, ground flaxseeds, cream of tartar, baking soda, cinnamon, salt, and nutmeg. Stir in the soy milk, corn oil, liquid stevia, and blackberry extract, if you are using it, being careful not to overmix. Stir in the blackberries and walnuts, being careful not to overmix.

2. Drop a few tablespoons of the batter onto a hot, oiled griddle and spread the batter into a circle. Cook each pancake until it is lightly browned underneath, and then flip it over with a metal spatula, and cook the other side until it is browned. Repeat until you've used up all the batter.

3. Serve Blackberry Pancakes with Wild Strawberry Sauce (page 208) or other fruit sauce, jam, or syrup.

MAKES 12 PANCAKES

WILD BLACK-AND-BLUE COBBLER

I used blackberries and blueberries when I made this cobbler, but other fruits work equally well.

FRUIT LAYER
4 cups wild blackberries
2 cups wild blueberries (page 260), picked over
for stems
½ cup sweet brown rice flour
¼ cup natural cherry juice concentrate
1 teaspoon ground cinnamon

1 teaspoon dried mint, finely crumbled

1 teaspoon blackberry extract (optional)

CRUMB TOPPING

2 cups fresh Bread Crumbs (page 40)

1 cup hazelnuts, chopped

2 tablespoons apricot oil or corn oil

1 teaspoon vanilla extract

½ teaspoon freshly ground coriander seeds

½ teaspoon ground dried wild ginger (page 111) or
regular ground ginger

½ teaspoon freshly grated nutmeg

¼ teaspoon liquid stevia or 2 tablespoons honey,
barley malt, or rice syrup

1. Preheat the oven to 350 degrees.

2. *To make the fruit layer:* Mix the fruit layer ingredients together in a large bowl. Transfer the fruit layer to a 14 x 9 x 2-inch oiled baking dish.

3. *To make the crumb topping:* Mix the crumb topping together in a medium-size bowl. Press the crumb topping onto the fruit layer. Bake the cobbler until bubbly, about 40 minutes. Serve hot or cold.

SERVES 8

WILD BLACKBERRY COBBLER

The first thing I do when I've collected more blackberries than I can devour raw is to bake some into this cobbler.

5 cups wild blackberries

2 tablespoons tapioca pearls, ground into powder

½ cup plus 1 tablespoon apple juice

1 teaspoon dried orange rind or ½ teaspoon orange
extract

1 teaspoon dried mint, finely crumbled

¼ teaspoon freshly ground cardamom seeds

1 ½ cups sweet brown rice flour or 7 ounces any
whole-grain flour

2 tablespoons apricot kernel oil, walnut oil, almond
oil, or corn oil

1 ¼ teaspoons cream of tartar

½ teaspoon baking soda

½ teaspoon ground cinnamon, plus more for
sprinkling

¼ teaspoon common spicebush berries (page 314),
finely chopped, or freshly ground allspice berries

½ teaspoon freshly grated nutmeg

¼ teaspoon salt

¼ cup corn oil

3 tablespoons soy milk, almond milk, or
unsweetened fruit juice, or as needed

1. Preheat the oven to 350 degrees.

2. Mix the blackberries, ground tapioca, ½ cup of the apple juice, the orange rind, mint, and cardamom together in a large bowl. Transfer the mixture to a 14 x 9 x 2-inch oiled baking dish.

3. Sprinkle the fruit mixture with 3 tablespoons of the flour and dot with the apricot kernel oil.

4. In a medium-size bowl, mix together the remaining flour, the cream of tartar, baking soda, cinnamon, spicebush berries, nutmeg, and salt. Mix in the corn oil, and then stir in the remaining 1 tablespoon apple juice and enough soy milk to make a dough that's neither sticky nor crumbly.

5. Using a rolling pin covered with a floured sleeve and working on a floured pastry sheet, roll the dough out ¼ inch thick in the shape of your baking dish. Transfer the rolled out pastry onto the berry layer, cut slits for steam to escape, and sprinkle on more cinnamon for color, if desired. Bake the cobbler until bubbly, about 40 minutes. Serve hot or cold.

SERVES 6 TO 8

BLACKBERRY DUMPLINGS

These corn-oat dumplings cooked in a wild blackberry sauce are an exceptional treat. This unusual dessert is one of my favorites, and I'm sure the same will be true for you.

DUMPLINGS

    1 ⅓ cups (5.5 ounces) oat flour, 1 cup plus
        2 tablespoons (5.5 ounces) buckwheat flour,
        and 1 ¼ cups (5 ounces) yellow cornmeal, or
        1 pound any whole-grain flour

    2 ½ tablespoons freshly ground flaxseeds
        (1 tablespoon seeds)

    1 teaspoon cream of tartar

    ½ teaspoon baking soda

    1 teaspoon dried mint, finely crumbled

    ½ teaspoon ground dried wild ginger (page 111) or
        regular ground ginger

    ½ teaspoon salt

    ¾ cup soy milk or nut milk

    1 tablespoon corn oil

    1 tablespoon vegetable glycerin, barley malt, or
        honey (optional)

    1 teaspoon vanilla extract

    1 cup cooked brown rice

    1 tablespoon lecithin granules

SAUCE

    4 cups unsweetened blackberry juice or other fruit
        juice

    ¼ cup kudzu or arrowroot

    ¼ cup vegetable glycerin, barley malt, rice syrup,
        or honey

    1 tablespoon Blackberry Spice Wine (page 279) or
        other wild or store-bought red wine

    ½ teaspoon amaretto extract (optional)

    ¼ teaspoon freshly ground cloves

    ½ teaspoon freshly grated nutmeg

    ¼ teaspoon liquid stevia (optional)

    2 cups wild blackberries

1. *To make the dumplings:* In a large bowl, mix together the flours, ground flaxseeds, cream of tartar, baking soda, mint, ginger, and salt.

2. In a medium-size bowl, mix together the soy milk, corn oil, vegetable glycerin, and vanilla. Mix the wet ingredients into the dry ingredients. Stir in the brown rice and lecithin. Shape the dough into about 32 balls, 1 inch in diameter.

3. *To make the sauce:* Mix together all the sauce ingredients, except the blackberries, in a large saucepan and bring the pot to a boil over medium heat, stirring often.

4. Add the dumplings, reduce the heat to low, and simmer, covered, for 15 minutes. Add the blackberries and simmer, covered, for another 5 minutes. Serve hot.

SERVES 6 TO 8

BLACKBERRY PASTRY SUPREME

The mellow flavor of the tofu cheese in this pastry contrasts perfectly with the tart flavor of wild blackberries.

FRUIT LAYER

    ½ cup apple juice or other unsweetened fruit juice

    3 tablespoons arrowroot or kudzu

    1 teaspoon blackberry extract (optional)

    ½ teaspoon orange extract

    ½ teaspoon liquid stevia or 2 tablespoons honey,
        barley malt, or rice syrup

    6 cups wild blackberries

PASTRY

1 cup plus 3 tablespoons (¼ pound) sweet brown
   rice flour and 1⅓ cups (¼ pound) buckwheat
   flour, or ½ pound any whole-grain flour

¼ cup arrowroot or kudzu

¼ cup walnuts, chopped

½ teaspoon freshly grated nutmeg

¼ teaspoon salt

¾ cup Tofu Cream Cheese (page 30)

3 tablespoons apple juice or other unsweetened
   fruit juice

½ teaspoon vanilla extract

½ teaspoon dried wild mint (page 129) or
   other mint, finely crumbled

¼ teaspoon liquid stevia or 2 tablespoons barley
   malt or honey

1 teaspoon ground cinnamon

1. Preheat the oven to 400 degrees.

2. *To make the fruit layer:* Mix together all the fruit layer ingredients, except the blackberries. Stir in the blackberries and transfer the mixture to a 14 x 9 x 2-inch oiled baking dish.

3. *To make the pastry:* In a large bowl, mix together the flours, arrowroot, walnuts, nutmeg, and salt.

4. In a medium-size bowl, mix together the Tofu Cream Cheese, apple juice, vanilla, mint, and liquid stevia. Mix the wet ingredients into the dry ingredients to make a dough that's moist enough so that it doesn't crumble when you pinch it, and dry enough not to be sticky. Add more apple juice if the dough is too crumbly, more flour if it is too sticky. Chill the dough to make it more workable, if desired.

5. On a floured pastry sheet with a rolling pin enclosed in a floured sleeve, roll out the dough ⅜ inch thick in the shape of your baking dish. Transfer the pastry by rolling it around the rolling pin along with

the pastry sheet. Position the pastry over the berry mixture and peel away the pastry sheet. Press the pastry down, seal the edges to the dish, and sprinkle cinnamon on top.

6. Bake the dessert until the liquid is bubbly and the top is lightly browned, about 40 minutes. Serve warm or cold.

SERVES 6

Note: You may also divide the filling and dough among six 4-inch tart pans.

BLACKBERRY JELLY ROLL

You can make this tempting sweet jelly roll with any kind of jam, using wild fruit, cultivated fruit, or even commercial jam.

4 cups (1 pound) oat flour and 3¾ cups (1 pound)
   barley flour, or 2 pounds any whole-grain flour

1 tablespoon plus 1 teaspoon ground cinnamon

1 tablespoon freshly ground fennel seeds

2 teaspoons freshly ground coriander seeds

½ teaspoon salt

One 19-ounce package silken tofu, drained

1⅓ cups pitted dates

¼ cup apricot kernel oil, corn oil, or other oil

6 cups Wild Blackberry Jam (page 272) or other
   jam

1 teaspoon ground cinnamon

1. Preheat the oven to 350 degrees.

2. In a large bowl, mix the flours, 1 tablespoon of the cinnamon, the ground fennel and coriander, and salt.

3. In a blender or food processor, combine the tofu, dates, and apricot oil and process until smooth. Mix the purée into the dry ingredients and knead the

dough until the ingredients are well combined.

4. Divide the dough into 6 equal balls. Roll each ball of dough into a ⅜-inch-thick rectangle on a floured pastry sheet with a rolling pin covered with a floured sleeve.

5. Spread 1 cup of the jam over the pastry, leaving 1-inch margins along the edges. Moisten the edges of the margins with water and roll up the pastry.

6. Place the rolls on an oiled cookie sheet seam side down. Sprinkle on the remaining 1 teaspoon cinnamon. Bake the jelly rolls until they are lightly browned, about 45 minutes. Let the jelly rolls cool on wire racks before slicing.

MAKES 6 LARGE ROLLS

BLACKBERRY CREAM PIE

The English of Shakespeare's day called the blackberry's bramble canes *lawyers*. They're thorny, they grab you, and they don't let go until they've drawn blood! Has anything changed in the legal profession in five hundred years? Fighting these bushes for their irresistible treasures is hard work, but this recipe makes it all worthwhile, and the nut cream stretches your hard-won fruit.

> 1 ½ cups apple juice
> 1 cup Cashew Butter (page 37) or other nut butter
> ¼ cup kudzu or arrowroot
> 2 teaspoons blackberry extract (optional)
> 1 teaspoon dried wild mint (page 129) or other mint, finely crumbled
> 1 teaspoon lemon extract or freshly grated rind of 1 lemon
> ½ teaspoon ground dried wild ginger (page 111) or regular ground ginger

> ½ teaspoon common spicebush berries (page 314), finely chopped, or freshly ground allspice berries
> ½ teaspoon liquid stevia or 2 tablespoons honey, barley malt, or rice syrup
> 6 cups wild blackberries
> Two 9-inch pie crusts, homemade or store-bought

1. Preheat the oven to 350 degrees.

2. In a blender, combine all the ingredients, except the blackberries and pie crusts, and process until smooth.

3. Transfer the mixture to a large bowl and mix in the blackberries gently.

4. Fill the pie crusts with the filling. Bake the pies until the filling is bubbling, about 35 minutes. Let the pies cool before slicing.

MAKES 2 PIES; SERVES 8 TO 12

BLACKBERRY BROWNIES

It may sound odd, but wild blackberries work surprisingly well in carob brownies. Cherry juice, which also complements carob, is the sweetener of choice.

ICING

> 1 cup pine nuts
> One 19-ounce package silken tofu, drained
> ½ cup carob powder
> 2 tablespoons corn oil
> 2 tablespoons natural cherry juice concentrate
> 2 teaspoons vanilla extract
> ½ teaspoon lemon extract
> ½ teaspoon ground dried wild ginger (page 111) or regular ground ginger
> ½ teaspoon common spicebush berries (page 314), finely chopped, or freshly ground allspice berries
> ½ teaspoon salt

BROWNIES

1 cup 3 tablespoons (5.5 ounces) sweet brown rice
   flour and 1 ¼ cups (5 ounces) oat flour, or 10.5
   ounces any whole-grain flour
1 cup carob powder
½ cup arrowroot or kudzu
½ cup plus 2 tablespoons freshly ground flaxseeds
   (¼ cup seeds)
¼ cup lecithin granules
1 teaspoon salt
1 teaspoon dried wild spearmint (page 59) or other
   mint, finely crumbled
1 teaspoon freshly grated nutmeg
½ teaspoon cream of tartar
¼ teaspoon baking soda
¾ cup natural cherry juice concentrate
¼ cup corn oil
2 teaspoons vanilla extract
1 ½ teaspoons liquid stevia
½ teaspoon blackberry extract (optional)
1 cup wild blackberries

1. Preheat the oven to 350 degrees.

2. *To make the icing:* Grind the pine nuts in a food
processor or by hand. Add the remaining icing ingredients, process until smooth, and set aside.

3. *To make the brownies:* In a large bowl, mix together
the flour, ¾ cup of the carob powder, the arrowroot,
ground flaxseeds, lecithin, salt, spearmint, nutmeg,
cream of tartar, and baking soda.

4. In a medium-size bowl, mix together the cherry
juice concentrate, corn oil, vanilla, liquid stevia, and
blackberry extract, if you are using it. Stir the wet
ingredients into the dry ingredients, being careful not
to overmix.

5. Roll the blackberries in the remaining ¼ cup carob
powder and fold them into the brownie batter.

6. Transfer the batter to an oiled 12½ x 9 x 2-inch
baking dish, pour the icing on top, and bake until a
toothpick inserted in the center emerges clean, about
40 minutes.

7. Cut the brownies into 32 rectangles while they are
still in the pan. Let the pan of brownies cool on a wire
rack, and then remove the brownies from the pan.

MAKES 32 BROWNIES

VANILLA ICE CREAM WITH BLACKBERRIES

When I gave up dairy products, I never thought I'd eat
ice cream again. Eight years later, I bought an ice
cream machine, started experimenting, and found
that vegan ice cream was easy to make. This low-calorie ice cream, my first success, tastes better than the
fatty, sugary ones in the store, and it's lots of fun to
make.

1 vanilla bean
2 teaspoons vanilla extract
2 ½ cups well-drained silken tofu
1 ½ cups soy milk or nut milk
½ cup canola oil or safflower oil
¼ cup vegetable glycerin
¼ cup lecithin granules
½ teaspoon liquid stevia or 2 tablespoons barley
   malt or honey
¼ teaspoon lemon extract or ½ teaspoon freshly
   grated lemon rind
1 ½ cups wild blackberries

1. Split the vanilla bean lengthwise with a knife and
scrape out the black pulp. Put the pulp in a blender
with all the other ingredients, except the blackberries,
and process until smooth.

2. Chill the mixture (or start with chilled ingredients) if required by your ice cream machine. Stir in the blackberries.

3. Pour the mixture into the ice cream machine and freeze it according to the manufacturer's instructions.

MAKES 6 CUPS; SERVES 6

BLACKBERRY ICE CREAM

Make a delightful, healthful ice cream with wild fruit, tofu, soy milk, and natural sweeteners. You'll be healthier, and your taste buds will thank you, too.

 2 cups soy milk or nut milk
 1 cup well-drained silken tofu
 ½ cup raw cashews
 ½ cup canola oil
 ¼ cup vegetable glycerin, barley malt, honey, or rice syrup
 ¼ cup lecithin granules
 2 teaspoons vanilla extract
 1 teaspoon blackberry extract (optional)
 1 teaspoon liquid stevia or 2 tablespoons honey, barley malt, or rice syrup
 ½ teaspoon salt
 2 cups wild blackberries

1. In a blender, combine all the ingredients, except for 1 cup of the blackberries, and process until smooth.

2. Force the mixture through a fine mesh strainer to remove the seeds.

3. Chill the mixture (or begin with chilled ingredients) if required by your ice cream machine. Stir in the remaining blackberries.

4. Pour the mixture into an ice cream machine and freeze it according to the manufacturer's instructions.

MAKES 5½ CUPS; SERVES 5 TO 6

BLACKBERRY SHERBET

Here's a great dessert you can transfer from the field to an ice cream machine in minutes.

 3½ cups water
 2 cups wild blackberries
 ½ cup raw cashews
 ½ cup canola oil
 ¼ cup vegetable glycerin, honey, barley malt, or rice syrup
 ¼ cup lecithin granules
 1 teaspoon liquid stevia (optional)
 1 teaspoon dried mint, finely crumbled
 ¼ teaspoon ground dried wild ginger (page 111) or regular ground ginger
 ½ teaspoon salt

1. In a blender, combine all the ingredients and process until smooth.

2. Strain out the seeds using a fine mesh strainer.

3. Chill the mixture (or begin with chilled ingredients) if required by your ice cream machine.

4. Pour the mixture into the ice cream machine and freeze it according to the manufacturer's instructions.

MAKES 6 CUPS; SERVES 6

BLACKBERRY SPICE WINE

Here's a traditional wild wine made in the traditional manner. Its robust flavor makes it a good companion to strong-flavored dishes. A small amount makes itself known as an ingredient in sauces and desserts.

 6 cups sugar
 1 gallon water
 6 cups wild blackberries

1 tablespoon common spicebush berries (page 314)
   or 1 teaspoon allspice berries

1 tablespoon cloves

Two 1-inch cinnamon sticks

½ teaspoon champagne yeast or other wine yeast

1. Dissolve the sugar in the water in a non-metal (plastic or ceramic) food container, add the blackberries, mashing them slightly with a hand blender or potato masher, and add the spices.

2. When the mixture is lukewarm, stir in the yeast and cover the container with a non-airtight cover, cheesecloth, or towel.

3. Allow the mixture to ferment for 7 to 10 days at room temperature, stirring it twice a day.

4. Strain the mixture through cheesecloth, transfer the liquid to a jug, and seal the jug with an airlock stopper (which lets carbon dioxide bubbles escape but keeps oxygen out).

5. When the bubbling stops and fermentation ends a few weeks later, seal the jug with a cork stopper and age the wine for 2 to 6 months before using it.

6. Siphon the wine to get rid of the sediment, if desired.

MAKES 1 GALLON

VOLUMINOUS-LATEX MILKY MUSHROOM
Lactarius volemus

LIKE ALL MILKY MUSHROOMS, THIS ONE HAS white gills under the cap that are attached to the stem, it grows on the ground near trees, it is somewhat funnel shaped, and it exudes a milky fluid when cut.

The voluminous-latex milky mushroom's orange-brown cap is 2 to 5¼ inches across. The gills, which are close together, are white, but they stain brown. The spores are white. The orange-brown stalk is 2 to 4 inches long and ⅜ to ¾ inch thick. The whole mushroom, which smells fishy, exudes large quantities of a sticky, white, milky latex when injured. Look for this fungus from early to late summer in deciduous woods throughout eastern North America.

This mushroom's cap and stem cook in about 15 to 20 minutes. Their flavor and texture are similar to those of ground beef, especially when you use appropriate seasonings. Use voluminous-latex milky mushrooms in recipes that call for a tasty, meaty-textured mushroom.

MUSHROOM-MILLET PILAF

The firm, chewy texture and meaty flavor of the voluminous-latex milky mushroom makes it a wonderful choice for cooking with grains.

4 ¼ cups Vegetable Stock (page 40)

2 cups millet

1 ½ cups voluminous-latex milky mushrooms, sliced

1 cup unsalted dry-roasted peanuts, chopped

1 ripe plantain, peeled and sliced

1 teaspoon dried basil, finely crumbled

1 teaspoon Vege-Sal or ½ teaspoon salt, or to taste

½ teaspoon freshly ground fennel seeds

½ teaspoon dried savory, finely crumbled

Combine all the ingredients in a large saucepan and bring the pot to a boil. Reduce the heat to low, and let the mixture cook, covered, until all the liquid is absorbed and the millet is tender, about 30 minutes.

SERVES 6 TO 8

HYGROPHORUS MILKY MUSHROOM

Lactarius hygrophoroides

ANOTHER MILKY MUSHROOM, THIS ONE HAS AN orange brown cap that is 1¼ to 4 inches across, and there is quite a bit of space between the gills (see page 279 for a description of this group). The orange brown stalk is 1¼ to 2 inches long and ¼ to ⅝ inch thick. It exudes a white milk when injured. You can find this fungus all summer long in deciduous woods throughout eastern North America.

This mushroom has a texture that's firmer than that of most other species, although it's never tough, and the flavor is always pleasant. Of course, you can use it in mushroom side dishes and in generic entrées, but its texture also makes it one of the best meat substitutes you'll ever come across. Use both the caps and stems, cooked. They will cook in 15 minutes.

HASHED MILKY MUSHROOMS

The hygrophorus milky mushroom provides the meaty texture to balance the potatoes and seasonings in a wild version of this familiar American dish.

> 6 tablespoons olive oil
>
> 6 cups hygrophorus milky mushrooms, sliced
>
> 4 medium-size red potatoes, thinly sliced
>
> 3 celery stalks, thinly sliced
>
> 2 medium-size onions, thinly sliced
>
> 4 cloves garlic, chopped
>
> ¼ cup Fakin' Bacon Bits
>
> 2 tablespoons chopped fresh basil leaves

> 1 teaspoon freshly ground black pepper
>
> (½ teaspoon peppercorns)
>
> 1 teaspoon dried sage, finely crumbled
>
> 1 teaspoon dried savory, finely crumbled
>
> ½ teaspoon freshly grated nutmeg
>
> 2 tablespoons Bragg's Liquid Aminos or tamari soy
>
> sauce

1. Heat the olive oil in a large skillet over medium heat. Add the remaining ingredients, except the Bragg's, and cook, stirring, for 10 minutes.

2. Add the Bragg's, reduce the heat to low, cover, and cook until the potatoes are tender, about another 10 minutes. Serve warm.

SERVES 6

SUMAC

Rhus species

SUMACS ARE SHRUBS OR SMALL TREES WITH lemon-scented alternate, feather-compound leaves (the leaves are divided into leaflets along an axis) that can grow to over 2 feet long. The paired, toothed, pointed leaflets turn a spectacular red in the fall. Erect cone-shaped flower heads with thousands of fragrant, tiny, greenish-yellow flowers appear at the tips of the branches beginning in midsummer. By fall, the flowers have transformed into hard, small, red, hairy berries. (The only dangerous species, poison sumac [Rhus vernix], has drooping flower and seed heads, and white berries.)

This uncommon plant grows in sandy swamps. Sumacs grow on dry, rocky, or sandy soil in overgrown fields, on hillsides, along roadsides, along the margins of woods, and in canyons and disturbed areas.

Sumac berries flavor water so it tastes like pink lemonade. Just swish the berries in cold water (hot water releases bitter tannin), then strain out the berries and sweeten the flavored water to taste (kids love this drink). You can follow up by making sumac concentrate, which can be used to replace lemon or lime juice or vinegar as a source of sourness in almost any recipe.

SUMAC CONCENTRATE AND WILD PINK LEMONADE

Here's a superior source of sourness you can make with any species of sumac that has red berries. Use it in any recipe that requires a sour liquid.

Clusters of ripe sumac berries
Cold or room-temperature water as needed

1. Cover a few clusters of sumac berries with water in a bowl. Squeeze, rub, and swirl the sumac in the water to release its flavor.
2. Strain the liquid through a cheesecloth-lined colander.
3. *To make wild pink lemonade:* Sweeten the concentrate to taste, if desired.
4. *To make sumac concentrate:* Repeat the process several times adding new clumps of sumac berries in the same water until the liquid tastes as sour as lemon juice. The concentrate will keep, tightly covered, in the refrigerator for up to 2 weeks. I freeze it in an ice cube tray and then pack the cubes into a freezer container. I then defrost the handy cubes, which last indefinitely, as needed.

SUMACADO VINAIGRETTE

This mouth-watering salad dressing, thickened with an avocado, and with sumac concentrate replacing the standard lemon juice, is sure to please.

2 cups Sumac Concentrate (page 281)
1 medium-size ripe avocado, peeled and pitted
⅓ cup mellow (light-colored) miso
⅓ cup canola oil or other vegetable oil
½ medium-size red onion, peeled
4 cloves garlic, peeled
1 tablespoon peeled and chopped fresh ginger
2 common spicebush berries (page 314), finely chopped, or ½ teaspoon freshly ground allspice berries

In a blender, combine all the ingredients and process until smooth. Sumacado Vinaigrette will keep in the refrigerator, tightly covered, for up to 10 days.

MAKES 4½ CUPS

PIQUANT SUMAC SAUCE

Sumac, concentrated to give it the sourness of lemon juice, has its own unique flavor—perfect for a piquant sauce. Use it on potatoes or other vegetables.

1 cup Sumac Concentrate (page 281)
One 19-ounce package silken tofu, well drained
½ cup corn oil or olive oil
¼ cup fresh parsley leaves
1 tablespoon mellow (light-colored) miso, or to taste
1 teaspoon freshly ground yellow mustard seeds (½ teaspoon seeds)
1 teaspoon freshly ground white pepper (½ teaspoon peppercorns)
½ teaspoon freshly grated nutmeg

¼ teaspoon turmeric

¼ teaspoon hot paprika

1 teaspoon Vege-Sal or ½ teaspoon salt

In a food processor or large bowl, combine all the ingredients and process or beat with a whisk or fork until smooth. Piquant Sumac Sauce will keep, tightly covered, in the refrigerator for up to a week, and indefinitely in the freezer.

MAKES 5½ CUPS

SKORDALIA

If you love garlic, this bread-thickened garlic mayonnaise is for you, and it's even better with sumac concentrate replacing the lemon juice. Use skordalia in sandwiches, as a dip, in salad dressings, on steamed vegetables, or to add flavor and creaminess to soups and stews.

10 slices any yeast-leavened bread, or 6 slices
*   bread and ¼ cup pine nuts (Greek version),*
*   lightly toasted*

1 cup olive oil

½ cup rice vinegar or other vinegar

2 tablespoons chopped garlic, or to taste

5 tablespoons Sumac Concentrate (page 281)

1. Place all the ingredients, except the sumac concentrate, in a blender and let them soak for 30 minutes.
2. Slowly add the sumac concentrate while running the blender on low speed. Blend until smooth. If you want a thinner mayonnaise, add more sumac concentrate or some water. Skordalia will keep, tightly covered, in the refrigerator for 1 week.

MAKES 4 CUPS

MOCK TURKEY GRAVY

This sauce is just like turkey gravy, only the turkey is still alive. And I'm sure the turkey would prefer being mocked to being eaten!

4 cups Vegetable Stock (page 40) or water

1 tablespoon chopped fresh basil leaves or
*   1 teaspoon dried*

½ teaspoon dried thyme, finely crumbled

½ teaspoon freshly ground black pepper
*   (¼ teaspoon peppercorns)*

¼ cup tamari soy sauce

3 tablespoons brewer's yeast

2 tablespoons Sumac Concentrate (page 281)

2 ounces any whole-grain flour

¼ cup olive oil

1. Place all the ingredients, except the flour and olive oil, in a medium-size saucepan and bring the pot to a boil over medium heat.
2. Meanwhile, cook the flour in the olive oil in a small skillet over medium heat, stirring constantly, until the mixture is fragrant and slightly browned, about 5 minutes.
3. Transfer the flour and oil mixture to another saucepan and slowly add the boiling stock mixture, stirring constantly. Simmer over low heat for 10 minutes, stirring often. If lumps form, carefully blend the mixture in small batches in the blender until smooth, beginning on low speed and holding down the blender cover with a towel to prevent eruptions. Mock Turkey Gravy will keep, tightly covered, in the refrigerator for 1 week, or in the freezer for 6 months.

MAKES 5 CUPS

SUMAC FALAFEL

These chickpea balls, flavored with sumac concentrate, are better for you than the ones you get in Middle Eastern restaurants because you bake them instead of deep-frying them.

> 2 cups cooked chickpeas, drained
> 4 large cloves garlic, minced
> ¾ cup soy flour or whole-grain flour
> ½ cup Vegetable Stock (page 40) or water
> ¼ cup olive oil
> 3 tablespoons finely chopped fresh cilantro or
>   parsley leaves
> 4 ramp bulbs (page 116) or ½ small onion,
>   finely chopped
> 1 tablespoon hot paprika
> 1 tablespoon freshly ground cumin seeds
> 2 tablespoons Sumac Concentrate (page 281)
> 2 teaspoons Vege-Sal or 1 teaspoon salt, or to taste
> 2 teaspoons freshly ground black pepper
>   (1 teaspoon peppercorns)

1. Preheat the oven to 350 degrees.
2. In a large bowl, combine all the ingredients, mashing everything as smooth as possible.
3. Shape the chickpea mixture into approximately 2 dozen balls and arrange the balls on an oiled cookie sheet. Bake the falafel until they are lightly browned underneath, about 35 minutes, turning them halfway through the baking time.
4. Serve the falafel with sprouts, lettuce, and Wild Hummus (page 132) in Pita Bread (page 38).

MAKES ABOUT 2 DOZEN FALAFELS

SUMAC RICE

The lemony flavor of sumac and the addition of Indian spices make this the perfect rice to serve with other Indian dishes.

> ¼ cup corn oil
> 4 teaspoons turmeric
> 2 teaspoons black or yellow mustard seeds
> 1 teaspoon Vege-Sal or ½ teaspoon salt
> 6 cups cooked brown rice
> ¼ cup Sumac Concentrate (page 281)

1. Heat the corn oil in a small skillet over medium heat. Add the turmeric, mustard seeds, and Vege-Sal and cook, stirring or shaking constantly, until the mustard seeds start to pop.
2. Mix the spice mixture into the rice, heat it through, and add the sumac concentrate.

SERVES 6

SUMAC ICE CREAM

Sumac's lemony flavor creates an ice cream that tastes like pink lemonade—unusual but addictive.

> 2 cups soy milk or nut milk
> ½ cup Sumac Concentrate (page 281)
> ½ cup canola oil
> ½ cup drained silken tofu
> ½ cup raw cashews
> ¼ cup vegetable glycerin
> ¼ cup lecithin granules
> 1 teaspoon liquid stevia or 2 tablespoons honey,
>   barley malt, or rice syrup
> ½ teaspoon salt

1. In a blender, combine all the ingredients and process until smooth.

2. Chill the mixture (or begin with chilled ingredients) if required by your ice cream machine.

3. Pour the mixture into the ice cream machine and freeze it according to the manufacturer's instructions.

MAKES 5 CUPS; SERVES 5

SUMAC-HAZELNUT PUDDING

Tart sumac concentrate and earthy hazelnuts in a creamy purée yield an irresistible pudding.

> 3 common spicebush berries (page 314) or
> ¼ teaspoon allspice berries
> 1 cup hazelnuts, toasted (page 158)
> ½ cup dried figs
> One 19-ounce package silken tofu, drained
> ¼ cup lecithin granules
> 3 tablespoons Sumac Concentrate (page 281)
> 2 tablespoons corn oil
> 2 tablespoons kudzu or arrowroot
> 1 teaspoon vanilla extract
> 1 teaspoon liquid stevia or 2 tablespoons honey,
> barley malt, maple syrup, or rice syrup
> ¼ teaspoon salt
> ½ teaspoon freshly grated nutmeg
> ¼ teaspoon orange extract
> ½ cup cultivated currants

1. Preheat the oven to 350 degrees.

2. In a food processor, grind the spicebush berries and hazelnuts together or chop them fine by hand.

3. Add the figs and grind again, or chop again by hand.

4. Add all the remaining ingredients, except the currants, and process or chop once more. Stir in the currants.

5. Transfer the mixture to a 1-quart oiled casserole dish and bake, uncovered, until bubbly, about 30 minutes. Serve hot or cold.

SERVES 4 TO 6

RINGLESS HONEY MUSHROOM

Armillariella tabescens

THIS IS A YELLOW-BROWN MUSHROOM WITH A cap that is 1 to 4 inches across and features distinct scales that look like tiny hairs toward the center. Under the cap are white gills that run down the stem, and the spore print is white. The fibrous stalk, which tapers toward the base, is 3 to 8 inches long and ¼ to ⅝ inch thick. From late summer to fall, large clusters of this mushroom, connected at their bases, can be found growing at the foot of living or dead trees or stumps, especially oaks, throughout eastern North America. Ringless honey mushrooms were the first wild mushrooms I ever identified on my own and ate. I went over every detail of the mushrooms with my mushroom field guide again and again, and I was still scared. But I survived, and I still enjoy these choice wild mushrooms whenever I find them.

With a meaty texture and savory flavor, ringless honey mushrooms are good in any dish that calls for mushrooms. Sauté or cook them in soups for 15 to 20 minutes. The stems tend to be tough, so use them for puréed dishes or stock.

Caution: Ringless honey mushrooms sometimes cause digestive distress in sensitive individuals. Eat a very small amount the first time you try them, and never undercook them.

RINGLESS HONEY MUSHROOMS WITH BROCCOLI

I hated broccoli when I was a child, and it was always prepared poorly. Now I love it. It's easy to avoid overcooking it, and the wild mushrooms and seasonings make it taste even better.

3 tablespoons olive oil

6 cups packed ringless honey mushrooms, sliced

6 cloves garlic, finely chopped

One and a half 19-ounce packages silken tofu, drained

¾ cup Wild Crabapple Blossom Wine (page 425) or white wine

3 tablespoons arrowroot or kudzu

3 tablespoons tamari soy sauce

1 tablespoon chili paste or 1 ½ teaspoons cayenne pepper, or to taste

1 ½ teaspoons freshly ground dill seeds or dillweed, finely crumbled

1 ½ teaspoons hot paprika

1 ½ teaspoons freshly ground star anise

¾ teaspoon freshly ground ajwain seeds (a spice that is available in Indian specialty stores; optional)

1 ½ heads broccoli, broken into florets

1. Heat the olive oil in a large skillet over medium heat. Add the mushrooms and cook for 5 minutes, stirring often. Add the garlic and cook, stirring, for another 5 minutes.

2. Meanwhile, in a blender, combine the remaining ingredients, except the broccoli, and process until smooth. Stir the wine and spice mixture and the broccoli into the mushroom mixture. Bring the pot to a boil over medium-high heat, stirring constantly. Reduce the heat to low and simmer, covered, just until the broccoli is tender, stirring often, 10 to 15 minutes. Serve hot.

SERVES 6

KOUSA DOGWOOD
Cornus kousa

THIS SMALL DOGWOOD TREE, WHICH GROWS 8 to 30 feet tall, has mottled ochre and brown bark, and opposite, narrowly heart-shaped, toothed leaves that are up to 4 inches long. The ball-shaped green flower head, covered with tiny four-petaled flowers, is surrounded by four large, petal-like white sepals (modified leaves), which bloom in the spring. In late summer and fall, the flower head develops into a warty, soft, globular, red fruit that can be up to an inch across, containing hard, small seeds. Look for this foreign ornamental in cultivated areas and parks throughout the United States.

The fruit tastes like apricots and mangoes, although the skin is sometimes unpleasantly bitter, and you can't eat the hard seeds. For years I tried to find a way to cook the fruit without increasing its bitterness. The solution: use it raw as a garnish.

KOUSA DOGWOOD PARFAIT

Here one berry tops a decadent-tasting but healthful parfait. It's best to warn your guests that they'll have to spit out the fruit's hard seeds.

> 1 ¼ cups Crunchy Almond Butter (page 38)
> 1 ½ cups Carob Cream (page 319)
> 1 ¼ cups Wild Apricot Jam (page 228)
> 5 kousa dogwood berries

1. Layer the ingredients in 5 of your most attractive looking 1-cup glasses. Start with ¼ cup of the almond butter, ½ cup of the carob creme, and ¼ cup of the apricot jam. Top the parfait with a kousa dogwood berry.

2. Repeat the process with 4 more glasses to use up all the ingredients. Serve chilled.

SERVES 5

FOREST AGARICUS MUSHROOM

Agaricus silvaticus

LIKE OTHER MEADOW MUSHROOMS (*AGARICUS* species), this mushroom grows on the ground, where it decomposes organic material; it has gills that are free from the stalk (there's a space between them), and the gills, which are white at first, soon turn brown owing to the brown spores (don't confuse this with potentially deadly *Amanitas*, which always has white gills). This species has a convex to flat, grayish cap that is 1 to 3 inches across. The stalk is 2 to 3 inches long, ⅜ to ½ inch thick, and there's a ring on the upper stalk. The whole mushroom bruises pinkish

when injured. You can find forest agaricus mushrooms on the ground in moist woods from summer to fall in the East, and from late fall to late winter in California.

The mushroom's deep, smoky flavor makes it ideal for a variety of savory dishes. It cooks in 15 to 20 minutes.

Caution: This mushroom doesn't agree with everyone, so try small amounts the first time.

RUSSIAN MUSHROOM PATTIES

The Russians have appreciated wild mushrooms for centuries, and so will you after you savor the way their flavor pervades these millet croquettes.

> 2 tablespoons olive oil
> 2 cups packed forest agaricus mushrooms, sliced
> 1 cup ramp bulbs (page 116), shallots, or onions, chopped
> 2 large cloves garlic, finely chopped
> 1 small chile (optional), seeds and ribs removed and finely chopped
> One 19-ounce package silken tofu, well drained
> ¼ cup lecithin granules
> 2 tablespoons corn oil or flaxseed oil
> 2 tablespoons mellow (light-colored) miso, 1 tablespoon Vege-Sal, or 1 ½ teaspoons salt
> 1 tablespoon Daylily Wine (page 69) or sherry
> 1 teaspoon hot paprika
> 1 teaspoon fennel seeds
> ½ teaspoon turmeric
> 1 teaspoon freshly ground yellow mustard seeds (½ teaspoon seeds)
> ¼ teaspoon freshly ground fenugreek seeds
> 2 cups cooked millet
> 1 cup fresh Bread Crumbs (page 40)

1. Preheat the oven to 350 degrees.

2. Heat the olive oil in a medium-size skillet over medium heat. Add the mushrooms, ramp bulbs, garlic, and chile and cook, stirring, for 5 minutes.

3. In a food processor, combine the tofu, lecithin, corn oil, miso, wine, paprika, fennel seeds, turmeric, and ground yellow mustard and fenugreek seeds and process until smooth.

4. Combine the puréed mixture with the cooked millet and bread crumbs in a large bowl. Stir in the sautéed vegetables. Shape the mixture into 12 patties, place them on an oiled cookie sheet, and bake them until they are lightly browned underneath, about 45 minutes, turning them halfway through the baking time.

5. Serve the patties with Sea Rocket Tartar Sauce (page 249), Healthy Hollandaise Sauce (page 130), Wild Tomato Sauce (page 94), Homemade Ketchup (page 37), or French Mushroom Sauce (page 346).

MAKES 12

LAMB'S-QUARTERS
Chenopodium album

HERE'S A VIRTUALLY ODORLESS, BRANCHING plant that grows 3 to 10 feet tall with stalked, alternate, diamond-shaped leaves that are up to 4 inches long and are whitish underneath. Dense spikes of tiny, ball-shaped, greenish flowers grow from the leaf axils (where leaves and stem join) and the upper plant in summer and fall. The flowers turn reddish in the fall and become filled with tiny black seeds. Lamb's-quarters grows from spring to fall on disturbed soil, in fields, along roadsides and trailsides, at the edges of woods, in vacant lots, urban parks, and backyards throughout the United States.

The leaves taste better than spinach, a related plant you can substitute for lamb's-quarters in the following recipes. Use the leaves raw or cooked. You can steam them, sauté them, or simmer them in soups. They cook in 5 to 10 minutes. You can also harvest the seeds and use them like a grain, but this is very labor intensive work.

LAMB'S-QUARTERS SPREAD

Lamb's-quarters is better than spinach, its relative, both for flavor and nutrition. And it contributes greatly to the flavor of this spread.

> *2 cloves garlic, peeled*
> *1 small red onion, peeled*
> *2 cups lamb's-quarters leaves*
> *1 ripe avocado, peeled and pitted*
> *1 cup walnuts*
> *One 6-ounce jar low-sodium pitted olives, drained*
> *3 tablespoons hedge mustard leaves or seedpods (page 78)*
> *2 tablespoons mellow (light-colored) miso*
> *1 tablespoon chili paste or 1 teaspoon cayenne pepper, or to taste*

1. Chop the garlic in a food processor or by hand. Add the onion and chop.

2. Add the remaining ingredients and process or chop until finely chopped. Lamb's-Quarters Spread will keep, tightly covered, in the refrigerator for 5 to 7 days.

MAKES 2½ CUPS

LAMB'S-QUARTERS LASAGNA NOODLES

Lamb's-quarters makes these lasagna noodles green and tasty. If you have a pasta machine (or a rolling pin and some patience), you'll love this pasta with any of the sauces in this book.

> ¾ cup plus 2 tablespoons water
> ¾ cup cooked lamb's-quarters
> 3 ⅓ cups (1 pound) sweet brown rice flour and
>   3 ⅓ cups (1 pound) buckwheat flour, or
>   2 pounds any whole-grain flour
> 2 teaspoons dried sage, finely crumbled
> 2 teaspoons dried oregano, finely crumbled
> 2 teaspoons dried waterleaf (page 105) or parsley,
>   finely crumbled
> ½ cup olive oil

1. In a blender, combine the water and lamb's-quarters and process until smooth.
2. In an electric pasta machine, combine the flour and dried herbs. Add 6 tablespoons of the olive oil and mix. Add the puréed lambs-quarters and knead the dough in the machine.
3. Use a lasagna die to turn out lasagna or cut the pasta by hand.
4. In a large pot of rapidly boiling salted water with the remaining 2 tablespoons olive oil, boil the pasta until it is *al dente*, about 7 minutes.

MAKES 54 LASAGNA NOODLES;
SERVES 5 TO 6

WILDMAN'S LASAGNA

When I omitted all dairy products from my diet in 1990, lasagna, an Italian favorite of baked layers of pasta, tomato sauce, and cheese, seemed forever out of my reach. Now I've created the dairy-free cheeses that I write about in this book, and at the moment of writing this, my mouth is watering as I wait for my first lasagna in many years to emerge from the oven.

> 5 ¼ cups Wild Tomato Sauce (page 94)
> ½ pound Lamb's-Quarters Lasagna Noodles
>   (opposite), uncooked
> 2 ½ cups Tofu Grated Cheese (page 32)
> 2 cups Tofu Cream Cheese (page 30)

1. Preheat the oven to 350 degrees.
2. Thinly cover the bottom of an oiled 12¼ x 9 x 2-inch baking dish with some of the tomato sauce.
3. Repeatedly layer the pasta, tomato sauce, Tofu Grated Cheese, and Tofu Cream Cheese until you've used up all ingredients, ending with the grated cheese.
4. Bake the lasagna until it is bubbly and the top is slightly browned, 45 to 60 minutes.

SERVES 6

TEMPEH AND LAMB'S-QUARTERS

When Emily, a participant of my tours, found huge quantities of lamb's-quarters growing on mounds of bulldozed soil on one of my tours in Brooklyn's Prospect Park, she combined this wild vegetable with tempeh (fermented soy cake, which is available in health food stores and Asian specialty stores) to share with her boyfriend for dinner. Here's her creation. Serve this dish as a main course or a side dish.

> 2 tablespoons olive oil
> 1 medium-size onion, chopped
> Two 8-ounce packages tempeh, cut into thin strips
>   or squares

2 cloves garlic, minced

One 2-inch piece fresh ginger, peeled and minced

¼ teaspoon dried basil, finely crumbled

⅛ teaspoon crushed red pepper, or to taste

*1 tablespoon Bragg's Liquid Aminos or tamari soy
sauce*

1 teaspoon brown rice vinegar

4 cups lamb's-quarters leaves

1. Heat the olive oil in a large skillet over low heat.
Add the onion, and cook, stirring, until it is translucent, about 10 minutes. Add the tempeh, garlic, ginger, basil, red pepper, Bragg's, and vinegar. Cook, stirring occasionally, until the tempeh is light brown on
both sides.

2. Stir in the lamb's-quarters, cover, and cook until
the lamb's-quarters are wilted, about 5 more minutes.
Serve hot, over rice, if desired.

SERVES 4 TO 6

WILD PINE NUT

Pinus species

P INES ARE FAMILIAR TREES WITH LONG, NARROW,
cylindrical needles and a familiar pine smell
(yews, *Taxus* species, which are poisonous, have short,
flat needles and no odor). In the late summer and fall,
the familiar cones containing seeds fall to the earth.
All you can do with East Coast pines is snip the needles into small pieces with scissors and steep them to
make tea (the seeds are minuscule), but the cones of
several West Coast species contain pine nuts, which
you can remove from their shells and eat raw or cooked.
They're similar to Italian pignoli nuts, with a high fat

content and wonderful flavor. Look for pinyon pines
in the mountains, in forests, and on hillsides.

TARATOR SAUCE

Turkish cuisine is usually mildly seasoned, but there
are exceptions: This uncharacteristically strong-tasting Levantine answer to pesto gets an extra kick from
American black walnuts, tempered with the mellow
flavor of wild pine nuts. You can serve it as a sauce or
condiment with vegetables, beans, or pasta, or on
bread or popcorn.

4 cloves garlic, peeled

¼ cup fresh dill leaves

½ cup black walnuts (page 375)

½ cup wild pine nuts

½ cup brown rice vinegar

½ teaspoon Vege-Sal or ¼ teaspoon salt, or to taste

¼ teaspoon Tabasco sauce, or to taste

1. In a food processor, chop the garlic and dill.
2. Add the remaining ingredients and process until
finely chopped. Tarator Sauce will keep, tightly covered, in the refrigerator for up to 2 weeks.

MAKES 1⅓ CUPS

WILD RISOTTO

This traditional Italian rice and cheese dish is even
better with homemade tofu cheese and wild pine nuts.

4 cups cooked brown rice or other grains

2 cups Tofu Grated Cheese (page 32)

2 cups wild pine nuts

½ teaspoon paprika

1. Preheat the oven to 350 degrees.

2. Mix the rice with 1 cup of the Tofu Grated Cheese and the pine nuts in a 3-quart oiled casserole dish.

3. Top with the remaining Tofu Grated Cheese and sprinkle on the paprika. Bake the risotto, uncovered, until it is lightly browned on top, about 40 minutes.

SERVES 6

WILD PINE NUT ICE CREAM

Pine nuts make anything taste good, so it's no surprise that they lend themselves to natural ice cream so well.

> 2½ cups soy milk or nut milk
> ½ cup canola oil
> ½ cup drained silken tofu
> ½ cup raw cashews
> ¼ cup lecithin granules
> ¼ cup vegetable glycerin, honey, barley malt, or rice syrup
> ½ cup pitted dates
> 2 teaspoons vanilla extract
> ½ teaspoon freshly grated nutmeg
> ¼ teaspoon praline extract (optional)
> ¼ teaspoon crème de menthe extract (optional)
> 1 teaspoon liquid stevia (optional)
> 1 cup wild pine nuts

1. In a blender, combine all the ingredients, except for ½ cup of the pine nuts, and process until smooth.

2. Chill the mixture (or begin with chilled ingredients) if required by your ice cream machine.

3. Pour the mixture into the ice cream machine along with the remaining ½ cup pine nuts and freeze according to the manufacturer's instructions.

MAKES 5½ CUPS; SERVES 5 TO 6

AUTUMN WILD FOODS

FALL IS THE BUSIEST TIME FOR WILD FOODS.
Those greens that are around for the entire growing
season are joined by a second burst of cold-weather
vegetables as the autumn season progresses. It's the main
season for nuts and seeds, and the best time for mushrooms.
Various fruits and berries also come into season, and root
vegetables, getting ready for next year by storing energy (food)
underground, become edible again.

ACORN

Quercus species

OAKS ARE COMMON (VARIOUS SPECIES GROW throughout North America in many wooded habitats), usually large trees with alternate, usually lobed, leaves. The early spring flowers are inconspicuous, tiny, green and hang en masse from long clusters called catkins. The familiar nuts, which ripen in autumn, are acorns. They're thin-shelled, oval, and partially surrounded by cups.

Oak trees come in two groups. The ones with blunt-edged leaves and acorns with shells that are hairless inside—the white oaks—are the ones to gather. Those trees with pointy-edged leaves and acorns with hair on the inside of the shells—the red oaks—contain so much bitter tannin that the process outlined below for getting rid of tannin isn't practical.

Acorns are among the easiest to recognize yet least appreciated food sources. These nuts have a rich, earthy flavor and a moist texture. They're good in soups and stews, and they provide a wonderful high-protein, dark flour that's superb in breads, muffins, cakes, and pie crusts.

BASIC ACORN PREPARATION

Acorns contain bitter, unhealthful tannin in varying concentrations. Here's how you leach it out and make the acorns from the white oak group of trees edible. Ignore this recipe if you're a squirrel or chipmunk, because you're already adapted to handling concentrated tannin.

1. Boil the acorns in water to cover for 1 to 2 minutes to loosen their shells.

2. Drain the acorns and, when they are cool, cut them into quarters with a paring knife. This makes them easier to shell.

3. Shell the acorns, discarding any insect-damaged, internally blackened ones. This part is labor intensive.

4. In a blender, place 1½ cups of acorns, fill the container almost to the top with water, and process until the acorns are finely chopped—the pieces should be the size of rice grains (to create more surface area for the boiling water to act on).

5. Boil the acorn bits for 5 to 10 minutes in water to cover, and taste one of the largest pieces. If it has any trace of bitterness, change the water and repeat this procedure until all the bitterness is gone and the water no longer discolors.

6. Drain the acorns and use them within a couple of days (acorns are perishable, raw or cooked), or freeze them for up to a year.

Note: You may also dry leached acorns in a food dehydrator. Or arrange them on a cookie sheet in an oven on the lowest setting and dry them overnight, with the door ajar to release the water vapor. Pack the dried acorns into a tightly closed jar to store and they will keep for a year.

When the acorns are dry, you can grind them into flour in a grain mill, spice grinder, or blender. Acorn flour will keep frozen for up to a year. One cup shelled acorns yields 5⅓ ounces or about 1⅓ cups flour.

ACORN NOODLES

Serve this recipe whenever you invite a squirrel over for dinner. Marinara or mushroom sauce is a good accompaniment.

1⅔ cups (½ pound) sweet brown rice flour and 2
cups (½ pound) oat flour, or 1 pound any
whole-grain flour

2 cups (½ pound) acorn flour (page 292)

½ cup arrowroot or kudzu

2 teaspoons freshly grated nutmeg

1 teaspoon dried marjoram, finely crumbled

1 teaspoon dried sage, finely crumbled

2 teaspoons Vege-Sal or 1 teaspoon salt

¼ cup corn oil

¾ cup plus 2 tablespoons water

1. In a pasta machine, combine the flours, arrowroot, nutmeg, herbs, and Vege-Sal.

2. Mix in the corn oil, then the water, and roll out noodles according to the manufacturer's instructions. Acorn Noodles will keep frozen for up to 6 months.

MAKES ABOUT 1½ POUNDS
(12 CUPS); SERVES 6 TO 8

ACORN TORTILLAS

Acorn flour provides these tortillas with an exceptional flavor and a delightfully soft texture. The tortillas can be filled with Tofu Cream Cheese (page 30) or Red Hot Chile Sauce (page 162) and rolled up. Sauces such as Ramp Guacamole (page 117) or Hot and Wild Sauce (page 122) are also suitable.

1½ cups sweet brown rice flour or 7 ounces any
other whole-grain flour

1 cup (¼ pound) Acorn Flour (page 292)

⅓ cup arrowroot

½ teaspoon Vege-Sal or ¼ teaspoon salt, or to taste

3 tablespoons corn oil

½ cup lukewarm water, or as needed

1. In a large bowl, mix together the flours, arrowroot, and Vege-Sal. Stir in the corn oil, then the water. Use enough water to make a soft dough that you can press into a very thin sheet between your fingers. If the dough is too sticky to work, add more flour.

2. Divide the dough into 6 balls. Roll the balls into flat, round disks about ⅛ inch thick between 2 sheets of waxed paper with a rolling pin, or flatten the dough into disks using a tortilla press.

3. Cook each disk on both sides on a very hot dry griddle until the tortilla is flecked with brown, less than 1 minute altogether. Don't overcook the tortillas or they will get hard.

MAKES 6 TORTILLAS

Note: You may keep cooked tortillas warm in a covered baking dish in an oven on the lowest setting, or refrigerate or freeze them and then reheat them briefly on a hot griddle before filling them.

Some cooks fry the filled tortillas in ¼ inch of oil, but although this tastes good, it creates a very high-fat food. A healthier alternative is brushing the outside of the rolled tortilla with corn oil and baking it for 10 to 15 minutes in a preheated 350-degree oven, and then filling it.

HOT CHEESE TACOS

When you fold or roll a tortilla around a filling, it automatically becomes a taco. Here's a simple but delicious example:

6 Acorn Tortillas (opposite)

¾ cup Tofu Cream Cheese (page 30), warmed to
serving temperature

6 to 12 tablespoons Red Hot Chile Sauce (page
162), to your taste, warmed at least to serving
temperature

1. If the tortillas are cold, heat them on both sides for a few seconds on a hot dry griddle. If the tortillas are too hard to roll, moisten them with a little water.

2. Spread 2 tablespoons of the Tofu Cream Cheese and 1 tablespoon of the Red Hot Chile Sauce on each tortilla and roll the tortillas up.

3. If you want fiery-hot tacos, spread another tablespoon of Red Hot Chile Sauce on each rolled-up taco. Serve hot.

SERVES 6

CHIMICHANGAS

This Mexican dish consists of tortillas stuffed with vegetarian ground beef and cheese substitutes plus vegetables.

> 10 Acorn Tortillas (page 293)
> 2½ cups Red Hot Chile Sauce (page 162), heated
> 2¼ cups Tofu Ground Beef (page 164)
> 1½ cups Tofu Cream Cheese (page 30)
> 1½ cups Tofu Grated Cheese (page 32)
> 1½ cups very young dandelion leaves (page 71), chopped, or shredded lettuce
> 1½ cups field garlic (page 57) leaves, scallions, or chives, finely chopped

1. Preheat the oven to 350 degrees.

2. If the tortillas are cold, heat them on both sides briefly on a hot dry griddle.

3. Put the Red Hot Chile Sauce in a shallow pan and briefly dip the tortillas in to moisten and soften them.

4. Put 3 tablespoons of the Tofu Ground Beef in the center of each tortilla and either fold the tortilla over the filling or roll it up. Place each filled tortilla, seam side down, in a 14 x 9 x 2-inch oiled baking dish. Pour the Tofu Cream Cheese on top and sprinkle on the

Tofu Grated Cheese. Bake the chimichangas until they are hot, 15 to 20 minutes.

5. Serve the chimichangas hot, garnished with the dandelion leaves and field garlic.

SERVES 6

ENGLISH OAK MUFFINS

The Druids of ancient England worshipped the oak tree. After you've tasted English muffins made with the fruit of the oak (from *ye corne of ye aike, or aike corne,* in Middle English), you just might become a born-again Druid.

> 4 teaspoons (2 packages) active dry yeast
> ¼ cup lukewarm water
> 5¾ cups plus 2 tablespoons (1¾ pounds) sweet brown rice flour and 1 cup plus 3 tablespoons (¼ pound) buckwheat flour, or 2 pounds any whole-grain flour
> ½ cup arrowroot or kudzu
> 2 teaspoons Vege-Sal or 1 teaspoon salt
> 1 teaspoon dried thyme, finely crumbled
> 1 teaspoon dried marjoram, finely crumbled
> 1¾ cups shelled white oak acorns, leached of their tannin (page 292)
> 1½ cups soy milk or nut milk
> ¼ cup corn oil
> 1 teaspoon baking soda
> ⅓ cup yellow cornmeal

1. Dissolve the yeast in the lukewarm water.

2. In a large bowl, mix together the flour, arrowroot, Vege-Sal, thyme, and marjoram.

3. In a blender, combine the leached acorns with the soy milk, corn oil, and yeast mixture and process until smooth. In another large bowl, mix these wet ingredients with two-thirds of the flour mixture. Cover the bowl and let the dough rise in a warm place (80 to 85 degrees) for 30 minutes.

4. Mix the remaining flour mixture with the baking soda and add this mixture to the risen dough. Knead the dough briefly and shape it into 12 flat, round muffins that are 3 inches across by ½ inch thick. Dust the tops and bottoms with the cornmeal. Cover the muffins with a damp towel and let them rise for 1 hour in a warm place.

5. Cook each muffin on an oiled hot griddle over low heat until the underside is dry, about 10 minutes. Turn it over with a metal spatula and cook it until the other side is dry, about another 10 minutes. Serve the muffins immediately or let them cool on wire racks.

MAKES 12 MUFFINS

BACK-TO-THE-FUTURE CHESTER BUNS

These ancient British buns are updated with healthful, whole ingredients, and then returned to pre-Roman days with acorn flour.

2 teaspoons active dry yeast

½ cup lukewarm apple juice

1 ¾ cups water

3 ⅓ cups (1 pound) sweet brown rice flour, 2 cups (½ pound) acorn flour (page 292), and 1 ½ cups (6 ounces) oat flour, or 30 ounces any whole-grain flour

½ cup arrowroot or kudzu

1 ½ teaspoons lecithin granules

1 teaspoon Vege-Sal or ½ teaspoon salt, or to taste

2 tablespoons fennel seeds

⅓ cup plus 1 tablespoon corn oil

½ cup drained silken tofu

1 teaspoon peeled and chopped fresh ginger

1. In a small bowl, mix the yeast with the lukewarm apple juice and let it dissolve for 5 minutes.

2. In a large bowl, mix together the flours, arrowroot, lecithin, Vege-Sal, and fennel seeds.

3. In a blender, combine the yeast mixture, ⅓ cup of the corn oil, the tofu, and ginger and process until smooth. In another large bowl, stir the wet ingredients into half the flour mixture. Cover the bowl and leave the dough in a warm place to rise for 45 minutes.

4. Mix in the remaining flour mixture and knead the dough for a few minutes. Divide the dough into 22 parts, shaping each piece into a ball, and place the dough balls into oiled muffin cups, one ball of dough per muffin cup. Brush the tops of the buns with the remaining 1 tablespoon corn oil.

5. Cover the buns with a damp towel and place them in a warm spot until they have risen by 50 percent, about 45 minutes.

6. Preheat the oven to 350 degrees. Set a pan of hot water on the bottom of the oven to keep the buns from becoming too crusty.

7. Bake the buns until they pull away from the sides of the tin slightly and sound hollow when you tap them, about 40 minutes.

8. Remove the buns from the oven and let them cool on wire racks.

MAKES 22 BUNS

REFRIED ACORNS

This recipe is a wild alternative to Mexican refried beans, with acorns replacing the beans. Serve it as a side dish with other Mexican foods.

¼ cup olive oil

4 cups leached acorns (page 292)

1 medium-size onion, chopped

6 cloves garlic, chopped

4 small chiles, seeds and ribs removed and chopped

2 tablespoons chopped fresh cilantro or parsley
leaves

1 teaspoon Chili Powder (page 36)

1 teaspoon dried sage, finely crumbled

1 teaspoon freshly ground cumin

1 teaspoon dried oregano, finely crumbled

2 tablespoons Bragg's Liquid Aminos or tamari soy
sauce

1. Heat the olive oil in a large skillet over medium heat. Add all the ingredients except the Bragg's Liquid Aminos and cook, stirring, for 15 minutes.

2. Stir in the Bragg's Liquid Aminos and serve.

SERVES 6 TO 8

ACORN ICE CREAM

Leached acorns contribute their earthy, nutty quality to a variety of ice cream you'll never find at Baskin Robbins.

2 cups soy milk or nut milk

1 cup well-drained silken tofu

½ cup canola oil or safflower oil

¼ cup vegetable glycerin, honey, barley malt, or
rice syrup

2 teaspoons vanilla extract

1 teaspoon liquid stevia (optional)

½ teaspoon salt

½ teaspoon freshly grated nutmeg

¼ teaspoon freshly ground coriander seeds

2 cups leached acorns (page 292)

1. In a blender, combine all the ingredients except for 1 cup of the acorns and process until smooth.

2. Chill the mixture (or start with chilled ingredients) if required by your ice cream machine.

3. Pour the mixture into the ice cream machine along with the remaining 1 cup acorns and freeze according to the manufacturer's instructions.

MAKES 6 CUPS; SERVES 6

BUTTERNUT

Juglans cinerea

THIS NATIVE TREE, WHICH GROWS UP TO 80 feet tall, has gray bark with shallow grooves and wavy ridges. The alternate, feather-compound leaves (divided along an axis) consist of 7 to 19 paired, lance-shaped, toothed leaflets that are 2 to 4 inches long. Inconspicuous, long catkins hang from the branches in early spring, threaded with many small, green, inconspicuous male flowers. Short, even more inconspicuous green female flowers grow at the tips of the branches. In late summer or early fall, sticky, oblong, green nuts that are 3 inches long and 1¼ inches wide fall to the ground. The tree grows in wooded areas throughout eastern North America.

Let the nuts dry out and mature for a couple of weeks. They'll turn brown. Then crack them with a heavy-duty nutcracker (some are specially made for black walnuts and butternuts), a vise, a heavy hammer, or rock, and remove the nutmeat with a nutpick (you can also roast the nuts in a roasting pan first, in a preheated 250-degree oven for about 40 minutes, stirring them occasionally). Enjoy them raw or cooked.

These large, little-known nuts are at least as good as any commercially available species, as you'll realize when you taste them. Use them in any recipe that calls for nuts. You'll be nuts about them.

CORN GRUEL

This is a quick, easy breakfast cereal to which you can add any wild fruits, berries, or nuts that are in season.

5 cups water
2 cups soy milk, nut milk, or water
2 cups (12.8 ounces) yellow cornmeal
1 teaspoon salt
2 teaspoons fennel seeds
2 teaspoons vanilla extract
2 teaspoons strawberry extract (optional)
1 teaspoon ground dried wild ginger (page 111) or
    regular ground ginger
4 cups blackberries or other fruit or berries
2 cups shelled butternuts
¾ cup lecithin granules (optional)
6 tablespoons oat bran (optional)

1. Bring the water to a boil in a large, heavy saucepan.
2. Thoroughly mix the soy milk with the cornmeal. Stir this mixture into the boiling water slowly enough so that the water doesn't stop boiling and no lumps form. Add the salt, fennel seeds, extracts, and ginger, reduce the heat to very low, and simmer, covered, for 10 minutes, stirring occasionally.
3. Add the blackberries and continue to simmer, covered, for another 10 minutes, stirring occasionally. Stir in the remaining ingredients. Serve hot.

MAKES 10 CUPS; SERVES 6

BUTTERNUT OATMEAL COOKIES

These cookies blend the wonderful essence of butternuts with the flavors of oats and sweet cicely.

¾ cup raisins
1⅞ cups apple juice
3½ cups (14 ounces) oat flour
½ cup plus 2 tablespoons (3 ounces) sweet brown
    rice flour
½ cup plus 2 tablespoons freshly ground flaxseeds
    (¼ cup seeds)
1 teaspoon baking soda
1 teaspoon salt
1 teaspoon ground cinnamon
½ teaspoon freshly ground star anise
½ cup corn oil
2 tablespoons fresh lemon juice
2 teaspoons vanilla extract
1 teaspoon walnut extract (optional)
½ cup sweet cicely taproots (avoid the gnarled,
    stringy underground stems; page 92) or carrots
1 cup shelled butternuts, chopped

1. Cover the raisins with ¾ cup of the apple juice in a small saucepan and bring the pot to a boil. Remove the pot from the heat, cover, and let the raisins steep for 1 hour. Drain the raisins, reserving the apple juice. (Or soak the raisins in the apple juice overnight without heating them, and then drain them.)
2. Preheat the oven to 375 degrees.
3. In a large bowl, mix the flours, ground flaxseeds, baking soda, salt, cinnamon, and star anise together.
4. In a blender, combine the remaining apple juice, including the apple juice drained from soaking the raisins, the corn oil, lemon juice, and extracts. Add the sweet cicely and blend briefly on low speed until

the sweet cicely is finely chopped.

5. Combine the wet ingredients with the dry ingredients, being careful not to overmix. Stir in the drained raisins and butternuts.

6. Drop the dough by the teaspoonful onto 2 oiled cookie sheets. Bake the cookies until they are lightly browned underneath and a toothpick inserted in the center emerges clean, 20 to 30 minutes.

MAKES 3 DOZEN COOKIES

BUTTERNUT FUDGE

Fudge is another dessert that doesn't have to be junk food. Healthy ingredients provide the sweetness and texture. Butternuts work best in this recipe, but you can use any wild or commercial nuts.

½ cup raisins

1 cup well-drained silken tofu

½ cup Cashew Butter (page 37) or Crunchy Almond Butter (page 38)

¼ cup carob powder

1 teaspoon salt

2 tablespoons walnut oil, canola oil, or safflower oil

1 tablespoon vegetable glycerin or barley malt

1 tablespoon lecithin granules

4 teaspoons vanilla extract

1 Kentucky coffee tree seed (page 52; optional), toasted and ground

1 teaspoon butter-pecan extract (optional)

¼ teaspoon liquid stevia or 2 tablespoons honey, barley malt, or rice syrup

¾ cup shelled butternuts, toasted (page 158)

1. In a food processor, combine the raisins and process until smooth or chop very fine by hand. Add the remaining ingredients except the butternuts and

process or mix by hand until smooth. Mix in the butternuts.

2. Press the mixture into an oiled 10 x 8¼ x 2-inch baking pan and chill until set. Cut the fudge into squares and serve.

SERVES 6 TO 8

BRILL'S BAKED APPLES

Butternuts and wild ginger add a special touch to this traditional holiday treat.

STUFFING

2 tablespoons butternuts, chopped

2 tablespoons chopped walnuts

¼ cup fresh Bread Crumbs (page 40)

¼ cup raisins

3 tablespoons unsweetened blackberry juice or apple juice

¼ teaspoon liquid stevia or 1 tablespoon honey, maple syrup, barley malt, or rice syrup

½ teaspoon Blackberry Spice Wine (page 278) or red wine

½ teaspoon ground cinnamon

¼ teaspoon ground dried wild ginger (page 111) or regular ground ginger

¼ teaspoon freshly grated nutmeg

⅛ teaspoon salt

6 large baking apples

2 teaspoons arrowroot or kudzu

¾ cup unsweetened blackberry juice or apple juice

1. Preheat the oven to 450 degrees.

2. *To make the stuffing:* In a large bowl, mix all the stuffing ingredients together.

3. Core each apple with an apple corer, leaving the

bottom ⅛ inch of the core intact. Fill the apples with the stuffing and place them in an oiled 3-quart casserole dish.

4. Combine the arrowroot with the blackberry juice and pour the mixture over the apples. Bake, covered, until the apples are tender, about 35 minutes. Serve hot.

SERVES 6

BUTTERNUT-FIG ICE CREAM

If you like the combination of fruit and nuts, this ice cream is for you.

2 ½ cups soy milk or nut milk
1 cup well-drained silken tofu
½ cup canola oil
¼ cup vegetable glycerin
¼ cup lecithin granules
2 teaspoons vanilla extract
1 teaspoon liquid stevia
½ teaspoon salt
1 ¼ cups packed fresh figs
1 cup shelled butternuts

1. In a blender, combine all the ingredients, except for ¼ cup of the figs and ½ cup of the butternuts, and process until smooth.

2. Add the remaining butternuts and figs and blend very briefly on low speed, to chop.

3. Chill the mixture (or begin with chilled ingredients) if required by your ice cream machine.

4. Pour the mixture into the ice cream machine and freeze it according to the manufacturer's instructions.

MAKES 5½ CUPS; SERVES 5 TO 6

HAZELNUT
Corylus species

THESE SHRUBS GROW 10 TO 20 FEET TALL, WITH alternate, oval to heart-shaped, toothed, leaves that are 2 to 6 inches long. In late winter, male catkins a few inches long, covered with yellow pollen, hang from the twigs, while tiny crimson, petal-less female flowers, only ¼ inch across, project from their flower buds. In late summer or fall, the stalkless nuts, covered with bristly husks that are open at the tip, ripen on the twigs. Get these nuts before the squirrels do. You can find wild hazelnuts growing in thickets, woods, and landscaped parks in eastern and western North America, but not in the Deep South.

The wild nuts are similar to the ones you can buy, only smaller and tastier. They're great in any recipe that calls for nuts, and they're also excellent ground into meal and added to flour.

HAZELNUT BIRTHDAY CHEESECAKE

This cake came into being during a lonely period of my life, when there was no one special with whom I could celebrate my birthday. And I even missed my birthday myself—I had planned to bake myself a cake, but didn't get around to it until three days later. I was surprised when the tofu vanilla icing tasted like cheese. After this, I began deliberate experiments to make cheese analogs with tofu, all of which appear in this book. And my personal life has greatly improved since then, too.

CAKE

> 1 ¾ cups plus 2 tablespoons (9 ounces) buckwheat
> flour and 2 cups (9 ounces) barley flour, or 18
> ounces any whole-grain flour
>
> ¼ cup arrowroot or kudzu
>
> 2 teaspoons ground cinnamon
>
> 1 teaspoon freshly ground coriander seeds
>
> ½ teaspoon salt
>
> 1 ½ cups apple juice
>
> ½ cup corn oil or other vegetable oil
>
> ½ cup raisins
>
> Freshly grated rind of ½ lemon
>
> 1 cup shelled wild hazelnuts, chopped

ICING

> One 19-ounce package silken tofu, drained
>
> ¼ cup arrowroot or kudzu
>
> 2 tablespoons natural cherry juice concentrate
>
> 1 ½ teaspoons vegetable oil
>
> 1 ½ tablespoons fresh lemon juice
>
> ½ teaspoon salt
>
> ½ teaspoon freshly ground star anise
>
> ½ teaspoon freshly grated nutmeg
>
> ¼ teaspoon freshly ground cloves
>
> ¼ teaspoon vanilla extract
>
> ¼ teaspoon Grand Marnier extract (optional)
>
> ¼ teaspoon cherry extract (optional)
>
> ½ teaspoon liquid stevia or 2 tablespoons honey,
> rice syrup, or barley malt

1. Preheat the oven to 350 degrees.

2. *To make the cake:* Mix together the flour, arrowroot, cinnamon, coriander, and salt.

3. In a blender, combine the apple juice, corn oil, raisins, and lemon rind and process until smooth. Mix the wet ingredients into the dry ingredients, being careful not to overmix. Stir in the hazelnuts. Pour the batter evenly into an oiled 13 x 9 x 2-inch baking dish.

4. *To make the icing:* In a food processor, combine all the icing ingredients and process until smooth. Spread the icing evenly on top of the cake.

5. Bake the cake for 45 minutes. Cut the cake into 8 even slices while it is still in the pan, and place the baking dish on a wire rack to cool.

SERVES 8

HAZELNUT BISCUITS

You can make these quick, easy biscuits with wild or commercial hazelnuts and wild or commercial allspice. They're wonderful either way.

> 5 ¾ cups plus 1 tablespoon buckwheat flour or 1 ¾
> pounds other whole-grain flour, plus more for
> rolling
>
> 2 teaspoons cream of tartar
>
> 1 ½ teaspoons baking soda
>
> 1 tablespoon fennel seeds
>
> ½ teaspoon salt
>
> 1 ½ cups drained silken tofu
>
> ¾ cup corn oil
>
> 1 ½ tablespoons fresh lemon or lime juice
>
> 2 teaspoons almond extract
>
> 2 tablespoons peeled and chopped fresh ginger
>
> 1 teaspoon common spicebush berries (page 314),
> finely chopped, or freshly ground allspice berries
>
> 2 cups shelled wild hazelnuts, chopped

1. Preheat the oven to 450 degrees.

2. Mix together the flour, cream of tartar, baking soda, fennel seeds, and salt in a large bowl.

3. In a blender, combine the tofu, corn oil, lemon juice, almond extract, ginger, and spicebush berries and process until smooth. Mix the wet ingredients into the dry ingredients, being careful not to overmix.

Stir in the hazelnuts.

4. Roll half the dough into a large rectangle ½ inch thick on a floured pastry sheet with a rolling pin enclosed in a floured sleeve. Cut the dough into 8 rectangles with a pizza cutter or butter knife. Use a metal spatula to transfer the dough to an oiled cookie sheet. Repeat with the remaining dough. Bake the biscuits until they are lightly browned underneath, 15 to 25 minutes. Serve hot.

MAKES 16 LARGE BISCUITS

AUTUMN OLIVE–HAZELNUT CAKE

Neither a main course, bread, nor dessert, the nut cake went out of style at the end of the Middle Ages. It's about time we revived it, so here it is, with a wild twist.

4 cups shelled wild hazelnuts

1 cup Autumn Olive Purée (page 416) or Wild Applesauce (page 341)

1 cup drained silken tofu

¼ cup arrowroot or kudzu

5 tablespoons freshly ground flaxseeds (2 tablespoons seeds)

1 tablespoon lecithin granules

1 teaspoon ground cinnamon

1 teaspoon dried pennyroyal (page 203) or other mint, finely crumbled

½ teaspoon ground dried wild ginger (page 111) or regular ground ginger

1 teaspoon freshly grated nutmeg

½ teaspoon salt

1. Preheat the oven to 350 degrees.

2. In a food processor or ½ cup at a time in bursts in a

blender, grind the hazelnuts into a meal. Add the remaining ingredients and process until everything is evenly distributed (or mix by hand).

3. Shape the dough into 15 cakes that are 2½ inches in diameter and 1 inch thick. Place the cakes on an oiled cookie sheet and bake them until an inserted toothpick emerges clean, about 35 minutes.

4. Serve the cakes hot or cold, with Super Strawberry Jam (page 208) or Tofu Whipped Cream (page 32).

MAKES 15 LITTLE CAKES

HAZELNUT ICE CREAM

The contrast between soft ice cream, sweet raisins, and crunchy hazelnuts yields an irresistible combination.

2 cups soy milk or nut milk

1 cup well-drained silken tofu

½ cup canola oil

¼ cup vegetable glycerin, honey, barley malt, or rice syrup

2 teaspoons vanilla extract

½ teaspoon salt

1 teaspoon liquid stevia

¼ teaspoon orange extract

½ cup shelled wild hazelnuts

½ cup raisins

1. In a blender, combine all the ingredients except the hazelnuts and raisins and process until smooth.

2. Chill the mixture (or begin with chilled ingredients) if required by your ice cream machine.

3. Pour the mixture into the ice cream machine along with the nuts and raisins and freeze the ice cream according to the manufacturer's instructions.

MAKES 6 CUPS; SERVES 6

WILD PECAN

Carya illinoensis

THE PECAN IS A SPECIES OF HICKORY TREE with reddish brown bark marked with vertical ridges, and with alternate, feather-compound leaves that are 12 to 30 inches long and consist of 7 to 17 glossy, lance-shaped leaflets (for a complete description of hickories, see page 306). The smooth, thin-shelled, oblong nuts, which are 1½ to 2 inches long, grow clustered in threes and sixes. This tall tree grows in moist bottomlands in the Southeast; it is the same species as commercially grown pecans.

WILD PRALINES

Here's a healthy version of a decadent dessert from the South, based on the flavor of pecans.

2 cups drained silken tofu

2 tablespoons corn oil

2 tablespoons flaxseed oil

¼ cup arrowroot or kudzu

¼ cup fresh Bread Crumbs (page 40)

¼ cup lecithin granules

1 teaspoon liquid stevia

1 teaspoon vanilla extract

1 teaspoon praline extract

½ teaspoon butter-pecan extract

½ teaspoon salt

1½ cups shelled wild pecans

1. In a food processor, combine all the ingredients, except the pecans, and process until smooth.

2. Transfer the mixture to a large saucepan and bring the pot to a simmer over medium heat. Reduce the heat to low, and simmer for 5 minutes over low heat, stirring constantly. Mix in the pecans.

3. Press the mixture into a 10 x 6¼ x 2-inch food container and chill. Cut the pralines into 24 squares.

MAKES 2 DOZEN PRALINES

BUTTER-PECAN ICE CREAM

With plenty of fresh pecans, flaxseed oil in place of butter, and soy products replacing milk and cream, you can make an unbelievably delicious nutty ice cream in no time.

2 cups wild pecans

2 cups soy milk or nut milk

1 cup well-drained silken tofu

6 tablespoons canola oil or safflower oil

2 tablespoons flaxseed oil or corn oil

2 teaspoons vanilla extract

¼ cup lecithin granules

¼ cup vegetable glycerin, honey, barley malt, maple syrup, or rice syrup

1 teaspoon liquid stevia

½ teaspoon salt

¼ teaspoon butterscotch extract or butter-pecan extract (optional)

1. In a blender, combine 1 cup of the pecans with the remaining ingredients and process until smooth.

2. Pour half the mixture into the ice cream machine.

3. Add the remaining pecans to the mixture in the blender and blend for 1 second on low speed, or just enough to chop the nuts. Pour the mixture into the ice cream machine and freeze it according to the manufacturer's instructions.

MAKES 5½ CUPS; SERVES 5 TO 6

BUTTER BOLETE
Boletus appendiculatus

A S A BOLETE, THIS MUSHROOM GROWS ON THE ground near trees, is shaped like an umbrella, and releases microscopic spores from tiny holes or pores on the underside of the cap. This one has a brown cap that is 2½ inches to 1 foot across, with yellow pores underneath. The spores are dark olive brown. The thick, firm, yellow flesh turns blue when injured. The yellow stalk is 2 to 6 inches long and ¾ to 2½ inches thick, with a fine web pattern near the apex. It grows under deciduous trees from summer to early fall throughout North America.

This is one of the best, but least-appreciated boletes. Its buttery texture and earthy flavor make it ideal for soups, stews, and sauces. Use the cap and stems, if they are insect-free.

SLOPPY JOES
The butter bolete is another choice species from a group that produces many top-rate wild mushrooms. Added to sloppy joes, it demonstrates that even greasy American junk food can be healthy, delicious, and easy to make if you prepare it properly and with the correct ingredients.

2 tablespoons olive oil

4 cups sliced butter boletes

4 cloves garlic, chopped

4 cups Wild Tomato Sauce (page 94)

1 cup chopped Spanish Sausages (page 316; optional)

1 tablespoon Chili Powder (page 36)

1 teaspoon hot paprika

1 teaspoon freshly ground mustard seeds (½ teaspoon seeds)

1 teaspoon freshly ground black pepper (½ teaspoon peppercorns)

2 teaspoons Bragg's Liquid Aminos or tamari soy sauce, or to taste

8 Daylily Bread Rolls (page 214) or other whole-grain rolls, split in half

1. Heat the olive oil in a large skillet over medium heat. Add the mushrooms and cook, stirring, for 4 minutes. Add the garlic and cook, stirring, for another minute. Add the remaining ingredients, except the rolls, and bring the pot to a boil over medium heat, stirring often. Reduce the heat to low, cover, and simmer for 10 minutes.

2. Pour the sauce over the rolls and serve hot or cold.

MAKES 8 SLOPPY JOES

BEECHNUT
Fagus species

B EECH TREES GROW 60 TO 80 FEET TALL, WITH smooth, gray bark, and alternate elliptical, coarsely toothed leaves that are 1 to 5 inches long. In the fall, the trees litter the ground with small burrs about an inch across enclosing 2 to 3 smooth-shelled, triangular, brown nuts.

Most years, the nutshells are empty, because an insect or other agent has interfered with the nuts' development, but other years, there's a bumper crop. The nuts, no larger than sunflowers, are delicious raw, toasted, or cooked in any recipe that calls for nuts. The larger trees growing in the sun have the most nuts. The smaller offspring of such trees usually offers you nothing. That's because it's a son-of-a-beech!

Beeches are planted in landscaped parks throughout the country, and they grow in rich, moist forests and upland forests in eastern North America.

GRANOLA FROM THE WILD

The beech seems to bear an abundant crop of nuts only once or twice per decade, but when it does, you're in for a treat. Beechnuts are great in virtually any nut recipe, especially granola. Here's a basic formula you can use as a starting point for your own granola experiments. The bran and lecithin are food supplements, the former helping your digestion and the latter protecting your cardiovascular system.

5 cups rolled oats (not instant)

5 cups shelled mixed wild nuts such as beechnuts, black walnuts (page 375), butternuts (page 296), or wild hazelnuts (page 299)

2 tablespoons any combination of sweet spices or herbs such as powdered sassafras root bark (page 44), ground cinnamon, ground dried wild ginger (page 111) or regular ground ginger, dried wild mint (page 129) or other mint, freshly grated nutmeg, or freshly ground cardamom seeds, star anise, coriander seeds, or allspice berries (your choice)

½ teaspoon salt

¼ cup oat bran or wheat bran (optional)

½ cup lecithin granules (optional)

1. Preheat the oven to 275 degrees.
2. Toast the oats in a roasting pan, stirring them occa-

sionally, until they are fragrant or slightly browned, about 1 hour.

3. Toast the nuts in separate roasting pans for 20 to 40 minutes at 275 degrees, stirring often, until crisp. Each nut takes a slightly different amount of time, and having all the ingredients toasted to perfection is what makes this recipe so good, whatever your choice of nuts and seasonings. Check the nuts often so that nothing burns. When the nuts are lightly browned and crisp, they're done.

4. If desired, chop the nuts in a food processor or by hand to whatever degree of fineness you prefer.

5. Mix together the nuts, oats, and the remaining ingredients. When the granola has cooled, refrigerate it. Serve granola with soy milk or nut milk, fresh fruit in season (or dried fruit), and the sweetener of your choice. Granola from the Wild will keep, tightly covered, in the refrigerator for up to 2 months.

MAKES 11 CUPS

BEACH PLUM
Prunus maritima

THE BEACH PLUM IS A THORNLESS SHRUB THAT grows 1 to 8 feet tall with dark reddish brown, streaked bark. Stalked, alternate, oval, finely toothed leaves grow 2 to 3 inches long and ½ to 1 inch across. Showy clusters of white, radially symmetrical flowers ½ inch across cover the many branches in the spring. The display is even more impressive since beach plums usually grow in dense stands. The round, purple-black plums, powdered with a waxy, white bloom, grow up to 1 inch across, contain a hard pit, and ripen in autumn. Look for these plums in the shrubs behind any beach along the Northeast or mid-Atlantic coast.

Beach plums are smaller and tastier than any commercial plum, so I can't help eating this sweet and tart fruit when I find it. But it's also great cooked, with a sweetener or thickener. Strain out the pits with a food mill, and you're ready to use these plums in virtually any kind of dessert.

DUCK-FREE DUCK SAUCE

You can cook wild or cultivated fruits with vinegar, tamari, and a sweetener to make a superior version of this familiar sauce. Use it on Asian dishes.

2 green apples, cored and chopped

2 ripe pears, cored and chopped

1 ripe peach, peeled, pitted, and chopped

½ cup pitted beach plums

1¼ cups apple juice or a mixture of any other unsweetened fruit juices

¼ cup cider vinegar

1 tablespoon tamari soy sauce

¼ teaspoon liquid stevia or 2 tablespoons honey, barley malt, or rice syrup

1 teaspoon chopped field garlic (page 57) or wild garlic bulbs (page 160) or 2 cloves garlic, finely chopped

⅛ teaspoon freshly ground cloves

1. Place all the ingredients in a large saucepan over medium heat and bring the pot to a simmer. Reduce the heat to low, and simmer, covered, until tender, 10 to 15 minutes.

2. Carefully transfer the mixture to a blender, if desired, and chop on low speed, holding down the cover with a towel to prevent eruptions. Use the sauce hot or cold. Duck-Free Duck Sauce will keep, tightly covered, in the refrigerator for up to a week, and frozen for up to 6 months.

MAKES 5 CUPS

SWEET-AND-SOUR DELIGHT

Here's a sweet-and-sour dish that brings out the best of fresh pineapple. Homemade duck sauce makes it even better.

¼ cup apricot kernel oil or peanut oil

1½ cups texturized vegetable protein (TVP), presoaked in hot water or vegetable stock

1 medium-size yellow bell pepper, seeded and sliced into strips

1 large chile, seeds and ribs removed and chopped

2 large cloves garlic, chopped

3 ripe plantains, peeled and sliced

1 ripe pineapple, peeled, cored, and diced (3 cups)

3 cups Duck-Free Duck Sauce (opposite)

Heat the apricot kernel oil in a large skillet over medium heat, add the TVP, bell pepper, chile, and garlic and cook, stirring, for 5 minutes. Add the remaining ingredients and bring the pot to a simmer. Reduce the heat to low, and simmer, covered, for 10 minutes. Serve hot over rice or noodles.

SERVES 6

BEACH PLUM JAM

Everyone who tries beach plums loves them. When you collect more than you can consume fresh, this is a good way to preserve them for future use. You can use the jam in pies, puddings, and parfaits.

7 cups beach plums

¼ cup natural cherry juice concentrate

¼ cup vegetable glycerin, barley malt, rice syrup, or honey

8 teaspoons agar powder

1 teaspoon dried pennyroyal (page 203) or other mint, finely crumbled

1 teaspoon freshly grated nutmeg

¼ teaspoon amaretto extract (optional)

⅛ teaspoon liquid stevia

1. Place all the ingredients in a large saucepan over medium heat and bring the pot to a simmer. Reduce the heat to low, and simmer, covered, for 10 minutes.
2. Test the jam for firmness (agar's thickening effect varies according to its fineness) by putting a large metal spoon with a small amount of jam in the freezer for a couple of minutes, until the jam is chilled. If the jam is thick enough, proceed to step 3. If it's too watery, stir in more agar, simmer the jam for another 5 to 10 minutes, and test it again. If the jam is too thick, stir in some fruit juice or water and test it again immediately.
3. Pass the jam through a food mill to remove the seeds. (If you don't own a food mill, remove the pits by hand before cooking.)
4. Store Beach Plum Jam, tightly covered, in the refrigerator for up to 10 days, or in the freezer for up to a year.

MAKES 4 CUPS

BEACH PLUM PARFAIT

When you've made plenty of beach plum jam from a large harvest of fruit, use some of the jam to make this perfect parfait.

2 cups Tofu Whipped Cream (page 32)

2 cups Cashew Butter (page 37), Crunchy Almond Butter (page 38), or other nut butter

2 cups Beach Plum Jam (page 305)

¼ cup black walnuts (page 375) or regular walnuts

1. Fill about 6 wine glasses or your most attractive-looking clear cups with even layers of cashew butter, beach plum jam, and Tofu Whipped Cream, until you've used up all the ingredients.
2. Top the parfait with black walnuts.

MAKES 6 PARFAITS

HICKORY NUT
Carya species

HICKORIES ARE TALL TREES WITH ALTERNATE, feather-compound (leaves divided along an axis) leaves. Five to seven opposite, lance-shaped, toothed leaflets make up each leaf. Inconspicuous long, slender catkins of male flowers hang from the twigs in early spring, and even more inconspicuous, short, green female flowers grow from the branch tips. Ball-shaped nuts ½ to 1½ inches long, their green husks cleft partially into four parts, fall to the ground in autumn. Various species grow throughout eastern North America. The shagbark hickory tree (*Carya ovata*), which is easy to recognize because strips of bark partially peeling from the trunk make it look shaggy, has the best nuts. The pignut (*Carya cordiformis*), with rough, tight, grayish bark, is usually much too bitter to eat (unless you're a pig).

Stomp on the husks to remove the nuts. Wear

rubber gloves when handling the nuts if you want to avoid staining your fingers. Crack the nutshells with a heavy-duty nutcracker, heavy hammer, or large rock. Remove the nutmeat with a nutpick (this can be labor-intensive work in species with contorted shell compartments), and enjoy the nuts raw or cooked. Use them in any recipe that calls for nuts, and you'll be glad you did.

If you can't find hickory nuts, substitute pecans.

VEGE-TURKEY LOAF

This vegetarian stuffed turkey loaf includes wild goutweed which tastes a little like celery, and parsley, along with wild hickory nuts. All that's missing is the turkey!

CRUST

    2 tablespoons chopped fresh basil leaves or
       2 teaspoons dried, finely crumbled

    2 cloves garlic, peeled

    6 cups drained soft tofu

    ½ cup brewer's yeast

    2 tablespoons any whole-grain flour

    1 teaspoon dried thyme, finely crumbled

    1 teaspoon dried savory, finely crumbled

FILLING

    2 tablespoons olive oil

    1 cup chopped celery

    2 medium-size red bell peppers, seeded and chopped

    2 cups fresh bread cubes or cooked brown rice

    ½ cup Wild Tomato Sauce (page 94) or other
       tomato sauce

    ¼ cup fresh goutweed (page 130) or parsley
       leaves, chopped

    1 teaspoon dried rosemary, finely crumbled

    1 teaspoon dried marjoram, finely crumbled

    1 teaspoon freshly ground black pepper
       (½ teaspoon peppercorns)

    ½ cup shelled hickory nuts, chopped

    ½ cup raisins

    ½ teaspoon Vege-Sal or ¼ teaspoon salt, or to taste

    1 teaspoon sweet paprika

    Mushroom Stem Gravy (page 269) or Mock
       Turkey Gravy (page 282)

1. Preheat the oven to 350 degrees.
2. *To make the crust:* In a food processor, finely chop the basil and garlic together or chop by hand. Add the remaining crust ingredients and process (or mash by hand) until smooth.
3. *To make the filling:* Heat the olive oil in a small skillet over medium heat. Add the celery and cook, stirring, for 10 minutes. Transfer to a large bowl and mix the celery with the remaining stuffing ingredients.
4. Press two-thirds of the crust mixture into the bottom and sides of 2 oiled 6½ x 4⅜ x 2½-inch loaf pans. Pour in the filling, top with the remaining crust mixture, and sprinkle the paprika on top. Bake the loaves until they are lightly browned, about 1 hour. Serve with the hot gravy or cranberry sauce.

SERVES 6 TO 8

APPLESAUCE SPICE CAKE

This naturally delicious cake gets its flavor from both wild and commercial ingredients and flavorings.

CAKE

    2 ½ cups (14 ounces) sweet brown rice flour and
       3 ½ cups (14 ounces) oat flour, or 1 ¾ pounds
       any whole-grain flour

    ½ cup arrowroot or kudzu

½ cup plus 2 tablespoons freshly ground flaxseeds
(¼ cup seeds)

2 teaspoons salt, or to taste

1 ½ teaspoons baking soda

1 teaspoon cream of tartar

2 teaspoons ground cinnamon

1 teaspoon ground dried wild ginger (page 111) or
regular ground ginger

2 cups Wild Applesauce (page 341)

½ cup corn oil

1 teaspoon liquid stevia

2 teaspoons vanilla extract

½ teaspoon almond extract

½ teaspoon orange extract

2 cups raisins

2 cups shelled hickory nuts, chopped

¼ cup lecithin granules

8 common spicebush berries (page 314), finely
chopped, or 1 ½ teaspoons freshly ground
allspice berries

FILLING

4 large green apples, peeled, cored, and chopped

1 cup apple juice

2 tablespoons fresh lemon juice

1 ½ tablespoons agar flakes

½ teaspoon liquid stevia or 2 tablespoons honey,
barley malt, or rice syrup

1 teaspoon freshly ground coriander seeds

1 teaspoon freshly ground star anise

½ teaspoon freshly ground cloves

1. Preheat the oven to 375 degrees.

2. *To make the cake:* In a large bowl, mix together the flour, arrowroot, ground flaxseeds, salt, baking soda, cream or tartar, cinnamon, and ginger.

3. In a medium-size bowl, mix together the applesauce, corn oil, liquid stevia, and extracts. Mix the wet ingredients into the dry ingredients, being careful not to overmix. Stir in the raisins, hickory nuts, lecithin, and spicebush berries, being careful not to overmix.

4. Divide the batter between 2 oiled rectangular baking pans. Set a pan of hot water on the bottom of the oven to keep the crust soft. Bake the cakes until a toothpick inserted in the center emerges clean, 35 to 40 minutes.

5. Invert the cakes onto wire racks and let them cool.

6. *To make the filling:* Bring all the filling ingredients to a boil in a medium-size saucepan over medium heat, stirring often. Reduce the heat to low and simmer, covered, for 10 minutes, then chill.

7. Place 1 layer cake on a cookie sheet, cover it with half the filling, top it with the other layer cake, and cover it with the remaining filling.

SERVES 8

HICKORY-POMEGRANATE CRUNCH ICE CREAM

An exotic fruit and a wild nut combine here to create a sublime dessert.

1 ½ cups soy milk or nut milk

1 cup drained silken tofu

½ cup canola oil

¼ cup vegetable glycerin, honey, barley malt, or
rice syrup

¼ cup lecithin granules

2 teaspoons vanilla extract

1 teaspoon liquid stevia

1 teaspoon fresh lemon juice

½ teaspoon salt

¼ teaspoon orange extract

1 cup pomegranate seeds

½ cup hickory nuts, chopped

1. In a food processor, combine all the ingredients, except the pomegranate seeds and hickory nuts, and process until smooth.

2. Chill the mixture (or begin with chilled ingredients) if required by your ice cream machine.

3. Pour the mixture into an ice cream machine and freeze it according to the manufacturer's instructions.

4. Stir in the pomegranate seeds and hickory nuts.

MAKES 6 CUPS; SERVES 6

CHICKEN-FAT SUILLUS

Suillus americanus

THERE'S NO WAY AROUND IT—THE CAPS OF bolete mushrooms (umbrella-shaped mushrooms that grow on the ground near trees and disperse spores through pores on the underside of the cap) in the genus *Suillus* are slimy, and the chicken-fat suillus is no exception. Its slimy bright yellow to ochre, reddish streaked cap grows from 1¼ to 4 inches across. Its yellowish flesh turns pinkish brown when injured. The pore surface, which attaches to the stem or runs down the stem slightly, is yellow, although it stains brown when injured. The spores are dull cinnamon. The yellow stalk is 1¼ to 3½ inches long and ⅛ to ⅜ inch thick. As with other *Suillus* mushrooms, the upper stem is dotted, and there's a ring on the upper stalk. This mushroom grows on the ground near white pine trees in the Northeast. Other edible *Suillus* species grow throughout the country.

Some people peel skins (which sometimes cause diarrhea) off the caps, but this is unnecessary if you test yourself by eating small amounts first, and notice no ill effects. The yellow cap may remind you of chicken-fat; it has a wonderfully savory mushroom flavor. Too slimy to sauté, these are great in soups, stews, and sauces. They thicken dishes slightly, the way okra does. You can bake them, because this dries them out and concentrates the flavor, or make spreads with them. Use the caps and stems, if they are insect-free.

SUILLUS SPREAD

The okra-like mucilaginous quality of chicken-fat suillus bolete mushrooms makes them especially good for spreads. Use this on bread or as a dip.

2 tablespoons olive oil

2 cups sliced chicken-fat suillus mushrooms

1 clove garlic, chopped

1 tablespoon chopped fresh parsley leaves

1⅔ cups well-drained silken tofu

1 tablespoon mellow (light-colored) miso

1 tablespoon fresh lemon juice

1 tablespoon umeboshi plum vinegar or red wine vinegar

1 teaspoon dried rosemary, finely crumbled

1 teaspoon freshly ground caraway seeds

1 teaspoon brewer's yeast

1 teaspoon freshly ground black pepper (½ teaspoon peppercorns)

½ teaspoon turmeric

½ teaspoon hot paprika

¼ teaspoon dried savory, finely crumbled

¼ teaspoon dried thyme, finely crumbled

½ teaspoon Tabasco sauce or ¼ teaspoon cayenne pepper, or to taste

1. Heat the olive oil in a medium-size skillet over medium heat. Add the mushrooms and garlic and

cook, stirring, for 10 minutes.

2. In a food processor, combine the remaining ingredients, except the cooked mushrooms, and process until smooth.

3. Add the mushrooms and continue to process (or chop by hand) until well chopped. Suillus Spread will keep, tightly covered, in the refrigerator for 5 days.

MAKES 2 CUPS

BALSAMIC BOLETES

When you bake the chicken-fat suillus or any of its relatives with herbs and balsamic vinegar, you'll understand why people prize wild mushrooms so highly.

6 cups chicken-fat suillus caps

3 tablespoons corn oil

2 tablespoons tamari soy sauce

1 ½ teaspoons balsamic vinegar

1 ½ teaspoons dried rosemary, finely crumbled

1 ½ teaspoons dried tarragon, finely crumbled

1 ½ teaspoons freshly ground black pepper
  (¾ teaspoon peppercorns)

¾ teaspoon Tabasco sauce, or to taste

1. Preheat the oven to 375 degrees.

2. In a large bowl, mix the mushrooms with all the other ingredients.

3. Place the mushrooms cap side down on a wire rack placed over an oiled cookie sheet. Bake the mushrooms until they are lightly browned, about 20 minutes. Serve hot.

SERVES 6

MACARONI 'N' MUSHROOMS

This traditional Italian casserole is terrific with wild mushrooms, homemade tomato sauce, and Tofu Grated Cheese.

2 tablespoons olive oil, or as needed

3 cups sliced chicken-fat suillus mushrooms

4 cloves garlic, finely chopped

2 teaspoons freshly ground black pepper
  (1 teaspoon peppercorns)

1 teaspoon Vege-Sal or ½ teaspoon salt, or to taste

1 teaspoon paprika

½ pound (3 cups) homemade macaroni (use the Buckwheat Noodles recipe, page 34, and use a macaroni die) or store-bought whole-grain macaroni or other pasta

1 ½ cups Wild Tomato Sauce (page 94)

½ cup Tofu Grated Cheese (page 32)

1. Preheat the oven to 375 degrees.

2. Heat the olive oil in a large skillet over medium heat. Add the mushrooms, garlic, pepper, Vege-Sal, and paprika and cook, stirring, for 10 minutes.

3. Meanwhile, cook the macaroni for 2 minutes less than directed in rapidly boiling salted water with a dash of olive oil. Drain the macaroni in a colander and then lower the colander into a bowl of cold water to stop the cooking.

4. Spread a few tablespoons of the tomato sauce over the bottom of a 2-quart oiled casserole dish. Layer one-third of the noodles, half the mushroom mixture, half the remaining tomato sauce, one-third of the noodles, the remaining mushrooms, the remaining tomato sauce, the remaining noodles, and the Tofu Grated Cheese.

5. Bake the casserole, uncovered, until bubbly, about 25 minutes. Serve hot, with homemade bread.

SERVES 6

WILD PEAR

Pyrus communis

THIS FAMILIAR TREE, WHICH GROWS 50 FEET tall, has oval to elliptical, toothed leaves that are 1½ to 3 inches long, plus cream white flowers that are 1 to 2 inches across that bloom in early spring. Unlike the similar apple tree, the twigs and leaf undersides aren't hairy. The pears, smaller and harder than cultivated pears, ripen in early fall (although many "wild" pear trees are forgotten cultivated ones).

Use the harder pears cooked, the softer ones may be eaten raw or cooked. Even cultivated pears you find "wild" taste better than the ones you buy in the store.

WILD PEAR SOUP

Although I lead field walks in spring, summer, and fall, I'm a cold-weather person. Sometimes very hot and humid weather persists into September (when wild pears ripen), and when I go out to gather wild foods I like to bring along a Thermos of this ice-cold fruit soup.

> 6 ripe large wild pears, cored and coarsely chopped
> 4 cups unsweetened pear or apple juice
> 1 ⅓ cups drained silken tofu
> 1 ½ tablespoons vanilla extract
> 1 tablespoon chopped fresh wild spearmint (page 59) or other mint leaves or 1 teaspoon dried, finely crumbled
> ½ teaspoon amaretto extract (optional)
> ⅓ cup raw cashews or Cashew Butter (page 37)
> 2 tablespoons fresh lemon juice
> ½ teaspoon salt

1. Place all the ingredients in a large saucepan and bring to a boil over medium heat. Reduce the heat to low, cover, and simmer until the pears are tender, 5 to 10 minutes.

2. Carefully transfer the mixture in batches to a blender and process until smooth, holding down the top with a towel to prevent eruption.

3. Chill the soup completely before serving.

SERVES 6

TOFU-PEAR PUDDING

Here's another dessert that's tasty and easy to prepare. You can make this pudding with wild or commercial pears.

> 6 cups pear sauce (make this the same way you'd make Wild Applesauce, page 341) or unsweetened applesauce
> 1 cup drained soft tofu, cut into cubes
> 1 cup raisins
> 1 cup shelled raw sunflower seeds
> 1 ripe banana, peeled and sliced
> ½ teaspoon common spicebush berries (page 314), finely chopped, or freshly ground allspice berries
> ½ teaspoon freshly ground cloves
> 1 teaspoon freshly grated nutmeg

Place all the ingredients in a large saucepan and bring the pot to a simmer over medium heat. Reduce the heat to low and simmer for 10 minutes. Serve hot or cold.

SERVES 8

WILD PEARS BAKED IN CREAM

Ideal for truly wild pears, which never ripen to a completely soft state, this simple dessert also works well with slightly unripe cultivated Bosc pears, as well as other varieties.

2 pounds wild pears, cored and sliced
2 tablespoons unsweetened pear or apple juice
½ teaspoon vanilla extract
2 ½ cups Tofu Whipped Cream (page 32)
½ teaspoon ground cinnamon

1. Preheat the oven to 375 degrees.
2. In a large saucepan, mix the pears with the pear juice and vanilla and bring the pot to a simmer over medium heat. Reduce the heat to low, cover, and simmer until the pears are tender, 10 to 15 minutes.
3. Transfer the pears to a 2-quart oiled baking dish. Spread the Tofu Whipped Cream over the pears, sprinkle the cinnamon on top, and bake the pears, uncovered, until most of the liquid is absorbed and a crust has formed on top, 10 to 15 minutes. Serve hot or cold.

SERVES 6

PAWPAW

Asimina triloba

THIS SHRUBBY TREE, WHICH GROWS 10 TO 40 feet tall, has alternate, large, oblong to lance-shaped, smooth-edged, leaves that are up to 1 foot long and 6 inches across. Six-petaled, bell-shaped, dull purple flowers about 1½ inches across bloom in the spring. The fruit, which ripens in early fall, is oblong, stubby, and bumpy, like a short, fat, yellow-green, pulpy banana with large, round, hard, flattened seeds inside. Pawpaws grow in the Southeast and in botanical gardens (I gather it every year in the Brooklyn Botanical

Garden when the guards aren't looking).

Try a small amount the first time—it makes some people throw up. Peel the skin and eat the pulp like a banana, or remove the seeds and cook the pulp for about 10 minutes in any fruit recipe. Its sweet flavor, like a combination of mangoes and bananas, makes it ideal for breads and cakes.

CHILLED PAWPAW SOUP

Here's another cold fruit soup for a hot summer day.

2 cups soy milk
2 cups amazake (a sweet fermented rice concoction
  that is available in health food stores) or any
  unsweetened fruit juice
½ cup drained silken tofu
¼ cup corn oil
2 teaspoons mellow (light-colored) miso
2 teaspoons arrowroot or kudzu
1 ½ teaspoons freshly grated orange rind or
  ½ teaspoon orange extract
¼ teaspoon liquid stevia or 2 tablespoons vegetable
  glycerin, maple syrup, barley malt, or honey
1 teaspoon vanilla extract
½ teaspoon freshly grated nutmeg
¼ teaspoon freshly ground cardamom seeds
4 pawpaws, peeled, seeded, and coarsely chopped

1. In a blender, combine all the ingredients, except the pawpaws, and process until smooth.
2. Transfer the mixture to a large saucepan, add the pawpaws, and bring the pot to a boil over medium heat, stirring constantly. Reduce the heat to low and simmer, covered, for 5 minutes, stirring occasionally. Chill completely before serving.

SERVES 6

PAWPAW CRISP

Pawpaws baked with a granola-like topping will be one of the best desserts you've ever tasted.

6 cups sliced pawpaws, peeled and seeded

1 tablespoon fresh lemon juice

1 teaspoon freshly ground cardamom seeds

⅓ cup brown rice flour or 2.2 ounces any other whole-grain flour

1 cup rolled oats (not the quick-cooking kind)

1 cup walnuts, chopped

½ cup raisins, steeped for 30 minutes in ½ cup apple juice just off the boil and drained

¼ cup almond oil or vegetable oil

2 tablespoons apple juice

½ teaspoon salt

2 teaspoons ground cinnamon

1 teaspoon freshly ground coriander seeds

1. Preheat the oven to 375 degrees.

2. In a 2-quart oiled casserole dish, mix the pawpaws with the lemon juice and cardamom.

3. Combine the remaining ingredients and press them on top of the pawpaws. Bake the dessert until it is lightly browned, about 35 minutes. Chill completely before serving.

SERVES 6

PAWPAW CREAM CAKE

It is a shame that the pawpaw, with its creamy, banana-like texture and its sweet flavor, was not cultivated beginning centuries ago, as you'll certainly agree if you taste the fruit, or this cake made with it.

CAKE

1½ cups (7 ounces) sweet brown rice flour and 7⅓ cups (7 ounces) buckwheat flour, or 14 ounces any whole-grain flour

¾ teaspoon cream of tartar

1⅓ teaspoons baking soda

5 tablespoons freshly ground flaxseeds (2 tablespoons seeds)

1 tablespoon lecithin granules

½ teaspoon salt

1 teaspoon freshly grated nutmeg

¼ teaspoon freshly ground cardamom seeds

¼ teaspoon freshly ground coriander seeds

¾ cup corn oil

¼ cup apple juice or other unsweetened fruit juice

1½ teaspoons vanilla extract

½ teaspoon banana extract (optional)

½ teaspoon liquid stevia or 2 tablespoons maple syrup, barley malt, or honey

1 cup peeled and seeded pawpaws

¾ cup walnuts, chopped

PAWPAW FROSTING

1¼ cups drained silken tofu

1 cup peeled and seeded pawpaws

2 tablespoons chopped pitted dates

1 teaspoon lecithin granules

1½ teaspoons flaxseed oil or corn oil

½ teaspoon banana extract (optional)

½ teaspoon vanilla extract

¼ teaspoon orange extract

⅛ teaspoon salt

¼ cup walnuts, chopped

1. Preheat the oven to 350 degrees.

2. *To make the cake:* In a large bowl, mix together the flours, cream of tartar, baking soda, ground flaxseeds, lecithin, salt, and spices.

3. In a medium-size bowl, mix together the corn oil, apple juice, extracts, and liquid stevia. Mix the wet ingredients into the dry ingredients, being careful not to overmix. Fold the pawpaw pulp and walnuts into the batter.

4. Pour the batter into an oiled 13 x 9 x 2-inch baking pan and bake the cake until a toothpick inserted in the center emerges clean, about 30 minutes. Remove the cake from the pan by inverting it onto a wire rack, and let it cool.

5. *To make the icing:* In a food processor, combine all the icing ingredients and process until smooth. Spread the icing on top of the cooled cake. Sprinkle with the walnuts.

SERVES 6

COMMON SPICEBUSH
Lindera benzoin

THIS SPREADING NATIVE SHRUB GROWS FROM 5 to 20 feet tall, with elliptical, toothless leaves that are 2 to 6 inches long; clusters of fragrant tiny yellow flowers in early spring, and oval red berries that are about ½ inch long, with one seed inside, in the fall. The whole plant is fragrant. The leaves and twigs smell lemony, and the berries smell like allspice. This shrub grows in partially shaded moist woods, hillsides, and along stream banks throughout the eastern United States.

You can make tea with the leaves, but the berries are invaluable. I use them to season so many recipes that I no longer know how I could get along without them. They taste like allspice, only better, and they're good ground up in main courses and desserts. They're especially good with carob. You can use the whole berry—flesh, seed, and all—finely chopped or puréed in a blender. Because they're oily, store them long-term in a freezer—don't dry them. If you're a kid, observe the spicebush carefully from behind a tree, just before sunrise, and you might see the missing Spice Girl!

GARDEN SPICE SPREAD

When my friend Ed presented me with fresh culinary herbs from his garden, I combined them with common spicebush berries, plus miso and tahini for thickness, to make an exotic-tasting herb spread. Use Garden Spice Spread as an herb butter, as a spread, or in cooking.

3 cups olive oil

½ cup mellow (light-colored) miso

6 tablespoons Tahini (page 38)

¼ cup fresh dill leaves

¼ cup fresh basil leaves

¼ cup fresh parsley leaves

¼ cup fresh oregano leaves

2 tablespoons fresh rosemary leaves or 2 teaspoons dried, finely crumbled

8 common spicebush berries, finely chopped

4 cloves garlic, peeled

1 teaspoon fresh thyme leaves

In a blender, combine all the ingredients and process until smooth. Garden Spice Spread will keep, tightly covered, in the refrigerator for up to a month.

MAKES 3½ CUPS

FRENCH HERB BUTTER

Corn oil and lecithin granules provide the butter flavor, while common spicebush berries enhance the flavor of the traditional French seasonings to create an outstanding mock butter spread. If you can get your hands on fresh rosemary, tarragon, and sage, use three times the amount specified for the dried herbs. Use French Herb Butter as a spread, on popcorn, or to sauté vegetables, tofu, or tempeh.

1 ½ cups corn oil

½ cup fresh parsley leaves

2 small chiles, seeds and ribs removed, or
   ½ teaspoon cayenne pepper

3 cloves garlic, peeled

¼ cup dark-colored miso

2 teaspoons common spicebush berries, finely
   chopped

1 teaspoon hot paprika

1 teaspoon dried rosemary, finely crumbled

1 teaspoon dried tarragon, finely crumbled

½ teaspoon dried sage, finely crumbled

In a blender, combine all the ingredients and process until smooth. French Herb Butter will keep, tightly covered, in the refrigerator for up to a month.

MAKES 2 CUPS

TAHINI-SPICEBERRY DRESSING

Here's a nutty salad dressing, seasoned with berries of the common spicebush—but there's nothing common about it.

1 cup olive oil

1 cup canola oil

½ cup balsamic vinegar

¼ cup raw peanuts, toasted (page 158)

¼ cup Tahini (page 38)

¼ cup mellow (light-colored) miso

8 common spicebush berries, finely chopped

2 large cloves garlic, peeled

In a blender, combine all the ingredients and process until smooth. Tahini-Spiceberry Dressing will keep, tightly covered, in the refrigerator for up to a month.

MAKES 3 CUPS

SPICEBERRY DRESSING

Common spicebush berries are as fabulous as a seasoning in a salad dressing as they are in many other recipes.

1 cup olive oil

1 cup canola oil

¼ cup balsamic vinegar

¼ cup mellow (light-colored) miso

2 tablespoons lecithin granules

2 tablespoons brewer's yeast

1 tablespoon chili paste or ¼ teaspoon
   cayenne pepper

4 teaspoons fresh lemon juice

3 cloves garlic, peeled

4 common spicebush berries, finely chopped

In a blender, combine all the ingredients and process until smooth. Spiceberry Dressing will keep, tightly covered, in the refrigerator for up to 6 weeks.

MAKES 2 ¾ CUPS

SPICEBERRY BUTTER SAUCE

Here's an authentic-tasting nondairy mock butter sauce flavored with common spicebush berries. It's great for vegans who miss the flavor of butter, or anyone who wants a more healthful buttery spread. You can even sauté with it.

> 1 cup canola oil
>
> ½ cup flaxseed oil or corn oil
>
> 6 tablespoons lecithin granules
>
> 3 tablespoons mellow (light-colored) miso
>
> 2 tablespoons chopped fresh parsley leaves
>
> 1 tablespoon common spicebush berries (32 berries)
>
> 1 clove garlic, peeled
>
> ½ teaspoon freshly ground white pepper
>   (¼ teaspoon peppercorns)

In a blender, combine all the ingredients and process until smooth. Spicebush Butter Sauce will keep, tightly covered, in the refrigerator for up to 2 months.

MAKES 2 CUPS

BRILL'S BAKED POTATO CHIPS

Why stuff yourself with the partially hydrogenated oil and salt on commercial potato chips when you can easily create your own healthy version? The tricks for making the best potato chips are slicing the potatoes very thin, baking them at a low temperature, and checking and turning them often, so they don't burn. Serve these chips with any of the dips in this book.

> 5 tablespoons olive oil or corn oil
>
> 2 tablespoons dark-colored miso
>
> 4 cloves garlic, peeled
>
> 1 teaspoon dried rosemary, finely crumbled

> 1 teaspoon paprika
>
> 1 teaspoon chili paste or ⅛ teaspoon cayenne
>   pepper
>
> ½ teaspoon turmeric
>
> 4 common spicebush berries
>
> 4 large potatoes, very thinly sliced (the
>   super-thin slicing disk of a food processor
>   is perfect here)

1. Preheat the oven to 250 degrees.

2. In a blender or food processor, combine all the ingredients, except the potatoes, and process until smooth.

3. Coat the potatoes evenly in the purée.

4. Arrange the potatoes in a single layer on cookie sheets and bake for 20 minutes. Check the potatoes often and if any chips look like they're getting overcooked, turn them with a metal spatula or tongs.

5. Bake the potatoes until they are lightly browned and crisp on both sides, another 20 minutes. Check the potatoes often and remove any chips that are done, to avoid burning them. Eat the potato chips hot or cooled to room temperature.

SERVES 6

SPANISH SAUSAGES

Because common spicebush berries taste like allspice, they make a perfect seasoning for these meatless Spanish sausage patties, also called chorizos.

> 5 cloves garlic, peeled
>
> 6 common spicebush berries
>
> 2 ½ cups cooked lima beans, drained
>
> ¼ cup olive oil
>
> 3 tablespoons hot paprika
>
> 3 tablespoons red wine vinegar
>
> 1 tablespoon freshly ground coriander seeds

*1 tablespoon Bragg's Liquid Aminos, tamari soy
sauce, or Vege-Sal or 1 ½ teaspoons salt, or
to taste*

2 teaspoons dried oregano, finely crumbled

*2 teaspoons chili paste or 1 teaspoon cayenne
pepper, or to taste*

*2 teaspoons freshly ground black pepper
(1 teaspoon peppercorns)*

½ teaspoon freshly ground cumin seeds

*2 cups fresh cornbread bread crumbs or other
Bread Crumbs (page 40)*

1. Preheat the oven to 350 degrees.

2. In a food processor, grind the garlic and spicebush
berries together or chop them fine by hand. Add the
remaining ingredients, except the bread crumbs, and
process until the beans are mashed, or mash the ingredients together in a large bowl with a potato masher
or fork. Mix in the bread crumbs.

3. Shape the mixture into patties and bake the patties
on an oiled cookie sheet for 30 minutes, or cook them
in an oiled frying pan with a raised grill until the patties are lightly brown, about 10 minutes on each side.

SERVES 6 TO 8

WILD BRAN MUFFINS

These high-fiber muffins, seasoned with wild herbs,
are as good for your taste buds as they are for your
digestive tract.

*2 ½ cups (11 ounces) barley flour and 1 ¼ cups
(5 ounces) oat flour, or 1 pound any other
whole-grain flour*

1 cup oat bran or wheat bran

1 tablespoon ground cinnamon

1 ½ tablespoons baking soda

1 tablespoon cream of tartar

½ teaspoon salt

*½ teaspoon common spicebush berries, finely
chopped*

¼ teaspoon freshly ground cloves

*¼ teaspoon ground dried wild ginger (page 111) or
regular ground ginger*

1 ¾ cups amazake, soy milk, or nut milk

¼ cup corn oil

1 tablespoon vanilla extract

*1 teaspoon liquid stevia or 2 tablespoons honey,
barley malt, or rice syrup*

2 cups cultivated currants

¼ cup lecithin granules

1. Preheat the oven to 375 degrees.

2. In a large bowl, mix together the flours, oat bran,
cinnamon, baking soda, cream of tartar, salt, spicebush berries, cloves, and ginger.

3. In a medium-size bowl, mix together the amazake,
corn oil, vanilla, and liquid stevia. Mix the wet ingredients into the dry ingredients, being careful not to
overmix. Stir in the currants and lecithin, being careful not to overmix.

4. Oil two 12-section muffin tins or a cookie sheet.
Using your hands, divide the dough into 24 pieces,
roll into balls about 1¾ inches across, and place each
ball of dough in a muffin cup or on the cookie sheet.
Bake the muffins until a toothpick inserted in the center of one of the muffins emerges clean and the
muffins are lightly browned underneath, about 20
minutes.

5. Let the muffins cool on wire racks before eating.

MAKES 24 MUFFINS

SOURDOUGH RYE BREAD

Here's the current version of a recipe I've been making since the early 1980s, with common spicebush berries and dulse complementing the more conventional rye bread seasonings. Because I don't live where I can harvest dulse, I have to buy it.

14¾ cups plus 2 tablespoons (3¼ pounds, 3 ounces) rye flour

5 cups lukewarm water

2 cups actively bubbling Sourdough Starter (page 42)

½ cup dulse flakes (page 174; optional)

¼ cup caraway seeds

4 cloves garlic, crushed

1 teaspoon common spicebush berries, finely chopped

1 teaspoon Vege-Sal or ½ teaspoon salt

½ teaspoon paprika

1. In a large bowl, mix half of the flour with 4 cups of the water and the Sourdough Starter. Cover the bowl loosely and allow the dough to rise at room temperature for at least 6 hours and as long as overnight. (Meanwhile, replenish your sourdough starter with 1 cup of the remaining flour and the remaining 1 cup water.)

2. Stir the remaining flour and the remaining ingredients, except the paprika, into the sourdough mixture until thoroughly mixed. Do not knead.

3. Shape the dough into loaves in 3 well-oiled 6½ x 4⅜ x 2½-inch loaf pans and sprinkle the paprika on top. Place the loaf pans inside supermarket plastic shopping bags without letting the bag touch the dough, or cover the loaf pans with damp towels, to keep the dough from drying out. Let the loaves rise for at least 6 hours and up to overnight at room temperature.

4. Preheat the oven to 350 degrees. Set a pan of water on the bottom of the oven to keep the crust soft. Bake the loaves until they pull away from the pan slightly and sound hollow when you tap them, about 50 minutes.

5. Remove the loaves from the loaf pans (running a butter knife or stiff plastic spatula along the sides to loosen the bread will make this easier) and let the loaves cool on wire racks so the bottom doesn't get soggy, or slice and serve the bread immediately.

MAKES 3 LOAVES

PEANUT SPICEBERRY BREAD

Here's a bread seasoned with common spicebush berries that all peanut lovers will appreciate. And if you're not a peanut lover, this bread will turn you into one. What spread goes best on peanut bread? Peanut butter, of course.

4 teaspoons active dry yeast

2½ cups lukewarm apple juice

4 cups plus 3 tablespoons (1¼ pounds) sweet brown rice flour and 4⅓ cups (1¼ pounds, 1 ounce) buckwheat flour, or 41 ounces any whole-grain flour

½ cup kudzu or arrowroot

½ cup lecithin granules

½ cup plus 2 tablespoons freshly ground flaxseeds (¼ cup seeds)

1 teaspoon common spicebush berries, finely chopped

1 teaspoon freshly grated nutmeg

½ teaspoon freshly ground cloves

1 teaspoon salt

1½ cups soy milk or nut milk

7 tablespoons peanut oil

2 teaspoons liquid stevia

⅔ cup Crunchy Peanut Butter (page 38)

1 teaspoon sweet paprika

1. Dissolve the yeast in the apple juice for 5 minutes.

2. In a large bowl, mix together the flours, kudzu, lecithin, ground flaxseeds, spicebush berries, nutmeg, cloves, and salt.

3. In a medium-size bowl, mix together the soy milk, 6 tablespoons of the peanut oil, the yeast mixture, and liquid stevia. Mix the wet ingredients into the dry ingredients.

4. Mix in the peanut butter and knead the dough briefly by hand, with an electric mixer, or in a bread machine.

5. Place the dough in an oiled bowl, cover the bowl with plastic wrap or a moist towel, and let the dough rise in a warm place (80 to 85 degrees) for 1 hour.

6. Punch down the dough, divide the dough among 3 oiled 6½ x 4⅜ x 2½-inch loaf pans, and shape it into loaves. Brush the loaves with the remaining 1 tablespoon peanut oil, sprinkle with the paprika on top, cover the loaves with a moist towel, and let the loaves rise for 1 hour in a warm place.

7. Preheat the oven to 375 degrees. Set a pan of water on the bottom of the oven to keep the crust soft.

8. Bake the loaves until they are lightly browned, 35 to 40 minutes. Let the loaves cool on wire racks before slicing.

MAKES 3 LOAVES

CAROB SAUCE

This sweet dessert sauce, based on soy milk with carob and seasonings and thickened with kudzu, gets extra flavor from common spicebush berries. Serve it hot over ice cream or other desserts, use it as a fondue and dip slices of fresh fruit into it, or chill it (with fresh fruit or nuts if desired) and serve it as a pudding.

2 ½ cups soy milk

¾ cup carob powder

¾ cup carob chips

½ cup canola oil or safflower oil

¼ cup vegetable glycerin

¼ cup lecithin granules

2 tablespoons kudzu or arrowroot

2 teaspoons vanilla extract

1 teaspoon common spicebush berries, finely chopped

1 teaspoon liquid stevia

½ teaspoon salt

¼ teaspoon almond extract

¼ cup butterscotch extract (optional)

1. In a blender, combine all the ingredients and process until smooth.

2. Transfer the mixture to a large saucepan and bring the pot to a boil over medium heat, stirring constantly. Reduce the heat to low, cover, and simmer for 10 minutes, stirring occasionally. Carob Sauce will keep, tightly covered, in the refrigerator for up to a week.

MAKES 5½ CUPS

CAROB CREAM

The best way to use carob as a substitute for chocolate is to sweeten it and include complementary flavors. This wild-seasoned, rich, healthful pudding can also be used in other recipes, such as parfaits, ice cream toppings, and icings.

½ cup pitted dates

One 19-ounce package silken tofu, well drained

½ cup carob powder

1 tablespoon vegetable glycerin, honey, barley
    malt, or rice syrup

2 teaspoons vanilla extract

1 teaspoon liquid stevia or 2 tablespoons honey,
    barley malt, or rice syrup

1 teaspoon dried wild spearmint (page 59) or other
    mint, finely crumbled

½ teaspoon common spicebush berries, finely
    chopped

¼ teaspoon freshly ground cloves

½ cup carob chips

1. In a food processor, combine all the ingredients,
except the carob chips, and process until smooth, or
chop the spicebush berries very fine by hand and combine them with the other ingredients with a whisk.

2. Mix in the carob chips.

3. Chill Carob Cream completely before serving. Carob
Cream will keep, tightly covered, in the refrigerator
for 1 week.

MAKES 3 CUPS

CAROB–PEANUT BUTTER BALLS

Here's a simple peanut-flavored candy that's made
even better thanks to the flavor of common spicebush
berries. Keep it away from kids, or there won't be any
left for you (or, if you're a kid, keep it away from
adults, for the same reason).

1½ cups Crunchy Peanut Butter (page 38)

½ cup pitted dates, chopped

¼ cup corn oil or peanut oil

2 teaspoons vanilla extract

1½ cups dry Bread Crumbs (page 40)

1 teaspoon liquid stevia

½ teaspoon common spicebush berries, finely
    chopped

¼ teaspoon freshly ground coriander seeds

¼ teaspoon salt

½ cup carob powder

1. Mix all the ingredients, except the carob powder,
together in a medium-size bowl and roll the mixture
into balls 1½ inches in diameter.

2. Roll each ball in the carob powder to coat. Chill
completely before serving.

MAKES 16 BALLS

CAROB-CHIP SPICE COOKIES

Wild herbs make these healthful, chocolate-like cookies so good that it's hard not to feel guilty when you
eat them. I always make a double batch so I can stash
away a supply in the freezer.

1¾ cups plus 2 tablespoons (9 ounces) sweet brown
    rice flour and 1⅔ cups (8 ounces) buckwheat
    flour, or 17 ounces any whole-grain flour

1 cup carob powder

2 teaspoons freshly ground star anise

1 teaspoon ground dried wild ginger (page 111) or
    regular ground ginger or 1 tablespoon peeled
    and chopped fresh ginger

1 Kentucky coffee tree seed (page 52), toasted and
    freshly ground, or 2 teaspoons ground coffee
    substitute

1 teaspoon cream of tartar

½ teaspoon baking soda

½ teaspoon salt

1 ½ cups apple juice

½ cup plus 2 tablespoons corn oil or flaxseed oil

2 teaspoons freshly grated orange rind or
   1 teaspoon orange extract

2 teaspoons vanilla extract

½ teaspoon Angostura bitters (optional)

2 cups chopped Brazil nuts or walnuts

2 cups carob chips

½ teaspoon common spicebush berries, finely chopped

1. Preheat the oven to 350 degrees.

2. In a large bowl, mix together the flours, carob powder, star anise, ginger, ground coffee tree seed, cream of tartar, baking soda, and salt.

3. In a medium-size bowl, mix together the apple juice, corn oil, orange rind, vanilla, and Angostura bitter, if you are using them. Mix the wet ingredients into the dry ingredients, being careful not to overmix. Stir in the Brazil nuts, carob chips, and spicebush berries.

4. Shape the dough into cookies with a teaspoon and arrange the cookies on 3 oiled cookie sheets. Bake the cookies until a toothpick inserted in the center of a cookie emerges clean, about 15 minutes. Let the cookies cool on wire racks.

MAKES 3 DOZEN COOKIES

SPICEBUSH-COCONUT ICE CREAM

Coconut lovers will go coconuts over this wild-herb-seasoned ice cream.

2 ⅔ cups unsweetened coconut milk

1 ¼ cups soy milk or nut milk

½ cup canola oil

¼ cup vegetable glycerin, rice syrup, barley malt,
   or honey

¼ cup lecithin granules

2 teaspoons vanilla extract

1 teaspoon coconut extract (optional)

1 teaspoon liquid stevia

½ teaspoon salt

½ teaspoon common spicebush berries

¼ teaspoon ground dried wild ginger (page 111)
   or regular ground ginger

½ teaspoon freshly grated nutmeg

½ cup unsweetened shredded coconut

1. In a blender, combine all the ingredients, except the shredded coconut, and process until smooth.

2. Chill the mixture (or use chilled ingredients) if required by your ice cream machine.

3. Stir in the coconut, and pour the mixture into the ice cream maker. Freeze it according to the manufacturer's instructions.

MAKES 5½ CUPS; SERVES 5 TO 6

CHICKEN MUSHROOM
Laetiporus sulfureus

THIS IS A POLYPORE—A SHELF-LIKE MUSHROOM with pores under the cap that grows on wood. The overlapping, flat, fan-shaped, bright orange to salmon caps are 2 to 12 inches across. The tiny pores may be bright sulfur yellow or white (there are two subspecies). The spores are white. The flesh is white, light yellow, or pale salmon, and it looks like chicken meat. It's soft when the mushroom is young (which is when you should collect it for food), and later becomes dry and crumbly (when the mushroom is too old to eat). And there are no poisonous look-alikes, although people sometimes confuse the dull orange-brown Berkeley's polypore (see page 199) with the chicken mushroom. Also called the sulfur shelf, this mushroom grows on trees, logs, or stumps, deciduous or coniferous, across North America. Most common in autumn, it also appears in spring and summer.

The chicken mushroom is one of the most common, the largest (I've found logs covered with 50-pound mushrooms), and the easiest to recognize choice species in the United States. It tastes like chicken, especially if it is prepared with customary chicken seasonings. Properly prepared, it's wonderful. To adapt it to traditional chicken recipes, include a source of protein (that is, grains or beans) to make the dish filling, plus some olive oil or vegetable oil, because unlike chicken, the mushroom contains no fat.

Unless the mushroom is so young and tender that it almost drips with juice, it's better to cook it in moist heat (that is, in soups, stews, or in grains) than to cook it in oil. Beginners seem to be subject to an irresistible compulsion to sauté middle-aged chicken mushrooms the first time they find them, making the mushrooms as tough as leather. That may be why many mushroom hunters in Europe wrongly consider this mushroom inferior.

The chicken mushroom freezes well after you cook it, but I've never had success dehydrating it because it seems to retain a papery texture when you try to rehydrate it.

VEGETARIAN CHICKEN SALAD

I was so proud to have made an authentic vegetarian chicken salad, and so disappointed when a journalist doing a story on me and having dinner in my home refused to eat it. He was a vegetarian, too. The prob-

lem was that the chicken mushroom made the mock chicken salad taste too much like the real thing!

2 cups steamed chicken mushrooms (see note below), chopped

1 cup thinly sliced celery

1 small head romaine lettuce, washed, spun dry, and torn into pieces

6 tablespoons sliced low-sodium pitted olives

6 tablespoons almonds, toasted (page 158) and slivered

½ cup Wild Mustard Seed Mayonnaise (page 206)

3 tablespoons finely chopped field garlic leaves (page 57), chives, or scallions

In a large bowl, mix together all the ingredients and serve immediately.

SERVES 4 TO 6

Note: To steam the mushrooms, place them on a steaming rack over boiling water or stock, cover the pot, and let the mushrooms steam for 20 minutes.

CHICKEN MUSHROOM FRUIT SALAD

This combination of mushrooms and fruit is unusual but good.

2 cups steamed sliced chicken mushrooms (see note above), diced

2 cups cored and diced green apples (2 large apples)

½ cup sliced celery

½ cup walnuts, chopped

6 tablespoons raisins

½ cup Wild Mustard Seed Mayonnaise (page 206)

In a large bowl, stir all the ingredients together until well combined. Chill the salad completely before serving.

SERVES 6

CHICKEN FRUIT SALAD

Simply cooked chicken mushrooms and fresh fruit with a lemon dressing balance themselves perfectly in this feast, which should be enjoyed cold.

SALAD

1 tablespoon sesame oil

1 ¾ cups packed very young, tender chicken
    mushrooms, sliced

1 teaspoon freshly ground fennel seeds or dried
    rosemary, finely crumbled

¼ teaspoon salt

1 celery stalk, sliced

1 cup walnuts, chopped

½ cup raisins

DRESSING

6 tablespoons water

6 tablespoons drained silken tofu

2 tablespoons lecithin granules

1 tablespoon corn oil

½ teaspoon dried wild spearmint (page 59) or
    other mint, finely crumbled

¼ cup fresh lemon juice

¼ teaspoon salt

1. *To make the salad:* Heat the sesame oil in a medium-size skillet over medium heat. Add the chicken mushrooms, fennel, and salt and cook, stirring, for 10 to 15 minutes or until tender.

2. *To make the dressing:* In a blender or food processor, combine the dressing ingredients and process until smooth.

3. Toss the chicken mushrooms and dressing with the remaining salad ingredients. Serve chilled.

SERVES 6

CHICKEN SANDWICH FILLING

Once you've tasted a chicken sandwich made with top-grade chicken mushrooms, you'll never want to bother with the old-fashioned kind of chicken sandwich again. It's even better with homemade mayonnaise and homemade bread. And you can also use the filling as a vegetarian chicken salad.

2 tablespoons olive oil

2 cups very young, tender chicken mushrooms cut
    into ½-inch-thick slabs

2 teaspoons fresh lemon juice

½ teaspoon Vege-Sal or ¼ teaspoon salt

1 ¾ cups lettuce torn into bite-size pieces

½ cup Wild Mustard Seed Mayonnaise (page 206)

1 small red onion, sliced

¾ cup sliced ripe tomatoes, olives, or pimientos

1 ½ tablespoons Fakin' Bacon Bits (optional)

12 to 16 slices toasted homemade whole-grain
    bread or commercial bread, or as needed

1. Heat the olive oil in a medium-size skillet over medium heat. Add the chicken mushrooms and fry them until they are lightly browned underneath, about 3 minutes. Turn the mushrooms over with a metal spatula or fork, sprinkle them with the lemon juice and Vege-Sal, and continue to fry them until the other side is lightly browned.

2. Dice the cooked mushroom slices and mix them with the remaining ingredients, except the bread.

3. Put a generous amount of filling between 2 slices of

toasted bread and repeat until you've used up all the ingredients and all the bread.

MAKES 6 TO 8 SANDWICHES

CHICKEN ASPIC

Vegetarians need not give up chicken with so many huge chicken mushrooms popping up on living and dead trees throughout the country every year. This gelled chicken salad, made with agar, a gelatin-like seaweed, will fool anyone who is not familiar with this mushroom.

> 3½ cups Vegetable Stock (page 40)
>
> 1 tablespoon agar powder
>
> ½ cup Wild Mustard Seed Mayonnaise (page 206)
>
> 1 tablespoon tamari soy sauce, or to taste
>
> ¼ teaspoon cayenne pepper, or to taste
>
> 2 cups steamed sliced chicken mushrooms (see
>   note on page 322)
>
> 1 celery stalk, sliced
>
> 2 Jerusalem artichokes or 1 large carrot, sliced
>
> 1 daikon (an Asian radish available in ethnic
>   stores and supermarkets), sliced
>
> 1 medium-size green bell pepper, seeded and sliced
>   into strips
>
> 1 small red onion, chopped
>
> 2 tablespoons chopped fresh parsley leaves
>
> 4 cups wild or cultivated salad greens, torn or
>   chopped, for garnish

1. Place the stock and agar in a medium-size saucepan and bring the pot to a boil over medium heat. Reduce the heat to low, and simmer for 5 minutes. Test the consistency by putting a spoonful of stock in the freezer for a few minutes. If the stock is too watery, add more agar. If it's too solid, add more stock and test the consistency again.

2. In a blender, combine the mayonnaise, tamari, cayenne, and gelled stock and process until smooth. Transfer to a large bowl and combine this liquid with the remaining ingredients, except the salad greens.

3. Pour the mixture into a 12-cup bowl or mold and chill.

4. Briefly place the mold in a bowl of hot water to loosen the aspic. Invert the mold over a platter, garnish with the salad greens, and serve.

SERVES 6 TO 8

INDIAN-STYLE VEGETABLE STEW

Here's a simple Indian stew that includes two kinds of wild mushrooms.

> 2 cups Vegetable Stock (page 40)
>
> ¼ cup olive oil
>
> 5 cups diced carrots
>
> 4 celery stalks, diced
>
> 2 cups honey mushrooms (page 356) or shiitake
>   mushrooms
>
> 1 cup drained and diced firm tofu
>
> 1 medium-size onion, minced
>
> 2 cloves garlic, crushed into a paste
>
> ½ cup buckwheat flour or 2.4 ounces any other
>   whole-grain flour
>
> 7 cups sliced chicken mushrooms
>
> 3 tablespoons Curry Powder (page 112)
>
> 2 dozen low-sodium pitted olives
>
> ¼ cup fresh parsley leaves, chopped

1. In a small saucepan, bring the stock to a boil.

2. Meanwhile, heat the olive oil in a large skillet over medium heat. Add the carrots, celery, honey mushrooms, tofu, onion, and garlic and cook, stirring, for

10 minutes. Stir in the flour and cook, stirring, for another 2 minutes. Stir in the chicken mushrooms, curry powder, and stock, reduce the heat to low, and simmer, covered, for 10 minutes, stirring occasionally. **3.** Add the olives and parsley and simmer for another 10 minutes. Serve hot over rice or with Indian bread.

SERVES 8

cook, stirring, for 10 minutes. Transfer to a stockpot, add the garlic and cook, stirring, for another 2 minutes. Add the remaining ingredients and bring the pot to a boil over medium heat, stirring often. Reduce the heat to low and simmer, covered, for another 10 minutes. **2.** Serve the stew hot, with grains or bread.

SERVES 6 TO 8

OLIVE–CHICKEN MUSHROOM STEW

This hearty recipe is good to make in the winter when you have precooked chicken mushrooms stockpiled in the freezer.

2 to 4 tablespoons olive oil, or as needed

3 cups sliced carrots

2 cups drained and grated extra-firm tofu

1 cup chopped onions or shallots

1 cup chopped celery

2 cloves garlic, finely chopped

2 cups steamed sliced chicken mushrooms (see note on page 322), chopped

1 cup soy milk or nut milk

1 cup Vegetable Stock (page 40)

½ cup low-sodium pitted olives, drained

2 tablespoons chopped fresh dill

1 tablespoon chili paste or 1 teaspoon cayenne pepper, or to taste

1 tablespoon tamari soy sauce

1 tablespoon Wild Crabapple Blossom Wine (page 425) or white wine

1 teaspoon sweet paprika

½ teaspoon dried tarragon, finely crumbled

1. Heat the olive oil in a large skillet over medium heat. Add the carrots, tofu, onion, and celery and

CHICKEN VEGETABLE STEW

Chicken mushrooms transform a simple vegetable stew into something special.

2 tablespoons olive oil

½ cup texturized vegetable protein (TVP)

2 medium-size red onions, chopped

3 celery stalks, sliced

1 medium-size red bell pepper, seeded and sliced into strips

1 medium-size carrot, sliced

2 cloves garlic, chopped

1 small chile, seeds and ribs removed and chopped, or ¼ teaspoon cayenne pepper, or to taste

½ teaspoon dried tarragon, finely crumbled

½ teaspoon dried oregano, finely crumbled

¼ teaspoon dried sage, finely crumbled

¼ teaspoon hot paprika

2 teaspoons kudzu or arrowroot

2 cups Vegetable Stock (page 40)

1 tablespoon tamari soy sauce, or to taste

1 teaspoon Vegetarian Worcestershire Sauce (page 56)

2 cups steamed sliced chicken mushrooms (see note on page 322)

Half of a 6-ounce jar low-sodium pitted olives, drained

½ cup raw cashews

2 cups Tofu Grated Cheese (page 32)

1. Heat the olive oil in a large skillet over medium heat. Add the TVP, onions, celery, bell pepper, carrot, garlic, chile, tarragon, oregano, sage, and paprika and cook for 10 minutes, stirring.

2. Mix the kudzu with the stock in a large saucepan, using a whisk.

3. Add the sautéed ingredients to the kudzu mixture, along with all the remaining ingredients except the Tofu Grated Cheese and bring the pot to a boil over medium heat, stirring often. Reduce the heat to low, cover, and simmer for 10 minutes.

4. Stir in the Tofu Grated Cheese. Serve hot with whole grain bread or brown rice.

SERVES 6

ＣOQ AU VIN

Here's a classic French dish adapted to include the chicken mushroom.

3 tablespoons olive oil, or as needed

3 cups water chestnuts, sliced

4 large onions, chopped

6 cloves garlic, crushed into a paste

2 ½ tablespoons peeled and finely chopped fresh ginger

4 common spicebush berries (page 314), finely chopped, or ½ teaspoon freshly ground allspice berries

18 cups diced chicken mushrooms

2 teaspoons dried thyme, finely crumbled

2 teaspoons dried rosemary, finely crumbled

2 teaspoons sweet paprika

2 teaspoons freshly ground white pepper (1 teaspoon peppercorns)

1 teaspoon freshly grated nutmeg

2 teaspoons Vege-Sal or 1 teaspoon salt, or to taste

Two 16-ounce packages firm tofu, drained and diced

2 cups sweet brown rice

2 cups Black Locust Blossom Wine (page 182) or white wine

2 cups liquid from the drained olives, Vegetable Stock (page 40), or water

1 tablespoon chopped fresh goutweed (page 130) or parsley leaves

1 teaspoon dried marjoram, finely crumbled

1 ½ teaspoons freshly ground celery seeds (1 teaspoon seeds)

4 medium-size ripe tomatoes, sliced

Two 6-ounce cans low-sodium pitted olives, drained, reserving brine if desired

1. Preheat the oven to 350 degrees.

2. Heat the olive oil in a large skillet over medium heat. Add the water chestnuts, onions, garlic, ginger, and spicebush berries and cook, stirring, for 10 to 15 minutes.

3. Remove the pot from the heat and mix the cooked vegetables with the chicken mushrooms, thyme, rosemary, paprika, white pepper, nutmeg, 1 teaspoon of the Vege-Sal, and the tofu.

4. Mix together the rice, wine, olive liquid or stock, goutweed, marjoram, celery seed, and the remaining 1 teaspoon Vege-Sal in a 3-quart oiled casserole dish.

5. Spoon the chicken mushroom mixture over the rice mixture and top with tomatoes and olives. Bake the casserole, covered, until most of the liquid is absorbed, about 1 hour. Serve hot.

SERVES 8

CREOLE CHICKEN GUMBO

Sassafras is a widespread tree that's very easy to recognize, and the powdered dried leaves, used to create filé powder, are available in gourmet stores and herb stores. The addition of chicken mushrooms makes this traditional sassafras-thickened stew special.

1 cup plus 1 tablespoon barley flour or 4 ounces
   any other whole-grain flour
5 tablespoons freshly ground flaxseeds
   (2 tablespoons seeds)
1 tablespoon lecithin granules
1 ½ teaspoons brewer's yeast
½ tablespoon bayberry leaves (page 185) or bay
   leaves, freshly ground
1 teaspoon sweet paprika
1 teaspoon ground chile or ¼ teaspoon cayenne
   pepper, or to taste
½ teaspoon dried oregano, finely crumbled
½ teaspoon dried thyme, finely crumbled
½ teaspoon dried marjoram, finely crumbled
1 teaspoon freshly ground yellow mustard seeds
   (½ teaspoon seeds)
½ teaspoon freshly ground cumin seeds
1 teaspoon Vege-Sal or ½ teaspoon salt, or to taste
1 teaspoon freshly ground white pepper
   (½ teaspoon peppercorns), or to taste
¾ cup olive oil or peanut oil
4 cups diced chicken mushrooms
2 medium-size potatoes, sliced
1 celery stalk, sliced
1 medium-size red onion, sliced
1 large carrot, sliced
4 cloves garlic, chopped
8 cups Vegetable Stock (page 40)
¼ cup filé powder (ground dried young sassafras
   leaves, page 45)

1. In a medium-size bowl, mix together the flour, ground flaxseeds, lecithin, brewer's yeast, bayberry leaves, paprika, ground chile, oregano, thyme, marjoram, ground mustard and cumin seeds, Vege-Sal, and white pepper.

2. Heat 2 tablespoons of the olive oil in a large skillet over medium. Add the chicken mushrooms and cook, stirring, for several minutes. Stir in half the flour mixture.

3. Add the potatoes, celery, onion, carrot, garlic, the remaining 10 tablespoons olive oil, and the remaining flour mixture and cook for 10 minutes.

4. Meanwhile, in a stockpot, bring the Vegetable Stock to a boil.

5. Carefully transfer the mushroom mixture to the stockpot, slowly stir, and bring the pot to a boil over medium heat, stirring constantly. Reduce the heat to low, cover, and simmer for 10 minutes, stirring often.

6. Remove the pot from the heat and stir in the filé powder. Serve Creole Chicken Gumbo hot over brown rice.

SERVES 6 TO 8

CHICKEN IN A HURRY

When you have pounds and pounds of this choice but perishable mushroom to prepare in a hurry, here's a method that is as good as it is quick. If you use very fresh, young chicken mushrooms, you'll make wild mushroom converts of anyone who tries this side dish.

¼ cup olive oil
Juice of 1 lemon
6 cloves garlic, finely chopped
3 tablespoons tamari soy sauce
1 tablespoon chili paste or any hot sauce
1 tablespoon paprika
12 cups sliced chicken mushrooms

1. Preheat the oven to 350 degrees.

2. In a small bowl, mix together the olive oil, lemon juice, garlic, tamari, chili paste, and paprika.

3. Place the chicken mushrooms in a 13 x 9 x 2-inch oiled baking dish, toss to coat well with the sauce, and bake, uncovered, until most of the liquid has cooked off, about 45 minutes. Serve hot.

SERVES 6

BAKED CHICKEN MUSHROOMS

No one believes how similar this mushroom is to chicken until they try it. The chicken seasonings in this dish further enhance the similarity. You may serve this as a side dish or use it in other recipes that call for chicken. It also freezes well. Be sure to use fresh, young chicken mushrooms. This species gets tough and loses flavor when it gets older. As Frank Purdue never said: "It takes a tough forager to find a tender chicken mushroom."

9 cups coarsely diced chicken mushrooms

¼ cup tamari soy sauce

¼ cup red wine vinegar

¼ cup olive oil

¼ cup red wine

2 tablespoons chili paste or 1 tablespoon Tabasco sauce

1 tablespoon paprika

1 teaspoon dried rosemary, finely crumbled

½ teaspoon dried sage, finely crumbled

1. Preheat the oven to 350 degrees.

2. Place the chicken mushrooms in a 3-quart oiled casserole dish.

3. In a small bowl, mix the remaining ingredients together and pour the mixture over the mushroom chunks. Bake, covered, for 30 minutes.

SERVES 6 TO 8

Note: You may also prepare this dish in advance and refrigerate it before baking—marinating the mushroom overnight and letting the flavors soak in.

CHICKEN MUSHROOM CURRY

This traditional-style Indian curry uses whole spices instead of curry powder, chicken mushrooms instead of poultry, and tofu with lemon juice rather than yogurt. This recipe is moderately hot. Feel free to increase or decrease the spices to taste.

SAUTÉ

2 tablespoons sesame oil

1 medium-size green bell pepper, seeded and chopped

¼ cup dried chiles, or to taste, freshly ground

5 cloves garlic, finely chopped

2 tablespoons peeled and chopped fresh ginger

2 tablespoons coriander seeds

2 tablespoons turmeric

1 tablespoon cumin seeds

1 tablespoon broken cinnamon sticks

1 tablespoon cardamom seeds

SAUCE

One 16-ounce package silken tofu, drained

½ cup Vegetable Stock (page 40) or water

Juice of 2 limes

½ tablespoon Vege-Sal or ¼ tablespoon salt, or to taste

4 cups chopped chicken mushrooms

½ head cauliflower, broken into florets

1 cup cooked lentils or beans, drained

½ cup raw cashews, coarsely chopped

¾ cup unsweetened shredded coconut

1. *To make the sauté:* Heat the sesame oil in a large saucepan over medium heat, add the bell pepper, and cook for 10 minutes, stirring often. Add the chiles and spices and cook, stirring, until the garlic is lightly browned, another 3 to 4 minutes, adding more oil if necessary. Don't let the garlic burn, or it will become bitter.

2. *To make the sauce:* In a blender, combine the sauce ingredients and process until smooth.

3. In a large pot, combine the sauce with the sautéed mixture and the remaining ingredients and bring the pot to a boil over medium heat, stirring often. Reduce the heat to low, cover, and simmer for 40 minutes, stirring occasionally. Serve over brown rice or with Indian bread.

SERVES 8 TO 10

SPICY CHICKEN MUSHROOM BAKE

Here's another wonderful recipe for the most common of all wild mushrooms. Serve it as a side dish, or use it in other recipes that call for cooked chicken. You may also freeze it.

12 cups chicken mushroom chunks

¼ cup olive oil

Juice of 1 lemon

6 cloves garlic, crushed

3 tablespoons tamari soy sauce

1 tablespoon chili paste or 1 teaspoon cayenne pepper

1 tablespoon hot paprika

1. Preheat the oven to 350 degrees.

2. Combine all the ingredients and bake, covered, in a 3-quart oiled casserole dish for 45 minutes. Serve hot.

SERVES 6 TO 8

SWEET-AND-SOUR CHICKEN MUSHROOMS

This is a Chinese sweet-and-sour recipe without unhealthful sugar, using chicken mushrooms to replace chicken.

¼ cup peanut oil, or as needed

1 tablespoon toasted sesame oil, or as needed

12 cups steamed sliced chicken mushrooms (see note on page 322)

4 medium-size red bell peppers, seeded and sliced

8 celery stalks, sliced medium-thick

5 cups snow peas, strings removed

6 scallions, sliced

2 cups walnuts

8 cloves garlic, crushed into a paste

One 29-ounce jar water chestnuts, drained

1 cup Homemade Ketchup (page 37)

⅔ cup Vegetable Stock (page 40)

1 tablespoon Five-Spice Powder (page 112)

2 tablespoons tamari soy sauce

2 teaspoons Angostura bitters

¼ teaspoon liquid stevia or 2 tablespoons honey, rice syrup, or barley malt

1. Mix the peanut oil and sesame oil together and heat over high heat in a wok or large skillet. Starting with 2 tablespoons of the mixed oil, consecutively stir-fry the following ingredients, removing each cooked ingredient and setting it aside, and adding more of the mixed oil as needed.

2. Stir-fry the red peppers for 3 minutes, the celery for

3 minutes, the snow peas for 2 minutes, the scallions for 2 minutes, and the walnuts with the garlic for 1 minute.

3. Transfer to a large pot and stir in the remaining ingredients along with the stir-fried ingredients and bring the pot to a boil. Reduce the heat to low, and simmer, covered, for 15 minutes. Serve with brown rice.

SERVES 8 TO 10

CHICKEN CROQUETTES

Chicken mushrooms provide the "meat" for these simple patties.

> 2½ cups steamed sliced chicken mushrooms (see note on page 322), finely chopped
>
> 1 cup fresh Bread Crumbs (page 40)
>
> ¼ cup arrowroot or kudzu
>
> ½ cup Béarnaise Sauce à la Brill (page 120), Wild Mustard Seed Mayonnaise (page 206), or Healthy Hollandaise Sauce (page 130)
>
> 4 cloves garlic, crushed into a paste
>
> 2 tablespoons chopped fresh parsley leaves
>
> 2 tablespoons lecithin granules
>
> 1 tablespoon chili paste or ½ teaspoon cayenne pepper, or to taste
>
> 1 tablespoon mellow (light-colored) miso, or to taste
>
> 2½ tablespoons freshly ground flaxseeds (1 tablespoons seeds)
>
> 1 teaspoon freshly grated lemon rind
>
> 1 tablespoon paprika
>
> 2 teaspoons freshly ground white pepper (1 teaspoon peppercorns)
>
> 1 teaspoon dried sage, finely crumbled

1. Preheat the oven to 350 degrees.

2. In a large bowl, combine all the ingredients and shape the mixture into 10 patties.

3. Arrange the patties on an oiled cookie sheet and bake them until they are lightly browned, about 40 minutes, turning them halfway through the baking time. Serve the croquettes hot, with any savory sauce in this book.

MAKES 10 CROQUETTES

CHICKEN MUSHROOM ALMONDINE

Chicken mushroom with broccoli, stir-fried with Asian seasonings, is a winning combination.

> 1 pound Buckwheat Noodles (page 34) or store-bought whole-grain fettuccine or other pasta
>
> 6 tablespoons toasted sesame oil
>
> 1 cup diced tender young chicken mushrooms
>
> 3 cups broccoli florets
>
> 1 tablespoon peeled and finely chopped fresh ginger
>
> 3 cloves garlic, finely chopped
>
> ½ cup Blackberry Spice Wine (page 278) or red wine
>
> ¼ cup tamari soy sauce
>
> 1 teaspoon chili paste or ¼ teaspoon cayenne pepper, or to taste
>
> ½ cup Tofu Grated Cheese (page 32)
>
> ½ cup almonds, toasted (page 158) and chopped

1. Cook the fettuccine in rapidly boiling salted water until it is *al dente*. Drain the pasta and keep it warm.

2. Meanwhile, heat the sesame oil over high heat in a wok or large skillet. Add the chicken mushrooms and stir-fry them for 2 minutes.

3. Add the broccoli, ginger, and garlic and stir-fry for another minute.

4. Add the wine, tamari, and chili paste, reduce the heat to low, and simmer, covered, for 10 minutes.

5. Toss the cooked vegetables with the drained pasta and the Tofu Grated Cheese, garnish with the almonds, and serve.

SERVES 4 TO 6

CHICKEN 'N' DUMPLINGS

This homey traditional American dish uses the most abundant, easy-to-recognize mushroom in the United States, the chicken mushroom. This mushroom is so tasty, it inspires me to enter politics: Vote for me, and I promise you two chicken mushrooms in every pot!

8 cups Vegetable Stock (page 40) or water

2 tablespoons olive oil

1 medium-size onion, sliced

1 medium-size carrot, sliced

1 celery stalk, sliced

2 small chiles, seeds and ribs removed and chopped,
*   or ¼ teaspoon cayenne pepper, or to taste*

3 cloves garlic, finely chopped

½ recipe Wood Sorrel Dumplings (page 183),
*   uncooked*

1 cup coarsely diced chicken mushrooms

2 small potatoes, sliced

1 medium-size turnip, peeled and sliced

2 tablespoons kudzu or arrowroot

1 tablespoon tamari soy sauce, or to taste

1 teaspoon dried savory, finely crumbled

¾ teaspoon freshly ground celery seeds
*   (½ teaspoon seeds)*

½ teaspoon freshly grated nutmeg

½ teaspoon freshly ground black pepper
*   (¼ teaspoon peppercorns)*

¼ cup fresh parsley leaves, chopped

1. Bring 6 cups of the stock to a boil in a large saucepan.

2. Meanwhile, heat the olive oil in a large skillet over medium heat. Add the onion, carrot, celery, chiles, and garlic and cook, stirring, for 10 minutes. Set aside.

3. Add the dumplings, chicken mushrooms, potatoes, and turnip to the boiling stock and simmer, covered, for 10 minutes.

4. In a blender, process the remaining 2 cups stock with the kudzu and stir the mixture into the simmering stock along with the tamari, savory, ground celery seed, nutmeg, and black pepper. Simmer for 5 minutes, stirring often.

5. Stir the sautéed vegetables and parsley into the pot with the stock mixture and simmer, covered, for 5 minutes, stirring often. Serve hot.

SERVES 6

MEXICAN CHICKEN FILLING

Thanks to the chicken mushroom's resemblance to the white meat of chicken, you can make this sweet and spicy chicken filling for Corn Tortillas (see page 39). Use this chicken filling for Mexican dishes such as enchiladas and chimichangas, stuffed peppers, stuffed squash, and avocados. This filling is especially good mixed with Tofu Cream Cheese (page 30), which softens the spiciness.

1 tablespoon olive oil

1 medium-size onion, chopped

4 cloves garlic, finely chopped

2 cups chicken mushrooms grated in a food
*   processor or finely chopped*

⅔ cup Red Hot Chile Sauce (page 162)

¼ cup raisins

2 tablespoons chopped low-sodium pitted olives

1 tablespoon finely chopped fresh basil leaves or 1
  teaspoon dried, finely crumbled
1 ½ teaspoons freshly ground celery seeds
1 teaspoon dried marjoram, finely crumbled
1 teaspoon paprika
½ teaspoon Vege-Sal or ¼ teaspoon salt, or to taste

1. Heat the olive oil in a large skillet over medium heat. Add the onion and garlic and cook, stirring, for 10 minutes.
2. Stir in the remaining ingredients, reduce the heat to low, and cook, covered, for 10 minutes, stirring occasionally.

MAKES 3 CUPS

STACKED CHICKEN MUSHROOM ENCHILADAS

This recipe transforms other recipes in this book into a wonderful Mexican dish, and it takes only a few minutes to assemble.

2 cups Red Hot Chile Sauce (page 162)
12 Corn Tortillas (page 39) or Acorn Tortillas
  (page 293)
3 cups Mexican Chicken Filling (page 331)
3 cups Tofu Cream Cheese (page 30)

1. Preheat the oven to 350 degrees.
2. Pour enough of the chile sauce onto the bottom of a 13 x 9 x 2-inch oiled baking dish to moisten it.
3. Add a tortilla, spread about 2½ tablespoons of chile sauce on top, followed by about 3 tablespoons of the chicken filling, and around 2½ tablespoons of the Tofu Cream Cheese.
4. Add another tortilla and continue to layer the casserole dish in this order until all the ingredients are used up, ending with the Tofu Cream Cheese.
5. Bake the enchiladas, uncovered, until the sauce bubbles, about 30 minutes.

SERVES 6 TO 8

CHICKEN MUSHROOM CASSEROLE

This casserole features one of the most common, tastiest, and easy-to-recognize wild mushrooms, in a creamy sauce.

6 tablespoons olive oil
6 cups sliced chicken mushrooms
2 celery stalks, sliced
¼ cup very thinly sliced burdock root (page 139)
  or carrots
4 scallions, sliced
4 cloves garlic, sliced
¾ cup tomato juice
2 tablespoons Black Locust Blossom Wine (page
  182) or sherry
1 tablespoon tamari soy sauce
1 teaspoon dried tarragon, finely crumbled
1 teaspoon dried sage, finely crumbled
1 teaspoon dried thyme, finely crumbled
2 teaspoons white pepper (1 teaspoon peppercorns)
1 teaspoon chili paste or ¼ teaspoon cayenne
  pepper, or to taste
3 cups cooked brown rice or Buckwheat Noodles
  (page 34)
1 cup shelled butternuts (page 296) or walnuts,
  coarsely chopped
2 ⅓ cups Tofu Sour Cream (page 33)
½ teaspoon paprika

1. Preheat the oven to 350 degrees.

2. Heat the olive oil in a large skillet over medium heat. Add the chicken mushrooms, celery, burdock, scallions, and garlic and cook, stirring, for 10 minutes.

3. Transfer the mushroom mixture to a large saucepan and add the tomato juice, wine, tamari, tarragon, sage, thyme, white pepper, and chili paste, reduce the heat to low, cover, and simmer for 10 minutes.

4. Layer a 3-quart oiled casserole dish with the cooked rice, mushroom mixture, butternuts, and Tofu Sour Cream. Sprinkle the paprika on top and bake, covered, until bubbly, about 40 minutes. Serve hot with whole grains.

SERVES 6 TO 8

CHICKEN HARISSA

This unusual side dish consists of the common chicken mushroom cooked in North African seasonings and a peanut sauce.

SAUTÉ

¼ cup olive oil

4 cups sliced very tender young chicken mushrooms

1 medium-size onion, chopped

2 cloves garlic, chopped

2 small chiles, seeds and ribs removed and chopped

1 ½ teaspoons freshly ground cumin seeds

2 teaspoon freshly ground coriander seeds

1 teaspoon freshly ground caraway seeds

1 teaspoon dried wild spearmint (page 59) or other mint, finely crumbled

SAUCE

2 tablespoons water

2 tablespoons Bragg's Liquid Aminos or tamari soy sauce

2 tablespoons fresh lemon juice

3 tablespoons Crunchy Peanut Butter (page 38)

1. *To make the sauté:* Heat the olive oil in a large skillet over medium heat. Add the rest of the sauté ingredients and cook, stirring, for 10 minutes.

2. *To make the sauce:* Mix the sauce ingredients together with a whisk or fork.

3. Stir the sauce into the sautéed ingredients and bring the pot to a boil. Reduce the heat to low, cover, and simmer for 10 minutes.

4. Serve Chicken Harissa hot, with noodles or homemade bread.

SERVES 6

CHICKEN WITH CAULIFLOWER

Here's another great way to dispose of a major harvest of large quantities of choice, young chicken mushrooms to advantage.

1 ½ cups Tofu Sour Cream (page 33)

6 tablespoons Garlic Butter Sauce (page 35)

1 teaspoon Vege-Sal or ½ teaspoon salt, or to taste

8 cups sliced chicken mushrooms

1 medium-size head cauliflower, broken into florets

1. Preheat the oven to 350 degrees.

2. In a large bowl, mix together the Tofu Sour Cream, Garlic Butter Sauce, and Vege-Sal; add the chicken mushrooms and cauliflower, and combine.

3. Transfer the mixture to a 3-quart oiled casserole dish and bake, covered, until the cauliflower is tender, about 30 minutes. Serve hot, over noodles.

SERVES 6

BAKED CHICKEN MUSHROOMS WITH VEGETABLES

You'll be highly gratified with the way chicken mushrooms taste baked with these complementary vegetables in a mild but tasty sauce.

> 4 cups sliced chicken mushrooms
> 2 medium-size zucchini, ends trimmed and sliced
> 4 medium-size ripe tomatoes, sliced
> 2⅓ cups Sassafras Peanut Sauce (page 45)

1. Preheat the oven to 375 degrees.
2. Combine all the ingredients in a large bowl.
3. Transfer the mixture to a 3-quart oiled casserole dish and bake until it is bubbly and the mushrooms are tender, about 50 minutes. Serve hot as a side dish, with rice or bread.

SERVES 6 TO 8

CHICKEN PILAF

American chicken mushrooms and wild rice with Mexican chili powder and South American quinoa seeds create a Pan-American delight.

> 3½ cups water
> 2 cups sliced chicken mushrooms
> ½ cup wild rice (page 353)
> ¾ cup quinoa
> 2 medium-size ripe tomatoes, sliced
> 1 medium-size red onion, chopped
> 1 medium-size red bell pepper, seeded and chopped
> 2 tablespoons Chili Powder (page 36)
> 4 cloves garlic, crushed into a paste
> 2 teaspoons Vege-Sal or 1 teaspoon salt, or to taste

Place all the ingredients in a large saucepan and bring the pot to a boil over medium heat. Reduce the heat to low, and simmer, covered, until all the liquid is absorbed and the grains are tender, 25 to 35 minutes. Serve hot.

SERVES 10

CHICKEN MUSHROOM PARMESAN

This familiar dish soars nutritionally and flavorwise when you use chicken mushrooms and tofu cheeses instead of animal products. Homemade tomato sauce improves it even more. If you want to impress nutritional skeptics or wild mushroom disbelievers, this is the dish to make! And it includes an original vegan coating that acts like beaten eggs to make bread crumbs stick to food. The liquid lecithin substitutes for egg yolks, acting as an emulsifier and allowing the water and oil to mix and thicken. The flaxseeds replace the egg whites and enhance the stickiness. The miso provides saltiness and more stickiness and thickness. The spices, commonly used for poultry, enhance the chicken flavor in the mushrooms.

COATING

> 1½ cups water
> ¼ cup peanut oil, corn oil, or olive oil
> ¼ cup mellow (light-colored) miso
> ¼ cup liquid lecithin
> 5 tablespoons freshly ground flaxseeds
>   (2 tablespoons seeds)
> 1½ teaspoons dried sage, finely crumbled
> 1 teaspoon dried thyme, finely crumbled
> 2 teaspoons freshly ground yellow mustard seeds
>   (1 teaspoon seeds)
> 1 teaspoon dried tarragon, finely crumbled

2 teaspoons freshly ground black pepper
  (1 teaspoon peppercorns)

½ teaspoon turmeric

½ teaspoon freshly grated nutmeg

1 teaspoon chili paste or ¼ teaspoon cayenne
  pepper, or to taste

8 cups chicken mushroom slabs

1 ½ cups fresh Bread Crumbs (page 40), or as
  needed

¼ cup olive oil

6 cups Wild Tomato Sauce (page 94)

5 cups Tofu Sliced Cheese (page 31)

3 cups Tofu Sharp Cheese (page 30)

2 cups Tofu Grated Cheese (page 32)

1. Preheat the oven to 350 degrees.

2. *To make the coating:* In a blender, combine the coating ingredients and process until smooth.

3. Stir the coating into the chicken mushroom slabs in a large bowl. Stir in the bread crumbs to coat all the chicken mushroom slabs.

4. Heat the olive oil in a large skillet over medium heat. Fry the breaded slabs in the hot olive oil until they are browned on both sides.

5. Layer a 14 x 9 x 2-inch oiled baking dish with half the tomato sauce, the chicken mushrooms, the Tofu Sliced Cheese, the remaining tomato sauce, and the Tofu Sharp Cheese. Top with Tofu Grated Cheese. Bake, uncovered, until bubbly, about 40 minutes. Serve hot.

SERVES 8

CHICKEN MUSHROOM CRÊPES

Traditional chicken crêpes vegan style are more than possible with wild chicken mushrooms.

CRÊPES

1 ½ cups plus 2 tablespoons (3 ounces) buckwheat
  flour and 1 cup plus 1 tablespoon (4 ounces)
  barley flour, or 7 ounces any whole-grain flour

5 tablespoons freshly ground flaxseeds (2 tablespoons seeds)

¼ cup kudzu or arrowroot

¼ cup lecithin granules

4 ½ cups soy milk or nut milk

2 tablespoons corn oil

1 teaspoon Vege-Sal or ½ teaspoon salt

1 teaspoon brandy extract (optional)

1 teaspoon freshly ground black pepper
  (½ teaspoon peppercorns)

FILLING

4 ½ cups sliced chicken mushrooms

1 ½ cups Tofu Sour Cream (page 33)

2 large mild chiles, seeds and ribs removed and
  chopped

2 tablespoons olive oil

2 tablespoons red wine vinegar

2 tablespoons olive oil

2 tablespoons Wineberry Wine (page 246)

2 tablespoons arrowroot or kudzu

1 ½ teaspoons sweet paprika

½ teaspoon dried tarragon, finely crumbled

½ teaspoon dried rosemary, finely crumbled

¼ teaspoon dried sage, finely crumbled

1. Preheat the oven to 350 degrees.

2. *To make the crêpes:* Whisk together the crepe ingredients in a large bowl until smooth.

3. Pour a circle of batter onto a hot oiled griddle and cook each crêpe until it is lightly browned on both sides, turning it once. Repeat the process until all the batter is used up, keeping the cooked crêpes warm.

4. *To make the filling:* In a large bowl, mix the filling

ingredients together.

5. Spread about 1½ tablespoons of filling along the edge of each crêpe and roll it up. Bake the crêpes on an oiled cookie sheet for 25 minutes. Serve hot, with additional Tofu Sour Cream, if desired.

MAKES 24 CRÊPES; SERVES 8

CHICKEN IN NESTS

This is a great place to settle down if you're a chicken mushroom—protected by a layer of bread crumbs and vegetables, mixed with a creamy soy mayonnaise, and hidden under Tofu Grated Cheese. What could be a better place to nest?

3 tablespoons olive oil

3 celery stalks, sliced

3 medium-size red bell peppers, seeded and sliced into strips

3 medium-size red onions, sliced

6 cloves garlic, chopped

2½ tablespoons chopped fresh parsley leaves

2 teaspoons dried tarragon, finely crumbled

1½ teaspoons dried sage, finely crumbled

1½ teaspoons Vege-Sal or ¾ teaspoon salt, or to taste

2 teaspoons freshly ground black pepper (1 teaspoon peppercorns), or to taste

6 cups dry Bread Crumbs (page 40)

1¼ cups Wild Mustard Seed Mayonnaise (page 206)

3 cup steamed sliced chicken mushroom (see note on page 322)

1½ cups low-sodium pitted olives, drained

1 cup Tofu Grated Cheese (page 32)

1. Preheat the oven to 375 degrees.

2. Heat the olive oil in a large skillet over medium

heat. Add the celery, red peppers, onions, garlic, parsley, tarragon, sage, Vege-Sal, and black pepper and cook, stirring, for 10 minutes.

3. In a large bowl, mix half the sautéed vegetables with the bread crumbs and 1 cup of the mayonnaise, and press this mixture onto the sides and bottoms of six oiled 1½-cup ramekins or custard dishes.

4. In a separate bowl, mix the remaining sautéed vegetables and the remaining ¼ cup mayonnaise with the chicken mushrooms and olives and spoon this mixture into the bread-crumb nests. Top with the Tofu Grated Cheese. Bake until bubbly, about 30 minutes. Serve hot.

SERVES 6

FETTUCCINE ALFREDO

In 1996 the Center for Science in the Public Interest bashed this classic Italian dish on national television, condemning it as one of the worst high-fat disasters you can eat in an Italian restaurant. Here's a version that is as nutritious as it is tasty.

1 pound Buckwheat Noodles (page 34) or store-bought whole-grain fettuccine or other pasta

Dash of olive oil

1½ cups Tofu Cream Cheese (page 30)

1⅓ cups water

¼ cup corn oil

2 cups steamed sliced chicken mushrooms (see note on page 322), diced

1 tablespoon olive oil

1½ teaspoons field garlic (page 57) or wild garlic bulbs (page 160) or chopped regular garlic, or to taste

1½ cups Tofu Grated Cheese (page 32)

¾ cup fresh parsley leaves, chopped

½ teaspoon Vege-Sal

¼ teaspoon freshly ground black pepper
(⅛ teaspoon peppercorns), or to taste

1. Cook the fettuccine until it is *al dente* in a pot of rapidly boiling salted water with a dash of olive oil. Drain the pasta.

2. Meanwhile, mix together the Tofu Cream Cheese, water, and corn oil in a large saucepan. Add the chicken mushrooms and heat the mixture through, covered, over low heat, stirring occasionally. Do not bring the pot to boil.

3. Meanwhile, heat the olive oil in a large skillet over medium heat. Add the wild onions and cook, stirring, until they are lightly browned. In a large serving bowl, toss the fettuccine with the sautéed wild onion. Pour the Tofu Cream Cheese sauce over the fettuccine, add the Tofu Grated Cheese and parsley, and toss lightly. Sprinkle with the Vege-Sal and black pepper and serve immediately.

SERVES 6 TO 8

CREAMED CHICKEN IN NOODLES

This French treatment features the chicken mushroom at its best without raising anybody's cholesterol levels. Use the youngest, top-quality chicken mushrooms, because older ones won't become tender when you sauté them.

4 cups Buckwheat Noodles (page 34) or store-
   bought noodles
¼ olive oil
2 cups sliced very young tender chicken
   mushrooms
4 cloves garlic, chopped
1 medium-size onion, chopped

SAUCE
   2 cups Vegetable Stock (page 40) or water
   ½ cup drained silken tofu
   2 tablespoons Redbud Wine (page 159) or red
      wine
   2 tablespoons Bragg's Liquid Aminos or tamari soy
      sauce
   2 tablespoons arrowroot or kudzu
   2 tablespoons lecithin granules
   1 teaspoon dried thyme, finely crumbled
   1 teaspoon dried tarragon, finely crumbled
   1 teaspoon dried sage, finely crumbled
   1 teaspoon freshly ground black pepper (1 teaspoon
      peppercorns)

2 medium-size ripe tomatoes, sliced
½ cup Tofu Sharp Cheese (page 30) or Tofu
   Grated Cheese (page 32)

1. Preheat the oven to 350 degrees.

2. Boil the homemade noodles for 5 minutes in rapidly boiling salted water with a dash of oil. If you're using store-bought noodles, cook them for 2 minutes less than the package directions indicate. Drain the pasta in a colander and immediately lower the colander into a bowl of cold water to halt the cooking. Drain the noodles again.

3. Meanwhile, heat the olive oil in a large skillet over medium heat, add the chicken mushrooms, garlic, and onion and cook, stirring, for 10 minutes.

4. *To make the sauce:* In a blender, combine the sauce ingredients and process until smooth.

5. Stir the sauce into the sautéed ingredients, along with the sliced tomatoes. Bring the pot to a boil, stirring often. Reduce the heat to low, cover, and simmer for 5 minutes.

6. Transfer the noodles to a 13 x 9 x 2-inch oiled bak-

ing dish. Top them with the mushroom-sauce mixture. Sprinkle on the Tofu Sharp Cheese. Bake until bubbly, about 35 minutes. Serve hot.

SERVES 6

CHICKEN MUSHROOM SOURDOUGH BREAD

When I brought this bread to a potluck dinner, I had to take home every slice at the end of the evening. The guests, all of whom were vegetarians, thought it contained chicken and mushrooms, and they missed a fabulous treat.

6¾ cups (2 pounds) sweet brown rice flour

4⅓ cups (1 pound) rye flour

½ cup dulse flakes (page 174)

5 cups water

2 cups Sourdough Starter (page 42), actively bubbling

¼ cup corn oil

¼ cup sesame seeds

1 tablespoon Vege-Sal or 1½ teaspoons salt

4 large cloves garlic, crushed into a paste

2 teaspoons dried oregano, finely crumbled

2 teaspoons dried tarragon, finely crumbled

1 teaspoon dried rosemary, finely crumbled

1 teaspoon dried sage, finely crumbled

2½ cups sliced chicken mushrooms

1 teaspoon paprika

1. Mix half of each of the flours with 4 cups of the water and the sourdough starter in a large bowl. Cover the bowl loosely and let the dough rise at room temperature for at least 6 hours and up to overnight. (Meanwhile, replenish your sourdough starter with 1 cup of the remaining flour and the remaining 1 cup water.)

2. Stir the remaining flour and the rest of the other ingredients, except for the paprika, into the sourdough mixture until the ingredients are thoroughly mixed. Do not knead the dough.

3. Shape the dough into 3 loaves in 3 well-oiled 6½ x 4⅜ x 2½-inch loaf pans and sprinkle the loaves with the paprika. Wrap the loaves inside supermarket plastic shopping bags so that the plastic does not touch the dough, or cover the loaves with damp towels, to keep the dough from drying out. Let the loaves rise for at least 6 hours and up to overnight at room temperature.

4. Preheat the oven to 350 degrees. Set a pan of water on the bottom of the oven to keep the crust soft. Bake the loaves until they pull away from the sides of the pan slightly and sound hollow when tapped, about 1 hour.

5. Remove the loaves from the loaf pans (running a butter knife or stiff plastic spatula along the sides to loosen the bread will make this easier) and let the bread cool on wire racks before slicing.

MAKES 3 LOAVES

Note: Avoid using metal containers or utensils to prepare the dough, since they can kill sourdough.

AMARANTH

Amaranthus species

THIS IS A GROUP OF COARSE, NONWOODY annual plants that can trail the ground or grow over 7 feet tall, with long-stalked, alternate, lance-shaped to oval, leaves that are 1 to over 3 inches long. Dense, erect bristly spikes of tiny green flowers and seeds arise from the leaf axils (where they emerge from the stalk) in late summer and fall, respectively.

Amaranth, a tasty Aztec staple, grows throughout North America.

Cut off dozens of stalks in the fall and store them in a paper supermarket bag for a few weeks until they dry out. To remove the seeds, hold the seed heads over a tray. Then you can blow away the lighter chaff with a fan and the seeds remain on the tray. Cook the highly nutritious seeds like a grain. They have a light, nutty flavor, which I use to supplement the grains in other dishes.

AMARANTH OATMEAL

This is one of my favorite breakfast recipes. You may substitute other fruit for the apples, but don't use wineberries, which don't work well in this context.

> One 33.8-ounce package soy milk or nut milk
> 1¾ cups rolled oats (not the quick-cooking kind)
> 4 wild apples (page 340) or 2 large green apples, cored and chopped
> 1 cup raisins or cultivated currants
> ¼ cup amaranth
> 1 tablespoon ground cinnamon
> 2 teaspoons vanilla extract
> 1 teaspoon almond extract
> 1 teaspoon salt
> ½ teaspoon liquid stevia or 1 tablespoon honey, rice syrup, or barley malt
> 6 tablespoons lecithin granules (optional)
> 3 tablespoons oat bran or wheat bran (optional)

1. Heat the soy milk in a heavy pot over medium heat, stirring often, until it reaches a boil (pay close attention or it will boil over and create the mother of all messes).
2. Stir in all the remaining ingredients except the lecithin and bran, reduce the heat to very low, and simmer, covered, for 10 minutes, stirring occasionally.
3. Remove the pot from the heat and let the cooked grains sit, covered, for 15 minutes. Stir in the lecithin and bran. Serve hot.

SERVES 6

AMARANTH-QUINOA PILAF

Amaranth increases the quality of protein in this recipe, and its delicious flavor blends well with that of quinoa.

> 4 cups water
> 1 cup amaranth
> 1 cup quinoa
> 1 cup sliced Japanese knotweed stems (page 98) or rhubarb stems
> 1 cup chopped carrots
> ¼ cup sliced tree ear mushrooms or other mushrooms
> 2 tablespoons freshly ground mustard seeds (1 tablespoon seeds)
> 1 tablespoon olive oil
> 1 tablespoon tamari soy sauce, or to taste
> 4 cloves garlic, minced
> 2 teaspoons freshly ground fennel seeds
> 2 teaspoons freshly ground coriander seeds
> 1 teaspoon freshly grated nutmeg
> 1 small chile, seeds and ribs removed and chopped, or ¼ teaspoon cayenne pepper, or to taste

Combine all the ingredients in a large saucepan. Bring the pot to a boil over medium heat, stirring often. Reduce the heat to low and simmer, covered, until all the liquid is absorbed and the grains are tender, 15 to 20 minutes. Serve hot.

SERVES 6 TO 8

WILDMAN'S PAELLA

Here's a famous Spanish dish simply made with healthful wild ingredients.

4 ¼ cups water

1 ¾ cups brown basmati rice

¼ cup amaranth

1 cup chopped chicken mushrooms (page 321) or other mushrooms

½ cup sun-dried tomatoes, chopped

½ cup dried ramp leaves (page 116) or chopped fresh chives

½ cup Chonce (page 162)

½ cup gingko nuts (page 435) or peas

4 cloves garlic, finely chopped

1 teaspoon Vege-Sal or ½ teaspoon salt, or to taste

1 teaspoon chili paste or ¼ teaspoon cayenne pepper

1. Preheat the oven to 350 degrees.

2. Combine all the ingredients in a 3-quart oiled casserole dish and bake, covered, until all the water is absorbed and the rice and amaranth are tender, 75 to 90 minutes.

SERVES 6 TO 8

AMARANTH CORNBREAD

Amaranth seeds provide the amino acid lysine, which is missing in corn, to create a complete protein, while adding just the right flavor.

DRY INGREDIENTS

5 cups (2 pounds) yellow cornmeal

1 cup amaranth

¾ cup arrowroot or kudzu

½ cup lecithin granules

1 ½ teaspoons dried tarragon, finely crumbled

2 teaspoons freshly grated lemon rind

1 ½ tablespoons cream of tartar

2 teaspoons baking soda

2 teaspoons salt

WET INGREDIENTS

2 ½ cups soy milk or nut milk

1 cup unsweetened cherry juice or other fruit juice

¾ cup corn oil

1 teaspoon liquid stevia (optional)

1. Preheat the oven to 350 degrees.

2. Mix together the dry ingredients in a large bowl.

3. Mix together the wet ingredients in a medium-size bowl. Add the wet ingredients to the dry ingredients, being careful not to overmix.

4. Pour the batter into 2 oiled 6½ x 4⅜ x 2½-inch loaf pans, shaping it into loaves. Set a pan of hot water on the bottom of the oven to keep the crust soft. Bake the loaves until a toothpick inserted into the center emerges clean, about 50 minutes.

5. Remove the loaves from the loaf pans and let them cool on wire racks before slicing.

MAKES 2 LOAVES

WILD APPLE

Malus species

APPLE TREES GROW TO JUST 30 FEET, WITH cracked gray bark. The alternate, oval, slightly toothed leaves, which are 2 to 3½ inches long, are wooly underneath, and the twigs are fuzzy, too. Showy, fragrant, long-stalked, white to pink five-petaled, radially symmetrical flowers bloom in early spring. The familiar red, green, or yellow fruit ripens in late summer and fall. Look for apple trees in thickets, at the edges of woods, and in landscaped areas throughout North America.

Apples take many forms in the wild. Some are abandoned large cultivated apples. Others are wilder—for example, the small and tart crabapples (see page 425) are especially good for cooking. If you're not sure about the identity of a small apple, cut it open along the "equator," and you'll see seeds in sets of five if it is an apple. Cut open larger apples too, to check for and remove any wormy parts (this is especially important if you're a vegetarian).

Use the apples unpeeled, unless the instructions say otherwise. If you can't find wild apples, substitute tart Granny Smith apples.

SPICED WILD APPLE CIDER

You can juice wild apples or use commercial apple juice to make a hot beverage that's wonderful to serve to guests on cold winter nights.

> *2 ½ cups apple juice*
> *1 orange, peeled and quartered*
> *½ teaspoon freshly grated nutmeg*
> *Three 2-inch cinnamon sticks*
> *4 cloves*

1. Bring all the ingredients to a boil in a medium-size saucepan over medium heat.
2. Remove the pot from the heat, cover, and let the mixture steep for 15 minutes before serving. Serve hot.

MAKES 3 CUPS; SERVES 4

WILD APPLESAUCE

This basic dish, which every cook must know, is excellent for beginning cooks and for beginning foragers, and it tastes a million times better than commercial canned applesauce.

> *6 medium-size wild apples*
> *½ cup apple juice*
> *2 tablespoons fresh lemon juice or red wine*
> *1 tablespoon ground cinnamon or ground dried sassafras root bark (page 44)*
> *1 teaspoon ground dried wild ginger (page 111) or regular ground ginger*
> *2 teaspoons freshly grated nutmeg*
> *Raisins and nuts to taste (optional)*

1. Core the apples, if desired. Grate them in the food processor or slice them by hand.
2. Put all the ingredients in a large, heavy saucepan and bring the pot to a boil over medium heat, stirring often. Reduce the heat to low, cover, and simmer until the apples are tender, about 15 minutes.
3. Transfer the mixture to a blender in batches and process until smooth, starting on low speed and holding the blender cover down with a towel to prevent eruptions.
4. Add nuts or raisins, if desired. Wild Applesauce will keep, tightly covered, in the refrigerator, for up to a week and frozen for up to 6 months.

MAKES 6 CUPS

CHAROSES

This was my favorite Passover dish as a child, and I love it just as much today. Use organic grape juice (or the juice of wild grapes) if possible. Commercial grapes are sprayed with very dangerous pesticides that migrant agricultural workers are forced to apply.

16 medium-size wild apples, cored and grated

1 cup almonds, toasted (page 158) and chopped

1 ½ teaspoons freshly grated lemon rind or
  ½ teaspoon dried

½ cup raisins

⅓ cup organic grape juice

1 tablespoon ground cinnamon

1 teaspoon freshly grated nutmeg

In a large bowl, combine all the ingredients. Serve cold.

SERVES 10 TO 12

WILD APPLE DELIGHT

Wild apples are usually tarter and chewier than commercial apples. Grating them, mixing them with compatible ingredients, and baking them tenderize them while bringing out the best of their flavor.

1 cup well-drained silken tofu

2 tablespoons corn oil or flaxseed oil

2 tablespoons fresh lemon or lime juice

1 ½ tablespoons vegetable glycerin, honey, barley
  malt, or rice syrup

2 teaspoons vanilla extract

1 teaspoon ground cinnamon

¼ teaspoon salt

¼ teaspoon almond extract

¼ teaspoon liquid stevia

4 cups cored and grated wild apples

½ cup black walnuts (page 375) or hazelnuts,
  chopped

½ cup regular walnuts, chopped

½ cup raisins

1. Preheat the oven to 350 degrees.

2. In a food processor or large bowl, combine the tofu, corn oil, lemon juice, glycerin, vanilla, cinnamon, salt, almond extract, and liquid stevia and process or beat with a whisk or fork until smooth. Stir in the remaining ingredients. Transfer the mixture to a 2-quart oiled casserole dish and bake, covered, until bubbly, about 45 minutes. Serve hot or cold.

SERVES 6

STEWED APPLES

There is nothing new about cooking apples with currants, nuts, and seasonings. This recipe is incredibly simple and wonderful.

12 cups cored and sliced wild apples

2 cups apple juice

1 cup raw cashews, chopped

¾ cup cultivated currants

⅓ cup tapioca pearls

¼ cup vegetable glycerin, honey, barley malt, or
  rice syrup

1 teaspoon liquid stevia (optional)

1 teaspoon ground cinnamon

1 teaspoon dried mint, finely crumbled

½ teaspoon ground dried wild ginger (page 111) or
  regular ground ginger

½ teaspoon freshly grated nutmeg

Place all the ingredients in a large pot and bring to a simmer over medium heat. Reduce the heat to low and simmer, covered, until the apples are tender, 10 to 20 minutes. Serve hot or cold.

SERVES 6 TO 8

STEWED WILD APPLES WITH WILD BLACKBERRIES

Here's a simple, sweet fruit compote made with ingredients that are easy to collect or buy. If you've just collected a huge haul of blackberries and you want to make something good in a hurry, this recipe is for you.

10 cups cored and sliced wild apples

2 cups apple juice

2 cups wild blackberries (page 271)

½ cup raisins

1 ½ tablespoons ground cinnamon

2 teaspoons peeled and finely chopped fresh ginger

2 teaspoons dried wild spearmint (page 59) or other mint, finely crumbled

1 cup black walnuts (page 375) or hazelnuts, chopped and toasted (page 158), if desired

1. Place all the ingredients except the walnuts in a large pot over medium heat and bring to a simmer. Reduce the heat to low and simmer, covered, for 15 minutes.

2. Stir in the walnuts. Serve hot or cold.

SERVES 8 TO 10

WILD APPLE TORTE

I loved this wonderful-tasting apple pastry when my grandmother used to make it when I was a very young child (she passed away just after my sixth birthday). Now I've re-created it with all-natural, healthy ingredients. It's quick and simple to prepare, and as good as ever.

PASTRY

1 ¼ cups (7 ounces) yellow cornmeal

¾ cup plus 3 tablespoons freshly ground flaxseeds (6 tablespoons seeds)

¼ cup lecithin granules

1 ¼ teaspoons baking soda

1 ½ tablespoons ground cinnamon

½ teaspoon salt

½ cup apple juice

2 ½ tablespoons fresh lemon juice

1 tablespoon vanilla extract

1 teaspoon maple extract (optional)

¼ teaspoon liquid stevia or 2 tablespoons barley malt

2 cups pecans or other nuts, chopped

FRUIT FILLING

4 cups cored and finely chopped wild apples

½ cup apple juice

1 teaspoon ground dried wild ginger (page 111) or regular ground ginger

2 teaspoons dried wild spearmint (page 59) or other mint, finely crumbled

1. Preheat the oven to 350 degrees.

2. *To make the pastry:* In a large bowl, mix together the cornmeal, ground flaxseeds, lecithin, baking soda, cinnamon, and salt.

3. In a medium-size bowl, mix together the apple juice, lemon juice, extracts, and liquid stevia. Mix the wet ingredients into the dry ingredients, being careful not to overmix. Stir in the pecans.

4. *To make the fruit filling:* Mix the fruit filling ingredients together in a medium-size bowl. Divide the filling between 2 oiled 9-inch pie tins.

5. Press the pastry layer over the fruit layer in both pie tins. Bake the torte until it is bubbly, about 35 minutes. Serve hot or cold, topped with Tofu Whipped Cream (page 32), if desired.

MAKES TWO 9-INCH PIES; SERVES 12

APPLE CHARLOTTE (APPLE-NOODLE CAKE)

I remember enjoying my grandmother's traditional Jewish version of this luscious recipe when I was five years old. I re-created it in her honor (and because I still missed it) when I first began cooking as an adult, when I still used milk, sugar, and eggs. Here's a healthier version of one of my life-long favorite desserts—even better, thanks to the wild apples.

1 cup oat flour or ¼ pound any whole-grain flour

¾ cup plus 3 tablespoons freshly ground flaxseeds
  (6 tablespoons seeds)

½ teaspoon salt

¾ teaspoon baking soda

1 teaspoon freshly grated nutmeg

½ teaspoon ground dried wild ginger (page 111) or
  regular ground ginger

½ teaspoon common spicebush berries (page 314),
  finely chopped, or ¼ teaspoon freshly ground
  allspice berries

1⅓ cups drained silken tofu

1½ cups soy milk or nut milk

6 tablespoons corn oil or flaxseed oil

¼ cup lecithin granules

1 teaspoon vanilla extract

¼ teaspoon liquid stevia or 2 tablespoons
  honey, rice syrup, or barley malt

1 pound wild apples, cored and sliced

1½ cup raisins

1 pound Buckwheat Noodles (page 34) or store-
  bought noodles

1 tablespoon poppy seeds

1. Preheat the oven to 350 degrees.
2. Sift together the flour, ground flaxseeds, salt, baking soda, nutmeg, and ginger.

3. In a blender, combine the spicebush berries, tofu, flour mixture, soy milk, corn oil, lecithin, vanilla, and liquid stevia and process until smooth. Stir the batter into the apples and raisins in a large bowl.
4. Meanwhile, cook the noodles in rapidly boiling salted water with a dash of oil until the pasta is nearly done. Drain the noodles and then combine them with the apple batter. Transfer the apple-noodle batter to a 3-quart oiled casserole dish, sprinkle the poppy seeds on top, and bake, covered, until thickened, about 45 minutes.
5. Serve hot or cold, topped with Super Strawberry Jam (page 208), Tofu Whipped Cream (page 32), or soy milk, if desired.

SERVES 8

WILD APPLE FRITTERS

What could be better than whole-grain pancakes flavored with natural seasonings and filled with apples? You won't be frittering away your time when you make these!

1¾ cups plus 2 tablespoons (½ pound) barley flour
  and 1 cup (¼ pound) oat flour, or ¾ pound any
  whole-grain flour

2 tablespoons arrowroot or kudzu

2½ tablespoons freshly ground flaxseeds
  (1 tablespoon)

¾ teaspoon freshly ground coriander seeds

1½ teaspoons freshly grated nutmeg

¾ teaspoon baking soda

1¾ cups soy milk or nut milk

¼ cup apple juice

2 tablespoons walnut oil or corn oil

1½ teaspoons liquid lecithin

1 teaspoon vanilla extract

¼ teaspoon liquid stevia or 1 tablespoon barley
   malt or maple syrup

3 ½ cups cored and sliced wild apples

½ cup pecans or other nuts, chopped

1 tablespoon freshly grated orange rind or
   1 teaspoon orange extract

1 ½ teaspoons lecithin granules

1. Mix together the flours, arrowroot, ground flaxseeds, coriander, nutmeg, and baking soda in a large bowl.

2. In a medium-size bowl, mix together the apple juice, walnut oil, liquid lecithin, vanilla, and liquid stevia. Mix the wet ingredients into the dry ingredients, being careful not to overmix. Stir in the apples, pecans, orange rind, and lecithin granules.

3. Ladle ¼ cup of the batter onto a hot oiled griddle and cook each fritter until the underside is lightly browned. Turn each fritter with a metal spatula and cook until the other side is lightly browned. Repeat until all the batter is used up. Serve with fruit jam, applesauce, or syrup.

SERVES 6 TO 8

WILD APPLE ICE CREAM

Wild apples impart an interesting tartness that contrasts with the sweetness of this ice cream.

   1 cup well-drained silken tofu

   1 cup apple juice

   1 cup soy milk or nut milk

   ½ cup canola oil

   ¼ cup vegetable glycerin, honey, barley malt, rice
      syrup, or maple syrup

   ¼ cup lecithin granules

   1 teaspoon ground cinnamon

1 teaspoon common spicebush berries (page 314),
   finely chopped, or ½ teaspoon freshly ground
   allspice berries

½ teaspoon salt

3 cups wild apples, cored and quartered

1. Place all the ingredients except for half the apples in a blender and process until smooth.

2. Chill the mixture (or begin with chilled ingredients) if required by your ice cream machine.

3. Pour half the purée into the ice cream machine and then add the remaining apples to the remaining purée in the blender and run it very briefly on low speed, just enough to chop the apples. Add this mixture to the machine and freeze according to the manufacturer's instructions.

MAKES 6 CUPS; SERVES 6

PRINCE MUSHROOM

Agaricus augustus

THIS ROYAL MEMBER OF THE FIELD MUSHROOM (Agaricus) group (see page 286 for common features of this group), the cover fungus (like a cover girl) of David Aurora's excellent Mushrooms Demystified, is one of the world's tastiest gilled mushrooms. The fibrous to scaly, yellowish brown cap is 4 to 10 inches wide. It bruises yellow and has an anise-almond fragrance, like the rest of the mushroom. The gills, which go from white (don't confuse this mushroom with the deadly Amanitas, which always has white gills and white spores) to pink and end up brown (colored by the brown spores), are free from the stalks. The scruffy stalk is 3 to 5 inches long and ¾ to 1¼ inches thick; it is larger toward the base. There's a membranous ring on the upper stalk, a remnant of a partial veil, a covering of the immature gills. This mushroom grows in spring and fall (late fall to spring in California) in the composted soil of parks and landscaped areas throughout North America.

Its almond/anise-tinged aroma and flavor is so attractive and strong, it's a good mushroom to use in recipes that are supposed to feature mushrooms. You can use virtually any method to cook this mushroom. It cooks in about 15 minutes. Use the cap and stem, if it is insect-free.

FRENCH MUSHROOM SAUCE

Some wild mushrooms, such as the prince, the honey mushroom (*Armillarellia mellea*), and many boletes, have caps that are more tender than the stems. You may want to sauté the caps or use them in entrées, and reserve the stems to make this superb sauce.

> 2 tablespoons olive oil, or as needed
>
> 1 medium-size onion, chopped
>
> 3 cloves garlic, finely chopped
>
> 6 tablespoons sweet brown rice flour or 1.8 ounces any other whole-grain flour
>
> 4 cups Vegetable Stock (page 40)
>
> 2 ¾ cups prince mushroom stems or other mushroom stems
>
> 1 ½ teaspoons Bragg's Liquid Aminos, tamari soy sauce, or Vege-Sal or ¾ teaspoon salt, or to taste
>
> ½ teaspoon chili paste or ¼ teaspoon cayenne pepper
>
> ¾ teaspoon freshly ground celery seeds (½ teaspoon seeds)
>
> ½ teaspoon freshly grated nutmeg

1. In a small pot, bring the stock to a boil.

2. Meanwhile, heat the olive oil in a large skillet over medium heat, add the onions and garlic and cook, stirring, until golden, 10 to 15 minutes. Add the flour and cook, stirring, for another 10 minutes.

3. Gradually stir in the stock, reduce the heat to low, add the remaining ingredients, and simmer for 10 minutes. French Mushroom Sauce will keep, tightly covered, in the refrigerator for 5 to 7 days; it also freezes well.

MAKES 7 CUPS

Note: If you incorporate the stock too quickly and the sauce becomes lumpy, purée the sauce in a blender in three batches until it is smooth, holding down the blender cover with a towel and beginning on low speed to prevent eruptions.

STIR-FRIED TOFU AND PRINCE MUSHROOMS

Here's a simple recipe that brings out the best of one of the tastiest of mushrooms.

STIR-FRY

> ¼ cup peanut oil
>
> 1 tablespoon toasted sesame oil
>
> 2 cups sliced prince mushrooms
>
> 2 celery stalks, sliced
>
> 1 medium-size red bell pepper, seeded and sliced into strips
>
> One 16-ounce package firm tofu, drained and diced
>
> 1 cup bean sprouts

SAUCE

4 cups Vegetable Stock (page 40)

¼ cup Wild Crabapple Blossom Wine (page 425)
or white wine

¼ cup kudzu or arrowroot

¼ cup dark-colored miso

1 tablespoon peeled and grated fresh ginger

2 teaspoons freshly ground white pepper
(1 teaspoon peppercorns)

2 teaspoons freshly ground fennel seeds

2 large garlic cloves, peeled

1. *To make the stir-fry:* Mix together the peanut oil and sesame oil and heat 1 to 2 tablespoons of the oil mixture over high heat in a wok or large skillet. Stir-fry the remaining ingredients consecutively. Use 1 to 2 tablespoons of the oil mixture at a time, removing and setting each ingredient aside when it is done. Add more of the oil mixture with each new ingredient.

2. Stir-fry the prince mushrooms for 4 minutes. Stir-fry the celery for 2 minutes. Stir-fry the red pepper for 2 minutes. Stir-fry the tofu for 3 minutes. Stir-fry the sprouts for 1 minute.

3. *To make the sauce:* In a blender, combine the sauce ingredients and process until smooth. Transfer the sauce to a large saucepan and bring the pot to a boil over medium heat, stirring constantly. Reduce the heat to low and simmer, covered, for 10 minutes, stirring often. Mix the cooked vegetables into the sauce and heat everything through. Serve over brown rice.

SERVES 6

PRINCELY PIZZA

Prince mushrooms and vegetarian cheeses make this outstanding pizza healthful and unique.

1 tablespoon active dry yeast

¾ cup lukewarm apple juice

1½ cups plus 3 tablespoons (½ pound) sweet
brown rice flour and 2 cups (½ pound) oat
flour, or 1 pound any whole-grain flour

1 cup arrowroot or kudzu

½ cup plus 2 tablespoons freshly ground flaxseeds
(¼ cup seeds)

1 teaspoon Vege-Sal or ½ teaspoon salt, or to taste

1 cup water

3 tablespoons olive oil

2 cups Wild Tomato Sauce (page 94)

1 cup Tofu Cream Cheese (page 30)

1 cup sliced prince mushrooms

½ cup Tofu Grated Cheese (page 32)

1 teaspoon dried oregano, finely crumbled

1 teaspoon crushed red pepper

1 teaspoon garlic powder

1. In a small bowl, dissolve the yeast in the apple juice for 10 minutes.

2. Mix together the flour, arrowroot, ground flaxseeds, and Vege-Sal in a medium-size bowl.

3. Mix the water and 2 tablespoons of the olive oil with the yeast mixture and combine these wet ingredients with the flour mixture. Knead the dough for 5 minutes, cover, and set in a warm place to rise for 1 hour.

4. Preheat the oven to 425 degrees.

5. Punch down the dough and roll it out into a 13-inch disk on a floured pastry sheet with a rolling pin enclosed in a floured sleeve. (You can also pat and stretch the crust.) Place the disk of dough in a 12-inch pizza pan, folding the edge inward and pressing it against the sides of the pizza pan. Brush the crust with the remaining 1 tablespoon olive oil.

6. Spread half the tomato sauce over the crust, followed by the Tofu Cream Cheese, the remaining

tomato sauce, the mushrooms, and the Tofu Grated Cheese. Bake the pizza until the crust is lightly browned, about 25 minutes.

7. Sprinkle on the oregano, crushed red pepper, and garlic powder and serve hot.

SERVES 6

CHESTNUT

Castanea species

CHESTNUT TREES HAVE SHALLOWLY GROOVED, dark brown bark, and simple, alternate, large spear-shaped, hairless leaves with sharp, coarse, recurved teeth. Long, drooping catkins bear fragrant, yellow-white flowers in early summer. In autumn, bristly husks containing two or three nuts, slightly flattened, drop to the earth.

Although American chestnuts (*Castanea dentata*) were almost wiped out by an imported blight in the early 1900s (scientists may soon succeed in reintroducing a blight-resistant breed), you may occasionally find Asian chestnuts, with nuts that are much sweeter than those of the commercial varieties, planted in backyards and landscaped areas throughout the United States.

Don't confuse chestnuts with poisonous horse chestnuts or buckeyes (*Aesculus* species), which are characterized by palmate-compound leaves (leaves divided into leaflets originating at the same point).

To shell chestnuts, cut an X on the shell with a paring knife (or the nuts might explode when you toast them) and toast them in a roasting pan in a preheated 450-degree oven for 20 minutes, stirring occasionally. When the chestnuts are cool, shell them (I use a paring knife and a serrated grapefruit spoon). You may also boil the chestnuts in water to cover until the nutmeat is tender, 30 to 40 minutes. Then shell the nuts. Use the nutmeat as is in stuffings, soups, or vegetable dishes. It's also great in desserts, and you can purée it to bring out its creamy quality.

CREAMY CHESTNUT DRESSING

Chestnuts and coconut milk make this salad dressing rich and creamy, while common spicebush berries add a bit of bite.

½ cup boiled shelled chestnuts (see above)

½ cup unsweetened coconut milk

¾ cup olive oil

2 tablespoons canola oil or safflower oil

½ cup brown rice vinegar or red wine vinegar

2 cloves garlic, peeled

2 teaspoons mellow (light-colored) miso

2 common spicebush berries (page 314), finely chopped, or ¼ teaspoon freshly ground allspice berries

1. Place the chestnuts and coconut milk in a medium-size saucepan over medium heat and bring the pot to a simmer. Reduce the heat to low, and simmer, covered, until tender, 5 to 10 minutes.

2. Carefully transfer the mixture to a blender, add the remaining ingredients, and process until smooth.

3. Chill the dressing completely before using it. Creamy Chestnut Dressing will keep, tightly covered, in the refrigerator for up to a week.

MAKES 2¼ CUPS

CAROB-CHESTNUT FUDGE

Whether you use wild chestnuts and pecans, or fudge things by buying the ingredients in the store, you'll love this nutritious candy.

1 ½ pounds boiled shelled chestnuts (page 348)

1 cup pecans or other nuts

½ cup unsweetened shredded coconut

6 tablespoons sesame oil

½ cup carob powder

1 teaspoon vanilla extract

1 teaspoon Angostura bitters

1 ½ teaspoons freshly grated orange rind or
*   ½ teaspoon dried*

¼ teaspoon liquid stevia or 2 tablespoons honey,
*   rice syrup, or barley malt*

1. In a food processor, combine all the ingredients and process until smooth.

2. Press the mixture into an oiled 10 x 6¼ x 2-inch baking dish. Chill completely. Cut into rectangles. Serve chilled.

SERVES 6 TO 8

CHESTNUT ICE CREAM

Wild chestnuts make this ice cream especially rich and creamy.

2 ½ cups soy milk or nut milk

1 ½ cups boiled shelled chestnuts (page 348)

1 cup well-drained silken tofu

½ cup canola oil

¼ cup vegetable glycerin, honey, barley malt, rice
*   syrup, or maple syrup*

¼ cup lecithin granules

1 teaspoon liquid stevia (optional)

2 teaspoons vanilla extract

½ teaspoon salt

1. In a blender, combine all the ingredients and process until smooth.

2. Chill the mixture (or begin with chilled ingredients) if required by your ice cream machine.

3. Pour the mixture into the ice cream machine and freeze it according to the manufacturer's instructions.

MAKES 5½ CUPS; SERVES 5 TO 6

COMMON SUNFLOWER

Helianthus annus

HERE'S A FAMILIAR PLANT THAT GROWS WILD and is also universally available commercially. An annual, it grows 3 to 8 feet high with a single, erect stalk and stalked, alternate, heart-shaped to triangular leaves that grow from 2½ inches to 1 foot long. The whole plant is rough, like sandpaper. The composite flowers (many small flowers fuse to make the flower head) are 2 to 6 inches across. The center is a brown or purplish disk, surrounded by golden rays. The seeds look like commercial ones, only smaller.

Smaller than commercial varieties and mainly restricted to the prairies and fields of the Midwest, wild sunflower seeds are great when you can find them: Pick the immature flower head before the birds eat the seeds, and let the flower head dry and ripen indoors. Like commercial seeds, you can toast these seeds in the shell and crack them with your teeth. The most efficient way to extract the seeds from the shells is to grind them coarsely, put them in water, and separate the floating shells from the sinking seeds.

CURRY SEEDS

Here's a foolproof recipe I make in quantity and pass out during lunch on my tours. Everyone who is partial to spicy foods goes crazy over this one. Infusing flavor into the sunflower seeds by boiling them with curry powder and then roasting them with more curry powder makes this recipe successful—especially if you use my curry powder formulation. And you can control the degree of spiciness by varying the quantities of curry powder and chili paste you use.

> *10 cups water*
> *Juice of 2 lemons*
> *8 cups shelled raw sunflower seeds*
> *6 cloves garlic, crushed into a paste*
> *1 cup Curry Powder (page 112), or to taste*
> *2 tablespoons Vege-Sal or 1 tablespoon salt, or to taste*
> *¼ cup chili paste or 1 tablespoon cayenne pepper, or to taste*
> *2 tablespoons olive oil*

1. Place the water, lemon juice, sunflower seeds, garlic, ½ cup of the curry powder, 1 tablespoon of the Vege-Sal, and 2 tablespoons of the chili paste in a large saucepan and bring the pot to a boil over high heat, stirring occasionally. Reduce the heat to low and simmer, covered, for 15 minutes stirring occasionally.
2. Meanwhile, preheat the oven to 300 degrees.
3. Drain the seeds in a colander. In a large bowl, mix the seeds with the olive oil and the remaining ½ cup curry powder, 1 tablespoon Vege-Sal, and 2 tablespoons chili paste. Transfer the mixture to 2 roasting pans and bake,

stirring every 20 minutes, until the seeds are dry and crisp, 3 to 4 hours. Curry Seeds will keep, tightly covered, for months in the refrigerator or indefinitely frozen.

MAKES 8 CUPS

FOXTAIL GRASS
Setaria species

THIS GRASS HAS LONG, NARROW LEAVES, TYPICAL of grass, and a single, dense, unbranched, bristly, cylindrical seed head that reminds one of a fox's tail. One species is erect; another bows. Both grow in fields and disturbed habitats across the United States.

When the blackish seeds come off easily in the fall, collect the heads, let them dry in a paper bag, and then rub off the loose seeds (don't rub hard, or you'll get unripe seeds and bristles). Place the seeds on a tray and use a fan to blow away the chaff. The seeds' crunchy texture (even cooking doesn't make them much softer) and nutty flavor make them an ideal alternative to poppy or caraway seeds in baking. You may also add them to grains when you cook them, grind them into flour, or use them in place of poppy seeds.

FOXY FRENCH BREAD

Foxtail grass seeds and whole-grain flours enrich this traditional bread.

> *1 tablespoon active dry yeast*
> *1 ½ cups lukewarm water*
> *¼ cup plus 2 tablespoons corn oil*
> *1 ½ teaspoons Vege-Sal or ¾ teaspoon salt*
> *2 cloves garlic, crushed into a paste*

⅛ teaspoon liquid stevia or 1 tablespoon barley
  malt
2 ¼ cups plus 1 tablespoon (11 ounces) buckwheat
  flour, 2 cups (8 ounces) oat flour, and 1 cup
  plus 3 tablespoons (4 ounces) sweet brown rice
  flour, or 23 ounces any whole-grain flour
¼ cup arrowroot or kudzu
2 tablespoons foxtail grass seeds

1. Dissolve the yeast in the warm water for 5 minutes in a medium-size bowl. Mix in ¼ cup of the corn oil, the Vege-Sal, garlic, and stevia.

2. Mix the flour, arrowroot, and foxtail grass seeds together in a large bowl. Thoroughly mix the wet ingredients into the dry ingredients. Place the bowl in a warm place (80 to 85 degrees) and let the dough rise, covered with a damp towel, for 1 hour.

3. Punch down the dough and roll it into a long, narrow shape, like a sausage. Place the dough in a French bread pan or on an oiled cookie sheet, brush it lightly with 1 tablespoon of the corn oil, and score it diagonally with a sharp knife. Cover the dough with a damp towel and let it rise in a warm place for 30 minutes.

4. Preheat the oven to 400 degrees. Bake the bread until it is lightly browned underneath, about 40 minutes. Brush the loaf with the remaining 1 tablespoon corn oil and let the bread cool on a wire rack before slicing.

MAKES 1 LOAF

BARLEY SPICE BREAD

Foxtail grass seeds add crunchiness and flavor to this simple yeast bread.

1 tablespoon active dry yeast
2 cups lukewarm apple juice
5 ¾ cups (25.2 ounces) barley flour

⅓ cup arrowroot or kudzu
2 tablespoons foxtail grass seeds
2 teaspoons Vege-Sal or 1 teaspoon salt, or to taste
1 teaspoon dried rosemary, finely crumbled
1 teaspoon dried oregano, finely crumbled
1 teaspoon dried marjoram, finely crumbled
3 tablespoons olive oil
2 cloves garlic, crushed into a paste
2 teaspoons chili paste or ½ teaspoon cayenne
  pepper, or to taste
½ teaspoon paprika

1. Mix the yeast with the warm apple juice in a medium-size bowl and let the mixture stand for 5 minutes.

2. Mix the flour, arrowroot, foxtail grass seeds, Vege-Sal, rosemary, oregano, and marjoram together in a large bowl.

3. Mix together 2 tablespoons of the olive oil, the garlic, chili paste, and yeast mixture. Combine the wet ingredients with the dry ingredients and knead the dough for 5 minutes. Cover the bowl with a damp towel and let the dough rise for 1 hour in a warm place (80 to 85 degrees).

4. Punch down the dough, place it in an oiled 6½ x 4⅜ x 2½-inch loaf pan, and shape it into a loaf. Brush the loaf with the remaining 1 tablespoon olive oil. Sprinkle the paprika on top. Cover the loaf with a damp towel and let the dough rise in a warm place for another hour.

5. Preheat the oven to 350 degrees. Set a pan of water on the bottom of the oven to keep the crust soft. Bake the loaf until it pulls away from the sides of the pan slightly and sounds hollow when you tap it, about 50 minutes. Remove the loaf from the loaf pan, brush it with more olive oil, if desired, and let it cool on a wire rack before slicing.

MAKES 1 LOAF

DOTTED-STALK SUILLUS MUSHROOM

Suillus granulatus

THIS *SUILLUS* MUSHROOM HAS A SLIMY, BUFF-colored cap that is 2 to 6 inches across, streaked with cinnamon color, which becomes more pronounced with age (see page 309 for a description of this group). The white flesh inside becomes yellowish with age. The pore surface underneath is cream to pale yellow, and the spores are a dirty cinnamon. The stalk is 1⅝ to 3¼ inches long, ⅜ to 1 inch thick, and pale yellow to dirty cinnamon from top to bottom. This mushroom grows under evergreens across the country from early summer to late fall in the East, and during the winter in California.

The slimy cap of all suillus bolete mushrooms turns some people off; others, afraid it may cause diarrhea (a relatively rare reaction), spend extra time peeling it. But the mushroom is very tasty, and the viscid layer on the cap creates a thickening effect similar to that of okra. Although they are too moist to sauté, I use the dotted-stalk suillus caps and stems in a wide variety of other kinds of cooked recipes. Other choice suillus species may be substituted if you can't find this one.

SCALLOPED SUILLUS

The dotted-stalk suillus mushroom's delicate flavor shines through the layers of noodles, sauce, and tofu cheese in this layered casserole.

¼ cup corn oil

8 cups sliced dotted-stalk suillus mushrooms

4 medium-size yellow bell peppers, seeded and sliced into strips

6 cloves garlic, finely chopped

4 small chiles, or to taste, seeds and ribs removed and chopped

2 teaspoons freshly ground caraway seeds

4 teaspoons freshly ground yellow mustard seeds (2 teaspoons seeds)

1 teaspoon freshly ground cumin seeds

1 teaspoon freshly ground coriander seeds

1 teaspoon turmeric

1 teaspoon Vege-Sal or ½ teaspoon salt, or to taste

6 cups homemade macaroni (use the Buckwheat Noodles recipe, page 34, and use a macaroni die) or store-bought whole-grain macaroni

1 cup Piquant Sumac Sauce (page 281) or Healthy Hollandaise Sauce (page 130)

2 cups fresh Bread Crumbs (page 40)

2 cups Tofu Sharp Cheese (page 30) or Tofu Grated Cheese (page 32)

1. Preheat the oven to 350 degrees.

2. Heat the corn oil in a large skillet over medium heat. Add the mushrooms, bell peppers, garlic, chiles, ground caraway, yellow mustard, cumin, and coriander, turmeric, and Vege-Sal and cook, stirring, for 10 minutes.

3. Meanwhile, cook the homemade pasta for 4 minutes in rapidly boiling salted water with a dash of olive oil. If you're using store-bought pasta, cook it for 3 minutes less than directed. Drain the pasta in a colander and immediately lower the colander into a bowl of cold water to halt the cooking. Drain the pasta again and mix it with the sumac sauce in a 3-quart oiled casserole dish. Cover the pasta layer with the sautéed

vegetables, then the bread crumbs, and finally with the Tofu Sharp Cheese. Bake the casserole, covered, until bubbly, about 30 minutes.

SERVES 6 TO 8

WILD RICE
Zizania aquatica

WILD RICE COMES MAINLY FROM LAKE COUNTRY, and you need a boat to collect it in the wild—which leaves me out. Fortunately, you can also purchase cultivated wild rice. (Should cultivated wild rice still be called *wild*?) Avoid buying light-colored "wild" rice, an inferior cultivated variety, bred because people tend to buy lighter-colored grains, no matter how bad they taste. Look for the tastier, dark-colored, truly wild types.

Growing from 3 to 10 feet tall, the side branches of this large grass, which is not related to rice, bear drooping, purple-tinged, straw-colored male flowers and erect plumes of yellow-green female flowers that can be over 2 feet long in the summer.

To collect the seeds, which ripen in late summer, you need to carry along a drop cloth in a boat (the plant grows in still freshwater and brackish water in the northern United States and Canada, from coast to coast) because, unlike cultivated grains, the seeds "shatter" when you touch them. Let the seeds dry, parch them in a preheated 300-degree oven for a couple of hours, and pound the seeds to separate the chaff. Transfer the seeds to a tray, and blow the chaff away with a fan. The seeds, which are heavy, remain on the tray.

Wild rice has a rich, nutty flavor. I often add it to brown rice for a richer flavor. It's also great in soups or stews.

INDIAN WILD RICE

You may cook wild rice with true rice, even though the two are unrelated. Here's a Bombay approach to combining the two.

2 tablespoons sesame oil or peanut oil
1 cup ramp bulbs (page 116) or onions, chopped
2 cloves
One 1-inch cinnamon stick
1 teaspoon Vege-Sal or ½ teaspoon salt, or to taste
¼ teaspoon freshly ground cardamom seeds
1½ cups brown basmati rice or other long-grain brown rice
½ cup wild rice
4 cups boiling water
2 common spicebush berries (page 314), finely chopped, or pinch of freshly ground allspice

1. Heat the sesame oil in a large saucepan over medium heat. Add the ramps and cook them, stirring, until they are lightly browned, about 10 minutes. Stir in the cloves, cinnamon stick, Vege-Sal, and cardamom. Add the brown rice and wild rice and cook, stirring, for 3 minutes.

2. Add the boiling water and simmer, covered, over low heat until all the water is absorbed and the rice is tender, about 40 minutes.

MAKES 6 CUPS; SERVES 6

THAI BAKED RICE

Chicken mushrooms, dulse flakes, and wild rice create an exceptional East Asian pilaf.

2 ¾ cups water

1 cup wild rice

1 cup brown basmati rice

1 cup sliced chicken mushrooms (page 321)

1 cup raw cashews

½ cup dulse flakes (page 174)

2 tablespoons flaxseed oil or corn oil

2 tablespoons Thai seasoning (available in health food stores)

2 tablespoons chili paste or ¼ teaspoon cayenne pepper, or to taste

1 tablespoon tamari soy sauce

Preheat the oven to 350 degrees. Mix all the ingredients together in a 3-quart oiled casserole dish and bake, covered, until all the liquid has been absorbed and the rice is tender, about 1½ hours.

SERVES 6 TO 8

PRICKLY PEAR

Opuntia species

THIS LOW-GROWING CACTUS HAS PADS THAT are separated by cylindrical joints. The showy, yellow 10- to 12-petaled, radially symmetrical flowers, 3½ inches across, bloom at the tops of the pads in the summer. The flowers are followed in the autumn by club-shaped red fruits that are 1 to 2 inches long and ¾ inch across. The prickly pear rules in the Southwest, but you can also find it in the Southeast and on the East Coast, in sunny, sandy areas (I collect it near the seashore in New York City, the northernmost part of its range). Always handle this plant with heavy-duty work gloves, or the nearly invisible prickles will make you wish you had. Then rub the young parts and fruit thoroughly with a wet towel to remove the thorns.

You can eat the mild-flavored young pads, peeled, in the spring, cooked like okra, but the best part is the fruit. It's somewhat sweet and watery, a little like watermelon. Remove the hard seeds (which you may grind into flour) and use the fruit raw, or cook it for 10 minutes and use it in a variety of fruit dishes.

PRICKLY PEAR ICE CREAM

Prickly pears provide another high-quality foundation for a dairy-free ice cream that looks and tastes a lot like strawberry ice cream.

6 prickly pear fruits, peeled and coarsely chopped

1 ½ cups soy milk or nut milk

1 cup drained silken tofu

½ cup canola oil

¼ cup vegetable glycerin, honey, barley malt, or rice syrup

¼ cup lecithin granules

2 tablespoons fresh lemon juice

2 teaspoons vanilla extract

1 teaspoon liquid stevia

½ teaspoon salt

¼ teaspoon lemon extract

1. Place the prickly pears and soy milk in a medium-size saucepan and bring the pot to a simmer over medium heat. Reduce the heat to low, and simmer, covered, for 5 minutes, stirring occasionally. Drain the

fruit, reserving the soy milk

2. Strain out the prickly pear seeds with a food mill or strainer.

3. In a blender, combine the prickly pear pulp, reserved soy milk, and the remaining ingredients and process until smooth.

4. Chill the mixture completely (1 hour in the freezer, 4 hours in the refrigerator).

5. Pour the mixture into an ice cream machine and freeze it according to the manufacturer's instructions.

MAKES 6 CUPS; SERVES 6

GIANT HORSE MUSHROOM

Agaricus osecanus

THIS MEMBER OF THE FIELD MUSHROOM GROUP is huge, with a white cap that is 4 to 15 inches across that's smooth—first convex, and eventually flattened (see page 286 for a description of this genus). The gills (which are free from the stem) are packed close together. They're white at first, becoming dull pink, reddish brown, and finally chocolate brown, colored by the chocolate-brown spores. (**Don't confuse this mushroom with the potentially deadly Amanitas, which have white gills and spores.**) The white stalk is 1½ to 6 inches long and ⅜ to 1 inch thick, with a membranous white veil that resembles a cogwheel covering the immature gills (in very young individuals), becoming a skirtlike ring on the upper stalk when the cap opens.

The giant horse mushroom grows in pastures, former pastures, lawns, and other grassy areas in the spring and fall. It's supposed to be a West Coast species, but I've definitely found it in New York City parks (no other field mushroom species has such a large cap), and it probably comes up in other regions in North America as well.

This large mushroom has all the flavor its relative the commercial white button mushroom lacks. It's not named after a giant horse, but after a smaller, similar-looking relative, the horse mushroom (*Agaricus arvensis*). Cook the cap and stem for 10 to 20 minutes and use it the same way you would the commercial white mushroom, cooked using virtually any method, but expect much better results. The rich, musky flavor and meaty texture are superb.

TURKISH ZUCCHINI PANCAKES

These traditional Turkish vegetable fritters take on an even more exotic character with the addition of giant horse mushrooms and purslane.

FILLING

¼ cup olive oil

2 cloves garlic, finely chopped

1 medium-size onion, chopped

4 cups sliced giant horse mushrooms

4 cups purslane leaves and stems (page 269) or seeded and chopped green bell peppers

1 medium-size zucchini, ends trimmed and chopped

SAUCE

¼ cup fresh dill leaves

1 clove garlic, peeled

2 tablespoons lecithin granules

2 tablespoons fresh lemon juice

2 tablespoons corn oil or flaxseed oil

One 19-ounce package silken tofu, drained

1 teaspoon Vege-Sal or ½ teaspoon salt

BATTER

- ¾ cup plus 3 tablespoons (4 ounces) buckwheat flour and ½ cup plus 3 tablespoons (3 ounces) barley flour, or 7 ounces any whole-grain flour
- ¼ cup kudzu or arrowroot
- 1 tablespoon poppy seeds
- ½ teaspoon freshly grated nutmeg
- ⅜ teaspoon freshly ground celery seeds (¼ teaspoon seeds)
- ½ teaspoon Vege-Sal or ¼ teaspoon salt
- 1¼ teaspoons cream of tartar
- ½ teaspoon baking soda
- 3 cups soy milk or nut milk
- 2 tablespoons olive oil
- ¼ cup lecithin granules
- 1 teaspoon Tabasco sauce or ¼ teaspoon cayenne pepper

1. *To make the filling:* Heat the olive oil in a large skillet over medium heat. Add the garlic, onion, mushrooms, purslane, and zucchini and cook, stirring, for 10 minutes. Allow the vegetables to cool to room temperature.

2. *To make the sauce:* In a blender, combine the mock yogurt sauce ingredients, process until smooth, and set aside.

3. *To make the batter:* Mix together the flour, kudzu, poppy seeds, nutmeg, ground celery seeds, Vege-Sal, cream of tartar, and baking soda in a large bowl.

4. Mix together the soy milk, olive oil, lecithin, and Tabasco in a medium-size bowl. Sir the wet ingredients into the dry ingredients. Stir in the sautéed vegetables, being careful not to overmix.

5. Pour a circle of batter 6 inches across onto a hot oiled griddle and cook each pancake over medium-low heat until it is lightly browned underneath. Turn the pancake with a metal spatula and brown the other side. Set the pancake aside and keep it warm. Repeat the process until you've used up all the batter.

6. Serve the pancakes with the sauce drizzled on top.

MAKES 12 PANCAKES; SERVES 6

HONEY MUSHROOM
Armillariella mellea

THE HONEY MUSHROOM FITS THE DESCRIPTION of the ringless honey mushroom (see page 284) in every way except for one particular: there's a white ring on the upper stalk. Actually a complex of species from a microscopic perspective, *the honey mushroom is abundant and widespread, but not easy for beginners to identify.* A parasite and saprophyte (meaning it lives off dead trees after killing them), the fungus can decimate an entire forest and fill it with mushroom clusters.

The honey mushroom is one of my favorite fall mushrooms. It tastes even better than its ringless cousin. Moist, rich, and meaty, it also adds a slight silkiness to soups, stews, and sauces, the way okra does. Use it as a meat substitute with those seasonings traditionally used for meat (see the Herb and Spice User's Guide, page 448), sauté it, or add it to noodle recipes, grain dishes, burgers, loaves, or stuffings. The stems are somewhat gritty, so some people discard them, but they're fine in soups and sauces if you purée them after cooking. Cook honey mushrooms for at least 15 minutes or you may become sick, and eat a small amount the first time; they don't agree with everyone. If you can't find honey mushrooms, the closest substitute is the shiitake mushroom (*Lentinus edodes*).

BASIC HONEY CAPS

Here's a quick way to bring out the best of honey mushroom caps. Use these caps in other recipes. Save the stems for sauces.

¼ cup olive oil

10 cups honey mushroom caps, sliced

4 cloves garlic, chopped

2 small chiles, or to taste, seeds and ribs removed
    and chopped

1 teaspoon paprika

¾ teaspoon freshly ground celery seeds
    (½ teaspoon seeds)

½ teaspoon freshly grated nutmeg

1½ tablespoons tamari soy sauce

1 tablespoon Blackberry Spice Wine (page 278) or
    red wine

Heat the olive oil in a large skillet over medium heat. Add the remaining ingredients and cook, stirring, until all the liquid is absorbed or evaporated, 15 to 20 minutes. Don't undercook the mushrooms.

MAKES 3½ CUPS; SERVES 4 TO 5

HONEY BURGERS

Similar to meat burgers, these patties feature tofu, texturized vegetable protein, and honey mushrooms in place of beef.

¾ cup Vegetable Stock (page 40) or water

¾ cup texturized vegetable protein (TVP)

2 tablespoons olive oil

½ cup ramp bulbs or greens (page 116) or 1 small
    onion, chopped

2 celery stalks, sliced

2½ cups honey mushroom caps, sliced

6 cloves garlic, finely chopped

One 16-ounce package soft tofu, drained

¼ cup fresh Bread Crumbs (page 40)

2 tablespoons lecithin granules

2 tablespoons Bragg's Liquid Aminos or tamari soy
    sauce, or to taste

2½ tablespoons freshly ground flaxseeds
    (1 tablespoon seeds)

1 tablespoon chopped fresh basil leaves

1½ teaspoons paprika

1 teaspoon common spicebush berries (page 314)
    finely chopped, or 1 teaspoon freshly ground
    allspice berries

1½ teaspoons chili paste or ½ teaspoon cayenne
    pepper

2 teaspoons freshly ground black mustard seeds
    (1 teaspoon seeds)

½ teaspoon dried oregano, finely crumbled

1 teaspoon freshly grated nutmeg

¾ teaspoon freshly ground celery seeds
    (½ teaspoon seeds)

½ teaspoon dried savory, finely crumbled

1. Preheat the oven to 350 degrees.
2. Place the stock and TVP in a small saucepan and bring the pot to a boil. Remove the pot from the heat, cover, and set it aside for 10 minutes. Drain the TVP in a colander, reserving the stock for another use.
3. Heat the olive oil in a large skillet over medium heat. Add the TVP, ramps, celery, mushrooms, and garlic and cook, stirring, for 10 minutes.
4. In a food processor or large bowl, combine the remaining ingredients and process or beat with a fork or whisk until smooth. Mix the tofu-and-spice mixture with the sautéed ingredients in a large bowl.
5. Shape the mixture into 12 patties and place them on an oiled cookie sheet. Bake them until they are

lightly browned underneath, about 30 minutes. Turn the patties over with a metal spatula and cook them for another 20 minutes to lightly brown the other side.

MAKES 12 BURGERS

HONEY MUSHROOMS BOURGUIGNONNE

This is basically French beef bourguignonne, but where's the beef? It's unnecessary, and the more tasty wild ingredients you include, the less you'll miss using animal products.

1 *pound extra-firm tofu, drained and diced*
½ *cup oat flour or 2 ounces any other whole-grain flour*
¼ *cup olive oil*
6 *medium-size onions, chopped*
4 *cloves garlic, crushed into a paste*
3 *cups honey mushroom caps, sliced*
1 ½ *cups sliced carrots*
4 *cups Vegetable Stock (page 40) or water*
3 ½ *cups watercress leaves (page 387), chopped*
8 *Jerusalem artichokes (page 361), peeled and sliced*
½ *cup any wild or red wine*
2 *tablespoons sweet paprika*
4 *bayberry leaves (page 185) or 2 bay leaves*
1 *tablespoon chopped fresh basil leaves or 1 teaspoon dried, finely crumbled*
2 *teaspoons freshly ground black pepper (1 teaspoon peppercorns)*
1 *teaspoon dried marjoram, finely crumbled*
1 ½ *teaspoons freshly ground celery seeds (1 teaspoon seeds)*
2 *tablespoons tamari soy sauce, or to taste*

1. Dredge the tofu in the flour, tapping off any excess.
2. Heat the olive oil in a large skillet over medium heat. Add the tofu, onions, garlic, mushrooms, and carrots and cook, stirring, for 5 minutes. Add the remaining ingredients and bring the pot to a boil. Reduce the heat to low and simmer, covered, for 10 minutes.
3. Remove the bayberry leaves and serve hot over grains or pasta, or with bread.

SERVE 6 TO 8

HONEY MUSHROOM LOAF

Honey mushrooms are so flavorful that this dish will become one of your favorites. They're especially good used as stuffing inside a loaf of flavored tofu.

STUFFING
¼ *cup olive oil*
8 *cups honey mushroom caps, sliced*
3 *cups hedge mustard leaves (page 78) or cultivated mustard greens*
4 *cloves garlic, crushed into a paste*
1 *cup fresh Bread Crumbs (page 40)*
½ *cup Tofu Grated Cheese (page 32)*
2 *tablespoons finely chopped fresh basil leaves*
½ *cup barley flour or 2 ounces any other whole-grain flour*
2 *teaspoons dried oregano, finely crumbled*
2 *teaspoons dried marjoram, finely crumbled*
2 *tablespoons tamari soy sauce*
1 *teaspoon freshly ground black pepper (½ teaspoon peppercorns)*
1 *cup Homemade Ketchup (page 37)*
TOFU LOAF
Four *19-ounce packages soft tofu, well drained*
½ *cup barley flour or yellow cornmeal*

¼ cup brewer's yeast

2 tablespoons Bragg's Liquid Aminos or tamari soy sauce

2 tablespoons olive oil

½ teaspoon dried rosemary, finely crumbled

½ teaspoon dried sage, finely crumbled

½ teaspoon paprika

½ teaspoon freshly ground white pepper (¼ teaspoon peppercorns)

1. Preheat the oven to 350 degrees.

2. *To make the stuffing:* Heat the olive oil in a large skillet over medium heat. Add the honey mushrooms, hedge mustard, and garlic and cook, stirring, until all the liquid is absorbed or evaporated, 10 to 15 minutes. Combine the cooked vegetables with the remaining stuffing ingredients in a large bowl.

3. *To make the tofu loaf:* In a large bowl, mix all the loaf ingredients together, mashing to combine.

4. Coat the bottom and sides of 2 oiled 8½ x 4½ x 3-inch loaf pans with one-third of the loaf mixture in each pan, reserving enough to cover the top of each loaf.

5. Fill each loaf with the stuffing.

6. Spread the remaining tofu loaf mixture on top of the stuffing. Bake the stuffed loaf until it is lightly browned, about 40 minutes. Serve hot.

MAKES 2 LOAVES; SERVES 8

SPAGHETTI 'N' MEATBALLS WILDMAN STYLE

Honey mushrooms and mock cheese transform this commonplace dish into an exciting, original treat.

7½ cups homemade spaghetti (use the Buckwheat Noodles recipe, page 34, and use a spaghetti die) or whole-grain spaghetti, freshly cooked

2 tablespoons Garden Spice Spread (page 314) or olive oil

18 meatballs made from the Honey Burgers recipe (page 357)

1½ cups Basic Honey Caps (page 357)

1½ cups Tofu Grated Cheese (page 32)

Toss the hot spaghetti with the spread, mix in the remaining ingredients, heat through, and serve.

SERVES 6

CREAMED HONEY MUSHROOMS

Honey mushrooms are one of my favorite species of mushrooms, and savoring them cooked in a French-style mock cream sauce will show you why.

¼ cup olive oil

16 cup honey mushroom caps, sliced

1 medium-size chile, seeds and ribs removed and chopped

4 cloves garlic, finely chopped

1¾ cups water

½ cup drained silken tofu

¼ cup corn oil

¼ cup White Oak Wine (page 176) or white wine

2 tablespoons dark-colored miso

2 tablespoons arrowroot or kudzu

2 tablespoons lecithin granules

1 teaspoon dried tarragon, finely crumbled

2 teaspoons dried parsley, finely crumbled

½ teaspoon freshly grated nutmeg

1. Heat the olive oil in a large skillet over medium heat. Add the mushrooms, chile, and garlic and cook, stirring, for 10 minutes.

2. Meanwhile, in a blender, combine the remaining ingredients and process until smooth. Pour the sauce over the sautéed ingredients and bring the pot to a boil over medium heat, stirring often. Reduce the heat to low, cover, and simmer for 10 minutes. Serve with bread or rice.

SERVES 6

SHEPHERD'S PIE

I'd been cooking for decades before I made my first shepherd's pie because the version the sadistic counselors regularly forced on me in summer camp still strikes terror in my gut. But this casserole of wild mushrooms, tofu, and fresh vegetables covered with mashed potatoes and baked in a casserole dish bears no resemblance to the culinary abomination—beyond the shared name.

> 2 tablespoons olive oil
> 2 medium-size onions, sliced
> 4 cloves garlic, chopped
> 1 head broccoli, broken into florets
> 1 cup walnuts, chopped
> ½ cup Spanish Sausages (page 316)
> ¼ cup Fakin' Bacon Bits
> 2 cups Creamed Honey Mushrooms (page 359)
> 1 teaspoon dried rosemary, finely crumbled
> ½ teaspoon dried sage, finely crumbled
> 1 teaspoon freshly ground black pepper
>   (½ teaspoon peppercorns)
> 3 cups mashed potatoes
> ¼ teaspoon paprika

1. Preheat the oven to 350 degrees.
2. Heat the olive oil in a large skillet over medium heat. Add the onions and garlic and cook, stirring, for

10 minutes. Add the broccoli, reduce the heat to low, cover, and cook for another 5 minutes.
3. Mix the cooked vegetables with the remaining ingredients, except the mashed potatoes and paprika, and transfer to a 3-quart oiled casserole dish.
4. Spoon the mashed potatoes evenly over the cooked vegetables and sprinkle the top of the casserole with the paprika. Bake the casserole until it is lightly browned, about 1 hour. Serve hot.

SERVES 6

HONEY MUSHROOM CASSEROLE

Sometimes the whole forest seems to erupt in honey mushrooms. Here's a way to prepare them quickly in a recipe you can freeze, if necessary, to enjoy at your leisure.

> 3 tablespoons olive oil
> 8 cups honey mushroom caps, sliced
> 4 cloves garlic, finely chopped
> 1 teaspoon Bragg's Liquid Aminos
> ½ teaspoon freshly ground black pepper
>   (¼ teaspoon peppercorns)
> 2 cups Healthy Hollandaise Sauce (page 130)
> 1 tablespoon kudzu or arrowroot

1. Preheat the oven to 350 degrees.
2. Heat the olive oil in a large skillet over medium heat. Add the honey mushrooms and garlic and cook, stirring, for 10 minutes.
3. Combine the mushrooms and garlic with the remaining ingredients in a 3-quart oiled casserole dish and bake, covered, for 30 minutes, or until bubbly. Serve hot.

SERVES 4 TO 6

JERUSALEM ARTICHOKE, SUNCHOKE

Helianthus tuberosus

HERE'S A PERENNIAL SUNFLOWER THAT USES tubers rather than seeds to spread. The sandpaper-like erect stem grows 6 to 12 feet tall, with branches only near the top. The long-stalked, lance-shaped to oval, three-ribbed, lightly toothed, pointed leaves grow from 6 to 10 inches long and 2 to 4 inches wide. They're opposite (paired) near the plant's base and alternate toward the top. The daisy-like flower heads, 2 to 3 ½ inches across, feature a yellow disk surrounded by 12 to 20 yellow rays. The firm beige underground tubers, connected by ropy rhizomes, look just like commercial Jerusalem artichokes.

Look for the Jerusalem artichoke in fields and thickets, along roadsides, and in disturbed areas in the Midwest, its native habitat. This sunflower has been planted and escaped into the wild from east of the Rockies to the East Coast, although I haven't found it growing in the wild in the New York metro area yet. Fortunately, you can buy Jerusalem artichokes in health food stores and supermarkets.

Misunderstanding the word *girosol*, which means "sunflower" in French, someone gave this sunflower, which neither grows in Jerusalem nor is an artichoke, its inappropriate name. The crisp, sweet, flavorful tubers, however, are great thinly sliced in salads. When cooked, they become very soft—ideal for sauces, soups, and purées.

BROWN SAUCE

Serve this Jerusalem artichoke–based sauce with vegetables, loaves, and casseroles. It's easier to make than are conventional sauces and gravies, and much more healthful because it's lower in fat and doesn't contain refined flour.

2 tablespoons olive oil

1 ½ cups sliced Jerusalem artichokes

4 cloves garlic, chopped

2 small chiles, seeds and ribs removed and chopped, or ¼ teaspoon cayenne pepper, or to taste

2 tablespoons sesame seeds

4 cups Vegetable Stock (page 40)

2 tablespoons kudzu or arrowroot

2 tablespoons Mulberry Wine (page 222) or red wine

2 tablespoons dark-colored miso

1 teaspoon dried marjoram, finely crumbled

1 teaspoon dried thyme, finely crumbled

1 teaspoon dried savory, finely crumbled

1 teaspoon freshly ground white pepper (½ teaspoon peppercorns)

1 teaspoon freshly ground yellow mustard seeds (½ teaspoon seeds)

1. Heat the olive oil in a medium-size skillet over medium heat. Add the Jerusalem artichokes, garlic, and chiles and cook, stirring, for 10 minutes.

2. In a small pot, bring the stock to a boil.

3. Carefully transfer the mixture to a blender, add the stock and remaining ingredients, and process until smooth. (Start on low speed and hold down the cover with a towel, to prevent an eruption.)

4. Bring the purée to a boil in a medium-size saucepan over medium heat, stirring often. Reduce the heat to low and simmer, covered, for 10 minutes, stirring often. Serve hot. Brown Sauce will keep, tightly covered, in the refrigerator for up to a week, and frozen for up to 6 months.

MAKES 5½ CUPS

JERUSALEM ARTICHOKES GREEK STYLE

Here's a simple, wonderful appetizer featuring the irresistible flavor of Jerusalem artichokes.

4 cups (1 pound) Jerusalem artichokes, sliced

2 cups Wild Tomato Sauce (page 94)

2 tablespoons olive oil

1 tablespoon fresh lemon juice

½ teaspoon dried tarragon, finely crumbled

10 drops liquid stevia or 1 tablespoon barley malt or rice syrup (optional)

2 tablespoons chopped fresh parsley leaves

2 tablespoons toasted (page 158) and ground hazelnuts

1. Mix all the ingredients, except the parsley and hazelnuts, together in a covered food container and let the mixture marinate in the refrigerator overnight.
2. Preheat the oven to 350 degrees. Drain the mixture and transfer it to a 1½-quart oiled casserole dish. Bake, uncovered, until the artichokes are tender, about 40 minutes. Garnish with the parsley and hazelnuts and serve.

SERVES 6

SUNCHOKE-DAYLILY CASSEROLE

Enjoy this casserole on a sunny day and you'll never choke, even if your name is Lily.

1 cup Vegetable Stock (page 40)

2 tablespoons kudzu or arrowroot

1½ teaspoons miso

2 cloves garlic, chopped

1 teaspoon turmeric

1 teaspoon dried mint, finely crumbled

1 teaspoon dried tarragon, finely crumbled

½ teaspoon chili paste or ¼ teaspoon cayenne pepper, or to taste

2 cups Jerusalem artichokes, sliced

1½ cups daylily shoots (page 64) or chopped scallions

1 cup drained and diced firm tofu

½ cup walnuts, chopped

1. Preheat the oven to 350 degrees.
2. In a blender, combine the stock, kudzu, miso, garlic, turmeric, mint, tarragon, and ground chiles and process until smooth.
3. Combine the stock mixture with the remaining ingredients in a 1½-quart oiled casserole dish. Bake, covered, until bubbly, about 40 minutes. Serve hot.

SERVES 4

SUNCHOKE LATKES

Jerusalem artichokes form the base of these Eastern European potato-free potato pancakes. Latkes are great smothered in hot homemade applesauce.

1 cup lukewarm soy milk, Vegetable Stock (page 40), or water

1 tablespoon olive oil

1 tablespoon active dry yeast

4 cloves garlic, peeled

1 teaspoon sweet paprika

1 teaspoon dried marjoram, finely crumbled

½ teaspoon Vege-Sal or ¼ teaspoon salt, or to taste

½ teaspoon freshly ground white or black pepper
 (¼ teaspoon peppercorns), or to taste

1 cup Jerusalem artichokes, coarsely chopped

1 ½ teaspoons lecithin granules

1 cup plus 2 tablespoons sweet brown rice flour or
 1 ¼ pounds any other whole-grain flour

½ cup arrowroot or kudzu

2 ½ tablespoon freshly ground flaxseeds
 (1 tablespoon seeds)

1. In a blender, combine the lukewarm soy milk, olive oil, yeast, garlic, paprika, marjoram, Vege-Sal, and pepper, and process until smooth.

2. Add the Jerusalem artichokes and lecithin and process until the Jerusalem artichokes are very finely chopped.

3. Mix the flour, arrowroot, and ground flaxseeds together in a large bowl.

4. Stir the wet ingredients into the dry ingredients and mix well. Divide the dough into 12 pieces and shape each piece into a ½-inch-thick disk. Cover the latkes with a damp towel and let them rise in a warm place (80 to 85 degrees) for 30 to 60 minutes.

5. Cook the latkes on both sides on a hot, oiled griddle or frying pan until they are browned, 5 to 10 minutes on each side. (Peanut oil, which tolerates heating best, is the first choice, although you may also bake the latkes for 20 minutes on an oiled cookie sheet in a preheated 350-degree oven.) Serve Sunchoke Latkes hot or cold.

MAKES 12 LATKES; SERVES 6

HEN-OF-THE-WOODS MUSHROOM, MAIITAKE

Grifola frondosas

THIS IS ONE OF MY FAVORITE POLYPORE MUSHROOMS (see page 199 for general features of this group). The clustered, overlapping, lateral, spoon- or fan-shaped, grayish brown caps grow ¾ to 2¾ inches wide, arising from short, white stalks that branch from the base. The surface of the tiny pores under the caps is whitish. The spores are also white.

The mushroom grows throughout most of the United States at the bases of deciduous trees, living or dead, often coming up year after year at the same place at the same time, in the fall. The hen-of-the-woods mushroom is very common, although it is easy to overlook owing to its camouflage colors. I live in a residential neighborhood. One hen-of-the-woods has been coming up from an oak tree in front of a school across the street from my apartment building since 1983. Another appears on an ornamental apple tree on my building's front lawn every year, and several come up around another oak tree one block away. And this is an expensive mushroom to buy. These mushrooms can be large. Three to four pounds per mushroom is usual, and I found one on Halloween of 1982 (not something you forget) that weighed 50 pounds.

Hen-of-the-woods (sold in health food stores under the name Maiitake and reputed to strengthen the immune system) has a deep, rich flavor and chewy texture. The only downside is that it can be a pain to clean unless it's very fresh. Grit gets ingrained in the dozens of little caps, and you have to cut gritty pieces

of the cap away with a paring knife. Prepare this flavorful fungus any way you like—sautéed, simmered in
soups, marinated, baked, or even pickled. It cooks in
15 to 20 minutes. Use both caps and stems.

SOLID CRAB SALAD

Here's a recipe in which hen-of-the-woods mushroom
is seasoned like crabmeat. It makes this solid salad
superior.

> 5 cups Vegetable Stock (page 40)
>
> 2 ½ teaspoons agar powder
>
> ⅔ cup Tofu Cream Cheese (page 30)
>
> 2 tablespoons mellow (light-colored) miso
>
> 1 clove garlic, peeled
>
> 1 teaspoon dried tarragon, finely crumbled
>
> ½ teaspoon turmeric
>
> ⅓ cup fresh dill leaves
>
> 2 cups Cajun Hen (page 365)
>
> 4 Jerusalem artichokes (page 361), sliced
>
> 1 celery stalk, sliced
>
> 1 medium-size carrot, grated
>
> 1 medium-size yellow bell pepper, seeded and
>   chopped
>
> ½ cup low-sodium pitted olives, drained and
>   chopped
>
> 1 small red onion, chopped
>
> 4 cups any salad greens, for garnish

1. Place the stock and agar in a medium-size saucepan
and bring the pot to a simmer over medium heat.
Reduce the heat to low and simmer, covered, until the
agar is dissolved, about 5 minutes.

2. Carefully transfer the stock mixture to a blender,
add the Tofu Cream Cheese, miso, garlic, tarragon,
and turmeric, and process until smooth. Add the dill

and briefly blend on low speed until it is chopped.

3. Combine the stock mixture with the remaining
ingredients, except the salad greens, in an oiled bowl
or mold and chill until the mixture jells.

4. Invert the bowl over a platter and tap the mold
to drop the jelled mixture onto the platter. Garnish
with the greens. Serve with Spiceberry-Ramp Salad
Dressing (page 122) or another dressing in this book,
if desired.

SERVES 8 TO 10

WILD VEGETABLE–MUSHROOM SOUP

Hen-of-the-woods mushrooms, sheep sorrel, watercress, and ramp bulbs all thrive in autumn. Here's a
hearty soup that contains all four. The soup is still
wonderful if you substitute store-bought ingredients.

> 1 ¾ cups barley
>
> 8 cups water
>
> 12 cups Vegetable Stock (page 40)
>
> 2 tablespoons olive oil
>
> 4 celery stalks, sliced
>
> ½ cup ramp bulbs (page 116) or shallots, chopped
>
> 5 cloves garlic, finely chopped
>
> 4 cups hen-of-the-woods mushrooms, chopped
>
> 3 cups watercress leaves (page 387), chopped
>
> 3 cups sheep sorrel leaves (page 138) or other leafy
>   greens, chopped
>
> ⅓ cup fresh dill leaves, chopped
>
> 1 tablespoon chili paste or ½ teaspoon cayenne
>   pepper, or to taste
>
> 2 teaspoons dried oregano, finely crumbled
>
> 1 teaspoon dried thyme, finely crumbled
>
> 1 teaspoon freshly ground fennel seeds
>
> ½ cup mellow (light-colored) miso

1. Place the barley, water, and stock in a soup pot and bring the pot to a boil. Reduce the heat to medium-low and simmer, covered, for 45 minutes.

2. Meanwhile, heat the olive oil in a medium-size skillet over medium heat, add the celery, ramps, and garlic and cook, stirring, for 10 minutes.

3. Add the hen-of-the-woods to the simmering stock and simmer for 10 minutes. Add the sautéed ingredients and all the remaining ingredients, except the miso, to the mushrooms and stock and simmer for another 5 minutes.

4. Turn off the heat, lower a strainer partway into the soup, and stir the miso against the sides with a whisk or wooden spoon until the miso dissolves. Serve hot.

MAKES 2 QUARTS; SERVES 8

CRAB BISQUE

Not even the crabbiest crab would ever crab about this lovely crab-free crab soup.

2 tablespoons corn oil
1 small red onion, chopped
4 cloves garlic, chopped
2 cups drained silken tofu
2 cups soy milk
2 tablespoons Redbud Wine (page 159) or red wine
4 teaspoons tamari soy sauce
1 teaspoon dried tarragon, finely crumbled
1 cup Cajun Hen (recipe follows)
¼ cup fresh parsley leaves, chopped

1. Heat the corn oil in a medium-size saucepan skillet over medium heat. Add the onion and garlic and cook, stirring, for 5 minutes.

2. In a blender, combine the onion, garlic, tofu, soy milk, wine, tamari, and tarragon and process until smooth. Add the Cajun Hen and blend briefly on low speed and chop fine.

3. Transfer the mixture to the saucepan, add to the onion and garlic, and bring the pot to a boil over medium heat, stirring often. Reduce the heat to low, cover, and simmer for 10 minutes. Serve hot, garnished with the parsley.

SERVES 6

CAJUN HEN

Here's a simple way to prepare hen-of-the-woods that makes it resemble spicy, Cajun-style crabmeat. You can enjoy it as a side dish, use it in recipes that call for crabmeat, or freeze it. When I come home with a gigantic mushroom, this is the way I like to prepare it in order to store it.

30 cups hen-of-the-woods mushrooms, sliced
½ cup Seafood Seasoning (page 257)
¼ cup chili paste or 1 tablespoon cayenne pepper, or to taste
¼ cup olive oil
¼ cup fresh dill leaves, chopped
2 tablespoons tamari soy sauce
Juice of 1 lemon

1. Preheat the oven to 350 degrees.

2. Mix all the ingredients together and bake for 45 minutes in a 14 x 9 x 2-inch oiled casserole dish until it is browned and fragrant.

MAKES 25 CUPS

EGGPLANT PARMESAN

This simple approach to a traditional dish replaces the cheese with tofu cheese, includes homemade tomato sauce, and adds the delicate flavor and chewy texture of hen-of-the-woods mushrooms. Could anything be better?

2 tablespoons salt

2 medium-size eggplants, sliced crosswise into
½-inch-thick slices

6 cups hen-of-the-woods mushrooms, chopped

¼ cup Vegetable Stock (page 40) or water

½ cup olive oil

6 cups Wild Tomato Sauce (page 94)

1½ cups fresh Bread Crumbs (page 40)

1 recipe (3 cups) Tofu Grated Cheese (page 32)

1. Salt the eggplant slices in a colander and set them aside for 30 minutes. Wash off the salt under running water and drain the eggplant in a colander. This process eliminates the eggplant's bitterness.

2. Meanwhile, bring the stock to a boil and steam the mushrooms over the boiling stock on a steamer rack for 20 minutes. Remove the mushrooms and save the stock for another use.

3. Heat the olive oil in a large skillet over medium heat. Add the eggplant slices and fry them on both sides until they are lightly browned. Blot them on paper towels.

4. Preheat the oven to 375 degrees.

5. Spread a thin layer of tomato sauce over the bottom of a 14 x 9 x 2-inch oiled baking dish and build layers of eggplant, mushrooms, tomato sauce, bread crumbs, and Tofu Grated Cheese, until you've used up all the ingredients, ending with the Tofu Grated Cheese. Bake until bubbly, about 45 minutes.

SERVES 6 TO 8

BRAISED EGGPLANT WITH MUSHROOMS

Most people cook eggplant in too much oil, and the eggplant absorbs oil like a sponge. In this simple, tasty vegetable side dish, the flavors and seasonings make such unhealthful cooking methods unnecessary.

⅓ cup olive oil

1 small young eggplant, thickly sliced

½ cup shallots, chopped

4 cloves garlic, minced

1 ¾ cups hen-of-the-woods mushrooms, sliced

¾ cup water

½ cup red wine vinegar

1 tablespoon freshly ground coriander seeds

1 tablespoon tamari soy sauce

2 teaspoons dried thyme, finely crumbled

1 teaspoon dried savory, finely crumbled

1 teaspoon freshly ground white pepper
(½ teaspoon peppercorns)

2 bayberry leaves (page 185) or 1 bay leaf

1. Heat the olive oil in a large skillet over medium heat. Add the eggplant, shallots, and garlic and cook, stirring, for 5 minutes.

2. Add the remaining ingredients, reduce the heat to medium-low, and simmer, covered, for another 15 minutes. Remove the bayberry leaves before serving.

SERVES 4 TO 6

CRAB CRÊPE FILLING

Hen-of-the-woods mushroom flavored with Cajun crabmeat seasonings adds distinction to this filling. Use the filing to stuff crêpes, with the batter from Chicken Mushroom Crêpes (page 335), or in any recipe that calls for stuffing.

3 tablespoons olive oil

2 medium-size zucchini, ends trimmed and thinly sliced

1 medium-size red bell pepper, seeded and chopped

1 medium-size onion, chopped

3 cloves garlic, chopped

1 ½ cups Cajun Hen (page 365)

1 ½ cups Tofu Cottage Cheese (page 30)

1 tablespoon Bragg's Liquid Aminos or tamari soy sauce

1. Heat the olive oil in a large skillet over medium heat. Add the zucchini, bell pepper, onion, and garlic and cook, stirring, until the onion is golden, about 10 minutes.

2. Mix in the remaining ingredients, heat the mixture through, and proceed as in Chicken Mushroom Crêpes (page 335), or use the mixture as a stuffing in other dishes.

MAKES ENOUGH FILLING FOR
24 CRÊPES; SERVES 8

CRAB IMPERIAL

In this classic gourmet casserole, I use seasoned hen-of-the-woods mushrooms in place of crabmeat, and it works perfectly.

4 cups Cajun Hen (page 365)

2 cups Wild Mustard Seed Mayonnaise (page 206) or store-bought vegan mayonnaise

2 cups low-sodium pitted olives, drained

1 ½ cups seeded and sliced red bell peppers

½ cup fresh Bread Crumbs (page 40)

2 teaspoons dried tarragon, finely crumbled

1. Preheat the oven to 350 degrees.

2. Mix all the ingredients together in a 3-quart oiled casserole dish and bake until bubbly, about 30 minutes. Serve hot on noodles.

SERVES 6

DEVILED CRAB

Hen-of-the-woods disguises itself so well in this crabmeat recipe, you'd have to already know it was there to recognize it. Serve Deviled Crab hot or cold as an appetizer with crackers.

2 cups Cajun Hen (page 365)

1 cup Tofu Cream Cheese (page 30)

¾ cup fresh Bread Crumbs (page 40)

2 cloves garlic, crushed into a paste

2 tablespoons chopped fresh parsley leaves

2 teaspoons freshly ground yellow mustard seeds (1 teaspoon seeds)

½ teaspoon freshly grated nutmeg

1 ½ teaspoons olive oil

1. Preheat the oven to 350 degrees.

2. Mix the Cajun Hen, Tofu Cream Cheese, ½ cup of the bread crumbs, the garlic, parsley, ground yellow mustard seeds, and nutmeg together in a 1½-quart oiled casserole dish.

3. Combine the remaining ¼ cup bread crumbs and the olive oil and sprinkle the mixture on top of the Cajun Hen mixture. Bake, uncovered, until hot, about 15 minutes.

SERVES 6

CRAB CAKES

Although this recipe contains many ingredients, it's very simple to make. And if you ever invite a crab over for dinner, this is the cake to serve, since crabs are, in fact, cannibalistic.

4 cups Cajun Hen (page 365)

1 large red onion, chopped

2 celery stalks, finely chopped

¼ cup fresh parsley leaves, chopped

2 cloves garlic, chopped

3 cups fresh Bread Crumbs (page 40)

½ cup arrowroot or kudzu

3 tablespoons plus 2 ½ teaspoons freshly ground
   flaxseeds (1 ½ tablespoons seeds)

2 teaspoons freshly ground yellow mustard seeds
   (1 teaspoon seeds)

1 teaspoon freshly ground dill seeds

1 teaspoon freshly ground coriander seeds

1 teaspoon freshly ground cloves

1 teaspoon ground dried wild ginger (page 111) or
   regular ground ginger

1 teaspoon common spicebush berries (page 314),
   finely chopped, or ½ teaspoon freshly ground
   allspice berries

6 bayberry leaves (page 185) or 3 bay leaves,
   freshly ground

1 teaspoon Vege-Sal or ½ teaspoon salt, or to taste

1 teaspoon freshly ground white pepper
   (½ teaspoon peppercorns), or to taste

½ cup Wild Mustard Seed Mayonnaise (page 206)

1 tablespoon corn oil

1 tablespoon fresh lime juice

2 tablespoons lecithin granules

½ teaspoon Tabasco sauce

1. Preheat the oven to 350 degrees.

2. Mix together all the ingredients and form the mixture into 23 patties.

3. Arrange the patties on an oiled cookie sheet and bake until they are lightly browned, about 30 minutes, turning them halfway through the baking time. Serve hot.

MAKES 23 PATTIES; SERVES 6 TO 8

MUSHROOM MEATBALLS

Mushrooms make a great substitute for meat. They have a similar chewy texture, and if you use super-flavorful wild mushrooms with the right seasonings, you'll get great results.

1 ½ cups Cajun Hen (page 365), finely chopped

3 cups fresh Bread Crumbs (page 40)

½ cup lecithin granules

½ cup water or Vegetable Stock (page 40)

5 tablespoons freshly ground flaxseeds (2 tablespoons seeds)

¼ teaspoon liquid stevia

2 tablespoons dark-colored miso

2 tablespoons Wineberry Wine (page 246) or red
   wine

2 tablespoons toasted sesame oil

¼ cup kudzu or arrowroot

2 teaspoons peeled and grated fresh ginger

⅛ teaspoon orange extract

1. Preheat the oven to 350 degrees.

2. In a large bowl, combine all the ingredients together thoroughly and shape the mixture into 20 meatballs.

3. Arrange the meatballs on 2 oiled cookie sheets and bake them until they are lightly browned, about 30 minutes, turning them halfway through the baking time.

4. Serve the meatballs with Buckwheat Noodles (page

34) or store-bought pasta and Wild Tomato Sauce (page 94).

MAKES 20 MEATBALLS; SERVES 4 TO 6

SESAME HEN

Tahini sauce and Middle Eastern seasonings provide an elegant setting for the sensational hen-of-the-woods mushroom.

3 tablespoons olive oil

7 cups hen-of-the-woods mushrooms, sliced

1 teaspoon dried marjoram, finely crumbled

1 teaspoon dried oregano, finely crumbled

1 teaspoon dried wild spearmint (page 59) or other mint, finely crumbled

½ teaspoon freshly ground cumin seeds

1 teaspoon freshly ground white pepper (½ teaspoon peppercorns)

4 cloves garlic, crushed into a paste

¼ cup fresh lemon juice

2 tablespoons Bragg's Liquid Aminos or tamari soy sauce

½ cup Tahini (page 38)

1. Heat the olive oil in a large skillet over medium heat. Add the mushrooms, marjoram, oregano, spearmint, cumin, and white pepper and cook, stirring, for 5 minutes. Add the garlic and cook, stirring, for another 3 minutes.

2. Meanwhile, mix the lemon juice and Bragg's Liquid Aminos with the tahini. Stir this mixture into the mushrooms, reduce the heat to low, and cook, covered, for another 5 minutes. Serve hot with bread or whole grains.

SERVES 6

HEN-OF-THE-WOODS SUPREME

Here's a wonderful main course that everyone will gobble up as soon as they taste it.

SAUTÉ

¼ cup olive oil

4 cups hen-of-the-woods mushrooms, sliced

2 medium-size yellow bell peppers, seeded and sliced into strips

2 medium-size onions, sliced

4 celery stalks, sliced

6 cloves garlic, chopped

1 teaspoon dried marjoram, finely crumbled

1½ teaspoons freshly ground celery seeds (1 teaspoon seeds)

1 teaspoon Vege-Sal or ½ teaspoon salt, or to taste

1 teaspoon freshly ground black pepper (½ teaspoon peppercorns)

SAUCE

4 cups Vegetable Stock (page 40)

½ cup red wine

3 tablespoons arrowroot or kudzu

3 tablespoons dark-colored miso

2 tablespoons corn oil

4 cups fresh Bread Crumbs (page 40)

4 cups Tofu Sliced Cheese (page 31)

2 cups Tofu Grated Cheese (page 32)

1. Preheat the oven to 350 degrees.

2. To make the sauté: Heat the olive oil in a large skillet over medium heat. Add the remaining sauté ingredients and cook, stirring, for 10 minutes.

3. To make the sauce: In a blender, combine the sauce ingredients and process until smooth.

4. In a medium-size bowl, mix the corn oil with the bread crumbs.

5. Layer a 14 x 9 x 2-inch oiled baking dish with half the sauce, all the sautéed vegetables, the Tofu Sliced Cheese, the remaining sauce, the oiled bread crumbs, and the Tofu Grated Cheese. Bake until bubbly, about 40 minutes.

SERVES 6 TO 8

SWEET-AND-HOT HEN

Here's a spicy Indian treatment of a great American mushroom. Enjoy as a mushroom side dish.

> 1 ¾ cups water
> ¾ cup drained silken tofu
> 6 tablespoons sesame oil or peanut oil
> ¾ teaspoon liquid stevia or 1 tablespoon honey, barley malt, or rice syrup
> 1 ½ teaspoons Vege-Sal or ¾ teaspoon salt
> 2 tablespoons arrowroot or kudzu
> 6 cups hen-of-the-woods mushrooms, chopped
> 1 teaspoon black mustard seeds
> 2 tablespoons Indian white split lentils (urad dal)
> 2 dried chiles, or to taste, seeds removed and chopped

1. In a blender, combine the water, tofu, 3 tablespoons of the sesame oil, the liquid stevia, Vege-Sal, and arrowroot, and process until smooth.

2. Heat the remaining 3 tablespoons sesame oil in a small skillet over medium heat and add the black mustard seeds. When the mustard seeds pop, add the lentils and cook them until they're light brown and the mustard seeds stop popping, stirring often. Stir in the chiles.

3. Transfer the lentil mixture to a large saucepan, add the tofu mixture, and bring the pot to a simmer over low heat, stirring constantly. Simmer until thickened,

about 1 minute. Add the hen-of-the-woods and simmer them over low heat for 10 minutes, stirring often. Serve hot with whole grains or Indian bread.

SERVES 6

MARINATED HEN-OF-THE-WOODS

Here's yet another way to prepare this versatile mushroom. Serve as a mushroom side dish, or use it in any recipe calling for cooked mushrooms.

> 4 cloves garlic, peeled
> 1 ½ teaspoons coriander seeds
> 2 teaspoons black mustard seeds
> 2 teaspoons dried sage, finely crumbled
> 1 teaspoon caraway seeds
> 1 teaspoon dill seeds
> 1 teaspoon black peppercorns
> 4 cups hen-of-the-woods mushrooms, coarsely diced
> 1 ¼ teaspoons corn oil
> ½ cup Vegetarian Worcestershire Sauce (page 56)
> ½ cup red wine vinegar
> ¼ cup tamari soy sauce
> ¼ teaspoon liquid stevia

1. Put the garlic, coriander, black mustard seeds, sage, caraway seeds, dill seeds, and peppercorns in a tea ball or tea bag or tie them up inside a piece of cheesecloth. Place the spices in a non-metal container with all the other ingredients, tossing to coat the mushrooms well with the mixture.

2. Refrigerate the mixture overnight, stirring it once or twice if possible.

3. Preheat the oven to 350 degrees.

4. Drain the mushrooms in a colander, transfer them to a 1½-quart oiled casserole dish, cover, and bake them for 30 minutes.

5. Drain the mushrooms and pat them dry with paper towels.

MAKES 2 CUPS; SERVES 2 TO 4

MUSHROOM-STUFFED PUMPKINS

Mini-pumpkins are sweet and tasty. They're even better filled with delectable hen-of-the-woods mushroom stuffing.

> Three 1-pound mini-pumpkins or kabocha
> squashes, stems removed
> 2 cups Marinated Hen-of-the-Woods (page 370),
> diced
> 2 cups fresh Bread Crumbs (page 40)
> 1 cup Tofu Grated Cheese (page 32)
> 1 tablespoon tamari soy sauce

1. Preheat the oven to 350 degrees.

2. Cut the mini-pumpkins in half along their equator and remove the seeds. Place the pumpkin halves cut side down on an oiled cookie sheet and bake them for 30 minutes. Leave the oven on.

3. Mix together the remaining ingredients in a medium-size bowl, and fill the pumpkins with the stuffing. Return the stuffed pumpkins to the oven and bake them for another 15 minutes. Serve hot.

SERVES 6

HEN-OF-THE-WOODS IN WINE SAUCE

Almost every type of cooking method works with this mushroom. Here's a French-style mushroom stew.

> ¼ cup olive oil
> 18 cups hen-of-the-woods mushrooms, sliced
> 2 medium-size bell peppers, seeded and chopped
> 3 medium-size zucchini, ends trimmed and sliced
> ½ cup walnuts, chopped
> 6 cloves garlic, finely chopped
> 2 cups Vegetable Stock (page 40)
> ½ cup Wineberry Wine (page 246) or red wine
> 2 tablespoons arrowroot or kudzu
> 1 tablespoon chopped fresh parsley leaves
> 1 teaspoon dried marjoram, finely crumbled
> 1 teaspoon dried tarragon, finely crumbled
> 1 teaspoon freshly ground black pepper
> (½ teaspoon peppercorns)
> 1 teaspoon peeled and chopped fresh ginger
> 1 teaspoon chili paste or ¼ teaspoon cayenne
> pepper, or to taste

1. Heat the olive oil in a large skillet over medium heat. Add the hen-of-the-woods, bell peppers, zucchini, walnuts, and garlic and cook, stirring, for 10 minutes.

2. Meanwhile, in a blender, combine the remaining ingredients and process until smooth.

3. Pour the purée into the skillet and bring the pot to a boil over medium heat, stirring constantly. Reduce the heat to low, cover, and simmer for 10 minutes, stirring occasionally. Hen-of-the-Woods in Wine Sauce will keep, tightly covered, in the refrigerator for 1 week.

SERVES 6

MUSHROOM-VEGETABLE FRITTATA

Here's a revolutionary eggless omelet. The combination of ingredients and seasonings provides a very close resemblance to eggs without the saturated fat, cholesterol, the inhumane conditions of factory farming, or even the necessity of breaking an egg to make an omelet! In Spanish omelets such as this one, the filling is incorporated into the omelet itself, instead of being enveloped as a stuffing. Hen-of-the-woods mushroom makes this frittata unbelievably good.

SAUTÉ

2 tablespoons olive oil

2 cups hen-of-the woods mushrooms, sliced

1 medium-size onion, chopped

1 medium-size yellow or red pepper, seeded and chopped

1 celery stalk, sliced

4 cloves garlic, chopped

1½ teaspoons chopped fresh basil leaves or ½ teaspoon dried, finely crumbled

1 teaspoon dried marjoram, finely crumbled

1 teaspoon dillweed, finely crumbled

½ teaspoon freshly ground fennel seeds

2 teaspoons tamari soy sauce

½ teaspoon chili paste or pinch of cayenne pepper, or to taste

OMELETS

5 cups drained silken tofu

6 tablespoons fresh Bread Crumbs (page 40)

6 tablespoons lecithin granules

¼ cup arrowroot or kudzu

3 tablespoons corn oil

1 tablespoon freshly ground black pepper (1½ teaspoons peppercorns)

1½ teaspoons freshly grated nutmeg

¾ teaspoon freshly ground fenugreek seeds

¾ teaspoon turmeric

¾ teaspoon Vege-Sal or ½ teaspoon salt, or to taste

1. *To make the sauté:* Heat the olive oil in a large skillet over medium heat, add the remaining sauté

ingredients, and cook, stirring, for 10 minutes.

2. *To make the omelets:* In a food processor or large bowl, combine the omelet ingredients and process or beat them with a whisk until smooth.

3. Stir the sautéed ingredients into the omelet mixture.

4. Pour one sixth of the combined mixture into a circle on a hot, oiled griddle (if you put a heat diffuser under the griddle and raise the heat to medium, the omelet will cook more evenly) and cook the omelet over medium-low heat until it is browned underneath. Turn the omelet with a metal spatula and brown the other side. Repeat with the remaining omelet mixture to make 6 omelets in all. Serve hot.

SERVES 6

HEN CASSEROLE EXTRAORDINAIRE

Hen-of-the-woods is a superb mushroom, fitting for an extraordinary casserole.

6 tablespoons olive oil

14 cups hen-of-the-woods mushrooms, sliced

6 cloves garlic, finely chopped

1½ teaspoons Vege-Sal or ¾ teaspoon salt

4 cups cooked diced squash

3⅓ cups Mock Egg Sauce (page 35)

5 cups Tofu Cottage Cheese (page 30)

4 cups fresh Bread Crumbs (page 40)

¼ cup corn oil

1. Preheat the oven to 350 degrees.

2. Heat the olive oil in a large skillet over medium heat. Add the mushrooms and garlic and cook, stirring, for 10 minutes.

3. Remove the skillet from the heat and mix the

cooked mushrooms and garlic with the squash, Mock Egg Sauce, and Tofu Cottage Cheese. Transfer the mixture to a 14 x 9 x 2-inch oiled casserole dish.

4. Combine the bread crumbs with the corn oil in a medium-size bowl and press the mixture on top of the mushroom mixture. Bake, uncovered, until bubbly, about 50 minutes.

SERVES 6

FOUNTAIN OF YOUTH

My friends Kathy and Joe discovered that if a choice polypore mushroom such as a chicken mushroom (page 321) or hen-of-the-woods is past its prime but not spoiled or infested with insects, marinating is one of the best ways to revive it. You can then bake the mushroom in a covered casserole dish, basting it often. I've used marinades myself to transform otherwise second-rate species, such as Berkeley's polypore (see page 199) into first-class fungi, but their original idea takes things one step further. (I do take credit for introducing them to wild mushrooms in the late 1980s.)

> 1 teaspoon coriander seeds
> 1 teaspoon dried oregano, finely crumbled
> 1 teaspoon dried sage, finely crumbled
> ½ teaspoon white peppercorns
> 8 cups middle-aged hen-of-the-woods mushrooms, sliced
> 2 cups corn oil
> 1 cup canola oil
> ½ cup red wine vinegar
> 1½ cups Blackberry Spice Wine (page 278) or red wine
> ¼ cup tamari soy sauce, or to taste
> 1 tablespoon chopped fresh dill or 1 teaspoon dillweed

> 1 teaspoon Tabasco sauce
> 1 tablespoon paprika

1. Place the coriander, oregano, sage, and peppercorns in a tea ball or tea bag, or tie them up inside a piece of cheesecloth. Combine the spices and the remaining ingredients, coating the mushrooms well, and refrigerate the mixture, covered, in a non-metal container overnight or longer.

2. Preheat the oven to 275 degrees.

3. Drain the mushrooms in a colander and then bake them, covered, in an oiled 3-quart casserole dish for 1½ hours, basting the mushrooms occasionally with the marinade.

4. Drain the mushrooms in a colander and press them between paper towels to remove the excess marinade.

SERVES 4 TO 6

HEN IN BUTTER SAUCE

This side dish doesn't sound very vegetarian, does it? But the hen is the hen-of-the-woods mushroom, and the butter sauce is the vegan version in this book. The two make a great combination.

> 3 tablespoons Spiceberry Butter Sauce (page 316)
> 2½ cups hen-of-the-woods mushrooms, sliced
> ½ teaspoon Vege-Sal or ¼ teaspoon salt, or to taste
> ½ teaspoon freshly ground black pepper (¼ teaspoon peppercorns), or to taste
> 2 tablespoons Blackberry Spice Wine (page 278) or red wine

1. Heat the Spiceberry Butter Sauce in a medium-size skillet over medium heat. Add the mushrooms, Vege-Sal, and pepper and cook, stirring, for 10 minutes.

2. Add the wine and cook for another 10 minutes.

Serve hot. Hen in Butter Sauce will keep, tightly covered, in the refrigerator for 1 week.

MAKES 1½ CUPS; SERVES 2 TO 3

GOLDEN PHOLIOTA MUSHROOM

Pholiota aurivella

THE GOLDEN PHOLIOTA HAS A SLIMY, OCHRE cap that is 2 to 6 inches wide, bell shaped to convex, and spotted with flat, brownish scales. Underneath, yellow-brown gills attach to the stalk. The spores are brown. The yellowish to yellow-brown stalk is 2 to 4 inches long, ¼ to ⅝ inch wide, and briefly encircled toward the top with an off-white ring that leaves a faint ring zone. The mushroom grows clustered on deciduous and coniferous trees, logs, and stumps in autumn, throughout most of North America. *Avoid Pholiota biemalis, a similar Pacific Northwest mushroom with slimy scales on the stalk, which is poisonous.*

Mushroom hunters consider the golden pholiota good, but a clear rank below the many choice mushrooms featured in this book. Yet it's so abundant in the second half of autumn, I've always wondered how to use it to make first-rate dishes. The trick is to take advantage of this mushroom's melt-in-your-mouth texture. Wash the slime off the cap and include the cap and stem in soups, stews, and sauces. Let other ingredients provide most of the flavor, and you can never go wrong.

STEVE'S SALSA

The golden pholiota mushroom's mild flavor and soft texture make it the perfect choice for this spicy Caribbean salsa. Use this as a dip for chips or as a condiment.

> 3 tablespoons olive oil
> 2 cups packed golden pholiota mushrooms, sliced
> 2 celery stalks, sliced
> 1 medium-size red onion, sliced
> 6 cloves garlic, chopped
> 6 small chiles, or to taste, seeds and ribs removed and finely chopped
> 2 teaspoons freshly ground cumin seeds
> 2 teaspoons dried oregano, finely crumbled
> 1½ teaspoons freshly ground celery seeds (1 teaspoon seeds)
> 4 medium-size ripe tomatoes, chopped
> ¼ cup fresh cilantro or parsley leaves, chopped
> 3 tablespoons Bragg's Liquid Aminos or tamari soy sauce
> ½ cup water

1. Heat the olive oil in a large skillet over medium heat. Add the mushrooms, celery, onion, garlic, chiles, cumin, oregano, and celery seeds and cook, stirring, for 10 minutes.

2. Add the remaining ingredients, bring the pot to a boil, reduce the heat to low, cover, and simmer for 10 minutes. Let the salsa cool before serving it. Steve's Salsa will keep, tightly covered, in the refrigerator for up to a week.

MAKES 4½ CUPS

BLACK WALNUT

Juglans nigra

THIS NATIVE TREE GROWS FROM 50 TO 120 FEET tall, with dark brown, deeply furrowed bark with flattened ridges. The alternate, feather-compound leaves consist of 12 to 24 narrow, lance-shaped, finely toothed, leaflets that are 3½ inches long on both sides of a midrib that is 1 to 2 feet long. Slender catkins of inconspicuous, green male flowers hang from the branches in the spring, while short, less noticeable female flowers grow at the branch tips. Walnuts resembling green tennis balls 2½ inches across fall to the ground in autumn. This tree and its edible close relatives grow in the Northeast, across the South, and into California.

Stomp on the nuts to remove the green husks. Wear rubber gloves when handling the husks and nuts or your hands will get stained. To eliminate the staining problems, let the nuts dry and mature in their shells for a week or so on newspapers. Crack the shell with a heavy-duty nutcracker, vise, heavy hammer, or large rock. Remove the nutmeat with a nutpick. Enjoy these nuts raw or cooked.

Black walnuts have a strong, rich, smoky flavor with a hint of wine. Use them in any recipe that call for nuts, but, unless you're featuring the black walnut's flavor, use it sparingly, or it will overpower everything else. I often combine one part black walnuts with three parts commercial (English) walnuts. If you can't find black walnut, substitute equal parts regular walnuts and hazelnuts.

BLACK WALNUT SPREAD

American black walnuts lend their rich, deep flavor to this Russian-style spread. Here is further proof that the cold war is over. Slather Black Walnut Spread on bread or use it as a dip.

> 1 cup well-drained silken tofu
> 2 tablespoons lecithin granules
> 2 tablespoons brown rice vinegar or red wine vinegar
> 2 tablespoons sweet white miso or other sweet miso
> 1 tablespoon corn oil, walnut oil, or flaxseed oil
> 2 teaspoons freshly ground yellow mustard seeds (1 teaspoon seeds)
> 1 teaspoon brewer's yeast
> 1 teaspoon dried tarragon, finely crumbled
> 1 teaspoon freshly ground white pepper (½ teaspoon peppercorns)
> 1 cup black walnuts
> 1 cup regular walnuts

1. In a food processor or large bowl, combine all the ingredients except the walnuts and process or beat with a whisk or fork until smooth.

2. Add the walnuts and process until they are finely chopped, or chop the nuts fine by hand and mix them with the remaining ingredients. Black Walnut Spread will keep, tightly covered, in the refrigerator for 1 week.

MAKES 2 CUPS

BLACK WALNUT–AVOCADO SPREAD

This tasty spread or dip features the flavor of black walnuts with the texture of avocado.

¼ cup fresh dill leaves

1 ripe avocado, peeled and pitted

⅓ cup black walnuts

¼ cup olive oil

2 tablespoons fresh lemon or lime juice

2 tablespoons mellow (light-colored) miso

2 tablespoons lecithin granules

1 tablespoon Crunchy Almond Butter (page 38) or
  Crunchy Peanut Butter (page 38)

½ teaspoon ground dried wild ginger (page 111) or
  regular ground ginger

¼ teaspoon orange extract or 1 teaspoon
  dried orange rind

1. In a food processor or by hand, chop the dill.

2. Add the remaining ingredients and continue chopping until the walnuts are finely chopped. Black Walnut–Avocado Spread will keep, tightly covered, in the refrigerator for 1 week.

MAKES 1¼ CUPS

BLACK WALNUT PESTO

Here's a mild pesto made with black walnuts and cooked garlic. Serve it on pasta, as a dip, or as a spread for crackers or bread.

1 head elephant garlic

1 cup olive oil, plus about 2 tablespoons for basting

½ cup fresh basil leaves

¼ cup fresh cilantro or parsley leaves

1 cup walnuts

1 cup pine nuts

½ cup black walnuts

¼ cup dark-colored miso

¼ cup lecithin granules

1. Preheat the oven to 375 degrees. In a covered, oiled casserole dish, bake the garlic for 40 minutes, basting occasionally with the 2 tablespoons of olive oil. Let cool and then peel.

2. Meanwhile, in a food processor or by hand, chop the basil and parsley. Add the garlic and process or chop again. Add the nuts and process or chop until finely chopped.

3. Add the miso, lecithin, and remaining cup of olive oil and process until well mixed. Black Walnut Pesto will keep, tightly covered, in the refrigerator for up to 3 weeks, covered with a thin layer of olive oil.

MAKES 3 CUPS

BLACK WALNUT SALAD DRESSING

Black walnuts blend right in with the other ingredients in this piquant salad dressing.

½ cup olive oil

½ cup canola oil or safflower oil

½ cup brown rice vinegar or red wine vinegar

¼ medium-size ripe papaya, peeled and seeded

¼ medium-size red onion, peeled

¼ cup black walnuts

Juice of ½ orange

1½ teaspoons fresh lemon juice

1½ teaspoons mellow (light-colored) miso

2 large cloves garlic, peeled

½ teaspoon chili paste or cayenne pepper, or to
  taste

In a blender, combine all the ingredients and process until smooth. Black Walnut Salad Dressing will keep, tightly covered, in the refrigerator for up to 2 weeks.

MAKES 2½ CUPS

BLACK WALNUT SAUCE

This pungent, savory garlic sauce is similar to pesto sauces in Italian cuisine. Serve it hot on pasta or vegetables, or serve it cold as a dip.

6 cloves garlic, or to taste, peeled
1 ½ tablespoons chopped fresh parsley leaves
⅓ cup black walnuts
⅓ cup walnuts or hazelnuts (page 299)
1 cup Tofu Cottage Cheese (page 30)
½ cup soy milk or nut milk
¼ cup olive oil
¼ cup corn oil
½ teaspoon Vege-Sal or ¼ teaspoon salt, or to taste

1. In a food processor or by hand, chop the garlic and parsley.
2. Add the remaining ingredients and process until well mixed, or chop the nuts by hand and mix them with the remaining ingredients. Black Walnut Sauce will keep, tightly covered, in the refrigerator for 5 to 7 days.

MAKES 2 CUPS

BLACK WALNUT BISQUE

You'll love this quick, simple, delicious soup.

5 cups Vegetable Stock (page 40) or water
¾ cup hazelnuts
½ cup black walnuts
1 cup drained silken tofu
1 celery stalk, sliced
2 tablespoons White Oak Wine (page 176) or sherry
1 small chile, seeds and ribs removed, or
    ¼ teaspoon cayenne pepper, or to taste
¼ teaspoon liquid stevia or 1 ½ teaspoons honey,
    barley malt, or rice syrup, or to taste (optional)

2 tablespoons corn oil
2 tablespoons mellow (light-colored) miso,
    1 teaspoon Vege-Sal, or ½ teaspoon salt,
    or to taste
2 tablespoons chopped field garlic (page 57),
    chives, or scallions
1 teaspoon freshly grated nutmeg

1. Place all the ingredients except the corn oil, miso, wild onion leaves, and nutmeg in a large saucepan and bring the pot to a simmer, covered, over medium heat. Reduce the heat to low, and simmer for 5 minutes.
2. Carefully transfer the mixture to a blender in 2 batches and process with the corn oil and miso until smooth, holding down the blender cover with a towel to prevent eruptions.
3. Serve hot, garnished with the garlic and nutmeg.

SERVES 6

MACARONI AND "CHEESE" CASSEROLE

Here's a simple Italian-style pasta casserole featuring black walnuts and tofu cheese.

2 cups homemade macaroni (use the Buckwheat
    Noodles recipe, page 34, and use a macaroni
    die) or store-bought whole-grain macaroni or
    other pasta
3 tablespoons olive oil
½ cup black walnuts
½ cup chopped walnuts
1 cup Tofu Grated Cheese (page 32)
1 ½ cups Tofu Cream Cheese (page 30)
3 tablespoons yellow cornmeal
½ cup fresh Bread Crumbs (page 40)

1. Preheat the oven to 350 degrees.

2. Cook the macaroni in rapidly boiling salted water with 1 tablespoon of the oil. Cook the pasta approximately 2 minutes before it is al dente. Drain the pasta in a colander.

3. Immediately toss the pasta with 1 tablespoon of the olive oil and all the walnuts, and transfer the mixture to a 2-quart oiled casserole dish.

4. Meanwhile, mix together the cheeses and cornmeal in one bowl, and mix the bread crumbs with the remaining 1 tablespoon olive oil in another bowl.

5. Pour the cheese mixture on top of the pasta in the casserole dish and spread the bread crumb mixture on top. Bake, covered, until bubbly, about 35 minutes. Serve hot.

SERVES 6

BAKED BLACK WALNUT–THREE-GRAIN CASSEROLE

If brown rice is a staple for you, here's a way to prepare it that will make it taste completely new.

> 4 cups water
> 1½ cups brown basmati rice or long-grain brown rice
> ¼ cup wild rice (page 353)
> ¼ cup amaranth (page 338)
> 1 cup black walnuts, chopped
> 1 tablespoon corn oil
> 2 teaspoons Vege-Sal or 1 teaspoon salt
> ½ teaspoon freshly ground cloves
> ½ teaspoon freshly ground black pepper
>   (¼ teaspoon peppercorns)

1. Preheat the oven to 375 degrees.

2. Mix all the ingredients together in a 3-quart oiled casserole dish and bake, covered, until all the water is absorbed and the rice and grains are tender, about 1½ hours.

SERVES 6

MEXICAN STUFFED PEPPERS

Black walnuts add distinction to the mock cheese stuffing in these chili peppers. Medium-size peppers may be hot or mild—choose the variety that suits your taste.

> ¼ cup raisins
> 10 medium-size chiles
> STUFFING
>   ¼ cup carob chips or unsweetened chocolate chips
>   ¼ cup black walnuts
>   1 cup Tofu Ricotta Cheese (page 31)
>   ½ teaspoon ground cinnamon
>   ½ teaspoon freshly grated nutmeg
>   ¼ teaspoon freshly ground cloves

1. Bring a medium-size saucepan of water to a boil, add the raisins to the water, and steam the chile peppers on a steamer rack for 30 minutes. Remove the chile peppers from the steamer and when they are cool enough to handle, slit one side of each pepper lengthwise and remove the seeds and ribs.

2. Strain the raisins from the water and mix them with the other stuffing ingredients. Fill the peppers with the stuffing. Chill completely before serving.

MAKES 10 PEPPERS; SERVES 5

BLACK WALNUT–PUMPKIN BREAD

Black walnut lovers, beware: You won't be able to stop eating this bread.

1 ⅓ cups apple juice

2 cups raisins

1 tablespoon active dry yeast (½ package)

2 ¾ cups plus 3 tablespoons (14 ounces) sweet brown rice flour and 3 ½ cups (14 ounces) oat flour, or 1 ¾ pounds any whole-grain flour

1 cup arrowroot or kudzu

1 teaspoon salt

2 teaspoons ground cinnamon

2 teaspoons freshly grated nutmeg

¼ cup walnut oil

½ cup corn oil

2 tablespoons liquid lecithin

½ teaspoon liquid stevia or 2 tablespoons honey, barley malt, or rice syrup

6 common spicebush berries (page 314), finely chopped, or 1 teaspoon freshly ground allspice berries

2 teaspoons freshly grated lemon rind

1 tablespoon peeled and chopped fresh ginger

2 cups cooked pumpkin

1 cup black walnuts

1. Bring the apple juice to a boil in a saucepan, remove the pot from the heat, add the raisins, and let them steep for 30 minutes. Strain out the raisins, reheat the apple juice to lukewarm, and dissolve the yeast in it for 5 minutes.

2. Meanwhile, in a large bowl, mix together the flours, arrowroot, salt, cinnamon, and nutmeg.

3. In a blender, combine the walnut oil, corn oil, liquid lecithin, liquid stevia, spicebush berries, lemon rind, ginger, cooked pumpkin, and yeast mixture and process until smooth. Mix the wet ingredients into the dry ingredients, add the black walnuts, and beat the thick batter for a few minutes. Cover the bowl and place the dough in a warm spot (80 to 85 degree) for 45 minutes to rise.

4. Punch down the dough, divide it among 3 oiled 6½ x 4⅜ x 2½-inch loaf pans, and shape it into 3 loaves. Cover the loaves with a moist towel and place them in a warm spot for 45 minutes to rise again.

5. Preheat the oven to 350 degrees. Set a pan of water in the bottom of the oven to keep the crust soft. Bake the loaves until they pull away from the edges of the pan slightly, about 1 hour.

6. Remove the loaves from the loaf pans and let them cool on a wire rack before slicing.

MAKES 3 LOAVES

BLACK WALNUT–PEACH CRÊPES

Gourmet cooks criticize health food crêpes for being too heavy. But the heaviness vanishes when you eliminate whole wheat flour. You can even do away with the eggs and milk. The filling for these dessert crêpes consists of black walnuts, Tofu Cottage Cheese, and peaches or nectarines.

CRÊPES

½ cup plus 2 tablespoons (3 ounces) buckwheat flour and ¾ cup plus 3 tablespoons (4 ounces) barley flour, or 7 ounces any whole-grain flour

5 tablespoons freshly ground flaxseeds (2 tablespoons seeds)

¼ cup arrowroot or kudzu

¼ cup lecithin granules

3 ½ cups soy milk or nut milk, or as needed

2 tablespoons corn oil

½ teaspoon salt

½ teaspoon liquid stevia or 2 tablespoons honey,
    barley malt, rice syrup, or maple syrup

1 teaspoon vanilla extract

½ teaspoon orange extract

FILLING

4 ripe peaches or nectarines, pitted and sliced

1 ½ cups Tofu Cottage Cheese (page 30)

½ cup black walnuts

2 tablespoons honey, barley malt, or rice syrup

1. Preheat the oven to 350 degrees.

2. *To make the crêpes:* In a blender, blend the crêpe ingredients together using enough soy milk to make a medium-thin batter.

3. *To make the filling:* In a large bowl, mix together the filling ingredients.

4. Spread a thin circle of the batter on a hot, oiled griddle and cook each crêpe over medium-low heat. Putting a heat diffuser under the griddle will help the crêpes cook more evenly. When the crêpe is lightly browned underneath, turn it over with a metal spatula and lightly brown the other side. Repeat the process until you've used up all the batter.

5. Spread some of the filling along an edge of each crêpe and roll it up. Continue until you have used up the remaining filling and crêpes. Bake the filled crêpes on an oiled cookie sheet until they are hot, about 20 minutes. Serve hot with a fruit sauce such as Wild Strawberry Sauce (page 208) or Tofu Sour Cream (page 33).

MAKES 21 CRÊPES; SERVES 7

BLACK WALNUT–CAROB CAKE

Here is a wonderful alternative to chocolate cake, and it is completely sin-free.

CAKE

1 ⅔ cups (½ pound) sweet brown rice flour and
    1 ⅔ cups (½ pound) buckwheat flour, or
    1 pound any whole-grain flour

1 cup carob powder

4 teaspoons cream of tartar

2 teaspoons baking soda

2 teaspoons dried mint, finely crumbled

2 teaspoons ground cinnamon

1 teaspoon freshly ground coriander seeds

1 teaspoon freshly ground star anise

2 cups apple juice

¼ cup corn oil or sesame oil

½ cup drained silken tofu

1 cup regular walnuts, chopped

½ cup black walnuts, chopped

CAROB ICING

2 cups almonds

½ cup carob powder

2 tablespoons natural cherry juice concentrate

1 tablespoon vanilla extract

½ teaspoon liquid stevia or 2 tablespoons honey,
    rice syrup, or barley malt

¼ teaspoon freshly ground cloves

⅛ teaspoon cognac extract (optional)

⅛ teaspoon almond extract

1. Preheat the oven to 350 degrees.

2. *To make the cake:* In a large bowl, mix together the flours, carob powder, cream of tartar, baking soda, mint, and spices.

3. In a blender, combine the apple juice, corn oil, and

tofu, and process until smooth. Mix the wet ingredients into the dry ingredients, being careful not to overmix. Add the walnuts. Press the batter into an oiled 12¼ x 9 x 2-inch baking dish. Bake the cake until a toothpick inserted in the center emerges clean, about 45 minutes.

4. *To make the icing:* In a food processor, process the icing ingredients using the chopping blade, until the nuts are well chopped (or chop the nuts and mix the ingredients by hand).

5. Remove the cake from the baking dish and let it cool on a wire rack.

6. When the cake is cool, cover the top with the icing.

SERVES 4 TO 6

BLACK WALNUT–PUMPKIN ICE CREAM TARTS

When you put a Wildman tofu ice cream into a pie crust, the results are spectacular.

ICE CREAM

1 cup cooked pumpkin

1½ cups well-drained silken tofu

½ cup canola oil or safflower oil

¼ cup vegetable glycerin, barley malt, or honey, or
to taste

1 teaspoon liquid stevia

2 teaspoons vanilla extract

2 tablespoons lecithin granules

1 teaspoon ground dried wild ginger (page 111) or
regular ground ginger

1 teaspoon ground cinnamon

1 teaspoon freshly grated nutmeg

½ teaspoon salt

½ cups black walnuts

CRUST

¼ cup (1.2 ounces) sweet brown rice flour and
¼ cup (1 ounce) oat flour, or 2 ounces any
whole-grain flour

2 tablespoons arrowroot or kudzu

1 teaspoon dried wild spearmint (page 59) or other
mint, finely crumbled

½ teaspoon salt

¼ teaspoon freshly ground cloves

½ cup apple juice

2 tablespoons corn oil

½ cup black walnuts, unsweetened shredded
coconut, or toasted sesame seeds (optional)

1. *To make the ice cream:* In a blender, combine all the ice cream ingredients, except the black walnuts, and process until smooth.

2. Chill the mixture (or begin with chilled ingredients) if required by your ice cream machine, and stir in the black walnuts.

3. Pour the mixture into the ice cream machine and freeze it according to the manufacturer's instructions. Store the ice cream in the freezer until you are ready to use it.

4. *To make the crust:* In a large bowl, mix together the flours, arrowroot, spearmint, salt, and cloves.

5. In a small bowl, mix together the apple juice and corn oil. Stir the wet ingredients into the dry ingredients. Chill the dough (or begin with chilled ingredients) to make the dough more workable.

6. Preheat the oven to 450 degrees.

7. Using a rolling pin covered with a floured sleeve, roll out the dough into a sheet ³⁄₁₆ inch thick on a floured pastry sheet. Cut the pastry into 4-inch circles using a cookie cutter or jar lid making 22 pastries or using up the dough. Press the circles into 2 oiled muffin tins. Bake the pastry shells for 10 minutes at 450 degrees, and then lower the oven temperature to 350 degrees, reducing the heat quickly by opening the oven door for a minute. Bake for another 10 minutes. Remove the pastry shells from the muffin tins and let cool on wire racks.

8. Fill the cooled pastry shells with the ice cream and sprinkle additional black walnuts, shredded coconut, or sesame seeds on top, if desired.

MAKES 22 TARTS; SERVES 11

BLACK WALNUT ICE CREAM

Black walnuts are one of the strongest-tasting nuts, and therefore they are ideal in ice cream, which softens their intensity.

2 cups soy milk or nut milk

1 ½ cups well-drained silken tofu

½ cup canola oil

¼ cup vegetable glycerin, honey, barley malt, or rice syrup

¼ cup lecithin granules

2 teaspoons vanilla extract

1 teaspoon liquid stevia

½ teaspoon salt

1 cup black walnuts, chopped

1. In a blender, combine all the ingredients, except ½ cup of the black walnuts, and process until smooth.

2. Chill the mixture (or begin with chilled ingredients) if required by your ice cream machine.

3. Pour the mixture into an ice cream maker, along with the remaining ½ cup black walnuts, and freeze the ice cream according to the manufacturer's instructions.

MAKES 6 CUPS; SERVES 6

KIWI–BLACK WALNUT SORBET

Black walnuts smooth out the sweet, tart flavor of kiwis in a dessert that will cool you off in hot weather.

6 kiwi fruits, peeled

2 cups apple juice or water

½ cup black walnuts

½ cup canola oil

¼ cup vegetable glycerin, honey, barley malt, or rice syrup

Juice of 1 lime

2 teaspoons vanilla extract

1 teaspoon liquid stevia or 2 tablespoons honey, barley malt, or rice syrup

½ teaspoon salt

¼ teaspoon orange extract (optional)

1. In a blender, combine all the ingredients and process until smooth.

2. Chill the mixture (or begin with chilled ingredients) if required by your ice cream machine.

3. Pour the mixture into an ice cream machine and freeze it according to the manufacturer's instructions.

MAKES 5½ CUPS; SERVES 5 TO 6

MEADOW MUSHROOM

Agaricus campestris

THIS MUSHROOM LOOKS LIKE THE COMMERCIAL white button mushroom (*Agaricus bisporus*) because that is its closest wild relative. The mostly smooth, convex to flat, white to brownish cap measures

1 to 4 inches across. As a member of the field mushroom group, it has gills that are free from the stem (see page 286 for details about this group's common characteristics). The gills are bright pink before the brown spores color them chocolate brown *(similar looking poisonous Amanitas and Lepiotas always have white gills and white spores)*. The whitish stalk is only 1 to 2 inches long and ⅜ to ⅝ inch thick and is usually smooth. A membranous white veil that covers the immature gills becomes a delicate ring, easily obliterated, on the stalk. A very similar-looking choice relative, the spring agaricus (*Agaricus bitorquis*), has a double ring, grows on hard, bare soil, and comes up in the spring and fall. The meadow mushroom grows in the grass, sometimes in great abundance, throughout North America, in late summer and fall, continuing through the winter in California.

My greatest success with this species was after I led a Columbus Day tour on the grounds of the Winterthur Museum, the former estate of the Du Ponts, in Wilmington, Delaware, in 1998. Former grass pastures stretching as far as the eye could see were smothered with meadow mushrooms. My friends and I just sat on our butts filling our bags. Then we'd scoot over a couple of feet and repeat the process, continuing until dark without collecting a fraction of what was there.

The meadow mushroom is much better tasting than its bland relative, the commercial mushroom. The caps and stems take to any cooking method, with spectacular results. This mushroom cooks in 10 to 20 minutes.

HUNGRY WILDMAN'S MUSHROOM SPREAD

Here is a superb spread made with puréed mushrooms and herbs.

2 tablespoons olive oil

2 cups packed meadow mushrooms, sliced

2 medium-size onions, chopped

2 large cloves garlic, finely chopped

¼ teaspoon common spicebush berries (page 314), finely chopped, or freshly ground allspice berries

1 cup drained silken tofu

2 tablespoons fresh lemon juice

¼ teaspoon freshly ground cardamom seeds

Vege-Sal or salt to taste

Freshly ground black pepper or cayenne pepper to taste

1. Heat the olive oil in a large skillet over medium heat. Add the mushrooms and onions and cook, stirring, for 10 minutes. Add the garlic and cook, stirring, for another 5 minutes.

2. In a food processor, combine the spicebush berries, tofu, lemon juice, cardamom, Vege-Sal, and pepper and process until smooth, or chop the spicebush berries fine and mix them with the remaining ingredients using a whisk or fork.

3. Add the mushroom mixture to the tofu mixture and chop fine. Hungry Wildman's Mushroom Spread will keep, tightly covered, in the refrigerator for 1 week.

MAKES 1½ CUPS

CREAMY BEET AND MUSHROOM CASSEROLE

I hated beets (and nearly all other vegetables) when I was a kid, but if you cook them correctly, they can be fantastic. This simple recipe is an example.

7 raw beets, sliced (5 cups)

4 cups cooked brown rice

4 cups packed meadow mushrooms, sliced

2 cups Wild Mustard Seed Mayonnaise (page 206)

1. Preheat the oven to 350 degrees.

2. Mix all the ingredients together in a 4-quart oiled casserole dish. Cover and bake for 1 hour. Serve hot.

SERVES 6 TO 8

WILD PASTA SUPREME

This basic pasta dish with vegetables and mushrooms tastes even better if you make it with wild ingredients.

2 tablespoons olive oil

1 cup packed meadow mushrooms, sliced

2 cloves garlic, finely chopped

2 ½ cups ramp leaves (page 116) or scallions, chopped

¼ cup preserved radish in chili (available in Asian grocery stores) or chopped fresh radish

4 cups Wild Tomato Sauce (page 94)

2 cups cooked Buckwheat Noodles (page 34) or store-bought pasta

1 cup cooked and drained unseasoned common milkweed (page 169) or chopped cooked broccoli

1. Heat the olive oil in a large skillet over medium heat. Add the mushrooms and garlic and cook, stirring, for 10 minutes. Add the ramps and preserved radish and cook, stirring, for another 5 minutes.

2. Add the tomato sauce, cooked pasta, and milkweed and heat through.

SERVES 4 TO 6

MEADOW MUSHROOMS ITALIAN STYLE

Italian cooks have excelled at wild mushroom preparation since ancient times. Here's my version of a traditional dish featuring the meadow mushroom.

2 tablespoons olive oil

1 ¼ cups packed meadow mushrooms, sliced

1 medium-size red bell pepper, seeded and sliced into strips

1 medium-size ripe tomato, chopped

1 celery stalk, sliced

¼ cup ramp bulbs (page 116) or shallots, sliced

SAUCE

2 cups Vegetable Stock (page 40)

¼ cup drained silken tofu

¼ cup fresh parsley leaves

¼ cup Wild Crabapple Blossom Wine (page 425) or sherry

2 tablespoons corn oil

1 tablespoon arrowroot or kudzu

1 teaspoon dried oregano, finely crumbled

1 teaspoon dried rosemary, finely crumbled

1 teaspoon dried thyme, finely crumbled

1 teaspoon Vege-Sal or ½ teaspoon salt, or to taste

1 teaspoon chili paste or ¼ teaspoon cayenne pepper, or to taste

½ pound (4 cups) Buckwheat Noodles using the spaghetti die (page 34) or store-bought whole-grain spaghetti

1 cup Tofu Grated Cheese (page 32)

1. Heat the olive oil in a large skillet over medium heat. Add the mushrooms, bell pepper, tomato, celery, and ramps and cook, stirring, for 5 minutes.

2. *To make the sauce:* In a blender, combine all the

sauce ingredients and process until smooth. Stir the sauce into the mushrooms and bring the pot to a boil over medium heat, stirring constantly. Reduce the heat to low and simmer for 10 minutes, uncovered, stirring often.

3. Meanwhile, cook the spaghetti in rapidly boiling salted water with a dash of olive oil until al dente. Drain the pasta in a colander and then toss it with the mushroom mixture. Sprinkle the Tofu Grated Cheese on top and serve hot.

SERVES 6

SAUTÉED MEADOW MUSHROOMS

Here's a quick, simple way to prepare a mushroom side dish with meadow mushrooms.

> 3 tablespoons olive oil
> 12 cups packed meadow mushrooms, sliced
> 6 cloves garlic, crushed into a paste
> 1 tablespoon dried rosemary, finely crumbled
> 1 tablespoon dried tarragon, finely crumbled
> 1 tablespoon dried marjoram, finely crumbled
> 1½ teaspoons Vege-Sal or ¾ teaspoon salt, or to taste
> 2 teaspoons freshly ground black pepper (1 teaspoon peppercorns), or to taste

Heat the olive oil in a large skillet over medium heat. Add the remaining ingredients and cook, stirring, for 10 minutes.

SERVES 6

DUKKA RICE

Meadow mushrooms and a Middle Eastern spice and nut combination make this rice dish outstanding.

> 2 tablespoons olive oil
> 4 cups packed meadow mushrooms, sliced
> 2 teaspoons freshly ground coriander seeds
> 1 teaspoon freshly ground cumin seeds
> 1 teaspoon dried thyme, finely crumbled
> 4 teaspoons Vege-Sal or 2 teaspoons salt
> 2 teaspoons freshly ground black pepper (1 teaspoon peppercorns), or to taste
> 3¾ cups water
> 1½ cups brown basmati rice
> ½ cup wild rice (page 353)
> ¼ cup sesame seeds, toasted (page 73)
> ¼ cup hazelnuts, toasted (page 158) and finely chopped
> 1 tablespoon chili paste or ½ teaspoon cayenne pepper, or to taste
> Juice of ½ lime

1. Heat the olive oil in a large skillet over medium heat. Add the mushrooms, coriander, cumin, thyme, 2 teaspoons of the Vege-Sal, and the black pepper and cook until all the liquid the mushrooms exude is evaporated, about 10 minutes.

2. Add the remaining ingredients and bring the pot to a boil over medium heat. Reduce the heat to low, cover, and simmer until all the liquid is absorbed and the rice is tender, about 40 minutes.

SERVES 6

SPICY MEADOW MUSHROOMS

This savory mushroom side dish will make your mouth water. By the way, garlic is supposed to keep Dracula away. Do you know why? Because it keeps everybody away!

2 tablespoons coriander seeds

1 tablespoon caraway seeds

1 tablespoon cumin seeds

1 ½ teaspoons black peppercorns

6 tablespoons olive oil

12 cups packed meadow mushrooms, sliced

6 cloves garlic, finely chopped

6 small chiles, or to taste, seeds and ribs removed and finely chopped

1 ½ teaspoons Vege-Sal or ¾ teaspoon salt, or to taste

1. Toast the coriander, caraway, and cumin seeds and peppercorns in a small skillet over medium heat until fragrant, 3 to 4 minutes, stirring constantly.

2. Grind the seeds into a powder in a spice grinder or coffee grinder (or with a mortar and pestle).

3. Heat the olive oil in a large skillet over medium heat. Add the mushrooms, garlic, chiles, Vege-Sal, and ground spices and cook, stirring, until all the liquid the mushrooms exude is evaporated, about 10 minutes. Serve hot.

SERVES 6

FRICADILLON

How can these meatballs suffer from lack of meat when they contain superlative meadow mushrooms instead?

2 tablespoons olive oil

4 cups packed meadow mushrooms, sliced

1 medium-size onion, sliced

4 cloves garlic, sliced

2 small chiles, or to taste, ribs and seeds removed and finely chopped

1 tablespoon Bragg's Liquid Aminos, or to taste

1 tablespoon fresh lemon juice

2 cups fresh Bread Crumbs (page 40)

¼ cup fresh parsley leaves, chopped

¼ cup lecithin granules

1 teaspoon dried savory, finely crumbled

1 teaspoon dried thyme, finely crumbled

1 ½ teaspoons freshly ground celery seeds (1 teaspoon seeds)

1 teaspoon freshly ground black pepper (1 teaspoon peppercorns)

1. Preheat the oven to 350 degrees.

2. Heat the olive oil in a large skillet over medium heat. Add the mushrooms, onion, garlic, chiles, Bragg's, and lemon juice and cook, stirring, for 10 minutes.

3. In a large bowl, combine the cooked vegetables with the remaining ingredients and shape the mixture into about 21 meatballs 2 inches in diameter. Arrange the meatballs on an oiled cookie sheet.

4. Bake the meatballs until they are lightly browned underneath, about 25 minutes. Serve with Buckwheat Noodles (page 34) and Wild Tomato Sauce (page 94).

MAKES 21 MEATBALLS; SERVES 7

CREAMY MEADOW MUSHROOMS

Mushrooms have been served to advantage with cream for centuries. Here's a dairy-free version that tastes too good not to be sinful.

¼ cup olive oil or corn oil

2 medium-size onions, sliced

12 cups packed meadow mushrooms, sliced

4 cloves garlic, chopped

2 teaspoons dried oregano, finely crumbled

1 teaspoon dried marjoram, finely crumbled

1 teaspoon freshly grated nutmeg

1 teaspoon freshly ground black pepper
*   (½ teaspoon peppercorns)*

2 tablespoons Bragg's Liquid Aminos or tamari soy
*   sauce, or to taste*

1 teaspoon paprika

2 cups Tofu Sour Cream (page 33)

1. Heat the olive oil in a large skillet over medium heat. Add the onions and cook, stirring, until golden, about 10 minutes.

2. Add the remaining ingredients, except the paprika and Tofu Sour Cream, and cook, stirring, until all the liquid is absorbed, about 10 minutes.

3. Stir in the paprika and Tofu Sour Cream and heat through. Serve with Buckwheat Noodles (page 34).

SERVES 6

FRESH TOMATO SAUCE

The meadow mushrooms and bayberry leaves included in this simple tomato sauce show how wild ingredients can make a traditional recipe special.

6 tablespoons olive oil

2 medium-size onions, sliced

8 cloves garlic, sliced

4 cups packed meadow mushrooms, sliced

12 medium-size ripe tomatoes, chopped

Two 6-ounce cans tomato paste

3 tablespoons chopped fresh basil leaves or
*   1 tablespoon dried, finely crumbled*

2 teaspoons dried marjoram, finely crumbled

2 teaspoons dried sage, finely crumbled

2 teaspoons dried thyme, finely crumbled

2 teaspoons dried oregano, finely crumbled

2 teaspoons Vege-Sal or 1 teaspoon salt, or to taste

4 bayberry leaves (page 185) or 2 bay leaves
*   (enclosed in a tea bag or tea ball if desired)*

½ teaspoon freshly ground black pepper
*   (¼ teaspoon peppercorns), or to taste*

1. Heat the olive oil in a large skillet over medium heat. Add the onions, garlic, and mushrooms and cook, stirring, until all the liquid is absorbed or evaporated, about 10 minutes.

2. Add the remaining ingredients and bring the pot to a boil over medium heat, stirring often. Reduce the heat to low, and simmer, uncovered, for 1 hour.

3. Remove the bayberry leaves before serving. Fresh Tomato Sauce will keep, tightly covered, in the refrigerator for 10 days, or in the freezer for 6 months.

MAKES 10½ CUPS

WATERCRESS
Nasturtium officinale

WILD WATERCRESS IS REALLY CULTIVATED European watercress gone wild. Its alternate, deep green leaves, 1½ to 6 inches long, are partially divided into increasingly large paired lobes, with the largest, unpaired lobe at the leaf's tip. Long, narrow clusters of tiny, white, four-petaled flowers appear in the summer and fall, followed by narrow, cylindrical seed capsules. Fine white roots emerge from the stem. Watercress grows in running fresh water throughout North America. You can find it almost all year, although there's often not enough in the winter to make harvesting worthwhile. Collect watercress only after you've had the water tested, or you run the risk of infecting yourself with parasites.

After only a few (human) generations in our streams, wild watercress has already evolved into a hardier, much tastier variety. Use this leafy vegetable in salads, sandwiches, soups, sauces, or stews. You'll also love it steamed, sautéed, or baked. It cooks in about 5 minutes.

WATERCRESS–GARLIC MUSTARD SALAD

As members of the mustard family, garlic mustard and watercress provide phytoestrogens, natural substances that help prevent cancer. These two related plants cooperate to prevent cancer in this salad.

> 2 tablespoons sesame seeds
> 2 ½ cups watercress leaves, chopped
> 1 ½ cups garlic mustard roots (page 61), finely
>   chopped
> 2 cloves garlic, crushed into a paste
> 1 tablespoon brown rice vinegar or red wine vinegar
> 2 tablespoons orange juice
> Vege-Sal or salt and freshly ground black pepper
>   to taste

1. Toast the sesame seeds in a small skillet over medium heat until they pop, become fragrant, and turn light brown, 2 to 3 minutes, stirring the seeds constantly.
2. Toss the toasted sesame seeds with the remaining ingredients in a medium-size serving bowl and serve. Serve the salad with any salad dressing in this book.

SERVES 6

DEBORAH'S FIRST SPRING SALAD IN FALL

Here's a salad you can make with the first plants of springtime (or again in late fall, when the same greens again come into season). The word *officinale* in the Latin name for watercress refers to the species' medicinal value, and this nutritious salad is "good medicine" when the days are short. Traditional herbalists recommend tonics, to strengthen all organ systems, at this time of year. And my niece, Deborah Drazen, a Ph.D. in behavioral neuroendocrinology, showed in research with hamsters that the immune system does produce fewer antibodies when challenged by infection during periods of shortened daylight. If this is also true for humans, the herbalists are right. And if not, I'm sure a hamster would enjoy this fresh green salad as much as you would.

> 2 cups beet leaves, chopped
> 2 cups walnuts, toasted (page 158) and chopped
> 1 ½ cups daylily shoots (page 64) or scallions,
>   chopped
> 1 cup common dandelion (page 71) or chicory
>   leaves (page 70), chopped
> 1 cup watercress leaves, chopped
> 1 medium-size green bell pepper, seeded and sliced
>   into strips
> 1 celery stalk, sliced
> 1 carrot, thinly sliced

Mix together all the ingredients in a large serving bowl. Toss the salad with any salad dressing in this book.

SERVES 6

WATERCRESS BISQUE

Here's a quick and easy soup made with watercress that's sure to please.

2 tablespoons olive oil

2 teaspoons freshly ground yellow mustard seeds
   (1 teaspoon seeds)

4 cups watercress leaves

4 cloves garlic, crushed into a paste

1 teaspoon dried tarragon, finely crumbled

1 teaspoon dried marjoram, finely crumbled

1 teaspoon freshly grated nutmeg

1 teaspoon freshly ground white pepper
   (½ teaspoon peppercorns)

2 cups Vegetable Stock (page 40)

1 cup peeled potato chunks, simmered in water to
   cover until tender and drained

1 tablespoon mellow (light-colored) miso

½ teaspoon Vege-Sal or ¼ teaspoon salt, or to taste

1. Heat the olive oil in a large skillet over medium heat, add the ground mustard seeds and cook, stirring constantly, until the seeds pop, 1 to 2 minutes. Add the watercress, garlic, tarragon, marjoram, nutmeg, and pepper and cook, stirring, for 5 minutes.

2. Carefully transfer the cooked watercress mixture to a blender, add the remaining ingredients, and process until smooth, holding down the blender cover with a towel at first to prevent eruptions. Reheat gently if necessary.

SERVES 4 TO 6

WATERCRESS SOUP

Here's a first-class soup featuring watercress.

¼ cup drained silken tofu

1½ teaspoons freshly ground celery seeds
   (1 teaspoon seeds)

1 tablespoon chopped fresh basil leaves or
   1 teaspoon dried, finely crumbled

½ teaspoon freshly ground white pepper
   (¼ teaspoon peppercorns)

1 teaspoon Vege-Sal or ½ teaspoon salt, or to taste

1 tablespoon paprika

4 cups Vegetable Stock (page 40) or water

2 medium-size potatoes, chopped

2 bayberry leaves (page 185) or 1 bay leaf

2 tablespoons olive oil

1 medium-size onion, finely chopped

2 cloves garlic, chopped

2 cups watercress leaves, chopped

2 tablespoons lecithin granules

1. In a blender, combine the tofu, ground celery seeds, basil, white pepper, Vege-Sal, paprika, and 2 cups of the stock and process until smooth. Start on low speed and hold the blender cover down with a towel to prevent eruption.

2. Transfer the stock mixture to a large saucepan, add the potatoes, bayberry leaves, and the remaining 2 cups stock, and bring the pot to a boil over medium heat. Reduce the heat to low and simmer for 15 minutes.

3. Meanwhile, heat the olive oil in a medium-size skillet over medium heat. Add the onion and garlic and cook, stirring, for 10 minutes. Add the onion and garlic to the potato-and-stock mixture along with the watercress and lecithin and simmer for another 5 minutes.

4. Discard the bayberry leaves before serving.

SERVES 6

WATERCRESS BUTTER

This healthful seasoned butter, flavored with wild watercress and herbs, contains no dairy products. Use it to impart a buttery flavor to your recipes, or as a spread, but don't sauté with it because it isn't oil-based.

1 cup well-drained silken tofu

⅔ cup watercress leaves

1½ tablespoons fresh lemon juice

1 tablespoon flaxseed oil or corn oil

1 tablespoon mellow (light-colored) miso

1 teaspoon wild garlic bulbs (page 160) or regular garlic, chopped

1½ teaspoons lecithin granules

½ teaspoon dried thyme, finely crumbled

½ teaspoon dried rosemary, finely crumbled

½ teaspoon dried marjoram, finely crumbled

⅛ teaspoon cayenne pepper, or to taste

In a food processor, combine all the ingredients and process until smooth. Watercress Butter will keep, tightly covered, in the refrigerator for 1 week.

MAKES 1⅛ CUPS

SALSA VERDE

No relation to the great classical composer (he was Italian anyway, not Puerto Rican, like this recipe), this green sauce, based on wild watercress, goes well with tofu, potatoes, cooked root vegetables, and pasta.

2 cloves garlic, peeled

2 cups watercress leaves

1 cup fresh parsley leaves

½ cup fresh dill leaves

½ cup olive oil

¼ cup fresh lemon juice

1 tablespoon mellow (light-colored) miso

1 teaspoon freshly ground pink or white pepper (½ teaspoon peppercorns)

1. Chop the garlic in a food processor or by hand.

2. Add and chop the watercress, parsley, and dill.

3. Add the remaining ingredients and process until finely chopped or chop by hand. Salsa Verde will keep, tightly covered, in the refrigerator for 1 week.

MAKES 1⅓ CUPS

SAFFRON MILLET

After Europeans brought watercress to our continent, it invaded many of our streams and waterways. Here it infiltrates a dish of millet that is flavored with saffron.

1½ teaspoons saffron threads, ground

2 tablespoons olive oil

1 tablespoon mellow (light-colored) miso

2½ cups water

2 cups millet

2 large Spanish onions, chopped

2 cups watercress leaves, chopped

1 cup almonds, chopped

2 tablespoons chopped fresh parsley leaves

2 cloves garlic, finely chopped

1. Mix the saffron with the olive oil and miso in a small bowl.

2. Combine the remaining ingredients in a large saucepan and bring the pot to a boil over medium heat. Reduce the heat to low, and simmer, covered, until all the water is absorbed and the millet is tender, about 30 minutes.

3. Stir in the saffron mixture and serve.

SERVES 6 TO 8

SHAGGY PARASOL

Lepiota rachodes

THIS LARGE LEPIOTA'S WHITISH CAP IS 3 TO 8 inches wide, convex to flat, with large pinkish to cinnamon brown patches (see page 248 for common characteristics of lepiotas). The cap's whitish flesh turns pinkish when cut. The broad, free, white gills are close together. The spores are white. The club-shaped to bulbous white stalk is 4 to 8 inches long and ⅜ to 1 inch thick, turning brownish where injured. The movable ring encircles the upper stalk. The shaggy parasol grows on the ground in wood debris under conifers in late summer and fall in eastern North America and from late fall to late winter on the West Coast.

This is not a mushroom for unsupervised beginners. You could confuse it with deadly Amanitas, and there are other deadly Lepiotas plus a poisonous look-alike with green spores. And some people have adverse reactions to this mushroom.

The shaggy parasol is a very strong-flavored, meaty, choice mushroom that goes well in hearty dishes. Cook the cap and stem 15 to 20 minutes using virtually any method you choose, and you won't be disappointed.

TEMPEH STROGANOFF WITH WILD MUSHROOMS

Beef stroganoff is a robust Russian combination of beef, sautéed mushrooms, and vegetables in a creamy sauce. After you try this easy-to-make vegetarian rendition with its outstanding wild ingredients, you'll never think of asking: "Where's the beef?" You can purchase tempeh, a fermented soy cake, in health food stores or Asian specialty stores.

4 to 6 tablespoons olive oil, or as needed

4 cups (1½ pounds) coarsely diced tempeh

4 cups sliced shaggy parasol mushrooms

⅔ cup common evening primrose roots (page 430) or carrots, sliced

2 medium-size onions, sliced

¼ cup fresh parsley leaves, chopped

1 tablespoon chopped fresh basil leaves or 1 teaspoon dried, finely crumbled

2 cloves garlic, crushed into a paste

1 teaspoon dried tarragon, finely crumbled

1 teaspoon dried rosemary, finely crumbled

1 teaspoon dried thyme, finely crumbled

2 teaspoons Vege-Sal or 1 teaspoon salt, or to taste

1 teaspoon freshly ground black pepper (½ teaspoon peppercorns), or to taste

1 cup Béarnaise Sauce à la Brill (page 120)

1 cup Wild Mustard Seed Mayonnaise (page 206) or other vegan mayonnaise

1. Heat the olive oil in a large skillet over medium heat. Add the tempeh, mushrooms, common evening primrose, onions, parsley, basil, garlic, tarragon, rosemary, thyme, Vege-Sal, and pepper and cook, stirring, for 15 minutes.

2. Add the béarnaise sauce and mayonnaise and heat to serving temperature. Do not boil. Serve on Buckwheat Noodles (page 34).

SERVES 6 TO 8

ABORTED ENTOLOMA MUSHROOM

Entoloma abortivum

THIS MISSHAPEN, FRAGRANT MUSHROOM COMES into being when the entoloma fungus parasitizes a developing honey mushroom (*Armillariella mellea*), aborting its normal development. So it comes in two forms, the unaborted form and the aborted form.

The unaborted form has a convex, grayish cap that is 2 to 4 inches across with an inrolled margin. The buff to pinkish gills attach to or descend the stalk. The spores are pink. The grayish white stalk is 1 to 4 inches long and ¼ to ⅝ inch thick, with white threads (the fungus) emanating from the base.

The distorted ball-shaped, spongy aborted form is 1 to 4 inches wide and 1 to 2 inches tall. Whitish outside, the whitish inside is marbled with pinkish veins. Aborted forms grow clustered or fused together.

Both forms grow together on the ground in leaf litter, or on or near rotting wood. Look for it in eastern North America west to Texas. It appears in the late summer and fall.

Pick this mushroom only when you find both forms growing together. Other similar Entoloma species that don't form abortions will make you throw up.

This top-rated mushroom is great sautéed; simmered in soups, stews, or sauces; baked; or even cooked in cocktail sauce as mock shrimp. Use the caps and stems of both forms.

SHRIMP-FREE COCKTAIL

When I noticed that the aborted entoloma tastes a little like shrimp, I tried cooking it in cocktail sauce, and it worked! Years later, when I had forgotten about this experiment, some friends served me mock shrimp cocktail for dinner, and I remarked how good it was. They had gotten the recipe from me!

9 cups aborted entoloma mushrooms, aborted form

2 teaspoons olive oil

1½ teaspoons Vege-Sal or ¾ teaspoon salt, or to taste

Two 25.5-ounce jars tomato sauce

2 tablespoons brown rice vinegar

3 large cloves garlic, crushed into a paste

Juice of 1 lemon

2 teaspoons freshly ground yellow mustard seeds (1 teaspoon seeds)

1 tablespoon dillweed, finely crumbled

1 teaspoon Tabasco sauce

1. Preheat the oven to 350 degrees.

2. Toss the mushrooms, olive oil, and ¾ teaspoon of the Vege-Sal together in an oiled baking dish and bake, covered, for 20 minutes.

3. Combine the mushrooms with the remaining ingredients in a large saucepan and bring the pot to a boil over medium heat. Reduce the heat to low, and simmer, covered, for 10 minutes.

4. Chill completely and serve cold with toasted whole-grain bread.

SERVES 6 TO 8

BROWN RICE WITH CASHEWS AND MUSHROOMS

If you like rice, you'll love this deluxe brown rice with its wild companions.

3 ¾ cups water

1 ½ cups long-grain brown rice

1 cup raw cashews

1 cup aborted entoloma, unaborted form

3 celery stalks, sliced

3 shallots, chopped

1 small red bell pepper, seeded and sliced into strips

6 tablespoons Herb Butter (page 58) or ¼ cup olive oil

¼ cup amaranth (page 338) or lamb's-quarters seeds (page 287)

¼ cup wild rice (page 353)

1 tablespoon dark-colored miso

2 teaspoons tamari soy sauce

2 teaspoons Vege-Sal or 1 teaspoon salt, or to taste

3 cloves garlic, crushed into a paste

½ teaspoon dried thyme, finely crumbled

½ teaspoon chili paste or ¼ teaspoon cayenne pepper, or to taste

Combine all the ingredients in a large saucepan and bring the pot to a boil over medium heat. Reduce the heat to low, and simmer, covered, until all the liquid is absorbed and the rice and grains are tender, about 40 minutes.

SERVES 8 TO 10

ABORTED ENTOLOMA CURRY

Aborted entoloma mushrooms take especially well to curries.

6 cloves garlic, peeled

4 small chiles, or to taste, ribs and seeds removed

1 ½ tablespoons peeled and chopped fresh ginger

½ cup fresh cilantro leaves

2 medium-size onions, peeled

2 teaspoons cumin seeds

2 teaspoons poppy seeds

1 teaspoon black mustard seeds

1 teaspoon turmeric

1 teaspoon Vege-Sal or ½ teaspoon salt, or to taste

¼ cup peanut oil

1 pound aborted entoloma mushrooms (either form)

¼ pound ripe tomatoes, chopped

1 cup unsweetened shredded coconut

1 cup water

1. In a food processor or by hand, chop the garlic, chiles, and ginger fine. Add the cilantro and chop. Add the onions, cumin seeds, poppy seeds, black mustard seeds, turmeric, and Vege-Sal, and chop as fine as possible.

2. Heat the peanut oil in a large skillet over medium heat. Add the spice mixture and cook for 5 minutes, covered, stirring often. Add the mushrooms and cook, covered, stirring, for another 10 minutes. Add the tomatoes, coconut, and water and cook, stirring, for another 5 minutes. Serve hot with brown rice or chapatis.

SERVES 6

NORTHERN WILD RAISIN, BLACK HAW

Viburnum prunifolium

THIS SHRUB, WHICH GROWS FROM 6 TO 40 FEET tall, has alternate, oval to elliptical, blunt-tipped, finely toothed leaves that are about 2 inches long. Umbrella-like clusters of white, five-petaled, radially symmetrical flowers bloom in the spring. Oval, bluish black berries with a single flattened seed inside ripen in the fall. The similar nannyberry (*Viburnum lentago*), which is also good to eat, has larger, pointed leaves. Both shrubs grow in thickets and landscaped areas throughout the eastern four fifths of the United States.

This fruit isn't related to the raisin it resembles. It has a flavor like prune butter and a texture like bananas. After removing the seeds (cook the fruit with fruit juice and strain out the seeds using a food mill), you can use the sweet, thick pulp in any recipe that calls for fruit purée (or as a substitute for prunes). It's one of my favorite pastry fillings, and it's also great in pies, cakes, and puddings.

WILD RAISIN–STUFFED SQUASH

Wild raisins go especially well with chestnuts, as one of my favorite Thanksgiving recipes demonstrates.

> 6 *butternut squash*
> 3 ½ *cups prune juice or other fruit juice*
> 2 *cups commercial dried chestnuts*
> 2 *tablespoons olive oil, or as needed*
> 4 *celery stalks, sliced*
> 1 *medium-size green or red bell pepper, seeded and sliced into strips*
> 8 *shallots, chopped*
> 1 *medium-size carrot, grated*
> 2 *cups wild raisins*
> ½ *cup fresh parsley leaves, chopped*
> ½ *cup fresh cilantro leaves, chopped*
> 1 *tablespoon poppy seeds*
> 1 *teaspoon dried tarragon, finely crumbled*
> 1 *teaspoon dried thyme, finely crumbled*
> 1 *teaspoon ground cinnamon*
> ½ *teaspoon freshly grated nutmeg*

1. Preheat the oven to 350 degrees.

2. Cut the butternut squash in half lengthwise. Remove the seeds (you can dry the seeds and prepare them as in Curry Seeds, page 350). Place the squash halves cut side down on oiled cookie sheets, and bake for 50 minutes. Leave the oven on.

3. Meanwhile, combine 1½ cups of the prune juice and the chestnuts in a small saucepan and bring the pot to a boil. Remove the pot from the heat and let the chestnuts steep for 1 hour to rehydrate them (or soak them in the refrigerator overnight without heating them first).

4. At the same time, heat the olive oil in a medium-size skillet over medium heat. Add the celery, bell pepper, shallots, and carrot and cook for 15 minutes, stirring often.

5. Drain the chestnuts, reserving the soaking liquid. Combine the chestnut soaking liquid with the wild raisins and the remaining 2 cups prune juice in a medium-size saucepan and bring the pot to a boil over medium heat. Reduce the heat to low, and simmer, covered, for 10 minutes, stirring occasionally.

6. Pass the wild raisin mixture through a food mill to strain out the seeds. Mix the wild raisin pulp with the sautéed ingredients and the herbs and spices. Pack this filling into the cut surface of the squash and bake, cut end up, until heated, 10 to 20 minutes. Serve hot.

SERVES 6

WILD HAMENTASCHEN

This Jewish pastry gets its name from the pockets (*taschen*) of Hamen, which traditionally were filled with prunes. Hamen is the anti-Semitic villain of the Purim festival. Wild raisin purée tastes even better than Hamen's prunes, especially in "pockets" of pastry.

CRUST

> *2 cups plus 2 tablespoons (10 ounces) sweet brown rice flour and 1¾ cups (7 ounces) oat flour, or 17 ounces any whole-grain flour*
>
> *7½ tablespoons freshly ground flaxseeds (3 tablespoons seeds)*
>
> *¼ cup arrowroot or kudzu*
>
> *1½ tablespoons lecithin granules*
>
> *1½ teaspoons cream of tartar*
>
> *¾ teaspoon baking soda*
>
> *¼ teaspoon salt*
>
> *1 teaspoon ground cinnamon*
>
> *½ teaspoon freshly ground cloves*
>
> *½ teaspoon freshly grated nutmeg*
>
> *1 cup apple juice or other unsweetened fruit juice*
>
> *½ cup corn oil*

FILLING

> *2 cups wild raisin purée (see Note)*
>
> *⅔ cup almonds, chopped*
>
> *2 tablespoons poppy seeds*
>
> *4 teaspoons fresh lemon juice*

> *6 common spicebush berries (page 314), finely chopped, or ½ teaspoon freshly ground allspice berries*

1. Preheat the oven to 400 degrees.

2. *To make the crust:* In a large bowl, mix together the flours, ground flaxseeds, arrowroot, lecithin, cream of tartar, baking soda, salt, cinnamon, cloves, and nutmeg.

3. In a small bowl, mix together the apple juice and corn oil. Mix the wet ingredients into the dry ingredients, being careful not to overmix.

4. Roll out the pastry ⅛ inch thick on a floured pastry cloth with a rolling pin enclosed in a floured sleeve. Cut the pastry into about 18 squares 4½ inches across using a pizza cutter or butter knife.

5. *To make the filling:* In a medium-size bowl, mix the filling ingredients together.

6. Place a heaping tablespoon of the filling inside each pastry square. Moisten the edges of the squares with water, fold the pastry over, corner to corner on the diagonal to form a triangle. Seal the pastry.

7. Bake the filled pastries on oiled cookie sheets until the undersides are lightly browned, 15 to 17 minutes. Let the pastries cool on wire racks.

MAKES 18 PASTRIES

Note: To make the raisin purée, simmer 3 cups wild raisins in 2 cups prune juice for 20 minutes, stirring occasionally. Remove the seeds using a food mill.

Pear-Shaped Puffball

Lycoperdon pyriforme

PUFFBALLS ARE ROUGHLY GLOBULAR ABOVE-ground mushrooms that contain spores within when they are mature. Any disturbance makes the spores erupt in a puff of smoky powder. There are two groups of puffballs. The smaller ones (*Lycoperdon* species) grow on wood and reach only a few inches tall. The larger ones (*Calvatia* species) grow on the ground and range in size from a hardball to a beach ball.

You can eat immature true puffballs; when you cut them open, they're white and soft inside, undifferentiated, like cream cheese (like tofu if you're a vegetarian). Other similar-looking mushrooms don't share those characteristics: *If there's a cap and stem inside, you have an immature* Amanita, *possibly deadly, and not a puffball. Or, if it's hard inside and goes from white to black, it's a poisonous earthball (*Scleroderma *species).* When the puffballs themselves mature and become colored and slimy inside, or get filled with powdery spores after that, you can't eat them anymore. If you observe these cautions, puffballs are among the safest mushrooms to eat.

The pear-shaped puffball is deep olive, ⅝ to 1¾ inches wide, ¾ to 1¾ inches high, and is pear-shaped. It grows, often in large numbers, on dead wood, mainly in the fall (sometimes also in the summer) throughout North America.

This fabulous, common, easy-to-recognize mushroom has such a strong flavor that you can add it to sourdough bread or other highly flavored dishes, and it will still stand out. Any cooking method works with this mushroom, and you can use it in virtually any main course, soup, or side dish. It cooks in about 10 to 20 minutes.

LAMB'S-QUARTERS AND PUFFBALL SALAD

Raw wild mushrooms may get you sick, and even commercial mushrooms contain carcinogenic hydrazines (similar to rocket fuel), which are dissipated only by cooking. But steamed puffballs are more than suitable in salads, here balanced with equally strong tasting lamb's-quarters.

> 6 tablespoons olive oil
> 1 tablespoon red wine vinegar
> 1 tablespoon fresh lime or lemon juice
> 2 cloves garlic, crushed into a paste
> Vege-Sal or salt and freshly ground black pepper
>   or cayenne pepper to taste
> ¾ cup lamb's-quarters leaves (page 287) or
>   spinach
> ½ cup pear-shaped puffballs, steamed for 15
>   minutes
> ⅓ cup field garlic bulbs (page 57) or onion,
>   chopped
> 1 tablespoon chopped fresh cilantro, parsley, or dill

Mix the olive oil, vinegar, lime juice, garlic, and seasoning in a small bowl. Place the vegetables in a medium-size serving bowl, toss with the dressing, and serve at once.

SERVES 6

PUFFBALL MARINARA

Puffball mushrooms and ramps dominate this Italian-style tomato sauce. Serve this with pasta, vegetables, loaves, or burgers.

¼ cup olive oil, or as needed

6 cups ramp leaves (page 116) or scallions, chopped

3 medium-size onions, chopped

3 celery stalks, sliced

4 cloves garlic, crushed into a paste

2 cups pear-shaped puffballs

Three 25.5-ounce jars tomato sauce

¾ cup any wild or store-bought wine

2 tablespoons chopped fresh basil leaves or 2 teaspoons dried, finely crumbled

1 tablespoon bayberry leaves (page 185) or bay leaves, enclosed in a tea bag or tea ball, if desired

1 tablespoon finely chopped fresh parsley leaves

1 teaspoon freshly ground black pepper (½ teaspoon peppercorns)

1½ teaspoons dried oregano, finely crumbled

1 teaspoon dried sage, finely crumbled

½ teaspoon dried rosemary, finely crumbled

1. Heat the olive oil in a large skillet over medium heat. Add the ramps, onions, celery, garlic, and mushrooms and cook, stirring, until the onions are lightly browned, about 10 minutes.

2. Meanwhile, bring the remaining ingredients to a boil over medium heat in a large saucepan, stirring often. Add the sautéed vegetables, reduce the heat to low, and simmer, covered, for 1 hour. Putting a heat diffuser under the saucepan will help prevent the bottom from scorching.

3. Remove the bayberry leaves before serving. Puffball

Marinara can be kept in the refrigerator, tightly covered, for 10 days or can be frozen for up to 6 months.

MAKES 12 CUPS

FANCY VEGAN LASAGNA

Here's a vegan lasagna with all the trimmings. The tofu cheeses set it apart from conventional lasagnas, and you can enhance this dish by using homemade pasta and homemade tomato sauce. Use Puffball Marinara (opposite) and you've got something unbelievably good.

6 cups homemade Buckwheat Noodles (page 34) or store-bought lasagna pasta

½ recipe Tofu Cream Cheese (page 30)

¼ cup fresh Bread Crumbs (page 40)

2 tablespoons arrowroot or kudzu

7 cups Puffball Marinara (page 397)

4 cups Tofu Grated Cheese (page 32)

1½ cups Tofu Ricotta Cheese (page 31)

1. Preheat the oven to 350 degrees.

2. Cook the homemade lasagna noodles for 1 minute or the store-bought pasta for 3 minutes in rapidly boiling salted water with a dash of olive oil. Drain the pasta in a colander and immediately plunge the colander into a bowl of cold water to halt the cooking. Drain the pasta again.

3. In a medium-size bowl, mix together the Tofu Cream Cheese, bread crumbs, and arrowroot.

4. Layer a 14 x 9 x 2-inch oiled baking dish with one-third of the marinara, half of the noodles, one-third of the Tofu Grated Cheese, half of the Tofu Ricotta Cheese, the remaining noodles, half of the remaining marinara, the remaining Tofu Ricotta Cheese, half of the remaining Tofu Grated Cheese, the remaining marinara, the bread crumb mixture, and the remaining Tofu Grated Cheese. Bake the lasagna until it is browned on top and bubbly, about 40 minutes.

SERVES 6

UNMEAT LOAF

In this mock meat loaf, texturized vegetable protein replaces the meat, and puffball mushrooms intensify the flavor.

  1 cup texturized vegetable protein (TVP)

  1½ cups Vegetable Stock (page 40)

  ¼ cup olive oil

  1 cup chopped shallots or onions

  4 celery stalks, sliced

  1 medium-size red bell pepper, seeded and sliced
    into strips

  1¼ cups pear-shaped puffballs

  1 cup bread cubes or Bread Crumbs (page 40)

  ¼ cup fresh parsley leaves, chopped

  2 tablespoons Bragg's Liquid Aminos or tamari soy
    sauce

  2 tablespoons chopped fresh basil leaves or
    2 teaspoons dried, finely crumbled

  5 tablespoons freshly ground flaxseeds
    (2 tablespoons seeds)

  2 tablespoons lecithin granules

  1 tablespoon chili paste or 1 teaspoon cayenne
    pepper

  1½ teaspoons dried thyme, finely crumbled

  1½ teaspoons dried sage, finely crumbled

  2 teaspoons freshly ground yellow mustard seeds
    (1 teaspoon seeds)

  2 teaspoons freshly ground black pepper
    (1 teaspoon peppercorns)

  1 teaspoon freshly grated nutmeg

  2 cups Homemade Ketchup (page 37)

1. Combine the TVP and stock in a medium-size saucepan and bring the pot to a boil over high heat. Remove the pot from the heat and let the TVP stand, covered, for 30 minutes.

2. Meanwhile, heat the olive oil in a medium-size skillet over medium heat. Add the shallots, celery, bell pepper, and mushrooms and cook, stirring, for 10 minutes.

3. Preheat the oven to 350 degrees.

4. Return the TVP and stock to the heat and simmer, covered, over low heat for 10 minutes. Drain the TVP, reserving the stock for another use.

5. In a large bowl, mix together everything except for 1 cup of the ketchup. Divide the mixture between 2 oiled 6½ x 4⅜ x 2½-inch loaf pans, spread the top of each loaf with the remaining ketchup, and bake for 1 hour, or until they are browned on top.

MAKES 2 LOAVES; SERVES 6 TO 8

MOOSE-FREE MOUSSAKA

Moussaka is a familiar Greek casserole topped with cheese sauce and containing layers of ground lamb or beef (no moose) and sliced eggplant. Here, Tofu Cream Cheese replaces the cheese, and puffball mushrooms and texturized vegetable protein stand in for the meat. You'll love the results.

  2 medium-size eggplants

  1¼ cups boiling Vegetable Stock (page 40)

  1¼ cups texturized vegetable protein (TVP)

  ¼ cup olive oil, or as needed

  2 cups pear-shaped puffballs, chopped

  2 medium-size onions, chopped

  4 cloves garlic, crushed into a paste

  1 medium-size green bell pepper, seeded and
    chopped

1 tablespoon chopped fresh basil leaves or

   1 teaspoon dried, finely crumbled

2 teaspoons dried rosemary, finely crumbled

1 teaspoon freshly grated nutmeg

1 teaspoon dried oregano, finely crumbled

1 teaspoon dried thyme, finely crumbled

1 teaspoon freshly ground black pepper

   (½ teaspoon peppercorns)

1 teaspoon Vege-Sal or ½ teaspoon salt

1 teaspoon paprika

3 cups Tofu Cream Cheese (page 30)

1. Preheat the oven to 375 degrees. Prick the eggplants with a fork and bake them on a wire rack set over a cookie sheet for 1 hour. Leave the oven on.

2. Meanwhile, combine the boiling stock and TVP, remove from heat, and let the TVP soak for 5 minutes. Drain the TVP in a colander, pressing out as much stock as possible with a spatula, and reserving the stock for another use.

3. Heat the olive oil in a large skillet over medium heat. Add the TVP, mushrooms, onions, garlic, green pepper, basil, rosemary, nutmeg, oregano, thyme, and ½ teaspoon of the black pepper and cook, stirring, for 10 minutes, adding the Bragg's Liquid Aminos toward the end of the cooking time.

4. When the eggplants are cool enough to handle, peel and slice them. Toss the eggplants with the remaining ½ teaspoon black pepper, the Vege-Sal, and paprika.

5. Layer the eggplant slices and sautéed vegetables and TVP in a 14 x 9 x 2-inch oiled baking dish and top with the Tofu Cream Cheese. Bake until a crust forms, about 1 hour.

SERVES 6

SHAGGY MANE MUSHROOM
Coprinus comatus

THE SHAGGY MANE IS AN INKY CAP. THESE gilled mushrooms release their spores by disintegrating into a stream of ink when they mature. This species has a cylindrical, white cap that is 1¼ to 2 inches wide and 1⅝ to 6 inches high, covered with flat, white scales that make it look shaggy. The mushroom turns into black ink from the edge inward as it matures. The crowded, white gills, free from the stalk (there's a space in between the two) also become black with ink as they mature and disintegrate. The spores are black. The hollow, bulbous, white stalk is 2⅜ to 8 inches long and ⅜ to ¾ inch thick, with a ring about two-thirds of the way down. Look for this mushroom in wood chips, grass, or on bare, hard-packed soil in the fall (also sometimes in the spring, as well as through half the winter in the Southeast) throughout North America.

The shaggy mane is the best of the inky caps, with a clear yet delicate flavor and the texture of fish. Its high water content makes it unsuitable for sautéing, but it's great steamed or in soups, stews, or sauces. If you season it with herbs traditionally used with fish, you can fool people into thinking they're eating fish dishes. The caps and stems cook in 10 to 20 minutes. Use this mushroom the same day you find it, when it's still completely white (or cut away any ink parts if they're not too extensive) before it degrades into ink. (You can also freeze it after cooking it.)

Don't drink alcohol soon after or before eating this mushroom or its similar relative, the alcohol inky cap (*Coprinus atramentarius*). (The alcohol inky cap also turns to ink, but it's gray and shorter, with faint, radial lines on the cap margin, and no shaggy scales.) *The combination may sometimes cause temporary but frightening symptoms that vanish after a few hours. (These symptoms include flushing, rapid heartbeat, fear, and the certainty that death is imminent.)*

QUINOA WITH SHAGGY MANES

Quinoa, a light, mild-tasting, high-protein South American relative of lamb's-quarters still hasn't received all the credit it deserves. Serve this dish, in which the delicate flavor of the shaggy mane mushrooms complements the grainlike quinoa seeds, and you'll discover why all of us should be more open to new foods.

> 3 ½ cups water
>
> 2 cups quinoa
>
> 4 cups packed shaggy mane mushrooms, chopped
>
> 1 medium-size onion, chopped
>
> 2 tablespoons sesame oil or any vegetable oil
>
> 2 cloves garlic, crushed into a paste
>
> 1 teaspoon Vege-Sal or ½ teaspoon salt, or to taste
>
> 1 teaspoon dried rosemary, finely crumbled
>
> 1 teaspoon freshly grated nutmeg
>
> 1 teaspoon ground dried wild ginger (page 111) or regular ground ginger
>
> ½ teaspoon dried thyme, finely crumbled
>
> 1 teaspoon cayenne pepper, or to taste

Combine all the ingredients in a large, heavy saucepan and bring the pot to a boil over medium heat. Reduce the heat to low, cover, and simmer gently until all the liquid is absorbed and the quinoa is tender, about 20 minutes.

SERVES 6 TO 8

ITALIAN BAKED RICE

Here's a rice dish that includes wild rice, amaranth, shaggy mane mushrooms, and Italian-style seasonings.

> 3 ¼ cups water
>
> 1 ½ cups brown basmati rice
>
> ¼ cup wild rice (page 353)
>
> ¼ cup amaranth (page 338)
>
> 2 cups sliced shaggy mane mushrooms
>
> 1 medium-size onion, sliced
>
> 4 cloves garlic, chopped
>
> ½ cup dried stinging nettles (page 83) or other leafy greens (optional)
>
> 2 tablespoons olive oil
>
> 2 tablespoons chopped fresh basil leaves
>
> 1 ½ teaspoons freshly ground celery seeds (1 teaspoon seeds)
>
> 2 teaspoons Vege-Sal or 1 teaspoon salt
>
> 1 teaspoon freshly ground black pepper (½ teaspoon peppercorns)
>
> 2 teaspoon dried oregano, finely crumbled

Preheat the oven to 375 degrees. Combine all the ingredients in a 3-quart oiled casserole dish and bake, covered, until all the water has been absorbed and the rice and grains are tender, about 1½ hours. Serve hot.

SERVES 6

SHAGGY MANE CASSEROLE

This mushroom tour de force features the delicate flavor of the shaggy mane mushroom at its best.

SAUTÉ

> ¼ cup olive oil
>
> ½ medium-size red onion, chopped
>
> 3 celery stalks, sliced

2 medium-size red bell peppers, seeded and sliced
   into strips
2 medium-size zucchini, sliced
1 small head cauliflower, broken into florets
2 cups snow peas, strings removed
4 cloves garlic, minced

SAUCE

1¼ cups Vegetable Stock (page 40) or water
2 tablespoons Wineberry Wine (page 246) or red
   wine
½ cup mellow (light-colored) miso
2 tablespoons kudzu or arrowroot
1 teaspoon chili paste or ¼ teaspoon cayenne
   pepper, or to taste
1 teaspoon turmeric
2 tablespoons chopped fresh dill
2 tablespoons chopped fresh cilantro or parsley
   leaves

2 cups chopped shaggy mane mushrooms or alcohol
   inky cap mushrooms (page 399), steamed for 10
   to 15 minutes
2 cups fresh Bread Crumbs (page 40)

1. Preheat the oven to 375 degrees.
2. *To make the sauté:* Heat the olive oil in a large skillet over medium heat. Add the onion, celery, red peppers, zucchini, cauliflower, and snow peas and cook, stirring, for 10 minutes. Add the garlic and cook, stirring, for another 5 minutes.
3. *To make the sauce:* Mix the stock, wine, kudzu, chili paste, and turmeric in a medium-size saucepan and bring the pot to a boil over medium heat, stirring constantly. (If lumps form, blend the mixture until smooth in the blender, holding down the blender cover with a towel when you first turn it on to prevent eruption.) Add the dill and cilantro, reduce the heat

to low, and simmer for 10 minutes, stirring often.
4. Mix the mushrooms with the sautéed vegetables and transfer one-third of this mixture to a large oiled casserole dish. Pour on one-third of the sauce and sprinkle one-third of the bread crumbs on top. Continue layering in this manner until you've used up all the ingredients. Bake until bubbly, about 40 minutes.

SERVES 12

SHAGGY MANE POLENTA PIE

Polenta is an Italian cornmeal mush traditionally mixed with Parmesan cheese. It makes a great crust on which to layer shaggy manes and vegetables.

4 cups cooked polenta (page 134)
¾ cup Ramp Pesto (page 121)
1 head cauliflower, stems and florets sliced
1 cup sliced shaggy mane mushrooms, steamed for
   10 minutes
1½ cups low-sodium pitted olives, drained
6 ripe plum tomatoes, thickly sliced
2 cups Tofu Sharp Cheese (page 30)

1. Preheat the oven to 375 degrees. Divide the polenta evenly between 2 oiled 9-inch pie tins and bake for 20 minutes. Leave the oven on.
2. Top the cooked polenta with half the pesto.
3. Mix the remaining pesto with the cauliflower.
4. Layer onto the polenta crust the cauliflower, shaggy manes, olives, tomatoes, and Tofu Sharp Cheese.
5. Bake for 40 minutes. Serve hot.

SERVES 8

SHAGGY MANE BERBERÉ

Shaggy manes have such a powerful flavor, you can cook them with tofu and potatoes, which absorb some of their flavor, and a pungent ethnic seasoning, to make a mushroom stew you'll want to make over and over again.

2 tablespoons peanut oil

4 medium-size red potatoes, sliced

One 19.5-ounce package soft tofu, drained and diced

1 medium-size onion, sliced

1 cup raw cashews

1 tablespoon chopped garlic

1 tablespoon peeled and chopped fresh ginger

4 small chiles, seeds and ribs removed and
*   chopped, or 1 teaspoon cayenne pepper, or*
*   to taste*

10 cups packed shaggy mane mushrooms, sliced

1 tablespoon freshly ground coriander seeds

1 tablespoon freshly ground cardamom seeds

2 teaspoons freshly ground white pepper
*   (1 teaspoon peppercorns)*

1 teaspoon freshly ground fenugreek seeds

1 teaspoon common spicebush berries (page 314),
*   finely chopped, or ½ teaspoon freshly ground*
*   allspice berries*

1 teaspoon freshly grated nutmeg

½ teaspoon freshly ground cloves

2 teaspoons Vege-Sal or 1 teaspoon salt, or to taste

1. Heat the peanut oil in a large skillet over medium heat. Add the potatoes, tofu, onion, cashews, garlic, ginger, and chiles and cook, stirring, for 10 minutes. Stir in the remaining ingredients, cover, reduce the heat to low, and simmer for 10 minutes.

2. Uncover the skillet and continue to cook the mixture until the liquid is reduced and somewhat thick-ened, about another 20 minutes. Serve over rice, bread, or noodles.

SERVES 8 TO 12

SHAGGY BAKED EGGS

Here's an egg-free dish similar to what I used to make when I was an ovo-lacto vegetarian, but better, thanks to the addition of shaggy mane mushrooms. Use already cooked shaggy manes because raw ones release too much liquid when you first cook them. The lecithin granules provide the egg yolk flavor; the bread crumbs give texture; and the wild mushrooms and herbs make the dish taste exotic.

2 cloves garlic, peeled

One 19-ounce package silken tofu, drained

2 cups fresh Bread Crumbs (page 40)

2 tablespoons lecithin granules

1 tablespoon arrowroot or kudzu

2 tablespoons flaxseed oil or corn oil

1 teaspoon Vege-Sal or ½ teaspoon salt

1 teaspoon brewer's yeast

1 teaspoon dried parsley, finely crumbled

½ teaspoon freshly ground white pepper
*   (¼ teaspoon peppercorns)*

½ teaspoon freshly ground yellow mustard seeds
*   (¼ teaspoon seeds)*

⅛ teaspoon ground mace or ¼ teaspoon freshly
*   grated nutmeg*

1 cup sliced shaggy mane mushrooms steamed for
*   10 minutes, chopped*

1. Preheat the oven to 350 degrees.

2. In a food processor, chop the garlic. Add all the remaining ingredients, except the mushrooms, and process until smooth.

3. In a medium-size bowl, combine the bread-crumb mixture with the mushrooms and transfer everything to a 1½-quart oiled casserole dish. Bake, uncovered, until set, about 40 minutes. Serve hot.

SERVES 4 TO 6

SHAGGY MUSHROOM SAUCE

Shaggy mane mushrooms, with their high water content, are perfect in sauces. With thickeners and minimal seasonings, they create an especially good, strongly flavored sauce. This sauce is ideal for serving on savory burgers and loaves, or steamed veggies and tofu.

2 ½ cups Vegetable Stock (page 40)

½ cup raw cashews

¼ cup miso

2 tablespoons arrowroot or kudzu

1 teaspoon dried marjoram, finely crumbled

1 teaspoon freshly ground black pepper

  (½ teaspoon peppercorns)

½ teaspoon freshly grated nutmeg

2 cups packed shaggy mane mushrooms

1. In a blender, combine all the ingredients, except the mushrooms, and process until smooth. Add the mushrooms and blend on low speed until they are finely chopped.

2. Transfer the mixture to a large saucepan and bring the pot to a boil over medium heat, stirring constantly. Reduce the heat to low, cover, and simmer, stirring occasionally, for 10 minutes. Shaggy Mushroom Sauce will keep, tightly covered, in the refrigerator for 1 week.

MAKES 4 CUPS

PURPLE-SPORE PUFFBALL

Calvatia cyathiformis

THE PURPLE-SPORE PUFFBALL IS A LARGE, roundish puffball in the group of larger puffballs called *Calvatia* (see page 403 for a description of puffballs). Often somewhat flattened, it grows from 2¾ to 7 inches across and from 3½ to 8 inches tall. Its beige surface, smooth at first, later develops cracks. The inside is soft and white at first. As the spores mature, they become violet-black to yellow-brown, then dark purple-black. Finally, the top of the puffball erodes and a large cup remains. It's hard to distinguish the immature purple-spore puffball mushroom from the similar skull-shaped puffball (*Calvatia craniformis*), which doesn't have purple spores, because by the time the spores are formed, you can't eat either mushroom anymore. But both are choice, as is the giant puffball (*Calvatia gigantea*), which is white, like Styrofoam, and can reach the size of a beach ball. Use all *Calvatia* puffballs the same way. There are no poisonous look-alikes.

Calvatia mushrooms grow in grassy pastures and suburban lawns throughout eastern and central North America, appearing in the summer and early fall and persisting through late fall. Their flavor is rich, slightly sweet, and smoky, and their texture is like that of a marshmallow. Trim away the cuticle (covering) if it's encrusted with dirt, and cut out any bad parts with a paring knife. Try not to wash this mushroom under water, or it will become too soggy to sauté. Brushing works only if the grit isn't engrained.

Slice the puffball and sauté it, steam it, or simmer

it in soups, like other mushrooms. It's also great baked or grilled. It cooks in 10 to 20 minutes. It doesn't dehydrate well. To store it long-range, cook it and freeze it.

PUFFBALL PARMESAN

Mock cheeses, homemade tomato sauce, and the purple-spore puffball topped with homemade bread crumbs make a heavenly combination.

6 tablespoons olive oil

4 cups packed purple-spore puffballs or other puffballs, sliced ¾ inch thick

2 ½ teaspoons Vege-Sal or 1 ¼ teaspoons salt

2 cups fresh Bread Crumbs (page 40)

2 tablespoons corn oil

2 cups Wild Tomato Sauce (page 94) or prepared tomato sauce

2 cups Tofu Ricotta Cheese (page 31)

1 ½ cups Tofu Grated Cheese (page 32)

1. Preheat the oven to 350 degrees.
2. Heat the olive oil in a large skillet over medium heat. Add the puffballs and fry them until they are brown on one side, about 5 minutes. Turn them over with a metal spatula or tongs, sprinkle on ½ teaspoon of the Vege-Sal, and brown the other side.
3. In a medium-size bowl, mix together the bread crumbs, corn oil, and the remaining 2 teaspoons Vege-Sal.
4. Layer a 14 x 9 x 2-inch oiled baking dish first with half the tomato sauce, then the cooked puffballs, the remaining tomato sauce, the Tofu Ricotta Cheese, the oiled bread crumbs, and finally the Tofu Grated Cheese. Bake until bubbly, about 35 minutes.

SERVES 6

OYSTER MUSHROOM
Pleurotus ostreatus

HERE'S A MUSHROOM THAT LIVES UP TO ITS name—it looks, smells, and tastes like oysters. With virtually no stalk, this mushroom's oyster-shaped caps usually grow in layers on dead deciduous wood (or are sold in some supermarkets), like clusters of oysters. The moist, fragrant, white to smoky gray, hairless caps are 2 to 8 inches wide. The white, hairless gills (which become tinged yellow with age) descend the short, stublike, lateral stalk, when it exists. The spores are white. Oyster mushrooms grow throughout North America. If it rains enough and it's not too hot or cold, you can find oyster mushrooms any month of the year, although they're most common in the second half of autumn.

Cut out any part near the stem that's so tough you can't pinch through, and save that part for making stock. Cook the tender parts for 10 to 20 minutes using any cooking method. These mushrooms have a soft, chewy texture and taste a little like seafood. Use seasonings suitable for seafood (see the Herb and Spice User's Guide on page 448) for a mock seafood effect.

Once my friend Joe found ten pounds of oyster mushrooms on a dead tree on a lawn by a house along the side of a road. He stopped his car, ran across the lawn with his pocketknife, cut down the mushrooms, returned to his car, and sped off with his prize. Ten minutes later, the state police came after him. He'd been spotted running across the lawn of the state prison warden's home waving a knife. Joe nervously explained that he was picking mushrooms, and wasn't an escaped prisoner bent on revenge. The police let him go.

But two weeks later, after a heavy rainstorm, Joe was driving along the same road when he spotted 20 pounds of oyster mushrooms on the same tree. This time he went and knocked on the door and asked the warden for permission to take the mushrooms.

The warden scratched his head and answered, "Sure, be my guest. You can have all the mushrooms you want. And thank you so much for stopping by to ask. You wouldn't believe the nerve of the last guy who found mushrooms on my tree!"

CHINESE OYSTER MUSHROOM DUMPLINGS

I don't expect you to go to China to get Chinese oyster mushrooms for this recipe. Fortunately, the same oyster mushrooms grow all over the world, and they're perfect in Chinese dumplings. You may form the dumplings by hand, but it's more fun to use an inexpensive ravioli press.

> 2 cups plus 1 ½ tablespoons (10 ounces) sweet
> brown rice flour, 2 ½ cups (10 ounces) oat flour,
> and 1 ¼ cups (6 ounces) buckwheat flour, or
> 26 ounces any whole-grain flour
> 1 cup arrowroot or kudzu
> 1 teaspoon freshly ground anise seeds
> 4 teaspoons freshly ground Szechuan or black
> pepper (2 teaspoons peppercorns), or to taste
> 1 teaspoon freshly ground coriander seeds
> 1 ⅞ cups boiling water or Vegetable Stock (page 40)
> 2 tablespoons peanut oil
> 1 teaspoon tamari soy sauce
> 5 cups sliced oyster mushrooms steamed for
> 15 minutes

1. In a large bowl, mix together the flours, arrowroot, the ground anise seeds, Szechuan pepper, and coriander. Stir in the boiling water. Stir in the peanut oil and tamari and knead a few minutes.

2. When the dough is cool, roll it out into a rectangle ³⁄₁₆ inch thick on a floured pastry sheet with a rolling pin enclosed in a floured sleeve. Cut the dough into about 40 squares 2¾ inches across with a pizza cutter or butter knife.

3. Put ½ tablespoon of the mushrooms in the center of a square, moisten the edges, place another square on top, and press the dough together with a ravioli press (or use a jar or a glass 2½ inches across). Repeat with the remaining squares and mushrooms until they are used up.

4. Cook the dumplings in a large pot of rapidly boiling salted water for 20 minutes. Drain the dumplings in a colander.

5. Serve hot with Chinese Sauce (page 176), or top with a mixture of tamari soy sauce, chili paste, and brown rice vinegar to taste.

MAKES 20 DUMPLINGS

OYSTER-VEGETABLE SOUP

The oyster mushrooms and seaweed in this Japanese-style recipe ensure that the otherwise-bland tofu will get filled with flavor, and you'll enjoy that flavor when you drink the soup.

> 1 cup arame or hiziki (sea vegetables sold in health
> food and Asian ethnic stores)
> 10 cups Vegetable Stock (page 40)
> 2 cups drained soft tofu, diced
> 3 cups oyster mushrooms, any tough stalks
> removed and sliced
> 2 cups field garlic leaves (page 57) or scallions,
> chopped

1 teaspoon dried savory, finely crumbled

1 ½ teaspoons freshly ground celery seeds
   (1 teaspoon seeds)

1 teaspoon dried rosemary, freshly crumbled

¼ teaspoon cayenne pepper, or to taste

1 cup alfalfa sprouts

1. In a small bowl, cover the seaweed with water and let it soak for 15 minutes.

2. Meanwhile, bring the stock to a boil in a large stockpot over high heat.

3. Drain the seaweed and discard the water. Add the seaweed to the stock along with the tofu, oyster mushrooms, field garlic, savory, celery seeds, rosemary, and cayenne, reduce the heat to low, and simmer for 15 minutes.

4. Add the sprouts, simmer for another 3 minutes, and serve hot.

MAKES 3 QUARTS; SERVES 12

OYSTER BISQUE

Bisque, which is especially popular in New England, is a rich, creamy soup that often contains seafood. Using oyster mushrooms to provide the "seafood" and cashew butter for creaminess, you can make this authentic-tasting vegetarian seafood bisque in minutes.

2 cups water

¼ to ½ cup Cashew Butter (page 37), depending on how thick you prefer your soup

2 teaspoons mellow (light-colored) miso, 1 teaspoon Vege-Sal, or ½ teaspoon salt, or to taste

½ teaspoon dried tarragon, finely crumbled

½ teaspoon chili paste or ¼ teaspoon cayenne pepper, or to taste

¼ teaspoon ground mace

½ teaspoon freshly ground black pepper
   (¼ teaspoon peppercorns)

2 cups sliced oyster mushrooms, steamed for 15 minutes

1. In a blender, combine all the ingredients, except the mushrooms, and process until smooth.

2. Add the mushrooms and blend a few seconds on low speed until the mushrooms are finely chopped.

3. Transfer the mixture to a large saucepan, heat to serving temperature over medium heat, and serve.

SERVES 4 TO 6

OYSTER-TOMATO SAUCE

Homemade tomato sauce always beats the commercial versions that skimp on herbs to save money. But tomato sauce that includes wild mushrooms, wild vegetables, and wild herbs is even better.

6 tablespoons olive oil

4 cups oyster mushrooms, any tough stalks removed and sliced

4 medium-size onions, chopped

½ cup sweet cicely taproots (avoid the gnarled, stringy underground stems; page 92), chopped, or 1 tablespoon freshly ground fennel seeds

2 celery stalks, sliced

1 cup sliced carrots

1 medium-size green bell pepper, seeded and sliced

6 cloves garlic, crushed into a paste

Four 25-ounce jars tomato sauce

1 cup Ramp Wine (page 129) or sherry

¼ cup fresh parsley leaves, chopped

¼ cup fresh basil leaves, chopped, or
   1 ⅓ tablespoons dried, finely crumbled

2 tablespoons dried oregano, finely crumbled

1 tablespoon dried sage, finely crumbled

*1 tablespoon bayberry leaves (page 185) or bay
leaves, enclosed in a tea ball or tea bag if
desired*

*1 tablespoon Vege-Sal or 1 ½ teaspoons salt, or to
taste*

*1 tablespoon chili paste or 1 teaspoon cayenne
pepper, or to taste*

*2 teaspoons freshly ground white pepper
(1 teaspoon peppercorns)*

2 teaspoons dried tarragon, finely crumbled

2 teaspoons dried rosemary, finely crumbled

1. Heat the olive oil in a large skillet over medium heat. Add the mushrooms, onions, sweet cicely, celery, carrot, bell pepper, and garlic and cook for 15 minutes, stirring often.

2. Transfer the sautéed vegetables to a large pot, add the remaining ingredients, and bring the pot to a simmer over low heat, covered. Simmer, stirring occasionally, for 1 hour.

3. Remove the bayberry leaves before serving. Oyster-Tomato Sauce will keep, tightly covered, in the refrigerator for 10 days or frozen for up to 6 months.

MAKES 25 CUPS

SIMPLY OYSTERS

Here's a quick, easy way to bring out the best of these common, top-grade wild mushrooms. It's a great mushroom dish you can make when you're overwhelmed by the amount of oyster mushrooms you've gathered. It freezes well, and you can use it in any of the recipes in this book that call for cooked oyster mushrooms.

¼ cup olive oil

*13 cups oyster mushrooms, any tough stalks
removed and sliced*

*4 small chiles, or to taste, seeds and ribs removed
and finely chopped*

8 cloves garlic, or to taste, finely chopped

Juice of 1 lemon

*1 tablespoon fresh dill or 1 teaspoon dillweed,
finely crumbled*

2 tablespoons tamari soy sauce or to taste

*2 tablespoons White Oak Wine (page 176) or
sherry*

Heat the olive oil in a large skillet over medium heat, add the remaining ingredients, and cook, stirring often, until all the liquid is absorbed or evaporated, about 10 minutes. Serve hot.

SERVES 6

STEAMED OYSTERS WITH TOFU

This side dish makes these mushrooms taste so much like oysters, you will be searching for the pearl!

½ cup Looing Sauce (page 118)

One 16-ounce package firm tofu, drained and sliced

*6 cups oyster mushrooms, any tough stalks
removed and sliced*

4 celery stalks, sliced

*2 cups arugula or watercress leaves (page 387),
chopped*

1 clove garlic, crushed into a paste

½ teaspoon peeled and grated fresh ginger

2 tablespoons peanut oil

1 tablespoon white wine or any wild wine

1 tablespoon tamari soy sauce

1. Pour the Looing Sauce into a medium-size saucepan. Set a steamer rack inside the saucepan and place the tofu, oyster mushrooms, celery, and arugula on the rack.

2. In a small bowl, mix together the garlic, ginger, peanut oil, wine, and tamari and pour this mixture over the mushroom mixture.

3. Bring the Looing Sauce to a simmer over low heat, cover, and steam the tofu and vegetables over the sauce for 20 minutes. Serve over whole-grain or bread, topped with the Looing Sauce, if desired.

SERVES 6

SCALLOPED OYSTERS IN BREAD CRUMBS

Stay away from all oyster mushrooms if you're a microscopic nematode (roundworm). The fungus will ensnare you, infiltrate your body, and absorb you. But if you're human, you can devour this tasty side dish.

16 cups oyster mushrooms, any tough stalks
  removed and sliced
6 cups fresh Bread Crumbs (page 40)
½ cup White Oak Wine (page 176) or white wine
½ cup olive oil
2 tablespoons dried goutweed leaves (page 130) or
  parsley, finely crumbled
5 cloves garlic, finely chopped
1 tablespoon tamari soy sauce
2 teaspoons freshly ground black pepper
  (1 teaspoon peppercorns)
2 teaspoons freshly grated nutmeg
½ teaspoon dried thyme, finely crumbled
½ teaspoon dried savory, finely crumbled
½ teaspoon Tabasco sauce or ¼ teaspoon cayenne
  pepper, or to taste

1. Preheat the oven to 350 degrees.

2. Combine all the ingredients in a 14 x 9 x 2-inch oiled baking dish. Bake, covered, for 45 minutes. Serve hot.

SERVES 6 TO 8

SCALLOPED OYSTERS WITH VEGETABLES

Oyster mushrooms make virtually any recipe shine, and this casserole is no exception.

2 small eggplants, sliced crosswise into ½-inch-
  thick rounds
1 tablespoon salt, or as needed
6 tablespoons olive oil
4 cups oyster mushrooms, any tough stalks
  removed and sliced
6 yellow crookneck squash, sliced
1 medium-size green bell pepper, seeded and
  chopped
4 cloves garlic, crushed into a paste
1 teaspoon dried sage, finely crumbled
1 teaspoon dried rosemary, finely crumbled
1 teaspoon dried oregano, finely crumbled
1 tablespoon tamari soy sauce, or to taste
1¾ cups fresh Bread Crumbs (page 40)
3¾ cups Tofu Cream Cheese (page 30)
1 tablespoon chili paste or 1 teaspoon cayenne
  pepper, or to taste

1. Place the eggplant slices in a colander and salt them to draw out the bitterness. Set them aside for 30 minutes.

2. Meanwhile, heat 3 tablespoons of the olive oil in a large skillet over medium heat. Add the mushrooms, squash, green pepper, garlic, sage, rosemary, and

oregano and cook for 15 minutes, stirring in the tamari toward the end. Set the vegetables aside until you are ready to use them.

3. Preheat the oven to 350 degrees.

4. Wash the salt off the eggplant slices under running water, drain them, and toss them with 1 tablespoon of the olive oil. Bake the eggplant for 45 minutes on wire racks set over 2 cookie sheets. Leave the oven on. (You may also sauté them for 5 to 10 minutes on each side in olive oil, but they will absorb so much oil that the calorie content will be increased significantly.)

5. Meanwhile, in a small bowl, mix the bread crumbs with the remaining 2 tablespoons olive oil.

6. In a 14 x 9 x 2-inch oiled baking dish, layer the baked eggplant, the sautéed vegetables, and the Tofu Cream Cheese, finishing up with the oiled bread crumbs. Bake until the bread crumbs are lightly browned, about 30 minutes.

SERVES 6 TO 8

OYSTER-CAULIFLOWER QUICHE

When I found oyster mushrooms in my neighborhood in the middle of January, I tried to make the most of this unusual winter bonanza by quadrupling this recipe. But when I served this dish at a potluck of the environmental organization Long Island EarthSave, I almost started an uprising as the first people on line gobbled it all up immediately, and the remaining members were angry because there was none left.

CRUST

1 ⅔ cups (½ pound) buckwheat flour and 1 ⅔ cups (½ pound) sweet brown rice flour, or 1 pound any whole-grain flour

¼ cup arrowroot or kudzu

1 teaspoon Vege-Sal or ½ teaspoon salt

1 teaspoon freshly ground fennel seeds

1 teaspoon dried marjoram, finely crumbled

1 teaspoon dried tarragon, finely crumbled

½ teaspoon freshly ground white pepper (¼ teaspoon peppercorns)

¼ cup corn oil

¾ cup water

FILLING

¼ cup olive oil

6 cups oyster mushrooms, any tough stalks removed and sliced

1 medium-size head cauliflower, broken into florets

2 celery stalks, sliced

6 cloves garlic, finely chopped

¼ cup Blackberry Spice Wine (page 278) or red wine

2 tablespoons chopped fresh dill

2 tablespoons caraway seeds

2 tablespoons tamari soy sauce, or to taste

2 teaspoons chili paste or ½ teaspoon cayenne pepper, or to taste

1 teaspoon freshly grated nutmeg

1 teaspoon freshly grated lemon rind

¼ cup kudzu or arrowroot

2 ¼ cups Tofu Cream Cheese (page 30)

1 cup Tofu Grated Cheese (page 32)

1 teaspoon sweet paprika

1. *To make the crust:* In a large bowl, mix together the flours, arrowroot, Vege-Sal, herbs, and pepper. Mix in the corn oil. Add the water and knead the dough for a few minutes, until smooth. Chill the dough in the freezer while you prepare the filling, but make sure the dough doesn't freeze.

2. *To make the filling:* Heat the olive oil in a large skillet over medium heat. Add the mushrooms, cauliflower, celery, and garlic and cook for 10 minutes, stirring often. Add the blackberry wine, dill, caraway seeds, tamari, chili paste, nutmeg, and lemon rind, reduce the heat to low, and cook, covered, for 10 minutes. Stir the kudzu into the cooked vegetables and then fold in the Tofu Cream Cheese.

3. Preheat the oven to 450 degrees.

4. Divide the dough into 2 pieces. On a floured pastry sheet, using a rolling pin enclosed in a floured sleeve, roll out one piece of dough into a disk about 9½ inches in diameter. Roll the dough around the rolling pin, along with the pastry sheet, to transfer it to an oiled 9-inch pie pan. Peel off the pastry sheet. Repeat the process with the other disk and another pie pan. Prick holes in the pastry with a fork to keep the crust from pulling away from the pan when it bakes.

5. Divide the filling between the two pie crusts, top with the Tofu Grated Cheese, and sprinkle the paprika on top.

6. Bake the quiches for 10 minutes to brown the crust. Reduce the oven temperature to 350 degrees and bake the quiches until they are bubbly and lightly browned on top, another 35 minutes, turning the pie pans so the crusts bake evenly.

7. Let the quiches cool before cutting each pie into 4 or 6 pieces. Serve hot or cold, but not at an EarthSave potluck!

SERVES 8 TO 12

OYSTERS IN SOUR CREAM

The oyster mushroom is one of the world's tastiest foods, and it's especially good smothered in Tofu Sour Cream, Russian style.

> 3 tablespoons olive oil
> 6 cups oyster mushrooms, any tough stalks
>   removed and sliced
> 6 cloves garlic, chopped
> ¾ teaspoon peeled and finely chopped fresh ginger
> 3 small chiles, seeds and ribs removed and
>   chopped, or ½ teaspoon cayenne pepper, or
>   to taste
> ¾ teaspoon Vege-Sal or ½ teaspoon salt,
>   or to taste
> 1½ cups Tofu Sour Cream (page 33)
> 1½ teaspoons sweet paprika

1. Heat the olive oil in a large skillet over medium heat. Add the mushrooms, garlic, ginger, chiles, and Vege-Sal and cook until the mushrooms are tender, 10 to 15 minutes, stirring.

2. Stir in the Tofu Sour Cream and continue to cook until the mixture is heated through. Sprinkle the paprika over the mushrooms. Serve hot over rice or pasta.

SERVES 6

STUFFED OYSTERS

Baked with this simple stuffing, oyster mushrooms are out of this world. Here's a natural appetizer you can serve with pride.

> 5½ cups oyster mushrooms, any tough stalks
>   removed
> 1 tablespoon olive oil

½ teaspoon Vege-Sal or ¼ teaspoon salt, or to taste

STUFFING

1⅔ cups Tofu Cottage Cheese (page 30)

1⅓ cups fresh corn kernels (cut from 2 ears of corn)

¼ cup fresh parsley leaves, chopped

2 cloves garlic, crushed into a paste

2 small chiles, seeds and ribs removed and finely chopped

1 cup fresh Bread Crumbs (page 40)

1. Preheat the oven to 350 degrees.

2. In a medium-size bowl, toss the mushrooms with the olive oil until they are coated. Place the mushrooms, gills up, on an oiled cookie sheet. Sprinkle them evenly with the Vege-Sal.

3. *To make the stuffing:* Combine the stuffing ingredients and press the mixture onto the mushrooms. Bake for 30 minutes. Serve chilled.

SERVES 6

Note: If the wild oyster mushrooms were so dirty that you had to scrub them under running water, squeeze each mushroom in your hand to remove excess water.

BAKED OYSTERS IN TAHINI SAUCE

Here's a casserole that's really appetizing, consisting of delicately seasoned oyster mushrooms and cauliflower, baked in a sesame sauce.

SAUTÉ

2 tablespoons olive oil

8 cups oyster mushrooms, any tough stalks removed and sliced

1 head cauliflower, broken into florets

4 cloves garlic, chopped

2 small chiles, or to taste, seeds and ribs removed and chopped

¼ cup fresh dill leaves, chopped

2 tablespoons Black Locust Blossom Wine (page 182) or sherry

1 teaspoon Vege-Sal or ½ teaspoon salt, or to taste

SAUCE

½ cup sesame seeds, toasted (page 73)

1 tablespoon sesame oil

1 cup drained silken tofu

2 tablespoons mellow (light-colored) miso

2 tablespoons lecithin granules

1 tablespoon fresh lemon juice

1½ teaspoons red wine vinegar

½ tablespoon brewer's yeast

½ teaspoon caraway seeds

½ teaspoon paprika

¼ teaspoon Tabasco sauce or pinch of cayenne pepper

¼ teaspoon turmeric

½ pound Buckwheat Noodles (page 34) or store-bought noodles

1 tablespoon plus ½ teaspoon corn oil

2 cups fresh Bread Crumbs (page 40)

1 cup Tofu Grated Cheese (page 32)

⅛ teaspoon liquid stevia or 1 teaspoon honey, barley malt, or rice syrup

1. Preheat the oven to 350 degrees.

2. *To make the sauté:* Heat the olive oil in a large skillet over medium heat. Add the mushrooms, cauliflower, garlic, and chiles and cook, stirring, for 5 minutes. Stir in the dill, wine, and Vege-Sal, reduce the heat to low, cover, and simmer for 10 minutes.

3. *To make the sauce:* In a food processor, combine the sauce ingredients and process until smooth, or grind

the sesame seeds in a blender, mix them with the remaining sauce ingredients, and mash everything together with a whisk or fork.

4. In rapidly boiling salted water with a dash of olive oil or other vegetable oil, cook the noodles for 2 minutes less than directed. Drain the pasta in a colander and lower the colander into a bowl of cold water to halt the cooking. Toss the noodles with ½ teaspoon of the corn oil in a 14 x 9 x 2-inch oiled baking dish.

5. Combine the sautéed ingredients with the sauce and pour the mixture over the noodles. Combine the bread crumbs with the remaining 1 tablespoon corn oil and spread this mixture on top of the mushroom-and-sauce layer. Top the casserole with the Tofu Grated Cheese. Bake until bubbly, about 40 minutes.

SERVES 6

OYSTERS NEWBURG

Lobster Newburg, a traditional gourmet dish, contains high-cholesterol egg yolks and detritus-eating shellfish, along with high-fat butter and heavy cream. It reminds me of my ex-girlfriend—beautiful but deadly.

This recipe, one of my favorites, substitutes oyster mushrooms for the lobster and features a luxuriant but healthful mock cream sauce. It reminds me of my fiancé—beautiful and all-around fantastic.

¼ cup canola oil or olive oil

¼ cup corn oil

12 cups oyster mushrooms, any tough stalks removed and sliced

SAUCE

1 cup water

½ cup Black Locust Blossom Wine (page 182) or sherry

⅔ cup drained silken tofu

¼ cup flaxseed oil or corn oil

6 tablespoons lecithin granules

2 tablespoons kudzu or arrowroot

2 teaspoons Vege-Sal or 1 teaspoon salt, or to taste

2 teaspoons freshly grated nutmeg

½ teaspoon sweet paprika

½ teaspoon liquid stevia or 2 tablespoons honey, barley malt, or rice syrup

¼ teaspoon cayenne pepper, or to taste

1. Heat the canola and corn oil in a large skillet over medium heat. Add the mushrooms and cook, stirring, for 10 minutes.

2. *To make the sauce:* Meanwhile, in a blender, combine the sauce ingredients and process until smooth.

3. Stir the sauce into the mushrooms and bring the pot to a simmer over low heat, stirring often. Reduce the heat to low, cover, and simmer for 10 minutes. Serve on toast.

SERVES 6

OYSTERS IN EGG SAUCE

With oyster mushrooms replacing oysters (which are coastal filter feeders, and sometimes accumulate pollution and pathogens) and vegan egg ingredients replacing the eggs, you can enjoy a healthy version of a scrumptious dish.

2 tablespoons olive oil

4 cups oyster mushrooms, any tough stalks removed and sliced

2 cloves garlic, chopped

½ teaspoon Vege-Sal or ¼ teaspoon salt, or to taste

¼ teaspoon Tabasco sauce

1 ¾ cups Mock Egg Sauce (page 35)

1. Heat the olive oil in a large skillet over medium heat. Add the oyster mushrooms, garlic, Vege-Sal, and Tabasco and cook, stirring, for 10 minutes.

2. Stir in the Mock Egg Sauce and bring the pot to a boil. Reduce the heat to low, and simmer, covered, for 5 minutes. Serve hot.

SERVES 6

OYSTER RICE

Oyster mushrooms will transform plain brown rice into one of the best grain dishes you've ever tasted.

> ¼ cup olive oil
>
> 3 cups oyster mushrooms, any tough stalks removed and sliced
>
> 3 cups ramp leaves (page 116) or scallions, chopped
>
> 2 celery stalks, sliced
>
> 4 cloves garlic, chopped
>
> 1 ¾ cups brown basmati rice or long-grain brown rice
>
> ¼ cup wild rice (page 353)
>
> ¼ cup amaranth (page 338)
>
> 1 tablespoon Bragg's Liquid Aminos or tamari soy sauce
>
> 2 teaspoons Chili Powder (page 36)
>
> 1 teaspoon dried marjoram, finely crumbled
>
> 1 teaspoon dried wild spearmint (page 59) or other mint, finely crumbled

1. Preheat the oven to 375 degrees.

2. Heat the olive oil in large skillet over medium heat. Add the mushrooms, ramps, celery, and garlic and cook, stirring, for 10 minutes.

3. Combine the cooked vegetables with the remaining ingredients in a 3-quart oiled casserole dish and bake, covered, until all the liquid has been absorbed and the rice and grains are tender, about 1½ hours.

SERVES 6

OYSTER STUFFING

This mushroom stuffing is great for filling veggie loaves, peppers, squash, ravioli, and even other mushrooms.

> 2 to 4 tablespoons peanut oil, or as needed
>
> 2 cloves garlic, peeled
>
> 2 cups drained firm tofu, diced
>
> 4 cups oyster mushrooms, any tough stalks removed and sliced
>
> 2 cups undercooked short-grain brown rice
>
> 2 cups shelled raw sunflower seeds, toasted (page 158)

1. Heat a couple of tablespoons of the peanut oil in a wok or large skillet over medium heat. Add the garlic and stir-fry it until it is slightly browned, 30 seconds to 1 minute. Remove the garlic from the wok and set it aside.

2. Add more peanut oil if necessary and stir-fry the tofu for 3 to 4 minutes. Remove it from the wok and set it aside.

3. Add more peanut oil if necessary and stir-fry the oyster mushrooms until they begin to release liquid, 3 to 4 minutes, adding more oil if necessary. Reduce the heat to low and add the rice.

4. Chop the reserved garlic and add it to the wok, along with the tofu. Cover and cook the stuffing over low heat for 10 minutes, stirring occasionally.

5. Remove the wok from heat, stir in the sunflower seeds, and serve.

SERVES 4 TO 6

BEAR'S HEAD
TOOTH MUSHROOM
Hericium coralloides

THIS IS A TOOTH MUSHROOM, CHARACTERIZED by slender teeth that hang from the side of the mushroom and release spores into the air. This species forms a large mass, 8 to 20 inches high and 6 to 12 inches across, with short, branching, white stems (discoloring beige with age) tipped with tufts of slender white spines. The spore print is white, and the whole mushroom gives off a sweet, mealy fragrance. You can find this mushroom growing on deciduous logs, stumps, and living trees from late summer to late fall in eastern North America. A larger relative that becomes salmon-buff to whitish when old and tastes just as good grows in the Pacific Northwest.

This is a great-tasting mushroom that lends itself to a variety of recipes. It is sweeter than any other mushroom in my experience, and its delicate flavor penetrates other ingredients exceptionally well. If you include the bear's head tooth mushroom in a recipe with many other items, its flavor will always shine through. It does very well in slow-cooked recipes such as soups or stews, although you can also sauté it for 15 minutes with superb results. Because it's so large, you can slice off large slabs, bread them, and prepare them as cutlets, or bake them smothered with stuffing. Remove the stems only if they're tough and use them in stocks.

I have collected this mushroom, which is uncommon in my area, only once so far, just before this book went to the publisher, although I've found it several times when it was past its peak. The trouble is, if you don't find this mushroom when it's fresh, it gets too bitter to use. (In that case, it looks old, brownish, and beat up. Take a tiny taste raw and spit it out; if it's bitter, come back to the same spot a week or two earlier the following year.)

BEAR'S HEAD SOUP

I had to wait 18 years to find this choice mushroom in a fresh state, but after I used it in a traditional mushroom-barley soup, it was obvious that it was worth every minute of waiting.

> *10 cups Vegetable Stock (page 40)*
> *1 cup barley*
> *¼ cup olive oil*
> *2 celery stalks, sliced*
> *1 cup grated carrots*
> *1 medium-size onion, chopped*
> *4 cloves garlic, chopped*
> *3 cups sliced bear's head tooth mushrooms*
> *3 tablespoons chopped fresh parsley leaves*
> *¾ teaspoon freshly ground celery seeds*
> *   (½ teaspoon seeds)*
> *1 teaspoon freshly ground white pepper*
> *   (½ teaspoon peppercorns)*
> *½ teaspoon freshly grated nutmeg*
> *¼ cup mellow (light-colored) miso*

1. Place the stock and barley in a soup pot and bring the pot to a boil over medium heat. Reduce the heat to low, cover, and simmer for 35 minutes.
2. Meanwhile, heat the olive oil in a medium-size skillet over medium heat. Add the celery, carrot, onion, and garlic and cook, covered, stirring, for 10 minutes.
3. Add the mushrooms, parsley, celery seeds, white pepper, and nutmeg to the barley and stock and simmer, covered, for another 10 minutes. Add the

sautéed vegetables and simmer, covered, for 10 minutes more.

4. Remove the pot from the heat. Put the miso into a strainer, lower it partially into the soup, and stir the miso against the sides of the strainer with a wooden spoon to incorporate the miso into the soup.

MAKES 3 QUARTS; SERVES 12

BEAR'S HEAD CUTLETS

The bear's head tooth fungus is large enough to slice into cutlets. But how can you make bread crumbs stick to the slices without dipping the slices into eggs in the traditional method? Liquid lecithin, which tastes like egg yolks (lecithin gives eggs their color and flavor), is an emulsifier that holds the water and peanut oil together. The ground flaxseeds act like egg whites, and the miso adds thickness to a sticky vegan coating that works even better than eggs.

COATING

> 1½ cups water
>
> ¼ cup peanut oil
>
> ¼ cup liquid lecithin
>
> ¼ cup mellow (light-colored) miso
>
> 5 tablespoons freshly ground flaxseeds
>   (2 tablespoons seeds)
>
> 1 teaspoon chili paste or ¼ teaspoon cayenne
>   pepper, or to taste
>
>
> 8 cups bear's head tooth mushrooms sliced about
>   ⅜ inch thick
>
> 1½ cups fresh Bread Crumbs (page 40)

1. Preheat the broiler.

2. *To make the coating:* In a blender, combine the coating ingredients and process until smooth.

3. Stir the coating ingredients into the mushroom slices in a large bowl. Stir in the bread crumbs and turn the mushrooms to coat them evenly. Place the mushroom slices in a single layer on an oiled cookie sheet.

4. Broil the breaded mushrooms until they are browned on top, 2 to 3 minutes, turning the cookie sheet if necessary to avoid burning the mushrooms. Turn the mushroom slices over with a metal spatula or tongs and broil the other side until it is browned. Serve hot.

SERVES 6

AUTUMN OLIVE
Elaeagnus umbellata

OVERLOOKED EVEN BY WILD FOOD FORAGERS, this sometimes thorny shrub grows 12 to 18 feet tall, in orchard-like stands. Its alternate, long-oval, toothless, leathery leaves are 2 to 4 inches long, ¾ to 1½ inches wide, and silvery underneath. Clusters of fragrant, small, tubular, radially symmetrical flowers that are ½ inch long crowd the leaf axils (where leaves join branches) in early spring. They're partially divided into four parts. Countless clusters of specked, round, red berries, the size of cultivated currants, with small, oblong, yellow seeds inside, crowd the branches in late fall. This prolific, invasive Asian shrub, related to the honeysuckle, grows in the Northeast now, but it's been planted and is spreading into the wild elsewhere. Look for it in sandy fields, thickets, and areas of poor soil.

The red berries have a mouth-watering, sweet-sour flavor, reminiscent of the flavor of raspberries, pomegranates, and cranberries.

Note: After you simmer the berries for 5 minutes (they release their own liquid, so you need not add any cooking liquid) and strain out the seeds using a food mill, you may thicken (using arrowroot, kudzu, agar powder, flour, or tapioca) or sweeten the purée and use it in pies, ice cream, fillings, puddings, toppings, ice cream, breads or fruit sauces. The purée will be half as much as the original volume of berries you started with.

If you can't find autumn olives, substitute cranberries.

AUTUMN OLIVE PANCAKES

Autumn olive berries add just the right flavor to these mouth-watering buckwheat-barley pancakes.

DRY INGREDIENTS

> 1⅔ cups (½ pound) buckwheat flour and 1¾ cups plus 2 tablespoons (½ pound) barley flour, or
> 1 pound any whole-grain flour
> ½ cup plus 2 tablespoons freshly ground flaxseeds (¼ cup seeds)
> 2½ tablespoons arrowroot or kudzu
> 2 tablespoons lecithin granules
> 1 teaspoon dried wild spearmint (page 59) or other mint, finely crumbled
> 1 teaspoon cream of tartar
> 1 teaspoon ground cinnamon
> ¾ teaspoon baking soda
> ½ teaspoon salt
> ½ teaspoon ground dried wild ginger (page 111) or regular ground ginger
> 1 teaspoon freshly grated nutmeg

WET INGREDIENTS

> 2½ cups soy milk, nut milk, or water
> 2 cups autumn olive purée (see Note, above)

> ½ cup corn oil
> 1 teaspoon vanilla extract
> ¼ teaspoon butterscotch extract (optional)
> ¼ teaspoon liquid stevia or 2 tablespoons maple syrup, honey, rice syrup, or barley malt

1. In a large bowl, combine the dry ingredients.
2. In a medium-size bowl, combine all the wet ingredients. Stir the wet ingredients into the dry ingredients, being careful not to overmix.
3. Pour 3 to 4 tablespoons of the batter onto a hot oiled griddle or frying pan. Cook each pancake until it is slightly browned underneath, turn it over with a metal spatula, and brown the other side.
4. Serve these pancakes with Autumn Olive Sauce (page 417), autumn olive purée, jam, or another topping.

MAKES 16 TO 18 PANCAKES;
SERVES 8 TO 9

CAROL'S AUTUMN OLIVE SURPRISE

My friend Carol just fed me this wonderful fruit dish she created. You can use it as a dessert, or as a relish in place of cranberry sauce for Thanksgiving.

> 16 cups autumn olive purée (see Note, above)
> ¾ cup agar flakes
> 2 cups peeled, cored, and chopped fresh pineapple
> 2 oranges, peeled, seeded, and chopped
> 2 apples, cored and chopped

Place the autumn olive purée and agar in a large, heavy saucepan and bring the pot to a simmer over medium heat. Reduce the heat to low, and simmer until the agar is dissolved, about 5 minutes. Add the remaining ingredients and chill completely before serving.

MAKES 4 CUPS; SERVES 4

PINK APPLESAUCE

How do you make pink applesauce? Include autumn olive berries.

8 large green apples, cored
4 cups autumn olive purée (see Note, page 416)
Juice of 1 lemon (optional)
1 tablespoon ground cinnamon
1 teaspoon freshly grated nutmeg
½ teaspoon ground dried wild ginger (page 111) or regular ground ginger
¼ teaspoon liquid stevia or 2 tablespoons honey, barley malt, or rice syrup

1. Grate the apples in a food processor or by hand.
2. Transfer the grated apples to a large, heavy pot and add the remaining ingredients. Bring the pot to a simmer over medium heat, reduce the heat to low, and simmer until the apples are tender, 10 to 15 minutes.
3. Carefully transfer the mixture in batches to a blender and process until smooth. Hold down the blender cover with a towel and begin on low speed to prevent eruptions.
4. Serve the applesauce hot or cold, with raisins or chopped nuts, if desired. Pink Applesauce will keep, tightly covered, in the refrigerator for up to a week, or frozen for up to 6 months.

SERVES 8 TO 10

TKEMALI

Cooks in the (former Soviet) Republic of Georgia use a local variety of sour plum in this sauce, but a purée of the autumn olive berry is an excellent alternative. Georgians use this sour sauce on vegetables.

4 cups autumn olive purée (see Note, page 416)
1½ cups fresh cilantro leaves
¼ cup arrowroot or kudzu
3 cloves garlic, finely chopped
1 small chile, seeds and ribs removed and finely chopped
½ teaspoon salt

1. In a food processor or blender, combine all the ingredients and process until smooth.
2. Transfer the mixture to a medium-size, heavy saucepan and bring the pot to a boil over medium heat, stirring constantly. Reduce the heat to low, and simmer, stirring often, for 5 minutes. Serve hot over vegetables. Tkemali will keep, tightly covered, in the refrigerator for 1 week.

MAKES 4 CUPS

AUTUMN OLIVE SAUCE

Here's a cousin of applesauce with a flavor all its own. Eat it as a pudding, serve with pancakes, or mix into fruit salads.

12 cups autumn olive berries
2 cups unsweetened pear juice or other fruit juice
½ cup kudzu or arrowroot
¼ cup fresh lemon juice
2 teaspoons ground cinnamon
2 teaspoons freshly ground star anise
4 teaspoons freshly grated nutmeg

1. Combine all the ingredients in a large, heavy saucepan and bring the pot to a boil over medium heat, stirring often. Reduce the heat to low, and simmer, covered, for 10 minutes, stirring often.

2. Strain out the seeds using a food mill or push the pulp through a colander. Serve hot or cold. Autumn Olive Sauce will keep, tightly covered, in the refrigerator for 1 week.

MAKES 8 CUPS

BANANA–AUTUMN OLIVE BREAD

Tart autumn olives combine with sweet bananas to produce a wonderful, sweet, high-fiber bread.

> 3 cups sweet brown rice flour or 1 ½ pounds any
>   other whole-grain flour
>
> 2 cups oat bran or wheat bran
>
> ½ cup plus 2 tablespoons freshly ground flaxseeds
>   (¼ cups seeds)
>
> 2 teaspoons baking soda
>
> 1 teaspoon salt
>
> 1 teaspoon freshly ground coriander seeds
>
> 1 teaspoon freshly ground cardamom seeds
>
> 3 cups peeled and sliced ripe bananas or pawpaws
>   (page 312)
>
> 1 cup autumn olive purée (see Note, page 416)
>
> ¼ cup fresh lemon or lime juice
>
> 2 teaspoons vanilla extract
>
> 1 teaspoon banana extract (optional)
>
> ½ teaspoon liquid stevia or ¼ cup honey
>   or barley malt
>
> 4 common spicebush berries (page 314), finely
>   chopped, or 1 teaspoon freshly ground allspice
>   berries
>
> 1 cup chopped walnuts

> 1 cup cultivated currants or raisins
>
> 2 tablespoons lecithin granules

1. Preheat the oven to 350 degrees.

2. In a large bowl, mix together the flour, bran, ground flaxseeds, baking soda, salt, and ground coriander and cardamom.

3. In a blender or food processor in 3 batches, process the bananas, autumn olive purée, lemon juice, extracts, liquid stevia, and spicebush berries together until smooth. Combine this mixture with the dry ingredients, being careful not to overmix. Stir in the walnuts, currants, and lecithin.

4. Pour the batter into two oiled 8½ x 4¼ x 2¾-inch loaf pans. Bake the loaves until a toothpick inserted in the center emerges clean, about 1 hour. If you prefer a less crusty bread, set a pan of water in bottom of the oven.

5. Remove the loaves from the loaf pans and let them cool on wire racks before slicing.

MAKES 2 LOAVES

PINK AUTUMN OLIVE MUFFINS

Autumn olive purée makes the lightest whole-grain muffins you've ever tasted.

DRY INGREDIENTS

> 1 ⅓ cups (5.5 ounces) oat flour and 1 cup
>   (5 ounces) buckwheat flour, or 10.5 ounces
>   any whole-grain flour
>
> 3 tablespoons plus 2 ¼ teaspoons freshly ground
>   flaxseeds (1 ½ tablespoons seeds)
>
> 2 tablespoons lecithin granules
>
> 1 teaspoon ground cinnamon
>
> 1 teaspoon salt

½ teaspoon ground dried wild ginger (page 111) or
regular ground ginger

1 ¼ teaspoons cream of tartar

½ teaspoon baking soda

WET INGREDIENTS

½ cup soy milk or nut milk

6 tablespoons corn oil

¼ cup apple juice or grape juice

¾ cup autumn olive purée (see Note, page 416)
or Pink Applesauce (page 417)

1 teaspoon liquid stevia

1. Preheat the oven to 400 degrees.

2. In a large bowl, mix together the dry ingredients.

3. In a medium-size bowl, mix together the wet ingredients. Stir the wet ingredients into the dry ingredients, being careful not to overmix.

4. Pour the batter into oiled muffin tins, filling each cup three-quarters full. Bake the muffins until they are lightly browned and a toothpick inserted in the center emerges clean, about 20 minutes.

5. Let the muffins cool on wire racks.

MAKES 18 MUFFINS

BAKED BANANAS IN AUTUMN OLIVE SAUCE

Tart autumn olives contrast especially well with baked bananas.

6 ripe bananas, peeled

1 ½ cups autumn olive purée (see Note, page 416)

1 tablespoon kudzu or arrowroot

1 tablespoon Redbud Wine (page 152) or red wine

1 teaspoon ground cinnamon

¼ teaspoon liquid stevia or 1 tablespoon barley
malt or honey, or to taste

6 tablespoons almonds, toasted (page 158) and
chopped

1. Preheat the oven to 350 degrees.

2. Arrange the bananas in a 10 x 6½ x 2-inch oiled baking dish.

3. In a blender, combine the autumn olive purée, kudzu, wine, cinnamon, and stevia and process until smooth, and pour over the bananas.

4. Bake the bananas, uncovered, until bubbly, about 40 minutes, basting them with the sauce every 20 minutes. Sprinkle the almonds on top. Serve hot or cold.

SERVES 4 TO 6

AUTUMN OLIVE PUDDING

Tart autumn olive berry purée, creamy cashews, and soft, absorbent bread crumbs combine to produce a simple bread pudding that you can't stop eating.

2 cups soy milk or nut milk

1 cup autumn olive purée (see Note, page 416)

1 cup raw cashews

½ cup corn oil or flaxseed oil

½ cup pitted dates

¼ cup lecithin granules

¼ cup kudzu or arrowroot

1 tablespoon fresh lemon juice

2 teaspoons vanilla extract

1 teaspoon liquid stevia

¼ teaspoon orange extract

½ teaspoon salt

1 cup fresh Bread Crumbs (page 40)

1. Preheat the oven to 350 degrees.

2. In a blender, combine all the ingredients, except

the bread crumbs, and process until smooth. Combine this mixture with the bread crumbs in a 1½-quart oiled casserole dish.

3. Bake, uncovered, until the pudding is thickened and bubbly, about 50 minutes. Serve hot or cold.

SERVES 6

AUTUMN OLIVE PIE

The autumn olive berry has a really strong flavor. In this pie filling, silken tofu tones down the berries and helps create a creamy filling; while ground nuts, bread crumbs, and dates serve as the base for an uncooked crust.

FILLING

    12 cups autumn olive berries
    ½ cup vegetable glycerin, honey, rice syrup,
        maple syrup, or barley malt
    One 19-ounce package silken tofu, drained
    1 cup agar flakes
    2 teaspoons dried pennyroyal (page 203) or other
        mint, finely crumbled
    1 teaspoon freshly ground coriander seeds
    1 teaspoon ground dried wild ginger (page 111) or
        regular ground ginger
    ½ teaspoon salt
    ½ teaspoon cranberry extract (optional)

CRUST

    2¼ cups walnuts
    4 cups dry Bread Crumbs (page 40)
    1½ cups pitted dates
    ¾ cup water
    1½ teaspoons vanilla extract
    3 tablespoons apricot kernel oil or corn oil
    ½ teaspoon salt
    ½ teaspoon walnut or almond extract

⅛ teaspoon amaretto extract (optional)

1. *To make the filling:* Place the filling ingredients in a large, heavy saucepan and bring the pot to a simmer over medium heat. Reduce the heat to low, and simmer, covered, for 10 minutes.

2. Remove the seeds from the mixture using a food mill or by pressing the mixture through a colander. Chill the filling in the freezer while you make the crust. Don't let it freeze.

3. *To make the crust:* In a food processor fitted with a chopping blade, combine all the crust ingredients and process until finely ground (or chop by hand).

4. Pinch a piece of the crust mixture between your fingers. If it's too crumbly to press into a pie pan, add more water. If it's too moist and sticky, add more bread crumbs or ground nuts.

5. Divide the dough among 3 oiled 9-inch pie pans and press the dough into each pan. Fill the crusts evenly with the filling. Chill the pies until the filling sets before serving.

MAKES THREE 9-INCH PIES;
SERVES 12 TO 18

PUMPKIN–AUTUMN OLIVE PIE

Here's a traditional-style recipe that includes wild berries for an added twist.

CRUST

    1¼ cups (6 ounces) sweet brown rice flour and
        1½ cups (6 ounces) oat flour, or ¾ pound any
        whole-grain flour
    ½ cup almonds, ground into meal
    ½ teaspoon salt
    ¾ cup apple juice

¼ cup almond oil

1 teaspoon vanilla extract

½ teaspoon almond extract

¼ teaspoon butterscotch extract (optional)

FILLING

7 cups pumpkin purée

3 cups autumn olive purée (see Note, page 416)

½ cup arrowroot or kudzu

2 ¼ cups pecans, chopped

1 cup raisins or cultivated currants

2 teaspoons liquid stevia

2 teaspoons ground cinnamon

1 teaspoon freshly grated nutmeg

½ teaspoon ground dried wild ginger (page 111) or
regular ground ginger

¼ teaspoon salt

1. *To make the crust:* In a large bowl, mix together the flours, almonds, and salt.

2. In a medium-size bowl, mix together the apple juice, almond oil, and extracts. Stir the wet ingredients into the dry ingredients to form a soft but not sticky dough, adding more apple juice or flour if necessary. Knead the dough. Chill it if you have the time.

3. Preheat the oven to 425 degrees.

4. *To make the filling:* In a large bowl, mix together the filling ingredients.

5. Divide the dough into 6 pieces. Using a rolling pin covered with a floured sleeve and working on a floured pastry sheet, roll out one piece of dough to fit a 9-inch pie pan. Transfer the pastry to the pie pan by rolling the pastry along with the pastry sheet around the rolling pin, and then unrolling it over the tin. Repeat the process with two more pieces of dough. Punch holes in the crust with a fork so the crust doesn't separate from the pan.

6. Divide the filling among the 3 pies. Roll out a top

crust for each pie. Moisten the edges of the bottom crust with water, transfer the top crust over the filling, and press the edges together. Repeat until you've used up all the dough and filling.

7. Bake the pies for 7 minutes. Reduce the oven temperature to 350 degrees and bake the pies for another 35 minutes, turning them occasionally so that the crust bake evenly. Let the pies cool before slicing.

MAKES THREE 9-INCH PIES;
SERVES 12 TO 18

AUTUMN OLIVE ICE CREAM

The autumn olive, a member of the honeysuckle family, is one of the most underappreciated of the wild fruits. Seeds removed and puréed, it's an ideal fruit for making ice cream.

1 ½ cups autumn olive purée (see Note, page 416)

1 ½ cups soy milk or nut milk

½ cup well-drained silken tofu

½ cup raw cashews

½ cup canola oil

¼ cup vegetable glycerin, honey, maple syrup,
barley malt, or rice syrup

2 teaspoons vanilla extract

1 teaspoon strawberry extract (optional)

½ teaspoon lemon extract

½ teaspoon almond extract

1 teaspoon liquid stevia (optional)

½ teaspoon salt

½ cup pecans, chopped

1. In a blender, combine all the ingredients, except the pecans, and process until smooth.

2. Chill the mixture (or begin with chilled ingredi-

ents) if required by your ice cream machine, and stir in the pecans.

3. Pour the mixture into an ice cream machine and freeze it according to the manufacturer's instructions.

MAKES 5½ CUPS; SERVES 5 TO 6

WINEBERRY–AUTUMN OLIVE ICE CREAM

Wineberries and autumn olives are wonderful together in ice cream and other desserts. Since they're in season at different times of the year, it's worthwhile freezing one or the other so you can combine them.

3 cups drained silken tofu

1 cup autumn olive purée (see Note, page 416)

1 cup soy milk or nut milk

½ cup canola oil

¼ cup vegetable glycerin

¼ cup lecithin granules

2 teaspoons vanilla extract

1 teaspoon dried wild spearmint (page 59) or other
   mint, finely crumbled

1 teaspoon orange extract

1 teaspoon strawberry extract (optional)

1 teaspoon ground cinnamon

1 teaspoon freshly grated nutmeg

½ teaspoon salt

½ teaspoon liquid stevia or 2 tablespoons honey,
   barley malt, or rice syrup

1½ cups wineberries (page 240) or raspberries,
   chilled or frozen

1. Working in 2 batches, in a blender, combine all the ingredients, except the wineberries, and process until smooth.

2. Chill the mixture (or begin with chilled ingredi-

ents) if required by your ice cream machine, and stir in the wineberries.

3. Pour the mixture into an ice cream machine and freeze it according to the manufacturer's instructions.

MAKES 7½ CUPS; SERVES 6 TO 8

AUTUMN OLIVE HOLIDAY SORBET

This is my most successful recipe failure. I was trying to make autumn olive ice cream, but instead I got the best sorbet I ever tasted.

2 cups autumn olive purée (see Note, page 416)

2 cups drained silken tofu

1 cup unsweetened pear juice or apple juice

½ cup canola oil

¼ cup vegetable glycerin

¼ cup liquid lecithin

½ teaspoon liquid stevia or 2 tablespoons barley
   malt, honey, or maple syrup

1 tablespoon lecithin granules

½ teaspoon ground cinnamon

½ teaspoon dried pennyroyal (page 203) or other
   mint, finely crumbled

½ teaspoon ground dried wild ginger (page 111) or
   regular ground ginger

1 teaspoon vanilla extract

1 teaspoon orange extract

1 teaspoon strawberry extract (optional)

½ teaspoon salt

1. Working in 2 batches, in a blender combine all the ingredients and process until smooth.

2. Chill the mixture (or begin with chilled ingredients) if required by your ice cream machine.

3. Pour the mixture into the ice cream machine and

freeze it according to the manufacturer's instructions. Serve immediately or store in the freezer. Before serving it, let it stand at room temperature until it is soft enough to eat.

MAKES 6 CUPS; SERVES 6

AUTUMN OLIVE WINE

This sweet-and-sour red berry, unrelated to the olive, usually turns recipes red, so it was quite a surprise when the wine it makes turned out to be colored yellow. Too pungent for drinking, it makes a wonderful dry cooking wine, especially suited to French and Italian dishes.

4 cups boiling water

Juice of 1 lemon

3 pounds sugar

4 ½ cups autumn olive berries

6 common spicebush berries (page 314) or
    1 teaspoon allspice berries

1 tablespoon dried pennyroyal (page 203) or other
    mint species

1 tablespoon poppy seeds

2 teaspoons coriander seeds

½ teaspoon champagne yeast

1. Bring the water and lemon juice to a boil in a large, heavy pot, add the sugar, and stir until it is dissolved.
2. Meanwhile, in a blender, briefly chop the autumn olives coarsely.
3. Stir all the ingredients except the yeast together in a large non-metal (plastic or ceramic) food container.
4. When the mixture is cooled to lukewarm, stir in the yeast and cover the container loosely with a non-airtight cover, cheesecloth, or towel.
5. Allow the mixture to ferment at room temperature for a week, stirring it twice a day.
6. Strain out all the solids through a cheesecloth-lined colander.
7. Pour the mixture into a large jug and seal it with an airlock stopper (which lets carbon dioxide bubbles escape but keeps oxygen out).
8. After the bubbling stops and fermentation ceases in 10 to 14 days, seal the jug with an airtight cap or cork.
9. Allow the wine to age for 6 months to 1 year before using it. The wine will be at its best after 2 years.

MAKES 5 QUARTS

WILD CRANBERRY

Vaccinium species

THESE NATIVE PERENNIALS FORM HORIZONTAL mats that are 2 to 3 feet long. The plants feature alternate, small, curved, oval, smooth-edged, leathery leaves and small, pink, flowers. With its four recurved petals and long yellow stamen, the flower resembles a bird's bill. The small, round, red fruit, which ripens in autumn, looks like its commercial descendants. Wild cranberries grow in the poor, acidic soil of bogs, and one species grows in acidic woodlands. The plants grow in the eastern half of northern North America and Canada. Domesticated in the late nineteenth or early twentieth century, commercial cranberries provide a good substitute for wild ones.

As a cook who avoids refined and concentrated sweeteners, I've always found cranberries difficult to work with because they're very sour. Using them in dishes that contain sweet fruits or sweet sauces thickened with bland silken tofu best solves the problem.

WILD CRANBERRY SAUCE

Here's a different version of the familiar Thanksgiving fare.

4 cups wild cranberries
¾ cup apple juice
2 ripe pears, cored and sliced
1 cup raisins
1 teaspoon liquid stevia

1. Combine all the ingredients in a medium-size, heavy saucepan and bring the pot to a boil over medium heat. Reduce the heat to low, cover, and simmer for 10 minutes, stirring occasionally.

2. Chill the sauce completely before serving. Wild Cranberry Sauce will keep, tightly covered, in the refrigerator for 2 weeks.

MAKES 4 CUPS

WILD CRANBERRY BREAD

Here's a moist, rich bread that is lightly flavored with cranberries.

3½ cups (14 ounces) oat flour and 2¾ cups plus 3
tablespoons (14 ounces) sweet brown rice flour,
or 1¾ pounds any whole-grain flour
½ cup plus 2 tablespoons freshly ground
flaxseeds (¼ cup seeds)
1½ teaspoons cream of tartar
1¾ teaspoons baking soda
1 teaspoon salt
½ teaspoon freshly ground cloves
1 teaspoon freshly grated nutmeg
¼ teaspoon freshly ground cardamom seeds
1½ cups cranberry juice
6 tablespoons corn oil

2 teaspoons liquid stevia
½ teaspoon orange extract
½ teaspoon cranberry extract (optional)
1¾ cups wild cranberries
½ cup walnuts, chopped
¼ cup lecithin granules

1. Preheat the oven to 375 degrees.

2. In a large bowl, mix together the flours, ground flaxseeds, cream of tartar, baking soda, salt, cloves, nutmeg, and cardamom.

3. In a medium-size bowl, mix together the cranberry juice, corn oil, liquid stevia, and extracts. Stir the wet ingredients into the dry ingredients, being careful not to overmix. Stir in the cranberries, walnuts, and lecithin, being careful not to overmix.

4. Divide the batter between 2 oiled 6½ x 4⅜ x 2½-inch loaf pans. Set a pan of hot water on the bottom of the oven to keep the crust soft. Bake the loaves until a toothpick inserted in the center emerges clean, about 45 minutes.

5. Let the loaves cool on a wire rack before slicing.

MAKES 2 LOAVES

WILD CRANBERRY ICE CREAM

This sour fruit works perfectly in an ice cream that includes other natural flavors, thickeners, and sweeteners.

2 cups soy milk or nut milk
1½ cups drained silken tofu
½ cup canola oil
¼ cup vegetable glycerin or barley malt
¼ cup lecithin granules
½ teaspoon salt

2 teaspoons vanilla extract

1 teaspoon dried wild mint (page 129) or other
   mint, finely crumbled

½ teaspoon orange extract

½ teaspoon cranberry extract (optional)

1 teaspoon liquid stevia

1 cup wild cranberries

1. In a blender, combine all the ingredients, except for ¼ cup of the cranberries, and process until smooth.

2. Chill the mixture (or begin with chilled ingredients) if required by your ice cream machine.

3. Pour the mixture into the ice cream machine and freeze it according to the manufacturer's instructions.

4. Stir in the remaining ¼ cup cranberries.

MAKES 6 CUPS; SERVES 6

CRABAPPLE

Malus species

CRABAPPLES ARE SIMPLY SMALLER VERSIONS OF wild apples (see page 340), often more tart than the larger versions. Because other ingredients can offset their tartness, the most tart crabapples, which have the strongest flavors, are often the best to cook with.

CRABAPPLE CUSTARD

The tartness of wild crabapples, the creaminess of Tofu Cottage Cheese, plus the crunchiness of almonds add up to a delicious pudding.

2 cups crabapples, cored and sliced

2 cups Tofu Cottage Cheese (page 30)

¾ cup apple juice

½ cup soy milk or nut milk

½ cup chopped almonds

¼ cup cultivated currants

2 tablespoons lecithin granules

1 tablespoon canola oil or corn oil

1 tablespoon arrowroot, kudzu, or tapioca pearls

2 ½ tablespoons freshly ground flaxseeds
   (1 tablespoon)

2 teaspoons vanilla extract

½ teaspoon ground dried wild ginger (page 111) or
   regular ground ginger

½ teaspoon freshly grated nutmeg

¼ teaspoon salt

1 teaspoon ground cinnamon

1. Preheat the oven to 375 degrees.

2. Mix together all the ingredients, except the cinnamon, in a 1½-quart oiled casserole dish. Sprinkle the cinnamon on top.

3. Bake the custard until it is thick and bubbly, about 40 minutes. (You may also bake the pudding in a pie crust, or cover the pudding with a pie crust dough and bake it.) Serve hot or cold.

SERVES 4 TO 6

WILD CRABAPPLE BLOSSOM WINE

Ornamental crabapple trees bloom every year in cultivated places throughout the United States. I first made wine with blossoms from trees planted in front of my apartment building, and it was as good as any I've ever tasted. Use this white wine as a universal table wine as well as a cooking wine in sauces, soups, side dishes, and entrées. Gather the short-lived blossoms when they've just opened, when they're at their best.

6 cups sugar

1 gallon boiling water

2 quarts crabapple or apple blossoms

1 lemon, including the rinds, chopped and crushed

1 orange, including the rinds, chopped and crushed

Two 2-inch cinnamon sticks

2 tablespoons star anise

2 tablespoons coriander seeds

½ teaspoon champagne yeast or other wine yeast

1. Dissolve the sugar in the boiling water in a non-metal (plastic or ceramic) food container and add the blossoms, fruits, and spices.

2. When the mixture is lukewarm, stir in the yeast and cover the container with a non-airtight cover, cheesecloth, or towel.

3. Allow the mixture to ferment for a week at room temperature, stirring it twice a day.

4. Strain the mixture through cheesecloth, transfer the liquid to a jug, and seal it with an airlock stopper (which lets carbon dioxide bubbles escape but keeps oxygen out).

5. When the bubbling stops and fermentation ends about 2 weeks later, seal the jug with a cork and age the wine for 6 to 12 weeks before using it.

6. Siphon the wine to get rid of the sediment, if desired.

MAKES 1 GALLON

WILD PARSNIP
Pastinaca sativa

THIS FRAGRANT GARDEN RUNAWAY IS A BIENNIAL, a plant that lives for two years. The first year, basal leaves 2 feet long emerge from the ground. They're feather-compound, divided into stalkless, coarse, ragged, toothed leaflets on both sides of a midrib. These leaves alternate along a flower stalk that grows 5 feet tall by mid-spring of the second year. The small clusters of stalked, tiny, yellow flowers, which bloom in the summer, are configured like an umbrella. They're followed by small, flattened, yellow-green seeds. Underground is a single, thick, white taproot, distinct from water hemlock (*Cicuta maculatum*), a deadly relative that grows in swamps, with finger-like bundles of fleshy roots. Look for wild parsnips on disturbed soil, along roadsides, and in wetlands, overgrown fields, and empty lots throughout the United States.

The root of the basal rosette stage in the plant's first year is good to eat from fall through early spring although if your winters are cold, there will be no leaves to indicate where to dig. Coarser and more gnarled than cultivated parsnip, the wild root tastes much sweeter when you cook it. Use it in soups, stews, and sauces. You'll love it.

WILD PARSNIP RELISH

This seasoned parsnip condiment will add zest to any meal.

½ cup Vegetable Stock (page 40)

1 pound wild parsnips, grated

½ cup red wine vinegar

¼ cup olive oil

6 cloves garlic, chopped

1 teaspoon ground cinnamon

1 teaspoon freshly ground cumin seeds

1 teaspoon freshly grated lemon rind

1 teaspoon Vege-Sal or ½ teaspoon salt, or to taste

¼ teaspoon cayenne pepper, or to taste

1. Combine the stock and parsnips in a large saucepan over medium heat and bring the pot to a simmer. Reduce the heat to low, and simmer, covered, for 15 minutes. Add the remaining ingredients and simmer for another 5 minutes.

2. Chill the relish completely before serving. Wild Parsnip Relish will keep, tightly covered, in the refrigerator for 10 days.

MAKES 3 CUPS

SCALLOPED WILD PARSNIPS

Scalloping vegetables by baking them with a sauce and bread crumbs works exceptionally well with wild parsnips, especially in combination with tofu cheese and other ingredients that diffuse wild parsnips' strong flavor.

4 cups sliced wild parsnips, steamed for 20 minutes
    over boiling water or Vegetable Stock (page 40)

1½ cups Tofu Cream Cheese (page 30)

¼ cup ramp bulbs (page 116) or shallots, diced

¼ cup fresh parsley leaves, chopped

2 cloves garlic, crushed into a paste

½ teaspoon freshly ground black pepper
    (¼ teaspoon peppercorns)

¾ cup Tofu Grated Cheese (page 32)

2 teaspoons paprika

1. Preheat the oven to 350 degrees.

2. Arrange the parsnips in a 2-quart oiled casserole dish.

3. Mix together the Tofu Cream Cheese, ramps, parsley, garlic, and pepper. Pour this mixture over the parsnips. Cover the vegetable mixture with the Tofu Grated Cheese and sprinkle the paprika on top.

4. Bake, uncovered, until the casserole is slightly browned and bubbling, about 50 minutes.

SERVES 6

RAMP-BAKED WILD PARSNIPS

Ramps and parsnips both have strong, distinctive flavors that can drown out weaker-tasting ingredients. Together, they make excellent partners in this baked vegetable dish.

2 tablespoons olive oil

2 tablespoons balsamic vinegar

1 teaspoon dried thyme, finely crumbled

1 teaspoon dried rosemary, finely crumbled

1 teaspoon chili paste or ¼ teaspoon cayenne
    pepper, or to taste

¾ teaspoon freshly ground celery seeds
    (½ teaspoon seeds)

1 teaspoon Vege-Sal or ½ teaspoon salt

2 pounds wild parsnips, thickly sliced

½ pound ramp bulbs (page 116) or shallots, sliced

1 head garlic, cut in half along the "equator"

1. Preheat the oven to 425 degrees.

2. Mix the olive oil, vinegar, thyme, rosemary, chili paste, celery seeds, and Vege-Sal together in a 1½-quart oiled casserole dish.

3. Mix in the parsnips and ramps until the vegetables are well coated.

4. Place the halves of the garlic head in the baking dish with the cut side down. Cover and bake the casserole for 15 minutes. Stir and continue to bake the casserole, uncovered, until the parsnips are tender, about another 15 minutes.

5. Remove and discard the garlic, or save it for another use, and serve warm.

SERVES 4

CURRIED WILD PARSNIPS

This traditional Indian cooking method works beautifully with wild parsnips.

  2 cups drained silken tofu

  ¾ cup water

  ¼ cup fresh lime juice

  1 ½ teaspoons corn oil

  2 ½ tablespoons peanut oil

  1 tablespoon black mustard seeds

  1 tablespoon cumin seeds

  ¾ teaspoon cardamom seeds, whole or ground

  ¾ teaspoon fenugreek seeds

  1 tablespoon turmeric

  6 cloves garlic, chopped

  2 small chiles, seeds and ribs removed and
   chopped, or ¼ teaspoon cayenne pepper, or
   to taste

  1 ½ teaspoons Vege-Sal or ¾ teaspoon salt, or
   to taste

  2 ½ cups thinly sliced wild parsnips

1. In a blender or medium-size bowl, combine the tofu, water, lime juice, and corn oil and process or beat with a whisk until smooth.

2. Heat the peanut oil in a large skillet over medium heat. Add the black mustard seeds, cumin seeds, car-

damom, fenugreek seeds, turmeric, garlic, chiles, and Vege-Sal and cook for 3 minutes, stirring constantly.

3. Stir the tofu mixture and parsnips into the skillet with the spices, reduce the heat to low, and cook, covered, until the parsnips are tender, about 20 minutes. Serve hot.

SERVES 6

PARSNIPPANY CASSEROLE

As long as you love parsnips, you won't have to live in Parsippany, New Jersey, to enjoy the Parsnippany Casserole.

  4 cups cooked lima beans, drained

  1 cup chopped or sliced onions

  4 cloves garlic, finely chopped

  ¾ cup sliced wild parsnips

  2 celery stalks, sliced

  6 tablespoons common blue violet leaves (page
   106) or seeded and chopped green bell peppers

  ½ cup Steve's Salsa (page 374) or tomato juice

  2 tablespoons olive oil

  1 tablespoon chopped fresh basil leaves or
   1 teaspoon dried, finely crumbled

  1 teaspoon dried oregano, finely crumbled

  1 teaspoon Vege-Sal or ½ teaspoon salt

  2 cups Tofu Sharp Cheese (page 30)

1. Preheat the oven to 350 degrees.

2. Mix together all the ingredients except the Tofu Sharp Cheese in an oiled 2-quart casserole dish.

3. Top the vegetable mixture with the Tofu Sharp Cheese. Bake, covered, for 30 minutes. Uncover the casserole and bake it for another 30 minutes. Serve hot.

SERVES 6

ENOKI MUSHROOM, VELVET FOOT

Flammulina velutipes

THIS MUSHROOM'S STICKY, CONVEX TO FLAT, reddish brown to tawny cap grows 1 to 2 inches across. Its white to yellowish white gills, which attach to the stalk, release white spores. The stalk is 1 to 3 inches long, ⅛ to ¼ inch wide, yellowish white above, and distinctly velvety black below. (Surprisingly, these features are different from the same species grown commercially and sold in Chinese markets: that mushroom is completely white.) The enoki grows clustered on dead deciduous logs and stumps across North America. You can find it from fall to early spring, even in mid-winter if it's above freezing and there's been enough rain.

Remove the stems, which are too tough to eat (but good for making stock—see page 40) and use the caps in soups or sauces. The caps will cook in 10 to 15 minutes, imparting a delicate, rich flavor and a silky texture.

ENOKI BURDOCK SOUP

Asian chefs prize the enoki mushroom (velvet foot) for the magic it imparts to soups. You'll certainly agree when you try this recipe—one of my best soups.

> 6 cups Vegetable Stock (page 40)
> 1 ¼ cups very thinly sliced burdock root (page 139) or sliced carrots
> 2 tablespoons sesame oil
> 6 cups enoki mushroom caps, sliced
> 3 celery stalks, sliced

1 tablespoon peeled and finely chopped fresh ginger

4 cloves garlic, chopped

3 tablespoons kudzu or arrowroot

½ teaspoon freshly ground anise seeds

¾ teaspoon freshly ground celery seeds (½ teaspoon seeds)

1 teaspoon freshly ground Szechuan pepper (½ teaspoon peppercorns) or ½ teaspoon freshly ground white pepper (¼ teaspoon peppercorns), or to taste

1 ¼ cups drained silken tofu, diced

1. Place 5 cups of the stock and the burdock root in a large stockpot and bring the pot to a simmer over medium heat. Reduce the heat to low, and simmer, covered, for 15 minutes.

2. Meanwhile, heat the sesame oil in a large skillet over medium heat. Add the mushrooms, celery, ginger, and garlic and cook, stirring, for 10 minutes.

3. In a small bowl, mix the kudzu into the remaining 1 cup stock with a whisk or fork. Then stir the kudzu mixture into the stock, along with the cooked vegetable mixture and the remaining ingredients. Bring the pot to a boil over medium heat, stirring often. Reduce the heat to low, cover, and simmer for 10 minutes. Serve hot.

SERVES 6

BLEWIT

Clitocybe nuda

THIS FRAGRANT, BLUISH-TINGED MUSHROOM has a violet-gray cap that is 2 to 6 inches across. It begins convex, flattens, and ends slightly funnel-shaped. The broad, violet buff gills connect to the stem with a notch. The spores are white. The violet-gray stalk is 1 to 3 inches long and ⅜ to 1 inch across, with a bulbous base. Look for the blewit in composted soil and evergreen debris from late summer through late fall throughout North America (or late fall to late winter in California).

The poisonous silver-violet cortinarius (Cortinarius alboviolaceus) is similar, but it has brown spores that eventually darken the gills (which are protected by a cobweb-like veil when young), plus a faint ring zone around the mature stem.

One of the most prized of wild mushrooms, the blewit is so strong tasting, it overpowers some people's palates. You may prepare it simply with few other ingredients, or include it in a recipe with many strong-flavored ingredients. Its rich flavor and meaty texture will always shine through. And virtually any cooking method suits this choice fungus. Cook the cap and stem for 15 to 20 minutes.

MACARONI AND CHEESE WITH BLEWITS

Blewit mushrooms and vegan tofu cheeses make this commonplace, high-fat dish exotic tasting and healthful.

> 8 cups homemade macaroni (use the Buckwheat
>   Noodle recipe, page 34, and use a macaroni die)
>   or store-bought whole-grain macaroni
> 4 teaspoons olive oil
> 4 cups packed blewits, chopped
> 4 cloves garlic, chopped
> ¼ cup arrowroot or kudzu
> Double recipe (4 cups) Tofu Cream Cheese
>   (page 30)

> 1½ cups Spanish Sausages (page 316)
> 2 cups Tofu Grated Cheese (page 32)

1. Preheat the oven to 375 degrees.

2. Cook the macaroni in rapidly boiling salted water for 2 minutes less than directed. Drain the pasta in a colander and immediately immerse the colander in cold water to halt the cooking.

3. Meanwhile, heat the olive oil in a large skillet over medium heat. Add the blewits and garlic and cook, stirring, for 10 minutes.

4. Mix the arrowroot with the Tofu Cream Cheese and then stir in the Spanish Sausages. Spread a third of this Tofu Cream Cheese mixture over the bottom of a 14 x 9 x 2-inch oiled baking dish.

5. Make the following layers: the macaroni, half the remaining Tofu Cream Cheese mixture, the mushrooms, the remaining Tofu Cream Cheese mixture, and the Tofu Grated Cheese. Bake until bubbly, about 40 minutes. Serve hot.

SERVES 6

COMMON EVENING PRIMROSE
Oenothera biennis

THIS BIENNIAL BEGINS WITH A BASAL ROSETTE of lanced-shaped to elliptical, raggedy edged, hairy leaves that grow almost 1 foot long, emerging from a white, fleshy taproot that may also reach almost 1 foot in length. Each leaf has a distinct whitish midrib. In mid-spring of the plant's second year, a stout, reddish flower stalk 4 to 7 feet arises. Long-stemmed, yellow, four-petaled flowers bloom in the leaf axils (where the leaf joins the stem) in the summer and fall. A cross-shaped stigma (where the pollen lands) stands out. Cylindrical, woody capsules that are 1½ inches long enclose many tiny, hard, reddish seeds in late summer and fall. Look for this native plant and its close (edible) relatives in fields, disturbed soil, along roadsides, in wetlands, prairies, and sandy soil across the United States.

Harvest the root of the low first-year plant (no flower stalk) in the fall and early spring (you can sometimes also locate it during mild winters). Simmer the sliced root in soups, stews, or sauces for 15 to 20 minutes. It adds a peppery, radish-like flavor and slightly thicken liquids, the way okra does. It's also great added to grains and beans.

Bring your date to where the plant grows late at night, and you'll get to lead her or him down the primrose path.

PRIMROSE AND NOODLE SOUP

This wonderful soup, based on common evening primrose, noodles, and wild watercress, uses almond butter as a thickener.

12½ cups Vegetable Stock (page 40) or water

¼ cup Crunchy Almond Butter (page 38)

¼ cup dark-colored miso

1½ tablespoons olive oil

1 cup sliced common evening primrose roots

2 celery stalks, sliced

1 medium-size red bell pepper, seeded and sliced into strips

½ cup wild enoki mushroom caps (page 429) or other mushrooms

½ cup ramp bulbs (page 116) or onion, chopped

2 cloves garlic, chopped

3 cups Buckwheat Noodles made with a macaroni die (page 34) or store-bought macaroni

2 cups watercress leaves (page 46), coarsely chopped

2 tablespoons chopped fresh dill

2 tablespoons chopped fresh parsley leaves

2 tablespoons chopped fresh basil leaves

1½ teaspoons sweet paprika

1 teaspoon dried tarragon, finely crumbled

1 teaspoon freshly ground yellow mustard seeds (½ teaspoon seeds)

1 teaspoon freshly ground white pepper (½ teaspoon peppercorns)

1. In a large stockpot, bring the stock to a boil. In a blender, process 1 cup of the stock with the almond butter and miso until smooth.

2. Heat the olive oil in a large soup pot over medium heat. Add the primrose roots, celery, bell pepper, mushrooms, and ramps and cook, stirring, for 10 minutes. Add garlic and cook, stirring, for another 2 minutes. Add the remaining 11½ cups stock to the soup pot and simmer for 5 minutes.

3. Add the noodles and continue to simmer the mixture for 2 more minutes. (If you're using store-bought noodles, check the package's cooking time and add the noodles to the pot at a point when they will just finish cooking when the recipe is done.)

4. Add the watercress, dill, parsley, basil, paprika, tarragon, ground yellow mustard seeds, and white pepper and let the soup simmer for another 5 minutes.

5. Stir in the almond butter and stock mixture. Serve hot.

MAKES 3½ QUARTS; SERVES 6 TO 8

CREAM OF WILD VEGETABLE SOUP

This nutritious puréed soup will warm you up, fill you up, and satisfy your taste buds.

1 cup sliced common evening primrose roots
¼ cup sweet cicely taproots (avoid the gnarled, stringy underground stems; page 92) or fennel bulb
10½ cups Vegetable Stock (page 40)
2 celery stalks, sliced
Kernels cut from 2 ears of corn (¾ cup)
1 large clove garlic, chopped
Half a 19-ounce package silken tofu, drained
2 cups chickweed (page 53) or alfalfa sprouts
1 tablespoon chopped fresh parsley leaves
¾ teaspoon freshly ground celery seeds
    (½ teaspoon seeds)
½ teaspoon dried tarragon, finely crumbled
2 tablespoons corn oil
¼ cup dark-colored miso

1. Place the primrose root, sweet cicely, and stock in a soup pot and bring the pot to a simmer over medium heat. Reduce the heat to low, and simmer, covered, for 10 minutes. Add the celery, corn, garlic, and tofu and simmer for another 7 minutes. Add the remaining ingredients and simmer for 2 more minutes.
2. Carefully transfer the mixture to a blender in batches (or use a hand blender) and process until smooth, beginning at low speed and holding down the cover with a towel to prevent eruptions. Then process the mixture at high speed. Rewarm if necessary.

MAKES 4 QUARTS; SERVES 12 TO 16

STEVE'S CURRY

I first made this multi-vegetable curry soup with commercial ingredients when I was teaching cooking classes in 1981, before I became the "Wildman." Here's an updated version that includes wild vegetables. Instead of using curry powder, this recipe follows the traditional Indian practice of using whole spices.

3 cups Vegetable Stock (page 40) or water
1 cup drained silken tofu
1 tablespoon peeled and chopped fresh ginger
1 tablespoon fresh lime juice
2 tablespoons chickpea flour or any whole-grain flour
2 tablespoons peanut oil
½ teaspoon black or yellow mustard seeds
¼ teaspoon cumin seeds
6 cloves
One 1½-inch cinnamon stick
1½ teaspoons coriander seeds
2 teaspoons Vege-Sal or 1 teaspoon salt, or to taste
1 teaspoon turmeric
1 teaspoon cayenne pepper, or to taste
1 ripe plantain or large green banana, peeled and sliced
1½ cups sliced common evening primrose roots
⅓ cup chopped carrot
¾ cup field garlic leaves (page 57) or scallions, sliced
½ cup drained firm tofu, diced
1 celery stalk, sliced
1 small bell pepper (green, red, or yellow), seeded and chopped
¼ cup cauliflower florets

1. In a blender, combine the stock, silken tofu, ginger, lime juice, and chickpea flour and process until smooth. Transfer the mixture to a medium-size

saucepan and bring the pot to a boil over medium heat. Simmer, covered, for 10 minutes, stirring occasionally.

2. Meanwhile, heat the peanut oil over medium heat in a large saucepan. Add the mustard seeds, cumin seeds, cloves, cinnamon stick, and coriander seeds and cook, stirring constantly, until the mustard seeds pop.

3. Add the simmering stock mixture, Vege-Sal, turmeric, cayenne, and plantains and simmer for 5 minutes, stirring occasionally. Add the primrose roots, carrot, and field garlic and simmer for another 5 minutes. Add the firm tofu, celery, bell pepper, and cauliflower and simmer until all the vegetables are fairly soft, about another 10 minutes.

4. Serve hot with brown rice, other grains, or Indian bread.

SERVES 6

COMMON EVENING DAL

Common evening primrose makes all the difference in this Indian lentil dish.

> 1 cup dried small red lentils, picked over, rinsed, and drained
> 2 cups water
> Juice of 1 lime
> 1 tablespoon sesame oil
> 2 cups thinly sliced common evening primrose roots
> 1 tablespoon wild garlic bulbs or bulblets (page 160) or regular garlic, chopped
> 1 teaspoon turmeric
> ½ teaspoon freshly ground coriander seeds
> ½ teaspoon freshly ground fenugreek seeds
> ½ teaspoon Vege-Sal or ¼ teaspoon sea salt
> 1 teaspoon chili paste or ¼ teaspoon cayenne pepper, or to taste

1. Place the lentils, water, and lime juice in a medium-size saucepan and bring the pot to a boil over medium heat. Reduce the heat to low, and simmer, covered, for 20 minutes.

2. Meanwhile, heat the sesame oil in a medium-size skillet over medium heat. Add the primrose roots, garlic, turmeric, coriander, and fenugreek and cook, stirring, for 10 minutes.

3. Transfer the lentils and any remaining liquid to a food processor or medium-size bowl and process or mash with a potato masher or fork until smooth.

4. Return the mashed lentils to a saucepan, add the sautéed vegetables, Vege-Sal, and chili paste, heat the mixture through, and serve. Serve hot as a side dish.

SERVES 4 TO 6

PRIMROSE RICE

The simple addition of common evening primrose root transforms this brown basmati rice–amaranth pilaf into an extraordinary dish.

> 2 ¾ cups water
> 1 ½ cups brown basmati rice
> ¼ cup wild rice (page 353)
> ¼ cup amaranth (page 338)
> ¾ cup sliced common evening primrose root
> 1 medium-size red onion, chopped
> 4 cloves garlic, finely chopped
> 5 teaspoons olive oil
> 2 tablespoons tamari soy sauce
> 1 teaspoon toasted sesame oil
> 1 teaspoon dried rosemary, finely crumbled
> 1 teaspoon dried tarragon, finely crumbled
> 1 teaspoon dried thyme, finely crumbled
> 1 teaspoon chili paste or ¼ teaspoon cayenne pepper

Combine all the ingredients in a large saucepan and bring the pot to a boil over medium heat. Reduce the heat to low, cover, and simmer until all the liquid is absorbed and the rice and grains are tender, about 40 minutes.

SERVES 5 TO 6

PRIMROSE BARLEY

The sweet-hot flavor of common evening primrose adds just the right touch to the nutty flavor of barley.

3 ⅞ cups water

1 ¾ cups barley

¼ cup wild rice (page 353)

1 cup sliced common evening primrose roots

2 celery stalks, sliced

1 medium-size onion, sliced

2 cloves garlic, chopped

2 tablespoons tamari soy sauce, or to taste

1 tablespoon chili paste or ¼ teaspoon cayenne
  pepper, or to taste

¾ teaspoon freshly ground celery seeds
  (½ teaspoon seeds)

½ teaspoon freshly grated nutmeg

Preheat the oven to 375 degrees. Combine all the ingredients in a 3-quart oiled casserole dish and bake until all the water is absorbed and the grains are tender, about 1¼ hours.

SERVES 4 TO 6

BRICK TOP MUSHROOM

Naematoloma sublateritium

THIS BRICK RED MUSHROOM CAP, 1⅜ TO 4 inches across, has a distinctive color that fades toward the edge. The whitish to purple-gray gills attach to the stalk. They release purple-brown spores. The whitish stalk is 2 to 4 inches long and ¼ to ⅝ inch wide, with a zone of fibrils toward the top. Clusters of this mushroom grow on deciduous logs and stumps in late fall. You can find it throughout eastern North America.

The brick top is a good-tasting mushroom, and I'm always happy to find stands of it in the woods, but it's not choice. Normally, many of the other species in this book surpass it in flavor, but you don't find them as late in the fall. And you can even the odds of producing some really fine dishes by using the same savory seasonings that people generally use with mushrooms. The cap is the best part to use, although the stems are good in puréed soups and sauces.

PICKLED BRICK TOPS

Pickling brick tops with savory ingredients elevates them to the level of the best of the wild mushrooms. Present these mushrooms as an appetizer.

10 cups brick top mushrooms

4 cloves garlic, peeled

1 ½ cups brown rice vinegar or red wine vinegar

1 cup Wineberry Wine (page 246) or red wine

⅓ cup tamari soy sauce

2 tablespoons green or white peppercorns

1 tablespoon coriander seeds

1 teaspoon dried rosemary, finely crumbled

1 teaspoon cloves

1 teaspoon dill seeds

1 cup almond oil or olive oil

1. Place the mushrooms, garlic, vinegar, wine, and tamari in a large pot and bring the pot to a boil over medium heat. Reduce the heat to low, and simmer, covered, for 20 minutes.

2. Stir in the remaining ingredients and chill the mixture, tightly covered, overnight. Pickled Brick Tops will keep, tightly covered, in the refrigerator for up to a month.

MAKES 6 CUPS

GINGKO

Gingko biloba

THE GINGKO TREE HAS GRAY BARK, BULLET-shaped twigs, and unique, alternate, fan-shaped leaves that are 2 to 3 inches across. Inconspicuous, slender whitish strands of flowers hang from the branches in early spring. The soft, dull orange, round fruit, about 1 inch across, ripens from mid- to late fall. It smells like vomit and must have acted as a dinosaur repellant 100 million years ago. A thin-shelled whitish beige, almond-shaped nut inside encloses an edible, soft, green kernel.

A relic from the Mesozoic era, the gingko has no living relatives, close or distant. Driven almost to extinction by the last ice age, it was rescued from oblivion in ancient times by Chinese monks who planted a few survivors in their monastery gardens. Westerners rediscovered this living fossil and planted it on city streets, in parks, and in cultivated areas throughout the world, where it's now common.

Good for promoting circulation and memory, the nut tastes unlike any other nut—like a combination of peas and limburger cheese. ***Don't eat the nuts raw, because they are poisonous until they have been cooked.*** Use cooked gingko nuts (the fruit and raw kernel can make you sick) as appetizers, in soups, stews, salads, rice, and Asian dishes.

BASIC GINGKO PREPARATION

Remove the beige nut from the foul-smelling fruit under running water wearing rubber gloves (some people get a poison ivy–like rash from handling the raw fruit). Discard the fruit, rinse the nuts, and prepare them as follows.

4 cups gingko nuts, well rinsed and fruit discarded

1. Preheat the oven to 275 degrees. Toast the nuts for 30 minutes in a baking dish, stirring them occasionally. (Asians also prepare gingkos by boiling them, but I prefer my method.)

2. When the nuts are cool, crack open the thin shells by tapping them with a drinking glass or hardcover book (not this one!). Don't rap on the shell too hard or the shell will shatter.

3. Remove the green kernel, which is covered with a brown skin. It's unnecessary to remove the skin.

4. Use the toasted, shelled nuts within a few days or freeze them for up to a year. Unshelled and shelled gingkos dry out, become hard, and don't rehydrate (you can buy dried gingkos in Asian markets, but I haven't discovered the secret of successful dehydration). *Caution: Some people have an allergic reaction to gingkos, so start by trying this food in small quantities.*

MAKES 2 CUPS; SERVES 6

GINGKO CHEESE DRESSING

Familiar to Asian palates, gingkos sometimes taste strange to westerners. Yet combined with other cheesy-tasting and fermented ingredients, these nuts contribute a realistic cheese flavor to this dairy-free salad dressing.

1 cup olive oil
1 ⅔ cups flaxseed oil or corn oil
½ cup toasted and shelled gingko nuts (page 435)
¼ cup mellow (light-colored) miso
¼ cup brown rice vinegar
¼ cup umeboshi plum vinegar or red wine vinegar
2 tablespoons brewer's yeast
1 tablespoon hot paprika
2 teaspoons Tabasco sauce or chili sauce

In a blender, combine all the ingredients and process until smooth. Gingko Cheese Dressing will keep, tightly covered, in the refrigerator for up to 2 weeks.

MAKES 2 ⅔ CUPS

BURDOCK AND GINGKO SOUP FOR NIKI

My friend Niki loves burdock root and ginkgo nuts, so I created this wild soup for her.

2 tablespoons olive oil
3 medium-size carrots, sliced
½ cup chopped scallions
¼ cup ramp bulbs (page 116) or shallots, chopped
4 cloves garlic, crushed into a paste
12 cups boiling water
3 cups very thinly sliced burdock root (page 139)
1 cup wakame seaweed (one 4-ounce package), soaked in water to cover for 10 minutes and drained
1 ½ cups toasted and shelled gingko nuts (page 435)
5 ½ cups curly dock leaves (page 109), coarsely chopped
2 tablespoons preserved radish in chili (available in Asian specialty stores; optional)
½ teaspoon cayenne pepper, or to taste
¼ cup dark-colored miso

1. Heat the olive oil in a large skillet over medium heat. Add the carrots, scallions, ramps, and garlic and cook, covered, stirring, for 10 minutes.
2. Add the vegetables to the boiling water in a large soup pot, along with the burdock, drained seaweed, and gingko nuts, and simmer, covered, for 20 minutes over low heat.
3. Add the curly dock, preserved radish, and cayenne and simmer, covered, for another 5 minutes. Remove the pot from the heat.
4. Dip a strainer into the pot, add the miso, and stir it against the sides of the strainer with a wooden spoon until the miso is dissolved. Serve hot.

MAKES 4½ QUARTS; SERVES 16

GINGKO RICE

Gingko nuts complement rice and seaweed perfectly. And you'll never forget how good they taste together— since gingko improves memory.

4 cups water

1 cup brown basmati rice

1 cup sweet brown rice

1 cup toasted and shelled gingko nuts
    (page 435)

½ cup dried wakame or any other edible seaweed,
    soaked for 5 minutes in water to cover and
    rinsed

1 ½ tablespoons olive oil

1 ½ teaspoons Vege-Sal or tamari soy sauce

1 teaspoon dried thyme, finely crumbled

Place all the ingredients in a large saucepan and bring the pot to a boil over medium heat. Reduce the heat to low, and simmer, covered, until all the liquid is absorbed and the rice is tender, about 45 minutes.

SERVES 6

BROWN RICE WITH GINGKOS AND RAMPS

These wild ingredients transform plain brown rice into a feast.

3 ¾ cups water

2 cups brown basmati rice or long-grain brown rice

2 cups ramp leaves (page 116), chives, or
    scallions, chopped

1 cup toasted and shelled gingko nuts (page 435)

4 cloves garlic, chopped

2 small chiles, seeds and ribs removed and chopped,
    or ½ teaspoon cayenne pepper, or to taste

1 tablespoon tamari soy sauce, or to taste

1 tablespoon olive oil

1 teaspoon dried thyme, finely crumbled

1 teaspoon dried rosemary, finely crumbled

1 teaspoon dried marjoram, finely crumbled

Mix together all the ingredients in a large saucepan and bring the pot to a boil over medium heat. Reduce the heat to low, cover, and simmer until all the water is absorbed and the rice is tender, about 40 minutes.

SERVES 6 TO 8

GOBI MATAR

This traditional Indian cauliflower and pea dish gets even more interesting with the addition of gingko nuts, beets, and some relatively mild Indian seasonings.

¼ cup peanut oil

2 medium-size red onions, chopped

4 cloves garlic, chopped

2 tablespoons peeled and chopped fresh ginger

1 teaspoon chili paste or ¼ teaspoon cayenne
    pepper, or to taste

1 teaspoon turmeric

½ teaspoon freshly ground cardamom seeds

½ teaspoon freshly ground cumin seeds

½ teaspoon freshly ground coriander seeds

1 medium-size head cauliflower, broken into florets

2 raw beets, peeled and chopped

1 cup toasted and shelled gingko nuts (page 435)

1 cup water

1. Heat the peanut oil in a large skillet over medium heat. Add the onions, garlic, ginger, chili paste, turmeric, cardamom, cumin, and coriander and cook, stirring, for 10 minutes.

2. Add the remaining ingredients and bring the pot to a boil over medium heat. Cover, reduce the heat to low, and simmer until the cauliflower and beets are just tender, 10 to 20 minutes. Serve hot over brown rice or with Indian bread.

SERVES 6

WILD PERSIMMON

Diospyros virginiana

THIS TREE, WHICH CAN GROW UP TO 100 FEET tall, has black bark broken into square blocks ½ inch across, like a mosaic. The stalked, alternate, long-oval, toothless pointed leaves grow up to 6 inches long and 3 inches across. They're glossy above and light green below. Fragrant, bell-shaped, pale yellow flowers about ¾ inch long bloom in the spring. Globular, orange, pulpy fruits 1 to 1½ inches across, containing 1 to 6 large, flattened, brown seeds, ripen in late fall. Persimmon trees grow in dry woods, rich bottomlands, at the edges of fields, and along roadsides in eastern North America (a similar edible relative grows in Texas). They've been planted in cultivated parks throughout the United States.

Make sure the fruit is ripe to the point where it looks rotten, or you'll experience a very unpleasant astringency (which you can cure by eating a ripe persimmon). The time to collect the fruit is usually in very late fall or early winter, although some varieties may ripen earlier. This sweet, pulpy, native fruit is smaller than its commercial Asian relative, but much more flavorful. Enjoy it raw, or remove the seeds and you can use it in nearly any dessert. It contains pectin, so it will thicken itself like applesauce. Because wild persimmons are sweet but not tart, sour ingredients such as lemon juice, lime juice, and Sumac Concentrate (page 281) complement this fruit effectively.

WILD WALDORF SALAD

Waldorf salad originated at the Waldorf Hotel, but they'll never serve you this late-fall wild salad there.

> 2 ½ cups cored and diced wild apples (page 340) or crabapples (page 425)
> 2 ripe avocados, peeled, pitted, and diced
> 1 cup seeded and diced wild persimmons
> 1 cup garlic mustard greens (page 61) or alfalfa sprouts
> ½ cup black walnuts (page 375) or other nuts
> ½ cup regular walnuts
> 2 tablespoons Sumac Concentrate (page 281) or fresh lemon or lime juice
> Dash of salt, or to taste

Toss together all the ingredients in a large serving bowl. Serve immediately.

SERVES 6

WILD PERSIMMON JAM

Wild persimmons contain so much pectin that turning them into jam involves no more than cooking them with fruit juice, seasonings, and sweetener.

> 1 cup seeded and chopped very ripe wild persimmons
> ½ cup unsweetened apricot juice or other fruit juice
> 1 tablespoon fresh lemon juice
> 1 teaspoon dried wild mint (page 129) or other mint, finely crumbled
> ½ teaspoon freshly grated nutmeg
> ¼ teaspoon freshly ground coriander seeds
> ⅛ teaspoon liquid stevia or ½ tablespoon maple syrup

Stir all the ingredients together in a medium-size, heavy saucepan and bring the pot to a simmer over low heat. Simmer, covered, for 5 minutes, stirring often. Wild Persimmon Jam will keep, tightly covered, in the refrigerator for 10 days or frozen for 6 months.

MAKES 1¼ CUPS

PERSIMMON-LEMON CAKE

Wild persimmons are great in all fruit dishes, and cakes are no exception.

CAKE

 2 cups plus 2 tablespoons (10 ounces) sweet brown
  rice flour and 2 cups (10 ounces) buckwheat
  flour, or 1 ¼ pounds any whole-grain flour

 ½ cup arrowroot or kudzu

 ¾ cup plus 3 tablespoons freshly ground flaxseeds
  (6 tablespoons seeds)

 2 teaspoons freshly grated lemon rind

 1 teaspoon ground cinnamon

 1 teaspoon freshly ground coriander seeds

 1 teaspoon baking soda

 ½ teaspoon salt

 2 cups unsweetened peach juice or other fruit juice

 1 cup corn oil

 ½ cup lecithin granules

 3 tablespoons fresh lemon juice

 2 teaspoons liquid stevia or ¼ cup honey, barley
  malt, or rice syrup

 1 teaspoon lemon extract

ICING

 1 recipe Tofu Sour Cream (page 33)

 2 teaspoons liquid stevia

 2 tablespoons arrowroot or kudzu

 1 ½ cups seeded and chopped wild persimmons

 ½ cup chopped pitted dates

1. Preheat the oven to 350 degrees.

2. *To make the cake:* In a large bowl, mix together the flours, arrowroot, ground flaxseeds, lemon rind, cinnamon, coriander, baking soda, and salt.

3. In a blender, combine the peach juice, corn oil, lecithin, lemon juice, liquid stevia, and lemon extract and process until smooth. Stir the wet ingredients into the dry ingredients, being careful not to overmix.

4. *To make the frosting:* In a large bowl, mix the Tofu Sour Cream, liquid stevia, and arrowroot together. Stir in the persimmons and dates.

5. Pour the cake batter into a 12¼ x 9 x 2-inch cake pan and top with the icing. Bake the cake until a toothpick inserted in the center emerges clean, about 50 minutes. Let the cake cool on a wire rack before serving.

SERVES 8 TO 10

PUMPKIN-PERSIMMON TORTE

Sweet wild persimmons complement the familiar flavor of pumpkin for this Halloween treat.

 8.75 ounces any whole-grain flour

 1 cup seeded and chopped wild persimmons

 1 cup hazelnuts, chopped

 ½ cup plus 2 tablespoons freshly ground flaxseeds
  (¼ cup seeds)

 2 tablespoons lecithin granules

 1 teaspoon ground cinnamon

 2 teaspoons freshly grated nutmeg

 ½ teaspoon ground dried wild ginger (page 111) or
  regular ground ginger

 ½ teaspoon dried wild mint (page 129) or other
  mint, finely crumbled

 ¾ teaspoon baking soda

 ½ teaspoon cream of tartar

½ cup corn oil

2 teaspoons vanilla extract

½ cup apple juice

½ teaspoon liquid stevia or 2 tablespoons maple syrup

1 ⅓ cups cooked pumpkin or squash purée

4 common spicebush berries (page 314), finely chopped, or ½ teaspoon freshly ground allspice berries

3 cups Tofu Whipped Cream (page 32) or Vanilla Ice Cream (page 277)

1. Preheat the oven to 350 degrees.

2. Mix ¼ cup of the flour with the persimmons and hazelnuts in a medium-size bowl and set aside.

3. In a large bowl, mix together the remaining flour, the ground flaxseeds, lecithin, cinnamon, nutmeg, ginger, mint, baking soda, and cream of tartar.

4. In a medium-size bowl, mix together the corn oil, vanilla, apple juice, and liquid stevia. Stir the wet ingredients into the dry ingredients, being careful not to overmix. Stir in the pumpkin, spicebush berries, and remaining ingredients, including the persimmon-and-hazelnut mixture.

5. Turn the mixture into a 10 x 6½ x 2-inch oiled baking dish and bake the torte until a toothpick inserted in the center emerges clean, about 30 minutes. Cut the torte into 8 pieces while it is still in the baking dish and then let the torte cool on a wire rack.

6. Serve topped with Tofu Whipped Cream or vanilla ice cream.

SERVES 6 TO 8

LEMON-GLAZED PERSIMMON LOAF

Tart lemon glaze contrasts with the rich, dense texture of wild persimmons, currants, and pecans in this sweet bread.

LOAF

1 cup plus 2 tablespoons (5.5 ounces) buckwheat flour and 1 cup plus ½ tablespoon (5 ounces) sweet brown rice flour, or 10.5 ounces any whole-grain flour

½ cup arrowroot or kudzu

2 ½ tablespoons freshly ground flaxseeds (1 tablespoon seeds)

1 teaspoon baking soda

½ teaspoon salt

1 teaspoon ground cinnamon

1 ½ teaspoons freshly grated nutmeg

¼ teaspoon freshly ground cloves

1 cup unsweetened apricot juice

¼ cup corn oil

1 cup seeded and chopped wild persimmons

1 cup pecans, chopped

1 cup cultivated currants

1 ½ teaspoons lecithin granules

GLAZE

5 tablespoons water

3 tablespoons fresh lemon juice

2 tablespoons agar flakes

⅛ teaspoon liquid stevia or ½ tablespoon barley malt or honey

1. Preheat the oven to 350 degrees.

2. *To make the loaf:* In a large bowl, mix together the flours, arrowroot, ground flaxseeds, baking soda, salt, cinnamon, nutmeg, and cloves.

3. In a medium-size bowl, mix together the apricot

juice and corn oil. Stir the wet ingredients into the dry ingredients, being careful not to overmix. Stir the batter into the persimmons, pecans, currants, and lecithin, being careful not to overmix.

4. Pour the batter into an oiled 6½ x 4⅜ x 2½-inch loaf pan and bake the loaf until a toothpick inserted in the center emerges clean, about 45 minutes.

5. Remove the loaf from the baking dish and let it cool on a wire rack.

6. *To make the glaze:* Simmer all the glaze ingredients together for 5 minutes in a small saucepan over low heat, stirring occasionally.

7. After the loaf has cooled, return it to the loaf pan and pour the warm glaze over it. When the glaze gels a few minutes later, remove the loaf from the loaf pan and cut it into 6 to 8 pieces.

SERVES 6 TO 8

APPLE-PERSIMMON SQUARES

The persimmon's generic name, *Diospyros*, means "food of the gods." When you taste this recipe, you'll know why.

> 2 ⅔ cups sweet brown rice flour or 10.5 ounces any other whole-grain flour
> 2 ½ tablespoons freshly ground flaxseeds (1 tablespoon seeds)
> 1 ½ teaspoons lecithin granules
> ¼ teaspoon salt
> ½ teaspoon freshly grated nutmeg
> ¼ teaspoon ground dried wild ginger (page 111) or regular ground ginger
> ½ cup unsweetened pear juice or other fruit juice
> ¼ cup corn oil
> 1 teaspoon vanilla extract

> ¼ teaspoon liquid stevia or 1 tablespoon maple syrup or barley malt
> 2 cups cored and finely chopped or grated wild apples (page 340) or 2 Granny Smith apples, cored and finely chopped or grated
> 1 cup seeded and chopped very ripe wild persimmons
> ½ cup pecans, chopped
> 1 teaspoon ground cinnamon

1. Preheat the oven to 350 degrees.

2. In a large bowl, mix together the flour, ground flaxseeds, lecithin, Vege-Sal, nutmeg, and ginger.

3. In a medium-size bowl, mix together the apple juice, corn oil, vanilla, and liquid stevia. Stir the wet ingredients into the dry ingredients. Add in the apples and persimmons and press the batter into a 10 x 6½ x 2-inch oiled baking dish.

4. Top the batter with the pecans and sprinkle on the cinnamon. Bake the dessert until a toothpick inserted in the center emerges clean, about 25 minutes.

5. Cut the dessert into squares or bars and remove from the pan to cool on a wire rack.

SERVES 6 TO 8

WILD PERSIMMON COOKIES

If you collect more wild persimmons than you can eat, turn some into these cookies and then eat them.

> 8 ounces silken tofu, drained
> ¾ cup unsweetened apricot juice
> ¼ cup corn oil
> 2 teaspoons freshly grated lemon rind
> ½ teaspoon almond extract
> ½ teaspoon salt

2 common spicebush berries (page 314), finely
chopped, or ¼ teaspoon freshly ground allspice
berries

1¾ cups (7 ounces) oat flour and 1½ cups (7
ounces) sweet brown rice flour, or 14 ounces
any whole-grain flour

1 cup arrowroot or kudzu

1 cup Wild Persimmon Jam (page 438)

1 teaspoon ground cinnamon

1. In a blender, combine the tofu, apricot juice, corn oil, lemon rind, almond extract, salt, and spicebush berries and process until smooth.

2. Mix the wet ingredients with the flours and arrowroot in a large bowl and chill.

3. Preheat the oven to 375 degrees.

4. Roll the dough into two ¼-inch-thick rectangular sheets on a floured pastry sheet with a rolling pin enclosed in a floured sleeve.

5. Spread half the jam over each sheet, moisten the edges with water, and roll up the dough. Slice each roll into ¾-inch-thick sections.

6. Place the sliced and filled dough on an oiled cookie sheet and bake it until it is slightly browned, about 25 minutes.

MAKES 24 COOKIES

PERSIMMON FOOL

The sweet, astringent taste of wild persimmons in a creamy pudding is enough to make a fool out of anyone.

3 cups drained silken tofu

3 tablespoons Crunchy Almond Butter (page 38)
or other nut butter

3 tablespoons corn oil

3 tablespoons sweet white miso or mellow (light-
colored) miso

2 tablespoons lecithin granules

1 tablespoon fresh lemon juice

1 tablespoon vanilla extract

½ teaspoon liquid stevia (optional)

1 tablespoon vegetable glycerin, honey, rice syrup,
or barley malt

1½ cups seeded and chopped wild persimmons

¾ cup walnuts

1. In a blender or large bowl, combine all the ingredients, except the persimmons and walnuts, and process or beat with a whisk or fork until smooth.

2. Add the persimmons and walnuts and process until they are well chopped (or chop by hand and mix in).

3. Chill completely before serving.

SERVES 6

PERSIMMON TAPIOCA PUDDING

Tapioca pudding was a great favorite for such a long time that it finally had to go out of style. Nearly forgotten today, it's still delicious, especially in this simple pudding containing wild persimmons.

4 cups soy milk or nut milk

1 cup seeded and chopped wild persimmons

½ cup tapioca pearls

⅔ cup pomegranate seeds or raisins

⅔ cup unsweetened pear, apple, or other fruit
juice

¼ cup unsweetened shredded coconut

5 tablespoons freshly ground flaxseeds
(2 tablespoons seeds)

1 tablespoon lecithin granules

2 teaspoons vanilla extract

1 teaspoon ground cinnamon

1 teaspoon dried wild spearmint (page 59) or other mint, finely crumbled

1 tablespoon freshly grated orange rind or 1 teaspoon dried orange rind or orange extract

½ teaspoon salt

¼ cup almonds, toasted (page 158) and chopped

1. Combine all the ingredients, except the almonds, in a large, heavy saucepan. Bring to a boil over medium heat, stirring often. Reduce the heat to low and simmer for 15 minutes.

2. Sprinkle the pudding with the almonds. Serve hot or cold.

SERVES 4 TO 6

PERSIMMON ICE CREAM

Wild persimmons are so tasty that it's well worth the effort to find trees growing in your region, or to buy them (the persimmons, not the trees) in gourmet stores. Combined with soy milk, sweeteners, and flavorings, they make a blue-ribbon ice cream.

3 cups soy milk or nut milk

½ cup canola oil

1 tablespoon lecithin granules

2 teaspoons vanilla extract

¼ cup vegetable glycerin, honey, barley malt, rice syrup, or fruit juice concentrate

4 common spicebush berries (page 314), finely chopped, or ¼ teaspoon freshly ground allspice berries

1 teaspoon dried wild spearmint (page 59) or other mint, finely crumbled

1 teaspoon fresh lemon juice

1 teaspoon orange extract or 1 tablespoon freshly grated orange rind

½ teaspoon liquid stevia (optional)

½ teaspoon salt

½ teaspoon freshly grated nutmeg

1 cup seeded and chopped wild persimmons

6 tablespoons pomegranate seeds (from ½ pomegranate; optional)

1. In a blender, combine all the ingredients, except the persimmons and pomegranate seeds, and process until smooth.

2. Add the persimmons and process until they are finely chopped.

3. Chill the mixture (or begin with chilled ingredients) if required by your ice cream machine, and stir in the pomegranate seeds.

4. Pour the mixture into an ice cream machine and freeze it according to the manufacturer's instructions.

MAKES 5 CUPS; SERVES 5

WILD RADISH

Raphanus raphanistrum

HERE'S YET ANOTHER WILD MUSTARD, THIS one closely related to a familiar commercial vegetable. In early spring (and again in late fall), it grows a basal rosette of long, fuzzy, toothed leaves that are deeply divided on both sides into lobes. The lobe at the leaf tip, the largest, is rounded. The leaves emerge in a circle from a slender, fleshy, white taproot. From early spring through late fall, a hairy flower stalk 1 to 2½ feet tall, with alternate leaves like the basal ones, bears pale yellow, purple-veined, 4-petaled flowers that are ½ to ¾ inch wide. Long, slender, beaded seedpods follow in the spring, summer, and fall. This invasive European plant grows in fields, disturbed habitats, and along roadsides throughout eastern North America.

The wild radish is a member of the mustard family I used to scorn (I even omitted it from my previous book). You could nibble on the radish-flavored flowers or add them to salads, but the leaves were too coarse and hairy, and the taproots were tough and stringy.

Then I discovered that very young plants, in early spring and late fall, have tasty leaves and taproots. The plants are plentiful and easy to collect in quantity—which is important for practical and conservation-minded foraging. And they taste like something halfway between the commercial radish and the Asian daikon. The young leaves are great in salads, soups, stews, and sauces, and you can use the taproots, raw or cooked (they cook in about 10 minutes) to add spiciness or crunchiness to a dish—just like commercial radishes.

CHINESE FRIED RICE

Wild radish roots, along with gingko nuts and Chinese-style seasonings, enhance this brown rice dish.

3 tablespoons sesame oil

1 tablespoon toasted sesame oil

2 cups brown basmati rice

¼ cup chopped wild radish taproots

4 cloves garlic, chopped

1 teaspoon yellow mustard seeds

3¾ cups water

1 cup toasted and shelled gingko nuts (page 435)

2 tablespoons tamari soy sauce

½ teaspoon ground dried wild ginger (page 111) or regular ground ginger

1 teaspoon freshly ground Szechuan or white pepper (½ teaspoon peppercorns)

1. Heat the sesame oils together over medium heat in a large saucepan. Add the rice, wild radish, garlic, and yellow mustard seeds and cook for 5 minutes, stirring often.
2. Add the remaining ingredients and bring the pot to a boil over medium heat. Reduce the heat to low, and simmer, covered, until all the water is absorbed and the rice is tender, about 40 minutes.

SERVES 6

CURRIED CASSAVA

The cassava (*Manihot esculenta*), also called the yucca (not to be confused with an oft-cultivated wild plant called the yucca) is a starchy tropical root vegetable that is common in Hispanic grocery stores. The source of tapioca, the root, looks like a small log. You peel off the bark, slice the root, and cook it like a potato. With the addition of wild radish roots and curry powder, it makes a side dish similar to curried fried potatoes.

¼ cup olive oil

1 cassava, peeled and sliced

¼ cup sliced wild radish root

4 cloves garlic, sliced

2 small chiles (optional), seeds and ribs removed and chopped

2 tablespoons Curry Powder (page 112)

½ teaspoon Vege-Sal or ¼ teaspoon salt, or to taste

½ cup water

Juice of 1 lime

1. Heat the olive oil in a medium-size skillet over medium heat. Add the cassava, wild radish, garlic, chiles, curry powder, and Vege-Sal and cook, stirring, for 10 minutes.
2. Add the water and lime juice, reduce the heat to low, cover, and simmer for 10 minutes. Serve hot.

SERVES 6

WILD RADISH GREENS IN CASHEW SAUCE

This is the newest wild green I've discovered in my decades-long quest for edible wild plants, and it's one of the best—if you harvest it when it's young enough. Prepared with other vegetables and a cashew sauce, it's sublime.

3 tablespoons walnut oil, canola oil, or olive oil
6 cups young wild radish leaves, chopped
3 small zucchini, ends trimmed and sliced
3 cloves garlic, chopped
4 medium-size ripe tomatoes, chopped
¾ cup raw cashews
6 tablespoons water
¾ teaspoon Vege-Sal or ¼ teaspoon salt, or to taste

1. Heat the walnut oil in a large skillet over medium heat. Add the radish leaves and cook, stirring, for 2 minutes. Add the zucchini and garlic and cook, stirring, for another 2 minutes. Add the tomatoes and cook over medium-high heat, stirring often, until the liquid is evaporated or absorbed, about 5 minutes.
2. Meanwhile, place the cashews and water in a blender and process until smooth.
3. Add the cashew purée and Vege-Sal to the greens in the skillet and bring the pot to a boil over medium heat, stirring often. Reduce the heat to low, cover, and simmer for 5 minutes. Serve hot.

SERVES 6

APPENDICES

Herb and Spice User's Guide

Here's everything I've been able to discover and compile about the uses of common and wild seasonings. I include those for animal products not to encourage carnivory, but to allow vegetarians like myself to create animal-free analog dishes.

Keep this chart handy (I have the pages taped inside the doors of my kitchen cabinets) so you can glance at it when you choose seasonings, to become aware of all the possibilities, and to find out how they work (see page 13 for more details about using seasonings).

Allspice and common spicebush berry (page 314)		
	Appetizers	Pickles, relishes
	Baked Goods	Various cakes, cookies, pies, pumpkin pie
	Beverages	Shakes
	Dairy Analogs	Cheese
	Desserts	Various custards, ice cream, pudding, pumpkin pie
	Entrées	Casseroles
	Fruit	Various, apples, pears, persimmon, pumpkins
	Grains	Barley
	Legumes	Lima beans, white beans
	Meat Analogs	Various, duck, fish, fish stew, meatballs, pot roast
	Miscellaneous	Marinades
	Salads	Fruit
	Sauces	Barbecue, Creole, gravies
	Soups	Various, fruit, sweet-sour
	Vegetables	Various, beets, carrots, common evening primrose, eggplant, onions, parsnips, potatoes, squash, tomatoes

---

Anise seeds, star anise, and sweet cicely (page 92)		
	Appetizers	Sweet pickles
	Baked Goods	Breads, cakes, candies, coffee cakes, cookies, Danish, rolls
	Beverages	Shakes, tea
	Desserts	Candies, fruit pies, ice cream
	Fruit	Jams
	Meat Analogs	Crab, fish stew, pork, poultry, scallops, shrimp
	Miscellaneous	Marinades, Chinese five-spice powder
	Salads	Fruit, vegetable
	Sauces	Fruit
	Soups	Fruit
	Vegetables	Leeks, pumpkin

Asafoetida	APPETIZERS	Indian pickles
	BAKED GOODS	Chapatis, parathas
	DAIRY ANALOGS	Herb cheese
	ENTRÉES	Indian dishes
	GRAINS	Various
	LEGUMES	Indian beans
	MEAT ANALOGS	Various
	MISCELLANEOUS	Garlic substitute
	SALADS	Vegetable
	SAUCES	Indian
	SOUPS	Various
	VEGETABLES	Various

Basil	BEVERAGES	Various, tomato cocktail
	DAIRY ANALOGS	Cottage cheese, cream cheese, cheeses, eggs, omelets, soufflés
	ENTRÉES	Curries, Italian dishes, pizza, stews
	GRAINS	Noodles, rice
	LEGUMES	Various beans, chickpeas, lentils, peas
	MEAT ANALOGS	Various, beef, chicken, duck, fish, lamb, poultry, veal, venison
	SALADS	Various, egg, potato, macaroni, poultry, seafood, vegetable
	SAUCES	Various, Creole, pasta, pesto, salad dressing, salsa verde, tomato
	SOUPS	Various, lentil, poultry, vegetable, seafood, tomato, vegetable
	VEGETABLES	Asparagus, bell peppers, Brussels sprouts, carrots, cattails, cauliflower, corn, cucumbers, eggplant, green beans, lamb's-quarters, mushrooms, onions, potatoes, salads, spinach, squash, tomatoes, zucchini

Bayberry leaves (page 185), **bay leaves**	APPETIZERS	Pickles
	BAKED GOODS	Herb breads, waffles
	BEVERAGES	Herb tea
	ENTRÉES	Casseroles, chicken mushroom stew, loaves, curries, shish kebab, stews
	GRAINS	Rice, stuffings
	LEGUMES	Beans
	MEAT ANALOGS	Various, beef, chicken, fish, lamb, pot roast, shellfish, veal, venison
	MISCELLANEOUS	Marinades

Bayberry leaves, **bay leaves** (*continued*)	SAUCES	Various, barbecue, gravy, salad dressing, spaghetti, tomato
	SOUPS	Various, bean, fish, chowder, vegetable, stock, tomato
	VEGETABLES	Beets, carrots, Jerusalem artichokes, onions, parsnips, potatoes, tomatoes
Black pepper	BAKED GOODS	Chapatis, onion bread
	DAIRY ANALOGS	Cheese, eggs, Indian spice ice cream
	DESSERTS	Indian spice pudding
	ENTRÉES	Various
	GRAINS	Noodles, rice
	LEGUMES	Various, chickpeas, peas
	MEAT ANALOGS	Various, chicken, ham, pot roast
	MISCELLANEOUS	Marinades
	SALADS	Various
	SAUCES	Various, barbecue, gravy, salad dressings, tomato
	SOUPS	Various
	VEGETABLES	Bell peppers, cabbage, carrots, celery, corn, cucumber, eggplant, green beans, lamb's-quarters, mushrooms, onions, potatoes, spinach, salads, tomatoes, zucchini
Caraway seeds	APPETIZERS	Pickles
	BAKED GOODS	Various, breads, cakes, cookies, crackers, rye bread
	DAIRY ANALOGS	Cheese, cottage cheese
	ENTRÉES	Vegetable pie
	FRUIT	Various, apples, pears
	GRAINS	Noodles, stuffing
	MEAT ANALOGS	Various, chicken, fish, kidneys, liver, pork, sausage, tuna
	MISCELLANEOUS	Sauerkraut
	SALADS	Various, cattail, cucumber, cole slaw, kimchi, potato
	SAUCES	Various, cheese
	SOUPS	Various, beet
	VEGETABLES	Beets, broccoli, Brussels sprouts, cattail shoots, cabbage, carrots, cauliflower, common evening primrose, cucumbers, green beans, milkweed, onions, parsnips, potatoes, squash, turnips, winter cress
Cardamom	APPETIZERS	Pickles
	BAKED GOODS	Breads, coffee cakes, cookies, spiced cakes, pastry, pies, rolls
	BEVERAGES	Shakes
	DAIRY ANALOGS	Cheese spreads

Cardamom	DESSERTS	Puddings, sweetmeats, ice cream
(continued)	ENTRÉES	Curries; Indian, Middle Eastern, and Scandinavian dishes; loaves
	FRUIT	Apples, bananas, blueberries, grape jelly, melons, pawpaws, pumpkins
	GRAINS	Granola, pilafs
	LEGUMES	Beans
	MEAT ANALOGS	Various, sausage
	MISCELLANEOUS	Garam masala, halvah
	SAUCES	Fruit
	SOUPS	Fruit
	VEGETABLES	Cauliflower, sweet potatoes, yellow squash, zucchini

Cayenne pepper,	APPETIZERS	Pickles, relish
chile pepper,	BEVERAGES	Tomato juice cocktail
crushed red pepper	DAIRY ANALOGS	Cheese, cottage cheese, cream cheese, stuffed eggs, eggs, omelet, sour cream, spreads
	ENTRÉES	Casseroles; chili; creamed dishes; curries; Cajun, Indian, Italian, and Mexican dishes; pizza
	FRUIT	Stews
	GRAINS	Corn, pasta, peas, rice
	LEGUMES	Beans
	MEAT ANALOGS	Various, beef, fish, poultry, pork, pot roast, seafood, sausages
	MISCELLANEOUS	Dips
	SAUCES	Various, barbecue, cream, French dressing, hollandaise, hot, mayonnaise, pasta, pizza, tomato, vinaigrette dressing
	SOUPS	Chowders (white), minestrone, tomato, vegetable
	VEGETABLES	Various, cattails, corn, cucumbers, green beans, lamb's-quarters, mushrooms, onions, potatoes, spinach, tomatoes, zucchini

Celery seeds	APPETIZERS	Dips, pickles
	BAKED GOODS	Breads, rolls
	BEVERAGES	Tomato juice, vegetable juice cocktail
	DAIRY ANALOGS	Cheese, eggs
	ENTRÉES	Burgers, casseroles, loaves, pot pies, stews
	GRAINS	Pasta, rice, stuffing
	LEGUMES	Chickpeas, peas

Celery seeds (continued)	MEAT ANALOGS	Various, beef, brisket, fish, pork, pot roast, poultry, seafood, tongue, veal
	MISCELLANEOUS	Spreads
	SALADS	Various, cole slaw, potato salads, vegetable
	SAUCES	Various, barbecue, cream, fish, ketchup, mayonnaise, salad dressings, spaghetti
	SOUPS	Various, chowder, cream, potato, vegetable
	VEGETABLES	Various, beets, bell peppers, cabbage, cauliflower, carrots, cattails, corn, cucumbers, green beans, onions, potatoes, tomatoes, zucchini

Chervil and goutweed (page 130)	APPETIZERS	Dips
	BAKED GOODS	Breads, rolls
	BEVERAGES	Vegetable juice cocktail
	DAIRY ANALOGS	Butter, cheese, cottage cheese, cream cheese, eggs
	ENTRÉES	Casseroles, curries, loaves, stews
	GRAINS	Various
	LEGUMES	Various, peas
	MEAT ANALOGS	Fish, poultry
	MISCELLANEOUS	Garnishes
	SALADS	Vegetable
	SAUCES	Various, butter, French and other dressings
	SOUPS	Various
	VEGETABLES	Various, celery, lamb's-quarters, spinach, wild greens

Chili powder	APPETIZERS	Bean dip, dips, guacamole
	BAKED GOODS	Cornbread
	BEVERAGES	Tomato juice cocktail
	DAIRY ANALOGS	Boiled and scrambled eggs, omelets, cheese
	ENTRÉES	Burgers, casseroles, chili, enchiladas, Mexican dishes, stews, tacos, tamale pie
	GRAINS	Spanish rice
	LEGUMES	Beans, pinto beans
	MEAT ANALOGS	Beef, chicken, pot roast
	SALADS	Bean
	SAUCES	Barbecue, cheese, cocktail, French dressing, gravies, oyster, tomato
	SOUPS	Bean, vegetable

Chives, field garlic, and the leaves of all wild onions (page 57)	APPETIZERS	Dips
	BAKED GOODS	Onion bread, rye bread
	BEVERAGES	Vegetable juice cocktail
	DAIRY ANALOGS	Butter, cottage, cream, and other cheeses; deviled eggs, eggs, omelets, scrambled eggs; sour cream and yogurt
	ENTRÉES	Burgers, casseroles, curries, stews
	GRAINS	Barley, crêpes, noodles, pasta, rice, stuffing
	LEGUMES	Various beans, baked beans
	MEAT ANALOGS	Beef, chicken, fish, any poultry, sausage, veal
	SALADS	Egg, cole slaw, crab, fish, ham, macaroni, pasta, potato, tuna, vegetable
	SAUCES	Various, butter, cream, salad dressing
	SOUPS	Various, chowders, cream, potato, tomato, vichyssoise
	VEGETABLES	Asparagus, beets, broccoli, carrots, cattail shoots and flower heads, cauliflower, celery, corn, cucumbers, green beans, potatoes, squash, tomatoes, turnips, zucchini
Cilantro	APPETIZERS	Guacamole, tortilla chips, spreads
	BAKED GOODS	Breads, cornbread, tacos
	DAIRY ANALOGS	Herb cheddar cheese, cheese, eggs
	ENTRÉES	Various; casseroles; enchiladas; Mexican, Turkish, and Russian dishes
	GRAINS	Barley, rice
	LEGUMES	Beans
	MEAT ANALOGS	Chicken, roast beef
	SALADS	Vegetable
	SAUCES	Cheese, salsa, salsa verde
	SOUPS	Various, gazpacho, chicken mushroom
	VEGETABLES	Various, cattail flower heads, corn
Cinnamon	APPETIZERS	Sweet pickles
	BAKED GOODS	Various, biscuits, brownies, spice breads, cakes, coffee cake, cookies, Danish, fruit breads, pies, rolls, spice cake, toast, waffles
	BEVERAGES	Various, cider, hot chocolate or carob, soymilk, tea
	DAIRY ANALOGS	French toast, ice cream, whipped cream
	DESSERTS	Various, applesauce, cobblers, compotes, crisps, puddings
	FRUIT	Various, apples, peaches, pears, preserves, stewed fruit
	GRAINS	Cereals, granola, rice, stuffing

Cinnamon (*continued*)	MEAT ANALOGS	Ham, lamb, stuffed pork, sweet-sour fish
	MISCELLANEOUS	Carob, chocolate
	SALADS	Fruit
	SAUCES	Curry, fruit sauces, ketchup, sweet-sour
	SOUPS	Fruit
	VEGETABLES	Various, beets, carrots, squash, sweet potatoes, yams
Cloves	APPETIZERS	Chutney, dips, pickles, relishes
	BAKED GOODS	Spice breads, spice cakes, gingerbread, pies
	DESSERTS	Carob, chocolate and other puddings
	ENTRÉES	Stews, curries, falafels, loaves
	FRUIT	Various, cranberries, pickles, plums, stewed fruit
	GRAINS	Pilafs
	LEGUMES	Baked beans, beans
	MEAT ANALOGS	Various, baked chicken, broiled fish, ham, pork
	MISCELLANEOUS	Garam masala, marinades
	SALADS	Fruit, dressings
	SAUCES	Barbecue, ham, chili, dessert, salsa, syrups
	SOUPS	Various, fruit, onion-tomato, stock
	VEGETABLES	Various, beets, bland mushrooms, carrots, onions
Coriander seeds	APPETIZERS	Pickles
	BAKED GOODS	Biscuits, breads, cakes, coffee cakes, cookies, Danish, gingerbread, pastries, spice cakes
	BEVERAGES	Various, liqueurs
	DAIRY ANALOGS	Cream cheese
	DESSERTS	Various, carob, chocolate
	ENTRÉES	Casseroles; curries; Indian, Moroccan, and Spanish dishes
	FRUIT	Various, apples, stews
	GRAINS	Noodles
	LEGUMES	Beans
	MEAT ANALOGS	Various, chicken, fish, poultry, seafood, lamb stew, tuna
	MISCELLANEOUS	Dips, vinegars
	SALADS	Various, cole slaw, vegetables
	SAUCES	Various, fish and meat, salad dressing, sour cream dressings, tomato
	SOUPS	Various, cream, seafood, pea
	VEGETABLES	Asparagus, beets, broccoli, Brussels sprouts, cattails, cauliflower, cucumbers, green beans, milkweed, potatoes, sauerkraut, tomatoes

Cumin seeds	APPETIZERS	Indian, pickles, relishes
	DAIRY ANALOGS	Cheese, eggs, omelets
	ENTRÉES	Asian, Mexican, and Indian dishes; burritos, chili, curries, enchiladas, loaves, pies, tacos, tamales, stews
	LEGUMES	Beans
	SAUCES	Tomato
	VEGETABLES	Tomatoes

Curry powder	APPETIZERS	Curried sunflower seeds, dips, samosas
	DAIRY ANALOGS	Creamed eggs, deviled eggs, scrambled eggs
	FRUIT	Compotes
	GRAINS	Cereals, rice
	LEGUMES	Lentils
	MEAT ANALOGS	Various, fish, herring, roast pork, salami
	MISCELLANEOUS	Liquors
	SALADS	Various
	SAUCES	Various, fish
	SOUPS	Various
	VEGETABLES	Parsnips, potatoes, sauerkraut, sweet potatoes

Dill seeds	APPETIZERS	Pickles
	BAKED GOODS	Breads, cakes, pastries
	BEVERAGES	Herb teas
	DAIRY ANALOGS	Cheese, eggs, sour cream
	ENTRÉES	Stews, Turkish dishes
	LEGUMES	Tofu
	MISCELLANEOUS	Marinades
	VEGETABLES	Various

Filé powder	BAKED GOODS	Muffins, rolls
	ENTRÉES	Gumbos, stews
	FRUIT	Stewed fruit
	LEGUMES	Lentils
	MEAT ANALOGS	Fish
	MISCELLANEOUS	Thickener
	SAUCES	Creole, tomato
	SOUPS	Gumbos

Garlic, wild and commercial species' bulbs	APPETIZERS	Dips
	BAKED GOODS	Biscuits, breads, rolls
	DAIRY ANALOGS	Herb cheese, eggs, herb butter, omelets
	ENTRÉES	Burgers; casseroles; chili; Chinese, French and Italian dishes; pizza; pot pie; stews
	GRAINS	Pasta
	LEGUMES	Beans, chickpeas, tofu
	MEAT ANALOGS	Various, beef, chicken, fish, lamb, pork, poultry, sausage
	MISCELLANEOUS	Marinades
	SALADS	Various, chicken, potato
	SAUCES	Various, butter, mayonnaise, salad dressings, spaghetti, tomato
	SOUPS	Various, tomato, vegetable
	VEGETABLES	Bell peppers, cabbage, carrots, chicory, dandelions, eggplant, green beans, lamb's-quarters, milkweed, onions, pokeweed, potatoes, spinach, squash, salads, tomatoes, winter cress, zucchini
Garlic mustard seeds (page 252)	APPETIZERS	Canapes, sushi
	DAIRY ANALOGS	Herb cheese
	ENTRÉES	Various
	GRAINS	Various
	LEGUMES	Various
	MEAT ANALOGS	Beef, ham, lamb, pork, sausage
	SALADS	Vegetable
	SAUCES	Various, mayonnaise
	SOUPS	Cream, onion
	VEGETABLES	Cabbage, mushrooms, purslane, tomatoes, zucchini
Garlic mustard (page 61) root, horseradish (page 80), wasabe	APPETIZERS	Dips, pickles, sushi
	DAIRY ANALOGS	Cream cheese, yogurt
	ENTRÉES	Casseroles, loaves, Asian dishes, stews
	MEAT ANALOGS	Roast beef
	MISCELLANEOUS	Spreads
	SALADS	Kimchi
	SAUCES	Cream, salad dressings
	VEGETABLES	Various, winter cress

Ginger, wild ginger (page 111)	APPETIZERS	Chutneys, egg rolls, pickles, relish
	BAKED GOODS	Various, breads, cookies, cakes, gingerbread, pies
	BEVERAGES	Various, shakes, wine
	DESSERTS	Confections, puddings, pumpkin pie
	ENTRÉES	Various, curries; Indian and Asian dishes; loaves; stir-fries
	FRUIT	Various, applesauce, conserves, compotes
	GRAINS	Fried rice, stuffings
	LEGUMES	Lentils, peas, tofu
	MEAT ANALOGS	Various, beef, chicken, fish, lamb, pork, pot roast, sauerbraten, sausage, steak, veal
	MISCELLANEOUS	Chutneys, marinades
	SALADS	Fruit
	SAUCES	Dessert, dipping, salad dressings, sweet-sour, teriyaki
	SOUPS	Bean, fruit
	VEGETABLES	Beets, bell peppers, cattail flower heads, corn, carrots, dandelions, green beans, onions, pilafs, pumpkin, sweet potatoes, tomatoes

Juniper berries	APPETIZERS	Pâtés
	BEVERAGES	Gin, wines
	ENTRÉES	Burgers, loaves, stews
	GRAINS	Pilafs, stuffings
	LEGUMES	Various, tofu
	MEAT ANALOGS	Beef, game, lamb, veal, venison
	MISCELLANEOUS	Marinades, with rosemary and marjoram
	SAUCES	Various
	SOUPS	Bean
	VEGETABLES	Cabbage

Lemon rind	APPETIZERS	Cheese balls
	BAKED GOODS	Cakes, cookies, fruit pies, tarts
	DAIRY ANALOGS	Panir cheese
	DESSERTS	Various, custards, puddings, dessert toppings, meringues
	ENTRÉES	Middle Eastern dishes
	FRUIT	Various compotes, sweet fruit
	LEGUMES	Adzuki beans, pinto beans, tofu, white beans
	MEAT ANALOGS	Beef, chicken, fish, ham, lamb, poultry, veal
	MISCELLANEOUS	Marinades
	SALADS	Fruit
	SAUCES	Various, fruit, mayonnaise

Lemon rind (*continued*)	SOUPS	Bean
	VEGETABLES	Various, asparagus, beets, bell peppers, broccoli, cabbage, cauliflower, celery, eggplant, green beans, milkweed, mushrooms, Solomon's-seal, zucchini

Mace	APPETIZERS	Dips, pickles, spreads
	BAKED GOODS	Various, cakes, pastries, pies
	BEVERAGES	Shakes
	DAIRY ANALOGS	Cheese, cheese soufflés, eggs
	DESSERTS	Cheese desserts, puddings
	ENTRÉES	Stews
	FRUIT	Various, apples
	GRAINS	Pasta, rice
	MEAT ANALOGS	Chicken stew, fish stew, shellfish, pot roast, preserved
	SALADS	Fruit
	SAUCES	Béchamel, Creole, onion
	SOUPS	Clear
	VEGETABLES	Cattail flower heads, corn, onions, oyster mushrooms, sweet potatoes

Marjoram	APPETIZERS	Dips
	BAKED GOODS	Breads
	DAIRY ANALOGS	Cottage cheese, eggs, omelets, soufflés
	ENTRÉES	Burgers, casseroles, Italian, loaves, ragouts, stews
	FRUIT	Salad
	GRAINS	Stuffings
	LEGUMES	Various, peas, tofu
	MEAT ANALOGS	Various, fish, lamb, pork, poultry, sausage, veal
	SALADS	Various, cole slaw
	SAUCES	Various, barbecue, brown, cream, fish, fruit, lasagna, pizza, salad dressings, spaghetti, tomato
	SOUPS	Various, bean soups, minestrone, seafood, vegetable
	VEGETABLES	Asparagus, broccoli, Brussels sprouts, eggplant, green beans, lamb's-quarters, mushrooms, parsnips, potatoes, spinach, squash, tomatoes, zucchini

Mints, wild and commercial	APPETIZERS	Canapé garnish
	BAKED GOODS	Breads, cakes, cobblers, cookies, pies, rolls
	BEVERAGES	Various, fruit drinks, shakes, tea
	DAIRY ANALOGS	Cheese, ice cream, yogurt
	DESSERTS	Chocolate, carob, puddings
	ENTRÉES	Middle Eastern dishes
	FRUIT	Various, fruit cups, jellies, salad
	GRAINS	Cereal, granola, pilafs
	LEGUMES	Beans, peas, tofu
	MEAT ANALOGS	Beef, fish garnish, lamb, poultry, veal
	MISCELLANEOUS	Garnishes
	SALADS	Various, cole slaw, fruit, vegetable
	SAUCES	Various, fruit, mayonnaise, mint, vinaigrettes, white
	SOUPS	Fruit, pea soup
	VEGETABLES	Various, beets, carrots, cattail shoots, celery, cucumbers, green beans, squash, turnips, zucchini

Mustard seeds, black, yellow, and wild species	APPETIZERS	Various, pickles, condiments, prepared mustard
	BEVERAGES	Tomato juice, vegetable cocktail
	DAIRY ANALOGS	Cheese, cheese dips and spreads, omelets, stuffed eggs, eggs, soufflés
	ENTRÉES	Various, curries, Indian
	GRAINS	Rice
	LEGUMES	Baked beans, lentils, tofu
	MEAT ANALOGS	Various, beef, burgers, cured meats, fish, franks, ham, pickled meat, pork, sausage, veal
	MISCELLANEOUS	Indian dips, dishes, glazes, spreads, marinades, vinegar
	SALADS	Various, potato, vegetable, cole slaw
	SAUCES	Various, barbecue, cheese, gravies, mayonnaise, mustard, salad dressings, sweet-sour, white
	SOUPS	Pea, potato
	VEGETABLES	Various, bell peppers, cabbage, cattail flower heads, celery, chicory, corn, cucumbers, dandelions, mushrooms, onions, sauerkraut, zucchini

Nutmeg	APPETIZERS	Crudités
	BAKED GOODS	Various, banana bread, brownies, cakes, cookies, fruitcake, pancakes, pies, spice cake, zucchini bread
	BEVERAGES	Cider, eggnog, shakes
	DAIRY ANALOGS	Cheese, eggs, French toast, ice cream, whipped cream, yogurt

Nutmeg (*continued*)	DESSERTS	Various, bananas, candies, custards, pies, puddings
	ENTRÉES	Potpies, stews
	FRUIT	Various, bananas, chutneys, conserves, pawpaws, stewed fruit
	GRAINS	Amaranth, granola, oatmeal, pasta, rice, stuffings
	LEGUMES	Beans
	MEAT ANALOGS	Beef, chicken, fish, ham, lamb, mutton, pork, pot roast, poultry, sausage, veal
	MISCELLANEOUS	Fillings, nut butters, shakes
	SALADS	Fruit
	SAUCES	Various, cream, white
	SOUPS	Cream
	VEGETABLES	Various, beets, cabbage, cauliflower, green beans, lamb's-quarters, mushrooms, onions, peas, potatoes, spinach, squash, sweet potatoes, tomatoes, zucchini
Orange rind	BAKED GOODS	Various, cakes, cookies, orange bread
	BEVERAGES	Shakes
	DAIRY ANALOGS	French toast, ice cream
	DESSERTS	Various, puddings, toppings
	FRUIT	Various
	MEAT ANALOGS	Fish, pork
	SALADS	Fruit
	SAUCES	Barbecue, duck, fruit
	SOUPS	Fruit
	VEGETABLES	Squash
Oregano	APPETIZERS	Dips, guacamole
	BAKED GOODS	Herb breads
	DAIRY ANALOGS	Cheese, eggs, omelets, soufflés
	ENTRÉES	Chili; Italian and Mexican dishes; pizza; stews
	GRAINS	Pasta, rice, spaghetti
	LEGUMES	Beans, chickpeas, lentils, peas, tofu
	MEAT ANALOGS	Various, beef, fish, pheasant, poultry, lamb, pot roast, pork, sausage, veal
	MISCELLANEOUS	Marinades
	SALADS	Various, vegetable
	SAUCES	Barbecue, gravies, meat, salad dressings, Italian, tomato
	SOUPS	Various, bean, vegetable

Oregano (*continued*)	VEGETABLES	Various, bell peppers, broccoli, cabbage, cattail flower heads, cauliflower, corn, eggplant, green beans, lamb's-quarters, mushrooms, onions, potatoes, spinach, tomatoes, zucchini

Paprika	APPETIZERS	Canapés, dips
	BAKED GOODS	Breads
	BEVERAGES	Vegetable juice cocktail
	DAIRY ANALOGS	Cheeses, eggs, stuffed eggs
	ENTRÉES	Burgers, casseroles, goulash, loaves
	GRAINS	Various, bread crumbs, noodles
	MEAT ANALOGS	Various, beef, chicken, fish, game, lamb, pork, poultry, sausage, shellfish
	MISCELLANEOUS	Coloring
	SALADS	Vegetable
	SAUCES	Various, cheese, cream, gravy, salad dressings, spice, sweet-sour
	SOUPS	Various, cream
	VEGETABLES	Asparagus, cabbage, cattail flower head, cauliflower, celery, common evening primrose, corn, cucumbers, mushrooms, onions, parsnips, potatoes, Solomon's-seal, turnips, zucchini

Parsley	APPETIZERS	Various
	BAKED GOODS	Stuffed breads
	BEVERAGES	Green drinks
	DAIRY ANALOGS	Cheese, cottage cheese, eggs, herb butter, omelets, stuffed eggs
	ENTRÉES	Burgers, casseroles, loaves, stews
	GRAINS	Pasta, rice, stuffing
	LEGUMES	Chickpeas, lima beans
	MEAT ANALOGS	Various, beef, chicken, fish, lamb, pork, poultry, sausage, veal
	MISCELLANEOUS	Garnishes, spreads
	SALADS	Various, chicken mushroom, vegetable
	SAUCES	Various, gravies, mayonnaise, stock, tomato
	SOUPS	Various
	VEGETABLES	Various, carrots, cattail flower heads, cauliflower, common evening primrose, corn, eggplant, parsnips, potatoes, tomatoes, turnips, yellow squash, zucchini

Poppy seeds, black and white	APPETIZERS	Canapés
	BAKED GOODS	Breads, cakes, cookies, fillings, pastries, rolls
	BEVERAGES	Shakes
	DAIRY ANALOGS	Ice cream, French toast
	DESSERTS	Halvah, toppings
	ENTRÉES	Curries, Indian
	FRUIT	Various, prunes
	GRAINS	Pasta, rice, stuffing
	LEGUMES	Peas
	MISCELLANEOUS	Thickener (ground)
	SALADS	Various, fruit
	SAUCES	Fruit, salad dressings, thickener
	VEGETABLES	Various, cauliflower, potatoes

Rosemary	BAKED GOODS	Biscuits, breads
	BEVERAGES	Various
	DAIRY ANALOGS	Deviled, scrambled and various egg dishes
	ENTRÉES	Pizza, stews
	FRUIT	Various, salad
	GRAINS	Rice, stuffings
	MEAT ANALOGS	Various, beef, chicken, ham, Italian sausage, lamb, poached fish, pork, poultry, rabbit, seafood
	SALADS	Various, fruit, meat
	SAUCES	Various, butter, cream, salad dressings, white
	SOUPS	Various, chicken, fish, stocks
	VEGETABLES	Beets, cattail shoots, cauliflower, common evening primrose, cucumbers, eggplant, green beans, greens, lamb's-quarters, mushrooms, peas, spinach, tomatoes, turnips, zucchini

Saffron	BAKED GOODS	Buns, coffee cakes, rolls
	DAIRY ANALOGS	Cheese
	DESSERTS	Almond halvah
	GRAINS	Pilafs, rice, risottos
	MEAT ANALOGS	Chicken, fish, poultry
	MISCELLANEOUS	Coloring, wines
	SAUCES	Various, curry
	SOUPS	Various, bouillabaisse
	VEGETABLES	Various

Sage	BAKED GOODS	Herb breads
	BEVERAGES	Various
	DAIRY ANALOGS	Cottage cheese, cheeses, creamed eggs
	ENTRÉES	Burgers, casseroles, curries, dumplings, loaves
	GRAINS	Various, rice, stuffings
	MEAT ANALOGS	Various, beef, fish, chicken, lamb, pork, poultry, sausage
	MISCELLANEOUS	Sandwiches, spreads
	SALADS	Various, vegetable
	SAUCES	Cheese, duck, salad dressings
	SOUPS	Various, chowders, consommé, vegetable
	VEGETABLES	Various, Brussels sprouts, cabbage, eggplant, green beans, onions, zucchini

Sassafras (page 44), **inner bark** (cambium)	BAKED GOODS	Cakes, cobblers, crisps, pies
	BEVERAGES	Various, root beer, tea
	DAIRY ANALOGS	Ice cream
	DESSERTS	Various
	FRUIT	Various
	MISCELLANEOUS	Marinades
	SAUCES	Creole
	VEGETABLES	Squash

Savory	APPETIZERS	Pâtés
	DAIRY ANALOGS	Cheese, deviled eggs, omelets, scrambled eggs
	ENTRÉES	Casseroles, German dishes, stews
	GRAINS	Stuffings
	LEGUMES	Beans, lentils, peas
	MEAT ANALOGS	Burgers, chicken, fish, lamb, lobster, poultry, roasts, seafood, sweetbreads, veal
	MISCELLANEOUS	Beef, pork, sausage
	SALADS	Various, bean, cole slaw, vegetable
	SAUCES	Various, butter, fish, salad dressings
	SOUPS	Various, bean, chicken, seafood, vegetable
	VEGETABLES	Asparagus, beets, Brussels sprouts, cabbage, cattails, cauliflower, corn, celery, cucumbers, green beans, green salads, mushrooms, onions, potatoes, sauerkraut, zucchini

Sesame seeds	APPETIZERS	Middle Eastern
	BAKED GOODS	Biscuits, buns, cookies, pie crusts, rolls
	DAIRY ANALOGS	Cheese, cheese balls, cottage cheese
	DESSERTS	Various
	ENTRÉES	Middle Eastern dishes, falafels
	FRUIT	Various
	LEGUMES	Hummus, peas, tahini
	MEAT ANALOGS	Beef, chicken, lamb, pork
	MISCELLANEOUS	Candies
	SALADS	Fruit, vegetable
	SAUCES	Tahini, white
	SOUPS	Cream of vegetable, tomato
	VEGETABLES	Asparagus, bell peppers, carrots, cattail flower heads, cauliflower, celery, corn, green beans, lamb's-quarters, mushrooms, spinach, turnips

Tarragon	BAKED GOODS	Breads, rolls
	DAIRY ANALOGS	Butter, cheese, eggs, sour cream
	ENTRÉES	Burgers, casseroles, French dishes, loaves
	GRAINS	Pasta
	LEGUMES	Peas
	MEAT ANALOGS	Various, beef, chicken, fish, pork, veal
	MISCELLANEOUS	Prepared mustard, vinegars
	SALADS	Various, fruit
	SAUCES	Various, béarnaise, hollandaise, mayonnaise, mustard, salad dressings, tartar, white
	SOUPS	Chicken mushroom, mock turtle
	VEGETABLES	Asparagus, beets, bell peppers, broccoli, cabbage, cattails, cauliflower, cucumbers, green beans, lamb's-quarters, mushrooms, potatoes, spinach, tomatoes, yellow squash, wild greens, zucchini

Thyme	BAKED GOODS	Various
	BEVERAGES	Tea
	DAIRY ANALOGS	Cheese, soufflés, sour cream
	ENTRÉES	Burgers, casseroles, loaves, stews
	GRAINS	Barley, rice, stuffings
	LEGUMES	Peas
	MEAT ANALOGS	Various, beef, fish, lamb, poultry, pork, rabbit, sausage, veal
	SALADS	Various
	SAUCES	Various, brown, Creole, curries, gravies, mayonnaise, white

Thyme *(continued)*	SOUPS	Various, chowders, fish, gumbos, mushroom, pea
	VEGETABLES	Various, asparagus, beets, bell peppers, Brussels sprouts, carrots, cattails, cauliflower, celery, cucumbers, eggplant, green beans, lamb's-quarters, onions, spinach, squash, tomatoes, zucchini
Turmeric	APPETIZERS	Pickles
	BAKED GOODS	Breads, cakes, cookies
	DAIRY ANALOGS	Creamed eggs, deviled eggs, tofu cheeses
	ENTRÉES	Curries, Indian dishes
	GRAINS	Rice
	LEGUMES	Beans, dal, lentils
	MISCELLANEOUS	Coloring, curry, dips, marinades, mustards
	SALADS	Seafood, cole slaw
	SAUCES	Various, basting, cream, mayonnaise
	SOUPS	Cream, curry
	VEGETABLES	Cattail flower heads, corn
Vanilla bean and extract	BAKED GOODS	Various, brownies, cakes, pancakes, pies
	BEVERAGES	Shakes
	DAIRY ANALOGS	Ice cream
	DESSERTS	Various, puddings
	FRUIT	Various
	GRAINS	Breakfast cereals, oatmeal
	MISCELLANEOUS	Carob, chocolate, syrups
	SAUCES	Carob, fruit
White pepper	BAKED GOODS	Spice cookies
	DAIRY ANALOGS	Cheese, eggs, sour cream
	ENTRÉES	Various
	GRAINS	Barley, millet, pasta, rice, stuffing
	LEGUMES	Various
	MEAT ANALOGS	Chicken, fish
	SAUCES	Various, gravy, salad dressings, stock, white
	SOUPS	Various
	VEGETABLES	Cabbage, cauliflower, celery, lamb's-quarters, onions, spinach, zucchini

Wild carrot seeds
(page 73)

BAKED GOODS	Rye bread
BEVERAGES	Tea
DAIRY ANALOGS	Cheese
ENTRÉES	Casseroles
GRAINS	Various
LEGUMES	Beans
SALADS	Potato
SAUCES	Cream, gravy
VEGETABLES	Broccoli, carrots, common evening primrose, parsnips, squash

A Quick Guide to Making Dairy-Free Cheese

Here's a distillation of all the tofu cheese recipes in this book (see page 17 for the principles of making mock cheeses).

Cottage Cheese
(page 30)

TOFU	Soft, grated
ACIDITY	Umeboshi plum vinegar, brown rice vinegar
FLAVORS	Lecithin granules, brewer's yeast, salt, paprika, corn oil, Tabasco sauce, liquid stevia
COOKING	Bake
YIELD	2 cups
TIME	10 minutes for preparation, and 20 minutes for cooking

Cream Cheese
(page 30)

TOFU	Silken
ACIDITY	Umeboshi plum vinegar, wine vinegar
FLAVORS	Olive oil or corn oil, paprika, brewer's yeast, salt, turmeric, lecithin granules, Tabasco sauce
COOKING	None
YIELD	2 cups
TIME	10 minutes

Grated Cheese
(page 32)

TOFU	Extra-firm, grated
ACIDITY	Umeboshi plum vinegar, brown rice vinegar
FLAVORS	Olive oil or corn oil, debittered brewer's yeast, turmeric, Tabasco sauce, salt, paprika
COOKING	Sauté
YIELD	3 cups
TIME	15 minutes for preparation, and 15 minutes for cooking

Herb Cheese
(page 131)

TOFU	Soft
ACIDITY	Brown rice vinegar
FLAVORS	Garlic, goutweed (*Aegopodium podagraria*) or parsley, lecithin granules, brewer's yeast, rosemary, sage, paprika, salt, white pepper, turmeric, olive oil, Tabasco sauce

Herb Cheese	COOKING	None
(*continued*)	YIELD	2 cups
	TIME	15 minutes

Panir Cheese	TOFU	Firm, creamy style
(page 32)	ACIDITY	Lime juice, wine vinegar, brown rice vinegar
	FLAVORS	Corn oil, brewer's yeast, fenugreek, mace, salt, vanilla, liquid stevia
	COOKING	Sauté
	YIELD	2 cups
	TIME	15 minutes

Ricotta Cheese	TOFU	Soft
(page 31)	ACIDITY	Wine vinegar
	FLAVORS	Lecithin granules, corn oil, salt, paprika, liquid stevia
	COOKING	Bake
	YIELD	2⅔ cups
	TIME	15 minutes for preparation, and 30 minutes for cooking

Sharp Cheese	TOFU	Extra-firm, grated
(page 30)	ACIDITY	Umeboshi plum vinegar, brown rice vinegar
	FLAVORS	Brewer's yeast, corn oil, salt, paprika, fenugreek, white pepper, mace, Tabasco sauce
	COOKING	Bake
	YIELD	2⅔ cups
	TIME	10 minutes for preparation, and 30 minutes for cooking

Sliced Cheese	TOFU	Extra-firm, sliced
(page 31)	ACIDITY	Red wine vinegar, brown rice vinegar
	FLAVORS	Corn oil, Tabasco sauce, paprika, turmeric, yellow mustard seeds, mace, fenugreek
	COOKING	Marinate, bake
	YIELD	7 slices
	TIME	15 minutes for preparation, 6 hours for marination, and 20 minutes for cooking

A QUICK GUIDE TO WILD WINE

Here's a condensed version of all the wild winemaking recipes in this book (see page 24 for the general principles of winemaking).

Wild Crabapple Blossom Wine (page 425)		
	COMMENTS	A great white wine for the table and for cooking
	INGREDIENTS	2 quarts fresh, young crabapple or apple blossoms
	CITRUS	1 lemon and 1 orange, chopped and crushed
	SEASONINGS	4 cinnamon sticks, 2 tablespoons star anise, 2 tablespoons coriander seeds
	AGING	6 to 12 weeks

Autumn Olive Wine (page 423)		
	COMMENTS	A dry wine that goes well with French and Italian dishes, and in many sauces
	INGREDIENTS	4½ cups autumn olive berries, slightly mashed
	CITRUS	Juice of 1 lemon
	SEASONINGS	6 common spicebush berries (page 314) or 1 teaspoon allspice, 1 tablespoon dried pennyroyal (page 203) or mint, 1 tablespoon poppy seeds
	AGING	6 months to 1 year

Blackberry Spice Wine (page 278)		
	COMMENTS	A hearty table wine good in savory and sweet dishes. Use sparingly in recipes.
	INGREDIENTS	6 cups wild blackberries, mashed
	CITRUS	None
	SEASONINGS	1 tablespoon common spicebush (page 314) berries or 1 teaspoon allspice, 1 tablespoon cloves, 2 cinnamon sticks
	AGING	8 weeks to 6 months

Black Locust Blossom Wine (page 179)		
	COMMENTS	A dry white wine to drink with light meals, or to use in any European-style cooking
	INGREDIENTS	2 quarts fresh, young black locust blossoms in room temperature water
	CITRUS	1 lemon and 1 orange, chopped and crushed
	SEASONINGS	2 tablespoons chopped fresh ginger, 2 tablespoons star anise, 2 tablespoons coriander seed
	AGING	2 to 6 months

Daylily Wine
(page 64)

COMMENTS	A very strong-tasting cooking wine; use in all amounts to season vegetables or grains.
INGREDIENTS	8 cups daylily shoots
CITRUS	Juice of 2 lemons
SEASONINGS	1 tablespoon tarragon, 1 teaspoon dill seeds, 1 tablespoon poppy seeds
AGING	6 months to 2 years

Mulberry Wine
(page 222)

COMMENTS	Halfway between a dry and red wine, this mild wine is good in all dishes.
INGREDIENTS	4 cups mulberries
CITRUS	Juice of 2 lemons
SEASONINGS	2 cinnamon sticks, 1 tablespoon dried spearmint (page 59)
AGING	10 weeks to 6 months

Ramp Wine
(page 116)

COMMENTS	A pungent white cooking wine; use it to impart an onion-garlic flavor to savory dishes and sauces.
INGREDIENTS	2 cups ramp leaves and bulbs, or other *Allium* species
CITRUS	None
SEASONINGS	6 cloves garlic, peeled but not chopped, 2 tablespoons celery seeds
AGING	6 months to 1 year

Redbud Wine
(page 156)

COMMENTS	An excellent red table wine and cooking wine, strongly flavored, but not overpowering
INGREDIENTS	1 quart redbud flowers
CITRUS	1 lemon and 1 orange, chopped and crushed
SEASONINGS	8 bayberry (page 185) leaves or 4 bay leaves, 2 tablespoons coriander seeds
AGING	8 to 12 weeks

White Oak Wine
(page 176)

COMMENTS	Surprisingly, one of the best wild table wines and cooking wines; use it universally.
INGREDIENTS	2 quarts young, white oak leaves, not fully developed
CITRUS	None
SEASONINGS	¼ cup each juniper berries, fennel seeds, celery seeds
AGING	2 months to 2 years

Wineberry Wine (page 246)	COMMENTS	A sweet red wine that is ideal for desserts and sweet sauces
	INGREDIENTS	6 cups wineberries or other raspberries, mashed
	CITRUS	None
	SEASONINGS	4 sticks cinnamon and 2 tablespoons dried mint (page 129)
	AGING	6 weeks to 6 months

Wisteria Wine (page 151)	COMMENTS	A heady wine to serve at dinner or use in dessert dishes
	INGREDIENTS	2 quarts fresh, young wisteria blossoms
	CITRUS	1 lemon and 1 orange, chopped and crushed
	SEASONINGS	2 tablespoons common spicebush (page 314) berries or 1 teaspoon allspice, 2 tablespoons each bayberry (page 185) or bay leaves and tarragon
	AGING	2 to 6 months

EQUIVALENTS

H ERE'S EVERYTHING I'VE BEEN ABLE TO DISCOVER, MEASURE, OR COMPILE TO HELP you substitute healthful ingredients for unhealthful ones (or vice-versa, if you're really perverse), interchange weights and volumes, and find out how the volume changes when you cook various common and wild foods.

Acorns (page 292)	1 cup, unshelled	6 ounces
	1 cup, shelled	5.33 ounces
Adzuki beans	1 cup dried	2 cups soaked; makes 2⅔ cups cooked
Agar powder	2 teaspoons	Jells 1 cup liquid
	1 bar	5 tablespoons flakes or ½ tablespoon powder
	1 tablespoon powder	¼ ounce
Alfalfa seeds	1 cup (7 ounces)	4 cups sprouts
Almonds, shelled	1 cup	7 ounces
Apples, average-size commercial apples or large wild apples (page 340)	1 medium	1 cup (⅓ pound); makes 3 tablespoons juice
Apricots, dried	1 cup (⅓ pound)	Makes 1⅔ cups cooked
Apricots, fresh	1 cup	Makes ¾ cup pitted
Arrowroot	1 cup	½ pound
	2½ tablespoons	Thickens 4 cups liquid
	3 tablespoons	Thickens one 9-inch pie
Autumn olive berries (page 415)	1 cup	7 tablespoons cooked and strained
Baking powder	1 teaspoon	¼ teaspoon baking soda plus either ½ teaspoon cream of tartar or ½ tablespoon lemon juice

Baking soda	1 teaspoon plus either 2 teaspoons cream of tartar or 2 tablespoons lemon juice	Leavens 28 ounces flour
Bananas, medium	1, sliced	¾ cup
Beans, dry	1 cup	2½ cups, cooked
Beans, cooked	1 cup	⅓ pound
Beans, pinto	1 pound	2⅔ cups
Beets	1 medium, sliced	1 cup plus 6 tablespoons
Bell peppers	1	Holds ½ cup stuffing
Black cherries (page 253)	1 cup	6 tablespoons cooked and pitted
Blueberries (page 260)	4 cups, whole	Makes 3 cups plus 1 tablespoon purée
Bran	1 cup	2 ounces
Brazil nuts	1 cup	2 ounces
Bread crumbs, dry	3½ slices bread	1 cup
Bread crumbs, fresh	1 slice bread	¾ cup
Bread, yeast	1 large loaf	Substitute 2 cups sourdough starter for 1 cup flour plus 1¾ cups liquid
Burdock (page 139)	1 cup, sliced	4 ounces
Butter	1 cup	½ pound or 2 sticks or ⅞ cup vegetable oil plus ½ teaspoon salt
Cabbage, shredded	1 cup	¼ pound
	1 head	8 cups
Caraway seeds	1 cup	6 ounces
Cornelian cherries (page 255)	1 cup	1.5 ounces ½ cup cooked and strained

Carob powder	1 cup	6 ounces
Carrots, wild (page 73)	1 cup	6 small commercial or large wild carrots (6 ounces)
Cattail shoots (page 189)	1 cup	¼ pound
Cauliflower	6 cups	1 pound raw
Celery	1 cup	6 stalks finely chopped
Cheese, grated	1 cup	¼ pound
Chestnuts	1 cup, unshelled	6.5 ounces
Chia seeds or flaxseeds	1 cup	6 ounces
Chicken fat	⅔ cup	⅞ cup vegetable oil
Chicken mushroom (page 321)	1 cup	3 ounces
Chile pepper, whole	1 small hot pepper	1 teaspoon dry, powdered
Chocolate	1 ounce (1 square)	1 teaspoon dry, powdered
Cinnamon	1 teaspoon	1 teaspoon dried, powdered sassafras (page 44) root bark
Cocoa	1 cup	⅔ cup carob powder
Coconut, shredded	1 cup	2.8 ounces
Common spicebush berry (page 314)	1 teaspoon	11 berries
Corn, fresh	1 medium cob	About 1 cup
Cornstarch	1 tablespoon as a thickener	1 tablespoon arrowroot or kudzu, 2 tablespoons flour or 4 teaspoons tapioca

Cottage cheese, dairy or tofu	1 cup	½ pound
Crabapples (page 425)	1 cup	¼ pound
Crabmeat	1 pound	2 cups cooked hen-of-the-woods mushroom with Seafood Seasoning (page 257)
Cream of tartar	1 tablespoon plus 1 teaspoon baking soda	Leavens 7 ounces flour
Currants, commercial	1 cup	5.5 ounces
Currants, wild	1 cup	5 ounces
Curly dock (page 109)	1 cup, dried	0.5 ounce
Dates, whole, pitted	1 cup	8 ounces
Egg, 1	Leavening power equal to	½ teaspoon baking powder plus 1½ tablespoon whole-grain flour plus ½ tablespoon oil
Egg	1 medium	Substitute 2 tablespoons lecithin granules plus 1½ tablespoons ground flaxseeds or chia seeds plus 2 tablespoons water plus 1 tablespoon corn or flaxseed oil
Egg yolk	1	2 tablespoons lecithin granules plus 1 tablespoon corn oil or flaxseed oil
Egg white	1	1½ tablespoons water plus ½ tablespoon flaxseeds or chia seeds
Eggplant	1 cup	⅓ pound
Enoki mushoom (page 429)	1 cup caps	5.33 ounces
Figs, chopped	1 cup	6 ounces
Figs, whole	1 cup	5.8 ounces
Flaxseeds	1 cup	6.5 ounces
Forest agaricus mushroom (page 286)	1 cup	2 ounces

Garlic, fresh	2 large cloves	1 teaspoon
Garlic powder	1 teaspoon	8 small cloves garlic
Gelatin	1 tablespoon	½ tablespoon agar powder
Gingko (page 435)	1 cup, shelled nuts	4 ounces
Golden pholiota mushroom (page 374)	1 cup	3 ounces
Hazelnuts	1 cup	5 ounces
Hedge mustard (page 78)	1 cup	1.5 ounces
Hen-of-the-woods (page 363)	1 cup, raw	½ cup, cooked
	1 cup, cooked	3.5 ounces
	1 cup, raw	⅙ pound
Herbs, fresh	1 tablespoon	1 teaspoon dried, not ground
		¼ tablespoon dried and ground
Honey mushrooms (page 356)	1 cup	¼ cup, cooked
Honey or other concentrated liquid sweetener (rice syrup, maple syrup, barley malt, glycerine, or fruit juice concentrate)	1 cup (¾ pound) less ¼ cup water	1 cup white sugar
	1 cup (¾ pound)	¾ cup sugar plus ¼ cup liquid
Japanese knotweed (page 98)	1 cup	¼ cup cooked
Jerusalem artichoke (page 361)	1 cup	4 ounces
Juneberries (page 223)	1 cup	1 pound

Kudzu	2½ tablespoons	Thickens 4 cups liquid
	3 tablespoons	Thickens one 9-inch pie
Lamb's-quarters (page 287)	1 cup	⅓ cup, steamed
Lemons	1 large lemon	3 to 4 tablespoons juice plus 2 teaspoons rind
Lemon rind	1 teaspoon dried	2 tablespoons lemon juice
Lentils	1 cup	½ pound
Limes	1	1½ to 2 tablespoons juice
Macaroni	1 pound, uncooked	6 cups
Maple sugar	1⅓ cups	1 cup white sugar
Meadow mushoom (page 382)	1 cup, uncooked	2 ounces 2 tablespoons, cooked
Milkweed shoots (page 169)	1 cup	⅓ cup, cooked
Mung beans	2¼ cup 6 tablespoons	1 pound Makes 2½ cups sprouts
Mushrooms, commercial	1 pound	3.2 ounces dried or 6 ounces canned
Mustard, prepared	1 tablespoon	1 teaspoon dried, powdered mustard seeds
Nuts	1 cup	5 ounces
Oats, rolled	1 cup	½ pound
Oil	1 cup	½ pound
Olives	1.5 cups (1 can), drained	6 ounces
Onions	1 medium	½ cup, chopped 12 shallots

Orange	1 medium	7 tablespoons juice plus 2½ tablespoons rind
Orpine (page 83)	1 cup, raw	¼ cup, cooked
Peanuts	1 cup	5 ounces
Peaches, wild (page 232)	1 medium 1 cup	9 tablespoons 12 ounces
Pears	1	1⅓ cups
Peas	1 cup, split 1 cup, cooked	6½ ounces 3 ounces
Pecans	1 cup	5 ounces
Persimmons, wild (page 438)	1 cup	½ cup, pitted
Persimmons, commercial	1	½ pound
Pie crust	1 double crust	3 cups flour
Pie filling	4 cups	Fills one 8-inch pie
Pineapples	1	3 cups
Pinto beans	1 pound	2⅔ cups
Plantains	1	1¼ cups
Polypore mushrooms, such as Berkeley's Polypore (page 199), or Chicken Mushroom (page 321)	1 cup, marinated	½ cup, baked
Pomegranates	1	½ cup seeds
Potatoes	1 medium potato 1 cup	5 ounces ½ pound

Prickly pears (page 354)	1 cup, whole	4 ounces ⅓ cup pulp
Prunes	1 cup (7 ounces)	1¾ cups, stewed
Pumpkin	1 cup, raw	½ cup, steamed
Pumpkin seeds	1 cup, dry, shelled	⅓ pound
Purple-spore puffball (page 403)	1 cup	2 ounces
Raisins	1 cup ¾ cup	½ pound 1 cup, soaked
Rice, brown	1 cup	2½ cups, cooked
Salt	1 teaspoon	1 tablespoon dark miso 2 tablespoons, mellow or sweet miso 2 teaspoons tamari soy sauce
Sesame seeds	1 cup (7 ounces)	½ cup Tahini (page 38)
Shortening	1 cup (½ pound)	⅔ cup vegetable oil
Sourdough starter	2 cups, omitting 1¾ cups liquid and 1 cup flour from a yeast recipe	Leavens 1 large loaf bread
Soybeans	1 cup	6 ounces
Stevia, liquid	1 teaspoon	1 cup sugar or ⅔ cup honey
Stinging nettles (page 83)	1 cup	⅓ cup, cooked
Sunflower seeds	1 cup	7 ounces
Sugar, white	1 cup	½ pound ⅔ cup glycerin, honey, maple syrup, or fruit juice concentrate, or 1 teaspoon liquid stevia less ¼ cup liquid; or 2 cups rice syrup or barley malt, 1⅔ cups date purée or 2⅔ cups fruit juice

Tapioca	2½ tablespoons	Thickens 4 cups liquid
	3 tablespoons	Thickens one 9-inch pie
Tofu, firm	1 cup	½ pound
	1 cake	2 ounces
Tomatoes	1, sliced	¾ cup
Tomato sauce	1 cup	6 tablespoons tomato paste plus 1 cup water
Walnuts, black (page 375)	1 cup, shelled	4.7 ounces
Walnuts, English	1 cup	4 ounces
Water	1 cup	8 ounces
White flour	1 tablespoon, as a thickener	½ tablespoon arrowroot, kudzu, or tapioca
Wild carrot seeds (page 257)	1 teaspoon	2 teaspoond caraway seeds
Wild raisins (page 394)	1 cup	5 tablespoons pulp (cooked, seeds removed)
Wild rice (page 353)	1 cup, raw	2¼ cups, cooked
Wine-cap stropharia mushrooms (page 150)	1 cup raw	¼ cup, cooked
Yeast, active dry	1 package or cake	2 tablespoons (0.6 ounce)
	1 cake, compressed	1 envelope (2 tablespoons) active, dry yeast dissolved in ¼ cup very warm water
Zest, lemon or orange	1 teaspoon dried	1 tablespoon fresh or ½ teaspoon extract

Flour Substitutions

Here's a chart that lets you substitute one flour for another. It spells out how many cups of various whole grain flours to substitute for 1 cup of white flour and whole wheat flour, and how much one cup of various flours weighs. To substitute one type of flour for another, simply use the same weight of flour, not the same volume (see Wildman's Bakery, page 20, for the principles behind whole-grain baking).

The chart also supplies the weights of various kinds of whole grains (plus acorns, which are nuts you can also use to make flour—see page 292), in case you grind your own flour in a grain mill. **Note:** The volumes and weights of all the flours were determined after sifting (sifting flour before you bake with it improves results).

Acorn	Weight of 1 cup of acorns	5 ounces
	Weight of 1 cup of flour	4 ounces
	Grain volume for 1 cup of flour	1 cup, 4.5 tablespoons
	Grain volume to replace 1 cup (7 ounces) white flour	1 cup, 6.5 tablespoons
	Flour volume to replace 1 cup (7 ounces) white flour	1¾ cups
	Grain volume to replace 1 cup (4 ounces) whole wheat flour	13 tablespoons
	Flour volume to replace 1 cup (7.5 ounces) whole wheat flour	1 cup, 14 tablespoons

COMMENTS: *Rich, moist, nutty flavored—a heavy flour best mixed with lighter flours*

Barley	Weight of 1 cup of grain	7.5 ounces
	Weight of 1 cup of flour	4.3 ounces
	Grain volume for 1 cup of flour	¾ cup
	Grain volume to replace 1 cup (7 ounces) white flour	1 cup, 6 tablespoons
	Flour volume to replace 1 cup (7 ounces) white flour	1 cup, 10 tablespoons
	Grain volume to replace 1 cup (4 ounces) whole wheat flour	8½ tablespoons
	Flour volume to replace 1 cup (7.5 ounces) whole wheat flour	1¾ cups

COMMENTS: *Light, dry, nutty—best mixed with moist, rich flours*

Buckwheat	Weight of 1 cup of grain	6 ounces
	Weight of 1 cup of flour	4.8 ounces
	Grain volume for 1 cup of flour	13 tablespoons
	Grain volume to replace 1 cup (7 ounces) white flour	1 cup, 3 tablespoons

Buckwheat	Flour volume to replace 1 cup (7 ounces) white flour	1 cup, 7 tablespoons
(continued)	Grain volume to replace 1 cup (4 ounces) whole wheat flour	⅔ cup
	Flour volume to replace 1 cup (7.5 ounces) whole wheat flour	1½ cups

COMMENTS: *Rich, nutty—ideal for pancakes and muffins*

Corn	Weight of 1 cup of grain	8 ounces
	Weight of 1 cup of flour	6.4 ounces
	Grain volume for 1 cup of flour	13 tablespoons
	Grain volume to replace 1 cup (7 ounces) white flour	14 tablespoons
	Flour volume to replace 1 cup (7 ounces) white flour	1 cup, 1½ tablespoons
	Grain volume to replace 1 cup (4 ounces) whole wheat flour	½ cup
	Flour volume to replace 1 cup (7.5 ounces) whole wheat flour	1 cup, 3 tablespoons

COMMENTS: *Familiar flavor, light texture*

Millet	Weight of 1 cup of grain	9 ounces
	Weight of 1 cup of flour	6 ounces
	Grain volume for 1 cup of flour	⅔ cup
	Grain volume to replace 1 cup (7 ounces) white flour	12 tablespoons, 1 teaspoon
	Flour volume to replace 1 cup (7 ounces) white flour	1 cup, 3 tablespoons
	Grain volume to replace 1 cup (4 ounces) whole wheat flour	7 tablespoons
	Flour volume to replace 1 cup (7.5 ounces) whole wheat flour	1¼ cups

COMMENTS: *Light texture, dry, somewhat bitter—use sparingly*

Oat groats	Weight of 1 cup of grain	12 ounces
	Weight of 1 cup of flour	4 ounces
	Grain volume for 1 cup of flour	⅓ cup
	Grain volume to replace 1 cup (7 ounces) white flour	9 tablespoons
	Flour volume to replace 1 cup (7 ounces) white flour	1¾ cups
	Grain volume to replace 1 cup (4 ounces) whole wheat flour	⅓ cup
	Flour volume to replace 1 cup (7.5 ounces) whole wheat flour	1 cup, 14 tablespoons

COMMENTS: *Sweet, moist, light—use with any other flour*

Oats, steel-cut	Weight of 1 cup of grain	6.25 ounces
	Weight of 1 cup of flour	3.75 ounces
	Grain volume for 1 cup of flour	9½ cups
	Grain volume to replace 1 cup (7 ounces) white flour	10 tablespoons
	Flour volume to replace 1 cup (7 ounces) white flour	1 cup, 14 tablespoons
	Grain volume to replace 1 cup (4 ounces) whole wheat flour	10 tablespoons
	Flour volume to replace 1 cup (7.5 ounces) whole wheat flour	3 cups

COMMENTS: *Sweet, moist, light—use with any other flour*

Rice, sweet brown	Weight of 1 cup of grain	7.25 ounces
	Weight of 1 cup of flour	4.75 ounces
	Grain volume for 1 cup of flour	⅔ cup
	Grain volume to replace 1 cup (7 ounces) white flour	15½ tablespoons
	Flour volume to replace 1 cup (7 ounces) white flour	1½ cups
	Grain volume to replace 1 cup (4 ounces) whole wheat flour	9 tablespoons
	Flour volume to replace 1 cup (7.5 ounces) whole wheat flour	1½ cups

COMMENTS: *Sweet, moist, sticky—use with drier flours*

Rye	Weight of 1 cup of grain	6 ounces
	Weight of 1 cup of flour	3.7 ounces
	Grain volume for 1 cup of flour	11 tablespoons
	Grain volume to replace 1 cup (7 ounces) white flour	14 tablespoons
	Flour volume to replace 1 cup (7 ounces) white flour	1 cup, 3 tablespoons
	Grain volume to replace 1 cup (4 ounces) whole wheat flour	⅔ cup
	Flour volume to replace 1 cup (7.5 ounces) whole wheat flour	2 cups

COMMENTS: *Heavy, rich, strong flavored, moist—use alone or with lighter flours*

Whole wheat	Weight of 1 cup of grain	7.5 ounces
	Weight of 1 cup of flour	4 ounces
	Grain volume for 1 cup of flour	8½ tablespoons
	Grain volume to replace 1 cup (7 ounces) white flour	15 tablespoons
	Flour volume to replace 1 cup (7 ounces) white flour	9 tablespoons
	Grain volume to replace 1 cup (4 ounces) whole wheat flour	1 cup
	Flour volume to replace 1 cup (7.5 ounces) whole wheat flour	1 cup

COMMENTS: *Heavy, rich, moist—best-rising flour for making breads*

AFTERWORD

I HOPE THIS BOOK HAS DEEPENED YOUR UNDER-standing of the food you eat, the ecosystems that produce it, and your body, which is an outgrowth of both. While I feel that the recipes in this book and the concepts behind them have broken new ground, I've only just scratched the surface. I urge you to continue experimenting with the many possible ways of using the wide range of wild and not-so-wild food ingredients that are available, to create new, healthy, delicious meals. Feel free to add your own variations to the recipes in this book when it seems apropos, or see what completely original dishes you can create after you've gained experience with the recipes, ingredients, and ideas in this book. I may write another cookbook in the future, and I would happily consider including some recipes created by my readers and students.

And carry on your efforts to safeguard the non-renewable resources of the planet upon which we and future generations of living things depend.

Happy Foraging!

To contact the author

E-mail address: **wildmansteve@bigfoot.com**

Web page: **wildmanstevebrill.com**

INDEX

flaxseeds, 15–16, 22
Flour Substitutions, 481–83
flours, non-wheat, 20
flowers, edible, 27–28
Forest Agaricus Mushroom, 286–87
    Patties, Russian, 286–87
Foxtail Grass, 350–51
    Barley Spice Bread, 351
    Foxy French Bread, 350–51
Fricadillon, 386
Fried Chicken Mushrooms, 168–69
    Sweet-and-Sour Power, 169
Frittata, Mushroom-Vegetable,
    371–72
Fritters, Wild Apple, 344–45
Fruit. *See also specific fruits*
    Bake, Locust, 180
    Carol's Autumn Olive Surprise,
        416–17
    Corn Gruel, 297
    Duck-Free Duck Sauce, 305
    Fruitberry Shake, 207
    Loaf, Stuffed, 232–33
    preparing, 27
    Salad, Chicken Mushroom, 322–23
    Salad, Mulberry, 215–16
    Sattoo, 215
    Wild, Soup, 210–11
Fudge, Butternut, 298
Fudge, Carob-Chestnut, 349

G

Garam Masala, 36
Garlic
    -Almond Paste, 57–58
    Black Walnut Pesto, 376
    Black Walnut Sauce, 377
    Butter, 132
    Butter Sauce, 35
    Ramp Dressing, 122
    Ramp Pesto, 121–22
Garlic Mustard, 61–62
    Cream Sauce, 61–62
    Remoulade Sauce, 62
    Salad, Watercress–, 388
    Sauté, 62
Garlic Mustard Seed, 252–53
    Garlicky Lemon Rice, 253
    Millet, 253
    Rarebit, 252
Giant Horse Mushroom, 355–56
    Turkish Zucchini Pancakes, 355–56
Ginger. *See* Wild Ginger
Gingerbread, Wild, 114–15

Gingko(s), 435–37
    Cheese Dressing, 436
    Chinese Fried Rice, 444
    Gobi Matar, 437
    Milkweed Soup, 170–71
    Preparation, Basic, 435–36
    and Ramps, Brown Rice with, 437
    Rice, 436–37
    Soup, Burdock and, for Niki, 436
Glasswort, 184–85
    Pickles, 184–85
    Sofrito, 185
Gobi Matar, 437
Golden Pholiota Mushroom, 374
    Steve's Salsa, 374
Goutweed, 130–32
    All-Purpose Herb Stuffing, 131–32
    Garlic Butter, 132
    Healthy Hollandaise Sauce, 130–31
    Tofu Herb Cheese, 131
    Wild Hummus, 132
Granola from the Wild, 304
Gravy, Mock Turkey, 282
Gravy, Mushroom Stem, 269
Greenbrier, 159–60
    Baba Ghanoush, 160
    Wildman's Five-Boro Salad, 159–60
Greens. *See also specific greens*
    Deborah's First Spring Salad in Fall,
        388
    Early Spring Stir-Fry, 64–65
    Last Chance/First Chance Green
        Salad, 46–47
    Ramp Bulb and Cheese Salad, 124
    Vegetarian Chicken Salad, 322
    Wild Garlic Salad, 163
    Wildman's Five-Boro Salad, 159–60
Grits, True, 105–6
Guacamole, Ramp, 117

H

Hamentaschen, Wild, 395
Hazelnut(s), 299–301
    Birthday Cheesecake, 299–300
    Biscuits, 300–301
    Black Walnut Bisque, 377
    Cake, Autumn Olive–, 301
    Ice Cream, 301
    Pudding, Sumac-, 284
Hedge Mustard, 78–80
    Cream of, 80
    Indian Eggplant, 78–79
    Masala, 79
    Sautéed, with Tofu, 79–80

Hen-of-the-Woods Mushroom(s),
    363–74
    Braised Eggplant with, 366
    Cajun Hen, 365
    Crab Bisque, 365
    Crab Cakes, 368
    Crab Crêpe Filling, 366–67
    Crab Imperial, 367
    Deviled Crab, 367
    Eggplant Parmesan, 366
    Fountain of Youth, 373
    Hen Casserole Extraordinaire,
        372–73
    Hen in Butter Sauce, 373–74
    Marinated, 370–71
    Meatballs, 368–69
    Sesame Hen, 369
    Solid Crab Salad, 364
    -Stuffed Pumpkins, 371
    Supreme, 369–70
    Sweet-and-Hot, 370
    -Vegetable Frittata, 371–72
    Wild Vegetable–Mushroom Soup,
        364–65
    in Wine Sauce, 371
Herb(s). *See also specific herbs*
    Butter, 58
    Butter, French, 315
    buying and using, 14–15
    Oil, 112–13
    and Spice User's Guide, 448–66
    Stuffing, All-Purpose, 131–32
Hercules'-Club, 115–16
    Curried Rice with, 116
Hickory Nut(s), 306–9
    Applesauce Spice Cake, 307–8
    -Pomegranate Crunch Ice Cream,
        308–9
    Vege-Turkey Loaf, 307
Hollandaise Sauce, Healthy, 130–31
Honey Mushroom(s), 356–60
    Bourguignonne, 358
    Burgers, 357–58
    Caps, Basic, 357
    Casserole, 360
    Creamed, 359–60
    Indian-Style Vegetable Stew, 324–25
    Loaf, 358–59
    Shepherd's Pie, 360
    Spaghetti 'N' Meatballs Wildman
        Style, 359
Horseradish, 80–81
    Dressing, 80–81
Huckleberries. *See* Wild Blueberry(ies)
Hummus, Wild, 132